FOURTH EDITION

◆ ◆ ◆

A History of Film

Jack C. Ellis

ALLYN AND BACON

Boston   London   Toronto   Sydney   Tokyo   Singapore

142 0803

Vice-President, Humanities: Joseph Opiela
Senior Editor: Steve Hull
Marketing Manager: Lisa Kimball
Production Administrator: Annette Joseph
Editorial-Production Service: Communicáto, Ltd.
Manufacturing Buyer: Megan Cochran
Cover Administrator: Linda Knowles
Cover Designer: Suzanne Harbison

This textbook is printed on
recycled, acid-free paper.

Library of Congress Cataloging-in-Publication Data
Ellis, Jack C.
  A history of film / Jack C. Ellis. — 4th ed.
    p. cm.
  Includes filmographies, bibliographical references, and index.
  ISBN 0-205-16711-X
  1. Motion pictures—History. I. Title.
PN1993.5.A1E4   1995
791.43'09—dc20   94-38924
                                                    CIP

Printed in the United States of America
10 9 8 7 6 5 4   99 98 97

See photo and permissions credits on page 488

CONTENTS

♦ ♦ ♦

Contents

PREFACE

♦ ♦ ♦

This is *a* history of film. As in Jean-Luc Godard's *A Married Woman* (1964), the indefinite article is meant to indicate that this is only one kind of film history. Though international in scope, it is limited largely to the narrative fiction film. The avant-garde, documentary, and animated film are dealt with only in part. Yet no two histories of the international narrative fiction film can be the same; there are many valid and illuminating ways to approach the subject. When Godard entitled another of his films *A Film Like All the Others* (1968), he was, of course, being ironic.

Since the first edition of this book, an increasing amount of historical research, especially on the American film, has appeared. Some of it has centered on the very early years in an effort to understand what the film forms and contents of the first decade actually were. Other researchers have looked into the practices of film exhibition in the nickelodeon era or later in the twenties; into the way the motion picture trust functioned and how it faced both competition from the independents and legal action in the courts; into the transition from silence into sound; and the like. This research has involved the screening of films preserved in archives and the scrutinizing of early trade journals, distributors' catalogues, and legal and corporate records. In addition to the increased scholarly digging, recent research has brought to film the application of rigorously thought-through ideas about the nature of history (historiography), neoclassical economics, and Marxist theory.

In the revisions of this book, I have attempted to incorporate the findings of this contemporary research. At the same time, the method and basic structure of the original edition have been preserved. If we have learned that earlier makers of films had motivations we had not previously acknowledged, their contributions were still part of an evolution, the outcomes of which they could not have imagined. If there are underlying economic forces and ideological underpinnings to be understood, they are still determined by men and women whose work can be identified, described, analyzed, and appreciated. Perhaps the approach to film history that most readily permits us to grasp and remember its parts in relation to its whole, initially anyway, remains the sort of chronological narrative offered in the following pages.

This is essentially an aesthetic history. The organizing thesis is what Arthur Knight once called the "moving spotlight" view of film history. Among film scholar and critics, it is generally agreed that for brief periods certain countries made semir contributions to the development of film form and content. Of course, there brilliant individual film makers who exist outside the construct and countries w' achievements are parallel. Even admitting the Procrustean limitations of any k' historical scheme, this one has proven serviceable and does permit variati amendment with relative ease.

Part of the present effort is directed toward trying to identify patterns in the unique and rampant growth of film during its first century. If there is anything original in this book, it has grown out of an attempt to understand the evolving practice of this young art. It may be too early to attempt an overall theory of film history (not until the late-nineteenth century was one enunciated for English literature by Frenchman Hippolyte Taine), but historians feel obliged to interpret, clarify, and connect. If our work is to be of value, we must undertake the chancy business of analysis and generalization, as well as assemble information.

Recognizing that we cannot yet take from a shelf the complete works of Robert Altman or move to a section labeled "The Soviet Film, 1925–1929," perhaps what a book like this can most usefully do is establish contexts for individual films that are usually viewed at random over a period of years. At any rate, the attempt here is to provide observations and inferences related to the films and culture surrounding major works and to note the special contributions and preoccupations of their creators. Throughout, the writing is more interpretive than descriptive or critical.

The early chapters are somewhat like separate essays, the content and structure of each being dictated by the special conditions that prevailed in the national period under consideration. General characteristics receive attention along with particular persons and their films. Later chapters extend from previous periods to the present in order to provide greater inclusivity and currency than a strict application of the thesis would permit. Interspersed are chapters on the American film by the decade—in the twenties, the thirties, the forties, and so on. These chapters are intended to keep track of major ongoing trends and contributions of the dominant Hollywood industry, even during those periods when the greatest artistic excitement seemed to be elsewhere.

Following the chapters are lists of significant films of each period and of recent books pertaining to the period. These are intended to suggest that many more films and film makers are worth attention than this limited space and the desire to simplify and explicate permit covering and that books exist that offer additional information and other interpretations. The caption under each film still accompanying the text lists title, country, year, and director and also actors shown (when known)—in that order.

The films discussed throughout are confined largely to those the author has seen which are also available to the reader on some basis, increasingly on video tape or disc. They are referred to by the titles most commonly used in the United States; the years listed for them are those of release rather than of production.

I would like to thank Joseph A. Daccurso, Los Angeles Valley College, and William C. Siska, the University of Utah, who provided useful suggestions for this fourth edition.

1

Birth and Childhood of a New Art

◆ ◆ ◆

1895–1914

The motion picture is one of two major arts to have evolved within modern history—the other art being still photography, upon which the motion picture is based. (Television is here regarded simply as a means for distribution and exhibition of moving images accompanied by sound.) We can only guess what first prompted people to express themselves in the various older artistic media, or how early modes and conventions developed and disappeared as aesthetic and social functions changed. The motion picture, however, is clearly the child of nineteenth-century scientific curiosity and technological ingenuity; it has grown up under our twentieth-century noses.

The most important of its original reasons for being had nothing to do with its artistic potential. The theory underlying the motion picture was demonstrated in a succession of optical toys. Its tools and materials were invented out of a desire to make visual records of life and to study the movements of animals, including humans. Its capacity to provide peep-show entertainment attracted impresarios and paying customers to what scientists and inventors had made available. Later, as the novelty of lifelike movement began to pale, the technicians and entrepreneurs who had discovered how to project moving images onto screens stumbled onto an old interest latent in audiences—the story. They began to offer simple narratives in a new form.

At first no one considered the storytelling potential of moving pictures, let alone their potential as an art form; but when still pictures began to move, they acquired duration, and the photographer was challenged to deal with that fourth dimension.

Temporal organization was demanded in addition to spatial composition. As in the novel, the play, music, or dance, an ordering of events into a beginning, middle, and end was required in even the simplest motion picture.

♦ BRIEF MOTION-PICTURE RECORDS OF ACTUALITY AND OF PERFORMANCES

Initially the moving picture was scarcely more than still photographs extended into motion. The brief duration of the short strips of film demanded little beyond the still photographer's concern that there be an interesting subject appropriately lit and composed. The early motion picture camera operator sought something that moved, but otherwise the concept was the same. The first films, made in the United States in the 1890s by the motion picture company founded by Thomas Alva Edison, the great inventor, were of vaudeville and circus acts. In France the Lumière brothers, Louis and Auguste, took their lighter-weight camera, developed from the Kinetoscope peep-show viewing machine manufactured by Edison from 1894 on, out into the

"Black Maria" ♦ The Edison Studio in West Orange, New Jersey, c. 1893.

Kinetoscopes in the Peter Bacigalupi Parlour ◆ San Francisco, c. 1894.

everyday world. In one of the early films, *Feeding the Baby* (France, 1895, Louis Lumière), rather than a fixed instant of Mama and Papa Lumière at breakfast with baby, we see the infant being fed successive spoonfuls of cereal. In a short from the Edison Company (U.S., c. 1894) we see two trained cats with tiny boxing gloves patting away at each other in a miniature ring, rather than standing in static pose. The novelty of captured motion was intriguing enough at first.

The Lumières began paid public performances of their films in a basement café in Paris in December 1895. In April 1896 the first commercial projection in a theater took place at Koster and Bial's Music Hall, New York City. The films shown were those made by the Edison Company.

As they chose the actions they would record, film makers soon discovered what painters and still photographers had already known: that some subjects have more intrinsic (or in another sense extrinsic) interest than others. While the motions of knocking down a wall or of a woman feeding chickens satisfied the earliest audiences, such everyday scenes were shortly supplemented by scenes of ships being launched and heads of state addressing large crowds. A strong man flexing his muscles (Edward Sandow) or a sharpshooter rapidly breaking targets thrown into the air ("Little Sure

Shot," Annie Oakley) were soon followed by a somewhat more eventful vaudeville skit, *Fun in a Chinese Laundry* (1894), and then by a piece of a popular stage success with Joseph Jefferson, *Rip van Winkle* (1896).

Even with more interesting subjects, however, the film makers' further choices were limited to two: where they set the camera and when they started cranking. They usually chose the ideal position of a human observer—straight in front, at eye level, and far enough back to take in all of the significant action. The amount of time was fixed by the length of the short film strips at half a minute or less.

In offering perfect reproductions of unmanipulated reality, Edison and Lumière succeeded (given the limitations of silence, black-and-white, and two dimensions) as well as anyone has since. The rowboat rounding the pier in early Lumière, or Fatima dancing for the Edison camera, are appealingly fresh, revealing the delight the first film makers and audiences must have felt when looking at natural movement in a new way. "It is life itself," one Frenchman is supposed to have exclaimed at a premiere

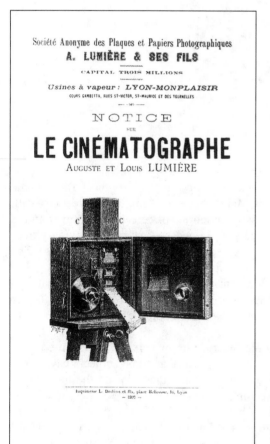

The Cinématographe, motion picture camera-projector-printer ♦ Invented by Louis Lumière, France, 1895.

screening; Lumière's train pulling into the station definitively established the way to record such an event—the camera low, stationary, and at an oblique angle.

As stripped to essentials as these primitive films seem, there were seminal differences between the programs of the Grand Café in Paris and those at Koster and Bial's in New York City. These differences suggest, in fact, the two main and divergent aesthetic impulses that have continued up to today, impulses that began in still photography—as Siegfried Kracauer emphasized in his *Theory of Film: The Redemption of Physical Reality.* One tendency, what Kracauer called the *formative,* was to strive for the "artistic," to use materials and models from the older arts. Even before the motion picture, certain photographers had begun to pose their subjects, arrange their decor and lights, and manipulate the photographic emulsion in various ways intended to make their photos look more like paintings, less like mere mechanical recordings. The other tendency, the *realistic,* was to take pride in the verisimilitude of photographic reproduction and in its ability to capture and preserve unadulterated actuality of events and views.

Perhaps largely because of the cumbersomeness of his camera, Edison started along the "artistic" way, in that he recorded performances that had originated on stage or in the circus ring. The pleasure afforded by a film of this sort depended almost entirely on the quality of the performance. Film merely preserved and made widely

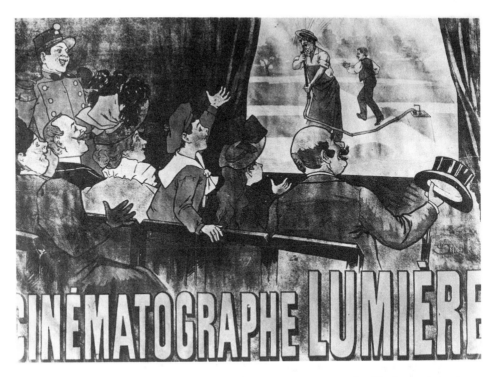

Poster advertising early Lumière showings ♦ *L'Arroseur arrosé* is the film being shown (France, 1895, Louis Lumière).

available what had been created and offered to the camera. In essence, this is the theatrical tradition, characteristic of fiction films in which actors perform roles in scripts that follow the time-honored rules of the earlier forms of storytelling.

The "realistic" tradition, the documentary impulse, was the more vigorous at first. Louis Lumière, with a portable camera, had no need for a studio or prepared material. He could wander the streets and set up his camera in front of any aspect of observed reality that took his fancy. The large projected image supported the illusion that the viewer was looking out a window (rather than into a room with one wall missing, as on the stage). Another key factor sustaining the illusion was that in Lumière's work the people, animals, and vehicles frequently moved toward and away from the camera, not just laterally in relation to it—as in many Edison films that duplicated stage-bound movement. As a result of his subjects and method, Lumière and his followers have left us a fascinating surface view of what the people and the world they lived in were like at the turn of the century.

Although film as record may not be film as art, these early topical and scenic views pointed to the capacity of film to find or to set its drama within real life. Lumière himself made a kind of fusion of the conceived and the actual, which seems to look way beyond Edison to the nonstudio fiction films of today. In the 1895

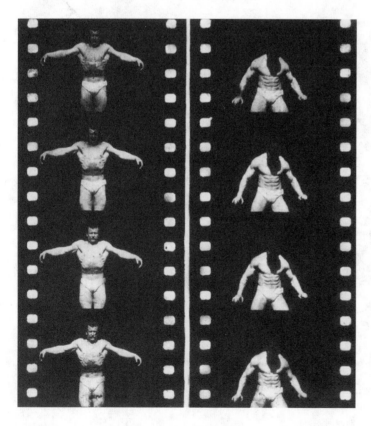

Early film taken at the Edison laboratory ◆ U.S., 1890/91, W. K. Laurie Dickson; Edward Sandow.

Workers Leaving the Factory ♦ France, 1895, Louis Lumière.

L'Arroseur arrosé (which means something like "the squirter is squirted") he set a concocted, vaudevillelike gag outdoors in an actual garden. A gardener is watering the lawn. When a boy steps on the hose, the water stops. The gardener peers into the nozzle to see what the trouble is. The boy takes his foot off the hose and the gardener is doused. In *A Game of Cards* (1896) Lumière made a somewhat similar attempt at a visual gag.

What *L'Arroseur* and *A Game of Cards* suggest, however, regarding an acted story in real settings would not be returned to for almost a decade. Instead screens were filled alternately with Lumière-type *actualités* and Edison-like stage attractions, and before the end of the decade both firms were producing both types of films. The films continued to be brief, with single shots from one camera position, and were shown characteristically as part of vaudeville programs. At first they were featured attractions; then, as the novelty began to wear off, they were reduced to the function of "chasers"—shown while one audience was leaving and another was entering the theater.

It is entirely possible that the art of the motion picture might have been stillborn, along with its capacity for entertainment, if the story ingredient hadn't been added. It is not possible, however, to establish when the first film to incorporate a story was made or who was responsible for it. Many of the early films have disappeared, so the "firsts" in film technique are subject to endless argument. National pride and individual partisanship further affect the writing of film history in this regard. But no one would deny the importance of Georges Méliès's contribution to the advance toward narrative full-length film, even though lesser contributions from his contemporaries must also be acknowledged. One of these was Alice Guy-Blaché, the world's first woman director, who began her career contemporaneously with Méliès when she joined the Gaumont film company in 1896.

◆ TELLING STORIES THROUGH STAGED AND FILMED PANTOMIME

Unlike other of the earliest film makers, Méliès had a background in the arts, which led him to think of the motion picture in a different way. At the time of the first Lumière showings he operated the Théâtre Robert-Houdin (named in honor of a renowned French magician, who also received homage from an American who called himself Houdini). In Méliès's tiny theater, fantastic sketches and magical acts were performed with the aid of trap doors, mirrors, invisible wires, and other trappings of stage illusion. As a magician it was only natural that Méliès would be fascinated by the unprecedented apparitions offered with such seeming ease by the motion picture. Immediately after seeing the first Lumière program in the small café near his theater, he asked the brothers Lumière to sell him one of their cameras. They refused, adding that Méliès would eventually thank them for saving him from a folly certain to be extravagant once the novelty lost public interest. Undeterred, Méliès obtained apparatus from the English pioneer Robert Paul, assembled a machine, and soon was, like the Lumières, out on the streets photographing.

In April 1896 (the month the Edison Vitascope opened in New York) Méliès began showing movies at the Théâtre Robert-Houdin. His brief skits and slices of life on the street were evidently quite indistinguishable from those of others. But according to Méliès's later account, it was during that first year as a film maker that he discovered quite by accident what would make his contribution most distinctive: the capacity of the motion picture to move beyond the real into the fantastic. One day, while photographing in the Place de l'Opéra, the film jammed. When he succeeded in getting the camera functioning again, he indifferently cranked the film on through. Fortunately, he developed it to see if any of the footage would be usable. When projected, the film offered a succession of images that brought instant joy to the heart of the conjurer: a horse-drawn tram on the street suddenly metamorphosed into a hearse. What had happened, of course, was that the tram was passing in front of the camera when Méliès had first started cranking; by the time the film had gotten stuck and unstuck the tram had passed on and been followed by a funeral cortege.

Méliès took deliberate advantage of this accidental discovery in *The Vanishing Lady* and *The Haunted Castle* (both 1896), starting an early genre of "trick films." Within the next few years he mastered most of the technical means for what today are called "special effects." Using fades and dissolves, superimpositions and mattes, fast and slow motion, animation and miniatures, and even hand coloring of each frame, he created a delightful phantasmagoric world. Though he had many imitators, it was years later before film makers were able to figure out how some of his remarkable results had been achieved.

In addition to introducing trickery, Méliès also made the most important beginning steps in screen narrative technique and helped increase the standard running time from less than a minute to ten to fifteen minutes—one reel. In 1897 he built France's first permanent film studio and founded Star Film Company, the first French firm devoted exclusively to making movies. By 1912 he had produced more than five hundred films of various types, but is best remembered for his fairy tales (beginning with *Cinderella* in 1900) and for a kind of fantastical science fiction (such as *An Impossible Voyage,* 1904; *The Conquest of the Pole,* 1912). Of the latter genre *A Trip to the Moon* (1902) is generally regarded as the master work; its enduring charm of conception and ingenuity of execution are easily appreciated today. It is one of the few early fiction films modern audiences laugh with rather than at. This man of the theater brought to film an innate taste for eccentric humor and a developed sophistication of visual embellishment.

A Trip to the Moon is vaguely based upon, but also parodies, a Jules Verne story; it lampoons scientific presumptions of the day as well. In making the film, an unprecedented thirty separate scenes were acted out by a sizable professional cast (including Méliès himself as the chief scientist) on the stage of his specially con-

A Trip to the Moon ♦ France, 1902, Georges Méliès.

structed glass-enclosed studio. Each scene was taken with an unbroken run of a stationary camera placed in an ideal position for viewing the whole—twelfth row center, as it were. The performers fully, not to say exaggeratedly, pantomime the action (intertitles were not yet in use), move laterally across the stage, make entrances and exits (for who was to know they didn't have to in this new medium?), and occasionally bow and gesticulate directly towards the audience (that is, the camera). The decor consists of painted canvas backdrops and highly stylized constructions and props; the robes and conical hats of the scientists, the shorts of the chorus-line guard of honor, and the devil suits of the moon men are all out of theater rather than life. Some of the trick effects are created by cinematic means; for example, scenes are joined by dissolves in place of opening and closing curtains. Other effects are achieved by such stage devices as scenery flats that are raised and lowered, trap doors, pulleys, and the like. What appears to be a dolly shot as the rocket ship approaches the moon (and lands right in the eye of its papier-mâché face) was achieved by moving the moon toward the camera rather than the camera toward the moon. In another shot, a matted drawing of the rocket enters an incongruously real ocean, proceeds down into an animated rendering of undersea life, then surfaces.

Méliès's marvelous contributions and ultimate limitations, in terms of film, are all clearly evident in *A Trip to the Moon.* He did manage to tell a complete story of many incidents in a coherent fashion; script, staging, and performances are carefully controlled to achieve a satisfying whole. The advance of what Méliès himself proudly called "artificially arranged scenes" over the single, undirected, and casually planned fragments which preceded him can only be admired. Where he stopped short, however, was in confining his camera to an uninterrupted view, making the photographic frame equivalent to the proscenium arch. Granting his intention "to push the cinema toward the theatrical way," we can say he succeeded too well. Though he achieved a theatrical sophistication of content and style, he failed to discover what the unique tools of the motion picture—camera and cutting shears—were capable of. No one would want to be without those creations of his that remain (hundreds of them no longer exist). But once Méliès had established larger ambitions for storytelling in film, it remained for others to make further contributions by using methods unique to the new medium.

One other aspect of Méliès's importance should be acknowledged before we move on. With his trick films he established the basis for what would become the avant-garde tradition, which began in France in the 1920s and has continued to today in the experimental/underground/independent film.

It is possible to say, then, that the three main artistic modes of film were present in embryo form almost from the outset: narrative fiction, documentary, experimental. The first represented a desire to tell stories with the new and increasingly rich effectiveness of moving pictures. The second had as its intention capturing the real world in a way that would help us to know and understand it more fully. The third creative impulse would lead beyond physical reality to humorous imaginings or frightful hallucinations, to the terrain of dream and the unconscious. The documentary and experimental possibilities were scarcely explored in the first decades of screen history; they did not evolve into mature forms until the early twenties, when they did so with curious simultaneity. Though given their proper value by the cognoscenti, the documentary and experimental modes have never been as widely popular as the fiction film. It was storytelling that first attracted a loyal audience and built an economic base, and the art continued to move along fictional lines.

◆ TELLING STORIES THROUGH FILMIC MEANS

Edwin S. Porter, an American who began film work in 1896, was much less well equipped in artistic background or sensibility than Méliès. In the history of the motion picture, a lack of experience with the traditional arts has frequently proved an advantage, artistically as well as commercially. In a medium seeking its own way, vigor and vulgarity have often stimulated rather than inhibited valuable innovation. A film maker without preconceptions about the nature of artistic function and form is free to try anything. By his own admission Porter was more mechanic than artist. In choosing a career he had considered both the horseless carriage and the "flickers," coincidental new engineering fields carrying unknown potential—of industrial expansion and cultural influence. (Henry Ford built his first car in Detroit in 1896; the last Model-T was manufactured in 1927, the year the silent film ended.)

At the time Porter was hired by Edison, in 1900, film makers were first of all camera operators, valued more for their technical ingenuity in keeping the camera operating properly than for their creative imagination. Unconscious genius though he may have been, Porter made the next and crucial step—through primitive and tentative editing—that set film on its main road of advance.

One of the favorite subjects for the early actuality film makers was horse-drawn fire engines rushing to a fire. It may have been commercial expediency that led Porter to use this available and conventional material in a new way, to "re-tread" what we would now call stock footage by adding some specially staged bits of action. At any rate, in late 1902 and early 1903 Porter made *Life of an American Fireman,* which raised the possibility of connecting different parts of a total action, all seeming to be happening at the same time but in various places. These segments were edited together in a more complex relationship than existed among Méliès's long, unbroken takes proceeding in strict chronological succession.

By employing a double line of action, Porter was forced into cutting from one setting to another, thus demonstrating for the first time that a film scene didn't have to be played through in its entirety before being followed by another (as is the usual practice in theater). Instead the scene could be left—while its action was still in progress—to go to the next, related scene. Given the greater mobility of film over theater, it is much easier to bring performers from one scene into another, thus joining the parallel lines of action. Furthermore, in Porter's scenes filmed at quite different times and places, the staged and the actual were intermingled to create a synthetic whole that never existed in real space or time. Editing, which appears in rudimentary form for the first time in Porter's films, was a potentiality that would excite the Soviet proponents of *montage* some twenty years later. Through Porter, film became simply but profoundly a new artistic entity rather than a reproduction of another art.

The opening scene of *Life of an American Fireman* is of a fire chief who has fallen asleep in his office and is dreaming (in superimposition) of a mother and baby trapped by fire in a bedroom. The next scene, very brief, is a closeup (perhaps the first, and what would later be called an insert) of a fire alarm box. A hand (and part of a body) enters the frame to send an alarm. The third scene (which begins the stock footage) is of the firemen asleep in their fire station. They leap from their beds, presumably as the alarm is sounded. Note the narrative linkage that Porter has managed to imply with these three separate shots. The fire chief dreaming of a woman and child in danger foreshadows what we will see, economically evoking the tension and responsibility of his job. The hand pulling the alarm tells us that at that very moment someone has observed such a fire. The alarm, turned on, goes to the firehouse and awakens the firemen.

This apparently interconnected and simultaneous action is followed by more stock footage: interiors of the firemen sliding down the pole, hitching up their apparatus, and starting off; then, the exterior of an engine house as fire wagons rush out; next, a splendid shot (from a moving vehicle) of horses galloping down a wide street with men and equipment. Now there appears what must have been a specially taken shot: A fire engine enters the frame, and the camera pans with it to reveal the house that is on fire. This is followed by a studio interior of the bedroom with mother and child amidst (rather unconvincing) wisps of smoke. There is some question about whether the extensive cutting that follows—from firemen on the exterior to victims in the interior, brought together as a fireman rescues first the unconscious mother and then the child—was as fully intercut in the original as in one (possibly reedited) version that has come down to us. Even in the less cut version, Porter, nevertheless, clearly demonstrates a grasp of the cinematic principle of simultaneous parallel lines of action by connectively cutting them together.

Porter's most famous film, *The Great Train Robbery* (1903), also exists in two versions with different amounts of cross-cutting. But even here the simpler version represents a substantial advance over *Life of an American Fireman* and everything else that had gone before. It is a remarkable achievement, containing virtually all of the elements that might be needed for a super-western released tomorrow, and it warrants repeated study. Unlike *Life of an American Fireman,* all of *The Great Train Robbery* was specially shot for the film, exteriors "on location," interiors in the studio. Though using "artificially arranged scenes," Porter dealt with a topical subject much in the headlines and built from realistic materials. In this respect his work was very different from Méliès's stylized theatricality; Méliès offered the first filmed fantasies, but realism became the main artistic style of the fiction film.

The plot of *The Great Train Robbery* progresses along three lines with three principal sets of characters. The first scene is in a railway telegraph office. Bandits enter and force the telegrapher to order the approaching train to stop for water. After binding and gagging him, the bandits leave. In scene two the desperadoes hide behind the water tank, then sneak aboard the train as it departs. Scene three takes place in the interior of the express car, which the bandits enter and rob. Scene four shows them commandeering the locomotive and forcing the engineer to stop the train. In scene five the engineer is made to uncouple the locomotive, pull ahead, and stop again.

Life of an American Fireman ◆ U.S., 1903, Edwin S. Porter.

Scene six furthers the course of the robbery as the passengers empty out of the train, line up while the bandits collect all their valuables, and then depart. The robbers board the locomotive in scene seven, and it moves off. In scene eight the locomotive comes to a halt and the bandits run off into the countryside. Scene nine shows them moving down a hill and across a stream to mount their waiting horses. Back in the telegraph office, scene ten, the telegrapher's daughter enters and frees her father, who then rushes out. In a dance hall, scene eleven, we see a number of couples square dancing; the telegraph operator staggers in; the men grab their rifles and leave. In scene twelve the robbers, and then the posse in pursuit, gallop by the camera. In the thirteenth and final scene the bandits, thinking they have escaped their pursuers, are inspecting their loot; the posse surrounds them, and shoots them all down. The famous epilogue, a medium closeup of one of the bandits firing directly at the camera, had no narrative function (as did the alarm box closeup in *Life of an American Fireman*); it was added simply to startle. In fact, the Edison catalogue of 1904 suggests that this scene "can be used to begin or end the picture."

Notice how neatly the thirteen scenes dovetail. The bandits enter the telegrapher's life, and then we follow them for the robbery and escape that constitute the bulk of the picture. The dance hall is introduced without explanation, Porter evidently counting on our being patient for a moment until the telegrapher arrives—thus bringing the dance hall men into the story and leading to the final dramatic action, the gunning down of the bandits.

The film's structure and characterization are so basically sound that one can easily imagine how its twelve minutes might be further expanded to ninety. The telegrapher would be a widower, let's say, whose daughter badly wants him to marry the local schoolteacher so she can have a new mother, and so her father won't be so lonely. The Eastern dude who has his heels shot at in the dance hall is really a fearless secret service agent whose job it is to track down train robbers. There is also the possibility of adding preceding events that explain how the gang's leader entered into a life of crime. The sturdy bones are all there; only flesh would be needed to give that first western large and full life today.

Note also how time and space are dealt with. Between most scenes brief or longer ellipses are suggested, and the order is straight succession as in *A Trip to the Moon*. When we cut from the mounted bandits back to the telegraph office, however, a reversal in time seems implied—since the bandits are still in the vicinity for the posse to catch them. There are instances of implicit simultaneity as well: In the beginning of scene three, in the express car, the bandits are evidently approaching as we watch the expressman's actions; or, at the start of scene eleven, in the dance hall, the telegraph operator is presumably on the way from his office as we see the dancing.

Each scene is still one continuous take—scene equals shot. Porter does not cut to varying distances or angles within scenes: The camera remains resolutely at eye level in long shot. But there are some interesting beginnings of camera variety, most likely forced on Porter by the exigencies of location shooting. First of all, in photographing the action of the robbers on the topside of a train in motion, a sort of moving camera results: The camera itself is stationary but the scenery passes by. Second, given the substantial number of "extras" lined up alongside the train, Porter probably couldn't get straight back far enough to include them all in the frame; and the side of the roadbed no doubt sloped down to a ditch. So he may have been required to move up the track for that effective oblique angle emphasized by the man who runs toward the camera to do a little dance of death at closer range. Finally, if horsemen are going to ride down a bluff and then left in front of the camera, the choice is either to pan and tilt with them or let them leave the frame. Though Porter's camera moves most hesitantly, the hesitation would be caused partly by a tripod head not constructed to accommodate such movement properly. It is possible also that he thought the odd angle and movement regrettable deviations from prevailing propriety rather than positive assets.

To us, if not to Porter, the conventionally painted canvas interiors mix poorly with the fine outdoor settings; they seem part of another and less innovative film. Looking back over the history of cinema we can find many valuable additions to technique forced on film makers by the requirements of nonstudio shooting. In the studio everything can be constructed and adjusted for the convenience of the camera; outside, the film maker must adapt to the world as is. With *The Great Train Robbery* it is the exteriors that are inventive in composition, depth, and movement; the interiors

The Great Train Robbery ◆ U.S., 1903, Edwin S. Porter.

are conventionally horizontal and unimaginative. Learning comes from the kind of improvisation demanded by the unanticipated.

This simplified account of the evolution of narrative film technique of necessity excludes other Porter films as well as hundreds of film makers and thousands of films that contained some of the same accidents and discoveries. These early films seem to evince a conscious pursuit of what would become standard narrative technique, but the motivation of the film makers at the time and what audiences were responding to may have been something quite different. Film historians are going back to the evidence of the films that still exist to try to understand better those original purposes. It seems evident, however, that Porter did not carry his remarkable discoveries much further than in the two seminal films discussed above; in fact, he seems not to have been altogether clear about what it was he had achieved. In the time between them he made a most uninspired bit of recorded theater in *Uncle Tom's Cabin*. After *The Great Train Robbery* he frequently lapsed into earlier and less interesting modes, and never surpassed that 1903 achievement. Even the seductively entitled and brilliantly ingenious *The Dream of a Rarebit Fiend* (1906) was a frank imitation of Méliès.

It was a group of English film makers, the "Brighton School" (subsequently rediscovered by French film historian Georges Sadoul), who first refined Porter's discoveries. It could even be that they had provided inspiration for some of Porter's most impressive achievements, most notably through the films of George Albert Smith and those of James A. Williamson. Robert Paul's *Plucked from the Burning* (c. 1898) and Williamson's *Fire!* (1901) may have been precedents for *Life of an American Fireman,* as *The Robbery of the Mail Coach* (1903) may have been for *The Great Train Robbery.* Of the Brighton School work succeeding Porter's two landmark films, Cecil Hepworth's *Rescued by Rover* (1905) is perhaps the most successful example. The care in the editing and the inventiveness of the exterior camera work, with movement angled toward and away from the camera, evidence full understanding of the new film principles involved. The use of a low angle and the presence of smooth panning are quite unprecedented. An improbable and not very interesting story, however, together with tedious repetition of the dog Rover's journeys, make it seem more of a thorough exercise in screen direction (lateral movement within the frame) and matching action (from shot to shot) than a signpost to the future.

The man who most effectively took over leadership from Porter, and whom Porter himself regarded with deference, was another American, David Wark Griffith. Griffith's introduction to film was in Porter's *Rescued from an Eagle's Nest* (1907); he played the father hero, calling himself Lawrence Griffith to keep his real name unsullied for anticipated fame as a playwright. Lack of success in the theater (as a dramatist he had only one play produced, and that unsuccessfully) kept Griffith tied to the movies. While acting in them for five dollars a day he learned that he could earn an additional ten to fifteen dollars apiece for story ideas. In 1908 he directed his first film, *The Adventures of Dollie.*

In a remarkably short time Griffith mastered what there was to know about the new medium and progressed beyond his contemporaries. Working with characteristically prodigious energy, his output of short films, the prevailing form, advanced virtually all aspects of technique. The one- and two-reelers contained experiments or

Rescued by Rover ♦ U.K., 1905, Cecil Hepworth.

refinements that carried forward the rudiments established by Porter; and by the time of Griffith's monumental feature *The Birth of a Nation* in 1915, the whole syntax of silent film had been laid out for use. The essential nature of Griffith's contributions can best be appreciated by comparing his work with the film making that preceded him. The extent to which Porter, the Brighton School, and others were able to develop the narrative aspects of cinematic expression was severely limited. Every development since Griffith had its origins in him, that most modern of film makers Jean-Luc Godard once said. Whether Godard's statement is hyperbolic or not, it is unquestionable that Griffith contributed more to the evolution of film as an art form than any other individual in its history to date.

♦ THE LANGUAGE OF FILM

Perhaps Griffith's single most important insight was that the shot rather than the scene should be the basic unit of film language. With this discovery came the possibility of varying the standard, stationary, head-on long shot. Gradually Griffith moved his camera to setups closer to the action or farther away, altered its angle for the most

David Wark Griffith directing.

effective view, let it follow a moving subject when appropriate or traverse a stationary scene for certain kinds of kinetic emphasis. These varied shots were then edited together to create the appearance of a continuous scene selectively viewed. Once understood, these options gave the film maker immeasurably greater control over the audience's emotional response, adding powerful connotations to the action itself. Méliès's framing, in unvaried long shot, had been emotionally neutral. Though Porter had begun to break away from fixed convention, the exceptions did not upset established rules even in his own films (and the deliberateness of his intentions is less than certain).

It was Griffith more than anyone who came to understand the separate psychological-aesthetic functions of the long shot, the medium shot, and the closeup, and who used this awareness consistently. In Griffith's work, and in that of his successors, the *long shot* usually begins a scene, establishing the action and its setting. It might be used to "reestablish," after closer and partial views, so that the parts could be kept related to the whole. Full of information—one could go on and on describing all the things seen in it—it is emotionally cool: We are literally distanced from the action. As the camera is placed closer, or a longer lens is used to achieve much the same effect, there are fewer things included within the frame, but we tend to be more interested in them, are closer to them emotionally as well as perceptually. The *medium shot* rather than the long shot became the standard framing from which the director departs for special purposes, just as we usually deal with life around us from middle distance. In it we are close enough to see and comprehend what is happening and what it means. Generally the stress of the medium shot is on relationships, on interaction: a person in conversation with another, or petting an animal, or cooking at a stove. When the camera is moved closer still, to a *closeup*, the visual information becomes quite limited—perhaps to one face, a hand stroking fur, a pot boiling over—but the emotional weight becomes very heavy. Our attention is directed to what we might not have noticed otherwise or might not have been able to discern at a distance. The closeup can also be used to draw us into strong identification with a character, and to suggest through facial expression what is being thought and felt. It is a freed visual statement that permits directors to show us exactly—and only—what they want us to see in the way they want us to perceive it.

Griffith called closeups "inserts," and he shot them after the scene had been filmed in long and medium shots. This frequently shifting point of view, especially to the closeup, offered a means of expression comparable to the use of spoken words in the theater. Though the stage director can block and light action in a way designed to lead our eye, we are still free to regard the whole proscenium—no more, no less—from one fixed position. Broad gestures and conspicuous props and symbolic settings may be employed, but most of what we learn comes from what the characters say to each other. Lacking the power of spoken words, Griffith substituted a kind of visual language with its own conventions and limitations. Though never as intellectually precise as words, the affective use of images can cause us to feel directly and deeply in a manner both unique and compelling.

Alternation of tempo through the editing of detached shots is something that Griffith came to understand from intuition and experiment, and that Porter understood not at all. Though Porter shifted from one scene to another, he did not break up the run of the camera within scenes. The pursuit of the bandits by the posse in *The Great Train Robbery* remains one of the slowest chases in memory as the first party of horsemen, and then the second, enters and passes through the frame. Griffith might extend screen time beyond actual time, as he would cut back and forth from shots of bandits to shots of a posse, building to a rhythmic climax; yet his chases (honored as "the Griffith last-minute rescue") seem incredibly more tense—and even faster. What he discovered, other film makers have learned and used since: Rapid cutting, or a succession of short shots, can create excitement; slow cutting, or shots held longer on the screen, will aid calm contemplation. Both the shifting spatial framing and the temporal alternation of shots give the film maker artistic resources extending well beyond the bare meaning of the action being recorded.

For transitions between shots, Griffith used a larger range of optical effects than is generally employed today. The *cut* is basic within scenes; virtually unnoticed in itself, it is necessary for the variable ordering and pacing of the action. The *dissolve* is a more noticeable transition in which one image is gradually superimposed over, and then replaces, the other. As in early Méliès, it is usually used between scenes rather than within them, and signals a change of place and/or of time. When one image *fades out* to darkness and a new image *fades in* to full exposure, a different place and lapse in time are usually being signaled also. (Griffith tended to favor fades over dissolves.) As the "heaviest" screen "punctuation," the only one in which we are given nothing to look at for a few seconds, fade-outs frequently indicate a larger break in the dramatic action as well, marking off groups of scenes that are called *sequences* by some critics. (Other writers and many film makers use *shot* and *scene* synonymously and *sequence* for what is here being called *scene,* leaving no term for a larger dramatic/narrative unit [comparable to an act or a chapter] short of the entire film.)

Griffith also liked *irises* as connective devices. An iris begins with a black screen containing only a small circle (or square or other shaped portion) of the total image: a girl's bowed head, for example. Then as the iris opens up it reveals the whole action and setting: a family standing over the girl at the dinner table in a farm kitchen. When the scene has run its course, with the girl explaining (in intertitles) how she has been orphaned and has come in desperation to these old friends of her parents, the final shot might iris out; within the contracting circle of black we see the girl's smiling, upturned face as she learns that the family will let her stay.

Griffith employed *masking* in several ways: the sides of the frame darkened to emphasize the height of a tower in the center; tops and bottoms darkened to form a CinemaScope-proportioned strip across the middle, stressing the horizontal movement and length of a column of galloping cavalry; or a cameo masking of the corners, to enhance the oval loveliness of Lillian Gish's face. He also experimented with *superimposition* and *split screen* for special effects—for the longing daydream in *Enoch Arden* (1911), or to make the awareness of burning Atlanta hang over the foreground of people fleeing in *The Birth of a Nation* (1915).

Griffith did not by any means confine his attention to the "grammatical" elements of screen language. Though of the theater, as Porter was not, Griffith soon began to sense that performance in film required a style quite different from that in fashion on the stage. If spoken words were lacking, the eloquence of body movement and gesture was magnified; in the new medium the camera registered and the projector projected. Actors on the screen appeared large, their every movement easily discernible from the back rows; as the camera came closer to them, its photographic authenticity rendered as false the prevailing theatrical histrionics. Griffith began to confine movement, dress, and makeup to an approximation of life; any exaggeration was kept small in scale and justified by character. Pantomime became more and more expressly tailored for the camera—the sad smile with only the face visible, the upper part of a body with hands plucking and fluttering in nervous excitement, the eyes revealing remorse or anger or frustrated passion. Richer and subtler characterizations began to replace the broad and simple performances of the first dramatic films. Faces and bodies, cut up and reassembled in edited sequence, were made to achieve a new precision of expression. Griffith commanded a thoughtfulness and invention from the actors in his developing stock company; with camera and cutting shears he shaped their performances into a dramatic entity that had existed initially only in his mind.

As for physical background to the action, Griffith's exterior locales were always carefully selected for their appropriateness to the events depicted and for their capacity to reinforce the mood of the story. Constructed sets in his films strike us as the real

The New York Hat ◆ U.S., 1912, D. W. Griffith; Mary Pickford.

thing even when they're not; the style is invariably naturalistic in solidity and detail. What he couldn't find on location he had carefully and fully re-created on the back lot or in the studio. Griffith was able to achieve a scale that had no theatrical precedents: real trains rushing across a wide prairie, enemy hordes encircling a besieged city. His lighting initially advanced along existing stage lines and then, as brighter lights and more sensitive emulsions became available, finally surpassed theatrical possibility. At first he and cameraman G. W. "Billy" Bitzer were content to light scenes with sharp, even clarity, using controlled sunlight for interiors as well as exteriors—standard practice at the time; yet photographically the earliest Griffith/Bitzer films stand out from those of most of their peers, as they somehow manage to look fresh and sharp even today. In addition to exact exposure and focus, this quality must have something to do with choice of emulsion and care in processing. In later work Griffith began to experiment with the effective possibilities of modulated and directional artificial light, breaking some taboos in the process. An interior night scene might be lit as if suffused by the flickering softness of the firelight, underexposed by standards then current, or what is called "low-key lighting" today. In another scene the heroine's head might be lit from behind by simulated morning light streaming in through a window so that it bounced off her blonde hair to form a halo of overexposure, "halation" in photographic terms. Some of these experiments would be expanded and refined by the Germans in the twenties, just as the Russians would further develop Griffith's editing.

Finally, Griffith was one of the leaders in the movement against the short length of films imposed by the American industry of the day. With few exceptions, the dominant companies were conservative in their adherence to established practice and their unwillingness to risk the capital that longer films would have required. At first Griffith was confined to the one-reel (ten to fifteen minutes) standard that Méliès and Porter had achieved. As film makers became more aware of the potential of the medium, they became increasingly ambitious in terms of subject matter. Larger subjects demanded more running time. In 1910 Griffith made a two-reeler entitled *His Trust,* which the studio released as two separate one-reel films. The same thing happened to his next two-reeler, *Enoch Arden,* but Griffith and others persisted until two reels became accepted as standard length. He continued to strive for more time and larger scale, and by the end of this first period of film history, he had reached a length of four reels, with *Judith of Bethulia* (1914). It was his last important film before *The Birth of a Nation,* and in narrative structure and historical spectacle it foreshadowed his even larger feature, *Intolerance.*

♦ INCREASING FILMS TO FEATURE LENGTH

In reaching feature length, Griffith had been passed by the French and the Italians. Free from the stringent limitation on running time imposed by the American industry, the Europeans had begun to exploit subjects that led naturally to films of an hour and more. Available to French film makers was a long and uniquely distinguished theatrical tradition. From as early as 1908, with *The Assassination of the Duc de Guise,* directed by Charles de Bargy, they began to turn out film versions of successful plays starring well-known players. A company called Film d'Art was the first in the field, bestowing its name on the entire shortlived subgenre. In most respects the idea was retrogressive, extending backward to Méliès, who had wanted to "push the cinema toward the theatrical way," and even to Edison, who had earlier recorded bits of popular theater. The principal difference of the *films d'art* was that the extreme deference paid to the older medium, however perverse, meant that whole plays rather than fragments were recorded exactly as performed. Intertitles were abridged substitutions for the unheard dialogue the actors mouthed. Except for the new length required, it was back to the camera in twelfth row center, the scene recorded in one shot, the theatrical sets and gestures. These films did attract a certain following, however, especially among the middle class who knew or thought they ought to know the theater; and the somewhat snobbish appeal and contemporary prestige helped to drag films as a whole toward greater length.

The most consequential of the series was *Queen Elizabeth* (1912), directed by Louis Mercanton and Henri Desfontaines, and starring Sarah Bernhardt and Lou Tellegen (her leading man offstage as well as on). The divine Sarah, though sixty-eight at the time, still commanded an international audience. Unlike many theatrical artists, she seems to have been extremely interested in film. "I rely on these films to make me immortal," she is supposed to have said. Alas, for Bernhardt and for us, much of her divinity must have resided in her reputedly remarkable voice and oral

Queen Elizabeth ◆ France, 1912, Louis Mercanton and Henri Desfontaines; Sarah Bernhardt.

interpretation. What remains in *Queen Elizabeth* now seems more nearly a cruel travesty of a great talent and an exhumation of dead theatrical convention. Such problems only vaguely troubled contemporary observers however. The film was acquired for distribution in the United States by the young Adolph Zukor and played with substantial and prophetic success in converted "legitimate" theaters at the unheard of price of one dollar a ticket. It provided the first capital as well as the precedent for Famous Players Film Company, which eventually became Paramount Pictures.

Though *Queen Elizabeth* opened up the possibility for successful American distribution and exhibition of feature-length films, it was the Italians who contributed more importantly to the form that features would take—along lines close to those Griffith had begun to explore in miniature. The inclination of the Italians was toward historical and religious spectacle set in their own glorious past. The first of these, *The Last Days of Pompeii,* was produced in 1908, the same year as the first of the films d'art. *The Fall of Troy* (1910) and *Dante's Inferno* (1911), at five reels in length, continued the trend. A static and dully literal illustration of the epic poem, the *Inferno* was followed by *Quo Vadis?* (1912), at nine reels. Both were road-shown in the United States, the latter even more successfully than *Queen Elizabeth.* Noteworthy among the like films were another *Last Days of Pompeii* (1913) and *Cabiria* (1914). Of the early Italian spectacles perhaps only *Cabiria* (twelve reels), a worldwide success at the time, is of more than historical interest today. From a script credited to Gabriele D'Annunzio and directed by Giovanni Pastrone, it is placed in the Punic Wars. The plot centers around Hannibal's crossing of the Alps and the siege of Syracuse. Vast sets were employed as well as plaster models. The action is directed and shot with an unusual amount of energy and movement, and an appropriate symphonic score was specially composed. Like its predecessor *Quo Vadis?*, *Cabiria* had a definite influence on American production.

Massive in all respects, these extravaganzas not only established feature length, but they demonstrated film's superior claim over the theater to this kind of spectacle. Patterns laid down in them would be followed by Griffith, Cecil B. De Mille, and by all those who have subsequently worked in the genre. They also moved the movies out of the nickelodeons and converted stores into large theaters and auditoriums, where they were often accompanied by full orchestra. The Italian lead was lost only with the outbreak of World War I.

Cabiria ♦ Italy, 1914, Giovanni Pastrone.

During its first two decades the motion picture had advanced from vaudeville turns and brief cinematographic records of life on the street to short film narratives using the rudimentary grammar of the medium. By the end of this period the length of films had increased until precedent had been established for the feature running over an hour, which would become the staple form around which the art and the industry further developed. The subsequent consolidation of these early advances and the move towards an expanded future initially occurred mainly in the United States.

FILMS OF THE PERIOD

1894
Fun in a Chinese Laundry
(U.S., Edison Company)

1895
The Arrival of a Train at the Station
(France, Louis Lumière)
L'Arroseur arrosé (France, Lumière)
The Execution of Mary, Queen of Scots
(U.S., Edison)
Feeding the Baby (France, Lumière)
Workers Leaving the Factory (France, Lumière)

1896
A Game of Cards (France, Lumière)
The Kiss
(U.S., Edison, starring May Irwin
and John C. Rice)
The Vanishing Lady (France, Georges Méliès)

1899
The Dreyfus Affair (France, Méliès)

1900
Attack on a China Mission
(U.K., James A. Williamson)
Cinderella (France, Méliès)
Grandma's Reading Glass
(U.K., George Albert Smith)

1901
Story of a Crime (France, Ferdinand Zecca)

1902
A Trip to the Moon (France, Méliès)

1903
The Great Train Robbery
(U.S., Edwin S. Porter)
Life of an American Fireman (U.S., Porter)

1904
An Impossible Voyage (France, Méliès)

1905
Rescued by Rover (U.K., Cecil Hepworth)

1906
The Dream of a Rarebit Fiend (U.S., Porter)

1907
Ben-Hur (U.S., Sidney Olcott)
Rescued from an Eagle's Nest (U.S., Porter)

1908
The Adventures of Dollie
(U.S., David Wark Griffith)
The Assassination of the Duc de Guise
(France, Charles de Bargy)
The Last Days of Pompeii
(Italy, Luigi Maggi)

1909
The Joyous Microbes (France, Emile Cohl)
The Lonely Villa (U.S., Griffith)

1911
The Lonedale Operator (U.S., Griffith)

1912
The Conquest of the Pole (France, Mèliés)

The Musketeers of Pig Alley (U.S., Griffith)
The New York Hat (U.S., Griffith)
Queen Elizabeth
    (France, Louis Mercanton and
    Henri Desfontaines)
Quo Vadis? (Italy, Enrico Guazzoni)

1913
The Battle at Elderbush Gulch (U.S., Griffith)

1914
Antony and Cleopatra (Italy, Guazzoni)
Cabiria (Italy, Giovanni Pastrone)

BOOKS ON THE PERIOD

Barnes, John, *Pioneers of the British Film* (Vol. 3, "The Beginnings of the Cinema in England, 1894–1901"). London: Bishopsgate Press, 1988

Barnes, John, *Filming the Boer War* (Vol. 4, "The Beginnings of the Cinema in England, 1894–1901"). London: Bishopsgate Press, 1992

Bowser, Eileen, *The Transformation of Cinema, 1907–1915 (Vol. 2, "History of the American Cinema").* New York: Charles Scribner's Sons, 1990

de Cordova, Richard, *Picture Personalities: The Emergence of the Star System in America.* Champaign: University of Illinois Press, 1990

Elsaesser, Thomas, ed., *Early Cinema: Space-Frame-Narrative.* London: British Film Institute, 1990

Fell, John, ed., *Before Hollywood: Turn-of-the-Century American Film.* New York: Hudson Hills, 1987

Gunning, Tom, *D. W. Griffith and the Origins of American Narrative Film: The Early Years at Biograph.* Champaign: University of Illinois Press, 1991

Jesionowski, Joyce E., *Thinking in Pictures: Dramatic Structure in D. W. Griffith's Biograph Films.* Berkeley: University of California Press, 1987

MacCann, Richard Dyer, *The First Film Makers.* (Vol. 2, "American Movies: The First Thirty Years"). Metuchen, NJ: Scarecrow Press, 1989

Musser, Charles, *Before the Nickelodeon: Edwin S. Porter and the Edison Manufacturing Company.* Berkeley: University of California Press, 1991

Musser, Charles, ed., *The Emergence of Cinema: The American Screen to 1907* (Vol. 1, "History of the American Cinema"). New York: Charles Scribner's Sons, 1990

Pearson, Roberta E. *Eloquent Gestures: The Transformation of Performance Style in the Griffith Biograph Films.* Berkeley: University of California Press, 1992

2

Rise of the American Film

♦ ♦ ♦

1914–1919

Except for the United States, the major film producing countries—France, Germany, Great Britain, and Italy—were involved in World War I from its outbreak. The United States did not enter the war until 1917, and then our participation was far less than total. Since some of the materials required for the manufacture of high explosives are the same as those for photographic film (cotton, and nitric and sulfuric acids), film stock was in short supply abroad. A much more serious effect of war on European film producers was the curtailment of international distribution of completed films. Nations were separated from each other by battle lines; transportation was unavailable for many nonmilitary purposes; and the large American audience lay three thousand miles across a submarine-infested ocean.

Though the French and the Italians had been the first to arrive at feature-length films, the United States was now in a position to pursue that development as no other country could. With its sizeable moviegoing public, an economy stimulated rather than drained by war, a tradition of business expertise, and film makers of considerable inventiveness and occasional genius, the United States had a crucial advantage at this important stage. The Americans made full use of their resources, and that is to their credit. If there had not been that four-year lead at exactly that historical moment, however, the subsequent domination of the world's screens by the United States might never have occurred, at least not to the extent that it has.

As it happened, during the second half of the teens, the Americans were the ones who expanded the art to a fuller expression, discovered the sorts of ingredients that would make the entertainment universally popular, and devised systems of manufacture, wholesaling, and retailing that could support the new expensiveness of feature production. In the United States during those years were three parallel develop-ments that deserve particular attention. First, was the culmination of Griffith's ear-lier experimentation in film form, his first features. Second, there began the quite special tradition of American screen comedy in the output of Mack Sennett and his co-workers, most notably Charles Chaplin. Finally, the new and prototypical systems of mass production, distribution, and exhibition evolved—with Thomas H. Ince among the leaders in organizing production—laying the groundwork for subsequent economic expansion.

◆ THE FIRST MASTERPIECES

We tend to apply the term *masterpiece* to artistic works of large size—to *War and Peace* first, and only then to *Pride and Prejudice*, which may even be qualified as a "small masterpiece." Griffith worked on both the large and the small scale. Many of his films that have aged well, or his scenes remembered with greatest pleasure, are close, intimate studies of character and feeling (for example, *Broken Blossoms*, 1919) or selective and heightened observations of everyday life in small-town America (*True Heart Susie*, 1919). Still, what was needed to shake film completely free from the stage, in a way so conspicuous that no one could fail to understand, was probably the kind of spectacular grandeur represented by Griffith's *The Birth of a Nation* (1915) and *Intolerance* (1916). Except for their length and expensiveness, any other single element of these two films could no doubt be found in one or more of the more than four hundred shorter Griffith films preceding them, especially in those produced from 1912 on. To bring together all these contributions, however, under complete control and on such a gigantic scale, was a truly staggering accomplishment. Nothing like these two films—in their size and intricacy of conception and in their mingling of history with passionate argument—had appeared before them.

The Birth of a Nation is the paradigm for the successful "big" Hollywood movie, through *Gone With the Wind* (1939) to Ridley Scott's *1492: Conquest of Paradise* (1992), and beyond. It also established the technique and style of film making that has come to be called classic Hollywood cinema. Today *The Birth of a Nation* may not be quite the fresh revelation of the breathtaking power of the screen that it was for its first audiences; still, it is an overwhelming experience, particularly when properly presented at silent rather than sound speed with a good print and the original music. It can come alive for those who can free themselves from unjustified feelings of superiority to any film not in a current idiom, those who can accept Griffith's artistic postulates and understand that his racial attitudes are embedded in the myths and memories that formed such a dominant part of his life.

After completing *Judith of Bethulia* in 1913 (four reels, twice as long as any film he had previously made), Griffith left his first employer, the Biograph Company. Apparently he was restive under commercial restraints that had prevented him from proceeding to even larger projects. It is not clear to what extent Griffith was influ-enced by the Italian features; internal evidence suggests that *Intolerance* may owe more to them than does *Birth*. Griffith claimed he was not influenced, and associates like Lillian Gish have testified that he was so busy making films he rarely took time to see any. He was working along lines similar to the Italian's, however, and their successes must have acted as competitive stimuli, if not as models, demonstrating that the kind of thing he was trying to do could be done. In any case, after joining the small independent firm called Mutual, where he directed some routine productions to meet the payroll, he began to plan the huge film on the Civil War and Reconstruction that became *The Birth of a Nation.* Most of the latter part of the film was based on Thomas Dixon's novel *The Clansman* and the successful play made from it; there are lesser borrowings from Dixon's *The Leopard's Spots* and other sources.

The Birth of a Nation broke all sorts of precedents. Even in production, its cost, approximately $110,000, was five times greater than the next largest sum spent on an American film up to that time. (*Judith of Bethulia* had cost $23,000—the most spent on a film prior to *Birth,* according to Seymour Stern, one of Griffith's biographers.) Having run through his backers' money, Griffith invested what he could raise and borrow on his own to finish it. There were six weeks of rehearsal; shooting extended from July into October of 1914; editing took another three months. This overall production time contrasted with the average in those days of six weeks or less. When completed, *Birth's* length was an unprecedented three hours. It was accompanied throughout by a symphonic score specially composed by Joseph Carl Briel, and was the first American film to be so treated.

In 1915 it opened as *The Clansman* in Los Angeles, and then as *The Birth of a Nation* in New York. This title change was suggested by Dixon, the author of the novel, who felt something was needed to suggest the epic scope of Griffith's achievement. The new title referred to the end of the sovereignty of the states, achieved by the victory over secession. Though it played in "legitimate" theaters for as much as two dollars per ticket, it has been estimated that the first six months of its national run drew more people than had attended all the performances of all the stage plays in the United States during any given five-year period. More than merely a motion picture, it was a cultural phenomenon that everyone felt obliged to witness. Because of its evident racial biases, it created enormous controversy, even riots, and the notoriety attracted still more customers.

Since it was distributed on a "states' rights" basis, with lump sums paid for regional distribution franchises, there are no accurate figures of what *Birth* earned at the box office. *Variety* estimated that it had grossed as much as $50 million, and until recent years it was acknowledged as the top money-maker of all time. It continues in active circulation among film societies and in nontheatrical series and academic courses, and receives occasional theatrical revivals. No doubt it is playing somewhere on the globe at this moment, and it is still capable of provoking picketing and threats of worse by civil rights groups who want to protect audiences from its depiction of African Americans.

Aside from the racial content (to be dealt with later), what may strike you most strongly about the film is the sheer massiveness of its subject. Part I deals with the North and South in the days before the War Between the States (as Griffith would have called it) and with the war itself; Part II covers the Reconstruction period in the South. The whole is much more than an "epic" in the vulgarized entertainment sense of a film loaded with extras; instead, it is a genuine effort to treat a national epoch in the fullest possible way.

Griffith's strategy included the portrayal of invented personalities who touch upon the salient aspects of national events. Partly through the social positions and vocations of the characters—who help shape the historical forces at work as well as representing those persons affected by the forces—a structural pattern was created that allowed for the large canvas to be colored and infused with personal drama. Historical tableaux frame and punctuate the fictional plot: the first slaves landing in Virginia, Lincoln brooding at night in the White House, Grant and Lee at Appomattox. (Griffith would use this sort of organization again in *Intolerance*, *Orphans of the Storm* [1921], and other historical works.) The fusing of fiction with history dates at least from Homer and was standard practice with Sir Walter Scott and other historical novelists; Griffith drew more or less consciously on nineteenth-century literary precedents for the shaping of his stories.

The dramatic parallels Griffith employed among his characters don't seem excessively schematic, given the full and lifelike detail of the incidents surrounding them. There are the two families, one northern and one southern, whose children become acquainted at a northern school—as they might well have done, given the southern aristocracy's practice of educating their sons in the North. The northern father, the Honorable Austin Stoneman, Leader of the House, is a powerful abolitionist politician (clearly modeled on Thaddeus Stevens, leader in the House of Representatives and a prime factor in the passing of Reconstruction legislation). He is a widower whose dead wife has been succeeded by a scheming, mulatto housekeeper. The southern father, Dr. Cameron, is an aging, wealthy planter with a gentle wife, thoroughly part of a chivalric tradition. Each family thus represents one of the strong causative elements in the impending conflict.

Because of their acquaintanceship, the invented characters can cross back and forth into each others' lives and surroundings: a friendly visit before the war, a fatal meeting on the battlefield, an encounter in a prisoner-of-war hospital, or the final merging through the postwar northern "occupation" of the South. They come in contact with actual personages at historical moments: when the Confederate mother approaches the Union president to plead for clemency for her captured son, or when a brother and sister attend the play at the Ford Theatre on the night the president is assassinated, and so on. The fictional characters' lives are lived within the re-created events and conditions of those times. Griffith's structuring is also strangely persuasive, drawing us into an understanding and sympathy, if we will allow it. President Woodrow Wilson, historian and southerner, is said to have exclaimed after seeing the film that it was "like writing history in lightning." After controversy arose over the film, the White House disavowed any approval on the part of the president.

It is the quality of passion that made *The Birth of a Nation* not only a *succès d'estime* but a *succès de scandale*. Though based in part on Dixon's novel, Griffith re-created the narrative world according to his own viewpoint. Born in Kentucky in 1875, he absorbed an understanding of the war and Reconstruction from his father—Colonel "Roaring Jake" Griffith of the Confederate Cavalry. The attitudes about black people in *Birth* are so much part of the total view of life the film encompasses that

Griffith was evidently shocked when he was accused of racism. Incidents like those in the film had in fact occurred, he argued (and had even footnoted some of the scenes in intertitles). He no doubt felt that many of the emancipated slaves had indeed been ignorant and shiftless by anyone's standards, and that it would be false to present them otherwise. On the other hand, his position was that he understood and loved black people better than did his attackers; some of his best friends were "colored," he seemed to be saying.

Thoroughly embodied in the film, however, is an assumption of innate inferiority of black people. The bad, usually those of mixed blood, are led by evil or misguided white men, are vicious and greedy for power, and line up with the northerners. The good are dependent and childlike, and support the white South. Bad or good, these blacks are given few individual attributes apart from caste role and function, and viewers today feel more uneasy with Griffith's approving patronization of "the faithful souls" than with his treatment of the villains.

Whatever documentation and evidence he might offer, it is the very unconsciousness of his assumption of black inferiority, that "that was how it was," that is most disturbing. The way in which this strand becomes an integral part of a credible whole makes it particularly effective "propaganda." The conviction of the film carries viewers along, and it is impossible to put aside one aspect of it as an aberration. Because the biases are so uncalculated and rawly emotional in their appeal, they may even get past our intellectual defenses. Given the film's enormous popularity, Griffith's assumptions must have been shared by a substantial number of his white contemporaries.

The nastiest aspect of Griffith's portrayal of black-white relationships is also the one closest to the national nerve—his obsession with possible sexual intermingling of the races. Would you want your sister to be molested by or married to a Negro? Griffith asks. For him the two possible fates exert an equally morbid fascination: Marriage to a black man is presented as unthinkable except as equivalent to rape. The much more prevalent forced submission of black women to white men is dealt with by Griffith only through the congressman's weakness for his housekeeper. This is presented as close to a pathological failing on his part, with the woman exercising what is clearly a sexually based power over him. Stoneman's horrified reaction to his black political protégé's asking for his daughter's hand is of a piece with the rest. Perhaps more than any other white character in the film, the congressman seems to exist solely for rhetorical purposes.

On the other hand, ambiguities are present in the attempted attack on Flora Cameron (Mae Marsh) by the renegade black, Gus, and in the behavior of mulatto politician Silas Lynch with Elsie Stoneman (Lillian Gish), as Lynch tries to force her into a marriage. Gus sets out to make advances of some sort to Flora; in fact, he has told her that he is interested in marriage. But his behavior seems to change gradually until it could be argued, from the evidence on the screen, that he ends by trying to calm her so that she won't cause harm to herself: "Wait, missie, I won't hurt yeh," Gus says. She answers, "Stay away or I'll jump!" He doesn't come any nearer, but she jumps. As presented, it is her hysterical fear, rather than anything Gus does, that motivates her fatal leap.

As for Elsie Stoneman's plight, her reactions seem so exaggerated that the hyperbolic irrationality of her response makes one aware of the obsessions underlying her fears (though Griffith surely didn't intend this implication). A false marriage could be annulled, you might well think, at least outside the spell of the film; it is the prospect of consummation that Griffith expects us to sweat over. Silas's behavior appears in part pathetic, as does Gus's, instead of seeming fixed as evil and cruel. In contrast, the climax of the film is entirely unambiguous: The white men prepare to bash in the skulls of their women if the black troops should break into the cabin. Here, it can only be conceded that if the action proposed seems tacitly approved by Griffith, it might also have been consistent with the feelings of the people upon whom the characters were based and those of the audience.

There are many who cannot accept the content of Griffith's films—not just the racial bias in *Birth*, but the sentimentality and melodramatics that color so much of his presentation and possibly his view of life. Even in his own time, his conception—rooted in nineteenth-century Victorianism—apparently came to seem increasingly old-fashioned and irrelevant to his audiences. Some critics—unable to allow for what is essentially a style, a set of conventions, a way of thinking about people and events—have tended to deplore the content while praising the form. Though other artists are infrequently subjected to this sort of dichotomy (such a separation is generally regarded as an aesthetic impossibility), perhaps a similar situation existed with the dramatists immediately preceding Shakespeare, those who fashioned the framework on which the great Elizabethan plays would be created.

In Griffith's case, it is evidently felt by some that so many unknown techniques had to be discovered and mastered in the early days of this new art form that little could be expected from what was being said. This position seems to imply, on the one hand, that any old material lying about could be pressed into service for purposes of formal experimentation; and, on the other, that Griffith was a generally silly and sometimes innocently vicious man with an innate and intuitive feeling for the language of the new medium. Perhaps a contrary proposition deserves more study: the possibility that Griffith developed the tools and materials of film precisely in order to deal, in the most effective manner possible, with what interested him. In either case, those who regard him as an artistically inspired child, and those who can see through the conventional artistic trappings of an earlier literature and theater to a validity and dignity in his view of humankind agree that in *The Birth of a Nation* his formal control over the medium achieved an unprecedented power.

From his overall conception of before, during, and after the war to the sequences that make up those parts, the scenes within the sequences, and the shots which comprise the scenes, the selection and balance are clearly and brilliantly thought out. The camera is positioned so that each shot is sure and precise in its meaning. The editing together of these shots leads an audience's perception; it tightens or loosens the emotional intensity with complete assurance and understanding of the aesthetic-psychological factors involved. Take, for instance, the scene at the Ford Theatre, which culminates with Lincoln's assassination. It begins with an iris of Elsie and her brother Phil taking their seats and speaking to acquaintances; the image opens up to a full screen of the front of the theater, taken from above and side, showing stage,

The Birth of a Nation ◆ U.S., 1915, D. W. Griffith.

orchestra, boxes, gallery (18 seconds). Then there is a medium closeup of Phil and Elsie as she looks through opera glasses (3 seconds). An intertitle announces, "The play: 'Our American Cousin,' starring Laura Keene" (4 seconds).

After this economical exposition, Griffith proceeds with the start of the perform-ance, leaving Elsie and Phil momentarily; he continues to vary the angle, distance, and duration of shots to give us a heightened sense of the mood and tempo of the public event. An intertitle states, "Time, 8:30. The Arrival of the President, Mrs. Lincoln, and party." With this, Griffith cross-cuts from the slightly ominous, dark and shadowy stairs in back of the boxes, as Lincoln and his party ascend, to the presiden-tial box as seen from the theater auditorium, with the first of the party entering. As Lincoln comes forward there is a medium shot of the box (4.5 seconds). Then Griffith returns to a medium closeup of Phil and Elsie, who evidently see the President, applaud and rise (6 seconds). This intimate framing is followed by a reestablishing long shot of the theater, with the audience now standing and cheering (2.5 seconds). And so it continues on through the tragic denouement.[1]

[1]This and the following shot lists are taken from Theodore Huff, *A Shot Analysis of D. W. Griffith's The Birth of a Nation* (New York: The Museum of Modern Art, 1961).

Consider, too, the shorter, simpler, but extraordinarily moving scene of Ben Cameron's return from the war. (Ben, the Little Colonel, is played by Henry B. Walthall.) After an intertitle, "The homecoming" (less than 1 second), there is a long shot of the street and the Cameron front yard: Everything is in need of repair; the columns are scorched, the fence is falling apart, the street and sidewalks are littered. Ben enters left background, shattered and weary; he pauses, leans against the fence, and looks about at the marks of war. Limping, he walks slowly and weakly forward along the fence (34.5 seconds). In medium closeup in the living room, his younger sister, Flora, is by a mirror admiring the effect of "southern ermine" (strips of raw cotton daubed with soot) decorating her dress. Ben's older sister, Margaret, and his mother hurry in, indicating that they have seen Ben coming; Margaret runs to the door and back; all run out of the room (18 seconds). Medium shot of the hall: The three rush forward, excited, joined by the father (6 seconds). Medium long shot of Ben pausing by the gate, opening it, supporting himself against it a moment and then going in (11 seconds). Medium long shot of the family, waiting in the hall breathlessly, smiling at Flora's excitement (3.5 seconds). Medium long shot of the front yard as Ben comes to the porch (7.5 seconds). Medium long shot of the family in the hall; Flora rushes forward (4.5 seconds). Medium shot of the porch as Ben climbs the steps; Flora comes out the door and meets him, smiling. They gaze at each other; she points to his worn and dirty uniform; he pulls off a piece of her "ermine." She explains, giggles, points to a hole in his hat. They both pause and gaze off into space, thinking

The Birth of a Nation ◆ U.S., 1915, D. W. Griffith; Mae Marsh and Henry B. Walthall.

of all that has happened. Suddenly they stop pretending. Flora starts to cry, and embraces Ben; he looks into the distance, kisses her hair, pats her. They start into the house arm in arm (57 seconds). Medium shot from side angle of the front door: Ben and Flora start in; a woman's arm comes from inside and encircles Ben's shoulders, gently drawing him and Flora in (17.5 seconds). Fade-out.

The shots in this latter example have a much longer average duration than those in the opening scene in the Ford Theatre. Here much more emotional content is conveyed by each shot, especially by the first two and last two. Only against Griffith's usual practice of presenting a scene from varying points of view in a rapid succession of shots did the tension of the Little Colonel's slow movement within that static frame (and the arm of the unseen mother appearing to encircle him) achieve the kind of eloquence it possesses. In the pre-Griffith years such a shot was the invariable standard in which an action took place, and thus it was not useful for special emphasis. An analogy might be made to silence, which had no dramatic meaning until the coming of sound: There had to be sound, and the cessation of sound, before silence had significance. Not until the camera was freed to interrupt the action, which would then be synthesized through editing, could a long-running wide-angle shot be used for contrasting emphasis.

As a final example, there is a famous single shot into which Griffith compresses a maximum amount of symbolic meaning. It opens with the screen dark except for an

The Birth of a Nation ♦ U.S., 1915, D. W. Griffith.

iris in the lower left-hand corner—in which we see a woman and three children huddled next to the ruins of a destroyed home on a hilltop. They look bedraggled and anguished. Then we are shown the cause in a slow pan to the right, while the iris gradually opens to reveal a column of troops stretching off into the distance, with burning and pillaging evident in the valley below. The shot lasts 34 seconds. In this complex and changing composition Griffith tellingly presents and protests the calculated ruthlessness of Sherman's march to the sea, giving individual human meaning to the large scale by starting with the poignant detail of the effects of this destruction on an innocent family. The shot ends with a pan back from the troops to the mother and children.

Performances in *The Birth of a Nation* are advanced well beyond the conventions of stage pantomime, and clearly grow out of a sense of real persons moving through the surroundings and incidents of life. Though simplified and heightened for dramatic communication without spoken words, the gestures and expressions are generally toned down in comparison with other contemporary films and Griffith's own earlier work. For example, the contrast with *The Battle* (1911—a sort of sketch for *The Birth*) is quite marked. There is some exaggeration in the young people's high jinks, which Griffith associates with youthful good spirits; Mae Marsh is fluttery—painfully so if projected at twenty-four frames per second; and the villainies or buffooneries of the blacks appear caricatured to modern eyes. But by and large, the acting style seems quite consciously created for the silent camera, rather than being a theatrical performance recorded by it. Henry B. Walthall and Lillian Gish rise considerably above minimum expectations to create characterizations unrivaled on the screen up to that time, comparable to the best that the mature silent film would offer. The subtlety and intensity of their playing do much to imbue the whole with its sense of loss and sadness, of feelings warped and impoverished by the cruel demands of the historic time.

The care in selection and design of interiors and exteriors surpasses historical re-creation to achieve a semblance of documentary veracity that makes the past seem present. So vividly real and particularized are the interior settings that the rooms look lived in. The huge, period tableaux grow out of a vision that makes them come alive: the ball on the eve of battle, the gigantic battlefield scenes, the gathering and ride of the Klan, the rioting and fighting in the streets. These sequences are staggering not only in their size but in their lifelike energy and the way their parts fit into the whole. Above all, we are impressed by the control Griffith exerts, even on this scale, to make the scenes function exactly as he wants them to, full of human meaning as well as historical spectacle.

Before *The Birth of a Nation* was released, Griffith had completed a feature to be called *The Mother and the Law*, its opening sequences based on an actual incident of conflict and violence in a contemporary labor dispute. After the grandeur of *The Birth*, however, particularly after its enormous success on the one hand and the angry criticism it provoked on the other, *The Mother and the Law* must have seemed an inadequate successor. As part of *The Birth* controversy, Griffith had published a pamphlet entitled *The Rise and Fall of Free Speech in America*. Then, apparently wanting to align himself clearly on the side of unquestionable social and moral rectitude to show his detractors how they had misunderstood him, and perhaps to castigate those he felt had been intolerant toward him, he conceived an even more elaborate narrative structure than that of *The Birth*. Added to *The Mother and the Law* were three other stories, set in widely disparate historical periods and cultures. These four stories, according to a title prefacing the multilayered whole, would show "how hatred and intolerance, through the ages, have battled against love and charity." This undertaking—perhaps the most ambitious in conception and largest in size of any film ever produced in the United States—became *Intolerance*, released in 1916.

The three stories added to the modern story were a re-creation of the fall of Babylon to the Persians (539 B.C.); vignettes from the life of Christ (27 A.D.), culminating in the crucifixion; and an account of the massacre of Protestant Huguenots in France on St. Bartholomew's Eve (1572). If the stories had been told consecutively (as in later anthologies of filmed short stories from Wilde, Maugham, or O'Henry), the task would have been difficult enough. But Griffith's design went even further, using intercutting so that narratives and characters became subservient to the overriding theme. He began with the modern story up to a certain point of development; then

Intolerance ♦ U.S., 1916, D. W. Griffith; Robert Harron and Mae Marsh, seated.

Intolerance ◆ U.S., 1916, D. W. Griffith.

he moved to Jerusalem and an episode from the life of Christ; then to the introduction of the plotting at court in sixteenth-century France; back to the modern story; on to the beginning of the Babylonian sequences; then to the modern story again; and so on.

These parts are announced, separated, and connected with an image of "The Woman Who Rocks the Cradle" (Lillian Gish) accompanied by Whitmanesque titles: "Endlessly rocks the cradle—Uniter of Here and Hereafter—Chanter of Sorrows," or "Out of the cradle endlessly rocking . . . " Later, as the tension in each of the stories increases, Griffith cuts ever more rapidly from one to another without interruption. Of this complex polyphonic form, with the separate parts all progressing simultaneously, he said:

> *[the] stories will begin like four currents looked at from a hilltop. At first the four currents will flow apart, slowly and quietly. But as they flow, they grow nearer and nearer together, and faster and faster, until in the end, in the last act, they mingle in one mighty river of expressed emotion.*[2]

[2] Quoted by Lewis Jacobs, *The Rise of the American Film* (New York: Harcourt, Brace, 1939), p. 189.

Intolerance ◆ U.S., 1916, D. W. Griffith; Lillian Gish.

In order to finance this colossal spectacle Griffith used all his profits from *The Birth of a Nation*, finally buying out the other backers when they lost their nerve. The total cost of the picture is said to have been $1.9 million; it has been estimated that it would cost well over $40 million to achieve the same results today. The sets of French streets, houses, and castle are all full scale, solid, and practicable. Babylon, constructed on a 254-acre site along Sunset Boulevard, is the most overwhelming: Its towers rise 200 feet; its walls are wide enough at their tops to allow two chariots to pass; and it took hundreds of extras to fill the courtyard and balconies in the film's victory celebration. *Intolerance* originally ran close to four hours, longer than *Birth*, and again Joseph Carl Briel composed a special score arranged to Griffith's specifications.

As he had done with *Birth*, Griffith followed *Intolerance* on its openings in Los Angeles and New York. Not satisfied with audience reactions, he continued to edit, rearranging and cutting the positive print being used for projection. Though some critics praised the film lavishly, the public seemed to find the disjunctive organization and unprecedented length confusing and exhausting. The final climactic passages become almost an assault on optical nerves as well as on emotions, as the cutting tempo increases to many shots no longer than five frames. Also, the thematic material was out of keeping with the national mood by the time the film was released.

Intolerance ♦ U.S., 1916, D. W. Griffith.

Brotherly love was going out of fashion. President Wilson, who had been reelected on an isolationist peace platform, asserting that the United States was too proud to fight, was soon moving with the country itself towards entry into World War I. Who could be tolerant of the loathesome "Hun" who was bayoneting Belgian women and children and was seemingly about to sweep over the whole face of Europe? The sentimental idealism of *Intolerance* carries nothing of the direct conviction of *The Birth of a Nation*, and was as dismal a financial failure as the preceding film had been an unrivaled success.

Griffith's career was deflected and probably permanently damaged by the necessity of paying the debts incurred with *Intolerance*. In a desperate effort to recoup some of the losses, he cut into the original negative, without printing a copy, to make versions of *The Mother and the Law* and *The Fall of Babylon*, which were subsequently released separately. As a result of these mutilations, copies of *Intolerance* that exist today are reduced approximations of the original. Even so, the overall effect is undeniably impressive. In many ways it is an advance on *The Birth of a Nation*. What it lacks in coherence and genuine passion it makes up in the sweeping imaginativeness of conception and increased perfection of technique.

Intolerance was to have an influence on film history quite disproportionate to its lack of popular appeal. After the war, Lenin arranged for it to tour the Soviet Union, where it ran continuously for ten years. Very likely Lenin was most interested in the portrayal of exploitative and repressive managerial classes in the modern story—Griffith's viewpoint being strongly anticapital and prolabor. But two future giants of Soviet cinema, Sergei Eisenstein and V.I. Pudovkin, saw much more in it than that. Griffith had shown them how argument (education and propaganda) could be conveyed through dramatic incident, and how its effectiveness could be heightened by the dynamics of editing. (Indeed, the strike in Pudovkin's *Mother* has some direct borrowings from *Intolerance*.) Most of what the Soviet masters formalized and articulated in theories of montage, Griffith had understood intuitively. In *Intolerance* the evolving unity rests on generalized idea and emotion—rather than solely on characters' decisions that forward a plot—and depends upon the unique resources of the film medium. Through skillful juxtaposition of images, disjunctive in physical place-time but related by each phase of the developing theme, the effect of the whole becomes greater than the sum of its parts.

In other respects *Intolerance* represents Griffith's growing mastery over the medium. The alternation between large vista and small human detail (the page boy sleeping in the throne room of Charles V, or the fat woman throttling her dance partner when he steps on her toes) is even more assured. Performances are completely non-stagelike and are carefully broken into shots, with especially forceful use of closeups (for example, the often cited shot of Mae Marsh's twisting hands in the courtroom, or Little Brown Eyes' face, enormous and haunting in the St. Bartholomew's Eve massacre). Griffith and Bitzer carried their experimentation with framing and lighting further than ever. Considerable camera movement was introduced: the long, cranelike dolly into Belshazzar's palace courtyard; the pan across the seated women in the marriage market, not to follow action but to compel our close attention to the women. There is some exterior night shooting in the Babylonian battle scenes which seems almost impossible at that time. The full range of irises, fades, superimpositions, and masking (a CinemaScope shape to present the sun court of Cyrus) are employed throughout—all done in the camera. In total, *Intolerance* is felt by many to represent Griffith's fullest achievement; for all it must stand as one of the great landmarks in the history of film.

◆ A TRADITION OF SCREEN COMEDY IS ESTABLISHED

At about the time Griffith was contributing a new flexibility and power to screen language, a distinctive line of American film comedy began that would produce its own geniuses and masterworks. Although contrasting strongly with Griffith's high seriousness and Victorian sentimentality (in fact, sometimes subjecting those qualities to parody), the early film comics nonetheless contributed importantly to solving some basic problems of the art form that preoccupied Griffith. Given funny-looking people behaving oddly in situations filled with humor, the amount of laughter obtained could still vary considerably, depending on how it was presented. The requirements of pictorial narrative, the selection and arrangement of shots, were as important to the effectiveness of the comedians as they were to Griffith. One of Griffith's former co-workers and informal students, Mack Sennett, came to understand this newly evolved technique and put it into practice for comic purposes. Like Griffith, Sennett didn't invent so much as he applied the insights gained from his own and others' experiments. His essential contribution was to fashion a kind of systematic, though unarticulated, comic aesthetic that would become a standard basis from which others would continue to develop.

As with most film genres, screen comedy was present in embryonic form from the very beginning—in fact, before the screen (for instance, *Fred Ott's Sneeze*, 1893, one of Edison's peep-show Kinetoscope fragments). Other early Edisons included visual records of comic vaudeville skits: *Fun in a Chinese Laundry* (1894) involved a chase, a policeman, and a thrown prop (not yet a pie), foreshadowing the later Sennett Keystone comedies—as did, even more clearly, the brief but fully developed *A Wringing Good Joke* (1896). Then there were the French "trick films" begun by Méliès and added to, most notably, by Ferdinand Zecca and Emile Cohl. In these the "trickery" was usually designed for humorous as well as fantastic effect; for example, pumpkins roll off a wagon and bounce around town creating all sorts of havoc (*The Pumpkin Race*, Cohl, 1907). Méliès's *An Adventurous Automobile Trip* (1905) in many ways foreshadows Sennett's later fun with Model Ts.

It was another Frenchman, Max Linder, who from 1905 on established most clearly a pattern for the kinds of visual incongruities and surprises that were to screen comedy what verbal gags were to stage vaudeville and burlesque. The comic figure he created was a dapper, upper-class man-about-town involved with a hard-hearted lady love. Sennett admitted to having studied Linder closely, and Sennett's most brilliant discovery, Charles Chaplin, was even more obviously in Linder's debt. In Chaplin's first films for Sennett, before he developed his tramp persona, his costume and mannerisms not only suggest his own English music-hall background, but also bear a resemblance to the smoothly maladroit and somewhat effete dandy that Linder had created. Sennett's work, however, which started a main line of film comedy lasting from 1912 (the year the Keystone Company was founded) on through the twenties and into the first years of sound, was vigorously and indigenously American. It was he who earned the broad popularity for the style known as *slapstick*, upon which Chaplin was to ring his own, subtler changes.

Whatever other influences there were, the precedents offered by Porter and Griffith would serve Sennett as a way of structuring his films. The chase, characteristic of the filmed action-melodramas, could be used for comedy as well as for pure suspense. With exciting action situations as backbone, comic muscle and flesh were added. Perhaps the essentials of the method can best be demonstrated by suggesting a composite Keystone comedy made up of remembered scenes from several of the actual comedies. It opens in a bungalow bedroom, with two seedy-looking robbers climbing through the window. They waken the rotund homeowner at gun point, gag him, tie him to a conveniently available hot water heater which they set at HOT (insert of gauge); they rifle his bureau, scoop up valuables, and leave. A freckle-faced, gaptoothed urchin peers in the window, sees the trouble, and sets off, presumably to summon help. (Note the similarity so far to Porter and Griffith.)

Cut to the interior of a police station, where an out-sized sergeant sporting a large brush of mustache (Mack Swain) is snoozing at the desk. He bounces awake, answers the phone, then shouts off screen. A gaggle of policemen stumble over each other through a door and line up in front of the desk. An odder collection of physical types would be hard to imagine. There's a tall skinny one (Slim Summerville), a fat one (Roscoe "Fatty" Arbuckle), a wildly cross-eyed one (Chester Conklin), and so on. A number of them are decorated with bizarre mustaches, beards, and sideburns. Uniforms are too large or too small, and parts are as apt to be on backwards as not. They twitch and weave in an irregular line as the sergeant shouts at them, then they rush toward a door leading outside. Emerging onto the sidewalk, they jump into a couple of open jalopies at the curb. The floor on the rear car gives way under the impact. Its occupants then leap in with the others in the front car, though one can scarcely believe it is holding them all. Starting up rapidly in reverse, they crash into the rear car, which then totally collapses. Roaring out into the street, they barely slip in front of an oncoming truck; zigzagging from one side to the other, they obliviously scatter

Unidentified Keystone comedy ♦ U.S., 1913, Mack Sennett; Sennett, with raised club, and Fred Mace, seated.

pedestrians and opposing traffic in their wake. An undercranked camera speeds up the movement to a surreal tempo.

Back in the bedroom, the nightgowned captive is still spread-eagled on a now swelling boiler. The needle of the gauge moves from HOT to BOILING and towards DANGER and EXPLOSION. Return to the police car, now careening along a highway at an improbable speed; the cops are all standing, overflowing the sides, peering ahead, gesticulating frenetically with their elbows in each others' faces.

Cut to a single file of laborers walking along a country road; the shovel on the shoulder of the last man catches a detour sign and turns it to point to a road other than the one it had been indicating. The police arrive in the patrol car, pause, zip backward and forward, then drive off on the route we know is not the detour. Coming down a hill at breakneck speed, they fail to stop as the road dead-ends into a lake; instead, they go straight off the end of a pier, and submerge. On the other side of the lake, they emerge unfazed, still going full tilt towards their destination; and so on, with other impediments, other cross-cuts to the bulging boiler distending the fat man's stomach, until the final rescue.

Several things are noteworthy about this kind of comic invention. For instance, it is clear that the same Porter/Griffith excitement and suspense of crime, chase, and rescue or capture are here turned into comedy by visual and emotional exaggeration. Also, a recognizably real world (unlike that of Méliès) is madly distorted as if certain

Keystone Kops in an unidentified comedy   ◆   U.S., ca. 1914–19, Mack Sennett.

physical laws (of gravity, acceleration, solidity of objects, and the like) operated eccentrically or not at all. The incongruity between what is expected in the real world and what happens in Sennett's universe extends throughout the films. The pleasure we get from this sportive tampering with the expected is the same as would later be offered in animated cartoons. We know that floorboards usually remain in cars, that boilers have no rubbery elasticity, that humans and machines move at predictable speeds, and that no one can drive along the bottom of a lake and come up on the other side; still, it's fun to have the unlikely made manifest. As for the people in Sennett's films, they are incredibly incompetent; also, it is highly improbable that a random sample of beings would include the widely variant physical types and appearances of his cast. Further, they are always inhumanly unflappable: They cope with the irregularities of nature with a maniacal seriousness, only dimly aware that anything is amiss.

These funny-looking, oddball characters could be expected to send a less sophisticated, or perhaps only less inhibited, audience into gales of laughter merely by their cross-eyedness or fatness. This suggests that a certain sadistic pleasure in others' misfortunes underlies the jokes of physical discomfort that are such an integral part of silent screen comedy, including the pratfalls and the pies in the face. We enjoy the robbery victim being grilled and splayed on the water heater; the car going off the end of the pier looks like a multiple drowning, and we howl with glee. An emotional catharsis of some sort is provided by this controlled display of aggression and violence. The magical power of the characters to survive annihilation is probably also an important cathartic element. There is no death; Sennett's people are invulnerable, and we are free to indulge in comic-hysterical relief and reaction to normally destructive actions. Our laughter no doubt arises from a feeling of comfortable superiority—we are not the ones afflicted.

In Sennett's films the powerful and socially exalted characters are comic butts, helpless in the face of an onslaught by nature or one of its minions. The choice of policemen is significant in this respect. Though he would turn in his grave at any suggestion of Freudian notions about authority figures as resented parental surrogates, Sennett evidently did realize that the incongruous and the uncomfortable were a lot more humorous when inflicted on types of people who were taken seriously by society and themselves. The indignities to which the grotesque and ineffectual policemen are subjected are funnier because they *are* policemen. And if soup spilled down a back is amusing, it is at least twice as funny if the back belongs to a plump dowager in evening gown at a formal function.

By puncturing pomposity and pretension, by making the leaders and guardians his victims, Sennett heightened our enjoyment. To this extent there is a social edge to his comedy. It is usually on the side of the little guy in the audience and directed against institutions and conventions outside his sympathies. This general satirical intention was even more pointed in the Sennett parodies of certain popular films he felt suffered from pretentiousness. *Barney Oldfield's Race for Life* (1913), for example, was an early kidding of the Griffith last-minute rescue. In the 1920s the first of the epic westerns, *The Covered Wagon*, became Sennett's *The Uncovered Wagon*; Erich von Stroheim's *Foolish Wives* was lampooned in *Three Foolish Weeks*; and there was nothing quite like Ben Turpin playing a Rudolph Valentino in *The Shriek of Araby* to put passion and heroics in proper perspective.

Slapstick was as natural to the silent screen as were the action-melodramas and spectacles, and for the same reasons: It utilized those aspects of the world best communicated through the moving image, those not requiring the supplement of language. Most of us who didn't grow up in the tradition of silent comedy have trouble getting back to its essence except through the works of the later and greater clowns—Buster Keaton, Harold Lloyd, Harry Langdon, Stan Laurel and Oliver Hardy, and post-Keystone Chaplin. One difficulty in our appreciation of early silent comedies is that we too frequently see them in excerpted and anthologized snippets, projected at a speed faster than intended (which undercuts Sennett's use of fast motion for precise effect). Exaggerated music and sound effects, and perhaps a commentator's condescending asides, act as further distractions.

The essential point to be understood is that the best of Sennett had a disciplined lunacy. His work is not merely a succession of unrelated inanities; though not intellectual, it is not mindless either. When properly constructed and executed, the rules of silent comic geometry are consistent, and a coherence is built from gag to gag to entire film. A great deal of skill and control was involved. Today's beginning film students and amateur movie makers who try to burlesque that style without understanding it, let alone loving it, end with films that are silly rather than funny—films with the comic logic missing. Frequently it is only these modern-day comic film makers themselves who think their work hilarious. Sennett's humor was for the audience, who rolled in the aisles.

Sennett and his colleagues were very serious about the business of being funny. Comedy is often hard work indeed, and some of the greatest comedians are known to lack a common garden-variety sense of humor, and to be anything but the life of the party off screen. Sennett's special genius lay in understanding the construction and timing of sight gags. Careful manipulation of the standard ingredients, plus a sure feeling for what each shot includes, at what point it appears, and how long it is held on the screen, make all the difference. Start with the basic comic situation of a man falling down; make that man a ridiculously pompous, rotund, middle-aged suitor on the way to his lady love's, carrying a dainty corsage, dressed in top hat, cutaway, and striped trousers; then select, quite properly, a small boy to deflate this dignity by placing a banana peel in the man's path. The comic effectiveness of character and incident may still be profoundly altered by whether we first see the man walking and falling in long shot, then the banana peel in closeup, then the boy peering around the fence in medium shot, or whether the order of these shots is reversed so we can share the boy's anticipation and sense of achievement. Of course, the film maker must judge when the audience will have gotten the full impact of a shot, and thus cut on the rising laugh—not before, not after.

In silent comedy the gag construction could advance unimpeded: No pause was needed for lines to be heard and laughs registered. The silent film maker could build steadily, milking the visual joke for all of the variations it offered. Roars of laughter crescendoed until the comic climax was reached; only then was there a slowing of pace, a transition, and a hooking into the beginning of the next gag—which started building all over again. Ideally, the audience was left weak and helpless, weeping with laughter. It was this kind of robust creation, one uniquely suited to silent film, that Sennett mastered. His work is directly related to the cinematic technique that concerned Griffith.

The early generation of American film makers who did not get their training from Griffith got it from Sennett. His transcendently brilliant protégé was, of course, Charles Chaplin, whom George Bernard Shaw called the only genius at work in motion pictures (as he thought himself the only genius at work in theater). Sennett and his partner Adam Kessel had seen Chaplin in the Fred Karno English music hall company, which had been touring the United States extensively between 1910 and 1913. Though Kessel didn't get the name quite right, he wired off for "Charlie Chapman" at a time when Keystone's then reigning star, Ford Sterling, was being difficult about salary. Charlie's first film—entitled *Making a Living* (1914), with prophetic understatement—was pure Sennett. *Tillie's Punctured Romance*, directed by Sennett in the same year, and featuring Chaplin, Marie Dressler, Mabel Normand, Mack Swain, and Charles Bennett, is generally considered the first feature-length comedy (six reels). It too represents Sennett's slapstick humor rather than the tragicomic elaboration of Chaplin's finest work.

From later accounts by Chaplin, and from the evidence of his early films compared to his subsequent successes, it is clear that he was not altogether comfortable in Sennett's broad, knockabout style. Gradually, especially after leaving Keystone, Chaplin would develop a comedy character rich and subtle beyond anything Sennett had conceived. Chaplin made that character into one of the great comic figures (along with Falstaff, Til Eulenspiegel, Don Quixote and Sancho Panza, and the creatures of the *commedia dell'arte*). The personality and costume of the little tramp, assembled through dozens of one- and two-reelers, evolved full-blown by the end of the teens. The little fellow, ingenuously and ingeniously triumphant while maintaining his cheerfulness and dignity in an adverse world, was quickly taken to the hearts of audiences everywhere.

In addition to the creation of this persona, rounded and complex enough to encompass strains of pathos, from *The Tramp* (1915) on Chaplin developed his unique pantomimic grace, evident early in *The Rink* (1916) and *The Cure* (1917). He handled his body as a dancer would, and there is an exuberant joy in merely watching him skip through the world, pirouetting to offer himself to the blondly beautiful Edna Purviance, bounding into and out of an open utility hole without apparent hurt, or running and gliding around a table, just out of reach of the giant Eric Campbell. From large movements to small (the dissection of a clock in *The Pawnshop*, 1916), there was a constant flow of invention. Charlie turned what could be done with arms, hands, legs, feet, and stiff backbones into unexpected and sometimes unimaginable physical potential, a playful and precise bodily commentary on the human condition. And this is not to mention his uses of a Murphy bed (*One A.M.*, 1916), a lamp shade (*The Adventurer*, 1917), and other props.

The social dimension implicit in Sennett was expanded by Chaplin, and tended to preoccupy him increasingly as his career progressed. Even in this early period his films generally included some pointed observations about people in relation to soci-

The Rink ♦ U.S., 1916, Charles Chaplin; Chaplin.

ety. *Easy Street* (1917) is a veritable catalogue: The main theme of law and order includes a delightful reversal of police brutality; revivalist religion, slums, poverty, welfare, anarchists, and drug addiction are all touched on along the way. *The Immigrant* (1917) is frequently quite sardonic as well as broadly amusing in its depiction of the experiences of new arrivals in the "Land of the Free." For example, as the ship passes the Statue of Liberty, the passengers are shoved and roped in like cattle; Charlie takes a quizzical second look at the statue. In *Shoulder Arms* the satirical treatment of military life and basic antiwar stance are all the more remarkable when you realize it was released before the armistice of 1918.

Chaplin's enormous popular success and shrewd handling of the income he earned from it allowed him, throughout his career, freedom for social-political comment and a degree of artistic autonomy (which Griffith lost after the failure of *Intolerance*). Chaplin's control over his films would become unique within the art-industry. From the early twenties on, he was his own producer; his artistic virtuosity permitted him to write the scripts for, direct, star in, compose the music for, and supervise all of the other creative functions of his films. To make fully certain that his works would reach the screen exactly as he intended, in 1919 he joined Griffith, Mary Pickford, and Douglas Fairbanks to form a distribution company called United Artists. Thus Chaplin not only succeeded in preserving his independence, but was able to proceed in a way quite opposite to the centrifugal, collective forces generally at work in the industry.

♦ EMERGING PATTERNS OF INDUSTRY

The feature length of *Tillie's Punctured Romance* proved something of an exception as far as comedies were concerned. Chaplin continued at two reels until 1918, when he left Mutual and joined First National. He then began a Griffith-like extension of running time (to three reels in 1918–1919) that would lead him to intermingle features and shorts in the early twenties. Though the short comedies held their own against features in popularity, the standard program by the late teens was organized around the feature attraction, with the preceding shorts adding variety.

It was the independent producers who introduced and rose with the features. The Motion Picture Patents Company, the fixedly conservative combine that had included all of the principal early producers—most notably Edison, Biograph, and Vitagraph—finally failed in its efforts to exert monopoly through its patent claims and its attempts

The Cure ♦ U.S., 1917, Charles Chaplin; Edna Purviance, Chaplin, and Eric Campbell, in front row.

to control the manufacture of equipment and film stock. Founded in 1908, the Trust, as it came to be known, consistently resisted longer films and stuck to the outright sale of prints—through its distribution arm, General Film Company, established in 1910. With the increasing acceptance of the more expensive features, a rental system evolved whereby after they had made the rounds of the theaters, the prints would return to the producers. By 1914–1915 the Trust was clearly being beaten by the amount and quality of its competition: The independents were too numerous, aggressive, and ingenious; there simply was no way to keep them from producing and distributing films. By 1917, through court decisions in a series of antitrust suits, the Motion Picture Patents Company was declared legally dead.

During those same years, partly as a result of the attempt by the independents to escape the legal harassment and goon squads of the Trust, the center of production shifted from New York to Southern California. (From about 1907 to 1917 Chicago was also a production center, with three large Trust firms—Essanay, Selig, and Kalem—located there.) With the feature film as the staple commodity, with the former independents becoming the newly dominant powers as the old Trust companies faded away or were absorbed, with Hollywood the production center, and with distribution controlled out of New York, the model was established for industrial expansion for the next decade and beyond.

The general lines followed were already standard in the manufacturing, wholesaling, and retailing of other products. The movie industry had the same requirements as any industry in which the annual costs of production were enormous—as its close contemporary, the automobile industry, for example. As far as manufacture was concerned, the motion picture and automobile industries were both geographically centered near raw materials and sources of power, with specialized labor pools developed around them (the workers often being imported from abroad). Detroit was within reach of coal, oil, iron ore, and the steel mills. Hollywood's distance from New York and proximity to asylum across the Mexican border were initially among its chief attractions to the independents who settled there. Later, Hollywood proved to have attributes similar to the raw materials and sources of power sought in other industries. The extraordinary variety of California's scenery meant that virtually any sort of locale—mountain, desert, ocean, forest, rolling fields—could be duplicated within a few hundred miles of Los Angeles. In those days when sunshine was still the principal source of illumination for movie making—even for interior scenes—Southern California had more of it than did the Eastern centers.

Gigantic Hollywood studios became the equivalents of Detroit's River Rouge plant; enormously expensive facilities and equipment were constructed and assembled in both. Motion picture projection was standardized throughout the world. Any change that required retooling involved vast sums, and only economic crisis would induce it. The assembly-line method devised by Henry Ford eventually would have its analogue in the Hollywood production process; tendencies in that direction were already manifest in the late teens.

It was Thomas H. Ince who first functioned as a studio head/production supervisor, planning and overseeing an entire production program. He supervised the making of hundreds of films, developing especially the western genre (and its early star,

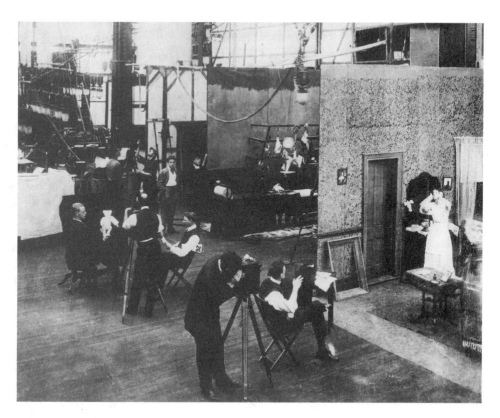

The Edison Company film studio in Menlo Park, New Jersey, in 1915.

William S. Hart) into a popularity that rivaled the melodramas of Griffith and the comedies of Sennett. In 1915 Ince joined Griffith and Sennett in the newly formed Triangle Film Corporation, named in honor of the three of them. When Ince left Triangle to form his own company, he built a big new studio at Culver City, which later became the M-G-M Studios.

The production methods that began with Ince would become standard Hollywood practice in the twenties. This piecemeal assembly—especially the practice of shooting out of sequence—however efficient and economical, tended to make the creative process disjointed and strained. The notion of separate specialists in charge of each of the many aspects of production seemed a bitter paradox to those who thought a work of art demanded, by definition, the absolute domination of a single personality. But there just wasn't enough individual genius around to supply the theaters with a steady and frequent change of bill. What generally resulted from this "art by committee"—as with American automobile manufacture—was a high level of standardized technical excellence.

The mass-produced films inevitably came to look pretty much alike, especially to the critical eye. A crucial problem for the motion picture industry thus became how

Thomas H. Ince, center with cigar, probably producing and perhaps directing.

to create the illusion of variety without fundamental differences involving wasteful experimentation and expense. One of the solutions was not unlike the development of automobile types—the sport roadster, the family sedan—and the offering of (slightly) different models each year. There evolved types of formula pictures (the "woman's picture," the comedy, the action-adventure) and cycles within each type (the vamp, the rural comedy, the war drama). Technicians could become expert at a particular kind of film making; one western, for example, could effortlessly follow the pattern of another. Audiences always had the choice of going to one of the popular genres one week and to another the next, keeping their entertainment sufficiently varied to obscure the similarities within the limited spectrum. Then too, the familiar had its own attractions. Repetition with variation is pleasurable: Nobody wanted a western so different as to seem unlike a western.

Another device that kept audiences coming back for more was the cultivation of the star personality. People would go again and again to see Mary Pickford or Mabel Normand, Charlie Chaplin or Doug Fairbanks, just to be in their screen presence for an hour and a half on a Friday night. In this case, too, the fans didn't want radical innovation any more than did the producers; they enjoyed their favorites in vehicles carefully tailored to exploit their appeal. The stars commanded an automatic audience. As long as the range extended from femme fatale Theda Bara to melodramatic heroine

Pauline Frederick, from robust comic John Bunny to matinee idol Francis X. Bushman, what more could be asked? Aspiring performers patterned themselves, or were patterned, along the lines of the already established, so that even the individuality of personality could be fitted into existing grooves.

Finally, the whole enterprise was enveloped in an unprecedented amount of promotion and advertising designed to whip up audience expectations. Each film, even if essentially indistinguishable from others preceding it, was presented as the most spectacular, the most action-packed, the funniest, the most heartwarming—in short, as something not to be missed. Press agentry soon encompassed the stars' lives off screen as well as on, and made them into demigods whose mythological existence commanded constant attendance and unswerving devotion. That was how the system came to work.

By the end of the first quarter-century, film production—which had begun in a tar-paper shack or out on the street—had moved into large, permanent studios, clustered for the most part around Los Angeles. Distribution initially was a simple and direct affair: The producers sold prints of films outright to those showing them—at so much per foot, like cordwood; ten cents per foot, or one hundred dollars per reel, was common, regardless of the quality of the entertainment. As audiences tired of seeing the same films over again, it occurred to someone to set up an "exchange" whereby exhibitors could trade in their prints and—for a small fee for the service—receive used prints of different films from other exhibitors. With increased competition among producers and discrimination on the part of the public, the practice of rental instead of sale gradually evolved; producers then received a share of the actual box-office drawing power of their films, greater for the more attractive and expensive, less for the others. This practice made for one of the singularities of the industry: The product is not bought or sold; customers merely pay to spend some time looking at it. The retailers (exhibitors) return a share of that income to the wholesalers (distributors), who in turn subtract their expenses and profits and pass the remainder on to the manufacturers (producers).

Exhibition, which had started as part of vaudeville programs, began to take place in nickelodeons from 1905 on, when films became longer and more of them narrative. Named for the price of admission, these first movie houses characteristically were converted store fronts, perhaps with chairs rented from a local funeral parlor. The nickelodeons showed continuous programs of assorted short films; the enormously successful *The Great Train Robbery* opened many of them. With the arrival of features and the increasing popularity of film, former stage theaters were converted for motion picture exhibition. The big era of showing movies in the town's "opera house" and competing with stage road shows dates from 1913 to 1916. At that time, there were perhaps as many as 28,000 movie theaters of all types in the United States. A new and more pretentious type of screen theater was initiated in 1914 with the opening of the Strand on Broadway, soon to be followed by others with equal ambitions. Widespread construction of theaters designed especially for movies did not occur, however, until the 1920s.

By the end of World War I in late 1918, the American film had achieved all the essentials necessary to ensure its success as an art-industry: a steady flow of features accompanied by shorts, especially by popular comedies; a national distribution in which prints circulated out of regional exchanges within a rental system that permitted the income to flow back through exhibitors and distributors to producers; and theaters gradually being formed into chains by enterprising exhibitors, accommodating larger and more demanding audiences paying higher prices. These fundamentals extended to an international scale gave the United States its lead in the conquest of the world's screens. Once the war was over, growth of the medium could resume unimpeded by national boundaries.

FILMS OF THE PERIOD

1914
A Fool There Was (Frank Powell)
Judith of Bethulia (David Wark Griffith)
Making a Living (Charles Chaplin)
The Squaw Man (Cecil B. De Mille)
Tillie's Punctured Romance (Mack Sennett)

1915
The Birth of a Nation (Griffith)
The Tramp (Chaplin)

1916
Civilization (Thomas H. Ince)
Intolerance (Griffith)

The Pawnshop (Chaplin)
The Rink (Chaplin)

1917
Easy Street (Chaplin)
The Immigrant (Chaplin)
Teddy at the Throttle (Sennett)

1918
Hearts of the World (Griffith)
Shoulder Arms (Chaplin)

1919
Broken Blossoms (Griffith)

BOOKS ON THE PERIOD

Koszarski, Richjard, *An Evening's Entertainment: The Age of the Silent Feature Picture, 1915–1928* (Vol. 3, "History of the American Cinema"). New York: Charles Scribner's Sons, 1990

MacCann, Richard Dyer, *The First Tycoons* (Vol. 1, "American Movies: The First Thirty Years"). Metuchen, NJ: Scarecrow Press, 1987.

MacCann, Richard Dyer, *The First Film Makers* (Vol. 2, "American Movies: The First Thirty Years"). Metuchen, NJ: Scarecrow Press, 1989

MacCann, Richard Dyer, *The Stars Appear* (Vol. 3, "American Movies: The First Thirty Years"). Metuchen, NJ: Scarecrow Press, 1992

MacCann, Richard Dyer, *The Comedians* (Vol. 4, "American Movies: The First Thirty Years"). Metuchen, NJ: Scarecrow Press, 1993

3

Great German
Silents

♦ ♦ ♦

1919–1925

Following the end of World War I, while the United States moved toward domination of the world motion picture industry, Germany led the art into newly urbane subject matter and refinement of technique. This brief period of cinematic ascendancy occurred at a time when the country itself was desperately unstable in its political, economic, and social life. The loss of the war and the humiliation of the Versailles Treaty peace terms were damaging to national pride. The shaky and directionless Weimar Republic faced rioting and anarchy. Inflation, unemployment, and food shortages crippled the economy and brought great hardship to the German people. Morale was lower than it had ever been during the war. The highest point of German silent film (1922–1924) was precisely the lowest point for the nation. French troops occupied the Ruhr industrial heartland; the Deutschmark was utterly worthless; revolt was incipient in Bavaria.

With the stabilization of the mark in 1924 and the election of war hero Field Marshal Paul von Hindenburg to the presidency in 1925, a kind of order was restored. Within German society, however, the amorality and decadence portrayed in the American musical *Cabaret* (based on stories by Christopher Isherwood), in Rainer Werner Fassbinder's *Berlin Alexanderplatz* (1980) television series, and reflected in Bertolt Brecht's and Kurt Weill's *The Threepenny Opera* (first produced in Germany in the late twenties) succeeded the immediate postwar years and formed the setting for the triumph of Naziism. At the same time, the German film began to lose its particular excellence, a loss caused in considerable measure by American infiltration and dominance within the German film industry.

During the first half of the twenties, however, there was a vitality in all the German arts, as if the national disease had caused a feverish counteractivity. Literature and, especially, drama and the visual arts, were released from the rigidities of a Hohenzollern monarchy and Prussian militarism. Prompted by the disillusionment of the war and the radically changed values that followed its end, newly expressive forms and styles were sought. At this time the plays of Brecht, Ernst Toller, and Georg Kaiser were first produced; Max Reinhardt, in his more conventional historical-romantic stagings, added elements of lighting and handling of crowds that would be translated directly into film. Lyonel Feininger, Vasily Kandinsky, and Paul Klee were among the many active painters. Others affiliated with the Berlin *Sturm* group became stage and then film designers. The general aesthetic impulses would feed into film and in some ways find their ultimate expression in the collective and composite film art.

In the United States, the West Coast center of film production was separated geographically (some would say culturally and spiritually as well) from the East Coast center of the other arts and communications media. In Germany, Berlin was not only the national capital, but the center for all the arts, including film. Those working in the traditional arts were free from feelings of condescension toward the movies that characterized many Americans; on the contrary, German artists expressed a lively curiosity about the new art form and demonstrated their interest by trying their hands at it. It was possible for them to do so without changing their place of residence or lifestyle, and German films owed much of their sophistication to those trained in the older arts.

Whereas American films had been populated by good guys, bad guys, funny guys, and pretty women, the Germans started probing complex and frequently disturbed characters along loosely Freudian lines, which stimulated the additions to technique noteworthy in their work. While the Americans had concentrated on action and melodrama, the Germans explored the psychological and pictorial. In their quest for means to objectify inner consciousness, they created a world on film that represents not so much a physical reality, as most of us perceive it, as a state of mind: the universe distorted and stylized to express what we might feel about it. Expressionism, as opposed to American realism and naturalism, was the prevalent style. First appearing in extreme and sustained form in *The Cabinet of Dr. Caligari* (1920), it is also manifest in subtle ways in much of the German production of the twenties, as will be noted.

◆ PREDOMINANT TYPES AND THEMES

Looking at these German films of 1919–1925 as a body, film historians have identified three prominent types with concomitant themes that make evident most of the major German contributions. **First** were the historical/mythological films in which architectural settings, careful costuming, and romantic lighting, as well as the handling of massed crowds, reflect Max Reinhardt's theories and experiments in stage production. In these films, history is treated psychologically and spectacularly, rather than realistically; they might be called historical fantasies. Ernst Lubitsch, who had acted in Reinhardt's stage company, was one master of this genre. His accounts of the Bourbons (*Passion/Madame du Barry,* 1919) or the Tudors (*Deception/Anna Boleyn,* 1920)

Madame du Barry/Passion ◆ Germany, 1919, Ernst Lubitsch; Pola Negri, kneeling.

center around a bedroom-keyhole view of the past, which suggests that great historical events can be seen as extensions of sexual intrigue. Someone once observed that Cecil B. De Mille, much indebted to Lubitsch, presented the Crusades as if they were fought for the sole benefit of Loretta Young; the same might be said about Lubitsch, the French Revolution, and Pola Negri. Onto gossipy biographies Lubitsch overlaid massive spectacles of the Bastille and the Tower of London, using hundreds of extras.

Allied to the Lubitsch pageants were Fritz Lang's less popular but more innovative and significant mythological/historical evocations. *Destiny* (1921), part legend, part fairy tale, includes three episodes placed in earlier times: one in a Moslem city, another in Venice during the Renaissance, and the final one in a charmingly fantastic China. Much of the pleasure in Lang's film is derived from the stylized settings. The dominant image is the enormous blank wall—in the connective story—that fills the whole screen and dwarfs the humans. Trained as an architect, Lang went on to even fuller expression of his themes in gigantic re-creations of the German saga *Die Nibelungen* (1924)—a film that became so vast it had to be released in two parts: *Siegfried* and *Kriemhild's Revenge.* (His *Metropolis,* 1926, though set in the future, is like the films about the past in that it re-creates another time and place through

Siegfried ♦ Germany, 1924, Fritz Lang.

predominantly architectural means.) Much more serious in intent than Lubitsch's, Lang's spectacles are nonetheless offered as feasts for the eyes. The careful visual patterns and breathtaking scale are designed to be enjoyed in their own right as well as to be the expression of what seems an especially Germanic imagination about a prehistoric or fantasied past. Static they may be; but monumental too.

Also set in the past, though frequently even less specific as to time, were **the second group:** the sinister, fantastic, macabre films in which expressionistic decor plays an important part and the subjects are often derived from old legends and ballads. *The Cabinet of Dr. Caligari* is the most famous of these. It could also be considered a precedent for the avant-garde film, predating the movement that would start in Berlin with Hans Richter's *Rhythmus 21* (1921) and Viking Eggeling's *Diagonal Symphony* (1925) and would then headquarter in Paris.

Originally Fritz Lang was to direct *Caligari.* When he withdrew to complete another film, Robert Wiene was appointed in his place. It was not the direction, however, so much as the eerily frightening story (by Carl Mayer and Hans Janowitz) and, particularly, the expressionistic settings, that made this film both seminal and enduring in its fascination. The names of the three painters who designed its sets— Hermann Warm, Walter Röhrig, and Walter Reimann—appear in various collaborations on the credits of many of the finest of the German films of this period. *Caligari* remains the purest and fullest use of the expressionist credo in film: "Films must be drawings brought to life," said Warm. The "exteriors" as well as the interiors were all constructed from wood, plaster, and canvas. The world created is that of a madman, a paranoid whose fears derive not only from the people and events around him, but also from the shapes of nature, the town, a fairground, and an insane asylum. Jagged irregularity dominates: trees like barbed spears; pools of black shadow cast by no discernible light (shadows and light were in fact painted in order to better control them); a maze of crooked streets; ramps and stairways foreshortened; and houses like clusters of strange geometrical blocks balanced precariously.

Scarcely the sort of film to inspire popular imitation (it was moderately successful), there was nonetheless a small group of films that reflected its influence. Perhaps best remembered are Paul Wegener's *The Golem* (1920) and F. W. Murnau's *Nosferatu* (1922). *The Golem* is based on a Jewish legend about a practitioner of black magic—a rabbi of great erudition—who brings to life a clay monster to aid the Jews against their governing Christian oppressors in Prague in the sixteenth century. As Doctor Frankenstein also discovered, such monsters often attack those who create them, punishing us for our presumption. The abstractly fashioned medieval town, with its skyline of sharply angled roofs and tilted chimney pots, looks like twisted ginger-

The Cabinet of Dr. Caligari ♦ Germany, 1920, Robert Wiene; Conrad Veidt and Lil Dagover.

The Golem ♦ Germany, 1920,
Paul Wegener; Wegener.

bread; not a straight line is visible. A gigantic gate into the walled ghetto dwarfs the
human beings. Irregular arches and inverted Vs predominate. The camera frequently
shoots through the archways, imposing their strange shapes on the frame itself. The
citizens—the males in tall conical hats and pointed beards—are again part of a
nightmarish world like that of *Caligari.*

In Murnau's *Nosferatu,* the themes of somnambulism, a man under another's
diabolical power, mass murder, madness, all recur, and the agent of death is destroyed
while attacking the young female loved one in her bedroom. Count Orlock, who is
Nosferatu-the-Vampire by night, strongly suggests Cesare of *Caligari* in appearance,
bodily movement, and facial contortions. Tall, thin, grotesquely made up and cos-
tumed, he moves in a trance (not unlike Cesare) when under the curse of his vampir-
ism. From real exteriors Murnau has selected the sorts of buildings (the deserted
castle, the town with its steep pointed roofs, the narrow twisting streets) and landscapes (rocky roads with abrupt inclines and turns, a deformed tree) that look as if
they could have served as models for the abstractions created in the studio for
Caligari. Going beyond the prototype, the expressionistic influence appears in specifically cinematic devices: fast motion, negative images, superimposition, and stop

Nosferatu ◆ Germany, 1922, F. W. Murnau; Max Schreck.

motion—which permits a tarpaulin to remove itself and a ship hatch to open of its own accord. The huge black shadow of Nosferatu, now created by light, moves horrifyingly toward and over his victims, unlike the painted theatrical shadows in *Caligari.* Unreal, irrational, and hauntingly disturbing, these expressionist works offered a totally new kind of film.

The third group of German films from this period, marked least obviously by expressionistic tendencies, and most important in advancing film technique, began with the *Kammerspielfilm* (literally "chamber play film"), which derived from Reinhardt theater. This style was marked by unity of time, place, and action, with virtually no intertitles; few characters, usually lower middle class; sparse decor, with objects given extraordinary importance; and intimate psychological content. Its characteristics are further described, lovingly and sensitively, by Lotte Eisner in *The Haunted Screen: Expressionism in the German Cinema and the Influence of Max Reinhardt.* Key films were Paul Leni's *Backstairs* (1921), Lupu Pick's *Shattered* (1921), and Murnau's *The Last Laugh* (1924). Scripts for all three were written by Carl Mayer.

The Last Laugh ◆
Germany, 1924, F. W.
Murnau; Emil Jannings.

Finest of the Kammerspielfilms, and arguably of all German silent cinema, is *The Last Laugh*. It chronicles the pathos of a proud and majestic doorman at an elegant hotel, who, having become too old to handle heavy baggage and perform his other functions adequately, is demoted to washroom attendant. Seemingly loved and respected by his family and neighbors in his earlier status, he is reviled and ridiculed when they learn of his demotion. In the epilogue, an eccentric American millionaire dies in the men's room, with a will in his wallet leaving his fortune to whomever is with him at his death. This whimsical conclusion, while lifting us out of the despair of the poor old man (played by Emil Jannings), by its very improbability reinforces the sense that real life is unhappy and that only stories have happy endings.

A genre related to the Kammerspielfilm is the "street film," a term used by Siegfried Kracauer in his *From Caligari to Hitler: A Psychological History of the German Film*. Beginning with Karl Grune's prototypal *The Street* (1923), street films include G. W. Pabst's *The Joyless Street* (1925) and Bruno Rahn's *Tragedy of a Street* (1927). In these films, most typically, the male protagonists are drawn away from home, family, and bourgeois life by the lure of the city, the seductive promise of excitement and sensual pleasures. These were individualized studies of lower-middle-class life, often set within or alongside entertainment, and sometimes vaguely underworld, milieus. If extracted from the frequently superb skill of their realizations, the plot themes might appear melodramatic or morbidly sentimental. Though rooted in contemporary reality, these films were concerned primarily with character study—frequently with the personality disintegration of an individual or group of individuals.

The Joyless Street, featuring Scandinavians Asta Nielsen, Greta Garbo, and Einar Hanson, deals more directly with economic and political problems in postwar Vienna (inflation, black market, stock manipulation, ineffectuality of government) than do other street films. Its realistic visual style is also quite different from the other street films; it was said at the time to be an example of the *Neue Sachlichkeit* (new objectivity). Showing how these national problems lead to general corruption and dislocation of moral and spiritual values, Pabst concentrated on the pressures exerted on a bourgeois father: The man faces old age and poverty, and his beautiful daughter is about to be forced into prostitution; they are saved by a *deus ex machina* in the form of a U.S. aid commission.

Variety (1925), directed by E. A. Dupont, though not exactly a Kammerspielfilm or a street film, embodies some of the characteristics of both. It concerns trapeze artists involved in a romantic triangle; the husband (played by Emil Jannings) murders the partner who has cuckolded him. The film proper is presented as a long flashback within the framework of Jannings in prison, telling his story to the warden. It was a great international success, especially popular in the United States.

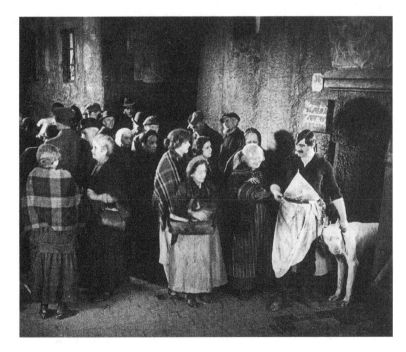

The Joyless Street ◆ Germany, 1925, G. W. Pabst; Werner Krauss, with hand on dog.

Variety ♦ Germany,
1925, E. A. Dupont;
Warwick Ward, Lya de
Putti, and Emil Jannings.

♦ PRINCIPAL TECHNICAL AND STYLISTIC ADVANCES

An underlying psychological function of all three major types of the German silent film is posited by Siegfried Kracauer in *From Caligari to Hitler.* According to him, they offered escape from contemporary social reality—into the past (historical or mythological), into fantasy (expressionist), or into the recesses of individual psyches (Kammerspiel and street films). Certainly it is true that German film makers were preoccupied with the psychological rather than the sociological, and that their new intentions brought innovations of technique to camera, lighting, set design, acting, and script construction.

To some extent the Germans, like the Soviets who would follow in the international spotlight, organized their industry as a vehicle of state. In 1917, when Germany's last great offensive in the West had failed, the giant firm Universum Film A. G. (Ufa) was founded by General Erich Ludendorff; over a third of its initial capital was supplied by the Reich. Mergers and affiliations with other large production firms and control of the biggest chain of first-run theaters led to its dominance. Unlike the Soviets, who used film directly for purposes of education and propaganda, the postwar German cinema was designed primarily to add to Germany's prestige through artistic accomplishment and to project Germany's image before the eyes of the world.

For these purposes, the huge Ufa studios at Neubabelsberg were erected. Its facilities were unrivaled, and the craftspeople working there were the finest known. Many of their names later appeared on screen credits outside Germany, especially in the United States, decades after this original brilliant period of experiment and training.

Probably the single most striking contribution by the Germans was their fuller use of the moving camera. The Kammerspiel and street films in particular developed this possibility in order to probe character, to follow and bore into protagonists, and to let the world be seen from subjective points of view. In this latter respect the moving camera became part of the general expressionist tendency.

As far back as Porter's *The Great Train Robbery,* the camera had panned and tilted; Griffith had used trucking and dollying as well; but moving the camera while shooting was relatively rare, and usually (not always) confined to the simple function of keeping a moving subject within frame. The standard Griffith method was to rehearse performances with actors, shoot them from the most effective angles and distances on a stationary tripod, then select and arrange the images, adjust the tempo of the action, and heighten the conflict through editing. Griffith thus transcended the spatial and temporal limitations of the stage, offering the varied filmic view rather than the fixed and continuous one available to the playgoer; but the viewpoint remained essentially objective, a recording of *dramatic* action.

The Germans made their camera part of the story in a more profound way. The camera became a *narrative* tool in addition to being a means of recording dramatic action. This potential was employed in two ways, both appearing together in many of the German silent films. First, the camera could become a narrator, like Joseph Conrad's Marlow, leading viewers into and through the story. *The Last Laugh,* for example, opens with the camera descending on an elevator, peering out through its wrought-iron grillwork at the passing floors of the hotel. In one continuous take it moves down to the lobby and across to the revolving door, where it offers a view of the street and of the doorman whistling up cabs, greeting guests, and unloading luggage. It is for all the world like a novelist writing "Evening was approaching at the fashionable Hotel Atlantic. On the upper floors maids scurried back and forth with fresh linen while guests moved toward the elevator and down into the lobby. There a string ensemble played to seated guests sipping aperitifs. If one crossed the lobby to the tall revolving door awhirl . . . ," and so on. Later, the camera follows at the shoulder of the little night watchman as he makes his rounds, permitting us to see what the light from his electric torch reveals as it bounces along the walls and floors of the corridors.

In the earlier sequences the doorman is viewed from a low camera angle, which exaggerates his size and importance in his splendid uniform and flowing mustache. When he is reduced to washroom attendant he not only moves lower in social status (and physically below the street level), but the camera is frequently placed at a high angle, further emphasizing the crushed spirit which makes the now stooped body seem small and pitifully vulnerable. Again, this kind of film making seems more analogous to a novelist's descriptive capabilities than to anything that can be achieved on a stage.

The other special use of the moving camera fully exploited by the Germans was the possibility of its taking on a character's point of view and even state of mind—what is called "subjective camera." In *The Last Laugh*, after a wedding party at his flat, the doorman is sitting alone amidst postparty debris, amiably bemused by drink. First he is seen to spin in the room as the camera moves around him (the "narrator's" viewpoint); then the room itself revolves as the camera takes on his own tipsy vision. In *Variety*, the camera is mounted on a swinging trapeze to let us experience the vertigo of the disturbed catcher as the audience below seems to approach and then recede. In the same Wintergarten scenes, specially constructed lenses fragment and distort images to suggest psychological states, those of the excited members of the audience as well as those of the principals.

Karl Freund was cinematographer for both *The Last Laugh* and *Variety*, and it was the German camera work that most strongly impressed Hollywood. Freed entirely from a fixed base on a tripod and from a strictly objective view, the camera now ran or stumbled, got dizzy or suffered from hallucinations, and "saw" the sounds of a reveler's horn blown at midnight or of a woman's footsteps going down a corridor. In the less important films this use of narrative/subjective camera placement and movement was a mere trapping, a "special effect." In the best work this subtly profound innovation opened a whole new range of screen technique, not only affecting the way subjects could be dealt with, but making accessible themes and kinds of characters never before treated.

The other vital component of the cinematographer's craft, lighting, was important to all three major types of German silent film. In the historical-costume films, it followed rather closely the stage lighting developed earlier by Reinhardt. The tableaux were bathed in pools of light and shadow, which enhanced the mood and fitted into the total composition of set design, massed extras, and featured players. In the expressionist films the lighting was one of the most evocative means of conveying the bizarre and the threatening as seen and felt by the characters. In the Kammerspiel and street films, often expressionistic in their subtler ways, lighting augmented camera movement to direct the viewer's eye where the film maker wanted it. Frequently the lighting was what most strongly evoked the feelings desired. Modeled lighting exposed a character's face (and soul) for examination. The essential significance of places and objects was rendered through the way they were lit. In these silent films things often seem to take on a life of their own, surrounding and commenting on the lives being led by the protagonists.

In all three types of German films the lighting was conceived and arranged specially to set the overall mood, and in the latter two types, to reflect the emotional states of the characters as well. Often eerie or sombre, at the same time romantic (softening) and decorative, it was vastly different from the consistent brightness and clarity of the American films (up until mid-Griffith, anyway). At its most basic level, of course, film, the medium, is simply film, the material: the response to illumination by a coating of light-sensitive emulsion on a cellulose base. The title of cameraman John Alton's book, *Painting with Light*, suggests the way the Germans learned to conceive of and use this primary factor.

Two specific lighting contributions can be noted as well. First was the new prevalence of *low-key* lighting. Suddenly the screen went dark, with candlelit rooms, gloomy stairways, streets at night, cabarets, and all the other environments that would be natural to the many "night people" of the German films. Sufficiently sensitive emulsions and expertness in laboratory processing had not been available before; nor, more important, had an understanding of the precise control that might be exercised over the cinematographic process. Second was the Germans' use of *key light* (not to be confused with low key, but often occurring in conjunction with it). The key light is the brightest light on the set, usually appearing to come from a source within the scene—a light fixture, a window, a street lamp. Griffith experimented with this possibility (notably in *Broken Blossoms*), but usually he led the eye and created emotional overtones by limiting the amount of area in the frame—cutting from long shot, to medium, to closeup—with the scene generally well and evenly lit.

The Germans came to realize that within a shot, if there is one brighter area amidst less brightly lit surroundings, it becomes the center of attention. They also sensed that it is much more satisfying aesthetically to have a variety of lighting intensities balanced around the frame—a monochromatic equivalent to the painter's placement of pigments. In short, they learned to lead the eye over the screen and to gratify it with the illumination, part of a total, ordered composition in which the main elements stand out and are reinforced by the lesser.

The importance of set design to the special effectiveness and unique qualities of the German silent film has already been noted, but can scarcely be exaggerated. Virtually all of the films were shot completely inside the studio, the painstaking "exteriors" frequently constructed on a mammoth scale. In *The Last Laugh,* for example, the huge Hotel Atlantic and the busy intersection in front of it, with autos, buses, and pedestrians flowing by, are studio creations. Even an exception like Arthur von Gerlach's *The Chronicle of the Gray House* (1923), shot in part out-of-doors, uses the East Prussian moors as Thomas Hardy used those of Dorsetshire. Nature is bent to human purposes and given an anthropomorphic coding to reinforce human conflicts. Most of the crucial action, however, takes place within large, ornate, and calculatedly oppressive sets of baroque rooms and castle courtyards.

Two prevalent impulses in German set design were rarely separate from each other. The pictorial beauty and grandeur of the historical films had psychological dimensions as well, especially in the work of Fritz Lang. The expressionist tendency offered visual design that was striking in its own right (*The Cabinet of Dr. Caligari*) and large in scale (*The Golem*) as well as being expressive of overall moods and subjective states. Even in the Kammerspiel and street films, which embodied a modified expressionism, the pictorial and psychological functions of the sets were commingled. The Wintergarten scenes in *Variety* dazzle us by their size and opulence, besides serving as the public setting for the private tensions of star performers.

In Lang's *Nibelungen* the huge re-creation of a forest is breathtaking, with its Klieg-light sunshine streaming through the branches of trees as big as sequoias. The blond Siegfried riding slowly into frame on a white horse approaches a sizeable, and palpably real, waterfall. Even the smoke-breathing dragon carries a rare conviction.

The Chronicle of the Gray House ♦ Germany, 1923, Arthur von Gerlach.

In a wide-angle long shot of a huge castle courtyard, human figures are placed on the checkerboard tiles to form part of a total visual pattern; Lang evidently intended that we study its vastness and ingenuity as the shot holds on the screen. The costumes, too, are geometrically patterned. This sense of persons being segments of a decorative whole is confirmed by a scene in a treasure cave: A large round table piled with ornaments and jewelry is supported by carved dwarfs in chains; when one of them moves slightly, we have an ultimate statement about person being interchangeable with object in a screen world remarkable for its nonhuman use of human beings. Lang seemed to like the idea of humans as statuary; he used it again in *Metropolis,* even more pointedly and ingeniously. The futuristic city of the latter film may have been Ufa's *magnum opus* as far as set construction was concerned. It also marks the last great burst of expressionism.

As for the acting, the monumental and mythological strands in German film did not call for any great change in the pantomimic tradition inherited from the theater; but the Kammerspiel and street films did, in their search for new psychological dimensions. Obviously there was no performance style except the theatrical when film came into being, and the evolution of screen acting included breaking away from stage tradition—a progress to which Griffith and contemporary Scandinavian film makers had contributed substantially. Griffith's intentions were to make his actors behave more nearly as their characters would in life, and the Scandinavians continued and advanced that approach. The more realistic style of film acting would in turn influence the theater.

Metropolis ♦ Germany, 1927, Fritz Lang.

In trying to delineate internal states without the help of dialogue, the Germans went beyond realism to a deliberate expressiveness. Actors began working out their characterizations by "becoming" as completely as possible the persons they were playing. Immersing themselves sufficiently in the roles, they would inevitably reveal the characters' feelings through small gestures, the slope of a back, the movement of a head, the eyes—especially the eyes. But to these intuitive physical responses was added an intellectual refinement to make fullest use of silent film limitations (in this sense, its strengths). Through closely observed facial expression and bodily movement, the camera can capture what is eloquent and seems true in the actors' understanding of the characters. This understanding is then "projected" effortlessly, to every seat in the house, by the projector shining a large likeness onto the screen. Gestures and expressions formed and shaped for the screen can reveal more than can actors on a relatively distant stage, or even people across a room.

The great actors in German silent film—Emil Jannings, Werner Krauss, Conrad Veidt, Lil Dagover, Asta Nielsen, Pola Negri, Greta Garbo—learned to retard and simplify their gestures to make precise psychological points. In *The Joyless Street* the neurotic intensity of Asta Nielsen and the radiant inward beauty of Greta Garbo are conveyed without any of the stagelike busyness of Mae Marsh or Lillian Gish (fine as she was) in the earlier Griffith films. Nielsen, who appeared in Danish films (beginning with *The Abyss,* 1910) before moving to Germany after the war, remains one of the great artists of the silent screen. Perhaps she was the first to suggest a dimension and complexity of feeling beneath the surface of the screen presence. Her style of passionate intensity would be developed to even greater expressiveness by Garbo, who began in Sweden and worked in Germany before coming to the United States. Jannings created remarkable portrayals through a kind of stylization that called for an absolute comprehension of the psychological makeup of his characters and an abstraction and heightening of the physical expression of feeling—an artfulness that did not so much conceal art as transcend life. Jannings lived a great number of screen lives in the studio world, and all of them consistent with the stylistic level of the carefully designed sets and lighting. The total creation evoked the essence of a reality filtered through the strong feelings of a character.

Given the complex interaction of the various elements of technique, the Germans needed more-detailed scripts than did the simpler, more open-air and improvised American films. (Neither Sennett nor Griffith used scripts at all.) If the camera was going to move in a sustained take down a studio street, lights had to be arranged along a predetermined path, sets built to accommodate the full range of its shifting angle and distance, and actors directed and rehearsed to move in relationship to it. Thus script writing, and the production planning growing out of it, achieved new importance. The German script writers could blueprint a film on paper, and the best of them, like Carl Mayer, could go beyond the mechanics to communicate a complete sense of a film. Through written descriptions of images, Mayer defined the kinds of emotional values required and suggested how to achieve them. He also understood clearly what sorts of themes, characters, and emotions lent themselves best to visual expression. The action in his scripts was invariably sparse and simple; the plots, tight in construction, required few intertitles—and ultimately, almost none at all (for example, *Shattered,* 1921, *New Year's Eve,* 1923, and *The Last Laugh*). It seems paradoxical that Griffith, without scripts, tended toward the literary, and required screen words to connect and explain his action. Mayer, working with words, used them to evoke self-explanatory images, which were given physical form by directors, set designers, cinematographers, and performers—the extraordinary collective of German talent in the 1920s.

◆ MIRROR OF THE CULTURE

E. W. and M. M. Robson, in their book *The Film Answers Back,* were possibly the first to note the ways in which German silent film reflected certain aspects of a nation suffering from social-political sickness that would ultimately lead to a cure worse than the disease. Siegfried Kracauer, in *From Caligari to Hitler,* systematized, elaborated, and extended their insights. His book is both a film history with a thesis and a provocative demonstration of the kinds of things that can be learned about a society by analyzing the content and style of a popular art form. Because of their collective creation and appeal to an anonymous multitude, Kracauer argues, the films of a nation reflect its "mentality," the "inner dispositions" of a culture, more directly than do other arts. In examining German films from the end of World War I to Adolph Hitler's accession to power, Kracauer finds revealed a steady succession of attitudes conducive to authoritarianism.

First, he observes that no alternative between tyranny and anarchic chaos is offered: Freedom is not depicted as a possibility. In *The Cabinet of Dr. Caligari,* the options are the asylum (tyranny) or the fair (chaos). This is by no means the only film example assessed by Kracauer. According to him, none of the major German films of this period suggests possible human control over destiny through rational, democratic action. He notes as well the studio construction of unreal worlds and the penchant for organization, which requires submission. Instinct and fate are shown to rule. This is as true of the strangely driven burgher of the street film, led down into corruption by his own vague lusts and longings, as it is of the haunted worlds of the expressionist films, in which an unknowable and malevolent destiny shapes the lives of the characters. The extent to which this particular worldview was held by the German people and could be invoked in a propaganda program was well understood by Hitler. Finally, Kracauer asserts that fantasy and retrogression were ubiquitous: the escaping of real problems in an unreal world, as in the expressionist films; the recurring image of a repentant man's head on a maternal woman's breast as in the street films. He reads these symbolic signs as indicating political paralysis and pointing ahead to the passive acceptance of Naziism.[1]

Some have accused Kracauer of bending the films to fit the theory and of ignoring those that don't fall neatly into one of his categories. There is, of course, a danger inherent in the application of any thesis to as diverse a body of data as a nation's films, and a summary condensation of Kracauer's inferences such as the above paragraph must make him seem especially vulnerable to the charge. But those who have pointed to some of his errors and hinted at other discrepancies have failed to offer an alternative understanding to replace his. George Huaco, in *The Sociology of Film Art,* and Paul Monaco, in *Cinema and Society,* deal with the same national period of film making as Kracauer. Though they use somewhat different methodologies and arrive at slightly different conclusions, their findings do not decrease the value or even fundamentally alter Kracauer's contribution. The three authors more or less agree on the very special and remarkably coherent qualities of this cinema. The more we look at the German films from the twenties, the more they seem to offer the kinds of social-psychological meanings Kracauer and others have discovered and to correspond with the findings of historians of the period.

◆ INFLUENCE ON HOLLYWOOD

An old Hollywood saw advises: "If you can't beat 'em, join 'em." In international terms this has often meant, "If you can't beat 'em, buy 'em up." There began in the twenties an emigration of German film makers to Hollywood, which would impover-

---

[1]See *From Caligari to Hitler: A Psychological History of the German Film* (Princeton, NJ: Princeton University Press, 1947), Chapters 5–10, pp. 61–130, for Kracauer's development of his thesis.

ish their native industry and further enrich the dominant American one. The entire principal cast and crew of *Variety* were imported—Erich Pommer (producer), E. A. Dupont (director), Karl Freund (cameraman), Leo Birinski (scenarist), and Emil Jannings and Lya de Putti (stars). Pommer, the production head of Ufa and arguably the man most directly responsible for the German "Golden Era" just surveyed, was lured by Paramount in 1927. Among other directors who emigrated were Ernst Lubitsch, Paul Leni, F. W. Murnau, and Fritz Lang. Cameramen Kurt Courant and Theodore Sparkuhl, along with Freund, brought German cinematography to American films. Actor emigrés also included Pola Negri and Conrad Veidt.

Germanic influence on American films was persistent, lasting decades after the first invasion. The imitation of German successes and the presence of German creative personnel combined to alter earlier American style in regard to moving camera, lighting, and the use of visual narrative transitions rather than titles. Often this "Germanization" was somewhat arbitrary, being applied to native plots and themes without the aesthetic logic that had made form and content so interdependent in the best of the German silent films. Certain film types that developed later in the United States had their roots in the earlier Ufa and became sturdy hybrids. The horror series of Universal Studios, which began with *Dracula* and *Frankenstein* (both 1931), is one example, depending as it did upon sinister and fantastic subjects; expressionistic lighting, makeup, and costuming; and special-effects cinematography. A later instance is the cluster of *film noir,* as the French called them. Reminiscent of the street films, these dark crime melodramas of the mid-forties also involve the probing of disordered psyches in a predominantly nighttime studio world. *The Woman in the Window* (1944) and *Scarlet Street* (1945) by Fritz Lang, *Phantom Lady* (1944) and *The Spiral Staircase* (1945) by Robert Siodmak, and *Double Indemnity* (1944) by Billy Wilder, were all made by directors who had worked in Germany.

In addition to the loss of talented creators, technicians, and performers, a kind of "internationalization" of German films, which began after the middle of the 1920s, vitiated the very distinctiveness that had made them popular as well as important. This marked the appearance of a recurring problem of commerce affecting art (which can also be observed in later productions from Italy and Britain). Once a country earns an international prominence through a special national contribution, it attempts to compete with Hollywood on its terms; that is to say, ingredients that are thought to make American films so successful are employed, in an effort to obtain an even larger piece of the global box office (which includes the huge American audience). At the same time, American studios set about to coproduce within countries that have demonstrated a successful competitiveness, contributing further to a blurring of national distinctions. In 1925 both Paramount and Metro-Goldwyn-Mayer negotiated with Ufa regarding joint production on the continent, using American-German casts and technicians. What Kracauer calls a "synthesis of Hollywood and Neubabelsberg" resulted in a further dilution of German themes and styles.

This is not to say that the German industry suddenly ceased to produce films of enduring value: With the arrival of sound, and before the Nazi government absorbed film into its total state, there was a flurry of innovative and valuable work. But the exceptions to a general decline have to be weighed against the dozens of uniquely fascinating films of the first half of the twenties. From about 1925 onwards the eyes of the film world shifted from Germany to a star rising in the east, a red star. Made for the new government in Russia, another remarkable body of work began to appear that could scarcely be more different from the German films in form, content, and purpose.

FILMS OF THE PERIOD

1919
Passion (Ernst Lubitsch)

1920
The Cabinet of Dr. Caligari (Robert Wiene)
Deception (Lubitsch)
Genuine (Wiene)
The Golem (Paul Wegener)

1921
Destiny (Fritz Lang)

1922
Dr. Mabuse, the Gambler (Lang)
Nosferatu (F. W. Murnau)
Vanina (Arthur von Gerlach)
Warning Shadows (Arthur Robison)

1923
The Chronicle of the Gray House (Gerlach)
The Street (Karl Grune)

1924
The Last Laugh (Murnau)
Die Nibelungen (Lang)
The Treasure (G. W. Pabst)
Waxworks (Paul Leni)

1925
The Joyless Street (Pabst)
Variety (E. A. Dupont)

1927
Metropolis (Lang)

BOOKS ON THE PERIOD

Murray, Bruce, *Film and the German Left in the Weimar Republic: From Caligari to Kuhle Wampe.* Austin: University of Texas Press, 1990

Petro, Patrice, *Joyless Streets: Women and Melodramatic Representation in Weimar Germany.* Princeton, NJ: Princeton University Press, 1989

Usai, Paolo Cherchi, and Lorenzo Codelli, eds., *Before Caligari: German Cinema, 1895-1920.* Madison: University of Wisconsin Press, 1991 [Distributed for Edizioni Biblioteca dell'Immagine]

4

Art and Dialectic in the Soviet Film

♦ ♦ ♦

1925–1929

The Russians were even more profoundly affected by World War I than were the Germans. While there had been no fighting within the borders of Germany, Russia had been a vast battlefield. It had suffered defeat at the hands of the Central Powers, and the peace treaty signed at Brest-Litovsk was even more vindictive than that of Versailles. While in Germany an abortive rebellion in 1919 was quickly suppressed, the Bolshevik Revolution of 1917 succeeded. At least five years elapsed, however, before it was clear that the new government of Russia, a communist government, could survive, and that a beginning stability would be achieved.

Not until 1925 did the Soviets fully launch into the final, and some would say most brilliant, phase of the silent film before the introduction of sound. The contrast between Soviet and German silent film, in both subject matter and technique, was even greater than that between the German film of the early twenties and American film preceding it. Though the German effort had been state-supported in part, it was directed toward the prestige of art. It can be valued precisely because of its extreme artificiality, but a prevailing aestheticism cannot be denied. There was an anarchic indifference to the social-political implications of content—which Kracauer interpreted as reflecting a kind of national neurosis. The introspection and morbidity of the major themes led to a slowness of tempo. As the veteran British director Anthony Asquith observed of German contributions, "while the film was gaining in its ability to convey mood, emotion, and character, it was gradually losing touch with its life-source—the movement."[1]

[1]Anthony Asquith, "The Tenth Muse Climbs Parnasus," *The Penguin Film Review,* no. 1 (August 1946): 10–26.

Soviet film, completely state-supported, was socially purposeful above all else: intended primarily to educate and indoctrinate the Russian people in the events and causes of the Revolution. Vigorous and optimistic, the films came out of the East like a blast of cold Siberian air, blowing away the hothouse atmosphere of the German studios. Objective in approach (as opposed to German subjectivism) and epic in form (as opposed to the personal dramas of the Germans), they brought rapid pace and physical action back to the moving picture and resumed the line that emphasized editing inaugurated by Porter and advanced by Griffith.

The German film makers' intellectual sources included Sigmund Freud. Their concern with the psychological led to expressionism and the subjective camera as means of portraying internal states. As used by the Germans, the moving camera became a kind of visual equivalent to the psychoanalyst's probing of the patient; the expressionistic design conveyed dreams, nightmares, and hallucinations.

In the Soviet Union the ideological basis was provided by Karl Marx and V. I. Lenin, and the film makers' concerns were social, political, and economic. The predominant aesthetic mode was futurism, which attempted to depict vividly the energetic and dynamic quality of contemporary life influenced by the motion and force of modern machinery. In film, pictorial realism rather than expressionism was the visual style required to portray the actual, external world. Cutting—paralleling the conflict and resolution of opposites in Hegelian/Marxian dialectic—was the principal formative method. A neat symbolic point is made by G. W. Pabst's having directed *Secrets of a Soul,* a popularization of Freudian psychology, in the same year, 1926, that V. I. Pudovkin made *Mechanics of the Brain,* explaining the Pavlovian scientific dialectic of stimulus-response. Even a comparison of the titles of the German and Soviet films is revealing: *secrets* versus *mechanics, a* versus *the, soul* versus *brain.*

♦ HISTORICAL SETTING

The first films to be seen in Russia were those sent in by the brothers Lumière in 1896, the year following the initial Paris screening, and shortly after the coronation of Czar Nicholas II—an event recorded by film makers from Europe and the United States. In the successful exploitation method the Lumières had developed around their "scenic views," a projectionist-cinematographer would visit a country and show short films of such sights as the Eiffel Tower, sidewalk cafés, the Zouaves in review, and other foreign attractions. In Russia, a troika ride, peasant dances, and the Kremlin domes would be filmed. These subjects would appeal to the national pride of the Russians and could be shown elsewhere throughout the world as scenes of exotic customs and faraway places.

It wasn't until considerably later that Russian film production commenced, pioneered by another French firm, however: Pathé Frères, with *Cossacks of the Don* in 1908. In that same year the first Russian studio began operation in Moscow, but all film supplies and equipment continued to be imported from France and Germany. By 1917 and the end of pre-communist Russia, there were more than twenty producers, with Moscow the main production center. Even so, more foreign than domestic films were shown.

In czarist Russia movies were not a popular art as they were elsewhere. There were few theaters, tickets were expensive, and the working classes couldn't afford to attend regularly. The high illiteracy rate made printed intertitles a general burden, and the literary-theatrical bent of the Russian silent films further helped confine their patronage to the educated middle classes. Somewhat equivalent to *films d'art* and Adolph Zukor's famous players in famous plays, the highly theatrical tradition of the Russian film (as opposed to the later Soviet film) is generally agreed upon and is borne out by the few examples existing in archives in the United States. After the Bolshevik Revolution, most of the film producers and actors emigrated, taking with them whatever equipment and film they could carry.

Those producers who chose to remain were at first allowed to continue along lines of private enterprise. Though they lacked revolutionary understanding, let alone zeal, not much attention was given to their output by a government preoccupied with more pressing matters. A Cinema Committee was set up, however, under playwright A. V. Lunacharsky, Minister of Education. With truly remarkable foresight, given the uses of film generally up to that time and the negligible Russian production, Lenin had said, "Of all the arts, the cinema is the most important for us." His statement contrasts as strongly as could be expected with one from the deposed Nicholas II, who had written: "I consider cinematography an empty, useless, and even pernicious diversion. Only an abnormal person could place this sideshow business on a level with art. It is all nonsense and no importance should be lent to such trash."[2] At the same time it is known that this last of the czars was an ardent moviegoer who spent many evenings at private screenings in the palace basement.

The national conditions that prevented Lenin and the other communist leaders from promptly turning film into the voice for the Revolution that it eventually became were not unlike those of postwar Germany, and considerably more severe. In the first year of the new government famine was widespread. During one of the cruelest Russian winters on record there was no fuel. Typhus raged in epidemic proportions. After participation in the war dragged to a halt, the Soviets faced Allied armies within their borders and continuing civil warfare with the counterrevolutionaries. One curious instance of the general instability was an episode in which some 50,000 escaped Czech prisoners of war ravaged the countryside unresisted along the route of the Trans-Siberian railway.

It took some five years (1918–1922) to fully establish the new political regime and two more years before the film industry was functioning with anything approaching productivity. (Even by the end of 1923 only 13 percent of the films shown in the country were Soviet.) In 1919 the industry had been completely nationalized when it became clear that the old capitalist economics and mentality would not serve the needs of a socialist state. In the same year the State Institute of Cinematography (VGIK)

[2]Quoted by Jay Leyda in *Kino* (New York: Macmillan, 1960), p. 69.

was established in Moscow to train new Soviet film makers; it is thus the oldest, as well as one of the largest and best, film schools in the world. In 1925 the Sovkino Trust was formed to try to bring some order into all aspects of the domestic industry and to reestablish distribution abroad.

The new Soviet cinema, which began its formative period about 1919, was thought of at the time as being divided into two creative camps. Though called the right and left wings, the labels weren't essentially political. At first the right wing carried on in the old theatrical tradition, using conventional methods and styles but substituting commissars, peasants, and Red Army soldiers for the upper-class characters of traditional theater. Romance, humor, and heroics persisted. The concerns of the new state motivate the action initially and appear as background, but scarcely replace standard dramaturgical elements: boy-girl, comic sidekicks, obstacles to be overcome, obstructive villains, and so on. *Kombrig Ivanov* (1923) is an example of this creative tendency; it was retitled *The Beauty and the Bolshevik* in the United States. Subsequently the work of the right wing achieved greater sophistication and addressed itself to sociological problems. Abram Room's *Bed and Sofa* (1927), for example, deals with a romantic triangle, but the shifting allegiance of the woman towards the two men involves the housing shortage and her attitude and theirs toward the role of women in the new society. The general methods of the right wing became the only officially sanctioned approach after "socialist realism" was imposed in the 1930s, and continued to dominate Soviet cinema. *The Cranes Are Flying* (1957) and *Ballad of a Soldier* (1959) are later popular examples.

The left wing was much more radical in its innovation, which involved form as well as subject. When we think of the Soviet silent cinema, it is usually of the films growing out of the theories and experiments of two left-wing pioneers. One of these was Dziga Vertov, who followed Lenin's advice that the first work of Soviet film makers should be with newsreels and documentaries. This seemed advisable partly because of the drain on resources that feature film production would have represented, but especially because of the urgency of communicating the history and spirit of the Revolution to the still largely apathetic and uninformed Russian public. In 1919 Vertov founded his Kino-Eye Group and began publishing manifestos.[3] "Life caught unawares" was Vertov's credo. What he meant by this was not exactly candid camera (since the subjects usually knew they were being filmed), but that nothing be staged or directed. Life in front of the camera was permitted to run its natural course; the only creative control the film maker exerted was through choosing what and how to shoot, and the placement of one shot in relation to another during the editing. In 1922 Vertov began to produce "Kino-Pravda," a series of monthly newsfilms that lasted for twenty-three issues. The title, incidentally, is synonymous with *cinéma vérité* (film truth), a term French anthropologist-film maker Jean Rouch coined in 1961 to apply

---

[3] Vertov's theories of film are available in *Kino-Eye: The Writings of Dziga Vertov,* edited and with an introduction by Annette Michelson, translated by Kevin O'Brien (Berkeley: University of California Press, 1984).

"Kino-Pravda" series ◆ USSR, 1922–25, Dziga Vertov.

to a new kind of documentary. What *cinéma vérité* added to *kino pravda* was essentially the lightweight, synchronous sound equipment that permitted the film maker to shoot and record virtually anything without interrupting or altering it for the benefit of camera or microphone.

Since Vertov had no control over the action he was filming, unlike a director of fiction films, editing took on a peculiarly central role in his work. Moreover, the shortage of raw stock in the Soviet Union in the early twenties (before the Soviets began to manufacture their own) meant that Vertov had to use pieces of film as he found them, frequently short ends left over from other projects. In an impulse not unlike Porter's in *Life of an American Fireman,* Vertov learned that by juxtaposing shots from old czarist newsreels with newly shot materials he could create new meanings. Russian tanks crossing a no-man's-land in the war could be followed by Soviet tractors breaking ground for cultivation. Juxtaposing a shot of the formal and elegant Nicholas stiffly reviewing his palace guard with a shot of a shirt-sleeved Lenin energetically addressing the workers added significance not inherent in either shot alone. In embryonic form this was precisely the kind of editing that Sergei Eisenstein would develop into montage; the title of his film *Old and New* (1929) concisely sums up a principal propaganda device of Vertov's. Beyond that, one can say of "Kino-Pravda" that all the subjects were socially purposeful: There are no beauty parades, no animals in the zoo. Inspirational in tone, the films seem to be urging that there's a job to be done. In general they show one region or aspect of national life to the rest of the country (a major mission of the documentary film later to be picked up in Britain, with proper credit always given to the Soviets). Vertov's reports are not all sweetness and light by any means; hard-hitting exposés are included. "Save the starving children" one title proclaims, as we see the pitiful young victims of famine. The directness of communication with the people is further revealed in end titles that encourage the audience to mail its "inquiries regarding traveling film shows" and "all film and photo work" to Kino-Pravda.

Another left-wing pioneer was Lev Kuleshov, film director, theorist, lecturer (from 1920 on) and later head of the State Institute of Cinematography.[4] As Sergei Eisenstein came out of the Vertov line, another great Soviet film maker, V. I. Pudovkin, was Kuleshov's star pupil. Eisenstein's impressively talented cameraman, Eduard Tisse, had worked for Vertov, as Pudovkin's cameraman, Anatoli Golovnya, had for Kuleshov. Kuleshov coped with the shortage of raw stock by conducting acting experiments performed for an empty camera. Also, he and his students spent much time analyzing and recutting existing motion pictures to learn filmic construction. When Kuleshov gained access to film stock he came to emphasize editing as heavily as did Vertov, but for different purposes. He discovered how, through cutting, to make nonactors appear to give skillful performances and how to give the acting of professionals meanings of which they were unaware at time of performance. Following Vertov and Kuleshov, Eisenstein and Pudovkin made editing for the Soviet silent film makers virtually synonymous with the creative process itself.

A third early creative and theoretical group contributed to the scope of Soviet cinema. In 1922 a youthful Grigori Kozintsev (age 17) joined Leonid Trauberg (17), and Sergei Yutkevitch (18) to form the Factory of the Eccentric Actor: FEX. The virtually unlimited freedom for experimentation in the arts during the hectic years of revolution and civil war unleashed the progressive spirit among the young. (In 1922 Vertov was 26, Kuleshov 23, Eisenstein 24, and Pudovkin 29.) This generation of Soviet artists, seeking new methods of expression, turned toward minor genres, "the kind of popular art which the aristocracy and bourgeoisie had scorned. To be precise: the music hall, the circus and the cinema."[5] Eisenstein's first film, *Strike* (1925), is very closely related to these aesthetic impulses. After seeing it, Kozintsev told the FEX group, "All that we're doing is childish nonsense, we must all see *Strike* again and again, until we can understand it and adopt its power for our own."[6]

---

[4] His theories are available in *Kuleshov on Film: Writings by Lev Kuleshov,* selected, translated, and edited by Ronald Levaco (Berkeley: University of California Press, 1974).

[5] Sergei Yutkevich in *Cinema in Revolution,* edited by Luda and Jean Schnitzer and Marcel Martin (New York: Hill & Wang, 1973), p. 16.

[6] Quoted in Leyda, *Kino,* p. 201.

By the Law ◆ USSR, 1926, Lev Kuleshov.

◆ THREE SILENT MASTERS

Ranked alongside Eisenstein and Pudovkin among the great Soviet silent makers would be **Alexander Dovzhenko.** Because he stands somewhat apart from the principal thrust of Soviet film making, his work will be discussed first. A Ukrainian from a family of uneducated farmers, Dovzhenko includes in his films strange ethnic and mystical elements that color his Marxism and make his silent work quite distinct from that of the other Soviet film makers. He was a painter before he became a film maker, and montage was not as important for him as it was for the others; at least his use of it is quite different.

In Dovzhenko's three major silent films—*Zvenigora* (1928), *Arsenal* (1929), *Earth* (1930)—the larger sequences seem separate from each other, circular in construction, and strangely complete in themselves. He emphasizes the relationships of scenes to scenes, within the sequences, rather than of shots to each other within the scenes. The numerous and varied scenes tend to be brief, but the shots (or even a single shot) that they comprise are often sustained. Contrasting and elliptical combinations involve quite extraordinary shifts of mood and statement. The connections of the parts to each other are often unclear or ambiguous on first viewing. In *Earth,* in a scene of the kulaks weeping and wailing, which follows the scene of the peasant grandfather dying, we assume initially that they are mourning his death. When we learn that it is a threatened loss of possessions that has provoked their grief, the comment about them becomes a negative one. Ambiguity of this sort is rarely allowed to occur in the more didactic main body of Soviet work. It is as if Dovzhenko were serenely indifferent to conventional continuity in his pursuit of evocative, many-layered imagery.

Marking Dovzhenko's visual style are extremely wide-angled long shots in which a complexity of action and composition builds up within a single frame like an evolving painting. Also, there are the painterly "still" shots—the striking silhouettes of *Arsenal,* the trees heavy-laden with fruit in *Earth*—which convey a sense of timelessness, of fixity. In thinking of Dovzhenko's work we remember its many images of the Ukrainian countryside composed of low horizons and small human figures moving under an enormous open sky. The shocking and beautiful balletic death of Vasily in *Earth,* as he moves down a curving moonlit road toward the camera, to be cut down almost casually by a murderer's bullet, is not likely to be forgotten. Throughout his early films Dovzhenko's intentions are clearly more poetic than narrative (as with Pudovkin) or dramatic (as with Eisenstein).

His symbols and metaphors are not forced or belletristic, however; they grow out of a conception of the closeness of the people to the soil. They also contain dialectical contradictions that advance the revolutionary argument; but because Dovzhenko sees life whole, there is nothing of the agitprop about his work. In *Earth* he is saying it is right for an old man to die (at peace) but wrong (against nature) for a young man to die (by violence). Yet death is followed by life in both cases. As the old man munches one apple, a child munches another, completing the cycle of generations. A woman gives birth during Vasily's funeral, and his comrades are clearly fulfilling the potential of his abbreviated life in building for the future. The autumn rain in the epilogue appears at first to be like tears, but it is also life-giving as it falls on the fullness of harvest. The tractor is regarded by the old as a replacement of themselves and their animals, and by the young as an extension of the people's productivity.

Though working in the service of the state, Dovzhenko's humanism causes him to extend sympathy to the old as well as the new. One can imagine that a Joseph Stalin might have regarded the ambivalence uneasily, and ultimately as subversive. To a modern American viewer, *Earth* carries a very optimistic tone and presents a remark-able argument for revolutionary change. But when it premiered in Moscow, it was attacked at length in *Izvestia* for being "defeatist" and "counterrevolutionary." Given its slowness of pace, ambiguities, obscurities, and dependence on the pictorial, it seems unlikely that it could have had the requisite popularity in Russia to do the indoctrinational job required of it by the sponsoring government. At any rate, after the brilliant experimental period of the twenties, the hard line of "socialist realism" appeared; Dovzhenko never again achieved anything equal to the unique visual lyricism of his silent films. Even in the earlier time he seemed out of step with his colleagues. What attracted him most strongly was clearly the human and natural beauty that could be captured by the camera, rather than the arguments that could be fashioned by an editor's shears.

Earth ◆ USSR, 1930,
Alexander Dovzhenko.

V. I. Pudovkin was educated as a physicist and chemist. (Dovzhenko's education, too, had been scientific and technological.) He became interested in acting for films, he said, as a result of seeing *Intolerance,* which had finally arrived in Russia in 1919. Though Pudovkin would appear as an actor in many of his own films as well as those of others, while studying under Kuleshov he came to see that the real creative fulfillment in motion pictures was for the director rather than the actor. Kuleshov, for his part, fully understood that Griffith had been working out of some of the same concepts that had begun to preoccupy him. A prominent concern of Kuleshov's was the difference between the actor's contributions to stage and to screen.

On stage, once the curtain rises the performer is in complete control of his or her performance. Direction and rehearsal are merely preparation to be used, or ignored for that matter, in interpreting a character in the presence of an audience. In film, the director is the principal "audience" of the live performance. The screen performance is constructed after the actor has finished his or her work, out of the selection made available by the camera: a long shot of the actor in a room full of people, a closeup of just the actor's profile, a reaction shot of someone else's face, and so on. It is no longer the actor's total performance that finally appears, no longer her or his rhythm or even whole body, but bits and pieces integrated into a synthetic whole. With systematic thoroughness Kuleshov began to test the possibilities of this basic cinematic technique.

His influence on Pudovkin was profound, and the latter participated in a series of Kuleshov's experiments that explored the potential of editing to create a time and

Mother ♦ USSR, 1926, V. I. Pudovkin; Nikolai Batalov, on left, and Vera Baranovskaya, on right.

space existing (or seeming to exist) only on film. For one of these experiments Kuleshov assembled five shots. In the first, a young man walks from left to right. In the second, a young woman walks from right to left. In a third, they meet and shake hands, and the young man points to something off screen. The fourth shot shows a large white building with a broad flight of steps. In the fifth, the couple ascends steps. A viewer would accept this scene as one uninterrupted action, but in actuality the five pieces had been shot in completely different times and places—the man and woman (shots one and two) in separate parts of Moscow, and the handshake (shot three) in yet another. The white building (four) was in fact the White House, snipped from an American film, and the steps (five) were those of a cathedral.[7] Rudimentary and obvious as such experiments may seem, they nonetheless isolated and held up for examination the most basic aesthetic underpinning of the medium.

Returning from their practical experiments to a further study of *Intolerance,* Kuleshov and Pudovkin began to see how to apply their discoveries to the requirements of a new Soviet cinema. Though as far from being a Marxist as is conceivable,

[7]V. I. Pudovkin, *Film Technique* (New York: Lear Publishers, 1949), pp. 60–61.

Griffith, in *Intolerance,* had carried on a moral and ethical argument through his separate historical episodes, and in the modern story, economic and social ones as well. (Not only the strike in Pudovkin's *Mother,* 1926, but Eisenstein's *Strike,* 1925, contain unmistakable borrowings from the Griffith film.) In a succession of master-works paralleling those of Eisenstein—warmer and more moving, if not as breathtakingly experimental and brilliant—Pudovkin gave full form to his learning. Unlike the highly intellectual appeal of Eisenstein's work, Pudovkin's films reach the emotions directly. They received instant acclaim and their power seems undiminished by the years. As with Dovzhenko, Pudovkin's major silent films—*Mother, The End of St. Petersburg* (1927), and *Storm over Asia* (1928)—stand as his finest and most personal achievements, though he too continued to work for several decades in the sound film. While he became a greater director than Kuleshov, Pudovkin also wrote theoretical work—*Film Technique* and *Film Acting*—which explained and showed the applications of his former teacher's insights. They remain among the best texts for beginning directors, especially for those interested in documentary film and work with nonactors.

Sergei Eisenstein, like Dovzhenko and Pudovkin, had a technical education (as a civil engineer) prior to defecting to the arts—first to theater in his case. Before beginning stage work, however, Eisenstein had developed an intense interest in Japanese language and culture, which would feed into his later profound and erudite theorizing about film. He was fascinated by the Japanese hieroglyphic writing, in which the word *weeping* is formed by combining the pictograph for *eye* with that for *water; singing* by combining that for *mouth* and *bird; listening,* for *ear* plus *door;* and so on. He came to feel that the two drawn symbols combined like film shots to provide a third meaning. Also, he noted a Japanese technique for teaching drawing, which limited the student to the composition of segments of a cherry tree branch within a frame. This attention to frame area and composition within it Eisenstein would find useful preparation for his own painstaking composing of images. Finally, Kabuki theater seemed to him to bring various artistic elements together in a balance not unlike that of film. In Kabuki, and in the Nō plays, spoken language is not the almost exclusive carrier of content that it is in Western drama. Japanese theater is visual as much as verbal. Words are part of an ensemble in which formalized gesture, choreographed body movement, music, even costumes, carry equal weight and add nuances and qualifications to a complex whole.

Eisenstein's theatrical beginning was as a scene designer for the Proletkult Theatre. From childhood he had been a prodigious sketcher and painter; the Proletkult, dedicated to the development of proletarian artists and the education of the working class, accommodated his sympathies for the revolution. From the Proletkult he learned to distrust the character-centered theater of the nineteenth century and to seek ways to make the masses the hero and to present social problems in place of bourgeois romantic triangles. Moving on to work with Vsevolod Meyerhold, a radically innovative theatrical producer and director, Eisenstein completed the theoretical education and practical experience that would propel him into film.

Meyerhold's theories of acting were in polar opposition to those of Konstantin Stanislavsky, the other great contemporary force in Russian theater. Whereas Stanislavsky started from within, in a psychological approach, instructing his actors to search out the emotions of their characters, Meyerhold began from without, in a theory he called biomechanics. Related to Pavlov's experiments in conditioned reflexes and consistent with the scientific spirit of the new Russia, Meyerhold's method was based on the idea that emotions could be stimulated in the actor (and conveyed to the spectator) through analysis of the emotive connotations of movement, and by developing the actor's body into a precise machine capable of producing the exact effects desired. This approach pulled the Meyerhold theater closer to the *commedia dell'arte* tradition and even to the technique of circus performers. It may have helped lay the groundwork for German revolutionary Bertolt Brecht's aesthetic stance; certainly it had a profound effect on Eisenstein.

Returning to the Proletkult, Eisenstein arrived at his own eclectic fusion of all he had come to understand up to that point. What he sought was a "montage of attractions"—a series of sensory experiences that would involve the spectators and carry them along a predetermined path of emotional response. His most successful realization of these theories on the stage seems to have been a parody production of Alexander Ostrovsky's *The Wise Man*. In it he combined acrobats, a tightrope walker, and satirical asides directed at foreign political figures with a caricatured religious procession bearing candles, chanting litany, and carrying placards inscribed "Religion is the opium of the people." A short comic film was specially produced for incorporation into the performance.

Eisenstein's final attempt to transform theatrical art and get closer to the emotional needs of contemporary audiences led him in a direction opposite from the circus and the music hall, toward the reality outside the theater. His production of *Gas Masks,* a play by Sergei Tretyakov, was performed by workers and staged in the actual Moscow Gas Factory. Eisenstein regarded this experiment as a failure. Rather than eliminating "art" and replacing it with "life," as he had intended by using real setting and nonactors, he had succeeded only in exposing the artificiality of conventions that would have seemed perfectly at home in the theater. Seeking a means of capturing the reality of factory and workers that so fascinated him, he arrived at film as the medium that could make art out of materials much closer to life than could theatrical drama. As he put it, "The cart fell to pieces and the driver dropped into the cinema."

Strike (1925), his first film, also used a factory setting, with the workers as the collective protagonists. The "montage of attractions" now became the rapid and rhythmic cutting together of shots, startling in their visual contrasts, physical in their impact. Though all of the elements of Eisenstein's mature silent work are present, traces of the kind of theater in which he had been working account for some excesses and discordances. The "circus" elements—caricatures, gross symbolism, and exaggerated action—though striking in themselves, fit rather strangely into the prevailing naturalism. On the other hand, there is a documentary-like looseness of structure that makes the film more successful within its sequences than it is as a whole. *Battleship Potemkin* (1925) advanced upon the first work by stripping away some of the flamboyance and disciplining the fertility of imagination. Built upon a tight and firm dramatic line, its five sequences proceed with the cumulative power of the acts of classical tragedy.

Strike ♦ USSR, 1925, Sergei Eisenstein.

Both films make essentially the same ideological points. Though *Potemkin* deals with the mutiny of the crew of an armored cruiser in the abortive 1905 Revolution, its officers are equivalent to the capitalists of *Strike;* its White Guards and Cossacks, who cut down the populace on the Odessa Steps, are like the army and police of the preceding film. In both films, the actions of the ruling class are arrogant and deceitful and lead to slaughter. The sailors and workers are simple and loyal to each other; except for their proletarian leaders, they are naive in the ways of the world. Incapable of evil unless duped into it by the authorities, they resort to violence only to counter unendurable oppression. The working classes are portrayed as the most productive resource of the nation and its only democratic force. A version of the desired dictatorship of the proletariat is offered in these two films. A recurrent image shows the revolutionary leaders haranguing the sailors or workers who then move together in a single group decision: "All for one, one for all!" the *Potemkin* titles shout.

The "hero" of both films is the masses—played by people who would have lived through situations much like those portrayed. In both cases, an epic scale of action is based on real or composite events. The viewpoint is broadly social-political and there is little delineation of characters except as types. Both films were shot on location

Battleship Potemkin ◆ USSR, 1925, Sergei Eisenstein.

rather than in studios; in the case of *Potemkin,* Odessa was the actual place of some of the incidents portrayed. Eisenstein seized upon and made full use of the accidents of setting: in *Strike,* the stairway tier of the workers' tenements; in *Potemkin,* the architectural characteristics of Odessa, a morning mist on the water, the stone lions, and the like. His play with mass, line, and movement is that of a dynamic painter; his handling of crowds is quite without peer. Always Eisenstein works through the kinetic. But, given the amount of movement within the frame and the rapidity of cutting, there is little moving camera. Instead there are an extraordinary number and variety of camera setups, as would be required by his kind of editing. At moments of climactic action some of the shots are as short as two frames, and their content is frequently horrifying: a Cossack's saber slashing downward, a woman's spectacles broken and her face bloodied. Through an intended physiological response, Eisenstein aimed to bring his viewers to a political attitude. Closeups abound and there is a prominent use of what in literature would be called synecdoche, the parts representing a larger whole. In *Potemkin,* the maggoty meat, the doctor's pince-nez which eventually dangle in the ropes, the pounding pistons of the ship's engines, and the final magnificent shot from below of its hull slicing through the water, all serve this function.

October (or *Ten Days That Shook the World,* 1928) marks the height of Eisenstein's "intellectual montage," but it lacks the passion and coherence of *Battleship Potemkin*—at least the versions of it that appear in the West. Like Griffith's *Intolerance,* in comparison to *The Birth of a Nation, October,* though in some respects Eisenstein's ultimate achievement, is on a canvas so large that the monumental conception remains only partially realized. *Old and New* (also known as *The General Line,* 1929) was his final silent film. In it, though his aesthetic sensibility and intelligence are as evident as ever, they seem essentially of the wrong kind for this account of Soviet farm life and collectivization.

Dovzhenko and Pudovkin adjusted to the conventions of socialist realism and continued a steady if scarcely distinguished output into the first decades of sound. Eisenstein could not adjust, and was frequently the target of criticism from bureaucrats, critics, and other film makers. The problem was not that he was unwilling to serve the state in ways deemed socially useful, but that he was innately and supremely what he was accused of being—a formalist. His released sound films—*Alexander Nevsky* (1938), *Ivan the Terrible,* Part I (1944), Part II (1958)—great though they are, are few. He spent much of the last fifteen years of his life teaching and writing. It may be that his theoretical writings, like George Bernard Shaw's prefaces to his plays, will

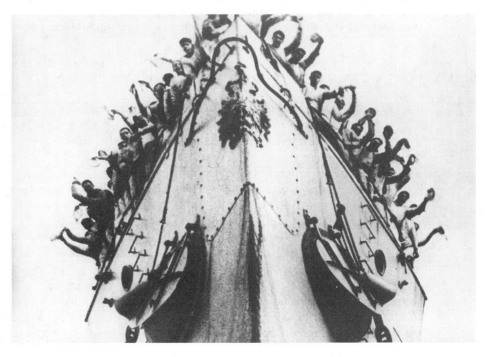

Battleship Potemkin ◆ USSR, 1925, Sergei Eisenstein.

retain a value beyond some of the creative work that grew out of them. In any event, Eisenstein's films and theories marked an enormous advance in a conscious and articulated understanding of how the cinema works as a means of communication—as a kind of language and as a form of art. Montage was the key concept.

♦ MONTAGE: THEORY AND PRACTICE

The word *montage* was borrowed from the French; *monter* simply means to mount or assemble. For the Soviet film makers, however, this assembling and mounting through editing became the ultimate creative act. Though they had learned from Griffith and were nudged into the most economic use of the shot by the shortage of raw stock, their practical experiments, published theories, and finally the great works of Soviet silent film, led them to a kind and level of accomplishment that has served to instruct film creators and critics ever since. Eisenstein and Pudovkin, friendly rivals as film makers, were also principal spokesmen in a running debate about the proper uses of montage. They agreed on the fundamental importance of editing, but for Pudovkin the cut was linkage, a joining of shots for the gradual accumulation of narrative meaning—the unfolding of a story. For Eisenstein its function was to achieve shock, the banging together of contrasting shots in a way that would force the audience into an understanding greater than the sum and different from any one of its parts. Eisenstein took particular satisfaction in what he regarded as the similarity of this process to the thesis-antithesis-synthesis of Hegelian dialectic. The argument is important as well as interesting, and worth pursuing through the words of the adversaries.

In *Film Technique,* Pudovkin, after acknowledging his indebtedness to Kuleshov and the importance of the concept of montage to Soviet film makers, writes:

> *Kuleshov maintained that the material in film-work consists of pieces of film, and that the composition method is their joining together in a particular, creatively discovered order. He maintained that film-art does not begin when the artists act and the various scenes are shot—this is only the preparation of the material. Film-art begins from the moment when the director begins to combine and join together the various pieces of film. By joining them in various combinations, in different orders, he obtains differing results.* [8]

Pudovkin continues by describing two more of the practical experiments (like the one with the couple, the steps, and the White House) that Kuleshov and his students were carrying out to test their theories.

The first involves three short strips of film. On one is the image of a smiling face, on another a hand pointing a revolver, on the third a frightened face. Pudovkin observes that if the shots are assembled in that order the impression we get is that the second man is facing the revolver and that he is a coward. If the order is reversed—

[8]Pudovkin, *Film Technique,* pp. 138–39.

frightened face, revolver, smiling face—the impression we get is that the man facing the revolver is very brave. Thus the meaning of precisely the same images is altered, even reversed, by changing their order.

In the second experiment recalled by Pudovkin, he and Kuleshov selected some closeups of the Russian actor Ivan Mozhukhin. They were static, neutral shots of Mozhukhin's face expressing no particular emotion. Those shots were then intercut with closeups of other material. First was a bowl of soup on a table; it seemed quite obvious that Mozhukhin was looking at the soup. Then the actor's face was followed by shots showing a coffin in which lay a dead woman. In the third instance the face was followed by a shot of a little girl playing with a funny toy bear. When the three combinations were shown without explanation to an audience, they raved about Mozhukhin's acting! They pointed out the heavy pensiveness of the mood created as he regarded the forgotten bowl of soup, the deep grief expressed as he looked at the dead woman, the light, happy smile that played across his features as he gazed at the little girl. In all three cases, according to Pudovkin, Mozhukhin's facial expression had been virtually the same, and expressing very little at that.

Pudovkin concludes his recounting of these experiments with an additional observation that:

The combination of various pieces in one or another order is not sufficient. It is necessary to be able to control and manipulate the length of these pieces, because the combination of pieces of varying length is effective in the same way as the combination of sounds of various length in music, by creating the rhythm of the film and by means of their varying effect on the audience. Quick, short pieces rouse excitement, while long pieces have a soothing effect.[9]

In other words, Pudovkin offers a sort of formula: Film creation equals (1) what is in the shots, (2) the order in which they appear, and (3) how long each is held on the screen. "To be able to find the requisite order of shots or pieces and the rhythm necessary for their combination," he summarizes, "that is the chief task of the director's art. This art we call *montage*—or constructive editing. It is only with the help of *montage* that I am able to solve problems of such complexity as the work on the artists' acting."[10]

Note the final emphasis given to performance. Unlike Eisenstein's silent films, Pudovkin's make heavy use of professional actors and contain some superb characterizations. He portrays the awakening of revolutionary consciousness through the microcosm of individual experience more than through the action of the masses; for example, Vera Baranovskaya as the title character in *Mother,* Ivan Chuvelyov as the peasant lad in *The End of St. Petersburg.* Still, Pudovkin regards actors as "plastic material" not unlike any objects that might be photographed. They move and gesture, stare and weep, but for Pudovkin the film "performance" is created by the director

[9]Pudovkin, *Film Technique,* pp. 139–41.
[10]Pudovkin, *Film Technique,* p. 141.

cutting together strips of celluloid registering these actions. As might be expected, this is a position that horrifies and infuriates actors.

Pudovkin began the "Introduction to the German Edition" of *Film Technique* with: "The foundation of film art is *editing*." Eisenstein, in an essay in *Film Form*, echoes Pudovkin: "To determine the nature of montage is to solve the specific problem of cinema." He goes on to explain:

> *The earliest conscious film makers, and our first film theoreticians, regarded montage as a means of description by placing single shots one after the other like building-blocks. The movement within these building-block shots, and the consequent length of the component pieces, was then considered as rhythm.*[11]

That was precisely what Pudovkin had written, as Eisenstein acknowledges with what is perhaps a feigned superiority of disbelief and an implied distinction between the theorist and the artist: "According to this definition, shared even by Pudovkin as a theoretician, montage is the means of *unrolling* an idea with the help of single shots: the 'epic' principle." (*Epic* is here used in the classical sense—narrative as opposed to dramatic.) In Eisenstein's opinion, however, "montage is an idea that arises from the collision of independent shots—shots even opposite to one another: the 'dramatic' principle."[12]

Elsewhere, in an essay in the companion volume, *The Film Sense*, Eisenstein continues the argument and expands upon his own position. As he sees the Soviet films, they are "faced with the task of presenting not only a narrative that is *logically connected*, but one that contains a *maximum of emotion and stimulating power.* Montage is a mighty aid to the resolution of this task," he asserts. Eisenstein goes on to ask rhetorically, "Why do we use montage at all?"

> *Even the most fanatical opponent of montage will agree that it is not merely because the film strip at our disposal is not of infinite length, and consequently, being condemned to working with pieces of restricted lengths, we have to stick one piece of it on to another occasionally.*
>
> *The 'leftists' of montage saw it from the opposite extreme. While playing with pieces of film, they discovered a certain property in the toy which kept them astonished for a number of years. This property consisted in the fact that two film pieces of any kind, placed together, inevitably combine into a new concept, a new quality, arising out of that juxtaposition.*
>
> *This is not in the least a circumstance peculiar to the cinema, but is a phenomenon invariably met with in all cases where we have to deal with juxtaposition of two facts, two phenomena, two objects. We are accustomed to make, almost automatically, a definite and obvious deductive generalization when any separate objects are placed before us side by side. For*

---

[11]Sergei M. Eisenstein, *Film Form* (New York: Harcourt Brace, 1949), p. 48.
[12]Eisenstein, *Film Form*, p. 49.

example, take a grave, juxtaposed with a woman in mourning weeping beside it, and scarcely anybody will fail to jump to the conclusion: a widow. *It is precisely on this feature of our perception that the following miniature story by Ambrose Bierce bases its effect. It is from his* Fantastic Fables *and is entitled "The Inconsolable Widow":*

"A Woman in widow's weeds was weeping upon a grave.

'Console yourself, madame,' said a Sympathetic Stranger. 'Heaven's mercies are infinite. There is another man somewhere, besides your husband, with whom you can still be happy.'

'There was,' she sobbed—'there was, but this is his grave." [13]

It is neatly coincidental that Pudovkin referred to a coffin in the experiment with the actor Mozhukhin. Both Eisenstein and Pudovkin are suggesting how the meaning of an action can be changed into something other than the actual or original through associative montage. But Pudovkin's addition of a coffin merely makes the actor's face seem sad when it was not necessarily. The attraction of Bierce's anecdote for Eisenstein is clearly that the normal additive principle is replaced by a combination of the unexpected, opposites in a sense, and the "widow" becomes an adulteress.

Eisenstein's use of an obscure piece of American literature to illustrate his conception, rather than a practical experiment with several pieces of film, represents fairly the difference between his critical method and that of Pudovkin. Eisenstein explored the arts of other cultures to show that montage as he understood it existed quite separately from film and had existed long before film appeared. His analyses of the shooting-script-like ordering of images found in passages from the poems of Pushkin and the novels of Dickens offer a contribution to literary criticism as well as provocative analogues for those studying film. For Eisenstein the form and sense of film aesthetic extended into a total philosophical view of the world. For Pudovkin the insights montage provided were carefully restricted to film technique and film acting.

In practice the argument between the two is happily muddled by some of the best examples of Eisensteinian shock montage appearing in films of Pudovkin and by Eisenstein necessarily having to resort to Pudovkinian narrative to hold together the brief pyrotechnical bursts of collision. Whether as linkage or juxtaposition, one result of this extreme fragmentation of the scene was that both film makers could use nonactors to a degree that more sustained takes would not allow. Any embarrassed self-consciousness could be stripped away and the usable moments selected and combined with other visual materials—like the actor Mozhukhin with soup, coffin, and child—to give the illusion of a performance that in fact never occurred. This new possibility led to theories of *typage,* of choosing people who looked the part regardless of their thespian skills.

Another characteristic of Soviet film technique was that the naturalistic materials of "real people" (as opposed to actors) and "actual locations" (in contrast to studio interiors or back lots) were subjected to an extreme degree of highly conscious manipulation through editing. Though the style is radically different from that of the

[13]Sergei M. Eisenstein, *The Film Sense* (New York: Harcourt Brace, 1942), pp. 4–5.

Germans', in their own ways the Soviet films are just as stylized. Finally, in order to construct their intricate mosaics from small pieces of the total action, the Soviets—like the Germans and unlike Griffith—relied on highly detailed scripts and preplanning. Eisenstein sketched virtually all of his shots in advance; a substantial portion of Pudovkin's *Film Technique* is devoted to a method of precise script construction.

Unlike the films of any nation that had preceded them, however, all the Soviet films had social-political purposes and government sponsorship. Most of them interpreted the revolution in ways designed to improve the understanding and win the loyalty of the Soviet people. When *Battleship Potemkin* first went out into the world as a revolutionary emissary—feared and hated by the reactionaries and philistines, elaborately praised by the liberals and aesthetes—its success was as much a surprise to the Soviets as to anyone. That many of the Soviet silent films are universal and enduring works of art as well as being indoctrinational is a tribute to the sincere enthusiasm the film makers felt for the gigantic social experiment of which they were part.

Though the significance of this body of work in the history of film is enormous, specific applications of its themes and techniques, unlike those of the Germans, were limited in the capitalist countries. Soon the formal concerns and innovations of the left wing would become unacceptable in the Soviet Union itself. Perhaps the one clear and direct link between Soviet silent films and films elsewhere is with the British social documentaries of the thirties, which were state-supported for purposes of broad citizenship education and which indulged in their own experimentation with form—especially the joining of sound and image.

In the fictional film the arrival of sound largely reduced the use of montage to brief transitional sequences—of spinning locomotive wheels superimposed over a succession of billboards as the young opera star progresses toward fame and heartbreak, or of crowded beaches, golfers, and children eating watermelon, to signal summer. To be sure, and for better or worse, every television commercial builds upon the kinds of persuasiveness the Soviets discovered lay in the combination of short strips of film. But the body of Soviet silent cinema stands with an integrity, eloquence, and beauty that require nothing more of it than continued availability. New audiences invariably marvel at the heights reached during this final national ascendancy in the silent film.

FILMS OF THE PERIOD

1925

Battleship Potemkin
    (Sergei Eisenstein)
Strike (Eisenstein)

1926

The Cloak
    (Grigori Kozintsev and Leonid Trauberg)
Mother (V. I. Pudovkin)

1927

Bed and Sofa (Abram Room)
The End of St. Petersburg (Pudovkin)
The Fall of the Romanov Dynasty
    (Esfir Shub)

1928

The Man with a Movie Camera
    (Dziga Vertov)

October/Ten Days That Shook the World
  (Eisenstein)
Storm over Asia (Pudovkin)
Zvenigora (Alexander Dovzhenko)

1929
Arsenal (Dovzhenko)

Fragment of an Empire (Friedrich Ermler)
The New Babylon (Kozintsev and Trauberg)
Old and New/The General Line (Eisenstein)
Turksib (Victor Turin)

1930
 Earth (Dovzhenko)

BOOKS ON THE PERIOD

Attwood, Lynne, ed., *Red Women on the Silver Screen: Soviet Women and Cinema from the Beginning to the End of the Communist Era.* San Francisco: Pandora Press, 1993

Kenez, Peter, *Cinema and Soviet Society, 1917–1953.* New York: Cambridge University Press, 1992

Lawton, Anna, ed., *The Red Screen: Politics, Society, Art in Soviet Cinema.* New York: Routledge, 1992

Mayne, Judith, *Kino and the Woman Question: Feminism and Soviet Silent Film.* Columbus: Ohio State University Press, 1989

Taylor, Richard, and Ian Christie, eds., *The Film Factory: Russian and Soviet Cinema in Documents, 1896–1939.* Cambridge, MA: Harvard University Press, 1988

Taylor, Richard, and Ian Christie, eds., *Inside the Film Factory: New Approaches to Russian and Soviet Cinema.* New York: Routledge, 1991

Tsivian, Yuri, ed., *Silent Witnesses: Russian Films, 1908–1919.* London: British Film Institute, 1990

Youngblood, Denise J., *Movies for the Masses: Popular Cinema and Soviet Society in the 1920s.* New York: Cambridge University Press, 1992

Youngblood, Denise J., *Soviet Cinema in the Silent Era, 1918–1935.* Austin: University of Texas Press, 1991

Zorkaya, Neya, *The Illustrated History of Soviet Cinema.* New York: Hippocrene Books, 1991

Hollywood
in the Twenties

♦ ♦ ♦

1919–1929

While German and Soviet films of the twenties commanded much of the early serious critical consideration, the American film began its domination of the international box office, a domination that has lasted until the present. Between the signing of the Versailles Treaty and the crash of the stock market, there began in the United States forms of economic expansion and cultural expression that signaled a new kind of empire. Though in its political and military stance the country became resolutely isolationist, its businesses and industries extended their sphere of influence. American automobiles, refrigerators, and countless other technological products were exported around the globe. While a succession of conservative presidents were elected to power, progressive stirrings in the arts that increased Americans' sense of national identity also attracted considerable attention abroad. It was in the twenties that modern American drama may be said to have begun—with the plays of Eugene O'Neill and Elmer Rice; that American literature achieved a new resonance—in the novels and stories of Sinclair Lewis, F. Scott Fitzgerald, John Dos Passos, William Faulkner, and Ernest Hemingway. Among America's contributions to the arts during that time, jazz is no doubt the most distinctive. But it was American movies, which connected art most firmly with commerce, that became the pervasive centurions in the new cultural conquest.

This is not to say that no fine films were made by important American film makers; but rather, that the American flair for mass production, promotion, and selling created and supplied a worldwide market for a particular kind of entertainment. From the outset, producing for a polyglot immigrant population, American film makers had been learning to make films satisfying to many nationalities. It is possible to state without chauvinism that "the movies" are more closely identified with the United States than with any other country, and that "Hollywood" holds a fascination for the entire globe. So, it is now proper to return from the rarefied atmosphere of European "art films" to the workaday Hollywood of gold bathroom fixtures, tame leopards, and white Stutz Bearcats. Since the basis for the success of the American film is industrial, the business of its art once again deserves attention.

♦ MOVIES BECOME BIG BUSINESS

The 1920s were characterized by intense competition among former independent companies that had become the new major studios. Old firms merged and disappeared; not one member of the Motion Picture Patents Company, with which the independents had competed between 1908 and 1915, survived.

In 1924 Metro-Goldwyn-Mayer was put together by Marcus Loew—president of Loew's, Inc., which had large theater holdings. Added to Metro Pictures Corporation (Loew's small production company) were the Goldwyn Picture Corporation and the Louis B. Mayer Pictures Corporation. Samuel Goldwyn had already left the Goldwyn Picture Corporation to become an independent producer; Mayer joined the newly created firm as studio head, beginning a reign that would last nearly thirty years. Also prominent were Universal (Carl Laemmle's outfit), Warner Brothers (Harry, Jack, Sam, and Albert), Paramount (which Adolph Zukor had brought along out of Famous Players-[Jesse] Lasky), Columbia (Jack and Harry Cohn), United Artists (Chaplin, Fairbanks, Pickford, Griffith), and the (William) Fox Film Corporation. The competition among these firms led to the need for increased capital—which was used to sign up stars, expand distribution and exhibition outlets, and buy out rivals. Public stock was issued, giving Wall Street a voice that would grow louder over the years.

The earlier economic battles had been fought largely in the field of production as the Motion Picture Patents Company trust attempted to stem the competition of the independents. During the first years after World War I, control of distribution was the major goal. National distribution became increasingly centralized and dominated by the major producing companies. The old "states' rights" franchise system, under which *The Birth of a Nation* and many of the first features had been distributed, faded away. For ultimate domination of the screen and long-term revenues, the struggle extended inevitably to ownership of the theaters themselves. There finally developed a pattern known as "vertical control," which lasted until it was outlawed by the federal courts in 1948. Under vertical control a few huge firms (eventually the roster became fixed at eight) produced, distributed, and exhibited their own films.

By the mid-twenties the fight for control of exhibition was being waged by three giants, which looked as if they might divide the whole pie, either forcing the other companies out or making them sit at table according to strict rules of etiquette. In 1919 Paramount had floated a $10 million issue of preferred stock, marking the beginning of the new phase. By 1921 that company was in virtual control of five hundred key theaters in the United States and first-run theaters in major cities around the world. By the end of the twenties Adolph Zukor had built up the most formidable combina-

Advertisement for the opening of the Paramount Theatre, New York City, in 1926.

tion in the industry: Paramount had the stars, the production outfit, the distribution channels, and control of two thousand theaters.

First National, the next largest production-distribution firm, had been formed by a group of theater chains to get access to the product on their own terms. The third contestant was Loew's, Inc., the vast firm of which Metro-Goldwyn-Mayer, the production-distribution arm, was only one part. Within a few years nearly all the major and first-run houses in the United States and Canada had been acquired by Paramount, Loew's, or the large circuits affiliated with the First National group. Fox and Universal also had theater outlets, but on a lesser scale.

By 1927 some four hundred to five hundred feature films a year were being produced. Ideally, each of the large companies would release no fewer than fifty-two a year, permitting a weekly change of program for its own theaters. Distribution involved close to six hundred exchanges (that is, regional offices handling prints of the films) in forty-six key American cities. Approximately twenty thousand theaters in the country were attended by some eighty million customers a week. The center of return on investment and of ultimate control was where distribution and exhibition were headquartered: New York City, not Hollywood. Any would-be new independents were effectively kept out of this closed system. If they wanted to produce, the screens weren't available to them; if they wanted to exhibit, they couldn't get access to films.

The emphasis on exhibition made the twenties the great decade of motion picture theater construction. The "movie palaces"—most of which have been torn down, divided into smaller theaters, or converted to other uses—stem from that era. The Capitol Theatre in New York City, for example, was built in 1919 and seated 5,300. *Photoplay* magazine wrote of it: "The mezzanine floor looks as if it had been designed for eight-day bicycle races."[1] Grauman's Egyptian and Chinese Theatres in Holly-wood along with large and ornate New York City theaters, including the fabled Roxy, were all part of this extraordinary architectural tradition.

My own recollections extend back to a "million-dollar theatre," the Rialto, in Joliet, Illinois. Architecturally it was a melange of imitation Byzantine, Venetian, classical Greek, and authentic midwestern Balaban & Katz (the Chicago-area chain, affiliated with Paramount Pictures). The Rialto offered more than movies: It provided a total cultural experience. On the weekends there were stage shows and a pit orchestra in addition to the films. The mighty Wurlitzer organ, with a console the size of a double bed and stops capable of producing every sound from canary peep to cannon roar, sufficed for weekdays. Objets d'art—sculpture, paintings, furniture, and even fountains—circulated around the B & K chain so that varied offerings of elegance were placed before the devotees at each temple. Perhaps most memorable of all was the scented Greco-Italian garden exiting audience members passed through on their way to the street: suffused in pink light, landscape murals lined the walls, and a simulated blue sky with fluffy white clouds moved overhead.

If the appeal of the films didn't always measure up to their surroundings, at least the increasing expensiveness of production kept pace with the new lavishness of presentation. Extravagance reigned, and the notion of spending money to make money was unquestioningly accepted. Salaries soared for directors, writers, and especially stars. While the epic *Birth of a Nation* had cost around $ 100,000 in 1915, *Ben-Hur* cost $6 million a decade later. By the end of the 1920s the average production expenditure on features was up to $200,000. The studios' steady incomes, however, came from the "program" or "B" pictures—unlike today, when television has taken over that kind of production, and theatrical features must offer something that seems special in order to attract an audience.

With such expenditures, and attendant financial concern, by the mid-twenties the director had been replaced by the production supervisor as the person in charge of film making. The production supervisor made many of the artistic decisions as well as all of the business ones. Developing out of the pattern first established by Thomas Ince, this function was most brilliantly exercised by the legendary boy wonder at M-G-M,

---

[1]Quoted by Lewis Jacobs, *The Rise of the American Film* (New York: Harcourt, Brace, 1939), p. 292.

Rialto Theatre, Joliet, Illinois.

Irving Thalberg, model for the hero of F. Scott Fitzgerald's uncompleted novel *The Last Tycoon*. Sometimes called production chief, head of studio, or vice-president in charge of production, this executive oversaw a whole program of pictures, deciding which ideas or literary and dramatic "properties" were to be developed into scripts, then casting players and assigning directors. With the cost and complexity of sound, added at the end of the twenties, the power of this position would become even more complete than in silent days. Film makers like D. W. Griffith and Erich von Stroheim were temperamentally incapable of working within this system and eventually were discarded by it. Griffith directed two sound films; von Stroheim one. Directors became "glorified foremen" and, with assembly-line specialization, were as much typecast as were the players. There were directors of westerns, of comedies, of romances, and so on, with second-rank directors hired to imitate the work of first-rank ones.

The easiest way to produce pictures rapidly, and to "sell" them in advance to exhibitors, was to imitate recent successes; thus the "cycle" was born, with the "formula picture" as the unit. Movies, once novelties, were now referred to as "products." In the early days it had been possible to experiment more freely, because there was no fixed idea of exactly what a film should be; there was no way of knowing for sure what would be appealing, except by trying and finding out. Now the conception of what was good film—that is, likely to be financially successful—had hardened.

Lewis Jacobs, in *The Rise of the American Film,* observed that all films had come to be assessed according to certain fixed criteria. The first things looked for were *names*—stars with drawing power; second, *production values*—elaborate sets, crowds of extras, and other evidence of great expense; third, *story value,* which tended to mean the huge price paid for the original, and its popularity as a novel or play. The next criterion was *picture sense*—a sort of conglomeration of the above elements plus any specific filmic qualities. Finally, there was *box-office appeal*—plenty of the standardized qualities that had proved successful in years past.

The industrial system described above would be in effect for the next thirty years. It has not yet been fully replaced.

♦ POPULAR GENRES

Perhaps more than the business acumen of the moguls or the technical resources of the big studios, more than the attractiveness of the stars and the skills of the directors, it is the popular genres that have most typified American film and given it its greatest strength and vitality. During the 1920s all the major types of American film were present except, of course, the musical, which required sound. The **western** was our most exclusive national contribution. It started at least with *The Great Train Robbery* (1903), and matured most notably in the films produced by Thomas Ince and starring

The Covered Wagon ♦ U.S., 1923, James Cruze.

The General ♦ U.S., Buster Keaton; Keaton (see "comedy" genre, page 104).

William S. Hart (for example, *The Gun Fighter* and *The Aryan,* both 1916). In the twenties the epic western was added to the line: *The Covered Wagon* (1923), directed by James Cruze, and *The Iron Horse* (1924), directed by John Ford. Hart continued to work until 1925 (*Tumbleweeds* was his last and probably finest film) and was succeeded in popularity by Tom Mix, Buck Jones, Tim McCoy, Hoot Gibson, Ken Maynard, and some lesser stars.

As for the meaning and function of this genre, French critic Jean-Louis Rieupeyrout put it this way:

> *Far from being glamorized fiction, the Western is rather a faithful representation of a too often unrecognized reality. It is the expression of a typically American mythology. Its heroes and its gods offer us a thousand epic pictures and unfold on the screens of the universe a new, gigantic, and vivid Bayeux tapestry.*[2]

[2]Jean-Louis Rieupeyrout, "The Western: A Historical Genre," *The Quarterly of Film, Radio, and Television,* 7 (Winter 1952): 128.

When the **comedy** genre moved from one- and two-reelers to include features, the 1920s became "Comedy's Greatest Era," as James Agee called it in a famous essay on the subject. The wonderful clowns—Charles Chaplin, Buster Keaton, Harold Lloyd, and Harry Langdon—created their masterworks during that decade. They confirmed and advanced the early discoveries and pioneering insights of Mack Sennett, making of silent film comedy an art form offering timeless and universal pleasure.

The features included Chaplin's *The Kid* (1921) and *The Gold Rush* (1925), Keaton's *The Navigator* (1924) and *The General* (1927), Lloyd's *Safety Last* (1923) and *The Freshman* (1925), and Langdon's *The Strong Man* and *Tramp, Tramp, Tramp* (both 1926). Along with the continuing shorts of Stan Laurel and Oliver Hardy, and others, these films gave American screen comedy an impetus that carried it through the 1940s and perhaps beyond.

If we include the work of Danny Kaye, Red Skelton, Jerry Lewis, Woody Allen, and Mel Brooks within that tradition, and maybe of Dan Ackroyd and Bill Murray as well, the influence of the comedies of the twenties has extended to the present. Though the introduction of sound required extreme modifications of style and introduced a new group of comics, the comedy, along with the western, the gangster film,

The Crowd ♦ U.S., 1928, King Vidor; Eleanor Boardman and James Murray (see "problem picture" genre, page 105).

and the musical, remains among the most distinctive, indigenous, and important American contributions to film forms.

The **"problem picture,"** dealing with social and moral concerns, had appeared among the first story films shortly after the turn of the century (for example, *The Ex-Convict,* 1905, *The Eviction,* 1907). This has always been a significant genre and includes some of this nation's most substantial work. Often the problem pictures look at society from the vantage point of a new generation and deal with the alarms and discomforts caused by social change. A number of films attacked Bolshevism at home and abroad, revealing American uneasiness over the successful Soviet revolution. Other films dealt with strikes, usually portraying them as resulting from misunderstanding between management and labor, rarely acknowledging real economic causes.

The overwhelming preponderance of "problems" considered in films of this genre had to do with morals and mores: the changing conception of marriage (*Wine of Youth,* 1924, *Trial Marriage,* 1929); women's increased independence (*Daring Youth, For Ladies Only,* both 1927); youthful rebellion (*Flaming Youth,* 1923, *Our Dancing Daughters,* 1928); promiscuity (*Husbands for Rent,* 1927, *Breakfast at Sunrise,* 1927); bootleg debauchery (*The House of Youth,* 1924, *The Mad Whirl,* 1925), and like subjects. From the attempts of De Mille and others to treat the "jazz age," postwar morality and the "modern generation" of the twenties, there runs a more or less straight line to the Depression films of the thirties.

Flesh and the Devil ♦ U.S., 1927, Clarence Brown; Greta Garbo and John Gilbert (see "love stories" genre, page 106).

In spite of a remark attributed to Samuel Goldwyn—"If you got a message, send it by Western Union"—the problem picture has been remarkably persistent in an industry presumably devoted to "escapist entertainment." This means, of course, that the problem picture has been good box office. Self-criticism and exposé form a strong thread that extends through American history beginning before Tom Paine and continuing past the "yellow journalism" of the twenties to Sunday night's *60 Minutes* on CBS. Films in this tradition—even if frequently exploiting as well as examining problems—have remained significant in reflecting and changing an awareness of our culture.

The **love stories,** vehicles for glamorous stars, were called "women's pictures" by the trade. Though they also go back to the beginning (*The Kiss,* 1896), they reached a romantic peak in the twenties. Since by then women constituted a majority of the movie audience, female as well as male stars were tailored to their expectations. Rudolph Valentino, Ronald Colman, and John Gilbert presented idealized characters in situations notably distant from the lives of those watching. Gloria Swanson, Pola Negri, and Greta Garbo offered models of allure for attracting those ideal males—or more modest realities closer to home. Romance has persisted on the screen, of course, but the changes over time have made it almost unrecognizable. Nowadays there isn't anything quite like the lives lived for love by Garbo and Gilbert in *Flesh and the Devil* (1926), *Love* (1927), or *A Woman of Affairs* (1928). We can't help but agree with Gloria Swanson in *Sunset Boulevard* (1950), when she stands in the beam of the

The Big Parade ♦ U.S., 1925, King Vidor; Renée Adorée, with her arm about John Gilbert (see "war dramas" genre, page 107).

Robin Hood ◆ U.S., 1922, Alan Dwan; Douglas Fairbanks, second from left (see "action and adventure" genre, below).

projector shining her own youthful image onto the screen and growls, "They don't make faces like that any more."

   War dramas were also common before the twenties, but had only the old-fashioned wars for subjects and treated those from a historical perspective. Moviegoers of the twenties had recently been through a world war, and the experience was influential to most of them. Though films about the war had been made during it, the "war is hell" prototypes were first offered in King Vidor's *The Big Parade (1925)* and Raoul Walsh's *What Price Glory?* (1926). A subspecies of the war dramas of the twenties was the air-war cycle, including *The Lone Eagle* (1927), *The Legion of the Condemned* (1928), *Lilac Time* (1928), and *Wings* (1929). The latter group suggest the impossibility of making an *anti*-war film—at least along standard lines. The ultimate drama of war cannot be denied: life and death, bravery and fear, selflessness and leadership, comradeship and love; they are present even within the impersonal slaughter of modern warfare. War may be hell; but on film, war has always been highly dramatic.

   Action and adventure—category, if not exactly a genre—takes various forms, most of which appeared in the twenties. Often the action-adventure films deal with a chase and pursuit, or with survival in some distant and colorful locale. There are adventures on the sea, under water, in the jungle (*Tarzan of the Apes* began the Tarzan

Ben-Hur ◆ U.S., 1926, Fred Niblo (see "spectacle" genre, page 109).

series in 1918), in the mountains, the desert, and in polar regions. Documentaries and semi-documentaries of the period appealed more factually to the same sort of interest—*Nanook of the North* (1922), *Grass* (1925), *Moana* (1926), *Chang* (1927). Another kind of action-adventure of the twenties (and thirties) was the animal picture, with animal stars; Rin-Tin-Tin and Rex, "King of the Wild Horses," were successful enough to have their imitators.

If you think of action-adventure films of the twenties, you might think first of the kind in which Douglas Fairbanks excelled. A star of considerable magnitude, his obvious attractions were a marvelous body, dazzling smile, acrobatic grace, and an ingeniously intricate way of moving about the world by scaling walls, sliding down draperies, leaping from roof to balcony and balcony to roof, and swinging on chandeliers. Those qualities and abilities, together with his enormous good cheer and easy superiority to the normal nagging concerns of the modern world, guaranteed the popular success of his films—*The Mark of Zorro* (1920), *The Three Musketeers* (1921), *Robin Hood* (1922), *The Thief of Bagdad* (1924), *The Black Pirate* (1926), and others. As the titles of the Fairbanks films suggest, their action and adventure were usually set in a past time as well as a distant place; the improbable could be given freest reign in exotic settings.

Another kind of historical film featured more **spectacle** than derring-do. *The Execution of Mary Queen of Scots* (1895) was the first of these, and it was Griffith who reached a level of spectacle—in *Intolerance* (1916)—that in some respects has never been equalled. De Mille, admitting his indebtedness to Griffith, took over the historical/Biblical extravaganza with *The Ten Commandments* (1923) and *The King of Kings* (1927), and intermittently pursued his own special form of it until his last film, the second *Ten Commandments* (1956). Other especially noteworthy historical/religious spectacles of the 1920s were Griffith's *Orphans of the Storm* (1921), about the French Revolution, and Fred Niblo's *Ben-Hur* (1926). *Variety's* annual listing of all-time box-office champions has a preponderance of the spectacular in its upper echelons. At the moment of this writing, someone is trying to put together a sequel to *Gone With the Wind*.

◆ SOME MAJOR DIRECTORS AND THEIR FILMS

Big business interests took over in the twenties and have remained dominant since. The popular genres became the established forms. But a number of talented film makers have always managed to create important, and even great, films working within (or briefly defying) the system and generic fixities. In sum total the American film stands unmatched in artistic quality as well as in quantity and commercial success (which is only to say popularity). Given that fact, perhaps there is something to be said for the system, which is rarely praised in critical circles.

With a chapter heading in *The Rise of the American Film,* Jacobs acknowledges that the decade of the twenties offered "A Throng of Directors." He chose to deal with Cecil B. De Mille, Erich von Stroheim, Ernst Lubitsch, F. W. Murnau, Victor Seastrom (né Sjöström), Robert Flaherty, John Stuart Robinson (now mostly forgotten), Henry King, James Cruze, Rex Ingram, and "others." Among the others held in particular esteem today are King Vidor, Josef von Sternberg (emerging late in the period), and Frank Borzage. Jacobs does not discuss the silent films of John Ford, Howard Hawks, Buster Keaton, or Raoul Walsh, all of whom worked in the twenties and have come to be valued highly.

The first three men on Jacobs's list not only made films of intrinsic worth; their collective output, radically dissimilar though the three bodies of work are, represents some general aspects of the American film of the twenties. De Mille's values were most clearly the system's values; von Stroheim was the rebel; Lubitsch, the whimsical subversive. Incidentally, the two who continued to work in the industry beyond the twenties—De Mille and Lubitsch—became producers in order to control their directorial efforts.

De Mille has often been disregarded or disapproved of by critics and historians on grounds that his films are generally superficial and frequently meretricious, that they add nothing to film art. In recent years, a reevaluation has occurred in some quarters, based on the visual (as opposed to intellectual) merits of his films. In either case, no one can deny their enormous success. Unparalleled as a showman, publicist, and businessman, De Mille also had a unique ability to move with the times. Though the artist in him may have been uncertain, the social psychologist was uncannily accurate in his intuitions. By examining De Mille's invariably successful pictures, today's social historians can infer much about the cultural climate of the American twenties. To some extent those films may have affected that climate.

De Mille's father and mother were of the theater; his brother was the playwright William C. De Mille. Cecil himself had been associated with David Belasco, the "Dean of the American Stage." De Mille's initial film effort, *The Squaw Man* (1914), was one of the earliest features and among the first films to be made in Hollywood; it established at the outset his ability to anticipate trends in the industry. From 1918 to 1924 he turned out a rapid succession of widely popular films aimed at middle-class audiences and reflecting postwar changes in manners and morals. As the titles themselves suggest, this was indeed the roaring twenties: *Old Wives for New* (1918); *Don't Change Your Husband, For Better or Worse, Male and Female* (all 1919); *Why Change Your Wife? Something to Think About* (both 1920); *Forbidden Fruit, The Affairs of Anatol, Fool's Paradise* (all 1921); *Saturday Night, Manslaughter* (both 1922); and *Adam's Rib* (1923). These were promoted as "typical De Mille productions—audacious, glittering, intriguing, superlatively elegant and quite without heart." Following these essays on contemporary mores (they were called the "divorce comedies"), a shift began to occur in De Mille's preoccupations. *The Ten Commandments* (1923) had a long Biblical prologue to a modern story, and *The King of Kings* (1927) was the first full work of the kind with which his name would subsequently become associated: religiosity cum sex and spectacle.

Except for the latter two mentioned, De Mille's films of the twenties were trivial in content. Nonetheless, they had considerable influence on the craft of motion picture making, and on the popular culture of the United States at large. While he made movies that were "production-conscious" (he was painstaking with details—clothes, makeup, lighting, properties, and sets), he also offered styles of interior decoration and clothing fashions for imitation. He is often given credit for inaugurating the tendency of American bathrooms to aspire to the sumptuousness of throne rooms. Theatrical in his direction, he rarely used camera or cutting obtrusively, except for "special effects." His historical spectacles are like a series of separate illustrations brought to life. The performances tend to be stiff, broad, and simple.

It must be conceded, however, that De Mille is one of a very few directors who have gotten their names onto marquees. People went to see a "De Mille picture." He achieved this star status partly from the size and dazzle of his productions, but also from a vigorous publicizing of his own personality. It is to De Mille that we owe the assumption that you could tell a motion picture director by his open-neck shirt, jodphurs, boots, and megaphone. Also, people went partly out of curiosity to see what all the other people were seeing. The consistency of De Mille's box-office record remains remarkable: Not one of his films lost money. When De Mille died, the prop Ten Commandments tablet used in his second film of that title was placed on a kind of altar under his lighted portrait in the Paramount commissary. The color of the tablet was gold.

The King of Kings ♦ U.S., 1927, Cecil B. De Mille; H. B. Warner, as Christ.

Erich von Stroheim resembled De Mille in flamboyance, meticulousness with details, and extravagance. But von Stroheim could not put those qualities to consistent commercial use. The iron will, artistic integrity, and rebelliousness for which he is respected by those who admire his films kept him from seeking out what the public wanted. Instead, he gave audiences the world as he saw it—in a style notable for scathing naturalism laced with irony—in place of the usual coating of reality covering a sentimental center.

Of the eight films von Stroheim made between 1918 and the end of his directorial career in 1928, *Greed* (1925) is unquestionably the masterpiece. It remains one of the most impressive films in the total history of the screen. The legend surrounding it contains omens pointing toward the end of his career as a director and his subsequent canonization: its staggering cost; its length of forty-five reels (over seven hours) cut to a conventional ten; von Stroheim's disavowal of the released version; and the power that remains in spite of the mutilation. Controversy about the film can still be heard, and there are still unshakable hopes and occasional rumors that a copy of the complete version may somehow have survived. There are those who defend von Stroheim (see biographies by Peter Noble, Joel W. Finler, Thomas Quinn Curtiss, and Richard Koszarski) and those who defend Hollywood (on the grounds that no industry, however benevolent, could be expected to tolerate such presumption and profligacy). The particular qualities of his art also raise arguments. At the time, critics faulted him for his decadence and cynicism or his slavish, plodding naturalism and lack of cinematic flair. Some argued that the fanatical literalness of his translation of Frank Norris's novel *McTeague* into the film *Greed* was not creation at all.

Today most would agree that a handful of his films (*Foolish Wives,* 1922, *The Merry Widow,* 1925, *The Wedding March,* 1928, and *Greed*) are original and extraordinary, powerful in a way and to a degree unlike anyone else's work. His camera-editing style rested on the long take/long shot not much in vogue during the ascendancy of montage, with its stress on fast cutting and closeups. (Others who shared von Stroheim's creative impulse were the silent comedians, who wanted to show that their

Greed ♦ U.S., 1925, Erich von Stroheim; Zasu Pitts and Gibson Gowland, center.

comic stunts really happened, and documentarian Robert Flaherty, who had a similar desire for different reasons to establish the authenticity of what was on the screen.) The sort of spatial-temporal coherence and realism represented by von Stroheim's style would later become a dominant aesthetic tendency. The resistance von Stroheim met from producers, critics, and public was caused not so much by his cinematic technique as by the awareness that his was an angry art. The mirror he held up to nature not only reflected warts and all, it emphasized the warts—the venality, selfishness, and perversity present in most of us.

Jacobs observes that all of von Stroheim's films are melodramas of lust; I would add, of obsession—fixed on sexual or material acquisitiveness. Sexuality is usually interwoven with money, station, or power in an uncompromisingly unpalatable view of life. Decadence and depravity are ubiquitous. In *Foolish Wives,* "Count" Wladislas Karamzin, played by Stroheim—"the man you love to hate"—evidently makes his way in the world through sexual enterprises based on seduction, blackmail, and the like. Enormously attractive, he obviously enjoys his work, which is accompanied by a fatal bit of recreational lechery with an idiot girl. Though he seems to be involved with five women, there is no suggestion of love in any of these relationships. This character, whom von Stroheim had created in his first film, *Blind Husbands* (1919), appears in intermittent variation throughout his work—including his last released film, *Queen Kelly* (1928). Though he doesn't appear in *Greed,* the consistent point is made most explicit as a romantic attachment gradually deteriorates into a single-minded pursuit of gold.

For the audacity of his themes, as well as for his arrogance and financial disinterest, von Stroheim was denied access to the tools of his art. His directorial career ended about the same time as that of D. W. Griffith, for whom he had first worked in film. The last decades of von Stroheim's life, like Griffith's, were spent in semiretirement outside the film industry.

Ernst Lubitsch's German films made within the romantic-historical tradition (*Passion/Madame du Barry* and *Deception/Anna Boleyn*) were discussed in chapter three. They were very popular in the United States and Lubitsch followed them here in 1922. But neither those films nor his earlier training as an actor in Max Reinhardt's company foreshadowed the kind of film Lubitsch would turn to and make peculiarly his own. After studying contemporary American production, Lubitsch moved into comedy and light drama of the sort De Mille was making so successfully. Before the end of the decade he had outstripped De Mille, in quality at least, while De Mille had moved to spectacles not unlike those Lubitsch had made earlier. But he is most amazing for his command of the medium: the subtlety and flexibility with which he was able to use silent film to communicate nuances of a situation, and later his experimental leadership in sound.

Though differences of style and outlook mask the similarities, the films of Lubitsch are like those of von Stroheim in one important respect: They are about sex and money. To increase his freedom for comment, and to add a bit of glamor and suavity, Lubitsch, like von Stroheim, tended to set his plots against European backgrounds. But in Lubitsch's films, sexual intrigue is merely frivolity engaged in by the

The Marriage Circle ◆
U.S., 1924, Ernst
Lubitsch; Adolphe
Menjou and Marie Prevost.

wealthy to occupy their leisure time. With few exceptions his pictures are comedies of manners, peopled entirely with the well-bred, urbane upper classes. He delineates their fads and foibles with a Viennese charm and worldliness that made them seem novel, fascinating, and a bit naughty to American audiences. His sophisticated humor came to be well known as "the Lubitsch touch." Of his American silent films, *The Marriage Circle, Forbidden Paradise* (both 1924), and *Lady Windermere's Fan* (1925) have best retained their charm.

◆ POSTSCRIPT

The convulsions brought on by sound would shake up and modify much about Hollywood of the twenties. Even so, the more things changed the more they remained the same. New corporate combines emerged, rather than altered business practices. Older silent film makers were sometimes replaced, but more often they were joined by new film makers. The popular forms and content carried on into sound, with some losses (silent comedies) and some gains (musicals). Patterns established in the twenties, in fact, seem to have become more fixed and rigid during the thirties and forties. But the breathtaking rapidity with which the almost entirely silent film of 1927 became the almost entirely sound film of 1929, a profound technological transmutation, was a sometimes harrowing but mostly exciting experience for all involved, including audiences and critics.

FILMS OF THE PERIOD

1919
Blind Husbands (Erich von Stroheim)
Male and Female (Cecil B. De Mille)

1920
The Last of the Mohicans (Maurice Tourneur
    and Clarence Brown)
The Mark of Zorro (Fred Niblo)
Way Down East (David Wark Griffith)

1921
The Four Horsemen of the Apocalypse
    (Rex Ingram)
The Kid (Charles Chaplin)
Orphans of the Storm (Griffith)
Tol'able David (Henry King)

1922
Foolish Wives (von Stroheim)
Nanook of the North (Robert Flaherty)
Robin Hood (Allan Dwan)

1923
The Covered Wagon (James Cruze)
Safety Last (Harold Lloyd)
The Ten Commandments (De Mille)
A Woman of Paris (Chaplin)

1924
The Iron Horse (John Ford)
The Marriage Circle (Ernst Lubitsch)
The Navigator (Buster Keaton)

Sherlock Junior (Keaton)
The Thief of Bagdad (Raoul Walsh)

1925
The Big Parade (King Vidor)
The Freshman (Lloyd)
The Gold Rush (Chaplin)
Greed (von Stroheim)
Lady Windermere's Fan (Lubitsch)
The Phantom of the Opera (Rupert Julian)

1926
Ben-Hur (Niblo)
Moana (Flaherty)
The Scarlet Letter (Victor Sjöström /Seastrom)
What Price Glory? (Walsh)

1927
The General (Keaton)
Hotel Imperial (Mauritz Stiller)
The King of Kings (De Mille)
Seventh Heaven (Frank Borzage)
Sunrise (F. W. Murnau)
Underworld (Josef von Sternberg)
Wings (William Wellman)

1928
The Crowd (Vidor)
The Docks of New York (von Sternberg)
The Last Command (von Sternberg)
The Wind (Sjöström/Seastrom)

BOOKS ON THE PERIOD

Koszarski, Richard, *An Evening's Entertainment: The Age of the Silent Feature Picture, 1915–1928* (Vol. 3, "History of the American Cinema"). New York: Charles Scribner's Sons, 1990

MacCann, Richard Dyer, *The First Tycoons.* (Vol. 1, "American Movies: The First Thirty Years"). Metuchen, NJ: Scarecrow Press, 1987

MacCann, Richard Dyer, *The Stars Appear* (Vol. 3, "American Movies: The First Thirty Years"). Metuchen, NJ: Scarecrow Press, 1992

MacCann, Richard Dyer, *The Comedians* (Vol. 4, "American Movies: The First Thirty Years"). Metuchen, NJ: Scarecrow Press, 1993

Naylor, David, *American Picture Palaces: The Architecture of Fantasy.* Englewood Cliffs, NJ: Prentice Hall, 1991

6

Sound Comes
to America

◆ ◆ ◆

1927–1935

In the United States, France, Great Britain, Italy, and elsewhere between 1895 and 1914, film makers had learned to tell a story with images in movement, and their films had become sufficiently long to tell a significant one. The consolidation and advance of techniques that established film as an art form, and the founding of an industry that enabled it to become popular entertainment, were achieved in the United States between 1914 and 1918. Refinements of visual expression in German films from 1919 to 1925 made possible a new intensity and unity of mood, emotion, and characterization. From 1925 to 1929 the Soviets further explored the dynamic shot-to-shot relationship Griffith had begun, and developed a systematic theory of editing which allowed an unprecedented eloquence and complexity of idea, feeling, and kinetic rhythm. Each of these national contributions marked an important addition to some aspect of the expressive possibilities of silent film. The end of this evolutionary stage was signaled on October 6, 1927, in New York City, when Warner Brothers presented *The Jazz Singer,* the first feature film with synchronized speech as well as music and other sound.

As with most technological innovations in film, sound was experimented with from the beginning. In fact, Edison seems initially to have conceived of the motion picture as illustration to go with his highly successful cylindrical phonograph—so that those purchasing the sound machines would have something to look at while they listened. W. K. L. Dickson, Edison's talented assistant (and the man most responsible for the development of motion picture equipment at the West Orange, New Jersey, laboratory), had joined sound to image prior to the first Lumière showings. A film made by Dickson shows a pair of Edison technicians dancing in eerie slow motion to a violinist, supposedly Dickson himself, playing into a huge phonograph horn. The further problem of amplifying sound sufficiently to fill a theater had been solved by 1914: primarily by Lee de Forest's invention of the silenium, or vacuum, tube which allowed for a "loud speaker" (audio amplifier).

◆ TECHNOLOGICAL AND ECONOMIC PROBLEMS

Like the later additions of color, wide screen, and 3-D, it took strong economic motivation to bring on sound. In 1924 and 1925 the comparatively small production firm of Warner Brothers, which owned no theater chains, was competing against the large companies that controlled distribution and exhibition. According to the Warners' account, accepted by many film historians, they decided in desperation to try the novelty of sound to see if it would help them out of their financial difficulties. Another, more credible and thoroughly documented explanation is offered in Robert C. Allen and Douglas Gomery, *Film History: Theory and Practice* (New York: Alfred A. Knopf, 1985, pp. 115–124). According to this version, Wall Street interests looking for a favorable opportunity for investment in the motion picture industry chose Warner Brothers. Though a small firm, it was tightly managed and well run financially. The infusion of new capital permitted competitive expansion along a number of lines, one of them being experimentation with sound.

For whatever reason, Warner Brothers added a sound track to a silent feature entitled *Don Juan,* starring John Barrymore, and released it in August 1926. Their Vitaphone system, as they called it, having acquired the Vitagraph company in 1925, used disc recordings mechanically synchronized with the projector. In the case of *Don Juan* the track consisted of a symphonic score plus some sound effects—especially the clanging of swords in the dueling scenes. To the feature they attached a few shorts of distinguished musicians in performance, including violinist Mischa Elman and Metropolitan Opera stars Giovanni Martinelli and Marion Talley.

Leading off this program was a short in which Will Hays appeared. Former Postmaster General and national chairman of the Republican Party, Hays had become president of the Motion Picture Producers and Distributors of America. This trade organization of the major studios (today called the Motion Picture Association of America) had come into being mainly as an attempt by the industry to protect itself—through public relations—from threats of censorship being provoked by the new frankness of the postwar films. Mr. Hays welcomed the public to the epochal event presented by the brothers Warner and predicted a glorious future for the motion picture accompanied by recorded sound.

Though the opening night audience was enthusiastic enough, the success of Vitaphone was limited because of the few theaters equipped for it. It was not altogether clear that *Don Juan* with Vitaphone was making more money than it would have without recorded sound. Two other programs of shorts and features with synchronized musical scores released in the following year met with only moderate success. The Warners had gambled so much on the innovation, however, that they couldn't consider abandoning it.

With the exception of William Fox, who had begun experimenting with his own sound system, the rest of the producers were annoyed with the Warners for rocking the industrial boat. Box office was down slightly and competition from the new sound entertainment of radio seemed one possible cause, but it was by no means certain that the addition of recorded sound to movies would bring larger audiences into the theaters.

The other studios held back because of general uncertainty and for several specific reasons. First, the expense of changing equipment and facilities for production and, especially, for exhibition (in the eighty thousand theaters throughout the world) loomed as ominous as the national debt. Second, the studios didn't relish paying royalties to Warner Brothers or Fox for use of their patented sound systems, and losing face to a competitor. Third, it was possible that sound might change production technique radically, and no one was yet trained to make sound features. Fourth, there was the backlog of silent films and others in production that might have to be written off as complete losses if they didn't conform to the new technology. Fifth, if the movies ever began to talk (a prospect only vaguely foreseen), the long-term contracts with silent stars, foreign stars, and directors might prove frozen assets if those individuals couldn't adapt themselves to the altered medium or to the English language. Finally, if the marvelous esperanto of the silent film were sacrificed, audiences abroad would be curtailed: Whereas titles could easily and inexpensively be translated and re-shot, what could the Hungarians, for example, make out of conversations in English? The industry continued to watch and wait.

For their fourth Vitaphone feature the Warners chose a popular musical play, *The Jazz Singer*, which had starred George Jessel on the Broadway stage. When they approached Jessel to repeat his performance for the film, negotiations broke down over the amount of money he asked. As it turned out, Al Jolson was hired for twice as much and insisted that his salary be in cash. Though the film's sound was thought of principally in terms of Jolson's six numbers (including his theme song, "Mammy"), two of his four sound scenes contain a little dialogue that seems scarcely to have been planned. In one scene, after finishing a song in a nightclub, Jolson utters the words that had become his trademark on Broadway: "Wait a minute, wait a minute, I tell ya. You ain't heard nothing." In this context the expression became unexpectedly prophetic. In the second scene, a bit of dialogue leading up to and intervening between two renditions of "Blue Skies" is certainly unscripted. It consists of Jolson joshing his little old screen mother, who is obviously embarrassed and can't think of a thing to say. It's almost as if the conversation had been recorded accidentally, or as a kind of test, and only afterwards did the Warners decide to include it. Whatever the intent, the response of the moviegoing public was emphatic.

There are something like 309 words of dialogue in *The Jazz Singer*, but it was clearly those spoken words more than the songs that had audiences queuing up four-deep around the block of the Warner Theatre. The comparative indifference to the sound in *Don Juan* had apparently occurred because it consisted solely of recorded music plus a few sound effects in place of the usual live orchestra, organ, or piano to which audiences were accustomed. With the ensuing success of *The Jazz Singer*, the "talkie" was born, and a new dramatic dimension in the spoken word was suggested.

Except for songs and fragments of dialogue, however, *The Jazz Singer* looks and sounds like the standard silent film of the time, with a recorded orchestral score (making heavy use of Tschaikowsky's overture to *Romeo and Juliet*) and with printed intertitles carrying the bulk of the verbal communication.

On the basis of *The Jazz Singer*'s success, the Warners extended what looks as if it had been intended as a two-reel short into a seven-reel feature. Entitled *The Lights of New York* and released in July 1928, it became the first "100 percent talkie." It begins with a prologue, which transports the young hero from "Main Street" to "Broadway." There he and his sidekick get mixed up with a couple of con men, and with a gang of bootleggers who use their barbershop as a front. The film contains what is surely the longest exposition in history; in fact, it is all exposition. The characters talk about what has happened, will happen, should happen, and might happen; very little except conversation does happen on the screen.

One of the subsidiary pleasures *The Lights of New York* now affords is in detecting where the stationary microphone is hidden—in a telephone, for instance, as Hawk orders his henchmen to "Take him for a ride." There is the marvelous moment in which the barber hero finishes a phone call and has to stride clear across the room—to another microphone (probably in the lamp overhead)—before he can tell his partner

The Jazz Singer ◆ U.S., 1927 Alan Crosland; Al Jolson and Eugenie Besserer.

The Lights of New York ◆
U.S., 1928, Brian Foy;
Cullen Landis and Helene
Costello.

that the call was from Kitty. An intriguing nightclub scene, including a bizarre master of ceremonies and a chorus line of dancing pirates, was obviously shot from a glassed-in booth which kept the noise of the camera from reaching the microphone. Because the camera was immobilized, the illusion of moving closer could be obtained only by changing lenses; a long shot (wide-angle lens), a medium shot (standard lens), and a closeup (telephoto lens) are all along an axis from a slightly right angle. Then, evidently, the action was stopped and the booth moved over to the center for the same progression of shots. The camera operator probably had to be hauled out and revived after each take.

We can feel a kind of morbid fascination in watching the limitations sound imposed at first on the brilliance of the best silent films. Everything is static, all is talk. The fluid camera work of the Germans is gone, along with Soviet montage. The flexible fluency of the mature silent film is reduced to a jabbering infancy. (The M-G-M musical *Singin' in the Rain,* 1952, provides a marvelously enjoyable account of the pains of this transition; it is funny because so true.) Though we can relish *The Lights of New York's* authentic "roaring twenties" flavor, it is impossible not to notice how much more dated it seems than many of its silent contemporaries (such as *The Crowd, The Wind,* or *The Last Command,* also released in 1928). Speech is more firmly rooted in the particularities of time and place than is image.

At first, some observers thought sound merely a fad, one that would pass away once audiences got over their fascination with lips moving and voices seeming to come from them. Others felt that the talkies might coexist with the silents, the one appealing to the rubes who liked the yackety novelty, the other for the more sensitive and intelligent. Whatever view was taken, the lines at the box office dictated that the rest of the industry could no longer afford to ignore the Warners' unsettling contribution.

By the close of the twenties there was no doubt that the synchronous sound film would be the universal form of the future. At the end of 1928 Hollywood had only 16 recording machines in use; by the end of 1929 there were 116, and almost half the more than twenty thousand theaters in the United States were equipped for sound reproduction. The consensus was that a sound system using optical patterns along the edge of the film (Fox Movietone), rather than discs (Warner Vitaphone), would provide more reliable synchronization. In 1931, in order to achieve standardization, the patents on the various sound systems held by most of the major studios and others were pooled and divided between Western Electric and Radio Corporation of America (RCA). The sound systems of those two firms became the only ones in use.

As the industry borrowed money to retool, the financial center of gravity, which had gradually moved eastward with the expansion of exhibition and the mergers, now rested firmly in the big banks of New York City and Boston. Among the major studios, there were shifts in power (Warner up, having absorbed First National; Paramount down) and new alignments (RKO and Twentieth Century-Fox). Incidentally the *R* in RKO stands for Radio Corporation of American, which had become involved in motion pictures because of sound; the *K* and *O,* for the Keith-Orpheum theater circuit, which stemmed from the days when vaudeville was still competing with film for popular audiences. As for the Fox (William) in Twentieth Century-Fox, he was forced out of his firm by the new large financial interests. He then commissioned a socialist author to expose the evils of capitalism, as he had experienced them, in the book *Upton Sinclair Presents William Fox.*

But during the first years of confusion and adjustment, as Hollywood learned to work in the augmented medium, the money kept rolling in. For awhile on the stock exchange, the movies were regarded as a Depression-proof industry. The public, attracted by sound, continued to enjoy Friday nights at the movies throughout hard times. Food for the spirit and escape from the daily realities of a painfully constricted economy were apparently as important as meat and potatoes to a large proportion of the country's millions.

♦ AESTHETIC DIFFERENCES

Sound was a somewhat mixed blessing for the art as well as for the industry. In a book entitled *Heraclitus; or The Future of Films* (1928) the young English author, Ernest Betts, went to the trouble and expense, of adding, after publication, a special footnote:

> *Since the above was written, speaking films have been launched as a commercial proposition, as the general pattern of the film of the future. As a matter of fact, their acceptance marks the most spectacular act of self-*

destruction that has yet come out of Hollywood, and violates the film's proper function at its source. The soul of the film—its eloquent and vital silence—is destroyed. The film now returns to the circus whence it came, among the freaks and the fat ladies.[1]

Betts was not alone among the critics in mourning the death of a great visual art. Exacerbated by the crudities of the early technology, certain basic aesthetic problems were raised when the spoken word was joined to the moving image. Rudolf Amheim, writing a foreword in 1957 to a new edition of his *Film as Art,* first published in 1932, saw no reason to change his mind about dialogue as corruption rather than addition. Some of the finest creators, too, resented and resisted the imposition and didn't know what to do with sound once they had it. Chaplin is the extreme case: He did not make a sound film (in the sense of using dialogue) until *The Great Dictator* (1940).

While the addition of sound brought film closer to a full rendition of physical reality, it also turned it into the sort of recorded theater it had been attempting to escape from its earliest days. All the efforts of the great film makers up to this point had been directed toward advancing the medium beyond mere photographic record, to make of it an expressive and distinctive art form. "Canned theater," as the early sound films were called by some, represented a mixed, reproductive art at best. Talkies slowed the editing pace and tended to restrict the use of closeup of anything but the faces of actors. In filmed conversation the words dictate what will be seen, and the choice of images becomes limited to the person speaking, the person(s) listening, or both together. This spatial limitation is accompanied by a temporal one: Words require natural time in which to be spoken, and they communicate much less in that amount of time than could images. To those who regarded editing and the closeup as the bases of film technique, sound seemed to bring losses rather than gains. With sound, emphasis shifted from the images and action—with which film was uniquely qualified to deal—to plot and performance—elements shared with theater.

As for the new realism added by sound, this too presented a kind of aesthetic danger. As art draws closer to life, it loses some of its value as art. The artist's function is to select from reality and arrange in significant form: to reduce and clarify the "blooming, buzzing confusion" that surrounds us. Art demands limitations and thrives upon them; to a degree, the more limited, the more pure and expressive. Music, that art to which all other arts are said to aspire, can say much more about the human spirit with its purely abstract tones than can the detailed accuracy of wax figures, for all their simulated lifelikeness.

Another loss was the universality of silent film art. Chaplin was well known not only as "Charlie," but also as "Charlot," "Carlino," "Carlos," or "Carlitos," and could be enjoyed equally by all. With sound, there is no really satisfactory means of presenting film dialogue to audiences who don't understand the language. Initially, multiple-language versions were produced with separate and/or multilingual casts. For example, *The Blue Angel* (1930), directed by Josef von Sternberg, with Emil Jannings and Marlene Dietrich, had an English as well as a German version; *Don*

[1]Ernest Betts, *Heraclitus; or The Future of Films* (New York: E. P. Dutton, 1928), unpaginated insert.

Quixote (1933), directed by G. W. Pabst and starring the renowned Russian basso Fyodor Chaliapin, was produced in French and English. But this practice proved cumbersome and expensive. Usually, only one version, the original, had a dynamic life of its own, the others being merely dutiful copies. Subtitles, superimposed on the images themselves rather than being placed between them on separate intertitle cards as in silent film, restrict and inevitably distort the meaning of the dialogue and distract attention from the visual. The "dubbing" of native voices for foreign ones became the accepted European practice; in Italy, for example, there developed a regular subindustry employing actors to supply Italian voices for James Cagney, Gary Cooper, Bette Davis, and the rest. But the personalities expressed through the original quality of voice and style of delivery could be only faintly approximated, as technically skillful as some of the dubbing became.

Finally, the much greater expense and technological complexity of the sound film limited artistic experimentation and increased the pressure to play it safe. The introduction of sound, more than anything else, ended the individual and small-group film making of the French avant-garde of the twenties. In Hollywood the standard-size crew increased to about sixty persons, and production by committee, with the producer as chair, prevailed.

But after all, we're glad to have sound; only a few FOOFS, as they're called (Friends of Old Films), cherish silence as golden anymore. In actuality, there never were silent films; there was always music and frequently sound effects—of horses' hooves and thunder claps, for instance. By the late twenties the titles, too, had pretty much abandoned the earlier narrative and expository functions to substitute for dialogue; it was as if the film makers, perhaps unconsciously, had already started to feel a need for "lip-sync" sound recording. In these silent films that weren't really silent, the means of providing sound was clumsy and approximate, an aspect over which film makers could have little control. Unless a complete score was provided, which was rarely done, the film maker was at the mercy of the theater musicians. Inappropriate or clichéd music can go a long way towards destroying the most effective scenes.

With the arrival of sound, the music, noises, and words were added by the people who made the film, and became an integral part of it. Sound also reduced the awkwardness of silent narrative and permitted films to flow more freely without interruption of titles or the tortuous circumlocutions of visual exposition. In the final shoot-out in von Sternberg's silent *Underworld* (1927) we are constantly being shown bits of wood chipping off and bottles breaking as reminders that a gunfight is being waged. Presenting a simple point—like a couple's intention to meet next day under the big oak—often challenged the ingenuity of silent film makers in ways that now seem wasteful of creative effort. In one of F. W. Murnau's last great silent films, *Sunrise* (released with a synchronized musical score in 1927), scriptwriter Carl Mayer and Murnau characteristically minimized titles. But following the film's climax it is necessary for an old fisherman to explain how he had rescued the young wife washed overboard during a storm; this is accomplished through a redundant flashback that slows and diverts the main narrative thrust.

There is no doubt that sound has permitted the tackling of more complex ideas and emotions. This is particularly evident in a greater depth of characterization and increased precision in communicating it. With sound, actors can reveal more nuance and ambivalence, even contradiction, through saying what they think and feel as well as showing it. Though dialogue didn't necessarily add emotional intensity (the moments of highest drama in the sound film tend often to be without dialogue), it certainly contributed a new intellectual weight.

Sound—noises and music as well as speech—offered an artistic resource in itself, and in support or counterpoint to the images. Rather than the single line of shot to shot, like unison Gregorian chants, there was a polyphonic blending of four separate lines—image, word, music, noise. This meant that films had to be created and understood in a totally different way: The sound film is not simply a silent film with sound added. Vertical montage, as Eisenstein called the relationships between sight and sound, offered a new source of expressiveness.

◆ EVOLUTION OF TECHNIQUE

The principal understanding that film makers had to arrive at was that movement and rhythm were as much the basis of the sound film as they had been of the silent. In silent film, composition depended upon the movement of people or things within the limits of the frame, and on the rhythmical relationship of one shot to another. The rhythm of the whole, however complicated in structure and detail, was simple in that it appealed to one sense only; it was purely visual. In the sound film, with its visual and aural streams, the movement of images had to be related to the movement of sound—whether music, dialogue, or incidental noises. Until these movements were related (not merely synchronized) in more than a casual, haphazard way, there were no true sound films.

These new problems attracted new people to aid in their solution, and some of the veterans did not make the transfer into sound. The turnover was especially marked among performers. Foreign film actors who had not mastered English sailed back to Europe—Emil Jannings, Pola Negri, and Vilma Banky among them. Greta Garbo, on the other hand, made a brilliant debut in the altered medium in *Anna Christie* (1930) under the triumphant slogan "GARBO TALKS!" The addition of her low, husky voice and accented speech complemented her extraordinarily attractive screen presence in *Grand Hotel* (1932), *Queen Christina* (1933), *Camille* (1937), *Ninotchka* (1939), and her other successes of the thirties. Some of the silent American stars couldn't or didn't choose to work in sound: Colleen Moore, Norma Talmadge, Corinne Griffith, and Mary Pickford all dropped out of pictures after a few early talkies. Ironically, the co-star of *The Jazz Singer,* May McAvoy, virtually disappeared from the screen with the coming of sound. John Gilbert, a talented and popular star whose high voice didn't record well in the crude technology, is often cited as an especially sad case: Heavy drinking and an early death followed the failure of his few sound films. (There is evidence suggesting that Louis B. Mayer, head of M-G-M, used sound as an excuse to end Gilbert's career.)

The silent comedians had a particularly difficult time. Their techniques bound them closely to pantomime. Not only had they no need for words (they used few titles), but dialogue had no place in their kind of comedy. Chaplin used only music, sound effects, and amusingly unintelligible gibberish in *City Lights* (1931) and *Modern Times* (1936). Keaton, Lloyd, and Langdon never quite succeeded in finding a style that would suit the new form. Among the top silent clowns, only Laurel and Hardy were able successfully to add their wryly inane dialogue to the earlier sight gags. Some who had been only modestly successful in the silents achieved a new eminence when verbal humor could be added. Most of these had had stage as well as screen experience. W. C. Fields was preeminent, of course, but there were also Will Rogers, Marie Dressler, and Wallace Beery. Their distinctive voices and delivery of lines were crucial to their kinds of comedy. Coming to films directly from the theater were the Marx Brothers, whose surrealist patter combined with plenty of zany action, and Mae West, of the superb sexual innuendo. Joe E. Brown, with siren wail, and Jimmy Durante, with his Brooklynese and raucous songs, also entered film from the stage.

In general, Hollywood turned to Broadway for people who had had experience with spoken words. For awhile, the Twentieth-Century Limited pulling out of New York City headed west with a load of actors, writers, and voice coaches. The silent directors were joined by a new crop who would carve their careers out of the possibilities opened up by sound; George Cukor, Leo McCarey, Rouben Mamoulian, Busby Berkeley, John Cromwell, Tay Garnett, all began to direct films in the first years of sound.

Three technical problems were solved during the early thirties, allowing the sound film to return to the movement of the silent film, reducing the dependence on dialogue, and regaining the visual richness. The first of these problems was to find a means of removing the camera from its soundproof booth. For that purpose a "blimp" was constructed: a metal cover filled with acoustic insulation that encased the camera. As heavy and large as the blimped cameras were, they still could be moved about quite freely on dolly and crane.

The second problem was to free the actors so they could move about without regard to the stationary microphones. Lionel Barrymore, who directed as well as acted in those days, claimed credit for solving this difficulty. As an actor he no doubt felt the performer's frustration in being rooted to one spot; he insisted, against technicians' protests, that a mike be swung overhead from a fishpole and moved around to follow the actors. The directional boom microphone, able to capture sounds from overhead while remaining out of frame, completely replaced the nondirectional fixed microphones that had been hidden about the set.

The blimped camera and boom microphone permitted more dynamic studio shooting, but they did not help the camera get outside the sound stages into the world of unwanted noises, bad acoustic conditions, and wind roaring in the microphone. *In Old Arizona* (1929), codirected by Raoul Walsh and Irving Cummings, was the first sound feature known to be recorded principally out-of-doors. "Location shooting" was made fully possible when sound technology advanced sufficiently so that sight and sound did not have to be recorded at the same time: Footage could be shot silent; sound could be recorded separately, then added to the images. Noteworthy early experiments included King Vidor's *Hallelujah!* (1929). In a frightening chase scene

Hallelujah! ♦ U.S., 1929,
King Vidor; Harry Gray
and Fannie B. DeKnight,
as Parson and Mammy.

at night in a swamp, snapping twigs, splashing water, and the heavy breathing of the actors are the principal sounds. The battle scenes of Lewis Milestone's *All Quiet on the Western Front* (1930) were shot with the sort of tracking camera movement and rapid cutting that marked the best silent work. The addition of rattling machine gun fire, the detonation of high explosives, and the screams of dying men made the images even more horrifying.

By 1932 sound effects, and even dialogue, could be added in "post-sync" recording and mixing. Rouben Mamoulian's *Dr. Jekyll and Mr. Hyde* (1932) was the first film to make use of synthetic sound, to amplify the unnatural transformation of Jekyll into the monstrous Hyde. By 1935 the fidelity of optical sound recording was quite acceptable. In fact, the frequency range fixed then (100 to 8,000 cycles per second) remained standard until the addition of the 35mm stereophonic optical tracks with the Dolby noise-reduction system in the late 1970s. As late as 1984, only 70mm magnetic striped tracks with the Dolby system used for science-fiction spectacles like *Return of the Jedi* (1983) could compare with the high fidelity of tape decks available for home use.

During the early sound years numerous American film makers added to conception and technique so that by the mid-thirties sound film had reached a level of artistic maturity at least comparable to its technological adequacy. The script writer, working in collaboration with the director, now made a much larger creative contribution. Dialogue, of course, was conceived, memorized, and rehearsed in advance of filming. Script writing became an absolute essential, and in some ways dominant, part of the

Hollywood sound film of the 1930s. Accordingly, certain writer-director teams emerged, like Jules Furthman with Josef von Sternberg, Robert Riskin with Frank Capra, Dudley Nichols with John Ford.

A look at two passages from a Nichols script based on a Liam O'Flaherty novel, *The Informer,* directed by Ford in 1935, may suggest how the power of an essentially visual conception could be increased by using sound to reinforce images and editing rhythm. Though there is virtually no speech in the excerpts following, the sorts of coordinated effects of sound in relation to sight that Nichols calls for could scarcely be trusted to improvisation. Some of the symbolic sight-sound linkages do not appear in the completed film, but its conception and style are essentially as called for in the script. As presented below, the scenes are in play-script form, with no reference to camera distance, angle, or movement.

The Informer takes place at the height of the Irish rebellion against the British in 1922, "The Troubles." The protagonist, Gypo Nolan (played by Victor McLaglen), is planning to betray his I.R.A. friend Frankie McPhillips to the British troops (Black-and-Tans) for £ 20 reward. The scene below is one in which Frankie is slipping into his mother's house. Emphasis has been added to the directions relating to sound to make them stand out.

> We see a doorway close to the lodging house steps and, looking out across the steps towards a lamppost in the fog, is FRANKIE in silhouette against the lamplight. As his dark figure starts furtively up the steps, **he hears footsteps tramping up the street,** and immediately he backs down the steps and glides around to the shelter of the doorway, so that he is in very close silhouette. . . . **Now the steps are loud** and through the fog in background, a patrol of eight BLACK AND TANS comes swinging along briskly.[2]

Note that sound motivates Frankie's action. In silent film an effect of this sort would most likely have required cutting to the soldiers, or having Frankie cup his ear with his hand, or inserting a title; in any case, weaker and clumsier. As it is, we hear and see just as he does, increasing our sense of identification with him and fear for his safety. Also, there is a kind of aesthetic tension created by the sound coming from an unseen source offscreen while we see a silent Frankie close up. In film, as in life, we more often see what we hear—and the closer it is, the louder it is.

Shortly thereafter Gypo enters Black-and-Tan headquarters to betray Frankie. But instead of letting us watch and listen to the betrayal, which we know is going to occur, Nichols calls for a cut from the sound of the door closing behind Gypo to a shot of those same loud, swinging marchers of the scene above. From that shot, there is then a cut to—

THE INNER OFFICE:
As the sound of the tramping continues . . . we see GYPO sitting hunched up beside a desk . . . at the desk beside GYPO, sits the officer; and two TANS, both officers, are standing beside him, their heads close together as they*

[2] "*The Informer:* A Screenplay by Dudley Nichols," *Theatre Arts,* 35 (August 1951): 61.

The Informer ◆ U.S., 1935, John Ford; Victor McLaglen.

ignore GYPO. GYPO faces a big clock and he stares at it numbly **as he listens to the tramping feet outside. Presently the tramping stops and the sound of two lorry engines starting across the street can be heard.** *GYPO never moves.* **The engines are raced and we hear voices;** *then the beams of light from the lorries come in through the windows as they start, and the beams sweep across GYPO's face. . . .* **And now there is neither tramping nor any other sound, only a deathly stillness in which the sound of the [clock's] ticking grows loud. The three officers are whispering in undertones we cannot hear,** *and nod to each other. GYPO stares at the clock and the slow swinging pendulum, which catches a flash of light on each swing and shoots it into his eyes with a hypnotic gleam. . . .* **Tick tock, tick tock goes the clock** *. . . . GYPO stares at the clock. Sweat comes out on his face and unconsciously he wipes it off with the sleeve of his coat.*[3]

Here the sounds of the swinging door, the marching soldiers, the lorry engines, the silence and unheard whispering, and the clock ticking, all complement the movement of the headlights, the nodding heads, the swinging pendulum. To express Gypo's growing tension and fear, the clock's tick is made increasingly louder than life.

[3]*"The Informer," Theatre Arts,* pp. 62–63.

There is a kind of sensory and symbolic richness here that couldn't be achieved in a silent film, even with the help of musical accompaniment. Note as well how powerfully silence and the absence of speech are used. It was toward this full and significant use of sound in relation to image that film makers had to make their way. Only gradually, and after considerable experimentation, were the essential differences between silent and sound films clearly seen.

Since it was to the United States that sound first came, the Americans were the first and the most prolific (given their output of four to five hundred feature films per year) in their successes and mistakes. Of course they were neither alone nor necessarily the most inspired in their contributions to the evolving form. The inventive and playful use of sound in Frenchman René Clair's delightful bits of proletarian whimsy laced with music—*Sous les toits de Paris* (1930), *Le Million,* and *À nous la liberté* (both 1931)—deserves special praise. Alfred Hitchcock, at work in England, provided what would become standard textbook examples: *knife* being the only word intelligible in a conversation as heard by a young woman who has murdered someone (*Blackmail,* 1929); a woman's mouth opening to scream, but seeming to emit a screeching whistle as a cut is made to a rushing train (*The Thirty-Nine Steps,* 1935). In Germany the American Josef von Sternberg made what many regard his masterpiece—*The Blue Angel* (1930)—and Fritz Lang, a German about to become an American, made what could be argued to be his—*M* (1931). G. W. Pabst, another of the great German film makers about to emigrate, did some of his best work during the early thirties—*Westfront 1918* (1930), *The Threepenny Opera* (1931), *Kameradschaft* (1931). By mid-decade the "100 percent all talking," "canned theater" had been largely transcended and the mature sound film achieved. Once this point had been reached, France in the latter half of the thirties made particularly full use of the new opportunities sound film offered.

FILMS OF THE PERIOD

1927
The Jazz Singer (Alan Crosland)

1928
The Lights of New York (Bryan Foy)
Steamboat Willie (Walt Disney)

1929
Applause (Rouben Mamoulian)
Hallelujah! (King Vidor)
The Love Parade (Ernst Lubitsch)

1930
All Quiet on the Western Front (Lewis Milestone)
Monte Carlo (Lubitsch)

1931
Dr. Jekyll and Mr. Hyde (Mamoulian)
The Smiling Lieutenant (Lubitsch)

1932
Love Me Tonight (Mamoulian)

1934
Our Daily Bread (Vidor)

1935
The Informer (John Ford)

For "Books on the Period," see Chapter 8, pp. 179–180.

7

Golden Age of French Cinema

◆ ◆ ◆

1935–1939

The economy of the French film has so persistently tended toward anarchy and chaos that it is easy to imagine its trade press keeping headline type standing to prophesy and then report "TOTAL COLLAPSE OF INDUSTRY." Made up of numerous small firms and individual impresarios, rather than a few huge studios, production companies have been born and laid to rest with a single film. Individual successes and fitful bursts of popularity have been supplemented by various forms of government protection and subsidy in efforts to achieve sustained good health. Since American movies have dominated in France as elsewhere as popular entertainment, the French have felt no need to produce large numbers of films each year. Instead, their relatively small output has included a high proportion of carefully crafted works that could compete with those of the Americans by virtue of artistic quality and distinctive national personality. During certain periods of rapid change the lack of economic ballast, which has otherwise been a liability, has given the French a peculiar advantage.

This was the case at the time sound was introduced. At first the greatly increased expense meant that only the two largest firms, Gaumont and Pathé, were capable of exploiting the new medium. When both collapsed from overextension of their resources, the situation reverted to French-normal. In part because they didn't have the heavy investments the American industry did, the French moved more readily into the experimental stage with sound, and hence exerted considerable leadership in the development of the altered art. In France the individual film maker frequently enjoyed a freedom of and control over expression seldom granted in Hollywood's major studios, or, for that matter, in the Ufa of Germany or the state-financed cinema of the U.S.S.R. A French film maker who could find a backer—wealthy lover, moribund aunt, reckless stock broker—could hope to make a film. With sound, French production returned to an international prominence it had relinquished after the first decade of the century.

First there was the delightful series of René Clair successes already mentioned— *Sous les toits de Paris* (1930), *À nous la liberté* (1931), *Le Million* (1931). Enchanting though these films are, Clair, coming from silence into sound, was a little like Méliès leaving the stage for the screen. Méliès gave us theater on film; Clair gave us silent film trimmed with delightful audio embellishments. He understood music and noises well and used them charmingly, often fantastically (a flower in the field bursting into song) or satirically (assembly-line work performed to the same music and monotonous sounds in the factory as in the prison). Dialogue had little place in his first sound works.

In those same early sound years Marcel Pagnol began his memorable trilogy of *Marius* (1931), *Fanny* (1932), and *César* (1936). In these a warmly human story about simple people is enacted in definitive performances against a Marseilles setting. For Pagnol dialogue was perhaps too important and the overall style remained "theatrical." Sharing Pagnol's predilection for the everyday, Julien Duvivier, in *Poil de carotte* (1932), and Jean Benoit-Lévy, in *La Maternelle* (1933), treated their subjects in a manner closer to documentary than to theater. Both films involve extraordinarily sensitive performances on the part of children. Both were also quite early and quite remarkable in breaking out of the sound stages to give a full sense of social and

Le Million ◆ France, 1931, René Clair; René Lefèvre and Annabella, as the lovers.

cultural particularities—of a country town in *Poil de carotte,* of a Paris suburb in *La Maternelle.*

Only a little later, Jean Vigo, the supreme poet of French cinema, made his two enduring and influential features before his tragically premature death. *Zéro de conduite* (1933), also concerning children, deals with life in a strangely surreal boys' school—a film to which Lindsay Anderson paid obvious and respectful homage in his own film *If. . .* (1968). *L'Atalante* (1934) is the tender and somewhat haunted, as well as haunting, love story of young newlyweds and a bizarre, elderly Caliban—set in a barge on the Seine. Both films are models for sparse and assured use of sound in support of images. The poetry is primarily visual rather than verbal, and the words, noises, and music coming from the loudspeakers add reverberations to what is already clear and rich on the screen.

Also before mid-decade, Jean Renoir's *Boudu Saved from Drowning* (1932) established the main elements of his later sound features. Already in *Boudu* there is the celebration of human life (of freedom and diversity) and the affectionate attention to the people who comprise it, loveable in spite of, and maybe even because of, their eccentricities and weaknesses. Renoir's *Toni* (1934), on the other hand, is a dark account of rural passion and crime among Italian migrant workers in Southern France. Brilliantly made, it seems to foreshadow Italian neorealism more than Renoir's own future development. Quite specifically it suggests *Ossessione* (1942), that harbinger of neorealism—whose director, Luchino Visconti, began in film in 1936 as Renoir's assistant on *The Lower Depths* and *A Day in the Country.* But *Toni,* as well as *Boudu*

Zéro de Conduite ♦
France, 1933, Jean Vigo.

and other pre-1935 Renoir sound films, showed an almost unique ease with the new medium. There is no sense of restraint or constriction imposed by the microphone, nor any self-conscious experimentation. Players and camera move freely in relation to each other, and the life portrayed is that of the world outside the sound stages, replete with its sounds.

In 1934, however, the year of *L'Atalante* and *Toni,* it looked to many as if the French industry *was* finally at an end, that it had reached that state of total collapse frequently predicted. Major cause of the catastrophe was the worldwide Depression that had by then hit France. Now no investment money was available for production, no films were being made, and film artists and technicians joined the millions of unemployed. Nineteen thirty-four was also a year of grave political unrest, not unlike 1919 in Germany. Demonstrations and riots preceded the formation of the Popular Front, a short-lived effort by the parties of the left to keep France from succumbing to fascism, as had Italy and Germany, and as Spain soon would. Perhaps this is yet another instance of periods of great national film expression growing out of troubled times. In any case, out of the ashes of 1934—and for reasons that aren't altogether clear in the general quirkiness of French film economics—a phoenix arose, becoming what is still referred to as the Golden Age of French Cinema.

One of the causes of revival seems more evident to the historian of today than it would have been to investors at the time. France was specially blessed with a cultural tradition that, though not fully accessible to the silent film, offered the stuff of which the best sound films are made. Whereas action-melodrama, spectacle, and slapstick comedy were ideal forms for the strictly visual requirements of the silent medium, the addition of dialogue demanded a new thoughtfulness, subtlety, and refinement of dramatic values. From 1935 until the end of the decade, French film makers utilized the resources of the new technology to emphasize intellectual content, to explore philosophical and psychological themes. Intelligent screenplays and superior screen acting were France's chief additions to the maturation of the sound film, contributed by some of its distinguished literary and theatrical talents. Those qualities, all of prime importance in the new medium, were often achieved without loss of visual brilliance—owing in no small measure to the well-known French affinity for the graphic arts. As tangible evidence of their excellence, it can be noted that French films of the late thirties became the first substantial body of foreign-language pictures to interest American audiences. In major American cities a few little "art theaters" sprang up to show them, somewhat as *The Great Train Robbery* had opened the nickelodeons in the earlier days. The first five annual New York Film Critics' Awards for the Best Foreign Film, which began in 1936, went to France: *Carnival in Flanders, Mayerling, The Grand Illusion, Harvest,* and *The Baker's Wife,* successively.

♦ LITERARY, THEATRICAL, AND PAINTING TRADITIONS

In the 1920s the French avant-garde film emerged from a nonfilmic line which began with the Impressionist painters of the late nineteenth century. The usually short, silent, avant-garde films are like visual poems, jokes, or dreams—more akin to modern poetry or to abstract or surrealist painting than to novels, plays, or feature films. At the end of the twenties, with the arrival of sound, many of the principal avant-garde film makers returned to the less expensive and more accessible traditional métiers: Fernand Léger (*Ballet mécanique,* 1924), Salvador Dali (*Un Chien andalou,* 1928), Marcel Duchamp (*Anemic Cinema,* 1928), and Man Ray (*Emak Bakia,* 1926; *L'Étoile de mer,* 1928) went back to painting and still photography. Others, however, found their way into commercial feature films. For example, René Clair (who had made the avant-garde *Entr'acte* and *Paris qui dort* in 1924), Luis Buñuel (*Un Chien andalou,* with Dali, and *L'Age d'or,* 1930, started with Dali but completed on his own), to an extent Jean Renoir (with *La Fille de l'eau,* 1924, and *The Little Match Girl,* 1928), and Jean Vigo (with *À propos de Nice,* 1930) had started in the avant-garde tradition. Jean Cocteau was the only one to bring avant-garde styles fully into sound features—in *The Blood of a Poet* (1930), *Beauty and the Beast* (1946), *Orpheus* (1950), and *The Testament of Orpheus* (1960).

Direct influence of the silent avant-garde tradition on French sound features of the thirties is evident in at least a few instances, however. Jean Vigo's *Zéro de conduite* and *L'Atalante* have strongly surrealistic overtones, which become quite explicit in the schoolboys' pillow fight of *Zéro* and in the hallucinatory underwater interlude of *L'Atalante.* Traces of the avant-garde also remain in the largely realistic and "theatrical" style of other fiction features. There is, for instance, the epileptic sequence in Julien Duvivier's *Carnet de bal* (1937), with its canted camera and exaggerated noises; also, there are the bizarre chase scenes (with echoes of Mack Sennett) in Jean Renoir's *The Rules of the Game* (1939).

In general, because of the avant-garde inheritance, the best of French cinema of the thirties was saved from the "staginess" that often marred Hollywood studio output. The avant-garde's attention to *cinéma pur,* and the fact that some of France's major directors came out of that informal school, kept the French aware that motion and picture was still the best two-word aesthetic of the motion picture, even when accompanied by sound.

But the French sound feature film, while showing the influence of a painterly tradition and of silent avant-garde film making, drew even more heavily upon literary and theatrical sources available to it. Historically, the French novel has been noteworthy for a kind of realism closely akin to the dominant style of the sound film. The works of Stendhal, Balzac, Flaubert, Zola, and de Maupassant comprise a main line in French literature; much of French cinema of the latter half of the thirties can usefully be seen as an extension of that inheritance. Often the films are set firmly within the provinces (*Carnet de bal,* 1937, *The Baker's Wife,* 1938), or amongst the urban working classes (*La Belle Équipe,* 1936, *Le Jour se lève,* 1939). Violence and crime frequently occur but, in French fashion, more out of passion than hatred or greed. Robust, sexually based humor alternates with worldly *tristesse.* The earthiness and honesty strike the viewer at once. Small important details of a scene are searched out; nearly tangible contact between characters and audience is established. Principal script writers were Jacques Prévert, Charles Spaak, and Henri Jeanson—all of whom had literary as well as filmic reputations—and they can claim a substantial share of the creative credit for films bearing their names. Most of the finest work of the period had scripts by one or another of them.

Excelling in psychological depth and intimate characterization, these films also depended to considerable extent upon the skill of French acting. Sound film was obviously more attractive than silent to actors trained in the theater. France had its great heritage of private and state-supported theatrical companies which for decades, even centuries, had provided one of the finest cadres of performers in the world. French cinema owes much of its luster and subtlety to the contributions of such actors as Arletty, Jean-Louis Barrault, Harry Baur, Pierre Blanchar, Pierre Brasseur, Jean Gabin, Louis Jouvet, Michèle Morgan, Raimu, Michel Simon, and Françoise Rosay. They approached the new medium with enthusiasm and quickly learned to adapt their talents and techniques to its special requirements.

◆ FIVE PROMINENT DIRECTORS

The quality of French films of the late thirties depended heavily upon the contributions of scriptwriters and performers. The directors who did the most important work in France from 1935 through 1939 came to film out of essentially theatrical or literary careers. Jacques Feyder began by acting in the theater; Julien Duvivier started as an actor as well; Marcel Pagnol had achieved distinction as a playwright and theatrical producer; Marcel Carné had been a journalist and film critic. Only Jean Renoir, younger son of the great Impressionist painter Pierre Auguste, had begun his artistic career with an interest in the visual/plastic arts (ceramics).

Jacques Feyder was a veteran commercial director, his career beginning far back in the silents with *Thérèse Raquin* (1928) the most enduring. After the coming of sound Feyder established the style of "poetic realism" that would become predominant in the late thirties. *Pension Mimosas* (1935), especially, became a prototype for later work, and Feyder's principal collaborators—Charles Spaak as scriptwriter and Marcel Carné as assistant director—would carry forward and elaborate on the themes, characterizations, and moody visual surface of that film.

Feyder's next effort, *Carnival in Flanders* (1935), was his greatest success. Essentially a richly amusing comedy about the battle between the sexes, it had certain political implications that gave it another kind of interest as well. Set in the Spanish Netherlands of the seventeenth century, it deals with the threat to a small Flemish town posed by an approaching military expedition led by the duc d'Olivarès. Pusillanimous and fearful of bloodshed, the men of Boom go into hiding, leaving the stalwart women to greet the conquerors. What develops between the women and the dashing Spaniards, with the Flemish men looking jealously on from their hiding place, is the main line of comic invention. Note, however, that Feyder (and the writer of the script and the novel from which it was taken, Charles Spaak) has the Flemish undergoing an invasion and occupation and, as it happens, indulging in fraternization and collaboration with the occupying power. (The ironic French title, *La Kermesse héroique*, means "the heroic village festival.") At the time, Feyder and Spaak, both Belgians, were attacked by Flemish nationalists among their fellow citizens for their unflattering portrayal. Subsequently, in World War II, the Flemish became notorious collaborators under German occupation, whereas Feyder and others who worked on the film were persecuted by the Nazis.

In *Carnival in Flanders* the arrival of the Spanish messengers in town—galloping horsemen shot from low angle with fluid camera movement and cutting to the music—is as lively a piece of cinema of that sort as can be found. Françoise Rosay gives a striking performance as the mayor's spirited wife, who takes command ("Femmes!" she shouts authoritatively from a balcony as she begins a speech to the assembled women below) and perhaps yields softly to the elegant duc. Louis Jouvet, in a lesser part as the cadaverous and wordly priest, is an equal delight; this is the first in a long series of such roles for him. The re-creation of the town and of the burghers themselves is a succession of Dutch paintings brought to life, reminiscent of Rembrandt, Vermeer, and particularly of Breughel in shots of the town square from an upper window in the burgomaster's house. The wit and sophistication, however, add a distinctly Gallic flavor.

Julien Duvivier, who also began directing in silent films, reached the height of his achievement between 1935 and 1939. He worked even more consistently and

Carnival in Flanders ♦ France, 1935, Jacques Feyder.

Carnet de bal ♦ France, 1937, Julien Duvivier; Fernandel and Marie Bell.

successfully within the style of poetic realism. Among his successes of the latter half of the thirties, most memorable (or perhaps merely most likely to be remembered in the United States) are *La Belle Équipe* (1936), *Pépé le Moko* (1936), and *Carnet de bal* (1937). The first two, starring Jean Gabin, explore the theme of escape; the third, in a way, deals with escape from self, escape to the past. *La Belle Équipe,* which means something like "the good gang," concerns a group of urban working-class buddies who win a lottery and attempt to establish a restaurant in the country. *Pépé le Moko* is set in Algiers, with Gabin as the fugitive who desperately wants to return to his native Paris but is safe only so long as he hides from the authorities in the Casbah. *Carnet de bal* began Duvivier's experimentation with the anthology film, which he continued in *La Fin du jour* (1939). (In Hollywood during the war he made *Tales of Manhattan,* 1942, and *Flesh and Fantasy,* 1943; and back in France, *Under the Paris Sky,* 1950—all employing a similar form.) A "carnet de bal" is a dance program, and the film revolves around a lonely widow who tracks down—some twenty years later—her partners from her very first dance. This scheme allowed for the stringing together of seven varied vignettes and a chance to display a galaxy of some of the most popular stars in French cinema: Françoise Rosay plays the demented mother of one of the old beaux, who has committed suicide; Harry Baur is a disillusioned musician turned monk; Pierre-Richard Willm is an Alpine guide; Raimu, the hen-pecked mayor of a little town; Louis Jouvet, a master criminal and nightclub proprietor; Pierre Blanchar, a one-eyed abortionist beset by a harridan mistress and epilepsy; Fernandel, a philosophical beautician.

Marcel Pagnol's *Marius* trilogy of the early sound years has already been mentioned. Before it was completed he produced *Joffroy* (1933), a charming anecdote about an aged Provençal peasant who sells his orchard land but claims that the fruitless old peach trees on it still belong to him. Perennial in its charm, it appeared in the United States nearly two decades later as one of three short films that formed *The Ways of Love*. (Renoir's *A Day in the Country* and Rossellini's *The Miracle* were the other two.) *Regain* (or *Harvest,* 1937) is also set in Provence and concerns an abandoned village. It has a back-to-the-earth theme and stars the popular comedian Fernandel in a role embodying a certain plaintiveness.

Pagnol's culminating achievement of the late thirties was *The Baker's Wife* (1938). Like *Regain* it is adapted from a Jean Giono story. The baker is played by the marvelously droll Raimu, one of the world's great comic actors, who has a distinctively French provincial quality. When his attractive young wife runs off with a handsome shepherd, he refuses to bake any more bread, thus involving the whole village in a search for the adulteress and in efforts towards reconciliation. Though

The Baker's Wife ♦ France, 1938, Marcel Pagnol; Raimu, center.

Raimu's style is in total contrast to Chaplin's, he has the same ability to edge comic situations with pathos.

Pagnol was resolutely a man of the theater who saw film as "a printing press for drama." If the pleasures he offers aren't essentially cinematic, they are very good theater indeed. His main preoccupations are with rural France—the simple and enduring way of life in the villages. His themes provide fascinating, if broad, understandings of traditional modes of French thought and behavior. With Raimu at their center, both the theatrical aspects of fine performance and the earthy wisdom and humor of provincial France are at their best.

Marcel Carné, a superb craftsman, did his best work in collaboration with the poet/screenwriter Jacques Prévert; in fact, it seems quite possible that Prévert was the *auteur* (author) in the filmic as well as the literary sense. Together they achieved an epitome of the poetic realism most characteristic of French film in the late thirties. The themes of doomed love, the tight dramatic structures, and the careful, evocative, and symbolic studio reconstructions of the real world mark their special aesthetic and give their work a sad beauty of lasting value. Their two greatest films of the period— *Quai des brumes* (*Port of Shadows*), 1938, and *Le Jour se lève* (*Daybreak*), 1939—are also remarkably consistent in the dark and despairing view they present of society. In them Carné and Prévert follow the ubiquitous Jean Gabin through urban lowlife on the fringes of the criminal world. Forced and led into a crime of passion that causes

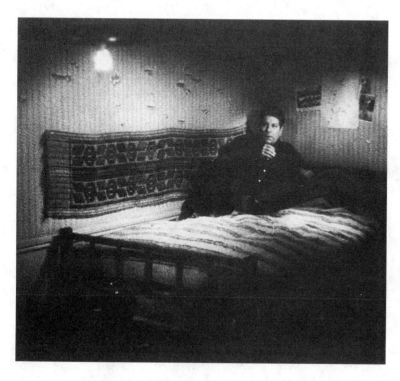

Le Jour se lève ◆ France, 1939, Marcel Carné; Jean Gabin.

his own destruction, Gabin meets his end with the special sort of stoicism that he carried with him from film to film. Even individual scenes seem almost interchangeable: The lighting and wallpaper in the forlorn hotel rooms look alike; a woman (Michèle Morgan or Arletty), with a kind of tired sensuousness, peels off a silk stocking; the same little bistro reappears, as do the same unadorned and cheerless flights of stairs. It's as if a bleak vision of the society had been frozen on the screen and Carné-Prévert insist that we see it over and over again with them. The social implications of this vision will be dealt with in the following section.

Then there was **Jean Renoir,** the giant figure among French film makers of that time. In fact, Renoir stands astride nations and periods in his long and fruitful career. His total corpus places him among the foremost film makers in the history of cinema to date; he is protean, experimenting in many forms and styles, yet usually saying essentially the same things. For Renoir life is fundamentally good—the life of the heart and of the senses. Sexual love and natural countrysides are to be celebrated along with food and wine. In Renoir's world there are no bores and few villains. (In *The Rules of the Game* one of his characters, played by Renoir himself, remarks, "Everyone has his own good reasons.") His people may cause themselves and others difficulties, but they are never less than human; always they are interesting, and ultimately verifiable in what we can recognize as one of humanity's possible aspects. Clearly enough, this celebratory view of life matched that of his father's paintings.

As observed earlier, Renoir's worldview had already been formed in his sound films preceding the high years of French cinema. *La Chienne* (1931), *Boudu Saved from Drowning* (1932), *Madame Bovary* (1934), and *Toni* (1934) can stand alongside his later work without apology. This is particularly true of *Boudu.* In it Renoir developed the notion of the social group, with the "outsider" (in one sense or another) serving as catalyst. This protagonist stirs up the group, unhinges it a bit; when he or she leaves, the group re-forms, changed by the experience. But the cohesiveness of the social unit, the need of people for each other, is one of the *idées fixes* in Renoir's universe of discourse.

In *The Crime of Monsieur Lange,* made in the landmark year 1935, Renoir restates these thematic materials in even fuller detail and more controlled form. Around the courtyard and within the offices of the publishing firm, a virtual microcosm of society at large is created, with basic human needs and weaknesses motivating the action. Yet, with Renoir, these social themes never seem schematic: They are made manifest through close observation of particular, idiosyncratic human beings rather than through reliance on types. His use of the camera (shots of considerable duration, wide-angled, composed in depth, and often inconspicuously panning) seems designed to capture what is happening to his characters without intruding upon them. The performances are so fresh and spontaneous they surpass an impression of improvisation to convey a sense of authenticity, of real persons at their core. Though the films are not life itself, they are definitive comments upon life as seen by one wise and humane artist.

Even the Gorky drama *The Lower Depths* is turned into a film (1936) that becomes part of Renoir's cosmos, and the viewer can't quite be sure how the alteration has taken place. *The Grand Illusion,* a year later, is unquestionably one of the director's masterworks. The script, which he wrote with Charles Spaak, is based on his own experiences during World War I and those recounted to him by others. Here the tale is that of French prisoners of war in German prison camps, of two of the prisoners who have escaped, and of a German woman and her child with whom they stay for awhile. The First World War was sometimes called The Great War, and that is the illusion referred to in Renoir's title. War may be big, it may also be pervasive, but it is scarcely grand. According to the film, it is an illusion that war can solve national problems; instead, it merely frustrates human needs. For the many soldier-prisoners, war is a deprivation—of freedom, primarily, and of women's love. For the two aristocratic professional soldiers, one French the other German, modern warfare doesn't even grant the traditional satisfactions of chivalry and comradeship.

It is also an illusion that war will ever end. (One of the characters says, in fact, that it is an illusion that this war will end all wars.) In fact the war itself may be an illusion—it remains offscreen throughout. What are not illusions? Friendship based on common humanity (cutting across national, economic, and ethnic differences), love (sexual, parental, and comradely), food and drink (which receive due attention) are real.

Renoir said that he was a pacifist, but this is not a clearly or at least a conventionally pacifist film. It contains no bloodshed, no atrocities, not even unbearable cruelties. (Punishment by solitary confinement comes closest; how like Renoir to regard being deprived of human companionship the cruelist of tortures.) If this is an antiwar film, it is even more profoundly a prohuman film, against all those restrictions placed on the human potential—nationality, class, military rank, religious prejudice—that keep us from solidarity.

After *La Marseillaise* and *The Human Beast* (both 1938) there came the final masterpiece of the thirties, *The Rules of the Game* (1939). It was completed just before French liberty was extinguished by the nation's collapse in the face of German onslaught.

The "game" of this title in an overall sense is the behavior of the upperclass hosts and guests during a house party. We see much of the servants of the estate as well. Their jobs are to serve the masters; the masters' jobs are to entertain themselves. The chief entertainment (game) is sexual intrigue, in which all the principal players indulge. In addition there are the host's collection of mechanical toys, a costume party, a rabbit hunt, a variety show.

The "rules" in general require that things be done properly, style taking precedence over feeling. (The feelings of the characters seem atrophied; or, at most, light and variable.) Passion is not permitted, sexual infidelity is accepted; embarrassment is avoided, decorum preserved; the appearance of friendship, frankness, and generosity is maintained. It is not just that the rules don't relate to human wishes and desires, they are in opposition to them (similar to the illusions of *The Grand Illusion*). Though essentially a comedy, the diagnosis of social illness is disturbing enough that the film was banned by the French during the Occupation. One of Renoir's few dark films, *Rules of the Game* became a requiem marking the end of an era.

The Rules of the Game ◆ France, 1939; Jean Renoir; Roland Toutain, Renoir, Nora Grégor, Pierre Magnier, Marcel Dalio, front row.

◆ REFLECTIONS OF A TROUBLED NATION

Just as Siegfried Kracauer saw evidence in German films of the twenties that that nation was ready to accept a Hitler, so it seems possible to infer from French films of the thirties certain attitudes that would contribute to the rapid and ignominious fall of France—signs of fatigue and demoralization. Examining French cinema of the late thirties against a backdrop of contemporary French politics and popular culture, Rod Whitaker found that the films of Carné-Prévert expressed most consistently and tellingly certain recurrent motifs. He analyzed them in especially great detail as they appear in *Quai des brumes*. Whitaker identified three major and two minor themes prominent in that film and reiterated, not only in additional Carné-Prévert work, but in a significant number of other films from that time and place.

First and strongest theme in *Quai des brumes* is the need for escape. This is also a major theme in *La Belle Équipe, Le Jour se lève, The Grand Illusion,* and *Pépé le Moko*—to name just a few other distinguished films of the period. (All starred Jean Gabin, who most closely among the French stars personified the average guy, the working-class man.) Second is the important role of a malignant fate. Whitaker found that the events and actions of *Quai des brumes* occur in a climate of fatalism, that the characters react as though they anticipated and accepted a certain malevolency in their destinies. The same can be said of Renoir's *Toni* and *The Human Beast,* in addition to the other films mentioned above. The third major theme is the ineffectiveness of action: Any attempts to achieve a goal by taking the initiative are either ineffectual or expose the characters to danger. This places the hero in a dilemma: On the one hand is the need to escape; on the other, to remain inactive. This situation may reflect what many French felt more or less consciously in the months leading up to and immediately following the outbreak of World War II. Perhaps crawling down underground and waiting in the reputedly impregnable Maginot Line seemed a way to embrace both horns of the dilemma.

The two minor themes may not extend so widely throughout French films of the late thirties, but are offered here so the reader can conduct a personal investigation in subsequent viewings. *Quai des brumes,* Whitaker observes, "presents fear as a constant condition of human existence." "One of the trademarks of the villain," he adds, "is to surrender to it, while one of the salient features of the hero is a victory over it."[1] Finally, Whitaker notes the pervasiveness of solitude in *Quai des brumes:*

> *The cosmos within which the events of the film take place is one in which man is essentially alone, but not independent in the sense that he controls his fate (as the cowboy prototype is alone and independent in the classic western). Nor can the hero depend upon friends; indeed, he cannot even rely on the mass as a cover under which to hide from avenging fate.*[2]

One last observation of Whitaker's does seem to apply to many French films of the late thirties mentioned in this chapter, and to others: "In the world of *Quai des brumes* there are . . . no children, no future, there is no joy, there are no homes, there are no great causes. There is, however, an innate dignity of man that seems to be worth preserving at all costs; but the final test and proof of this dignity lies not in the life of the man, but in his death."[3] The unhappy ending tended to be as typical of French films of the late thirties as the happy one was of American. It was Jean Gabin who most consistently (and satisfyingly) embodied that particular kind of tragic dignity. Romantic, anarchic, predestined, and pathetic, he believes in nothing but love and comradeship. Though his appeal is universal, Gabin developed a character of great and special meaning for his own culture.

At first glance, many of Renoir's films of the thirties may seem to be the great exceptions in any attempt to extend Whitaker's observations. Renoir was committed to the Popular Front, which came into power in 1936, when Léon Blum of the Socialist Party was elected president, and lasted until 1938. In fact his films of that

[1]Rodney Whitaker, "The Content Analysis of Film: a Survey of the Field, an Exhaustive Study of *Quai des brumes,* and a Functional Description of the Elements of the Film Language" (Ph.D. dissertation, Northwestern University, 1966), p. 238.

[2]Whitaker, "The Content Analysis of Film," p. 238.

[3]Whitaker, "The Content Analysis of Film," p. 228. Elizabeth Grottle Strebel, *French Social Cinema of the Nineteen Thirties: A Cinematographic Expression of Popular Front Consciousness* (New York: Amo Press, 1980), identifies similar themes.

Quai des brumes ♦ France, Marcel Carné;
Jean Gabin and Michèle Morgan.

brief, hopeful period are among those most clearly reflecting its liberal, egalitarian values. And in general we would expect Renoir's humanism and *joie de vivre* to be at war with the fatalism and defeatism so pervasive in other films—particularly in those of Carné-Prévert. But Renoir is an exception only in his treatment of the themes; the themes themselves remain as prominent in his work as in that of others. The need for escape is just as prevalent (*Boudu Saved from Drowning, The Crime of Monsieur Lange, The Lower Depths, The Grand Illusion*), but in Renoir's case the emphasis falls on an escape *to* as well as *from* something, and the escapes are apt to succeed.

Fate functions through coincidence in Renoir's films, as in those of others; but in his case fate tends to be benign rather than malignant. For example, in *The Lower Depths*—a version that has as much to do with Renoir as with Gorky, and is definitely French rather than imitatively Russian—the plot frequently turns on chance, but the outcomes are favorable. The thief and the baron are brought together by accident; Pepel (Jean Gabin assuming his archetypal role for the first time) happens to be at the outdoor restaurant to save the girl from dishonor; the death of the old landlord staves off catastrophe and offers escape to the tenants. Then too, with Renoir action *is* effective. In *The Crime of Monsieur Lange* the title character helps create a cooperative and then saves it by killing the former owner and escaping across a border. As for fear, Renoir's films are as remarkable for its absence—even in situations that would

The Grand Illusion ◆ France, 1937, Jean Renoir; Jean Gabin, Pierre Fresnay, and Marcel Dalio, front row.

seem to call for it (the prisons of *Grand Illusion*)—as those of Carné-Prévert are for its presence. Finally, Renoir's *oeuvre* is consistently and conspicuously redolent with solidarity and friendship; solitude or aloneness are almost entirely excluded from his screen world. Carné-Prévert and Renoir are equally concerned with the need for human warmth and companionship. But whereas Carné-Prévert present a world in which these qualities exist tenuously if at all, Renoir cannot conceive of existence without them.

If Renoir had the greatness and individuality of vision to withstand a common attitude, he still chose to look at the same things other French film makers did in the late thirties. He simply saw them in the positive light that permeates most of his major work rather than in the darkness and despair that was descending on his country and the rest of the world. If France had done no more than give tools and working space to this great film maker in the thirties, we could be grateful.

Renoir may be the supreme talent of that time and place, but he is first among equals. The group of creative film artists and cluster of brilliant films produced during that national flowering were influential and remain memorable. In retrospect they seem to have been the first to put the sound film to its full mature use. Though some of the work would be later criticized by the New Wave critics—the young removing the old to make way for themselves—it would be criticized as the "tradition of quality," which seems fair enough.

FILMS OF THE PERIOD

1935
La Bandera (Julien Duvivier)
Carnival in Flanders (Jacques Feyder)
The Golem (Duvivier)
Pension Mimosas (Feyder)

1936
La Belle Équipe (Duvivier)
César (Marcel Pagnol)
The Cheat (Sacha Guitry)
The Crime of Monsieur Lange (Jean Renoir)
A Day in the Country (Renoir)
The Lower Depths (Renoir)
Pépé le Moko (Duvivier)

1937
Carnet de bal (Duvivier)
The Grand Illusion (Renoir)
J'accuse (Abel Gance)

1938
The Baker's Wife (Pagnol)
The Human Beast (Renoir)
La Marseillaise (Renoir)
Quai des brumes (Marcel Carné)

1939
Le Jour se lève (Carné)
The Rules of the Game (Renoir)

BOOKS ON THE PERIOD

Buchsbaum, Jonathan, *Cinema Engagé: Film in the Popular Front.* Champaign: University of Illinois Press, 1988

Buss, Robin, *The French Through Their Films.* New York: Continuum Publishing, 1988

Crisp, Colin, *The Classic French Cinema, 1930–1960.* Bloomington: Indiana University Press, 1993

Slide, Anthony, *Fifty Classic French Films, 1912–1982: A Pictorial Record.* New York: Dover Publications, 1987

Williams, Alan, *Republic of Images: A History of French Filmmaking.* Cambridge, MA: Harvard University Press, 1992

8

Hollywood in the Thirties

◆ ◆ ◆

1929–1939

The 1930s in the United States were the years of the Depression and of the New Deal: of business collapse and bank failure, of unemployment and poverty; and of the WPA, the CCC, and the NRA (Works Progress Administration, Civilian Conservation Corps, and National Recovery Administration). They were years of economic stagnancy, industrial strife, and individual frustration. At the same time, they were years of rediscovery of American tradition, of affirmation of an American character, of un-earthing and preserving folklore and folk music, and of attempts at restoring and conserving our land and water through federal government efforts after decades of neglect and despoilation.

During these years the movies continued as a vital form of popular culture. Usually they seemed to avoid direct confrontation with the problems of the time, but inevitably they carried along its themes and concerns—even into seemingly escapist entertainment. Sometimes social stance was implicit in what was omitted or dis-guised. In other instances the movies spoke more or less directly to national fears and aspirations. The populist rhetoric and symbols of the first government documentaries, Pare Lorentz's *The Plow That Broke the Plains* (1936) and *The River* (1937), had their analogues in the fiction films of Frank Capra, *Mr. Deeds Goes to Town* (1936) and *Mr. Smith Goes to Washington* (1939).

American entertainment films of the 1930s were designed to function in a way quite different from theatrical feature films of today, at which attendance becomes something of a special occasion. Those earlier movies were more like current televi-sion series, and with similar audience expectations. Admission prices were much lower then; theaters were more easily accessible; and they were attended with greater casualness, more frequently—by 80 million customers a week. The men and women who created films for that mass audience conceived of themselves as making entertainment. They didn't think of their work as art.

A standard technique for screen narrative became fixed—what is now sometimes called classic Hollywood cinema. It involves a master long shot covering the whole scene, which introduces it and is returned to from time to time to reestablish spatial orientation. Within it are inserted medium shots and closeups in shot/reverse shot order, back and forth between action and reaction to it, speaker and listener(s). Screen direction and screen action are matched perfectly from shot to shot, and sight lines are carefully observed: When an actor looks, we see what she or he is looking at from approximately the same angle and distance. American film makers working within that style aspired to the well-made film, and the best of them had very high standards for their craft. But to regard the motion picture as a means for personal expression would generally have been considered a somewhat peculiar idea. Art existed in the movies of course; but in comparison to other more self-conscious artistic endeavors it was arrived at surreptitiously, sometimes unconsciously. We can tell this from the evidence of the five thousand or so features produced during the decade, and from an understanding of the industrial system within which they were made and marketed.

The thirties were the years of the giant studios having nearly complete control over the careers of their employees, more absolute than that of today's professional football teams over their players. The studios assembled their rosters of creators, performers, and technicians who, as they worked together over the years, became expert indeed. Because of this continuity of personnel, which extended from top management to lowliest grip, each studio had its own "look." In some ways we can deal with the American films of the thirties more adequately by identifying them with their studios rather than with individual film makers.

As much as we have come in recent years to think of the director as principal creator of a film, we must remember that in Hollywood in the thirties producers and stars would generally have been considered the major factors in each production. Producers, with a stable of script writers at their disposal, put together vehicles for stars. Producers like Irving Thalberg, Hal Wallis, and Darryl F. Zanuck left strong imprints on films they produced. Actors such as Katharine Hepburn, Clark Gable, Marlene Dietrich, or James Stewart had their wishes carefully attended to. The director was sometimes merely a supervisor who oversaw the recording of images and sounds. It makes sense, then, to look first at the industrial system before considering its product and the work of a few powerful creative figures who emerged.

♦ THE INDUSTRY

Rising out of the twenties, after seismic upheavals and shifts during the transition from silence to sound, the Hollywood economic terrain hardened into a pattern that would remain virtually unchanged for two decades. In fact, vestiges of the modus operandi of the thirties still characterize what is left of the once mighty feature film industry.

The system was built around eight major companies—five more major than the other three—and around the *vertical control* exerted by those firms over distribution and exhibition as well as production. Chains of theaters were owned by the five largest studios: Metro-Goldwyn-Mayer (M-G-M, the production arm of Loew's, Inc.), Twentieth Century-Fox, Paramount Pictures, Warner Brothers, Radio-Keith-Orpheum (RKO). Each studio produced upward of fifty features a year for its theaters and for those of the others. "Program," or "B," pictures might play only within their producing company's chain as weekly or semiweekly filler between hits. The more popular films were sought by all the exhibitors, regardless of which studios produced them. Whatever part of the country you are from, chances are that names of local theaters still pay tribute to their former owners: the RKO Grand, the Paramount, Loew's, and so on. The three smaller studios—Universal, Columbia Pictures, United Artists—produced and distributed, but to survive had to have their films shown in the theaters owned and controlled by the big five. Besides the eight major studios there were also those producers called independents. Some of them were reasonably large and well established (Samuel Goldwyn Productions, Walt Disney Studio, Republic, Monogram); others were individual entrepreneurs working out of one of the major studios (David Selznick at M-G-M, Walter Wanger at Paramount).

In 1939 the eight majors were responsible for 76 percent of feature films released, and took in 86 percent of total rental income. These studios were the members of the Motion Picture Producers and Distributors of America—the trade organization that self-censored the content of the films produced, bargained with foreign governments regarding export abroad, and performed other functions on behalf of the industry as a whole. Through the MPPDA (now the MPAA—Motion Picture Association of America) the majors dominated the industry. If control of exhibition was crucial to their power, they also controlled distribution.

The distribution branches of the majors undertook to "sell" the films to exhibitors and to physically handle and circulate prints to theaters. Selling involved advertising and promotion, which took two forms. First, each film was presented through advertisements and reviews in the trade press, and by sales representatives and advance screenings at regional offices. Second, the distributor developed a promotional campaign to attract general public attention to the new release—through the national press, radio, billboards, sky writing, and any other means available or thinkable. The budget allocated for promotion of each film was a key factor in determining the rental the exhibitor would pay for it. The more important the studio thought the picture, the more money it spent on the campaign, and the more the exhibitor might expect to take in at the box office.

The distributor worked out the kinds of appeals thought to be best suited and most effective for selling each picture. Its staff designed the graphics, wrote advertising copy, even prepared canned "reviews" for those newspapers that didn't choose to hire their own reviewers. Often the approaches to the public and to the trade were strikingly different. We are all aware that sex and violence are not only staples of popular entertainment but of the advertising for it. It may be less obvious that novelty is stressed almost as often: "For the first time on the screen . . . ," "At last it can be told . . . ," "Never before in the history of the motion picture. . . . " Usually pains were taken to disguise the probability that the film would be rather like the ones shown last week and a month ago, and to promise a unique experience no one could conceivably miss. To the exhibitor, however, the exact opposite (and a bit more honest) appeal was more often used: "The studio, the director, and the star who gave you *Dark Victory,*" "Judy and Mickey together again in the kind of story that made *Babes in Arms* a smash." The exhibitor sought known quantities in relation to audience tastes as demonstrated by their purchase of tickets in the past.

Some two hundred to four hundred prints of each film, costing around $250 apiece, were shipped from the laboratories to the regional film "exchanges." There were roughly thirty distribution centers in the country—Chicago, Dallas, Spokane, Atlanta, and so on, the same cities used as wholesale outlets by the garment manufacturers, meat packers, and other industries. Each distributor had an exchange along "film row." Prints were delivered from the exchanges to the theaters in time to open; prints of the closing program were returned for inspection and repair, then made available to other theaters in the region. In the eighteen to twenty thousand theaters across the country (estimates vary), nine thousand bookings were considered a good average for individual pictures. The first thirty-five hundred to four thousand bookings were scrutinized carefully to determine likelihood of success. If the projected income looked hopeful, more money might be spent on promotion. If not, the film was allowed to die quietly; prints would be kept in the exchanges, but no more money would be spent on promotion. Many fine films, particularly some small ones with quiet tone and subtle appeal, met this fate without being given a chance to reach the audience that might have existed for them.

The flow of money that started at the box office moved from the exhibitor to the distributor and finally back to the producer. Each took a cut to cover costs and make a profit, if any. With a looseness of accounting that flabbergasted people in other businesses, the distributor had to trust the exhibitor's report, and the producer the distributor's. Everyone cheated, it was said, and yet there was usually enough income to go around.

Helping to ensure the profits of distribution and production were certain characteristic trade practices. *Block booking,* for example, meant the exhibitor had to rent films in packages that included the "dogs" along with the "hits." This assured some return on even the weakest items in a studio's annual program. *Blind buying* occurred when an exhibitor was forced to book films unseen—sometimes even before they were made—to guarantee an advance market that would cover at least some of the considerable production and distribution costs. Block booking and blind buying led to *overbuying.* In those days of surplus product, the exhibitor might have to book more films than could be shown in order to get those that would attract the largest audiences. In return for what might be regarded as economic harassment (in 1940 the federal courts ruled the practices illegal), the exhibitor got *clearance* and *zoning.* If the theater was a downtown first-run "house" in a city, the exhibitor was assured that the film booked would not be shown in any other theater downtown or in the neighborhoods or suburbs until a certain time had elapsed—six months, say; or, if the theater was in a small town, the exhibitor knew that the film would not be shown in a town closer than perhaps twenty miles away.

In the days of vertical control this set of ungentlemanly agreements successfully kept out independents in any of the three phases—production, distribution, exhibition—except by tolerance of the major studios. Since profits could be made at any of the three levels, competition was largely internal within a single company: among its production, distribution, and exhibition branches. As for competition among the eight firms, since the members of the MPPDA parceled out their spheres of influence (kinds of production, regions in which theaters were owned), they competed with one another only in somewhat the manner of the several divisions of General Motors Corporation—Buick with Oldsmobile with Pontiac. Vertical control also meant that the industry could thoroughly police itself in terms of kinds of screen content it felt would be acceptable to the public. By self-censoring it was able to forestall outcries of moral indignation that might hurt the box office and invite government intervention.

◆ CENSORSHIP, SELF-REGULATION, PRESSURE GROUPS

To some creators, the system of self-regulation that developed was an even more onerous feature of the industrial organization than was the single-minded pursuit of profits by front office and stockholders. Certainly it had substantial effect on what would appear on the screen or, more accurately, what would not. This "production code" remained in operation with only minor revisions until 1968, when the industry adopted the practice, common abroad, of regulating attendance (the G/PG/R/X ratings) rather than content. The United States is almost unique among nations in never having had federal censorship of motion pictures.

As noted earlier, the move toward self-regulation began in the years immediately following World War I. It came in response to public criticism and the industry's fear of increased state and municipal censorship, and perhaps even federal government involvement. Eight states and a number of cities had passed film censorship laws by the early twenties. Public indignation had been provoked by films reflecting (exacerbating, some argued) a new, freer morality that featured hip flasks, knee-length skirts, and petting in the rumble seats of roadsters. Rocked by scandals surrounding the death of a starlet after an orgy (comedian Roscoe "Fatty" Arbuckle was accused of having caused her death), and by the unsolved murder of director William Desmond Taylor, Hollywood became the subject of particularly violent criticism.

In 1922 the Motion Picture Producers and Distributors of America hired Will H. Hays, Postmaster General and former national chairman of the Republican Party, to become its head. The choice was a shrewd one in several ways. Given his political clout, Hays could be expected to fend off government censorship. As an elder in the Presbyterian Church, he was regarded as a pillar of morality; his photograph alone, with high starched collar and ascetic features, was enough to attest to his virtue. The public relaxed, certain that Mr. Hays (dubbed the "Czar" of motion pictures) would launder the dirt out of the movies and prevent members of the industry from flouting conventional mores in their private lives.

This public-relations effort succeeded well enough for a number of years, until the public began to notice that the content of films had changed little. By the late twenties the tide of moral outrage was again rising. The response of the "Hays Office" to new threats of economic boycott and government intervention was the Motion Picture Production Code. Adopted in 1930, this curious document was drafted by Father Daniel Lord, S. J. (professor of dramatics at St. Louis University), assisted by Martin Quigley (publisher of the *Motion Picture Herald* and prominent Catholic layman).

Like the Ten Commandments, the Code's language was largely negative. Restrictions on what could be dealt with and how appeared under twelve main headings: crimes against the law, sex, vulgarity, obscenity, profanity, costume, dances, religion, locations (that is, bedrooms), national feelings, titles ("salacious, indecent, or obscene"), and repellent subjects (actual hangings or electrocutions, third degree, brutality, branding of people or animals, apparent cruelty to children or animals, the sale of women, surgical operations). Totally forbidden were presentations of drug traffic or the use of drugs, sexual perversion, "white slavery," sexual relationships between the white and black races, and nudity. The authors' detailed knowledge of human peccadilloes was at its most impressive under the heading profanity, the potential for which was now expanded with the talkie. Proscribed were "alley cat," "bat" or "broad (applied to a woman)." Also prohibited were: "Bronx cheer (the sound); . . . cripes; fanny; fairy (in the vulgar sense); finger (the)." A cryptic "in your hat" was banned from the screen, as were "nance; nerts; nuts (except when meaning crazy [one wonders about when meaning almonds]) . . . tom cat (applied to a man)," and so on, and on.

Once again everyone settled down, feeling that the Hays Office had a firm grip on Hollywood's transgressions—until, once again, the more observant observed that what was seen on the screen and heard from the loudspeakers had changed little as a result of the Code. In *Red Dust* (1932) Clark Gable gazes admiringly into the rain barrel in which Jean Harlow is bathing. In *Baby Face* (1933) Barbara Stanwyck sleeps her way to the top. And then there was the dialogue: witty, maybe, and risqué, certainly. In *International House* (1933) W. C. Fields, arriving at the rooftop restaurant of that establishment, to Peggy Hopkins Joyce: "Well, sweet buttercup, now that I'm here and see what's to be had, I shall dally in the valley, and believe me I can dally." And in *Jimmy the Gent* (1934), James Cagney: "Look, baby, what would you do for 500 bucks?" Alice White: "I'd do my best."

In 1932 a resolution was introduced into the U.S. Senate to investigate the motion picture industry. In 1933 the first large-scale social-scientific studies of the effects of mass media on the social attitudes and behavior of audiences were published: the twelve-volume *Motion Pictures and Youth,* sponsored by the Payne Fund. (The results of this research were popularized in Henry James Forman's *Our Movie-Made Children,* published in 1935, which emphasized and even exaggerated potential harmful effects.) In 1934 Catholic forces, particularly unhappy about Hollywood flouting a Code drafted by two of their own, formed the Legion of Decency.

Since the Legion's program rested on boycotting films that violated the Code (their titles to be announced from pulpits across the country), the industry finally became sufficiently alarmed to institute a mechanism to enforce adherence: the Code seal, to be applied by the Production Code Administration. Joseph I. Breen, a young Catholic newspaperman, was appointed director. The members of the MPPDA agreed not to release or distribute films unless they carried the seal. A $25,000 penalty was instituted for producing, distributing, or exhibiting any picture that had not received it. Given vertical and nearly complete control of the industry by the major studio members of the association, not a single important feature was released without the seal in the next two decades.

This enforced, official morality imposed on the creative personnel by the business leaders resulted in a screen world that many found more than a little removed from life. Though it was argued to be "self-regulation," the Code was embraced much more warmly by studio heads than by those who actually made the pictures. Writers, directors, and actors—who often came out of theater and the other less financially encumbered traditional arts whose audiences were smaller and more select—felt particularly inhibited by it. One principal problem was that the Code sapped creative energy at its source. Staying within the Code's standards of conventional, conservative middle-class mores became at least as important as creating a fine work. Another problem was the patent hypocrisy involved. The real reasons for the Code and the seal were financial rather than moral. If organized pressure groups succeeded in keeping audiences away from theaters, a substantial loss of income would result. If local and state censorship bodies increased in number and were joined by a threatened federal agency, the considerable expense of providing several versions of a film to meet the varying standards might be entailed.

Naturally film makers working within the Code tried to suggest what they could not show; the leer replaced a frank look at many of life's realities. Since restrictions were greatest on sexual matters, sexuality was replaced by violence (regarded with more equanimity by the society as well as by the Production Code Administration). Our popular genres contain more crime and violence than the films of any other nation; as Robert Warshow pointed out in two brilliant essays reprinted in *The Immediate Experience,* the gun is the central symbol of both the western and the gangster film. It is possible that we are the most criminal and violent nation on earth; but even if that much of the image were accurate, it became distorted by the Code's overall insistence that virtue be rewarded and vice punished.

On the other hand, the synthetic morality may have been appropriate, even aesthetically, to the world of the studio films of the thirties, created as they were out of imagination, plaster, lath, and klieg lights, From this distance in time, at least, considering what those films are generally about and the characters who usually inhabit them, it seems that reality is not so much excluded (as was argued by the social critics of the thirties) as dealt with obliquely and within the fixed rubrics of the popular forms. In *Trouble in Paradise* (1932), for example, after Gaston and Lily embrace passionately on a couch, the culmination of that embrace is expressed by a dissolve to the same couch, now empty, followed by a cut to Gaston's hand hanging a "Do Not Disturb" sign on the bedroom door. The indirection of content, like the stylization of technique, frequently adds to rather than detracts from the charm and resonant effectiveness of the best films of the thirties.

◆ EMERGENT GENRES

Until fairly recently, critics tended to discount or ignore the importance of genres to the history of the American film. A case could be made, however, that the conventions of genre—fixed yet capable of infinite variation—have supported and given strength to the work of many of the finest script writers and directors (as Shakespeare had built upon the conventional revenge tragedy introduced by Thomas Kyd). Though genres came about because of the requirements of mass production and popular appeal, they have nonetheless been consistently developed by American film makers. Howard Hawks's films, though they vary widely, all fit within conventional genres: war drama (including flying pictures), gangster, comedy, private eye, the western, sea and jungle action-adventure, historical spectacle (*Land of the Pharaohs,* 1955), even the musical (*Gentlemen Prefer Blondes,* 1953), and science-fiction (*The Thing,* 1951). We tend to identify John Ford with westerns, D. W. Griffith with historical spectacles, Alfred Hitchcock with mystery and suspense. The latter genre, because of plot intricacies requiring dialogue, did not develop fully until sound arrived. Though his silent *The Lodger* (1927) and early sound *Blackmail* (1929) are memorable, Hitchcock didn't hit full (British) stride until the mid-thirties, when the inadequacies of early sound technology and technique had been largely overcome.

Of the popular genres that had formed into recognizable patterns during the twenties, silent comedy was affected most radically by the introduction of sound. While lamenting the loss of comic pantomime and the great clowns who made it the universal and timeless form it is, we would still want to welcome the new kinds of comedies and the creators who entered with sound. Westerns, of course, could only be hampered by the sound stages; during the the first half of the thirties they were relegated largely to "B" and "C" production budgets and comparable prestige. They became the "oaters" beloved by rural adult populations and small boys everywhere on Saturday afternoons, but had little to do with the advance of the motion picture generally. With only a few exceptions (for instance, *Cimarron,* 1931), not until the mid-thirties was there a return to the earlier epic western: *The Texas Rangers* (1936), *The Plainsman* (1936), *Wells Fargo* (1937). Not until the end of the decade did *Stagecoach* (1939) establish a model for the "modern" western that has survived to this day.

Of the narrative forms emerging with the new sound medium, most vigorous and characteristic of the thirties were the musical, the gangster film, the horror film, the sound comedy, and the animated cartoon.

The **musical** was dependent on sound for its existence. In such harbingers as *The Merry Widow* of 1925, von Stroheim's most popular film, audiences had to be content with a live pit orchestra or organist providing a potpourri of Lehar melodies to accompany the pantomimed action and printed titles. Fittingly, the film that caused the revolution, *The Jazz Singer* (1927), foreshadowed the backstage musical, an important early subgenre. What it lacked most essentially was dancing, for the appeal of the musical came to depend as much on choreography as on music. From *The Hollywood Revue of 1929* through *Saturday Night Fever* (1977), *All That Jazz* (1979),

Flashdance (1982), and *Dirty Dancing* (1987), the creators of musicals have been men and women of dance as well as of song.

The Hollywood Revue of 1929 was a prototype for one line of musical, the revue, which flourished in the thirties and first half of the forties. It disappeared after World War II, with only a few exceptions (*Ziegfeld Follies,* 1946; *New Faces,* 1952). Consisting of separate "acts" unconnected by narrative linkage, like its stage counterpart, the screen revue let audiences throughout the world see the great entertainers whose performances had formerly been confined to Broadway and infrequent tours. Generally presented very much as they might have been on a superstage (by impresario Florenz Ziegfeld, let's say), the film revues substituted the possibility of perfection—ideal performers in their best performances—for the special excitements of live theater.

Another early film musical form deriving from theater was the filmed operetta. It began with the romantic comedies-cum-music of Ernst Lubitsch (starting with *The Love Parade,* 1929) and Rouben Mamoulian (*Love Me Tonight,* 1932). These operetta-like screen originals were made at Paramount and starred Maurice Chevalier and/or Jeanette MacDonald. Moving to M-G-M, in 1934 Lubitsch directed the same stars in his version of *The Merry Widow.* It was at M-G-M that the operetta continued, in a series of standard stage favorites beginning with *Naughty Marietta* in 1935. In them Chevalier was replaced by Nelson Eddy; he and MacDonald helped make a great deal of money for everyone concerned.

If the filmed operetta came out of Paramount and M-G-M, the backstage musical began at Warner Brothers. In 1930 Warner imported Broadway veteran Busby Berkeley, who became master of the production number. His ranks and clusters of chorines moving with military precision through elaborate patterns are understandably the subject of "camp" appreciation today. Those extravagant creations nonetheless contain an authentic if frequently exotic charm. Early in the period Berkeley's spectacular staging and bravura use of camera, cutting, and special effects were brought together in the narrative musical.

First of the stories with music and dance (which the term *musical* now generally means) was *42nd Street* (1933). Directed by Lloyd Bacon (with "Dances and ensembles created and staged by Busby Berkeley"), the story revolves around production of a Broadway musical, "Pretty Lady." The tough director of the show (Warner Baxter) is dependent on an "angel" (Guy Kibbee) who has put up $70,000 because of his infatuation with its star (Bebe Daniels). The night before opening she breaks her ankle, permitting the young unknown (Ruby Keeler) to take her place. As a result of the crisis, the established star realizes her love for her former vaudeville partner (George Brent), and the newcomer hers for the junior lead (Dick Powell). Una Merkel and Ginger Rogers play seasoned chorines—Rogers as Anytime Annie ("She only said 'No' once—and then she didn't hear the question").

The prototypical content elements work largely because of the pace and dazzle of the film. The lines are witty and delivered in rapid-fire staccato. Characterizations are deftly etched, stereotypical as they should be. The performers take themselves only seriously enough to blend in with what would become the conventional hard-boiled-

42nd Street ♦ U.S., 1933, Lloyd Bacon/Busby Berkeley; Ruby Keeler.

exterior, soft-on-the-inside view of show biz. Climaxing the film, and what it's all building toward, are the three production numbers: "Shuffle Off to Buffalo," "I'm Young and Healthy," and the title song, "42nd Street." After the numbing exhaustion of rehearsals and the nervous tension of the young heroine, we are given an enormous release in the polished extravaganza, which goes considerably beyond what could be created on any stage. Each of the numbers exceeds the preceding one in terms of spectacle, and each pulls farther away from the possibilities of live theater into strictly cinematic manipulations of space and time, of image and movement.

In *42nd Street,* Berkeley started full scale on that special kind of creation we associate with his name. The massed lovelies of the chorus are viewed by the camera from almost any position except a stationary one in front of a theater stage. They are seen from overhead as they form floral patterns or strange concentric rings suggesting interconnecting gears. Or the camera gets down on the floor and moves through their spread legs in as slyly elegant a bit of erotica—funny in a way, but lovely too—as one could imagine. Costumes and settings are designed to support and underscore the extravagant fantasy of the total choreographic conception; or, to put it the other way around, the dances grow out of and take full advantage of every suggestion provided by the visual decor. The chorus line performs a jerky, syncopated march up stairs, they turn toward the camera and raise cardboard profiles of skyscrapers, covering themselves and becoming a miniature Manhattan. Berkeley would later sustain and elaborate on delights of this sort at their most breathtaking (and bizarre) in the *Gold Diggers* series (*of 1933, 1935, 1937*).

If on one level *42nd Street* can be seen as the most purely escapist kind of entertainment, on another it seems to be dealing with the insecurity and paralysis of the Depression. It's not just the apple vendor, that symbol of the unemployed, in the "42nd Street" number; in a way the whole film is about lack of money and joblessness. The director insists that the only reason he's doing the show is for the money. Portrayed as a driving entrepreneurial type, he says he's been called a machine, producing a steady succession of hits. Sure he's made a lot of money in the past, but he's spent and lost it all on friends and high living and the stock market. As he delivers these lines he is standing against a window high above the street, suggesting the many suicidal leaps of those who had lost their money in the crash. This time, he says, he's going to sock away his earnings so hard they can never be taken from him. The control exerted by the unattractive and stupid, but wealthy, angel over all members of the production—and on the quality of the show itself, when he insists that Anytime Annie replace the injured star—is made pointedly clear. That two hundred jobs depend on the success of the show is insistently reiterated. Keeping cast and crew from falling back into the ranks of the unemployed is the strongest point made in the pep talk the director gives the young replacement for the star just before she goes on. Surely there was a special poignancy to that plea in 1933.

In this same narrative line, a series of films starring Fred Astaire and Ginger Rogers were the first to drop the theatrical setting as excuse for music and dancing. Though they play professional dancers, thus making their terpsichorean skill plausible, they move from the theater out into the world, breaking into song and dance whenever the emotional charge is sufficient. This observation covers all ten of their costarring films to one degree or another. In *Shall We Dance* (1937), for example, Astaire (as the great Petrov, a Russian Ballet dancer) is first seen tap dancing in his room to a jazz record. (Really he's Peter Peters from Philadelphia, PA.) Returning from Paris on board the *Queen Anne,* he wanders down into the (extraodinarily stylized) engine room, and sings and dances with the black crew and the rhythmically pumping, eccentrically designed machinery. That number suggests a benign and jazzy *Metropolis,* with the ebullient individual replacing the deadened mass, and the machines beating it out in swing-time. Another number on board ship has Rogers and Astaire walking their dogs to the Gershwin music. In New York they are seen roller skating with a group of extras in a soundstage Central Park. Soon they wander off to sing a song, and traject themselves into an energetic and skillful dance on skates. Astaire and Rogers, whose films together extend from 1933 to 1949, served to link the backstage musical inaugurated by *42nd Street* (same year as *Flying Down to Rio,* the first Rogers and Astaire) and the vintage cluster of M-G-M musicals beginning with *On the Town* (same year as the last Rogers and Astaire, *The Barkleys of Broadway*), which offered song and dance as the normal response to life. But of course the

Swing Time ◆ U.S., 1936, George
Stevens; Ginger Rogers and Fred Astaire.

grace and charm, the subtle and sophisticated virtuosity of Fred and Ginger gives its
own lasting pleasure, which transcends their place in the history of Hollywood
musicals. Their appeal remains as inimitable as it is irresistible.

Of the popular American genres, the musical remains one of the most indigenous
and enduring. Surely it is the loveliest, offering aesthetic pleasures that by comparison
cause many of the more "serious" films valued contemporaneously to fall behind in
lumbering earnestness. As long as a simple and sensible Aristotelian notion is accepted—that art offers beauty and beauty is a good in itself—the musical is assured
its deservedly important place in the history of the American film. Long may it talk,
and sing, and dance.

Though there were many films about gangsters in the twenties (von Sternberg's
Underworld, 1927, is one example), the **gangster film** was really a product of the
thirties. To make it viable, perhaps it needed the growling of limousines in low gear,
the squealing of tires and the screeching of brakes, the ratchet noise of tommy guns,
the explosions and tinkling glass. In its conventional form it was born, brought up,
and buried within that decade. *Little Caesar* (1930) began the cycle.

In film generally, and in the forms, styles, and subject matters of the popular
American genres particularly, it frequently happens that the prototypical films remain

the strongest and best of type. It's as if Elizabethan drama started with *Hamlet* and *Much Ado About Nothing* rather than building to them. In film, documentary commenced with *Nanook of the North; Battleship Potemkin* and *Mother* led off the high period of Soviet silent film, as *Open City* and *Shoeshine* did that of postwar Italian neorealism. In the American film, *On the Town* (1949) began the vibrant cluster of M-G-M musicals of the early fifties; *Destination Moon* (1950), the futuristic science-fiction genre; *Rebel Without a Cause* (1955), a succession of problem pictures dealing with misunderstood teenagers. So it was with the gangster film of the thirties. The three prototypical films—*Little Caesar* (1930), *The Public Enemy* (1931), and *Scarface* (1932)—so richly explored the potential of the genre that little was left for other film makers to do immediately except repeat and vary. One study, *The Gangster Film,* by Stephen Karpf, makes this point in its subtitle: *Emergence, Variation and Decay of a Genre, 1930–1940.* It is true that the thirties-type gangster film disappeared during the years of World War II. The genre itself, however, like the western, has remained sufficiently strong and healthy to give us a succession of important works such as *White Heat* (1949), *Bonnie and Clyde* (1967), *The Godfather* (1972/74), *Once Upon a Time in America* (1984), and *Goodfellas* (1990), to name but a few.

If musicals sometimes offered masked representations of the Depression society of the thirties, gangster films seem to present metaphorical explications of what had gone wrong with the country. The attitudes in them are quite amoral. The goals of the gangster protagonists are confined to acquiring wealth and power. They are the ones who understand the system and how to succeed within it. Others, those who believe in honest work, loyalty, affection, and decency, are ineffectual dupes. In these films gangsterism can be seen as supercapitalism, just as war was seen by military strategist Karl von Clausewitz as an extension of diplomacy. If gangsters are businessmen as well as criminals, might it not be equally true that businessmen are gangsters? Couldn't utilities magnate Samuel Insull be seen as a legitimized Al Capone? In any case, the ordinary citizen was caught in a corrupt system controlled by the greedy and the unconscionable. How come the banks couldn't pay back their investors? Why was it that profits made on the stock market suddenly became losses? In a later example of a related subgenre, *The Asphalt Jungle* (1950), the outwardly respectable lawyer secretly involved in criminal activity remarks to his wife, "Crime, my dear, is merely a left-handed form of human endeavor." In the initial gangster films the police are no better nor worse than the gangsters, and the methods of both are more or less interchangeable. When the first tough phases of the cycle came under severe public criticism and the studios were pressured by the Production Code Administration, the producers simply changed their gangsters into G-men, Treasury agents, and other law enforcement officers.

Though perhaps not the best aesthetically of the first three prototypical films, *Little Caesar,* directed by Mervyn LeRoy, contains the essential thesis of the gangster film in its simplest and clearest form. Rico (Edward G. Robinson), the hero, or antihero if you prefer, begins as a gun-toting thug with ambition—the toughest, most ruthless of the lot. What motivates him is the exercise of power. The film's makers don't feel obliged to justify their dramatic premise: It is presented as a given. Those on top are enviable because they are rich and powerful. But as you climb upward there's a danger of becoming soft. Refinement and sentiment make people vulnerable and lead to destruction through "loss of nerve." The film begins with Rico murdering a robbery victim and ends with Rico being gunned down by the police after he fails to shoot his friend, Joe Massara (Douglas Fairbanks, Jr.), who becomes indirectly responsible for his death.

In *Little Caesar* there are no "good guys." The detective Flaherty is simply on the other side, a nasty character with his own strong-arm men, who carries on a personal vendetta with Rico. McLure, the crime commissioner, is an unrealistic and ineffectual snob. The Big Boy represents a corrupt and criminal high society. But Rico, for all his viciousness, is not a sadist. He doesn't torture, doesn't get pleasure from killing. His view is presented as pragmatic, up to a point. Like Hitler in *Mein Kampf,* he pronounces on human behavior and values, and acts effectively as long as he follows his own cynical understanding. The world is a jungle, and the most effective predator kills fast and without compunction. When he fails to kill, he himself is killed.

Given the nature of artistic experience, something more than the relevance of these thematic statements to contemporary attitudes must have accounted for the wide and continuing appeal of gangster films. As with the musical, in the gangster genre formal elements and creative personalities command our attention. At a time when films generally were bound to the theater by the confines of the sound stage, gangster

Little Caesar ◆ U.S., 1931, Mervyn LeRoy; Edward G. Robinson, center right.

films seemed to break out into the real life behind the headlines, to be situated within recognizable slums, penthouses, streets, and speakeasies of big-city America during the Prohibition era. Indeed, they were full of life, driven forward by action, violence, and competition for the highest stakes. They were also frenetic in their pace, clipped and colorful in their language. With their usual tightness of construction, economy of means, and the fact that they deal with matters of life and death, at their best they provide satisfactions that are classic, that resemble Greek dramas—though the film makers themselves apparently had no self-conscious pretensions. More fascinating and credible than anything else, perhaps, are the conceptions of their roles and the dynamic performances by Edward G. Robinson, James Cagney, and Paul Muni as the first protagonists. Though painfully limited in education and outlook, these characters have stature. Within their small and evil world they are the tragic kings doomed by flaws, ambition and pride usually the dominant ones. Their inevitable deaths provoke pity and fear, as they should.

While the musical and gangster genres flourished at Warner's, **horror films** were the specialty of Universal. The appearance of these successors to *The Golem* and *Nosferatu* seems to have had less to do with the advent of sound technology than with American mastery of the lighting techniques originated earlier in Germany. Chiaroscuro lighting was crucial to the evocation of terror, and the names of German emigrés dot the technical credits of this series. Also, as in Germany, it may be that audiences respond especially to horror on the screen during times of national instability. At any rate, as with the gangster films, the two prototypical American horror films set forth fully the traits of their progeny. *Frankenstein* and *Dracula,* both released in 1931, are still in active circulation on video and in college series and courses. Of the two, *Frankenstein* is the more satisfying aesthetically, and remains a very fine film aside from generic considerations.

The opening graveyard scene, with its low-angled shots among the tombstones, an iconic cross, and a figure of death, establishes the mood. The desolate landscapes, remote ancestral castle, forbidding stone tower in which Henry Frankenstein conducts his experiments, the laboratory interior with its flashing electrodes—all would become familiar images of the Gothic horror movie. A sense of impending doom hangs over the film like a pall. Stylized Ruritanian settings and the bleak black-and-white cinematography create the visual atmosphere of shadowy gloom that dominates successive films of the genre.

Frankenstein's cast of characters includes several archetypal figures of the horror film. Frankenstein is the demonic scientist whose obsessive thirst for knowledge has misdirected the humanistic aim of his work. In his feverish search for the source of life, morality is forgotten: He desecrates both the grave and the hangman's gibbet in order to obtain specimens for his experiments. As a result, he is ostracized by his friends and colleagues. As the misfit scientist who defies the conventions of society in his quest for knowledge, he stakes his reputation on one major breakthrough that will bring him fame and power. His presumption, of course, is the original sin of Adam in seeking to know more than humans should. Frankenstein goes even beyond this in attempting to rival God as creator—an ultimate blasphemy. For his arrogance he is punished by the creature of his creation.

Frankenstein ♦ U.S.,
1931 James Whale; Boris
Karloff.

Other archetypal figures include the heroine whose true affection heals the ravages of Frankenstein's soul. The conflict of love and faith (feeling) with science (reason) is a popular theme in later films of this genre. The scientist's malevolent assistant is another standard figure; the same actor played a similar role in *Dracula*. The central archetype, however, is the monster himself. As played by Boris Karloff, he takes on a dimension of pathos. The scenes in which he raises his arms to the light and plays with the little girl contrast strongly with, and give added power to, those in which he is possessed by an inhuman fury. The terror evoked by this myth is all the more penetrating because of the sympathy aroused by the monster's dignity and by the anguish expressed in his tormented eyes. As an outcast of society, he prompts an empathic response in our own feelings of loneliness and alienation. Perhaps a Depression-ridden society, economically and culturally deprived, was particularly attuned to this appeal—and also to the suggestion that there is madness in high places, which can set loose a monstrous, impersonal, uncontrollable, destructive force.[1]

In any case, the archetypical horror film, like the gangster film, waxed in the thirties and waned after that decade, degenerating into more simplistic tales of horror, and finally even to self-parody (the series of *Abbott and Costello Meet* films: *Frankenstein,* 1948; the *Invisible Man,* 1951; and others). Though ailing, the genre didn't die with the thirties. Instead, the horror films produced by Val Lewton in the

---

[1]Much of this description and interpretation of *Frankenstein* is borrowed from a CinemaTexas program note written by Courtenay Beinhorn.

forties—such as *Cat People* (1942), *I Walked with a Zombie* (1943), *The Body Snatcher* (1945)—mark a sharp departure from the earlier patterns and are noteworthy for their intelligence and taste. Later the horror film was restored to something like full health by Roger Corman in his series of Edgar Allan Poe adaptations (such as *The Fall of the House of Usher,* 1960; *The Masque of the Red Death,* 1964) made in England. Though not as distinctively American as the musical or gangster film, like the other genres, the horror film has been worked at consistently by Americans including Corman, Brian De Palma, George Romero, and John Carpenter. It is another lasting contribution of the American thirties.

One line of **sound comedy** took advantage of the new possibilities for repartee and double entendre. Though like drawing room comedies of the theater, in the best film examples (Lubitsch's *Trouble in Paradise,* 1932) visual interest was retained and sight and sound were worked into counterpoint. A second line, out of vaudeville and stage, and replacing the silent clowns, featured talking comic stars in vehicles tailored to their special talents and the verbal styles associated with them. The Marx Brothers, for example, merely transferred to film their theatrical hits *The Cocoanuts* and *Animal Crackers,* in 1929 and 1930. W.C. Fields had been a popular vaudeville performer whose most memorable film bits (for instance, the crooked cue-stick routine) had

My Little Chickadee   ♦   U.S., 1940, Edward Cline; W. C. Fields and Mae West.

frequently been worked out before on stage. Mae West, long before she appeared in movies, had played her particular version of herself on stage. The point is that the great comic movie stars of the thirties were experienced with sound, especially with their own distinctive voices, as supplement to pantomime. In fact, they required sound for full comic effect.

Take as illustration a Fields short, *The Barber Shop* (1933). In addition to his gin-honed voice and throwaway delivery, there are sound gags acompanying verbal and sight gags. The poor unfortunate customer being shaved accounts for some droll lines. Fields: "I didn't recognize your face when you first came in." Man: "No, it's all healed up since I was in here last." At the same time, Fields wields the razor as if it were some sort of harvesting tool. While the man's back arches in discomfort we are able to share his feelings along our own spines because of the sandpapering noise that accompanies each stroke. Fields's solo work with his bass fiddle, Lena, is funny to look at; his comments about his ability are amusing; but the whole is bound together by our hearing that he is merely banging the bow against the strings in toneless percussionistic thumping.

The Marx Brothers used sounds in much the same way, and combined them with rapid-fire dialogue full of non sequiturs and malapropisms. The delivery of the lines augments their humorous content: the timing, Groucho's Lower East Side accent, and Chico's phoney Italian one. Harpo's feigned muteness, his honking of horns, beating on pans, and the like would make sense only in a sound medium. Obviously, the same is true for his harp and Chico's piano playing.

Mae West confined herself almost entirely to verbal humor, except for the ribald smirk and undulating walk. Though Fields and the Marxes expanded the scope of their comic jousts with society to take advantage of the variety of backgrounds and situations that could be encompassed within a single film, West used film mostly to record her great self in a room talking to a man. Given her marvelous way with talk and men, this seems quite enough.

A third kind of comedy developed in the thirties in which, rather than being a projection of a single or team comic persona, the plot dictated the personalities of the actors (who, to some extent, became interchangeable). It was like the first line mentioned above except less genteel and more energetic, and it originated in film rather than in theater. Called the "screwball" comedy, this style combined intellectual sophistication with slapstick behavior. It depended on fast, witty dialogue and a battle of the sexes in which male and female roles were often reversed (in terms of traditional expectations of male strength and dominance). The performers most frequently inhabiting the screwball world were Claudette Colbert, Gary Cooper, Irene Dunne, Cary Grant, Jean Harlow, Katharine Hepburn, Carole Lombard, Rosalind Russell, Barbara Stanwyck, and James Stewart.

Frank Capra's enormously successful *It Happened One Night* (1934) may have been the first of the screwball comedies. Howard Hawks also directed effectively in this subgenre (*Twentieth Century,* 1934; *Bringing Up Baby,* 1938; *His Girl Friday,* 1940; *Ball of Fire,* 1941). Other directors who did memorable work in this style were Gregory La Cava (*My Man Godfrey,* 1936), William Wellman (*Nothing Sacred,* 1937), and Leo McCarey (*The Awful Truth,* 1937). The distinctive series of comedies written

A Night at the Opera ◆ U.S., 1935, Sam Wood; Groucho Marx, Chico Marx, Sig Rumann, and Harpo Marx.

as well as directed by Preston Sturges are also of this type (*The Lady Eve,* 1941; *The Palm Beach Story,* 1942; *The Miracle of Morgan's Creek,* 1944; and others).

Scripts, even more than direction or performance, seem to provide the basis for the screwball cycle; the writers (especially Ben Hecht, Robert Riskin, Charles Brackett, Billy Wilder, and Sturges) worked out the typical patterns of theme, plot, and dialogue. Ludicrously improbable situations were devised and then dealt with as if they were everyday occurrences. In *Bringing Up Baby,* screenplay by Dudley Nichols and Hagar Wilde, the plot is furthered as Katharine Hepburn, playing an heiress, has her dress torn off while in an elegant dining room—much to the embarrassment of Cary Grant, a paleontologist. Subsequently: (1) they collide with a truck full of chickens; (2) Grant chases her aunt's dog around a country estate, to find a brontosaurus bone; and (3) a wild leopard is mistaken for a tame one (Baby of the title). The dialogue has speed and sparkle, is filled with unmistakably American exuberance. These films all evidence a close and sensitive attention to the native idiom—wisecracks, slang, and wrenched clichés are rapped out with uproarious effect. *Ball of Fire* points up this aspect neatly. It is about a group of professors compiling a dictionary of American slang who become involved with gangsters and a tough-talking burlesque queen.

Bringing Up Baby ♦ U.S., 1938,
Howard Hawks; Cary Grant and
Katharine Hepburn.

The live-action comedies and other feature films of the thirties were often preceded on the program by the newly emergent and enormously popular cartoon shorts. **Animated cartoons,** which had appeared intermittently from Winsor McCay's Gertie the Dinosaur (1914 on), seemed also to need sound, perhaps color, and evidently Walt Disney to propel them into the popularity they achieved during the 1930s. Disney's first big hit, Steamboat Willie (1928), was also the first animated film with synchronized sound. Soon cartoon shorts, provided by Disney and his imitators, became almost obligatory in theater programs, and Disney's ambitions carried him on to animated features.

The animated cartoon is not a genre, of course, even in the loosest sense of that term. It is a special film technique having as much to do with painting as with the motion picture. Yet, as developed at the Walt Disney Studio during the thirties it did contain standard genrelike elements, the anticipation of which set off delighted screams and whistles whenever the titles and familiar music announced Mickey and Minnie, Donald, Pluto, Goofy, and the rest. It was the mouse upon whom the empire was founded. Among twentieth-century comic figures only Charlie's Tramp could rival the universal affection in which Walt's Mickey was held.

Steamboat Willie ◆ U.S., 1928, Walt Disney; Mickey Mouse.

Disney's talking animals, like Aesop's, are caricatured human beings. They inhabit a world recognizable as an extension of Mack Sennett's, with the comic violence and destruction, the fanciful manipulation of time and space now given free reign in artists' drawings. Not only do the animals behave like humans, but distinct personalities are developed for each. Mickey, jaunty and optimistic, afflicted with less able companions for whom he assumes responsibility, performs heroic feats through a combination of pragmatism and ingenuity. Minnie is naive and coy, trusting and appreciative, with some resourcefulness and more than a little spunk of her own. Pluto, plagued by conscience, almost suffocating in his canine loyalty and affection, remains rambunctiously good humored as he commits one blunder after another. Goofy, the country bumpkin protected by his own innocence, is given to hiccups and half-witted ruminations. Donald, the irascible Duck, sputters a steady stream of nearly unintelligible expletives.

Even more than the live-action sound comedies the Disney creations rely heavily on sound. The voices are almost as important as the drawings in establishing characterizations (Mickey's was provided by Walt himself initially). Sound effects are given a new status and freedom of invention, detached from realistic sources. A whole range of crashes, bangs, and screeches accompany the bumps and thumps of the frantic action. As for the music, in Disney animation the score was recorded first and the pictures drawn to it, unlike live-action production where the score is the last element to be added. Music provides the audible continuity, punctuation and commentary. "Mickey Mousing" is a term still applied to a style in which music sounds like and is exactly synchronized to the action on the screen.

The importance of music to Disney's conception led him to alternate the Mickey shorts with the ambitious and innovative "Silly Symphonies." They began in 1929 with *Skeleton Dance,* set to Saint-Saëns's *Danse Macabre.* In that series the experimentation of Disney's technicians was allowed to develop most fully. In the best examples the animation is richly complex and breathtakingly inventive. The multiplane cel animation technique designed to give a greater sense of dimensionality and depth remains infused with flowing, rhythmical movement. Particularly lovely are *Flowers and Trees* (1932) and *The Old Mill* (1937). Most popular was *Three Little Pigs* (1933), whose cheery song "Who's Afraid of the Big Bad Wolf?" was interpreted as a defiance of the Depression. Perhaps it was linked in popular consciousness with the new President Franklin Delano Roosevelt's famous aphorism, "The only thing we have to fear is fear itself."

Though the Silly Symphony shorts ended in 1939, the impulse to illustrate music imaginatively, which they made manifest, carried over into other and later work. *Snow White and the Seven Dwarfs* (1937), Disney's first feature-length cartoon, is virtually an animated musical. Its human characters sing, and the animals and the rest of nature join in what can only be called dances. *Fantasia* (1940), also feature-length, is the apogee of the "Silly Symphonies." Its seven separate episodes are animated ballets set to classical music. In visual style *Fantasia* ranges from total abstraction (for Bach's *Toccata and Fugue in D Minor*) through more typical Disney romanticization and prettification (for Tschaikowsky's *Nutcracker Suite* and Beethoven's *Pastoral Symphony*) to horrification (for Moussorgsky's *Night on Bald Mountain*). Even Mickey appears, as the bedeviled servant in Dukas's *The Sorcerer's Apprentice.*

Accompanying Disney's stylistic experimentation was the constant employment of new technological means as they became available. His quickness to seize upon sound and his unparalleled exploitation of its untried and limitless relationships with images place his films among those most fully using the newly augmented medium. *Flowers and Trees* was the first film to employ the three-color Technicolor process, and color throughout the Disney animation, particularly in the Silly Symphonies, is handled in highly stylized and controlled ways for emotional effect impossible in live-action color cinematography. *Fantasia* introduced stereophonic sound, an addition not picked up by other film makers until more than a decade later. *Toot, Whistle, Plunk, and Boom* (1953), an amusing conjecture about the origins of the instruments of the orchestra, was an apt exploration of the recently arrived CinemaScope screen.

What Disney started, others continued. Ub Iwerks seems to have become the principal creative force at the Disney Studio as Walt concerned himself more and more with administration. In the forties Chuck Jones, who had worked with Iwerks and Disney, moved to Warner Brothers and created a rival menagerie in Bugs Bunny, Tweetie Pie, Daffy Duck, Speedy Gonzalez, Road Runner, and Wily Coyote. Others who left Disney about the same time, following the studio strike of 1941, later established United Productions of America. UPA offered the first radical departure from Disney in the extreme simplification and stylization of its drawings, much in the manner of modern French painting, and in the use of the human characters Mr. Magoo and Gerald McBoing Boing.

Animation for the theaters lost its reason for being when its cost, especially the laborious process perfected by Disney, and the disappearance of short subjects in movie programs made it financially unfeasible. Creative leadership passed from the Disney Studio to UPA, and to government film making like that of the National Film Board of Canada, with Norman McLaren, and especially to animation units in Poland, Czechoslovakia, and Yugoslavia (with the studio in Zagreb particularly noteworthy). In this country Ralph Bakshi has tried to create an audience for adult animated features, which have included *Fritz the Cat* (1972), *Heavy Traffic* (1973), and *Lord of the Rings* (1978). In 1979, Don Bluth, who had exerted animation leadership at the Disney Studio, left it to try independently to bring animation back to the sort of exquisitely detailed style that Disney earlier pursued. *The Secret of N.I.M.H.* (1982) was the first feature of his group. *Who Framed Roger Rabbit?* (1988), produced by the Disney Studio, live action directed by Robert Zemeckis, animation by Richard Williams, is a technically extraordinary fusion of live action with animation. Along the way cartoon characters created by animators at Disney, Warner Bros., M-G-M, and other studios in the forties are reintroduced.

With *Beauty and the Beast* (1991) and *Aladdin* (1992) the enthusiastic critical as well as popular response that had greeted earlier Disneys was repeated, perhaps even exceeded. For better or worse the standard techniques and predominant styles and content of animation were established at the Disney Studio during the 1930s. Everything that has happened in animation since has either grown out of that work or been a conscious reaction against it.

In the live-action features of the thirties, what weren't genres and originally conceived for the screen were adapted from literature, drama, history, or a combination of those sources, and included the most expensive and prestigious productions of the decade. In 1935 alone there were: the spectacular *Mutiny on the Bounty;* Max Reinhardt's production of Shakespeare's *A Midsummer Night's Dream; Becky Sharp,* the first feature in three-color Technicolor; *Captain Blood,* with some marvelously conceived and executed sea battles; *David Copperfield;* and *Lives of a Bengal Lancer.* All manifested the scale and skill associated with the big-studio Hollywood film of the thirties. They cost a lot and made a lot. Created by experts at that special sort of opulent illusion they were enjoyed by audiences who responded to it unselfconsciously and in large numbers. The kinds of pleasures offered by *Captains Courageous* (1937), say, or *The Adventures of Robin Hood* (1938), once regular if not routine, are no longer available except as those films and others of the thirties may still be replayed in reduced form on television or video. They don't make pictures like that the way they used to; or, when they do, the exceptions only prove the rule.

Mutiny on the Bounty ♦ U.S., 1935, Frank Lloyd; Clark Gable and Charles Laughton, white shirts center.

♦ NOTEWORTHY DIRECTORS

Given five hundred feature films a year, the conventions of genre and hybridism of adaptation, and the emphatic collectivity of Hollywood production in the thirties, it is not altogether easy to distinguish the work of particular directors most worthy of study. Within recent years, thanks at first to a few critics writing for *Cahiers du Cinéma* in France, the young English group associated with *Movie* magazine, and especially to Andrew Sarris in this country (his *The American Cinema: Directors and Directions 1929–1968* is discussed later), substantial progress has been made on this huge task. We have begun to identify those directors who were able to impose their own personalities on the assembly-line output in spite of the system and all of the forces that would seem to have militated against that possibility. The phenomenon may testify to the irreducible nature of human individuality and the unquenchable desire to create. At any rate, out of those walled-fortress-like factories, with their guards and huge cement blocks of soundproof stages (thought by the literati of the time to be idea-proof as well), there came some works of wit and beauty, of effervescent charm and lasting power.

The process of sifting continues, but to date, and partly with the aid of hindsight, certain major figures seem to stand tall. If the number of names were arbitrarily limited to four, Josef von Sternberg, Howard Hawks, Frank Capra, and John Ford would appear on the lists of many historians as preeminent. Each is very much his own man, with an identifiable personal style evident in both the themes he is drawn toward and the visual treatment of those themes, in his direction of the camera and of what's in front of it. Though all four men started in silent film in the twenties and continued to work fruitfully for decades after the thirties (Hawks and Ford more so than von Sternberg and Capra), they all reached creative maturity in the thirties.

Von Sternberg is the supreme visual stylist. With him the shadow is the substance. In a series of films starring Marlene Dietrich—*Morocco,* 1930; *Dishonored,* 1931; *Shanghai Express,* 1932; *The Scarlet Empress,* 1934; *The Devil Is a Woman,* 1935—he fashioned and perfected his own unique, exotic screen world. A film ought to be capable of offering an aesthetic experience when projected upside down and backwards, von Sternberg felt. He had a thorough background as an editor and cameraman, and there is evidence suggesting he did much of the cinematography on the films he directed. Certainly he understood lighting and used it for extraordinarily intricate and consistent effect. During the last few years of his life, on a campus tour, von Sternberg was asked by a beginning film production class at the University of

The Scarlet Empress ◆ U.S., 1934, Josef von Sternberg; Sam Jaffe and Marlene Dietrich, standing.

Iowa to show them how he would light a set. What was intended as a courteous gesture to this old man provoked gasps of astonishment as, with limited and simple portable lights, von Sternberg began to create his chiaroscuro. It was as if at any moment Dietrich would enter, the lights falling precisely to model those famous features and flare the blonde hair.

It may be a mixed compliment to observe that a still from a von Sternberg film gives a fuller sense of its essence than would a still from any other director's work. John Grierson, leader of the British documentary movement, wrote of him: "When a director dies, he becomes a photographer." What von Sternberg's films may lack in reality or even in drama, they make up in the sort of transcendent vision associated with certain very special painters—those who seem to create worlds to inhabit rather than art objects to be contemplated—like Paul Delvaux, for example. Von Sternberg's work is obsessive and strange, and perhaps stiff, but it is also exquisite and, above all, haunting.

Hawks is a quite different sort of artist. His is the art that conceals art. Working within genre conventions he nonetheless managed to state and restate what evidently were for him persistent preoccupations having to do with professionalism, individual courage (and cowardice, its complement), loyalty to the group, friendship among men, and battle between the sexes. He began and ended the thirties with films dealing with flying (*The Dawn Patrol,* 1930; *Only Angels Have Wings,* 1939) and he himself had been a flyer in World War I. In both films Hawks is obviously admiring and loving in

Only Angels Have Wings
♦ U.S., 1939, Howard Hawks; Cary Grant (seated at table in dark jacket), Thomas Mitchell, and Jean Arthur (standing close to table).

his treatment of the aviators. Dangerous flying can be senseless and frightening, but the camaraderie, pride, and bravery it allows for are to be honored. In *Dawn Patrol* there are no women (not even a mention of them except for the mothers of dead aviators), and their absence is filled by a "female" tenderness among the flyers toward each other. *Only Angels Have Wings* sets Jean Arthur off in pursuit of Cary Grant; but, since she is a woman, she can't really understand why the men behave as they do, and she represents a tacit threat to the group. These are some of the consistent thematic materials of Hawks the action director, the director of men's pictures.

Visually there is the notable kinetic energy of his films. *Scarface,* arguably one of the finest of the gangster cycle, moves with a controlled power evident in all aspects, from the details of the actors' performances to the cutting. *Twentieth Century* and *Bringing Up Baby,* two of his screwball comedies, are also explosive with frenetic activity. In the former an egomaniacal Broadway producer (John Barrymore) and his star/mistress (Carole Lombard) batter and rant at each other as the famous train of the title carries the producer from disastrous failure in Chicago to an ingeniously fraudulent attempt at comeback in New York. Money and jealousy are the two motivating factors in this cockeyed love story of sorts. In *Bringing Up Baby* a domineering, scatterbrained Katharine Hepburn has her way finally with scientist Cary Grant through upstoppable energy and wacky charm.

Peter Wollen, in *Signs and Meaning in the Cinema,* acknowledges the dynamism and stress prevalent in all of Hawks's work, its force. He also sees what he calls the crazy comedies as the inverse of the adventure dramas. "They are the agonized exposure of the underlying tensions of the heroic dramas," he writes. "Whereas the dramas show the mastery of man over nature, over woman, over the animal and childish; the comedies show his humiliation, his regression. The heroes become victims; society instead of being excluded and despised, breaks in with irruptions of monstrous farce."[2] The two strata must be taken together, Wollen argues, if we are to get a full sense of the meanings Hawks offers in the recurrent motifs of his films.

Though **Frank Capra**'s *It Happened One Night* is of the screwball type, and though others of his films share stylistic similarities, his comedies are essentially social. They present an explicit view of American society, its economy and its politics—a view uniquely Capraesque. In *Mr. Deeds Goes to Town* (1936), *You Can't Take It with You* (1938), and *Mr. Smith Goes to Washington* (1939), he celebrates the "little guy" (played by Gary Cooper or James Stewart)—not as dumb as he seems and, once aroused, able to defeat the city slickers and the power figures. His victories are achieved through pluck, persistence, Jean Arthur, and his overwhelming decency, which is matched by the decency of the American people when they see the true situation. Frequently even the villains are redeemed in Capra's films, since at heart they too are usually well intentioned.

Capra country is essentially an idealized small-town America (no matter that *You Can't Take It with You* ostensibly takes place in New York City and *Mr. Smith* is set in Washington). He celebrates lovable eccentricities and homely virtues. Even in the

---

[2]Peter Wollen, *Signs and Meaning in the Cinema* (London: Secker & Warburg, 1972), p. 91.

Mr. Smith Goes to Washington ♦ U.S., 1939, Frank Capra; James Stewart.

thirties his view was clearly nostalgic. Perhaps it would be more accurate to say that the society Capra depicts never existed at all except in his imaginings which, through great artistry, he was able to share with the moviegoing public. Similarly, his notions of economics and political action rest on a kind of folksy populism: If the little people would get together and help each other in cooperative endeavors, they could defeat the Depression and unemployment and live in peace and harmony. Richard Griffith, in *The Film Till Now,* labels Capra's conception the "fantasy of goodwill." The huge popular success of his pictures attests to the appeal his vision had in those troubled times. The corollary box office failure of *It's a Wonderful Life* (1946), made with exactly the same ingredients and as finely crafted as any of his films (it's Capra's favorite and has become a television tradition at Christmastime), suggests that the country in the mid-forties was a radically different place after the experience of World War II. In spite of his own contribution to the war effort in the "Why We Fight" series of documentaries made for the Armed Forces, Capra's own thinking and feeling seem to have remained in the earlier time. Be that as it may, the warmth and affection, the whimsical and engaging charm of his films of the thirties are readily available to anyone who approaches them with sympathy. His mastery as a director should be evident to all.

Finally, **John Ford,** who, like Hawks and unlike Sternberg and Capra, continued to do some of his finest work after the thirties, nevertheless shaped his art into personal and full expression during those precedent-setting years. *The Informer* (1935), dealt with earlier in regard to its use of sound, though a fine film, relates chiefly, among Ford's preoccupations, to his Irishness. It is not one of his favorites, and the creative strengths it seems to have come from the script by Dudley Nichols and the overlay of studio expressionism. Instead it was the cycle that began with *Steamboat 'Round the Bend* (1935) and continued with *The Prisoner of Shark Island* (1936), *Stagecoach* (1939), and *Young Mr. Lincoln* (1939) that showed Ford most clearly as the chronicler of American history, the reworker of American folklore, especially of its frontier West, that he became. *Stagecoach* lifted the non-epic western up to a kind of dignity and mythic evocation that has made it a viable form ever since. Classic in its proportions (the script by Nichols again), it is set in the West of the 1870s, when the frontier was disappearing. It picks up those elements of the gunfighter and his gun, of the moral and ethical decisions, of the kind of courage and code of honor that Robert Warshow wrote about so eloquently in his essay "The Westerner" (in *The Immediate Experience*). From that powerful progenitor stemmed Ford's later *My Darling Clementine* (1946), Hawks's *Red River* (1948), Henry King's *The Gunfighter* (1950), Fred Zinnemann's *High Noon* (1952), George Stevens's *Shane* (1953), Sam Peckinpah's *Ride the High Country* (1961), the westerns of Anthony Mann and Budd Boetticher, and many other important works within this most vigorous and indigenous tradition.

In his own westerns that followed *Stagecoach,* Ford was always concerned with the antithetical forces represented by the human desire to tame the wilderness. In *Signs and Meaning in the Cinema,* again, Wollen ticks off the "pairs of opposites" that run throughout Ford's work: " . . . ploughshare versus sabre, settler versus nomad, European versus Indian, civilised versus savage, book versus gun, married versus unmarried, East versus West."[3] "The master antinomy in Ford's films," Wollen suggests, "is that between the wilderness and the garden."[4]

Ford offers no Rousseau-type arguments for a return to nature, but it is clear in his films that he feels something is lost once the first stages of civilization have been achieved. Though he has dealt with the horse soldier of the U.S. cavalry even more sympathetically than with the more conventional figure of the gunfighter, it is the same story. Ford's past is a brief epoch that is forever ending and yet stands for us in much the same way that the time and events of the Trojan War did for the ancient Greeks. Looking to our past frontier Ford reminds us of what is best (and also worst) in our society, sings the praises of the heroes, and tries to help us understand the villains. The lessons Ford draws from American history are mythical and poetic rather than didactic, however; taken together they tell a very large story from a viewpoint

[3]Wollen, *Signs and Meaning,* p. 94.
[4]Wollen, *Signs and Meaning,* p. 96.

Stagecoach ◆ U.S., 1939, John Ford.

that is more than a little Homeric. This is so not out of academic imitation but because he shares some of the same simple and enduring concerns about the survival of a culture. Ford is more romantic than Homer, of course, but the romance is of strong people and a big country.

In addition to the pleasures they may offer individually, the paradoxes of the American films of the thirties taken as a whole can fascinate endlessly. There is the studio system with its big bosses and front office, mass production and distribution. It allowed and surely in some ways must have encouraged the scattering of master-pieces among those thousands of films. There is the repressive self-regulation that attempted to bleach art into the palest imitation of life. In the face of this, with ingenuity and energy, the creators managed to retain their robustness and abide only by the letter of the law, sometimes playing with the prim conventions in ways that became fresh and inventive. There are the genres, cycles, and formula pictures with their fixed patterns which at the same time permitted some of the finest directors in all cinema to create some of their best work. Though most of us wouldn't want a return to that kind of film making if it were possible, the films produced out of that special conjunction of system and circumstance continue to provide enjoyment for audiences and inspiration for film makers. One can ask no more of a national period.

FILMS OF THE PERIOD

1929
The Cocoanuts
    (Joseph Stanley and Robert Florey)
The Virginian (Victor Fleming)

1930
Little Caesar (Mervyn LeRoy)
Morocco (Josef von Sternberg)

1931
City Lights (Charles Chaplin)
Dracula (Tod Browning)
Frankenstein (James Whale)
The Front Page (Lewis Milestone)
The Public Enemy (William Wellman)
Tabu (F.W. Murnau and Robert Flaherty)

1932
I Am a Fugitive from a Chain Gang (LeRoy)
Scarface (Howard Hawks)
Shanghai Express (von Sternberg)
Trouble in Paradise (Ernst Lubitsch)

1933
Duck Soup (Leo McCarey)
42nd Street (Lloyd Bacon)
Gold Diggers of 1933 (LeRoy)
King Kong
    (Merian C. Cooper and Ernest B.
    Schoedsack)

1934
It Happened One Night (Frank Capra)
The Scarlet Empress (von Sternberg)
Twentieth Century (Hawks)

1935
A Night at the Opera (Sam Woods)

1936
Fury (Fritz Lang)
The Great Ziegfeld (Robert Z. Leonard)
The Green Pastures
    (Marc Connelly and William Keighley)
Mr. Deeds Goes to Town (Capra)
Modern Times (Chaplin)
The Story of Louis Pasteur (William Dieterle)
Swing Time (George Stevens)

1937
The Awful Truth (McCarey)
Camille (George Cukor)
The Life of Emile Zola (Dieterle)
Snow White and the Seven Dwarfs
    (Walt Disney)
A Star Is Born (Wellman)
You Only Live Once (Lang)

1938
Angels With Dirty Faces (Michael Curtiz)
Bringing Up Baby (Hawks)

1939
Gone With The Wind (Fleming)
Mr. Smith Goes to Washington (Capra)
Ninotchka (Lubitsch)
Only Angels Have Wings (Hawks)
Stagecoach (John Ford)
Young Mr. Lincoln (Ford)

BOOKS ON THE PERIOD

Balio, Tino, *Grand Design: Hollywood as a Modern Business Enterprise 1930–1939* (Vol. 5, "History of the American Cinema"). New York: Charles Scribner's Sons, 1993

Fine, Richard, *West of Eden: Writers in Hollywood, 1928-1940.* Washington, DC: Smithsonian Institution Press, 1993

Jenkins, Henry, *What Made Pistachio Nuts? Early Sound Comedy and the Vaudeville Aesthetic.* New York: Columbia University Press, 1992

Leff, Leonard, and Jerold L. Simmons, *The Dame in the Kimono: Hollywood, Censorship, and the Production Code from the 1920s to the 1960s.* New York: Grove Weidenfeld, 1990

Schatz, Thomas, *The Genius of the System: Hollywood Filmmaking in the Studio Era.* New York: Pantheon Books, 1988

9

Wartime and Postwar Hollywood

♦ ♦ ♦

1940–1952

Along with other social and economic abrasions, the 1930s contained the beginnings of World War II in military conquest and imperialist expansion. Japan gobbled up chunks of a China weakened by internal factionalism. Italy overran a defenseless Ethiopia. Germany joined Italy in testing weapons and tactics and helping to defeat the Republicans in Spain. The Germans continued to bluff their way through a series of territorial acquisitions culminating in the notorious Munich agreement concluded between Reichskanzler Adolph Hitler and Prime Minister Neville Chamberlain. On September 1, 1939, German dive bombers took to the skies, and tanks and trucks rolled across the Polish border, causing England and France to declare war on Germany. By some ten months later, not only Poland but France (along with Denmark, Norway, the Netherlands, and Belgium) had been ignominiously defeated. Germany's occupation of virtually all of Western Europe was complete and England was left to fight on alone against that massed power.

If the notion of history by decades is an arbitrary one, it becomes particularly so in regard to the forties in the United States. Though the preceding decade ended with the outbreak of World War II in Europe, for the United States 1940 and 1941 were really a continuation of the thirties. We had been backing into the war, pushed by the commitment President Roosevelt and other opinion leaders felt to Great Britain and its struggle against Nazi Germany. But the majority of the American public remained isolationist, preoccupied with ongoing domestic difficulties. When the Depression finally ended, it didn't die of natural causes; it was merely replaced by the artificial boom of a wartime economy after the Japanese attack on Pearl Harbor pulled us into the conflict in December 1941.

The United States would continue to provide the Allied and neutral countries with the bulk of their screen entertainment. The Hollywood films of wartime, for the most part, were more an extension of those of the thirties—appropriately trimmed with references to the war—than a prelude to those of the second half of the forties. The memorable *Casablanca* (1943) is one prominent example, its bittersweet romance tinged with antifascist idealism. To be sure, Orson Welles's exceptional *Citizen Kane* (1941) and *The Magnificent Ambersons* (1942) looked even beyond the forties in their seminal contributions to the evolution of film language and art. The remarkable social satires of Preston Sturges—including *Sullivan's Travels* (1941), *Hail the Conquering Hero,* and *The Miracle of Morgan's Creek* (both 1944)—would have been astonishing at any time for their irreverent wit and were especially so in wartime. Some of the films dealing directly with the war, derived from popular genres and toughened by wartime realities, antedated the realist postwar tendency to be discussed. Among the most popular were: *Wake Island* (1942); *Air Force, Bataan, The Moon Is Down* (all 1943); *Lifeboat, Thirty Seconds Over Tokyo* (both 1944); and *The Story of G. I. Joe* (1945). But it has been estimated that fewer than a third of the wartime films dealt with the war. More characteristic was the continuation, with home-front themes or military ruffles and flourishes added, of the comedies, the light romantic or family dramas, and the musicals, now increased in number and vitality.

Still, the bulk of American films of World War II undoubtedly contributed to the war effort. When not inspirational and hortatory, they were wholesomely entertaining and supportive of the culture the war was being fought to preserve. The top box-office hits of the war years (films that grossed more than $4 million in rentals in the United States and Canada, according to *Variety*), which also won major awards, were: *Mrs. Miniver* and *Yankee Doodle Dandy* (in 1942); *The Song of Bernadette* (in 1943); *Going My Way, Meet Me in St. Louis,* and *Thirty Seconds Over Tokyo* (in 1944); *The Bells of St. Mary's, Lost Weekend,* and *Spellbound* (in 1945). Of these nine films only one directly treated American involvement in the war, *Thirty Seconds Over Tokyo;* another concerned Britain's home front before the United States entered the war, *Mrs. Miniver.* Of the rest, four were musicals and/or comedies; one was a biography of a French Catholic religious figure; two of the comedies, *Going My Way* and *The Bells of St. Mary's,* were about Catholic priests and nuns in the United States (there are no atheists in the foxholes, a phrase of the time asserted); one was about an alcoholic and alcoholism; one was a suspense-mystery with psychoanalytical trappings.

◆ FILM NOIR

The last two films in the list above, especially *Lost Weekend,* offer evidence of a sort of substratum, or a kind of counterforce, that existed amidst wartime patriotism and wholesomeness. The subgenre or style subsequently identified by French critics as *film noir* was referred to in the close of the chapter on German silent cinema. These dark melodramas of crime and corruption, of psychological dislocation and aberration, reveal a Germanic influence (curious that they should appear during a war with Germany) in their intricate and artificial visual style and their preoccupation with disordered psyches. Austrian-born Billy Wilder, who coscripted as well as directed *Lost Weekend,* was one of the masters of the black film. His *Double Indemnity* (1944), which preceded *Lost Weekend,* was coscripted with Raymond Chandler. It is about a murderous pair of adulterers (Barbara Stanwyck and Fred MacMurray). His *Sunset Boulevard* (1950) and *Ace in the Hole/The Big Carnival* (1951) followed it. *Sunset Boulevard* deals with a decaying part of contemporary Hollywood peopled by a megalomaniac silent star (Gloria Swanson), her present butler and former director and husband (Erich von Stroheim), and an opportunistic young screen writer (William Holden). *Ace in the Hole* concerns a cynical and ruthless newspaper reporter (Kirk Douglas) who exploits human tragedy in an effort to regain his lost professional status. The latter was the only Wilder film up to that point that was not successful commercially, and it came near the end of the noir impulse. Wilder himself turned to comedies in which the black touches could be made more palatable.

Noir, an attitude as well as a style, descended not only from German expressionism of the 1920s but from French poetic realism of the 1930s, especially the films of Marcel Carné-Jacques Prévert. In Hollywood in the mid-forties it emerged in the work of a few German and Austrian expatriates. Along with Wilder there were Robert Siodmak (*Phantom Lady,* 1944; *The Spiral Staircase,* 1945; *The Killers,* 1946), Otto Preminger (*Laura,* 1944; *Fallen Angel,* 1945), and Fritz Lang (*The Woman in the Window,* 1944; *Scarlet Street,* 1945). It spread to include films of a number of other distinguished Hollywood professionals, among them Alfred Hitchcock (*Shadow of a Doubt,* 1943; *Rope,* 1948; *The Paradine Case,* 1948) and Michael Curtiz (*Mildred Pierce,* 1945; *The Unsuspected,* 1947). And it cut across genres: private eye (*The Maltese Falcon,* John Huston, 1941; *Murder, My Sweet,* Edward Dmytryk, 1944; *The Big Sleep,* Howard Hawks, 1946), gangster (*Kiss of Death,* Henry Hathaway, 1947; *Cry of the City,* Siodmak, 1948; *White Heat,* Raoul Walsh, 1949), and even the fight picture (*The Set-Up,* Robert Wise, 1949).

The fantasies the noir films offered were wrought with intelligence, misanthropy, and considerable skill. Theirs is a nightmare hallucination full of indecipherable complications, a pervasive sense of threat, of fear and helplessness in the face of enigmatic human malevolence. The protagonists are typically trying to comprehend the incomprehensible motives that exist within their subterranean world; they are trapped, seeking to find their way out of a tortuous labyrinth of unpleasantness, violence, and evil. It's Dick Powell, as Raymond Chandler's Philip Marlowe in *Murder, My Sweet,* who is drugged and beaten, endlessly it seems, as he tries to trace the whereabouts of a missing woman someone doesn't want him to find. He encounters a dimwitted amorous giant, an aging drink-sodden floozy, an ailing millionaire and his lecherous and lethal young wife, as well as other denizens of this shadowy netherworld in a succession of late-night bars and sleazy apartments. Or, it's the weak, lonely, middle-aged Edward G. Robinson in *The Woman in the Window* (quite literally a nightmare of lust, crime, and entrapment) and *Scarlet Street* as he reaches out for the unobtainable and deceptive appearance of young loveliness in a corrupt and rapacious Joan Bennett. Or it's Ella Raines of the hollow cheeks and shoulder-length

Murder, My Sweet ♦
U.S., 1944, Edward
Dmytryk; Dick Powell.

hair, more wraith than actress, in *Phantom Lady,* trying to find the persons and the reasons behind the frameup of her lover. The scenes with the hopped-up jazz drummer (Elisha Cook, Jr.), with the swirling cigarette smoke, the glaring lights and harsh shadows, the oblique camera angles, the tension of the editing, and the brittleness and vulnerability of the human figure, are characteristic of noir.

As opposed to the idealism of the society fighting together to combat the political evil of fascism, film noir dealt with individuals conspicuously antisocial in their greed and selfishness, driven to betrayal, violence, and crime (usually including murder) out of an incurable sickness (often ending in death or incarceration). Their malaise was presented as endemic to the human species, and the world they inhabited was a dark one literally as well as morally. The films seem to take place mostly at night, in seedy furnished apartments and on rain-washed streets of big cities. A jungle atmosphere was created in those studio sets (a human jungle, an asphalt jungle, a neon jungle), with predators stalking prey and danger lurking in the shadows, intermittently re-vealed by flashing electric signs. Perhaps even more than most other cinematic styles, film noir depends for its impact on nonverbal, essentially visual effects, where form far outstrips content.

The noir films eschewed the direct social meanings of the gangster films of the thirties, just as they remained in opposition to the liberal films of good causes of the late forties, though they shared realist aspects with both. They were clearly popular, perhaps appealing to something in audiences that distrusted the official rhetoric and optimism espoused by the dominant political forces. If not among the big hits, for the most part, the noir films continued as a steady stream.

◆ REALISM

The prestigious pictures of the postwar forties were not the noir films, however. Among those part of that tradition only *The Killers* (1946), *Kiss of Death* (1947), and *Sunset Boulevard* (1950) received major awards for their years. On the other hand, films with a heightened realism and/or dealing with social problems appeared frequently among those honored by the New York Film Critics, the National Board of Review, and *Film Daily,* or were nominated for Academy Awards as best picture of the year. The 1946 award winners included *The Best Years of Our Lives* (readjustment to civilian life by returning servicemen) and *A Walk in the Sun* (authentic portrayal of an infantry combat mission). In 1947 there were *Boomerang* (justice for the individual under the law), *Crossfire* and *Gentleman's Agreement* (both dealing with anti-Semitism in the United States). Among the award winners of 1948, *Call Northside 777* was a re-creation of an actual criminal investigation, and *The Naked City* offered a detailed, on-location account of the work of a New York City police homicide squad. *The Snake Pit* dealt with treatment of the insane; *State of the Union* with the functioning of American national party politics. In 1949 *All the King's Men* was about a Southern political demagogue unmistakably modeled on former Louisiana governor Huey Long; *Home of the Brave, Intruder in the Dust,* and *Pinky* were about prejudice and discrimination directed against African-Americans. In 1950 there were *No Way Out,* also about racial discord, *The Men,* a painfully realistic drama of the rehabilitation of war casualties, and *Panic in the Streets,* concerning the responsibility of government officials for protecting the citizenry from epidemic disease, much of it shot on location in New Orleans. In 1951, *Fourteen Hours* was based on actuality, in which a disturbed young man on a window ledge high above Manhattan threatens to jump while friends and police try to dissuade him. *Death of a Salesman,* a transcription of Arthur Miller's play, indicted the ways in which America's economic system and values cramped and warped the lives of some of its citizens.

If the British were able to hang onto certain aspects of documentary within their comedies, the Americans were drawn toward a tradition of exposé that had special need for a kind of fiction film making that stayed close to actuality. The American postwar equivalent to the British wartime semidocumentary began with *The House on 92nd Street* (1945), produced by Louis de Rochemont, former creative chief of "The March of Time" series.

Of three more or less distinct subspecies of the American fictional film with documentary tendencies, *The House on 92nd Street* fits into the one of films based on fact, on real persons or incidents. It re-created an actual FBI investigation that had uncovered a German espionage ring centered in New York City. It also contained many documentary-like stylistic characteristics, and even some blown-up 16mm footage of the German agents taken surreptitiously by the FBI. *House on 92nd Street* was followed by *Boomerang* (1947, also produced by de Rochemont), based on events

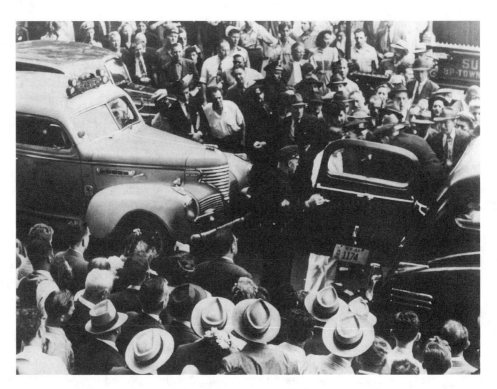

The House on 92nd Street   ◆   U.S., 1945, Henry Hathaway.

in the life of Homer Cummings, who had become Attorney General of the United States under Franklin Roosevelt. *Call Northside 777* (1948) is another example. It recounted the efforts of a crusading Chicago newspaperman that led to the exoneration of a prisoner who had already served ten years of a life sentence for the murder of a policeman.

Closely allied to the based-on-fact picture was "the inside story": how a police department works, for example. In *The Naked City* (1948, produced by former newspaperman Mark Hellinger) the emphasis and most of the running time are given to the dogged, dull, day-to-day routine of trying to track down a murderer living somewhere among New York's millions. *The Frogmen* (1951) devotes at least two-thirds of its footage to clear and interesting exposition of how Navy underwater demolition teams are trained. Only the final scenes of a mission into a Japanese-held harbor seem within the more familiar mode of screen heroics. The same documentary emphasis on how a thing is done pervades the opening passages of *13 Rue Madeleine* (1946, de Rochemont again producer), which deals with the training and a mission of Office of Strategic Services personnel.

Finally there were the "problem pictures," which sometimes didn't look as real as the above two categories but which did attempt to come to some sort of grips with social issues. It was in this line that the exposé tendency was strongest—films dealing with alcoholism (*The Lost Weekend,* 1945), prisons (*Brute Force,* 1947, Hellinger producer), and mental health (*The Snake Pit,* 1948), for example. A whole cycle concerning race relations began in 1947 with *Crossfire* and *Gentleman's Agreement,* both concerning anti-Semitism, and quickly moved to relations between blacks and whites. In 1949 alone there were *Home of the Brave* (produced by Stanley Kramer, who specialized in the problem picture), *Lost Boundaries* (de Rochemont once more), *Pinky, Intruder in the Dust* (the finest of the cycle), and others.

The trend toward realism of treatment, and social problems as subjects in American film lasted from the immediate postwar years to the early 1950s. It ceased in an outbreak of political paranoia that came to be known as McCarthyism, named for Joseph R. McCarthy, Republican Senator from Wisconsin.

◆ LIBERALISM, COMMUNISM, AND ANTICOMMUNISM: THE HOUSE UN-AMERICAN ACTIVITIES COMMITTEE AND BLACKLISTING

Though in some ways World War II was a cataclysmic event in the history of this nation, in other ways it proved to be only an interruption of some of the tensions of the thirties, especially the political ones. In the decade before the war, left-wing activities in the United States had achieved an unprecedented vigor and popularity. While the forces of conservatism and reaction feared the "communist influence" at home and abroad, and attempted to check it through the power of capitalist business and government, they were ultimately ineffectual in halting a leftward swing. Some felt the New Deal itself represented a kind of totalitarian communism, with its powerful presidential leader and its sweeping program of social change. Even more unsettling, during the war the preeminent communist state, the Soviet Union, became our ally in the fight against fascism.

In the United States following the war, after a brief period of optimism about the recently established United Nations and attempts to ameliorate racial and ethnic discrimination and class and partisan differences, a new climate, or return to an older climate, developed. By the late forties we were locked into a fierce struggle with the U.S.S.R. and international communism, and had become prey to fears of communist subversion in our midst. Now the reactionaries, supported by great numbers of unthinking conservatives and some frightened liberals, led us into a period of military belligerence and political repression that would climax in the early fifties in the Korean War and in congressional investigating committees.

Films of the time reflected the prevailing shift in political sentiment. When the Soviet Union had been our ally during World War II, Hollywood had made some pro-Soviet films, most notably *Mission to Moscow* (1943), *The North Star* (1943), and *Song of Russia* (1944). By 1951, one of the increasing number of anticommunist films, *I Was a Communist for the FBI,* was nominated by the Academy of Motion Picture Arts and Sciences as best feature-length documentary. In 1952 another anticommunist film, *The Hoaxters* (more properly categorized as documentary), received a nomination for the same award, and the anticommunist fiction feature *My Son John* was named by the National Board of Review among its ten best for the year. The rest of the films receiving major awards in 1952 were noticeably removed from contemporary domestic reality and its problems.

The appearance of the first anticommunist films after the war occurred following an investigation in 1947 by the House Un-American Activities Committee (HUAC) into alleged communist influence in Hollywood. Initially, the industry united to oppose such an inquiry as unnecessary, punitive, and itself un-American in infringing civil liberties. In Hollywood a Committee for the First Amendment (which guarantees freedom of speech and opinion) was organized by film directors William Wyler and John Huston, and screenwriter Philip Dunne. A sizeable delegation from the industry, headed by Eric Johnston, president of the Motion Picture Association of America, and including such celebrities as Lauren Bacall, Humphrey Bogart, John Huston, Gene Kelly, Danny Kaye, and Jane Wyatt, appeared before HUAC in Washington to protest its activities.

They weren't called upon immediately, however. Instead, the committee called on a series of witnesses whose ties or sympathies with the Communist Party had been suggested by its earlier investigations. John Howard Lawson, screenwriter and leader in Hollywood guild and union organizing, was first to be heard. He angrily denounced the committee and refused to answer its questions. His prepared statement, which he was not allowed to read, began: "For a week this committee has conducted an illegal and indecent trial of American citizens, whom the committee has selected to be publicly pilloried and smeared." Lawson was followed by nine other "unfriendly" witnesses, who also refused to answer the committee's questions about their political beliefs and associations and invoked the First Amendment to the Constitution. The "Hollywood Ten," as they came to be known, comprised, in addition to Lawson, screenwriters Alvah Bessie, Lester Cole, Ring Lardner, Jr., Albert Maltz, Samuel Ornitz, and Dalton Trumbo; directors Herbert Biberman and Edward Dmytryk; and producer Adrian Scott. All were cited for contempt of Congress.

In the face of the unfavorable publicity occasioned by the truculent defiance of these ten witnesses and the allegations of communist infiltration made by "friendly" ones (including actors Adolphe Menjou, Robert Taylor, Robert Montgomery, George Murphy, Ronald Reagan, and Gary Cooper; producer-directors Sam Wood, Leo McCarey, and Walt Disney; and executives Jack Warner and Louis B. Mayer), the Committee for the First Amendment collapsed. The studio heads and principal independent producers hastily met at the Waldorf-Astoria Hotel in New York City. The Waldorf statement, which resulted, deplored the action of the ten Hollywood men who had refused to testify. Its key concession, a complete reversal from the producers' earlier opposition to the intentions and procedures of HUAC, read as follows: "We will not knowingly employ a Communist or a member of any party or group which advocates the overthrow of the Government of the United States by force or by any illegal or unconstitutional methods" (aims alleged to be those of the Communist Party U.S.A.).

That sentence was followed by a paragraph which, ironically, while arguing for reasonableness and humanitarianism, described what already had happened and predicted precisely the situation that would arise as a result of the industry's changed stance.

In pursuing this policy, we are not going to be swayed by hysteria or intimidation from any source. We are frank to recognize that such a policy involves dangers and risks. There is the danger of hurting innocent people. There is the risk of creating an atmosphere of fear. Creative work at its best cannot be carried on in an atmosphere of fear. We will guard against this danger, this risk, this fear.[1]

The Hollywood Ten were sent to prison, and the industry moved into the era of blacklisting, in which people who were suspected of opinions and activities on the political left were denied employment. Failing to establish the presence of communist propaganda in the Hollywood film, HUAC sought to remove from the industry those who might have been able to support communism through their incomes and prestige. The studio heads were not concerned primarily with either possible communist subversion or with violation of democratic principles. What rendered them compliant with the committee's wishes was the fear of boycott and picketing of theaters by indignant citizens. Such picketing did actually occur and numerous pressure groups joined HUAC in attacking the industry. The largest, most energetic, and most powerful of these was the American Legion, which insistently demanded that Hollywood "clean house."

In 1951 and following, in the Hollywood "mass hearings," more than two hundred motion-picture workers were named by HUAC as suspected communists or communist supporters. These congressional investigations into communism became, in fact, trials of the witnesses called. Those appearing before the committee who claimed protection under the Fifth Amendment to the Constitution (designed to protect witnesses from incriminating themselves) were automatically assumed to be "guilty." A bizarre extralegal system of "clearances" was set up by the industry and representatives of the pressure groups to "rehabilitate" those accused individuals who were willing to meet the requirements made of them. Public confession and recantation, including the naming of former political associates, was required from the admitted communists. Noncommunists with suspicious liberal tendencies had to repudiate their past political attitudes and behavior and promise to sin no more in a letter to the studio executive employing them. Those who were named by HUAC or one of the anticommunist organizations and were unwilling to take such steps could no longer find employment in the Hollywood industry. Some screenwriters were able to sell their work under assumed names, at greatly reduced rates; some directors worked under pseudonyms on low-budget productions abroad. The blacklisted actors and actresses, whose presence on the screen could not be concealed, had no recourse.

The blacklisting continued even after HUAC's final Hollywood hearing in 1954. The economic damage suffered by hundreds of individuals and their families—with

[1]Quoted in John Cogley, *Report on Blacklisting I. Movies* (Santa Barbara, Calif.: The Fund for the Republic, 1956), p. 22.

accompanying anger and fear, bitterness and humiliation—was matched by the corrosive effect on the morale of the industry as a whole. The inhibiting and vitiating influence of the political climate became evident in the films as Hollywood headed into the fifties. The documentary residue of World War II was washed away, replaced by glossy wrappings and bland content. Meaningful statements about contemporary American society were sometimes made within modest genre pictures or might appear in cryptic form in more ambitious productions; but, in general, the integrity, assurance, and purposefulness that had begun to mark the work of a few of the American film makers coming out of the war years was missing in the decade that began with the election of Dwight Eisenhower as president in 1952 and will be dealt with in Chapter 13.

♦ SIX DIRECTORS

The choice of Alfred Hitchcock, William Wyler, Preston Sturges, Orson Welles, Michael Curtiz, and John Huston is at least as arbitrary as such choices usually are. All six continued to direct after the 1940s, several doing especially noteworthy work later. In addition, the directors dealt with in Chapter 13, on the American fifties, directed in the forties as well. And the forenamed directors are only some of those who were important during this period, and only some of their films are discussed here. At the time these six were regarded generally—by the Hollywood community, by critical and box-office responses—as worthy of attention.

Alfred Hitchcock begins the list partly because his American career (following his British one) began in 1940, when he was imported by producer David O. Selznick to direct *Rebecca*. That film was followed by the much more characteristic *Foreign Correspondent* (1940), produced by Walter Wanger. As an espionage thriller, it connects back to Hitchcock's British successes (*The Man Who Knew Too Much,* 1934; *The Thirty-Nine Steps,* 1935; *The Lady Vanishes,* 1938); and ahead to later American ones, such as *Saboteur* (1942) and *Notorious* (1946). The latter film, invoking recent memories of German espionage (Claude Rains as master spy), American counterespionage (Ingrid Bergman and Cary Grant, the agents), and atomic secrets, is a most expert blend of sex, suspense, and humor, with Hitchcock in full control of the medium.

A second line, which also had British precedents (*The Lodger,* 1926; *Blackmail,* 1929), combined murder mystery (or mystery of suspected murderous intent) with psychological probing. It includes *Suspicion* (1941), *Shadow of a Doubt* (1943), *Spellbound* (1945), and *Strangers on a Train* (1951). Of these, *Shadow of a Doubt* and *Strangers on a Train* seem darkest and most disturbing. The first involves a multiple murderer (Joseph Cotton); his namesake niece (Teresa Wright), who has incestuous feelings for him; and a very real small California town. In the second, an exchange of killings—of a wife by one stranger for a father by the other—is engineered by an equally evil, charming, and psychotic villain (played by Robert Walker).

Not only do Hitchcock's films contain ambiguities, they have provoked still-continuing arguments over whether they are merely conventional, rather mechanical entertainments contrived by a cynical manipulator of audience expectations, or

Shadow of a Doubt ♦ U.S., 1943, Alfred Hitchcock; Teresa Wright and Joseph Cotton.

whether they are, beneath their cleverness and skill, moral meditations stemming from their maker's strict Catholic upbringing and emotionally repressed adulthood. In either case, they are about life and death, guilt and punishment, temptations to innocence and tortured pleasures of sin, and the omnipresence and commonplaceness of evil. In either case, also, they reveal their creator's considerable experience and careful study of movie making (or "pure cinema," as he would prefer it).

Whatever their maker's true creative intentions, Hitchcock's films have been extraordinarily attractive to both pit and gallery. Huge audiences have gone to see each film because it was a Hitchcock film. As much serious critical writing has been published about the Hitchcock films—also because they are Hitchcock films—as about those of any other film maker. As both popular and critical successes, he and his films stand out prominently in the history of cinema.

When Hitchcock helped prepare a script for *Rebecca*, Selznick complained that he had turned Daphne du Maurier into Alfred Hitchcock. Selznick would not have been troubled in this manner by **William Wyler,** whose tendency would have been to turn Wyler into du Maurier. If Wyler is faulted in any way by the critics, it is usually only as lacking his own identity as an artist; he is universally praised as being among the finest of interpreters and most expert of directors.

Wyler's directorial career began in the 1920s with westerns. In the 1930s he directed a number of noteworthy films, frequently based on dramatic or literary works (*Dead End,* 1937; *Jezebel,* 1938; *Wuthering Heights,* 1939). He began the 1940s as his career had begun, with a western called *The Westerner.* It is his only film of this period that was not an adaptation of an already successful play or novel. The plays are: Somerset Maugham's *The Letter* (1940); Lillian Hellman's *The Little Foxes* (1941); the play made from Henry James's novel *Washington Square, The Heiress* (1949); Sidney Kingsley's *Detective Story* (1951). The novels are: Jan Struther's *Mrs. Miniver* (1942); MacKinlay Kantor's *Glory for Me,* which became *The Best Years of Our Lives* (1946); Theodore Dreiser's *Carrie* (1952).

Of these films, the much-awarded *The Best Years of Our Lives* would seem most to embody Wyler's personal response to life in addition to his response to another artist's art. It followed wartime service in the Air Force and the making of the documentary *Memphis Belle* (1944), which provided Wyler an opportunity to know bombardiers like the one played by Dana Andrews. The script, by Robert E. Sherwood, centers on three servicemen returning to civilian life at the end of the war (the other two played by Fredric March and nonactor amputee Harold Russell). It examines varied and representative problems faced by each with honesty and compassion.

The Best Years of Our Lives ♦ U.S., 1946, William Wyler; Dana Andrews, Myrna Loy, Fredric March, Hoagy Carmichael, and Harold Russell.

Details of time and place, situation and attitude, are exact. In terms of visual style, many of the scenes involve complex compositions in great depth, including multiple planes of action. One that sticks in mind takes place in a bar. A group at the piano, including two of the protagonists, is in the right foreground; several persons at the bar are in left middle ground reacting to the piano playing; the third protagonist is telephoning in center background. The cinematography is by Gregg Toland, who was important to a number of Wyler's finest films. *Best Years* was produced by Samuel Goldwyn, for whom Wyler did much of his best work.

Like Hitchcock, Wyler was admired by the Hollywood community for his professionalism. His direction was also admired by many distinguished foreign film makers—some whose approaches seem quite different from his (Akira Kurosawa and Satyajit Ray, for example)—who recognized his great skill and learned from it. Audiences went in large numbers to films directed by William Wyler, but they went to see a movie of a play they had heard about or a book they had read, or to see stars they liked, rather than to a Wyler film. No harm in that if the movie was an expert and moving rendition and the stars' performances were fully rounded, rich, and satisfying. Wyler frequently met these requirements.

Preston Sturges was not dependent on others for his material; he wrote his own. In fact he began as a writer (of plays before films), directing his first film, *The Great McGinty,* in 1940. It is the writing—the idiosyncratic, not to say wacky, behavior and dialogue of his characters—that provides the special charm of his films. The behaving and talking were done by character actors assembled by Sturges at Paramount. They appear again and again—for instance, William Demarest and Franklin Pangborn. If the technique of his films is not as "cinematic" as that of Hitchcock or Wyler, the content has a consistency and coherence that mark him as a distinctive film maker. Within his frames are enclosed representations of the United States of America in the early 1940s as it looked to him.

The Lady Eve (1941) and *The Palm Beach Story* (1942) cover the upper classes. In the former Barbara Stanwyck plays a professional gambler (who becomes Lady Eve), in feigned then real amorous pursuit of Henry Fonda, as Charles "Hopsy" Pike, heir to an ale fortune, but almost exclusively interested in snakes. The latter film offers a satirical commentary on success and marital tension, exposing the unrivaled effectiveness of sexual manipulation in a supposedly puritanical society, and the American ideal of luxurious ease as it is lived by the jovially senile members of the Ale and Quail Club.

The Miracle of Morgan's Creek and *Hail the Conquering Hero* (both 1944) take care of the middle class, the American small town, parenthood, marriage, and patriotism, in one fell (or should it be fallen) swoop. The "miracle" is the birth of sextuplets; the comic problem is that the father/husband seems to be a GI who had met and married the wife/mother on his last night before going overseas and whose name she has forgotten. The "hero" is Woodrow Lafayette Pershing Truesmith (Eddie Bracken), discharged from the Marines for chronic hay fever, who is presented to his home town as a genuine Marine hero by a bunch of genuine Marine heroes.

Sullivan's Travels (1941) surveys the whole social scene from the posh elegance of a (perhaps Beverly Hills) mansion to the deprivation and brutality of a (perhaps

Hail the Conquering Hero ♦ U.S., 1944, Preston Sturges; Ella Raines, Eddie Bracken, and Franklin Pangborn.

Georgia) chain gang, including movie makers and the making of movies about the social scene. The conclusion reached by Sullivan, and presumably by Sturges, is that the most socially useful thing a film maker can do is to make audiences laugh. Sturges makes us laugh a lot; but if we laugh with him, it is always at ourselves.

Orson Welles came to Hollywood following a phenomenal burst of creative leadership and experimentation in theater and radio. He was twenty-six when his first film, *Citizen Kane* (1941), was released. It became a landmark in the history of film, like *The Birth of a Nation* or *Battleship Potemkin* before it. What *Kane* did was to move film into the modernism present in the other arts. With its unconventional approach to theme, character, and narrative, as well as its range of cinematic technique, it would become a source book for future film makers. If, as Rick Altman has observed, modernist narrative "is usually associated with the foregrounding of filmic language, multiple levels of narration, and estrangement of the spectator,"[2] *Citizen Kane* might be said to be fully if not overly qualified for modernity.

The fictional Charles Foster Kane, played by Welles, was modeled closely enough on the real William Randolph Hearst to make him furious and vengeful. At the time

---

[2]Rick Altman, ed., *Genre: The Musical* (London: Routledge & Kegan Paul, 1981), p. 159.

of Kane's death, with which the film begins. Kane is a lonely and egocentric man of vast wealth and failed political ambition. He had built a newspaper empire, and his life is now investigated by a reporter for a new form of the press, a "March-of-Time"-like screen magazine. The edited work print of an issue of "News on the March" gives us our first account of Kane.

Using investigative journalism as a device, scriptwriters Herman J. Mankiewicz and Welles track back through Kane's life with interview and flashback recollection from his banker-guardian, his business manager, his best friend, his second wife, and his butler. From their divergent points of view, we are presented with different Kanes. Though we learn about the complexity of his activities, neither we nor the reporter get at Kane's essence. We do find out what "rosebud," his final word, referred to, as the reporter does not, but we are left standing at just as much distance from him—the sort of distancing or estrangement of the spectator employed by Bertolt Brecht.

As for filmic language, it is pushed very much into the foreground, obviously and brilliantly used to dazzling effect. The great depth of field of the images was provided by cinematographer Gregg Toland and made possible by improvements in film stock, light sources, and optics. It introduces a kind of intricacy in the relationship of characters to setting and to each other. It permits, in fact demands, a fuller "reading" than the selectivity and emphasis of image practiced by Griffith and Eisenstein, which

Citizen Kane ◆ U.S., 1941, Orson Welles; Welles.

had been developed into the standard technique of filmed narrative. Ceilings are present in *Kane's* rooms, as they usually are not in film rooms; low angles and chiaroscuro lighting abound. The soundtrack takes on the acoustical character of the surroundings. Sound montage, growing out of Welles's radio work, includes a character beginning a sentence in one scene and completing it later in a different location; or, in a famous sequence, wittily and concisely suggesting through breakfast conversation and then lack of it the deterioration over a period of time of Kane's first marriage.

In Welles's second film, *The Magnificent Ambersons* (1942), many of the characteristics of *Kane* are present—deep-focus cinematography, innovative uses of sound, exceptional performances from members of Welles's Mercury Theatre troupe (Joseph Cotton, Agnes Moorehead, Roy Collins, with Welles as narrator)—but RKO terminated his contract before he finished it and he exerted no control over the editing of the final version. The *Lady from Shanghai* and *Macbeth* (both 1948) are both accomplished and both very Wellesian, each in its own way.

Welles's career continued until his death in 1987. As a film maker, he had some inspired flashes and some partially realized creations. There was also his exploitation of a highly theatrical personality and impressive girth, as performer and celebrity; and much discussion with interviewers and by critics, especially French ones, about his film making. But of his work, it is for *Citizen Kane* that he will be most remembered. If Charles Foster Kane's fortune came out of a silver lode, the film that contains him has yielded its own kind of riches to generations of viewers.

Welles has been the darling of those critics who regard the director as "author" of the work; **Michael Curtiz** confounds them. His films offer no evident signature, as do those of Hitchcock, Sturges, and Welles, nor even consistent professional expertise, like Wyler's. Most of the extraordinary number of films Curtiz directed—beginning in Hungary (1912–19), continuing in Austria (1919–26), then in the United States (from 1926 until his death in 1962)–seem to have been unmemorable. His American films, some forty-five in the 1930s alone, range as widely across genres as one could conceive, the misses more or less balanced by the hits, with some particularly effective and lasting historical action-adventures starring Errol Flynn: *Captain Blood* (1935), *The Charge of the Light Brigade* (1936), *The Adventures of Robin Hood* (1938, codirected by William Keighley), *The Sea Hawk* (1940).

But in the 1940s he directed three films that are quite special, markedly different from each other, and very much of their time and place. Although the extent of Curtiz's contribution to their creation cannot be determined, their commercial and critical success are unquestionable.

Yankee Doodle Dandy (1943) is a biography of that most popular and most American of theater people, playwright, producer-director, and performer George M. Cohan. James Cagney plays the role, Walter Huston that of his father. This is as satisfying a bit of nostalgia, as charming and cheering a tribute to American vaudeville and musical theater, as has been created. Was it Michael Curtiz (*né* Mihály Kertész) who was responsible for this very native accomplishment? Who is/are saying all those splendid things about the Cohans, about an earlier period in this country, about its popular musical forms?

Yankee Doodle Dandy was followed by that ultimate romantic Hollywood delight, *Casablanca* (1943). In it Dooley Wilson tinkling away at the piano and growling "As Time Goes By" leads us all to believe in and care what happens to Rick, Humphrey Bogart, and Ilsa, Ingrid Bergman, as much as we've cared for any screen lovers, and maybe to confuse them with ourselves. In this instance the themes and settings are European and North African; its charm is thoroughly contemporary, topical even, and engagingly cosmopolitan.

But if we were to think that Curtiz had finally settled into his own true sensibilities, *Mildred Pierce* (1945) put the thought to rest. This film, from the novel by James M. Cain, is at one and the same time a masterful example of film noir, a vehicle for presenting its star Joan Crawford's persona as directly and forcefully as it has ever appeared, and a dark, complicated, devastating commentary on American materialism, sexuality, and parenthood. These ingredients, plus the great style and control evident, have ensured its survival, and account for its power with audiences today.

Each of these three films of Curtiz is a singular achievement; taken together—and one could add other fine films he directed—they seem to represent as well the studio

Casablanca ◆ U.S., 1943, Michael Curtiz; Claude Rains (in dark uniform), Paul Henreid, Humphrey Bogart, and Ingrid Bergman.

system within which they were made (Warner Brothers in Curtiz's case). A system instead of, or at least as well as, artistic genius would seem to be required for varied excellence of this sort.

John Huston worked both inside and outside that system, and many observers feel his finest work was done inside. Certainly the films he made between 1940 and 1952 represent him at his best and virtually bracket the period we've been dealing with. All of them have to do with groups of people undertaking dangerous enterprises at great risk, even involving death; all but one end in failure. In them Huston demonstrates special talent for a kind of sentimental realism and observation of the particularities of human behavior that have literary analogues in the writing of Ernest Hemingway.

The Maltese Falcon (1941) was Huston's first direction—he had been a screenwriter before that—and its success established a private-eye formula and the beginning of film noir. The performances of the cast—Humphrey Bogart, Mary Astor, Peter Lorre, Sydney Greenstreet—are definitive, for the genre and for each of them, and would often be repeated.

Huston's documentary work during World War II seemed to strengthen his qualities as an American realist. *The Battle of San Pietro* (1945) is a close and sensitive study of infantry combat, accurate in fact and feeling, a film of permanent value. Following the war, Huston directed a succession of what are his most representative features.

The Treasure of the Sierra Madre (1948), from a novel by B. Traven, is about three men (played by Bogart, Tim Holt, and Huston's father, Walter) prospecting for gold in Mexico in the 1920s. They find it and then lose it. *The Asphalt Jungle* (1950) is similar in many ways, though set in contemporary urban United States. In it a group of men come together to commit a big jewel robbery. They obtain the jewels, but suspicion and treachery and their own psychological weaknesses lead each to his death or capture. *The Red Badge of Courage* (1951), an adaptation of the Stephen Crane novel of the Civil War, deals with a young man's initiation into the terrors of warfare, its stupidities, brutalities, and pointlessness.[3]

In *The African Queen* (1952) the group consists of two (Katharine Hepburn as the missionary's prim sister and Bogart as the hard-bitten riverboat captain), unless one counts the rickety, quirky steam launch of the title on which they escape down river from German East Africa at the outbreak of World War I. This is the adventure, from the C. S. Forester novel, with a script by James Agee and Huston, that ends in success: They do escape, their lives have been changed for the better as a result of their enforced intimacy under perilous conditions over a period of weeks. But perhaps the success is qualified. Though it seems churlish to ask it, given the satisfaction of the ending, a question remains: What will become of them and their love for each other?

---

[3]The making of this film and the reasons and ways in which it was not completed as Huston had intended are chronicled by Lillian Ross in *Picture* (New York: Rinehart, 1952), the most perceptive and illuminating diary of Hollywood feature film making at the end of the big studio era.

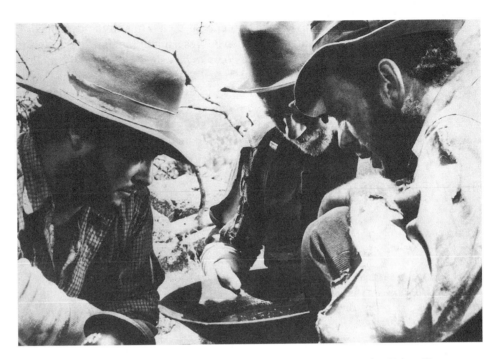

The Treasure of the Sierra Madre ♦ U.S., 1948, John Huston; Tim Holt, Walter Huston, and Humphrey Bogart.

In 1952, the year *The African Queen* was released, Huston moved from Hollywood to Ireland, because he could not abide McCarthyism, he has said. His subsequent films were made mostly abroad. As a matter of fact, *The African Queen,* shot in Africa and London, was a British picture in spite of its American creative personnel and its producer, Sam Spiegel. Increased internationalization was only one of the new tendencies that started to become apparent in the American film beginning about 1952.

If "the thirties" in Hollywood extended into the early forties, as argued at the beginning of this chapter, "the forties" extended into the early fifties, 1952 being a key transitional year that will be returned to in Chapter 13. By 1952 the wave of realist/problem pictures of the late forties had virtually ceased, as had film noir. It is probable that both cycles ended partly as a result of the House Un-American Activities Committee's investigations and the pressures being applied by militant anticommunist groups then at their height. Perhaps the realist/problem pictures were too explicitly liberal in their portrayal of the inadequacies and inequities existing in this society. The noir films, on the other hand, may have been too dark and pessimistic in their view of humanity and too critical, implicitly, of American society to be popular or even safe in the American fifties. Individual film makers of talent, such as Hitchcock, Wyler, Sturges, Welles, Curtiz, and Huston, had to, one way or another, adjust themselves and the styles and contents of their films to the demands of the period. Though not many persons could have foreseen it at the time, the forties turned out to be the last decade of what would come to be called the old Hollywood.

In 1940 David Selznick had brought Alfred Hitchcock from London to Hollywood to direct *Rebecca,* which is set in England; by 1953 Selznick went to Italy to have Vittorio de Sica direct *Indiscretion of an American Wife.* In the late forties and early fifties it was Italy in the spotlight, stage center of the realist tendency so prominent in the postwar years. Neorealism it was called there.

FILMS OF THE PERIOD

1940
Fantasia (Walt Disney)
Foreign Correspondent (Alfred Hitchcock)
The Grapes of Wrath (John Ford)
The Great Dictator (Charles Chaplin)
The Great McGinty (Preston Sturges)
His Girl Friday (Howard Hawks)
The Letter (William Wyler)
The Philadelphia Story (George Cukor)
Rebecca (Hitchcock)

1941
Citizen Kane (Orson Welles)
High Sierra (Raoul Walsh)
How Green Was My Valley (Ford)
The Lady Eve (Sturges)
The Little Foxes (Wyler)
The Maltese Falcon (John Huston)
Sergeant York (Hawks)
Sullivan's Travels (Sturges)
Suspicion (Hitchcock)

1942
Casablanca (Michael Curtiz)
The Magnificent Ambersons (Welles)
Mrs. Miniver (Wyler)
The Palm Beach Story (Sturges)
To Be or Not to Be (Ernst Lubitsch)
Wake Island (John Farrow)
Yankee Doodle Dandy (Curtiz)

1943
Air Force (Hawks)
Bataan (Tay Garnett)
The More the Merrier (George Stevens)

Ox-Bow Incident (William Wellman)
Shadow of a Doubt (Hitchcock)

1944
Double Indemnity (Billy Wilder)
Gaslight (Cukor)
Going My Way (Leo McCarey)
Hail the Conquering Hero (Sturges)
Laura (Otto Preminger)
Meet Me in St. Louis (Vincente Minnelli)
The Miracle of Morgan's Creek (Sturges)
Thirty Seconds Over Tokyo (Mervyn LeRoy)

1945
The Bells of St. Mary's (McCarey)
The House on 92nd Street (Henry Hathaway)
The Lost Weekend (Wilder)
Mildred Pierce (Curtiz)
The Southerner (Jean Renoir)
Spellbound (Hitchcock)
The Story of G.I. Joe (Wellman)

1946
The Best Years of Our Lives (Wyler)
It's a Wonderful Life (Frank Capra)
The Killers (Robert Siodmak)
My Darling Clementine (Ford)
Notorious (Hitchcock)
A Walk in the Sun (Lewis Milestone)

1947
Boomerang (Elia Kazan)
Brute Force (Jules Dassin)
Crossfire (Edward Dmytryk)
A Double Life (Cukor)

Gentleman's Agreement (Kazan)
Miracle on 34th Street (George Seaton)
Monsieur Verdoux (Chaplin)

1948
Call Northside 777 (Hathaway)
Louisiana Story (Robert Flaherty)
The Naked City (Dassin)
The Quiet One (Sidney Meyers)
The Search (Fred Zinnemann)
The Snake Pit (Anatole Litvak)
The Treasure of the Sierra Madre (Huston)

1949
Adam's Rib (Cukor)
All the King's Men (Robert Rossen)
Battleground (Wellman)
The Champion (Mark Robson)
The Heiress (Wyler)
Home of the Brave (Robson)
Intruder in the Dust (Clarence Brown)
A Letter to Three Wives (Joseph Mankiewicz)
On the Town (Gene Kelly and Stanley Donen)
The Set-Up (Robert Wise)
White Heat (Walsh)

1950
All About Eve (Mankiewicz)
The Asphalt Jungle (Huston)
Born Yesterday (Cukor)
Father of the Bride (Minnelli)
The Men (Zinnemann)
Panic in the Streets (Kazan)
Sunset Boulevard (Wilder)
Twelve O'Clock High (King)

1951
An American in Paris (Minnelli)
Detective Story (Wyler)
Fourteen Hours (Hathaway)
A Place in the Sun (Stevens)
Quo Vadis (LeRoy)
The Red Badge of Courage (Huston)
Strangers on a Train (Hitchcock)
A Streetcar Named Desire (Kazan)

1952
The African Queen (Huston)
My Son John (McCarey)
Carrie (Wyler)

BOOKS ON THE PERIOD

Dick, Bernard, *Radical Innocence: A Critical Study of the Hollywood Ten.* Lexington: University Press of Kentucky, 1988

Koppes, Clayton R., and Gregory D. Black, *Hollywood Goes to War: How Politics, Profits, and Propaganda Shaped World War II Movies.* New York: Free Press, 1987

10

Italian
Neorealism

♦ ♦ ♦

1945–1952

The eruption of a brilliant cluster of Italian films that began with Roberto Rossellini's *Open City* (1945) was stimulated by the removal of Fascist power after nearly a quarter century and the release of bottled-up feelings of frustration and humiliation generated by Italy's ambiguous and shifting position in World War II. Beginning as a nominal equal to the other two Axis powers, Germany and Japan, Italy subsequently was reduced to a subservient role. When Mussolini was overthrown, a separate peace was signed with the Allies. The Germans in Italy then turned into an occupying force, retreating slowly as the Allies advanced up the peninsula to replace Germany as the new occupier. It is against this background that *Open City* is set, at the point when Allied forces were approaching Rome and had already begun bombing its outskirts. An agreement was then reached whereby the Germans did not attempt to hold the Eternal City, thus averting its destruction.

♦ THREE MAJOR DIRECTORS

In *Open City* Rossellini chronicles in cross-sectional form the activities of the partisans, the raids and reprisals of the German military and the Italian police, the painful tensions among collaborators, resisters, and the great majority of people who simply wanted enough bread and wine, and an end to the killing and misery of war.

The film begins with German soldiers arriving outside the building lived in by Manfredi (Marcello Pagliero), a partisan activist. After he flees, his former lover (Maria Michi), now dependent on the Gestapo to supply her with drugs, tries to reach him by phone. Manfredi goes to the apartment of a friend and fellow partisan, whose fiancée (Anna Magnani) takes him in and sends for a Catholic priest who is aiding the resistance. The friend returns from work and the action proceeds with the Gestapo net closing in on Manfredi and the priest. But equal attention is given to the daily lives of the Roman people under the stress of a foreign presence, from child resistance-fighters to an irritable old man who scarcely comprehends what is happening but attempts to supply his needs nonetheless.

Scriptwriters Sergio Amidei and Federico Fellini, and director Rossellini, make as good a case as they can for the instances of courage, heroism, and martyrdom that occurred in a generally demoralized Italy. *Open City* seems in part an attempt to ease the national conscience in regard to the immediate past and, for the grim postwar problems yet to be solved, to provide models of behavior. The Catholic priest and the professional communist revolutionary unite in their efforts and sacrifice their lives in the fight to free their country from Fascist rule. The film is a passionate requiem, like Verdi's for his novelist friend Alessandro Manzoni, and its rough beauty and emotional intensity carry all before it.

No tyro, Rossellini had been working in films since 1934. The Italian industry was heavily controlled and subsidized by the government, and Mussolini used it as a relatively harmless field in which to place some of his less able relatives. After a few unsuccessful attempts to use the fiction film for direct propaganda—invoking the glories of ancient Rome and associating them with the contemporary Italy of the black shirts, for example—the fascists had to accept the evidence that audiences would simply stay away. Instead, the authorities became content to keep films from making any significant statement whatever about modern reality; the filmed opera, costume melodrama, and romance built around a box-office idol became ubiquitous. The latter type were known as the "white telephone films," since an ultimate in luxurious dalliance was frequently portrayed as a langorous heroine lounging in negligee on an elaborate bed cooing to her lover on the phone. Knowing Rossellini's political and humanitarian convictions we can imagine his private rebellion at the restraints placed on him.

That *Open City* was made at all is something of a marvel. (Vernon Jarratt, who lived in Italy at the time, recalls the travail in his excellent *The Italian Cinema*.) Rossellini filmed secretly between 1943 and 1945, scraping together funds from various sources. The money kept running out and at one point Rossellini and Magnani, who plays her first great screen role in the film, sold all their clothes to obtain enough lire to carry on for a few more days. Production conditions were incredibly primitive. Shooting was done on odds and ends of raw stock of various manufacturers. Studios weren't available to them, and nearly all the scenes were enacted on the actual locations they represent in the film. Even the electrical power in wartime was so erratic that maintaining consistent exposure was a constant problem. In spite of the technical and financial difficulties (dead broke, Rossellini is said to have sold the rights for $28,000; *Open City* grossed $5 million in the United States alone), the film emerged as a towering achievement that would inspire other Italian film makers to emulate its concepts and its method of dealing with contemporary reality.

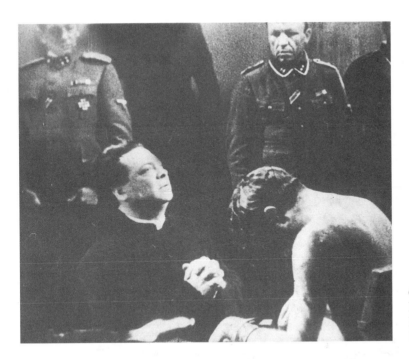

Open City ◆ Italy, 1945, Roberto Rossellini; Aldo Fabrizi and Marcello Pagliero, foreground.

Of the three major directors of the neorealistic period—Rossellini, Vittorio de Sica, **Luchino Visconti**—the first two better represent the characteristics of the movement as a whole in its techniques and commitments. At the same time it must be acknowledged that Visconti's *Ossessione* (1942), an unauthorized version of James M. Cain's novel *The Postman Always Rings Twice,* can be seen as a harbinger of neorealism even before the appearance of *Open City.* This is true more because of its naturalistic style (purposefully drab and unlovely) than its thematic content (passion, jealously, and greed). With *La Terra Trema* (1948) Visconti offered one of the accepted masterpieces of neorealism but, curiously, in that case it is largely the thematic materials and method of production that qualify it rather than the style. It is about a family of Sicilian fishermen being ground down into poverty by the dealers, who exert a monopolistic control over the prices and conditions under which the fish can be marketed. Sponsored initially by the Communist Party, shot entirely on location, the film uses nonactors exclusively. But having said that, it must be added that the realistic and ideological elements are molded into a kind of operatic form. Visconti was a Marxist, and in many ways his work is reminiscent of Eisenstein's silent films, especially, in this instance, in the extreme stylization imposed on the materials of actuality. The fishermen are grouped carefully, decoratively, their movements choreographed; the lighting is exquisite in its rich contrasts and as carefully controlled and patterned as if the film were made in a studio. There are also the emotionally surcharged scenes of passion and drunkenness that would fit better into classical Greek drama, perhaps, than into the films of the other neorealists. In *Rocco and His Brothers* (1960), in some ways a sequel to *La Terra Trema,* Visconti returned briefly

La Terra Trema ♦ Italy, 1948, Luchino Visconti.

to his own version of the neorealist canon. But as his subsequent work confirmed, he was really more at home with what Walter Korte called "the scenographic baroque."[1]

Rossellini, on the other hand, quickly followed *Open City* (see beginning of this section) with his other major film fully within the general terms of neorealist style and intention, *Paisan* (1946). In six separate episodes it traces the Allied campaign up the long boot of Italy, exploring the contacts between the conquerors (principally American) and the conquered. Maps and newsreel footage connect the parts, suggesting that the dramatic vignettes are incidents happening within the larger historical context. Each episode sketches one aspect of the complex and changing American-Italian relationships, which move from an initial distrust to a growing closeness.

The first episode takes place during the initial phase of the campaign, the invasion of Sicily. In it mutual suspicion and fear of treachery between a patrol of GIs and a group of peasants lead to the death of two likeable young people who were trying to get to know each other—a Sicilian Carmela and a Joe from Jersey. The second episode, set in Naples, is concerned with the black market, thievery, homeless children, poverty, and a military government—all characteristics of that devastated port

---

[1]Walter F. Korte, Jr., "Marxism and Formalism in the Films of Luchino Visconti," *Cinema Journal,* 11 (Fall 1971): 2–12.

city. It centers around an African-American MP who, while dead drunk, has his boots stolen by one of the countless urchins who survived on the streets of Italian cities during the war. The third story takes place in Rome and deals with prostitution and disillusionment in the wake of liberation. Thousands of young women from families broken up by the war gravitated to Rome. There was little work for which they were qualified, and what there was didn't pay enough to live on; so, for a fee they slept with the troops coming into Rome on rest leave. Nice young girls and lonely boys were forced by the situation into unfulfilling and sometimes hurtful liaisons, as the Rome episode indicates.

The Florentine sequence suggests the prewar ties between the United States and Italy through an Army nurse who tries to find her former lover, a painter, now leader of the partisans fighting to free Florence from the retreating Germans. Next, in a monastery near Bologna three U.S. Army chaplains gain understanding and respect for a cloistered order of monks as they try to achieve acquaintanceship through their common service to God. In the final episode, members of American OSS and British Intelligence fight beside courageous Italian partisans in the Po valley in the last days of the war. But courage, shared trust, and growing comradeship are incidental concomitants; the whole meaning of war is suffering and death, Rossellini is clearly saying. This last episode, the finest, is the most documentary-like; it is also the most grim and tragic.

Paisan ♦ Italy, 1946, Roberto Rossellini.

Rossellini worked the stories out as he went along, with the aid of a group of writers that included Federico Fellini. Each incident is particularly representative of that phase of the campaign. Taken together they treat, with extraordinary comprehensiveness as well as precision, the significance of the American presence in Italy. The camera and editing techniques are as sparse and unprettified as the stories. Of *Paisan's* large cast only four members had had previous acting experience (the GI and the prostitute in Rome, the nurse in Florence, the Catholic chaplain in Bologna); the others were picked up by Rossellini as he found them on location. The whole achieves a directness and power through its spontaneity. Rossellini's style is in perfect keeping with the material and his attitude toward it.

Vittorio de Sica and his scriptwriter, Cesare Zavattini, continued this national saga with an examination of the immediate postwar years. Before directing, de Sica had been a well known screen actor in the thirties. His first important film as director, *The Children Are Watching Us* (1943), was also his first collaboration with Zavattini. Roughly contemporary with Visconti's *Ossessione,* it was somewhat comparable in its realistic tendencies. In the main line of postwar neorealism, de Sica's *Shoeshine*

Shoeshine ♦ Italy, 1946, Vittorio de Sica; Rinaldo Smordoni and Franco Interlenghi, standing left rear.

(1946) is concerned with the Roman *ragazzi* who eked out a living shining GIs' shoes, pimping, and dealing in black market American cigarettes, candy bars, and, in this instance, blankets. Two boys are apprehended, tried, convicted, and sent to a reformatory, where their affection for each other is turned into hatred, resulting in the death of one of the boys. There are no villains, however, simply a bad system. We are not sure why there aren't enough staff and money to run this institution properly, except that there never are in institutions of this sort. Nor are we told what steps might be taken to obtain adequate resources. Though the neorealist films dealt with social problems, they tended to hold them up for examination in terms of their effects on individual lives rather than explain causes or propose solutions.

Zavattini's and de Sica's most successful collaboration, and among those films closest to the neorealist ideal, was *The Bicycle Thief* (1948). It deals with the simplest possible situation. An unemployed laborer with his first chance to work for some time has the bicycle stolen that he must have in order to keep his job. The events leading up to the theft and the attempt to recover the bicycle provide sufficient "plot" for a complete and significant work of art, even including implied social and political criticism. In following the man's and his young son's search for the bicycle, various aspects of Italian society are sketched, with apparent casualness it may seem at first; on reflection the highest degree of economy and skill become evident. *The Bicycle*

The Bicycle Thief ♦ Italy, 1948, Vittorio de Sica; Enzo Staiola and Lamberto Maggiorani.

Thief was shot almost entirely outside the studio, in the streets and apartments and offices of Rome. The father in the film was in real life a machinist in the big Breda steelworks. The boy who plays his son was a Roman newsboy. The performances elicited from the pair can only be described as miraculous. De Sica's work with nonactors, especially children, is always sensitive and sure; here he surpassed himself. Though methods formerly found only in documentary are basic to its conception, the emotional richness of *Bicycle Thief* depends to considerable extent upon the portrayals of its Everyman and his small son.

◆ THEORY

The working principles of the neorealist films which Rossellini had first improvised partly by necessity and accident, partly out of conviction, in turn became loosely codified into a theory of cinema. The premises underpinning neorealism were most forcefully articulated by scriptwriter Zavattini, who became spokesman for, as well as one of the principal creators in, the movement. Perhaps the only other screenwriter to have achieved a comparable intellectual-aesthetic dominance in a period of national excellence is Carl Mayer, in relation to the German-expressionist films of the twenties.

In a famous interview, Zavattini had the following things to say about the content and purposes of neorealism:

> *The most important characteristic, and the most important innovation, of what is called neorealism, it seems to me, is to have realised that the necessity of the "story" was only an unconscious way of disguising a human defeat, and that the kind of imagination it involved was simply a technique of superimposing dead formulas over living social facts. Now it has been perceived that reality is hugely rich, that to be able to look directly at it is enough; and that the artist's task is not to make people moved or indignant at metaphorical situations, but to make them reflect (and, if you like, to be moved and indignant too) on what they and others are doing, on the real things, exactly as they are.*[2]

Asking himself what effects on narrative structure the neorealist style had, Zavattini answered:

> *To begin with, while the cinema used to make one situation produce another situation, and another, and another, again and again, and each scene was thought out and immediately related to the next (the natural result of a mistrust of reality), today, when we have thought out a scene, we feel the need to "remain" in it, because the single scene itself can contain so many echoes and reverberations, can even contain all the situations we may need. Today,*

---

[2]Cesare Zavattini, "Some Ideas on the Cinema," *Sight and Sound,* 23 (October-December 1953): 64, 65.

in fact, we can quietly say: Give us whatever "fact" you like [a stolen bicycle, for example], and we will disembowel it, make it something worth watching.

Frequently Zavattini sounds exactly like a documentarian rather than a fiction film maker, and many of his statements could fit quite comfortably into the polemical writings of John Grierson, founder and leader of British documentary. In the same interview Zavattini said:

Substantially, then, the question today is, instead of turning imaginary situations into "reality" and trying to make them look "true," to make things as they are, almost by themselves, create their own special significance. Life is not what is invented in "stories"; life is another matter. To understand it involves a minute, unrelenting, and patient search.

Grierson had written about his efforts in the 1930s as attempts to find "drama on the doorstep."

♦ PRACTICE

Like the American semidocumentaries and problem pictures dealt with in Chapter 9, the newly realistic Italian films were based on a real incident, a composite of several, or a representative event; they had factual rather than fictional bases. For example, a film might be based on an actual situation of a staircase collapsing under the weight of hundreds of unemployed young women applying for jobs as typists (*Rome, Eleven O'Clock*, 1952), or on a typical one like that of an old man finding it difficult to live on his pension (*Umberto D*, 1952). The problems treated by these films had some degree of immediacy and broad concern. Their themes were not necessarily universal and timeless, as those of the arts tend to be; they were more tied to the here and now, like documentary: sociological as much as psychological in their approach. Among the prevalent concerns were poverty (*Miracle in Milan*, 1951; *Two Cents Worth of Hope*, 1952), prostitution (*Without Pity*, 1948), collaboration with and resistance to occupying military forces (*Outcry* and *To Live in Peace*, both 1947), exploitative agricultural conditions (*The Tragic Hunt*, 1947; *Bitter Rice*, 1949).

Works of this sort were split in the attention they gave to the social problem and to individual character and conflict. An effort was made to fuse the characters and the problem. Roles were created not so much for what the persons were like as for what they did (a resistance leader in *Open City*, 1945) or did not do (an unemployed worker in *The Bicycle Thief*, 1948). The personality of the protagonist could be of any sort—grouchy, or an unfaithful spouse (since the film was not about exclusively personal qualities)—as long as the public function was performed. Various aspects of the problem were represented by individuals, but its social (anonymous) nature was kept to the fore.

To put much the same thing another way, in these semi-documentary-like films there *is* a plot and there *are* characters, but they are less fully developed than in pure fiction, and are used quite directly to embody the theme and ideas. The conflict and

Umberto D ◆ Italy, 1952, Vittorio de Sica; Maria-Pia Casilio and Carlo Battisti.

resolution are apt to be drawn out of the larger situation rather than out of interpersonal relations. A poor fishing family is in contention with the boat owners; when the owners win, the fishermen are forced to work the boats on the owners' terms. The family that had been resisting is broken (*La Terra Trema,* 1948). In other words, in films of this sort the characters and their lives (plot incidents) are used deliberately to express an ideology.

Finally, in these films the film-making methods are drawn from both fiction and documentary. They tend to depend less on performance and dialogue than do conventional fiction films. Actors may appear in principal roles, but frequently nonactors are used in lesser roles and as extras (*Open City,* 1945; *The Tragic Hunt,* 1947), and even as leads (*Shoeshine,* 1946; *The Bicycle Thief,* 1948; *Umberto D,* 1952). In any event there is usually an avoidance of stars. Considerable location shooting (exteriors) is combined with studio (interiors). Sometimes candid or newsreel footage is interpolated. Frequently commentary, montage, even maps, suggest a broader scope and help bridge a less-tight plot. Lighting, costumes, makeup, sets are actual, or naturalistic in style. The editing is less "smooth" than in the usual story picture, being dictated by the subject-matter requirements. The cutting pace is frequently more rapid, too, as it tends to be when ideas more than emotions are being dealt with, and when film makers (as in documentary) are working with persons (nonactors) who cannot sustain performances. There tends to be emphasis on source sounds and avoidance of heavy musical scoring.

◆ AFTERWARDS

It must be admitted that cosmic meaning arising from the ordinary was not always, and seldom completely, attained in neorealist films. Melodrama superimposed on reality was still the rule. But films of the neorealist style attracted Italy's most talented directors, writers, and performers; received the widest foreign distribution; and exerted the strongest influence on the film production of other countries during the immediate postwar years. Incidentally, this seems to be another instance of a film movement growing out of troubled times, like the post-World War I German and Soviet cinemas. The neorealist films began in a defeated and occupied country, with a badly disorganized economy and political life, widespread poverty and unemployment, and uncontrolled inflation.

Problems of national identity, political turmoil, economic misery, and social dislocation continued, but by 1949 neorealism had begun to wane as the predominant force in Italian film making. Pressure from the Roman Catholic Church and the Italian government in the early 1950s resulted in a decline of the export of "social problem" films to the United States, the chief source of economic support for neorealism. A realization by the film makers themselves that the neorealist conception of reality, with its externalized nonpsychological approach, was limiting, led to an enlargement or alteration of their scope of concern. An often quoted comment by Michelangelo Antonioni about *The Bicycle Thief* is revealing. He said that if he had directed the film, he would have told more about the people and less about the bicycle.

If neorealism began with Rossellini's *Open City* in 1945, it ceased, or changed direction anyway, after the de Sica-Zavattini *Umberto D* of 1952. The latter is about an old man whose fixed income had become insufficient to support life with any dignity let alone pleasure. After that last great neorealist film, Italian film makers began shifting their attention from the lower classes and poverty to the upper classes and the unsatisfying and corrosive values of much of modern life that are most evident among them. Some of Rossellini's films of the middle and late fifties look ahead to a later kind of cinema, exerting great influence on the upcoming generation of French as well as Italian film makers. His *Voyage to Italy* (1953) especially is startlingly predictive; Antonioni's *L'Avventura* (1960) seems to grow directly out of it.

Fellini also can be considered a transitional figure who moved from the essentially materialistic concerns of the neorealist films to the, for want of a better word, spiritual concerns of the next generation of Italian film makers. "For me," he said, "neorealism means looking at reality with an honest eye—but at any kind of reality; not just social reality, but also spiritual reality, metaphysical reality, anything man has inside of him." His *La Strada* (1954) might in many ways be regarded as a pivotal film. Though set among the lower classes, it is not concerned with poverty but with inadequacies in human relationships, the inability to communicate and most of all to love.

De Sica attempted to return to neorealism with *The Roof* (1955), but this tale of a young couple trying to obtain their own place to live seemed strangely old fashioned and inessential in the newly prosperous Italy. Rossellini's *General delta Rovere* (1959) and de Sica's *Two Women* (1960) are also efforts to recapture some of the themes of the immediate postwar films. In spite of the professional polish, in part because of it of course, and some excellent things in each, both seem anachronistic. It may be fitting that in the former film Rossellini is directing de Sica, playing the lead as the General's impersonator who dies a hero. Those two films were a kind of final reprise, not so much for the two directors—because by then even those stalwarts of neorealism were making other kinds of films—but for the original movement.

The practice and the theory of neorealism did not cease to exist, however, and its influence has been discernible ever since the initial period. In Italy the films of Ermanno Olmi (*Il Posto,* 1961; *The Fiancés,* 1962) embodied it most directly. Also the works of Vittorio de Seta (*The Bandits of Orgosolo,* 1961) and Pier Paolo Pasolini (*Accatone,* 1961), in their methods and explicitly Marxist ideologies, recalled the earlier films, as did the films of Francesco Rosi (*Salvatore Giuliano,* 1961; *Hands Over the City,* 1963). The French New Wave, Eastern European cinema, and the British social-realist features, to be dealt with later, all owed something to the kind of film making practiced in Italy between 1945 and 1952.

FILMS OF THE PERIOD

1945
Open City (Roberto Rossellini)

1946
Paisan (Rossellini)
Shoeshine (Vittorio de Sica)

1947
Germany, Year Zero (Rossellini)
Outcry (Aldo Vergano)
To Live in Peace (Luigi Zampa)
The Tragic Hunt (Giuseppe de Santis)

1948
The Bicycle Thief (de Sica)
La Terra Trema (Luchino Visconti)
Under the Sun of Rome (Renato Castellani)
Without Pity (Alberto Lattuada)

1949
Bitter Rice (de Santis)
In the Name of the Law (Pietro Germi)

1950
The Mill on the Po (Lattuada)
The Road of Hope (Germi)

1951
Bellissima (Visconti)
The Forbidden Christ (Curzio Malaparte)
Miracle in Milan (de Sica)

1952
The Overcoat (Lattuada)
Rome, Eleven O'Clock (de Santis)
Two Cents Worth of Hope (Castellani)
Umberto D (de Sica)

BOOKS ON THE PERIOD

Bondanella, Peter, *Italian Cinema: From Neorealism to the Present.* New York: Continuum Publishing, 1990

Marcus, Millicent, *Italian Film in the Light of Neorealism.* Princeton: Princeton University Press, 1987

11

British Film
after the War

♦ ♦ ♦

1945–1963

To have kept Britain sidetracked up to this point seems characteristic of the treatment often afforded the British film—not least by the British themselves. About their own cinema, British critics habitually complain that it lacks a distinctive tradition like that of the French or Italians and that it is dominated and subsumed by the Americans.

American money and personnel are so inextricably interwoven with British production and distribution that it is difficult to determine where one industry leaves off and the other begins. In an article entitled "Tomorrow the World: Some Reflections on the un-Englishness of English Films" (*Sight and Sound,* Spring 1974), John Russell Taylor suggested that, with only a little simplification, the whole history of British cinema could be seen in terms of the fluctuating relations with the United States and the American market. If in the days of gunboat diplomacy commerce followed the flag, in modern economic imperialism culture follows the dollar.

The problem that British films present, then, is one of national identity, not of artistic quality. British technicians and the technical level of Britain's films are generally conceded to be among the best in the world; the acting talent available is unsurpassed. And there are kinds of films the British have made with a particular excellence. Films drawn from their literary or dramatic or historical heritage, or a type of sophisticated crime or espionage thriller are examples. The David Lean versions of Noël Coward and Charles Dickens (*Blithe Spirit,* 1945; *Brief Encounter,* 1945; *Great Expectations,* 1946; *Oliver Twist,* 1948), the Laurence Olivier adaptations of William Shakespeare (*Henry V,* 1944; *Hamlet,* 1948; *Richard III,* 1955), the Carol Reed collaborations with Graham Greene (*The Fallen Idol,* 1948; *The Third Man,* 1949) distinguish its immediate postwar history.

Then there were the films about World War II growing out of the wartime experience: *The Cruel Sea* (1953, Charles Frend), *The Dam Busters* (1953, Michael Anderson), *The Battle of the River Plate* (1956, Michael Powell and Emeric Pressburger). There were many other fine individual works within a sort of "academic" tradition: significant subjects treated with self-effacing expertness. But prestigious ventures of this sort became increasingly multinational in conception, financial backing, and creative personnel. John Huston's *The African Queen* (1952), *Moulin Rouge* (1953), and *Moby Dick* (1956), and David Lean's *Summertime* (1955) and *The Bridge on the River Kwai* (1957) are prominent examples.

Alongside these transcendent international successes there developed three popular native genres or film types which also proved exportable on a more modest scale. First were two series of specifically British comedy. One came out of Ealing Studios, and in a curious way out of the distinctive documentary tradition that had developed in the thirties and reached its height during the war in the semidocumentary features (like *Target for Tonight* [1941] and *Fires Were Started* [1943]) that combined fact and fiction. The other was the "Carry On" series, the origins of which could be traced back to the English music hall. Second were the social-realist features that complemented the plays and novels of the Angry Young Men (and women) of the late fifties and early sixties—films of criticism and protest. Third was the Gothic horror series of Hammer Films, which fitted into a British literary tradition that included the nineteenth-century novels of Mary Shelley (*Frankenstein*) and Bram Stoker (*Dracula*).

◆ POSTWAR COMEDIES

If the British semidocumentary became as rare soon after the war as it had been prevalent during wartime, it might be argued that it didn't so much cease as go underground and come up looking and sounding like the **Ealing comedy.** Michael Balcon, head of Ealing Studios, had always been a friend of the documentary movement and favored fiction films that were distinctively British rather than imitatively American. When the documentarians began to cross over into feature film making via the wartime semidocumentary it was to Ealing that they came. Alberto Cavalcanti, former production head of the government Crown Film Unit, as well as Harry Watt, one of its star directors, were among these. Three of the principal directors of the Ealing comedies, Charles Crichton, Charles Frend, and Alexander Mackendrick, had had considerable documentary experience. The result of these biases and this personnel, plus the fine writing talents Balcon acquired, especially T. E. B. Clarke, gave the string of comedies their distinctive flavor.

The first of the series was *Hue and Cry,* directed by Crichton in 1947. The lower- and middle-class milieu, location shooting, bumbling crooks and police, and fast pace all typify the Ealing manner. There followed, in fairly rapid succession, *Whiskey Galore* (1949, Mackendrick; *Tight Little Island* in the United States), *Passport to Pimlico* (1949, Henry Cornelius), *A Run for Your Money* (1949, Frend), *The Lavender Hill Mob* (1951, Crichton), *The Man in the White Suit* (1951, Mackendrick), *Genevieve* (1953, Cornelius), *The Titfield Thunderbolt* (1953, Crichton), *The Maggie* (1954, Mackendrick; *High and Dry* in the United States), *The Ladykillers* (1955, Mackendrick). In 1952 financial problems caused Ealing to sell its studios to BBC-TV; in 1955 the company itself was dissolved. Between 1951 and 1955 similar kinds of comedies were being made at Group 3, a government-financed experiment in feature production headed by John Grierson, former leader of the documentary movement.

These British comedies have much in common with the documentary tradition as well as with each other. They simply turn documentary seriousness on its ear. The themes of the Ealing films are notably social, economic, political, or at least cultural (in the anthropologist's sense), designed to bring out a particular facet of national life. They deal with the Scots' fondness for a wee drop, strict Calvinism, dislike of the English (*Tight Little Island*), the bureaucratic entanglements in which the British found themselves after the war (*Passport to Pimlico*), the expected honesty and trustworthiness of the English middle class (*The Lavender Hill Mob*), the collusion among management and labor, government and opposition within the English system (*The Man in the White Suit*). Laughter is provoked only through the incongruities and exaggerations with which these subjects are treated; even so, the comic style is noteworthy for its deadpan seriousness, underplaying, and throwaway delivery of lines.

Casting called on nonglamorous, quintessentially British actors (rather than stars)—Alistair Sim (*Hue and Cry*), Stanley Holloway (*Passport to Pimlico*), Alec Guinness (*The Lavender Hill Mob, The Man in the White Suit, The Ladykillers*)—and used local citizens as extras. The films were shot largely on location, the humor in every case being heightened by realistic background and detail—of cockney London as well as of the Scottish Hebrides.

In *Tight Little Island* the documentary influence is especially pervasive. The novel on which it is based—by Compton Mackenzie, who appears in the film in a small part as Captain Bucher—was drawn from an actual disaster to a whiskey-laden ship during World War I. Mackenzie was assisted on the screenplay by Angus MacPhail. (There is a preponderance of Scottish names in the credits.) The cast is a blend of well-trained actors, many of them Scottish by birth, and local inhabitants. Alexander Mackendrick, who directed, was trained in wartime documentary; this was his first feature.

The story is indigenous to the people it is about. It seems to stem from a series of questions. What if Scottish islanders during World War II rationing ran out of whiskey? How would they be affected? What if they had a chance to steal as much of 50,000 cases as they could carry away? What if this chance occurred late on a Saturday night among people whose respect for the Sabbath vies with their love of good whiskey? How would government officials—home guard, regular army, customs inspectors—react to all this? And so on, with acute insights and hilarious comedy being drawn from seemingly ordinary people in conceivably real situations.

Tight Little Island was shot almost entirely on location, interiors as well as exteriors. A kind of mobile studio unit was established on the Hebridean island so that no time would be lost waiting for good weather. Mackendrick even set up processing equipment so he could look at the rushes without undue delay, just as Robert Flaherty had done for his famous documentary feature *Man of Aran,* shot on an island off the coast of Ireland some fifteen years earlier.

Whiskey Galore/Tight Little Island ♦ U.K., 1949, Alexander Mackendrick.

Though its indebtedness is apparent, *Tight Little Island* pointedly kids the style of British documentary in its opening post-card shots of the Hebrides (almost identical with those of the General Post Office Film Unit's *The Islanders*) and voice-over commentary. This gentle kind of spoofing is well within an old and honorable British tradition, enjoyed abroad as well as at home. If we would not expect the British to kill the thing they love, their famous sense of humor could be aimed at it. From their documentary of the thirties has come a lot that is finest and most British in British cinema, and the rest of the world has shared in their achievement.

The *Carry On...* films, which began shortly after the Ealing comedies ended, were even more popular if less valued by critics. They too started from a basis in contemporary reality, with a kind of social commentary built in; but, rather than a documentary-like style, they employed the broad brush of burlesque caricature and knockabout farce. The series was created by a collaboration of Peter Rogers, its producer, Gerald Thomas, its regular director, and writer Norman Hudis (and later Talbot Rothwell), along with a stock company of actors. Drawing its inspiration from music hall, circus, radio comedy, seaside postcards, and working-class leisure culture generally, it ran uninterruptedly for some twenty years at the rate of one or two films a year beginning with *Carry On Sergeant* in 1958. Following the box-office success of that first film, about attempts to make comic misfits into soldiers, was the even more successful *Carry On Nurse* (1959), which offered patients versus hospital staff in a struggle for authority. Later titles included *Carry On Teacher, ... Constable, ... Cruising, ... Cabby, ... Camping,* and so forth.

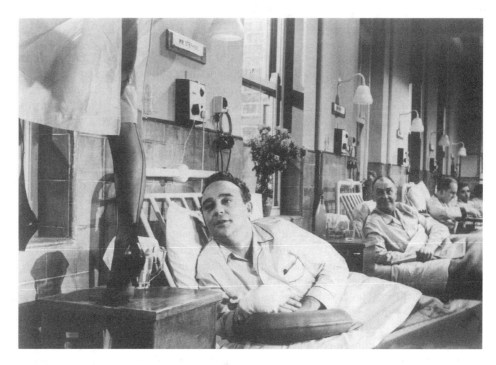

Carry On Nurse ◆ U.K., 1959, Gerald Thomas.

Evidently it was their formulaic nature that bored the critics—and attracted the public. Standard ingredients of the early films included institutional setting, episodic plot with comic set-pieces, robust vulgarity (sexual innuendo and double entendre, much made of large bosoms and backsides), and situations of physical discomfort and sexual embarrassment. There was also a running subtext regarding the English class system and the ineptitudes and inefficiencies of public institutions. A good idea of their attractions is available to those who remember the English television series *Are You Being Served?,* which met with widespread and sustained popular response on American public television.

After the period under consideration the series turned to parodies of other film genres (in *Carry On Spying* and *Carry On Cleo* [both 1964] for example). But, as author John Hill remarked, "what had often been best about the early *Carry On* films . . . [was] the closeness to contemporary realities and relative freshness of social observation."[1] And at the time British culture itself was changing. Another line of films was developing that would be more directly involved in those changes than were the "Carry On" series, and would grow even more directly out of British documentary than had the Ealing comedies.

[1]John Hill, essay on *Carry On Nurse, International Dictionary of Films and Filmmakers* (Chicago: St. James Press, 1990), vol. 1, pp. 152–53. I am indebted to this essay for other insights into the series as well.

◆ SOCIAL-REALIST FEATURES

For their one most indigenous kind of film, which has taken various forms within an overall continuity, the British have sometimes shown a peculiar lack of pride. The line referred to, of course, is the realistic one which extends from the documentaries of the thirties, into the wartime semidocumentaries, on to the Ealing comedies and war dramas of the postwar years. The next emergence of that tradition began in the mid-fifties with a documentary movement called Free Cinema. Combined with the work of new young playwrights and novelists, the Free Cinema spirit inspired a noteworthy cycle of feature films that began with *Room at the Top* (1958) and *Look Back in Anger* (1959). They grew out of the sort of social-realist impulse the British keep rediscovering from time to time and which has inspired some of their most vital as well as most characteristic contributions to the history of film. They also grew out of a sort of bloodless cultural revolution beginning in the mid-fifties which affected British life generally. With the advent of commercial television and a vitality in the political left that extended into the arts, new popular values ("vulgar" they were thought to be in some quarters) came to the fore.

Early in 1956 a program of three short films was shown at the National Film Theatre under the Free Cinema banner. *O Dreamland* (1954), by Lindsay Anderson, castigated the dull and synthetic pleasures being offered the bemused masses at a seaside amusement park. *Momma Don't Allow* (1955), by Karel Reisz and Tony Richardson, celebrated a lively London jazz club patronized by working-class teenagers. *Together* (1955), by Lorenza Mazetti and Denis Horne, described the emotionally impoverished lives led by two deaf-mute dock workers in the East End. The films' makers stated in their program notes for the occasion that Free Cinema was free from serving the sponsor's purpose (as in documentaries) and free from pandering to the demands of the box office (as in fiction features). It was to be an "entirely personal cinema," socially committed but also poetic. "Implicit in our attitude," they wrote, "is a belief in freedom, in the importance of people and in the significance of the everyday."[2]

The year 1956 was a crucial one in the political and cultural life of Britain. It was the year of a last gasp of imperial arrogance in the foolish and failed invasion of Suez. As a result of that debacle the whole governmental system was discredited. To many on the Left, the Labour Party, which worked within the system, seemed as culpable as the ruling Conservatives. Nineteen fifty-six was also the year of the Khrushchev attack on the cult of personality under Stalin, and of the Soviet invasion of Hungary, which caused many Marxist intellectuals finally to become disillusioned with Stalinist communism. Partially in reaction to those events, a politically sophisticated younger generation of dissidents arose around the universities—particularly Oxford, which most of the Free Cinema group had attended. The label "New Left" was attached to them, and their publication was entitled *New Left Review* (originally *Universities and Left Review*). The New Left wanted to go beyond the old-line socialists, with their

[2]As quoted in Elizabeth Sussex, *Lindsay Anderson* (New York: Frederick A. Praeger, 1969), p. 31.

basis in dialectical materialism, trade unionism, nationalization of industry, and social welfare. They were concerned more with theory and a fundamental reorganization of society that would affect the total quality of people's lives. As an intellectual movement which also encompassed the arts, the New Left in Britain was more like the continental Left.

The artists in various media who arose out of the spirit of the time, many of them from the working classes, were dubbed the Angry Young Men for their attacks on the establishment and the rigidities and inequities of the class system. In 1956 John Osborne's play *Look Back in Anger,* directed by Tony Richardson, opened at the Royal Court Theatre. At about the same time Joan Littlewood's Theatre Workshop was started. Playwrights such as Arnold Wesker and Shelagh Delaney soon joined Osborne to create an outpouring of plays set among the lower classes that were articulate and sometimes strident in their social criticism. A new crop of actors—Albert Finney, Rita Tushingham, Rachel Roberts, Tom Courtenay, Richard Harris, Ronald Fraser—also came out of that sort of theater and later worked in film. Novels of a similar tone began to appear as well, with John Braine's *Room at the Top* in 1957 followed by Alan Sillitoe's *Saturday Night and Sunday Morning,* Stan Barstow's *A Kind of Loving,* and David Storey's *This Sporting Life,* among others.

Though Free Cinema had in fact appeared slightly before the explosions in the other arts, it wasn't until it connected with the new drama and literature that its kind of expression moved over into the feature film and became economically viable. Following *Nice Time* (Claude Goretta and Alain Tanner) and *Every Day Except Christmas* (Anderson) in 1957, the Free Cinema movement as such virtually ceased with *We Are the Lambeth Boys* (Reisz) in 1959. Nonetheless, the attitudes and some of the rough-hewn style of Free Cinema were carried into the new social-realist features which began as the Free Cinema shorts ended. It was *Room at the Top,* however, much more conventional than Free Cinema in both content and form, that launched the new phase. It was directed by Jack Clayton, who had come up through the commercial industry and had no connection with Free Cinema.

Set in an industrial northern town, *Room at the Top* deals with the compulsions and confusions of a cynical young arriviste determined to climb up out of his slum origins. Its romantic conflict is class-based—to marry the daughter of a local industrialist in order to get ahead, or to stay with the mistress he loves but who would impede his chances for success—yet scarcely without precedent. It calls to mind Stendahl's *The Red and the Black* or Dreiser's *An American Tragedy.* Audiences in the United States could be excused for considering it extraordinary that this sort of class thing was still bothering the British after all these years. But there it was, up on the screen for the first time, and creating a huge stir.

Look Back in Anger put some of the same matters, and others, in a clearer and less ambiguous way. Through the Jimmy Porter character's brilliant and paranoiac monologues, we could begin to understand what the anger was all about. At least it was clear what he was trying to tear down (the Establishment, personified by his wife's parents) and what he was trying to preserve (the working-class virtues represented by his friend Ma Tanner). It was not so clear (if at all) what the replacement society would be like, and certainly not how it might come about.

In any case, these two films, double-billed in the United States, began the social-realist cycle that dealt with various aspects of working-class character and problems. As a body the films tended to be set in the industrial regions north of London. Thus they contrasted with British entertainment films up to that time which, according to the Free Cinema group at least, had reflected almost exclusively the outlook of metropolitan southern English culture and the middle and upper classes. Here were efforts to include "the rich diversity of tradition and personality which is the whole of Britain" called for in one of Free Cinema's manifestoes.

Of the Free Cinema trio of Anderson, Reisz, and Richardson, it was Richardson who first entered the feature field, with *Look Back in Anger.* Those three were joined by John Schlesinger, an Oxford classmate of Richardson's. Together they constituted the main directorial talent of the social-realist features of the early sixties. All of their films were based on the writings of the so-called Angry Young Men (or Women, as the case might be).

With the profits from *Look Back in Anger,* Richardson and Osborne set up Woodfall Productions, responsible for many of the social-realist features. In addition to his role as producer, Richardson directed three more of those features in rapid succession. *The Entertainer* (1960), from another Osborne play and script, was seen as offering evidence of collapse within British society. Laurence Olivier starred as the down-at-heel music hall comic in a seedy seaside town. Aging and hollow, his life lacks significance in his own eyes and those of others; his social alienation is matched by his messy and unsatisfying personal relationships. *A Taste of Honey* (1961) was from a play by Shelagh Delaney, who worked on the screenplay as well. The remarkable location cinematography in Lancashire was by Walter Lassally, one of two key technicians on the Free Cinema shorts and social-realist features; John Fletcher was the other. *A Taste of Honey* also deals with the complex psychological relationships and unfulfilled needs of a group of individuals existing below the level of middle-class respectability. *The Loneliness of the Long Distance Runner* (1962)—from a story by Alan Sillitoe, who also did the script—portrays the life, frustrated ambitions, and resentments of a lower-class youth who wanders into crime and is sent to prison. The causes of his problems are portrayed as societal, and sympathy as well as understanding is offered for his form of rebellion. All four of Richardson's social-realist features, interesting and modestly important, are marked by especially fine performances. His *Tom Jones* (1963), while remaining more or less faithful to Fielding's eighteenth-century novel, includes some of the same themes of youthful rebelliousness, plus a playfulness with the film medium clearly owing to the French New Wave.

Though Karel Reisz directed only one of the social-realist features (Richardson produced it), his *Saturday Night and Sunday Morning* (1960) is in many ways the most exemplary of their tendencies as a whole. From Sillitoe's popular novel (and he again did the script), it focuses on a working-class rebel. "Don't let the bastards grind you down," is his slogan. Hostile to the system, the young lathe operator finally lacks the resources—the imagination and understanding—to fight free from it. Proudly indigenous as the film is, we don't have to know England to sense that the rows of identically drab houses, the father glued to the telly, the job without meaning, and the inadequate release of a Saturday night drunk and tumble in the hay must be how it is

The Loneliness of the Long Distance Runner ♦ U.K., 1962, Tony Richardson; Tom Courtenay.

for a large segment of the population (as it is elsewhere). The documentary intention dominates. It is served equally by a story that grows out of the situation rather than being imposed on it and by convincingly natural performances. The ending, conclusive in spite of seeming inconclusive, consists simply of the protagonist (played by Albert Finney, in his first starring role) walking down into a new housing estate with his girl. It flies in the face of accepted demands of both box office and dramatic convention, as does much else in this uncompromising picture. If an epilogue were to be added to it, it could borrow from Dylan Thomas, as did the Free Cinema film makers for their first program: "This is the world/Have faith."

Lindsay Anderson, though acknowledged as leader and spokesman of the Free Cinema group, was the last to arrive at features. Curiously, his first, *This Sporting Life* (1963), if it marked a high point in the social-realist cycle, also indicated a turning away from the sources that had given that demimovement its character and strength. From a novel and script adaptation by David Storey, it has the requisite general characteristics of northern industrial town and working-class background. Where it departs from the other films is in its concentration on the tortured love affair between

Saturday Night and Sunday Morning ◆ U.K., 1960, Karel Reisz; Albert Finney, right rear.

the miner-turned-footballer and his widowed landlady, and in its flashback sequences of surrealist exaggeration. At the time of its release Anderson was complimented by British reviewers for having broken out of the confines of the social-realist films, with their air of objectivity and use of the representative to make their criticism stick, into richer areas of individual feeling, the traditional concerns of great art. Perhaps what was by then being referred to as the "kitchen sink" school of film making was limited in certain important ways and had run its course. Whatever the reasons, *This Sporting Life* along with *Billy Liar* (directed by John Schlesinger in the same year) proved to be the last films directly connected with the line that had begun with *Room at the Top*. Of the directors who worked in it, Anderson stuck closest to the earlier commitments (and made the fewest features). *If . . .* (1969), *O Lucky Man!* (1973), and *Britannia Hospital* (1982), though different in subjects and settings, grew out of the same impulses of social criticism as the earlier films.

It was Schlesinger who proved to be the real transitional figure leading on to the next phase of British film. His *A Kind of Loving* (1962) belongs in the social-realist line, with its young draftsman protagonist who gets a woman pregnant and enters reluctantly into marriage. *Billy Liar,* on the other hand, though set in the North and about a young man of the middle class and the thwarting of his ambitions, is more concerned with his amusing neurotic eccentricities and Walter-Mitty-like fantasies than with class-based causes. It also introduced Julie Christie, who would star in Schlesinger's next film, *Darling* (1965). It was the success of this latter film that confirmed the end of the social-realist cycle and heralded a new "swinging London." About a spoiled and charming model who sleeps around more and enjoys it less,

Darling could have been made anywhere. To the extent that it is about the loss of values and the restlessness among the affluent, and given the modish direction, you might have thought it came from France or Italy. In the brief boom of which it was part, "British" films as often as not had American or Italian, French or Polish directors. And the subjects, well the subjects had merely become part of an undifferentiated cinematic Esperanto. The "mid-Atlantic films" (for example, *Casino Royale* and *You Only Live Twice* in 1967), which seemed to come from no culture of their own, were compounded out of American capital and diverse ingredients taken from recent international successes.

In the past the documentary influence contributed to some of the most interesting and distinctive cycles of British fiction production. In each instance, once the documentary impulse was lost much of the significance and quality seemed to disappear as well—at least the succeeding films tended to lose their national character. It might be argued that the quiet genius of British cinema has always pointed most surely in the direction of realism and what John Grierson called the documentary idea.

It is as exciting as it is rare when the cumbersome and expensive machinery of the entertainment film can be geared to problems of national concern. When this happens, as in the Soviet silent films of the late twenties or the Italian neorealist films of the late forties, the resulting aesthetic richness and experimentation is accompanied by evolving theory which opens up still other areas of this relatively unexplored medium. In Britain in the early sixties something of the sort occurred briefly on a small scale with the social-realist features. For a while, as the young members of Free Cinema came together with the young men and women of theater and literature who had been tackling similar themes, the veracity of documentary detail was warmed and strengthened by the addition of story and character. Perhaps those who made the social-realist features between 1958 and 1963 got some of the older documentarians' preoccupations and methods more widely and effectively before a larger public.

♦ GOTHIC HORROR FILMS

Paralleling the developments out of documentary that began in the mid-fifties with Free Cinema and culminated in the early sixties with the social-realist features, there appeared a completely contrasting but equally distinctive line of British cinema. The horror series from a small studio named Hammer Films followed the tradition of the Gothic horror story, every bit as indigenous as the impulses towards social-realism and self-improvement which had given rise to the documentary. In fact the Gothic tradition had its beginnings in the eighteenth- and nineteenth-century English novel, appearing full-blown in Mary Shelley's *Frankenstein* and Bram Stoker's *Dracula*. In hindsight it seems curious that the Americans rather than the British were the first to make sustained screen use of this heritage, but the Universal horror series of the thirties already discussed was rather more indebted to German expressionism than to English literary models. By the mid-fifties the Americans had virtually abandoned conventional horror movies in favor of science fiction, leaving the field open to the British.

No one seems to know exactly how Hammer happened onto the horror genre, but its entrance occurred in that year of 1956 which witnessed the Suez debacle as well as the appearance of Free Cinema and the first stage production of Osborne's *Look Back in Anger.* There is no obvious, let alone necessary, connection between the rise of the horror films and the rest of those events. Superficially, at least, the Hammer series would seem as far removed from contemporary reality and seriousness of purpose as one could imagine. The British critics found the films meretricious in style; in search of redeeming social value, they found none. Their reviews were hostile in the extreme, especially toward what appeared to them to be gratuitous and excessive violence and gore. The public, of course, loved the horror cycle from the outset. The critics, eventually, would be faced with a series at the National Film Theatre devoted to Hammer Films.

The first of the Hammer horrors, *The Curse of Frankenstein,* produced in late 1956 and released in early 1957, became a phenomenal success, not only in Britain but abroad, including especially in the United States. It was followed by *Dracula,* which also became enormously popular throughout the world. These two films staked out Hammer's claims, never seriously challenged, on the two prototypical horror stories. The immediate progeny (*The Revenge of Frankenstein,* 1957; *The Brides of Dracula,* 1960) were soon joined by many other close and distant relatives. David Pirie, in his appreciative study, *A Heritage of Horror: The English Gothic Cinema, 1946–1972,* points to *The Devil Rides Out* (1968, entitled *The Devil's Bride* in the United States) as one of the most masterful achievements within the general field. Though not dealing with either of the prototypical stories directly, it includes many of the most significant thematic and stylistic elements of the genre as a whole.

Pirie insists that the films of Hammer and its imitators are distinctively English Gothic as opposed to European. He attributes the attraction of English audiences to the earlier Gothic literature and the later films to the repressions of Victorian morality. These forms fed a fascination with death and violence and sexuality by cloaking them in the exoticism of distant places, supernatural powers, and fanciful scientific imaginings. The English treatment of the mythic elements in these tales has a robustness and conviction, Pirie contends, devoid of the self-conscious artiness of certain European Gothic strains. He also makes the point that the horror genre, as developed by Hammer and its rivals, "remains the only staple cinematic myth which Britain can properly claim as its own, and which relates to it in the same way as the western relates to America."[3]

The principal director at work in the horror films was Terence Fisher. He inaugurated the entire cycle with *The Curse of Frankenstein* and worked almost exclusively for Hammer from that point on. Most interesting, in part because most representative, Fisher's work in the Horror genre rests securely on the archetypal struggle between good and evil. The dualities of light and darkness, spirit and matter, are rigidly maintained as the trappings of ritual formulae, sacred books, crucifixes, and the like

---

[3]David Pirie, *A Heritage of Horror: The English Gothic Cinema, 1946–1972* (London: Gordon Fraser Gallery, 1973), p. 9.

The Devil Rides Out/The Devil's Bride ◆ U.K., 1968, Terence Fisher.

are set in opposition to the vampires, werewolves, and monsters of all kinds who populate the films. Pirie argues that Fisher more than any other British director can lay claim to a recognizable and coherent worldview presented throughout his work. He was greatly aided in this by the repertory acting company at Hammer. Two male stars closely identified with the horror films contributed much to their success: Peter Cushing and Christopher Lee. Both appeared in the initial *Curse of Frankenstein* and *Dracula* and alone and together throughout much of the series.

The earlier concentration of key personnel and artistic elements in the Hammer production subsequently became diffused into other sorts of films, some of the appealing simplicity and clarity becoming lost in an increasing sophistication on the part of film makers and audiences alike. Noting this perhaps inevitable evolutionary process, Pirie concludes his study with the following observation:

> *Perhaps the highest compliment that can be paid to any popular form is to acknowledge some of England's most powerful and idiosyncratic myth-cycles, using the most exciting medium yet for fantasy and dream—the cinema—to rediscover crucial elements of the Romantic experience.*[4]

[4]Pirie, *A Heritage of Horror,* p. 168.

But by this time artistic traditions completely unfamiliar to western audiences had become available as films from Japan, then India, then China began to circulate globally. This cultural expansion of cinematic experience began at the Venice International Film Festival as another country stepped into the spotlight. The year was 1951, the country Japan. The film was *Rashomon,* and its director, Akira Kurosawa, would soon be recognized among the world's great film makers, along with a number of his compatriots.

FILMS OF THE PERIOD

1947
Hue and Cry (Charles Crichton)

1949
Passport to Pimlico (Henry Cornelius)
A Run for Your Money (Charles Frend)
Whiskey Galore/Tight Little Island
      (Alexander Mackendrick)

1951
The Lavender Hill Mob (Crichton)
The Man in the White Suit (Mackendrick)

1953
Genevieve (Cornelius)
The Titfield Thunderbolt (Crichton)

1954
The Maggie/High and Dry (Mackendrick)

1955
The Lady Killers (Mackendrick)

1957
The Curse of Frankenstein
      (Terence Fisher)

1958
Carry on Sergeant (Gerald Thomas)
Dracula (Fisher)
Room at the Top (Jack Clayton)

1959
Carry on Nurse (Thomas)
Look Back in Anger (Tony Richardson)

1960
The Entertainer (Richardson)
Saturday Night and Sunday Morning (Karel
      Reisz)

1961
A Taste of Honey (Richardson)

1962
A Kind of Loving (John Schlesinger)
The Loneliness of the Long Distance Runner
      (Richardson)

1963
Billy Liar (Schlesinger)
The Leather Boys (Sidney Furie)
This Sporting Life (Lindsay Anderson)

BOOKS ON THE PERIOD

Barr, Charles, ed., *All Our Yesterdays: 90 Years of British Cinema.* London: British Film Institute, 1987
Hutchings, Peter, *Hammer and beyond: The British Horror Film.* Manchester, UK: Manchester University Press, 1993
Landy, Marcia, *British Genres: Cinema and Society, 1930–1960.* Princeton, NJ: Princeton University Press, 1991

12

Asian Film

◆ ◆ ◆

1951–

We in the West have been slow in becoming familiar with eastern cinema. Our acquaintance has generally begun at international film festivals—especially those held at Cannes, Venice, Berlin, and Edinburgh. On these occasions work of film makers from countries around the world is seen, reported in the press, and sometimes acquired for distribution. At the time of *Rashomon*'s appearance, we knew little about film production in Asia except that reputedly large and heavily commercial industries seemed to be turning out entertainment aimed mainly at huge domestic audiences, at other countries in Asia, and at Asian populations living elsewhere in the world. Along with Japan, eventually India, Hong Kong, China, and Taiwan, in roughly that order, caught our attention with world-class films that have received some distribution internationally.

◆ JAPAN

Rashomon was particularly astonishing in that, not only was it clearly the work of an impressive individual talent, it suggested a whole industry and film culture able to support the sophistication of its conception and technique. This indeed proved to be the case. Subsequently we learned that *Rashomon* was by no means the only important Japanese film nor Kurosawa the sole great film maker; on the contrary, Japan had a distinguished cinematic history and many other film artists of considerable eminence. In 1952, the year after *Rashomon*, the American military occupation of Japan ended. The Japanese were then free to pursue their film destiny without foreign supervision. By the fifties Japan was producing over five hundred films a year, more than any other nation.

The structure of the Japanese industry was curiously like the "classic" American one of the thirties and forties (which was breaking up in the fifties): six major production companies controlled distribution and the theater circuits as well. Japanese film also had popular genres, some with close American counterparts. In a general way Japanese films were divided into two main categories: *jidai-geki*, or historical films, and *gendai-geki*, or contemporary films. The division between "historical" and "contemporary" times was marked by the year 1868, when the Emperor Meiji acceded to the throne and first opened Japan to commercial and cultural exchange with the West. It was during his reign that the country passed from feudalism to a modern way of life. Because the change was both sudden and radical, Japanese society in the contemporary period offered a striking contrast to that of the historical period. The two categories of films were also in sharp contrast to each other because each faithfully depicted the mores, thought, and feeling of the two periods. Each category had its own conventions, not only in regard to sets and costumes, but also production style and even acting. Studios, directors, and actors tended to specialize in one or the other of the two modes. The *jidai-geki* (historical) accounted for only forty percent of Japanese production, but it enjoyed constant popularity with the domestic audience and achieved the first successes abroad.

After its victory at Venice, *Rashomon* was distributed internationally. Daie Motion Picture Company, which had produced it, was Japan's most prestigious studio, like an earlier M-G-M. Daie followed *Rashomon* with other films sent out into (and possibly in part produced for) world distribution. Masaichi Nagata, the Irving Thalberg of Daie, to pursue the analogy, was producer of many of these. *Ugetsu* (1953) came next, directed by the veteran Kenji Mizoguchi. *Gate of Hell* (1953), the first Japanese film in the new Eastman Color, was directed by Teinosuke Kinugasa. Kurosawa's *Seven Samurai* (1954) reached the United States in a truncated version: two-and-a-half rather than three-and-a-half hours long. His *Ikiru*, though produced earlier (1952), followed. The latter was the first of the *gendai-geki* (contemporary films) to be seen here. The lovely Machiko Kyo, who appeared in the first three Japanese films to be imported, was much appreciated abroad, and Toshiro Mifune, whose finest work has been done with Kurosawa, established an international reputation with *Rashomon* and *Seven Samurai*.

Yet when the Japanese films began to arrive they seemed considerably more foreign than the films of other, western nations; perhaps they still do. It was not that the Japanese had invented a separate cinematic language; their films were as intelligible to American audiences as any others requiring subtitles. If the world hadn't seen Japanese films until the early 1950s, the Japanese had been seeing the world's films since the late 1890s, and their use of the medium had developed along lines parallel to those of other countries. The differences appeared to be more cultural, or in any case stylistic, than grammatical or syntactical.

Even when the themes were universal in significance, they received an interpretation and emphasis embodying unfamiliar assumptions and artistic conventions. In treatment there often seemed to American audiences a sentimentality, different in kind, no doubt, more than in degree from our own. This sentimentality was not so evident in the first, carefully selected exports and occurs more in the modern than in the period films. A didactic quality also seemed common (and presumably generally accepted) in Japanese cinema.

A final major difference was the pacing, which appeared generally slower than that of the West, Kurosawa usually an exception. Shots and scenes were allowed to extend beyond the requirements of the narrative point being made, seemingly to let audiences savor the feelings just expressed. If American film makers most frequently concerned themselves with action and Europeans with the psychology of character, as was sometimes said, the Japanese seemed to be more interested in overall mood and atmosphere.

Other, more precise formal characteristics were equally noteworthy, especially in contrast to the immediately preceding Italian neorealism. Many of the Japanese films are very beautiful, visually elegant. If one of them were stopped at random during projection, any frame held on the screen would probably be perfect in terms of composition and lighting. Long passages without dialogue give emphasis to the image. With a cultural tradition that places great importance on the visual arts, Japanese directors and cinematographers thought as painters. Their frame lines always serve as organizational matrices for graphic design as well as for enclosing chunks of content. Planes of action seem constantly to be considered and shots painstakingly composed in depth—foreground in relation to middle ground in relation to background.

These visual characteristics are especially striking in *Ugetsu* (and in Mizoguchi's work generally, we later discovered). In it images were designed not only to create feelings of unease or of calm security, but also to offer aesthetic pleasure in the very arrangement and balance of the blacks, whites, and grays. The full-color palette of *Gate of Hell* allowed for the most dynamic and dramatic use of color film anyone had seen up to that point—especially in its first glowing orange-red scenes of violent action in a civil war. Camera movements, too—for these films are full of kinetic energy along with their careful pictorial qualities—had a calculation and control in relation to subject movement that frequently results in a kind of cinematic dance. In *Rashomon* the shots of the woodsman moving through the forest, the camera tracking with him and tilting up into the sunlight glinting down through the tall trees, are a breathtaking example. *Rashomon* suggested what would be confirmed by *Seven Samurai*: that Kurosawa was a special master of camera movement. Another even more extraordinary instance in *Rashomon* occurs when Machiko Kyo weaves about after yielding to the bandit, confronting her husband's accusing stare as the camera swoops, backs, and glides with her. Reviewers resorted to phrases like "painting in motion" to describe the visual riches the Japanese films offered, and after the deliberate austerities and rough irregularities of the Italian neorealists, this was heady stuff indeed.

Stylistically still, but in terms of performance, the Japanese films drew on another ancient artistic tradition—that of the theater. Classical Nō plays, which go back for centuries, and the popular Kabuki have both reflected and influenced Japanese culture generally. They seem to represent a true expression of national sentiment and belief, at least of the older Japan, which evidently were giving way more slowly and less fundamentally than appeared on the surface. Donald Richie, American authority on Japanese cinema, has insisted that Kabuki hasn't really affected the Japanese film to any great extent. Kurosawa has said much the same thing in regard to his own work, with an obvious exception in a film like *The Men Who Tread on the Tiger's Tail* (1952). That may be, and yet there is something very different from western perform- ance styles in the Japanese historical (not the contemporary) films. A composite outline of the conventional samurai films (of which *Gate of Hell* is one example; *Samurai*, 1954, directed by Hiroshi Inagaki, another) may suggest some of the differences.

A young warrior is in love with his lord's wife. Out of loyalty to his master he does not show that love. The acting in the first two-thirds of the picture would be not only restrained but extremely formalized. We can infer that each gesture and every movement (as well as costumes, makeup, and hairdos) have some sort of fixed and known meaning. An enormous tension is built up through this constraint of powerful feeling expressed in behavior limited by rigid, social/aesthetic convention. Then, when the young warrior can bear it no longer and his passion overleaps those self- and societally-imposed bounds, he pursues the lady, fights the lord, and gives vent to his charged-up store of emotion. There never had been seen such full-blown repre- sentation of lust and anger, such lunging and sweating, crawling and panting. The cold, inscrutable Oriental indeed! *Rashomon* first showed us these two extremes of performance—theatrical stylization in the trial scene, earthy naturalism in the bandit's behavior—within a single film. How important the Japanese theatrical tradition is to the themes and characters and style of the historical films is impossible for an uninitiated westerner to say. That the elements described above add to their exotic charm in the West is undeniable.

Exotic charm is part of the problem in evaluating these films that come out of a culture and tradition so vastly different from the Greco-Judeo-Christian one. We cannot always be certain to what extent they are offering new filmic possibilities that might be incorporated into international cinema at large, or to what extent we are merely responding to things Japanese seen for the first time through their films. Perhaps the distinction is unimportant, yet I am intrigued by reports that the Japanese films most valued in the West are frequently not those that have found high favor with Japanese audiences and critics. Evidently there is a greater difference in this regard than between, say, Italian and American response to Italian films. We are told that the historical films usually are based on ancient legends well known to the Japanese audience. The stories about The Forty-Seven Ronin (masterless samurai), for exam- ple, have been the source for a good many films, those of Inagaki among the most popular. What can seem a lack of plausibility or of character motivation to us—a difficulty in *Gate of Hell*, for example—may be attributable to the film makers' assumption that viewers will be familiar with the source material or at least the attitudes of an earlier time. Japanese film makers may feel they can jump over certain connecting incidents, or omit supporting ideas and emotions, and that their audience will still be with them at the next juncture. Classical Greek dramatists did something of the sort in their segmentation and interpretation of Greek history and legend. But in addition, and much more basic, isn't it inevitable that Japanese literary and dramatic conventions and even life itself would operate by different rules and psychological understandings than they do in the West? Joseph Anderson, in comparing "Japanese Swordfighters and American Gunfighters," stated that "The Japanese unities are not those of plot, time and place, character, viewpoint, or thesis but are rather those of mood, tone, rhythm, effect."[1] From the period films we learn that the Japanese historical experience has had certain similarities to that of western nations, feudalism for instance, as well as certain differences, such as religion. It is the differences that fascinate most.

A philosophical stance, growing out of the Japanese historical experience, appears in the modern as well as the period films. It is distinctively and characteristically Japanese and is identified by one of those terms for which translators offer a sensible-enough English explanation but add that the concept remains essentially untranslatable. The phrase in this case is *mono no aware*. According to Richie, in *Japanese Cinema*, it means something like "that awareness of the transience of all earthly things, the knowledge that it is, perhaps fortunately, impossible to do anything about it: that celebration of resignation in the face of things as they are."[2] Mizoguchi's films have this attitude in abundance, and the opening and closing shots of *Ugetsu* are its visual expression. The original title, *Ugetsu Monogatari*, translates as "Tales of the Pale and Mysterious Moon after the Rain." Set in the sixteenth century, the film begins with a slow overhead pan across the countryside, then a tilt down and dollylike movement toward two couples. They are frantically loading a cart with pottery, while the noises of war are heard in the background. This is exceptionally economical exposition, to be sure. The shot also manages to suggest that the lives and events with which we will be concerned are embedded in a universal and timeless whole—the land and the people which go on—made up of ephemeral human existences and changing historical conditions. *Ugetsu* ends with the camera moving up and away from the potter's small son (while his dead mother's voice is heard on the sound track), back across the landscape. (Mizoguchi's *Sansho Dayu/The Bailiff*, 1954, employs much the same device.)

That initial cluster of five films opening the world's screens to Japanese cinema introduced us to two of Japan's greatest film makers: Akira Kurosawa and Kenji Mizoguchi. Both carry their personal concerns from film to film whether the setting is modern or feudal. The work of the third, Yasujiro Ozu, is even more resolutely fixed on certain themes and is always set in contemporary Japan. Of the three, in terms of content and style, **Kurosawa** is the most easily appreciated by Westerners.

Rashomon, for example, seems to require no special sense of Japanese culture or sympathy for a foreign point of view. It is based on two stories by the popular author Ryunosuke Akutagawa, who was much influenced by western culture. Though set in the Heian period (794 to 1184), its four-times-told tale of a rape (or seduction), murder (or suicide), and robbery (or disappearance) is indebted to Robert Browning's novel-length poem *The Ring and the Book*, while the musical score is a close imitation of Maurice Ravel's *Bolero*. This acknowledgement is not meant to detract from the originality and power of Kurosawa's film; but rather, simply to point out that it was

[1] J. L. Anderson, "Japanese Swordfighters and American Gunfighters," *Cinema Journal*, 12 (Spring 1973): 21.

[2] Donald Richie, *Japanese Cinema: Film Style and National Character* (Garden City, NY: Doubleday, 1971), p. 77.

Rashomon ♦ Japan, 1950, Akira Kurosawa; Toshiro Mifune, Masayuki Mori, and Machiko Kyo.

made in a cinematic *lingua franca* available to all. According to reports it was at first more fully appreciated in the West than in Japan. *Rashomon* was subsequently redone in the United States by Martin Ritt as *The Outrage* (1964).

Seven Samurai brings out even more remarkable, because pervasive, parallels between the samurai films and the American western. This is especially true in films of Kurosawa, and quite directly in relation to the westerns of John Ford, which Kurosawa is known to admire. Substitute swords for six-guns and samurai warriors for professional gunslingers, and much else remains the same. In 1960, *Seven Samurai* was remade into *The Magnificent Seven* by John Sturges. Kurosawa's *Yojimbo* (1961) and *Sanjuro* (1962), along with their other meanings, are obviously deliberate parodies of the western, although Joseph Anderson, in the article referred to earlier, is no doubt more accurate in stating that what is being parodied are the conventions most common to both the *jidai-geki* and the American western.

Seven Samurai is set in the sixteenth century at a transitional time when the ancient and honorable profession of the samurai was coming to an end as gun powder and new military tactics appeared. The samurai we see have fallen on hard times, and in their unemployment a group of them accept a proposal by a committee of peasants to protect their village from bandit raids. The film combines discerning psychological observation with stunningly choreographed action and violence. Each of the seven warriors is carefully delineated. The leader and eldest (Takashi Shimura, who also plays the woodcutter in *Rashomon* and the lead in *Ikiru*) is a compelling personality. He eschews wasteful bloodshed, advocates strategy over force, is wise, calm, and compassionate, with a sad acceptance of his destiny for leadership. Of the others, one samurai is tired of fighting, another is cool and skillful, a third bloodthirsty, a fourth a frightened youth, and so on. Crammed with action, the larger scenes of the bandits attacking the village are shot and cut with immense dynamism. The film is meant to be enjoyed for the kind of empathic release such material can provide when formally controlled; the separate shots are intricate and precise in their composition, movement, and rhythm. The insistently used telephoto lens compressed the images in a way that gives them a strange muted power. Kurosawa has no superior at this kind of film making. His *Throne of Blood* (1957), a version of *Macbeth*, offers more of the same.

In *Seven Samurai* the action of the smaller, more intimate scenes carries with it fuller emotional meaning. But even then Kurosawa worked through physical movement, and camera and cutting in relation to it. For example, there is the scene in which the preeminent swordsman is introduced. He is challenged by another samurai to a test of skill, using staffs in place of swords. The result is contested: The challenger says that their blows landed at the same time; the master says the other would be dead. The former foolishly insists they fight again, with swords. When the great swordsman cuts his adversary down, he shows little emotion, simply having proved what he already knew. His interest is solely in further perfecting his awesome skill. The two seduction scenes between the youngest samurai and a peasant girl—one on a sunny

Seven Samurai ♦ Japan, 1954, Akira Kurosawa.

flower-covered hillside, the other in the dark interior of a hut dappled by light—are also played largely with their bodies. His intense shyness and uneasy attraction and her almost wild abandonment to awakened sensuality are portrayed wordlessly, with beautifully exact gesture and movement. A final instance of Kurosawa's exceptional ability to transmute the physical into the emotional occurs in the scene of the raid on the bandits' fort. In the eerie early morning light amidst a surrealist, Dantesque inferno of fire, torn bodies, and steaming pool, there is a haunting exchange between a husband and wife. She has come out of the burning fort after having been kept there as a concubine since the last raid. As she stands at the door, he runs to her; they look at each other for a full minute; nothing is said; then she turns and runs back into the flames.

In Kurosawa's films set in contemporary times, he tends to subdue this kind of direct sensory appeal. Instead he keeps us focused on the subtler, more complex characters and on the sorts of social problems that more clearly show his dimension as a humanist. *Ikiru*, made in the same year as de Sica's and Zavattini's *Umberto D*, bears some resemblance to the Italian film. It concerns an inconsequential petty official who, after learning he has cancer, tries to instill some meaning into his life as he faces death. His final positive act of helping create a playground in a poor section allows him to die satisfied, but it sets off social and political reverberations that are reviewed and discussed in a crazy drunken Joycian wake. In its complicated and experimental structure *Ikiru* descends in personal tragedy during the first two-thirds and then ascends back over the same material throughout the last third, with wry social comment and a sort of bitter comedy reinterpreting on a broader scale what we have seen. *Red Beard* (1965) is regarded by Richie as Kurosawa's masterpiece. At the same time he concedes that we must be able to look through and beyond its sentimental surface to get at the greatness of the film. The title character (played by Toshiro Mifune) is a crotchety, selfless, driven physician who devotes his whole life to treating the poor. His qualities are revealed to us as they are discovered by a young intern who comes to study under him. The film follows the young man's maturation and final success in finding his true self—his vocation, almost in the religious as well as practical sense. The kind of spiritual journey and discovery at the core of these two contemporary films appear frequently in Kurosawa's work. Even in his historical pieces he is always commenting on contemporary life, and the concerns are profoundly social and moral.

A similar use of historical material containing lasting cultural values and psychological truths typifies the films of **Kenji Mizoguchi**, though the ratio of historical to contemporary in his work is much higher than in Kurosawa's. Also, Mizoguchi's attitudes, subjects, and style are more traditionally Japanese, and therefore his films have been less widely appreciated in America and Europe. *Ugetsu* tackles the big themes with disarming simplicity—a kind of elementariness. Also set in the sixteenth century, it deals with war and peace in relation to work and love; or perhaps, even more simply and broadly, war as it affects the total human condition. It centers around two brothers, a potter and a farmer, and their wives. The profiteering that wartime makes possible goads both men into an inordinate desire for gain. The potter wants money to buy extravagant presents for his wife and child, the farmer to equip himself as a samurai in order to impress his wife. While in the city selling his pots, the potter is seduced (partly through flattery about the aesthetic qualities of his pottery) by a mysterious and finally sinister Lady Wakasa. She causes him to abandon his wife for the sensuality and luxury she seems to offer. During the same time the farmer comes to be regarded as a military commander through a faked heroic exploit. But the potter is no more an artist (nor should be) than the farmer is a warrior, Mizoguchi seems to be saying. Work ought to be for its own sake, not for money (or false praise for creativity), nor for glory (based on feigned valor). Also, it should be part of the family, not done away from home with the results brought back.

In *Ugetsu* both work and war have for goals material wealth and women's love. But false ambitions are suggested and made possible by war, leading men away from true satisfactions. They are carried away from their wives and proper married love to erotic refinement (Lady Wakasa) on the one hand or animal lust (raping and whoring) on the other. The wives are destroyed by wartime conditions of hunger and rapine and by the husbands' desertion. The end of the film marks a return to the original state: work in peace, and conjugal and parental love.

Stylistically Mizoguchi's films are even more "painterly" than Kurosawa's. His shaping of the visual-dramatic content takes place within the shot more than through juxtaposition of shots. Composition is always conceived in depth, often with objects at the side of the frame in foreground to accentuate the perspective. Also, he uses the long shot quite deliberately to frame action at a distance; for example, there are the repeated views across the courtyard of Lady Wakasa's house, the scenes of the soldiers pillaging the village, the shot of the farmer shopping for armor seen at a distance and from behind the armorer. Mizoguchi's frequent pans, too, are used pointedly as a compositional device rather than merely to follow action. One particularly memorable usage of the sort is the high-angled pan across the refugees from the village as they are camping for the night. In constructing his scenes he typically allows the camera to pick up action and then follow it remorselessly to its conclusion. But unlike the films of the German silent film makers who worked this way, there is an enormous amount of action within Mizoguchi's shots, and sharp contrasts—calm to frenetic, lyrical to horrifying—from scene to scene. He likes to have action explode into frame. Looting soldiers move around a corner and emerge in the middle of the frame, the potter's wife rushes directly toward the camera (shot from low angle with short-focal-length lens) and scoops up her child right under our noses. Entrances are frequently from behind the camera—from right or left and sometimes from below— which creates a startling, disruptive effect.

Mizoguchi seems equally concerned with the sound track. In *Ugetsu* the music is extremely important. More of it is oriental than western, the opposite of Kurosawa's usual practice, and it is fully integrated with the visuals. It complements and frequently takes precedence over the dialogue. In part it is used in place of natural sounds; elsewhere as *leit motif*, evocative and symbolic. The bright piercing bell of Lady Wakasa's theme is matched by a gently melodic ensemble of bells in the return of the potter's wife. On the other hand, cries in the background sometimes supply an almost musical accompaniment to the action. When the two men and the farmer's wife

Ugetsu ♦ Japan, 1953
Kenji Mizoguchi; Kinuyo
Tanaka and Masayuki
Mori.

leave the potter's wife and child on the shore of the lake, the farewells become a melancholy round. The ghost of Lady Wakasa's father groans in eerie and wordless recitative accompanied by strange and discordant instrumentation.

Thematically rich as they are, Mizoguchi's films may finally be most valuable for their total, combined use of sensory resources. He can create a mood, an atmosphere that encapsulates characters and ideas, making them seem truly and fully representative of the culture and its history. Inevitably, therefore, his films must at first appear somewhat exotic to us. At the same time they can be seen as both universal in the significance of their artistic statements and uniquely beautiful in themselves.

In contrast not only to the work of Mizoguchi and Kurosawa but to that of almost any other film maker of any country you might think of, the style of **Yasujiro Ozu** is marked by the most rigorous austerity. In later films he rarely moved the camera, and then slightly and slowly solely to accommodate the action. Interiors predominate in his films and the action consists almost entirely of conversation among a few people. He worked exclusively in the formerly standard three-by-four screen ratio; though he used color when it became available to him for his last pictures, it was always muted and unemphatic, as if he were trying to keep the full palette from distracting. Characteristically, his camera sits at seated eye level, as if part of a formal tea ceremony, unblinkingly observing two of his characters reacting to each other. Very often the pair is made up of one old person and one young adult—an old man and a young woman perhaps most frequently in the final films. For above all Ozu was concerned with the relationships between the traditional ways and the newer ones in a changing Japan. Implicit in all his films is an awareness of the extraordinary cultural dislocations that began to occur when Japan was opened to the West in the late nineteenth century and have increased in geometric progression with each passing decade. Ozu observed these changes and tensions not on a broad social scale but within the intimacy of the family unit—parents and children, husband and wife—where they finally have their deepest effect. His view is a calm and balanced one. Though sad to see the old go, he has to acknowledge its passing, with sympathy but without complaint—*mono no aware*. Of the three giants of Japanese cinema, Ozu is unquestionably the most "Japanese."

What Ozu's films are incalculably rich in is the observation of human behavior in the most ordinary and universal of situations. In *Late Autumn* (1960), for example, he is concerned with a widow, her twenty-four-year-old daughter, and the deceased husband's three old college friends who involve themselves with trying to find suitable mates for both mother and daughter. At the emotional center of the film is the mother's reluctance to lose her daughter, which she tries to check, and the daughter's growing desire to marry, stubbornly denied even to herself out of loyalty and affection for her mother. The so subtly changing situation is observed most dis-

Late Autumn ◆ Japan, 1960, Yasujiro Ozu; Setsuko Hara and Yoko Tsukasa.

creetly—we learn no more about the characters than they know about each other—but for all of the quietness and control of Ozu's people, they possess a wonderful amount of robustness. Practical and realistic, they are willing to restrain their desires when necessary; at the same time they know the pleasures to be found in this world are those of the senses and feelings—eating, drinking, sex, and most of all, love and companionship.

Abundant humor is interlaced throughout with tenderness and sadness; bawdy talk can exist within the confines of good manners. Ozu's narratives are like those of a kindly and merry old grandfather who doesn't need the large and exceptional events and characters conventionally required by storytellers. With astounding clarity and economy, through a few words, a tentative gesture, a partial smile, he makes a viewer feel "Yes, I know that person," or "Yes, something like that has surely happened countless times in many cultures." Ozu's genius was very special: an ability to put life back together whole out of closely observed bits and pieces. His films, in total, form an extraordinary tapestry, depicting the everyday, the intimate, the habitual, the lived-in world of unglamorous work and a few enduring relationships that comprise life for most of us. How many tapestries can there be that so celebrate the ordinary?

Accompanying and succeeding the work of Kurosawa, Mizoguchi, and Ozu are the films of a small host of other noteworthy directors. Among those whose films have elicited the most sympathetic and sustained appreciation abroad are Kon Ichikawa, Masaki Kobayashi, Nagisa Oshima, and Masahiro Shinoda. The major works of all four contain elements of social criticism, one of the characteristics of modern Japanese cinema.

In the films of **Ichikawa** that have been shown in this country, he seems consistently concerned with dramatizing the conflict within people under peculiar stress. His films combine visual refinement—many of the images are memorable for their extraordinary beauty—with philosophical, even political statement; they tend toward allegory, or at least metaphor. *The Burmese Harp* (1956), his first international success, takes place at the end of World War II. The protagonist, a Japanese soldier separated from his unit, becomes converted to Buddhism. The values that had sustained him during the war are now meaningless to him, and he remains on alone in Burma to bury his fallen comrades. *Enjo* (1958) is about a young monk who, tortured by the hypocrisy and evil he sees around him, sets fire to and destroys a temple he loved more than anything else in the world. *Odd Obsession* (1959), a dark comedy, is an even more convoluted psychological study, centering on the hypereroticism, bizarre sexuality, and voyeurism of a kind of *ménage à quatre* made up of a middle-aged husband, younger wife, daughter, and her fiancé. *Fires on the Plain* (1959) returns to the Japanese army in defeat. Suffering the horrors of starvation while straggling across a hostile and alien landscape, some of the soldiers are finally driven to cannibalism. *Alone on the Pacific* (1963) deals with the obsession of a single man who attempts to cross the Pacific in a small sailboat. *An Actor's Revenge* (1963) is the story of a female impersonator in Kabuki theater. The subject of *Tokyo Olympiad* (1965), a gigantic documentary tribute to that athletic event, permitted Ichikawa to continue the themes of obsession and unusual stress. In it he humanized the competition with emphasis on the athletes and individuals in the crowds rather than on the events;

The Burmese Harp ♦
Japan, 1956, Kon
Ichikawa; Shoji Yasui.

Ichikawa's splendid visual flare and superb imagery of human bodies being pushed
to their utmost raise sports to the level of poetry.

Of **Masaki Kobayashi's** films, *Kwaidan* (1964), an elegantly beautiful anthology
of three period ghost stories, has been most popular in the United States. It does not
represent the main thrust of his work, however. He is especially noted for the consistent criticisms his films have leveled at aspects of Japanese social tradition, especially
as it extends into political and military systems. *Black River* (1957) exposed the crime
and corruption surrounding American military bases in occupied Japan. His massive
trilogy, "The Human Condition" (comprising *No Greater Love, Road to Eternity*, and
A Soldier's Prayer), was made between 1958 and 1961. The action takes place in
Japanese-occupied Manchuria from 1943 to 1945. It chronicles the fate of a young
pacifist intellectual forced into military service. He survives combat and, after the
Japanese collapse, is captured by the Russians. Escaping from prison, he dies on his
way to rejoin his wife. Antimilitary as well as antiwar, the trilogy aroused enormous
controversy in Japan. Though *Harakiri* (1962) is a *jidai-geki* samurai film, it presents
the traditional code of honor as senseless and destructive, a system ruled by a
corporate class that wreaks the cruelest of punishments on the individual (an impoverished young samurai is forced to disembowel himself with a bamboo sword blade)
in their efforts to keep themselves in power and the feudal system intact. The message
is clearly directed toward contemporary Japan.

Of the Japanese film makers discussed in this chapter, **Nagisa Oshima** is the most
"modern." Using narrative structures and techniques comparable to those of the
French Jean-Luc Godard, Oshima is yet profoundly Japanese in his sensibility, at least

Harakiri ◆ Japan, 1962, Masaki Kobayashi; Tatsuya Nakadai.

so it seems from the limited evidence available from his prolific output. The gentle, humanist criticism implicit in Ichikawa, the direct social-realist confrontation apparent in Kobayashi, become radical and revolutionary statements in Oshima. He challenges the moral assumptions underpinning Japanese society as well as its institutions. The values of the older generation are seen as neither valid nor relevant to the problems faced by youth, with whom he identifies.

Death by Hanging (1968) not only attacks capital punishment but goes further to suggest that the very concept of crime (and punishment) is a conception of the police, at considerable variance with actual human conduct and the motives behind it. It is the police rather than the criminal who are obsessed with crime. *Diary of a Shinjuku Thief* was made in the same year. Within an extremely fragmented structure and a mixture of modes, from the actuality of student riots to the artificiality of a ghost play, it links themes of sex as performance with theft as a revolutionary act. The film is dense and difficult; the actions of its individuals are intended to be read as symbolic statements about Japan. *Boy* (1969), based on a real incident, as was *Death By Hanging*, is about a child trained by his parents to run in front of moving autos to be hit and injured slightly so they can collect damages. It is about that particular situation, but the indictment, as Oshima has said, is not of the parents, but of a society that makes it necessary for them to live in that manner. In *The Ceremony* (1971), the plot revolves around a family for a period of twenty-five years since the end of the war.

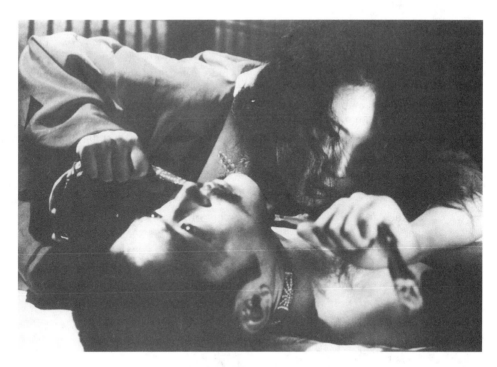

In the Realm of the Senses ♦ Japan, 1976, Nagisa Oshima; Tatsuya Fuji and Eiko Matsuda.

As they come together for weddings and funerals their traditional attitudes become increasingly divorced from the realities of modern life, their behavior ever more ritualistic, abstract, and finally strange.

However particular films of his may be interpreted, it can be said in general that, like other modern political film makers, Oshima has fashioned new forms to express new ideas. Disjunctive narrative, diverse styles within a given film, reality mingled with surrealist fantasy, formalized patterns achieving the effect of ritual—all are present in his work. His vision is frequently uniquely personal and difficult to comprehend in its complexity. As a Japanese film maker Oshima also offers images of exquisite beauty, especially unnerving (and thus suitable for his purposes) when they are of events horrifying in their human meanings.

Together with Oshima, **Masahiro Shinoda** is the most famous of Japan's Ofuna New Wave directors, who began their careers with the same sort of defiant modernism that characterized the contemporaneous and better-known French movement, discussed in Chapter 14. Oshima and Shinoda were assistant directors at the Ofuna branch of Shochiku studios, whose specialty in the highly stratified Japanese film industry was roughly equivalent to Hollywood's "women's pictures."[3] Shinoda's *Pale*

[3]"Dialogue on Film: Masahiro Shinoda" (interview, translated by Audie Bock), *American Film*, 10 (May 1985): 10–13.

Flower (1964) is said to be his first important film. Though it was not shown in this country, his *With Beauty and Sorrow* (1965), *Punishment Island* (1966), and *The Scandalous Adventures of Buraikan* (1970) were. It was *Double Suicide* (1969), however, that swept the festivals and earned him international notice. Based on a classical play about the conflict between love and duty, the stylistic devices of the traditional puppet theater from which the story was taken are fused with a fluid moving-camera style. The black-garbed puppeteers from the opening scenes in the theater remain hovering about the human characters throughout as a strange chorus heightening the sense of destiny and impending doom.

The "golden age" of Japanese cinema of the 1950s and 1960s came to an end by the mid-1970s. The situation in Japan paralleled developments in the United States, which will be dealt with in the next chapter. Television broadcasting began in 1954; by the early 1980s, ninety-nine percent of Japanese homes had color television sets. The old studio system broke down in the 1960s as the major companies faced declining audiences. Significant films from established directors were few in number and exceptions to the general scramble to match popular taste.

Double Suicide ◆ Japan, 1969, Masahiro Shinoda; Kichiemon Nakamura and Shima Inashita, right of black-garbed figure.

Of the three leading directors during the golden age, Mizoguchi died in 1956 and Ozu in 1963. From 1970 to 1985 Kurosawa made only three films. *Dersu Uzala* (1975), a Soviet-Japanese coproduction, is visually stunning in wide-screen color. Its title character and protagonist is a native hunter living in the wilds of Siberia. In *Kagemusha* (*The Shadow Warrior*, 1981) Kurosawa returned to the period of change in the last quarter of the sixteenth century, when Japan was beset by ceaseless internal wars. A poor thief is chosen for his resemblance to the dying leader of the Takeda clan to take the latter's place—to become a "kagemusha" (shadow warrior). At first frightened, the thief gradually becomes the man he is impersonating. Replete with large-scale period recreation and battling armies, the film moves from history to myth. *Ran* (1985), which translates as "chaos," Kurosawa made at the age of seventy-five. It is a version of *King Lear* (who is presented in Shakespeare's play as being that age). Transposed to the same period in which *Kagemusha* is set, Lear's three daughters become warlord sons.

As for the film makers of the subsequent generation, in 1985 Ichikawa remade *The Burmese Harp*. Though extremely popular at home, abroad it was generally thought to be excessively sentimental, anachronistic, and redundant. Kobayashi's *The Empty Table*, also 1985, received some praise at the Venice International Film Festival but little international distribution. Oshima and Shinoda, on the other hand, fared much better.

Oshima received his greatest international attention, not to say notoriety, with *In the Realm of the Senses* (1976). It centers exclusively on a couple obsessed with each other and with sensual experience; sexual activity, varied and sustained, is its content. It ends in death (for him) and madness (for her). *Realm of Passion* (1979), dealing with a pair of rural lovers, is a companion piece, though more restrained emotionally, less explicit sexually, and more social in its content. *Merry Christmas, Mr. Lawrence* (1983), with dialogue half in Japanese, half in English, is about life in a Japanese prisoner-of-war camp in Java in 1942.

Though these last three Oshima films mentioned contain much sex and violence—especially sexual violence—individual passions are set within political contexts, sometimes clearly evident, sometimes seeming to be more in Oshima's mind than on the screen. More recently, Oshima has worked in Europe; *Max, mon amour* (1986), made in France, is an example of this work. Max is a chimpanzee with whom a British diplomat's wife is having an affair of some sort.

Shinoda, in 1984, made *MacArthur's Children*, about Japan's postwar generation. (Shinoda was fourteen in 1945 at the time of Japan's defeat. General Douglas MacArthur was supreme commander of the Allied powers that ruled Japan until 1952.) With *Gonza the Spearman*, in 1987, Shinoda returned to another *bunraku* puppet play, written in 1717 by Chikamatsu, the source for his earlier *Double Suicide*. It too is a drama of sexual attraction and violent death; in this case a samurai and his master's wife, though innocent of suspected adultery, are tracked down and killed by the husband.

In the eighties a new genre of Japanese film appeared—irreverent satire focusing on contemporary society—made by new film makers. The cycle seems to have begun in 1983 with *Family Game*, directed by Yoshimitsu Morita. That film's main targets were the shortcomings of a family in which false standards for achievement and lack of communication prevail. Following its success, the actor who starred in it, Juzo Itami, then wrote and directed four brilliant satires in rapid succession: *The Funeral* (1984), *Tampopo* (1985), *A Taxing Woman* (1986), and *A Taxing Woman Returns* (1988).

The Funeral is said to have evolved out of Itami's own experience in handling his father-in-law's funeral rites. It is a concentrated study of the three days of a Buddhist wake seen from a comic perspective. The arcane intricacies of the ritual, scarcely remembered, and the cross-purposes, misunderstandings, and hypocrisies among the mourners provide the basis for a subdued sort of farce with an admixture of tenderness.

Tampopo does for food what *The Funeral* did for death. The story centers around the title character, whose name means Dandelion, and her efforts, aided by others, to cook a perfect noodle. An assortment of characters and situations, all of them related to food, are added to this main line, and film conventions, especially those of the American film, are parodied throughout. (It was promoted in the United States as the first noodle western.)

The Funeral ◆ Japan, 1984, Juzo Itami; Nobuko Miyamoto and Tsutomu Yamazaki, first row of black-clad mourners.

All four of these Itami films star his wife, Nobuko Miyamoto. In *A Taxing Woman* she plays the role of a resourceful government tax auditor obsessed with her job, who substitutes the satisfaction of bringing tax evaders to justice for sexual relationships, including in particular with an attractive, corrupt tax dodger she relentlessly pursues. The sequel also is a hilarious exposure of the corruption and inherent criminality of the patriarchal-capitalist power structure.

It seems significant and encouraging that *Family Game* and all three of Itami's films have been released in the United States. Other films in the same vein—*Crazy Family* and *Comic Magazine*, for example—have received more limited distribution. Though Japanese films don't move as freely about the globe as American or even French, they do appear frequently at international festivals and some play with modest success in the cities of the West. Each new work of Kurosawa continues to be required viewing by those who care seriously about the cinema. He has been followed by several generations of valuable and varied film makers since *Rashomon* surfaced in Venice more than forty years ago. Whereas before the fifties Japan was barely mentioned, if at all, in world film histories (written by Europeans and Americans), since that time we have come to realize that respectful attention is due.

♦ INDIA

In the number of films produced annually Japan was followed by India. (By the fifties the United States had become the third largest producer.) The Indian industry, even less known abroad than the Japanese, was apparently even more commercial and parochial in its outlook, with only a very occasional film of interest to anyone outside its own vast population. Indian cinema gained western consideration through another single entry in an international film festival. In 1956 at Cannes, *Pather Panchali* was voted the "best human document." It was the first film of a young director named Satyajit Ray. Appropriately, its screening followed right after a Kurosawa film, *I Live in Fear*. Unlike Kurosawa's works, however, Ray's film was created completely apart from his national film industry and was not representative of it. Whereas *Pather Panchali* made viewers think of the Italian neorealist films, in its deep social concern as well as in its use of nonactors and location shooting, in the rest of Indian film it seemed that the big studios turned out the most resolutely escapist entertainment in the world.

This output is currently in the range of 750 to 800 features a year, more than that of any other nation. Studios located in Bombay, Bangalore, Bhubaneswar, Calcutta, Hyderabad, Mysore, and Trivandrum contribute to that total in the sixteen officially recognized languages as well as in the others. Though most Indian popular films are based on contemporary social problems such as class conflict, caste, political corruption, and dowry, the formalistic and genre conventions are exceptionally restrictive. In their history, *Indian Film,* Erik Barnouw and S. Krishnaswamy observe that every film requires "a star, six songs, three dances." Running times are long—typically three hours—to give as full an evening's entertainment as possible. These conditions have to be met in order for the public to feel it is getting its rupees' worth. The Indian film audience is huge—roughly thirteen million a day—but the fixed low admission price and greed of the big studios keep film makers in petty competition with each other and their unadventurous films within the fixed mold. There are, of course, creative figures in the commercial sector who try to push the boundaries, but the standard approach is more of the same instead of something different.

From the outset **Satyajit Ray** was a maverick. A commercial artist by profession, he was one of the founders of the Calcutta Film Society and a passionate student of film. In his free time he saw as many movies as he could and paid particular attention to the work of such American directors as John Ford, William Wyler, Frank Capra, John Huston, and Billy Wilder. He was influenced strongly, he has said, by Flaherty's *Nanook of the North*, Jean Renoir's *The Southerner*, and "of course, all the Chaplins."[4]

In 1950 Ray met Renoir, who was in Calcutta shooting *The River*. Renoir encouraged him and permitted him to observe production. Later that year Ray was sent by his advertising agency employers to their headquarters in London for six months. While there he talked with leading British film critics and theorists and attended movies daily. He was especially inspired, he said, by de Sica's-Zavattini's *The Bicycle Thief*.

On the boat going home he wrote the first draft of the script for *Pather Panchali*, adapted from a popular novel. The film was almost an amateur production—in personnel as well as scale. Only two of the cast and only one of the crew of eight—the art director—were professionals. The cinematographer was an amateur still photographer. To show him what he wanted, Ray, who had never directed a film before, drew pen-and-ink sketches from the camera's viewpoint. Shot on weekends over a period of almost four years, production was frequently halted for lack of funds. Eventually the money ran out. Ray was about to give up when the West Bengal government agreed to back him in return for ownership of the film.

First of a trilogy (followed by *Aparajito*, 1956, and *The World of Apu*, 1958), *Pather Panchali* (1955) begins the account of a Bengali family of five during the 1920s, which extends from the time the boy Apu is about twelve, until he himself has a son about that age. In spite of its total three-feature length (each of the films can stand by itself, of course), the trilogy is not an epic in conception; or, at least, it is epic only by implication. When social, religious, and economic themes and problems appear it is within the detailed texture of the family's daily life. Out of the microcosm a true and accurate picture, of one kind of India at least, seems to emerge—from the inside out as it were. Yet Ray also achieves a rare degree of universal validity and timelessness because these people, as most people, are concerned primarily with the conflicts and loyalties of generations, familial and marital love, the necessity of maintaining existence (frequently at odds with the pursuit of an ideal), and fulfillment through satisfying work. He speaks for humankind as well as for Bengalis.

Pather Panchali, and *Aparajito* even more, is made up solely of diverse incidents from the life of the family. It has no story in the usual sense, nor is it documentary, obviously. If (maybe because) it lacks beginning, middle, and end, it flows as life itself

---

[4]Paul Grimes, "Indian Moviemaker Who Flees Escape," *The New York Times Magazine* (June 26, 1960): 42–43.

Pather Panchali ◆ India, 1955, Satyajit Ray; Karuna Banerji, Uma Das Gupta, and Subir Banerji.

to a degree scarcely equaled, even in the greatest of the Italian neorealist films. It ends when the father, who has been away trying to earn enough money to support the family, returns home. In his absence the aged aunt has died, and more recently and cruelly, his older child, a lovely adolescent girl, died of pneumonia caught while playing in the first of the rains. Father, mother, and Apu—their grim and intractable economic situation unresolved—load their few belongings onto an ox cart and depart for Benares.

Early in *Aparajito* the father dies, and the remainder of the film, with its sustained note of moving sadness, concerns the gentle and loving tension created by Apu's ambition for an education (which also means westernization) and his mother's conflicting need for his affection and the traditional ways. *The World of Apu* deals with his early manhood—his life in Calcutta, his marriage—and concludes with his relationship to his young son after his wife dies in childbirth.

Following the trilogy, Ray moved toward more strictly Indian and personal concerns. Somewhat like the Italian film makers, he shifted from the poorer to the middle and upper-middle classes of which he was a member and away from material to spiritual (even religious) and psychological themes. In *Devi* (*The Goddess*, 1960), a deeply religious feudal landlord becomes obsessed with the notion that his daughter-in-law is a goddess.

Kanchanjungha (1962), his first film in color, *Charulata* (1964), *Days and Nights in the Forest* (1970), *The Home and the World* (1984) are all concerned with complicated and shifting family, marital, and sexual relationships among the well-to-do and well educated. Frequently, like Ozu in Japan, Ray treated the old in a changing India, and the peculiar and fascinating mixture of East and West left as a legacy of the British raj. *The Music Room* (1958), for example, deals with a vanishing feudal culture, the protagonist being the last in a line of landed aristocrats in British India. *The Chess Players* (1977) is set amidst nineteenth-century expansion of British colonial power. Ray has also been consistently concerned with the role of females. *Mahanagar (The Big City*, 1963), addressing attitudes about women and work and independence from male-dominated households and traditional roles, is one example.

In the totality of his work Ray was neither the "Indian neorealist" nor the "Flaherty of Bengal" that he was called. Instead, he was a strong, highly individualistic film maker who achieved a position from which he pursued his own artistic preoccupations. Going his own deliberate way, averaging a film a year, he successively explored aspects of his own culture with something of the same kind of preoccupation and concentration that marked the greatest of the Japanese directors. While his films became less easily universal, demanding more understanding of Indian cultural and social traditions and problems, they also became more polished and theatrical, noteworthy for their brilliant acting. (This tendency first became evident in *The World of Apu*.) The post-trilogy films offer both less and more than the trilogy, but Ray remained an Indian film maker who continued to command worldwide attention until his death in 1992.

Around 1969–1970 there developed what was called, in reference to the commercial mainstream of Indian film making, New Indian Cinema, or Parallel Cinema, financed in part by the government's National Film Development Corporation. Along with Ray, Ritwik Ghatak and Mrinal Sen are considered its founding fathers. Except for Ray's work, New Indian Cinema has scarcely been distributed in the West, however. Films discussed below were shown in a series under that heading that toured museums and campuses in the United States in 1982–1983 and in another called "New Hindi Cinema" in 1986–1987.

Ritwik Ghatak, who died in 1976, directed only eight feature films, though he made a good many documentaries and wrote scripts for others' features. A Marxist activist, it is said of his films that practically all are about the social stress and turmoil in Bengal. Perhaps one of the most gentle and one of the few to arrive in the West, *Ajantrik (Pathetic Fallacy*, 1958) is about a taxi driver in a small provincial town and his ancient and decrepit Ford. The taxi is his only, and highly valued, companion, except for his brief encounters with the varied fares who join him in it. The film ends with the death and dismemberment of his faithful friend, the taxi; his sense of loss is shared by the audience, thanks to the special blend of enchantment and realism that Ghatak managed to create.

Mrinal Sen's features, some twenty-five or more in number, are quite different from those of either Ray or Ghatak, though all three are Bengalis. A Marxist, Sen experimented for awhile with form as well as content, in the manner of Frenchman Jean-Luc Godard, in an effort to create a revolutionary cinema. *Bhuvan Shome* (*Mister Shome*, 1969), Sen's biggest success, was the first low-budget feature financed by the Indian government. Its title character is a stuffy senior executive of the Indian railways. During a holiday in rural India he is transformed by his experience of country people and country ways, especially those of the cheeky young wife of a lowly railway clerk. It is both funny and lyrical. *In Search of Famine* (1980) is about film makers visiting a rural settlement in order to get the villagers to reenact the terrible famine of 1943 (also the subject of Ray's *Distant Thunder*, 1973). The interaction between the urban film crew and their rural subjects generates tension and ultimately forces the crew to abandon the actual and retreat to the security of the make-believe world of the studio. Biting irony is the prevailing tone. *The Ruins* (1983), less didactic than Sen's work generally, also concerns urban in relation to rural. A city-bred photographer spends a country weekend with some friends at a ruined estate where a lonely girl, foresaken by her betrothed, tries to keep her ailing mother alive with the hope that he will return. *Genesis* (1986), too, is set amidst ruins, but those of a town long deserted, which two men and a woman try but fail to bring back to life.

Among the other directors of New Indian Cinema, **Shyam Benegal**, who lives and works in Bombay, is perhaps best known abroad. *Ankur* (*The Seedling*, 1974), his

Bhuvan Shome/Mister Shome ♦ India, 1983, Mrinal Sen; Suhasini Mulay.

first feature, was a considerable success. Evidently it is a strong, tragic protest against the feudal society that has persisted in rural India. *Manthan* (*The Churning*, 1976) was financed by individual contributions from the farmers of Gujarat State and deals with the attempts of an Indian government administrator to set up a milk cooperative in a little village. The official becomes ensnared in caste and hierarchical entanglements that arise to thwart his efforts. The film seems extraordinarily honest in its portrayal of the difficulties, misunderstandings, and cross purposes that surely would face an outsider attempting to bring about change in a tradition-bound society. *Bhumika* (*The Role*, 1977), another considerable success, is based on the biography of an actual female star of theater and film in the 1940s, dubbed the "Joan Crawford of India." It reveals much about the world of popular entertainment and the constrictions placed on the life of even a successful woman in Indian culture. Benegal's concerns seem to embody feminism and Marxism; his style is more extravagant and sensuous than that of other directors of the New Indian Cinema. In fact one of his films, *Trikal* (1986), was said to fit into a Middle Cinema category, somewhere between the commercial mainstream and the small-budget, small-audience Parallel Cinema. In any case, Benegal seems to have kept steadily at work and to continue to attract attention at international film festivals as well.

♦ CHINA

The heading for this section is and is not correct. There are three centers of Chinese film production: Hong Kong, the People's Republic of China, and Taiwan. Separated geographically and politically, they share a common culture and language, and a lingering sense of nationalism. The films of Taiwan don't travel out into the world very often or very far. The films of China proper are just beginning to be seen abroad. Actually, it is Hong Kong, the tiny British crown colony perched on China's southern coast, that is the world's largest and most widely known producer of Chinese films. (Hong Kong will become part of China in 1997.)

The staples of **Hong Kong** production are the popular genres of martial arts, crazy comedies, gangster films, and soft-core pornography. They are distributed mostly within Asia, but at Cannes in 1975 Hong Kong's *A Touch of Zen* won the Grand Prix. Large in scale, three hours in length, it added Buddhism to martial arts. It was directed by King Hu. His *Legend of the Mountain* and *Raining in the Mountains*, shown at Edinburgh in 1979, also evoke the legends of ancient China and contain much visual elegance and a philosophical dimension along with their balletic fight scenes. King Hu is the acknowledged master of this sort of film making.

A few Hong Kong films falling outside the standard genres have won a modest degree of acceptance from the western film establishment as "art movies." Allen Fong's *Father and Son* (1982) and *Ah Ying* (1983) have had festival screenings and been sold for distribution in some western countries. In them the characters' experiences are said to become ciphers for the feelings, dreams, and contradictions of modern Hong Kong. Also admired at international festivals were the first three features of Ann Hui. (Though born in Hong Kong she received training at The London

A *Touch of Zen* ♦ Hong Kong, 1975, King Hu.

International Film School.) *The Secret* (1979) offers a speculative solution to a real-life murder mystery; stylistically it is reported to be heavily westernized. *The Spooky Bunch* (1981) deals with ghosts loose amongst the members of a Chinese opera touring company. *The Story of Woo Viet* (1982) concerns Manila's Chinatown. *Boat People* (1982), an account of the communist takeover of South Vietnam after U.S. withdrawal in 1975, was shot on location in China. *Song of the Exile* (1990) is a semiautobiographical exploration of the emotional and cultural gap between a British-educated Hong Kong girl and her Japanese mother. *My American Grandson* (1991), a Taiwanese production, about a Chinese-American child parked with his grandfather in Shanghai for the summer, is her most recent film known at time of writing. Though quite a number of Hong Kong films have been shot in China since the 1950s, and coproduction deals between China and Hong Kong and even Taiwan have increased, this huge neighbor remains a less well-known and, until recently, less active film producer.

Until 1949, **China's** film industry, based in Shanghai, was overwhelmed by American and British imports. The People's Republic of China (PRC), established in that year, had first produced films mainly for revolutionary indoctrination and education, much as had its communist predecessor, the Soviet Union. An exceptional fiction feature made later was *Two Stage Sisters* (1964), directed by Xie Jin, who continued to be China's most highly regarded veteran director. It chronicles the parallel lives of two actresses during the political turmoil of 1935–1950, intermingling melodramatic and dialectic treatment, bravura camera style, and fine performances. But during the "cultural revolution," 1966–1976, very few films were made and those were mostly

Two Stage Sisters ◆ China, 1964, Xie Jin; Cao Tindi and Xie Fang, left rear.

confined to themes of the "revolutionary operas" approved by the authorities. Studios were closed; writers, directors, actors, producers, technicians (and millions of others) were sent off to the countryside to be "reeducated." Since 1977 Chinese film production has resumed on a larger scale with a more sophisticated approach to the needs of the nation and its vast population.

Beijing and Shanghai are the main production centers; between 130 and 140 films a year are produced. In 1982 the People's Republic was represented for the first time in the official competition at Cannes with *The True Story of Ah Q*. The first movie from mainland China to receive widespread distribution in the United States was *Rickshaw Boy* (1983).

For the past ten years some of the films attracting most attention at the Hong Kong International Film Festival, and more recently in Cannes, Venice, and Berlin, have come from the PRC. These have been directed by graduates of the Beijing Film Academy—especially by members of the class of 1982, the so-called Fifth Generation. Though they vary widely from director to director, of course, what they have in common are stories set in the past and a brilliant pictorial sense. In the first class to enroll when the Academy was reopened in 1978, following the Cultural Revolution, were Chen Kaige and Zhang Zimou, who have become renowned internationally. Kaige's *Yellow Earth* (1984), the first of their films out to the festivals, is most widely known abroad and most influential at home. It tells the story of an encounter in the late 1930s between a soldier of the communist Eighth Route Army and peasants in Shaanzi Province in Northwestern China. Anthropological notations on the feudal culture and the superstition of the tradition-bound community are combined with observation of the ways in which some of the characters become "liberated" and react positively towards revolution.

The second feature by Kaige, *The Big Parade* (1986), has also been seen in this country in a cultural exchange with the film maker present. It is about a group of military cadets who train and rehearse for the huge celebration in 1984 of the Chinese Revolution's 35th anniversary. *Life on a String* (1991), Kaige's first film made with foreign backing, is a folkloristic tale of the lifelong quests of a master musician and his pupil. Its narrative is abstract, even metaphysical; its visual displays of choreographed camera virtuosity in relationship to breathtaking scenery are stunning. *Farewell My Concubine* (1992) was made with Taiwanese money by a producer based in Hong Kong. It concerns a Beijing Opera star's fifty-year unrequited passion for his costar. Both characters are male. A reformed prostitute is the wife of the lover, romantic rival of the loved one.

Yellow Earth ♦ China, 1984, Chen Kaige; Xue Bai and Wang Xueqi.

Kaige's relationship to his homeland appears equivocal, or in any case has transcended nationalism. His films have become increasingly personal and idiosyncratic. While dealing resolutely with Chinese subjects and themes, they are surely veering from political correctness. Though his background includes passionate commitment to Maoist policies in the sixties (he was, in fact, a Red Guard), he has subsequently spent much time in New York, living there for more than three years.

Cinematographer for Kaige's first two films was Zhang Yimou, who directed his first feature, *Red Sorghum*, in 1988. It won the Golden Bear at the Berlin festival, thus becoming the first PRC film to achieve the highest honor at one of the leading international festivals, was selected as the closing-night film of the New York festival, and was subsequently released in the United States. The story is set in the 1930s and is based on a Northern Chinese legend of a young woman sold into wifehood by her unfeeling father.

His second feature, *Ju Dou* (1990), wholly Japanese financed, is an earthy sexual melodrama of an old and vicious owner of a textile factory who buys a lovely bride and mistreats her. His nephew and she become lovers and violence and revenge ensue. The film met with considerable success abroad, including the United States. *Raise the Red Lantern* (1991), set in northern China in the 1920s, concerns a beautiful young woman from an impoverished family who becomes the fourth wife of the elderly master of a powerful clan. Yimou's portrayal of the oppression of women may be a metaphor for the larger social and political conditions in today's China. *The Story of Qiu Ju* (1992) uses a contemporary setting for the first time but the central figure is again a young woman of fierce will. The actress Gong Li has starred in all of Yimou's films (and is featured in Kaige's *Farewell My Concubine* as well); as a result, she has become China's best-known performer internationally. It may be that Yimou, who, unlike Haige, has never lived abroad, has become mainland China's director of films most accessible to audiences of the West.

The loosening of restrictions and seeking of coproduction and foreign audiences that began in the 1980s was abruptly halted, in fact reversed, with the brutal military crackdown on a prodemocracy student demonstration in Beijing's Tiananmen Square in 1989. The present situation is particularly anomolous in that coproduction with other countries continues, thus preventing Chinese authorities from completely controlling the content but being able to prevent films from being shown in the PRC. Thus Kaige's *Life on a String* and Yimou's *Ju Dou* and *Raise the Red Lantern* and films of other Fifth Generation film makers were mounted with foreign backing but were never shown in mainland theaters.

In **Taiwan,** on the other hand, martial law was lifted in 1987 and it became possible to show previously taboo aspects of the island's history and to continue coproduction with mainland China (though officially forbidden). *A City of Sadness* (1988), directed by Hou Hsiao-hsien, was Taiwan's first international artistic success (awarded the Golden Lion at Venice) while doing very well commercially at home.

Taiwanese films have been honored at international film festivals but not shown in the United States (except probably on unsubtitled cassettes available from the proliferating video stores serving immigrant Asian populations). The most interesting

A Brighter Summer Day ◆ Taiwan, 1991, Edward Yang.

director at work seems to be Edward Yang, member of a younger generation born and raised in Taiwan. Yang received his graduate education in this country (Florida State University and University of Southern California). Though he has made a good many features, his most important to date seems to have been *A Brighter Summer Day* (1991). Set in Taiwan in the early 1960s, it concerns teenagers who have no memory of life as lived on the mainland, are alienated by the totalitarian nationalist Chinese government, and gravitate toward gangs as they reject the ideals of their parents.

If the caveat is accepted that much of our evidence so far is second-hand—reports from festivals and visitors to Hong Kong, the People's Republic, and Taiwan—it does seem clear that these three nations have emerged as producers of important cinema. As our economy and politics focus increasingly on the Pacific Rim, it seems likely that we will want to know and deal with Chinese films during the years ahead more than we have yet done.

At the same time we must remember that when Asian films reach international audiences they fall within the orbit of the American film industry. Though what we call Hollywood changed radically in many ways during the fifties, when the Japanese and Indian film first began attracting world attention, one way Hollywood did not change so much as become more so was its dependence on and domination of world distribution. The next chapter is a return to the United States and what happened here during the decade following 1952, the year we left it at the end of Chapter 9.

FILMS OF THE PERIOD

China
1964
Two Stage Sisters (Xie Jin)

1984
One and the Eight (Zhang Junzhao)
Yellow Earth (Chen Kaige)

1986
The Big Parade (Kaige)
The Black Cannon Incident (Huang Jianxin)

1987
The Horse Thief (Tian Zhuangzhuang)

1988
King of the Children (Kaige)
Red Sorghum (Zhang Yimou)

1990
Ju Dou (Yimou)

1991
Life on a String (Kaige)
Raise the Red Lantern (Yimou)

1992
Farewell My Concubine (Kaige)
The Story of Qiu Ju (Yimou)

Hong Kong
1975
A Touch of Zen (King Hu)

1979
Legend of the Mountain (Hu)
Raining in the Mountains (Hu)
The Secret (Ann Hui)
The Spooky Bunch (Hui)

1982
Boat People (Hui)
Father and Son (Allen Fong)
The Story of Woo Viet (Hui)

1983
Ah Ying (Fong)

1989
The Killer (John Woo)

1990
Song of Exile (Hui)

1992
Hard-Boiled (Woo)

India
1955
Pather Panchali (Satyajit Ray)

1956
Aparajito (Ray)

1958
Ajantrik/Pathetic Fallacy (Ritwik Ghatak)
The Music Room (Ray)
The World of Apu (Ray)

1960
Devi/The Goddess (Ray)

1962
Kanchanjungha (Ray)

1963
Mahanagar/The Big City (Ray)

1964
Charulata/The Lonely Wife (Ray)

1969
Bhuvan Shome/Mister Shome
    (Mrinal Sen)

1970
Days and Nights in the Forest (Ray)
Uski Roti/Daily Bread (Mani Kaul)

1973
Distant Thunder (Ray)
Kaadu/The Forest (Girish Karnad)

1976
Manthan/The Churning (Shyam Benegal)

1977
Bhumika/The Role (Benegal)
The Chess Players (Ray)

1978
Ondanondu Kaladalli/Once Upon a Time
   (Karnad)

1980
Aakaler Sandhaney/In Search of Famine
   (Sen)

1983
The Ruins (Sen)

1984
The Home and the World (Ray)

1986
Genesis (Sen)
Trikal (Benegal)

1988
Salaam Bombay! (Mira Nair)

1989
Piravi/The Birth (Shaji)

1991
The Stranger (Ray)

Japan
1950
Rashomon (Akira Kurosawa)

1952
Ikiru (Kurosawa)
The Life of O'Haru
   (Kenji Mizoguchi)

1953
Gate of Hell (Teinosuke Kinugasa)
Tokyo Story (Yasujiro Ozu)
Ugetsu (Mizoguchi)

1954
Chikamatsu Monogatari (Mizoguchi)
Sansho Dayu/The Bailiff (Mizoguchi)
Seven Samurai (Kurosawa)

1955
Princess Yang Kwei Fei (Mizoguchi)

1956
The Burmese Harp (Kon Ichikawa)

1957
The Lower Depths (Kurosawa)
The Throne of Blood (Kurosawa)

1958
Enjo (Ichikawa)

1959
Fires on the Plain (Ichikawa)
Floating Weeds (Ozu)
Odd Obsession (Ichikawa)

1961
An Autumn Afternoon (Ozu)
The Human Condition
   (1958–1961, Masaki Kobayashi)
The Island (Kaneto Shindo)

1962
An Actor's Revenge (Ichikawa)
Harakiri (Kobayashi)

1964
Kwaidan (Kobayashi)
Onibaba (Shindo)
Woman of the Dunes (Hiroshi Teshigahara)

1965
Red Beard (Kurosawa)

1968
Death by Hanging (Nagisa Oshima)
Diary of a Shinjuku Thief (Oshima)

1969
Boy (Oshima)
Double Suicide (Masahiro Shinoda)

1970
Dodeska-den (Kurosawa)

1971
The Ceremony (Oshima)

1975
Dersu Uzala (Kurosawa)
Kaseki (Kobayashi)

1976
In the Realm of the Senses (Oshima)

1979
Realm of Passion (Oshima)

1981
Kagemusha/The Shadow Warrior (Kurosawa)

1983
Family Game (Yoshimitsu Morita)

1984
The Funeral (Juzo Itami)

1985
Ran (Kurosawa)
Tampopo (Itami)

1986
A Taxing Woman (Itami)

1987
Gonza the Spearman (Shinoda)

1990
Dreams (Kurosawa)

Taiwan
1986
The Terrorizer (Edward Yang)

1988
A City of Sadness (Hou Hsiao-hsien)

1991
A Brighter Summer Day (Yang)
My American Grandson (Ann Hui)

1993
The Wedding Banquet (Ang Lee)

BOOKS ON THE PERIOD

Asia
Dissanayke, Wimal, ed., *Cinema and Cultural Identity: Reflections on Film from Japan, India, and China.* Lanham, MD: University Press of America, 1988
Dissanayake, Wimal, ed., *Melodrama and Asian Cinema.* New York: Cambridge University Press, 1993
Lent, John A., ed., *The Asian Film Industry.* Austin: University of Texas Press, 1990

China
Berry, Chris, ed., *Perspectives, on Chinese Cinema.* London: British Film Institute, 1991
Clark, Paul, *Chinese Cinema: Culture and Politics Since 1949.* New York: Cambridge University Press, 1988
Semsel, George Stephen, ed., *Chinese Film: The State of the Art in the People's Republic.* New York: Praeger, 1987
Semsel, George S., Chen Xihe, and Xia Hong, eds., *Film in Contemporary China: Critical Debates, 1979–1989.* Westport, CT: Greenwood Press, 1993

India
Banerjee, Shampa, and Anil Srivastava, *One Hundred Indian Feature Films: An Annotated Filmography.* New York: Garland Publishing, 1988
Valicha, Kishore, *The Moving Image: A Study of Indian Cinema.* Bombay: Orient Longman, 1988

Japan

Buehrer, Beverley Bare, *Japanese Films: A Filmography and Commentary, 1921–1989*. Jefferson, NC: McFarland, 1990

Desser, David, *Eros Plus Massacre: An Introduction to the Japanese New Wave Cinema*. Bloomington: Indiana University Press, 1988

Hirano, Kyoko, *Mr. Smith Goes to Tokyo: Japanese Cinema under the American Occupation, 1945–1952*. Washington, DC: Smithsonian Institution Press, 1992

Nolletti, Arthur, Jr., and David Desser, eds., *Reframing Japanese Cinema: Authorship, Genre, History*. Bloomington: Indiana University Press, 1992

Richie, Donald, *Japanese Cinema: An Introduction*. New York: Oxford University Press, 1990

13

Hollywood
in Transition

♦ ♦ ♦

1952–1962

In the history of motion pictures, 1952 marked the beginning of a transition that would lead the American film industry from the hardened confines of a production-distribution-exhibition pattern that had lasted for over two decades into uncertainty and changing forms and functions. In film, what affects the industry affects the art; what happens in the United States influences the world.

Richard Dyer MacCann, in his perceptive book from which the title for this chapter has been borrowed, refers to the major changes that began in Hollywood about 1952 as "expanded freedoms." He lists freedom from censorship, from centralized studio production, from domination by the domestic box office, and from the tyranny of the assembly line. In what follows, much the same matters will be organized and dealt with in a way somewhat different from MacCann's, but 1952 remains the key year. That was the first full year in which the whole nation was blanketed by network television. It was also the year that brought wide screens and stereophonic sound, and more practicable and less expensive (Eastman) color. About that time, too, cracks began to show in the major studios and a new growth of independent production sprouted. Concurrently, the making of American films abroad and the dependence of Hollywood on foreign revenue increased. Finally, 1952 was the year of a Supreme Court decision that marked the beginning of a loosening of the social controls on film content.

Central factors accounting for and accompanying these changes were the decline in theater attendance from the booming war and postwar years (from 90 million weekly in 1948 to 51 million in 1952) and the breakup of the single, mass audience into separate specialized audiences—youths, intellectuals, African Americans, and so on. The former "family audience" was now a minority audience, administered to mainly by Walt Disney Productions. Going to the movies, once the staple form of entertainment, became more of a special occasion somewhere between staying home to watch TV and attending live theater or a concert. With increased public affluence, motion pictures were competing for leisure time with spectator sports, bowling, motorboating, hi-fi sets, and a whole range of new activities. Whereas in 1946, as *Variety* noted, almost $1.7 billion (or almost 20 percent of all U.S. expenditures for recreation) were paid in movie admissions; by 1962 that figure had plummeted to $930 million (or about 4.5 percent)—in spite of inflating ticket prices.

By 1952, the major studios had had to divest themselves of their theater holdings. After a decade of litigation, from 1938 to 1948, the Supreme Court had finally ruled, in *U.S.* v. *Paramount Pictures et al.*, that the practice of "vertical control" was in restraint of trade and tended toward monopoly. The majors might continue to produce and distribute but not exhibit. In the mid-forties about 400 features had been produced annually—300 by the major studios, 100 by independents. Every week between 80 and 100 million persons had paid admission to see them in 18,719 "hard-top" theaters and 300 drive-ins. By 1960 the average weekly attendance—in 13,200 indoor and 4,600 outdoor theaters—had dropped to an estimated 46 million. Of the 136 features produced that year, only 70 came from the major studios while 66 were from the independents. Those trends—fewer pictures, more of which were by independents; smaller audiences; and a decrease in the number of theaters, with the proportion of drive-in theaters increasing—would continue throughout the sixties and into the seventies.

♦ TELEVISION

It was TV, of course, that occupied most of the leisure time of the public who formerly would have gone to the movies. The shifting relationship between motion pictures and broadcasting is one of the main chapters in the history of those two industries during the fifties and sixties. Television had begun on an experimental basis just before World War II, but wartime priorities and shortages had frozen its development until the postwar years. From five stations and a few hundred sets in 1946 it expanded rapidly to the first year of big-time television in 1948, when Milton Berle and Ed Sullivan were seen and heard in the large urban centers. Between 1948 and 1952 approximately seventeen million TV sets were sold. In 1951 coaxial cable and microwave relay had connected the nation coast to coast. In that year major TV production began its move to Hollywood. From the early fifties on the audience continued to expand. Today there are more television sets than persons in the country. The most popular television series (*Roseanne*, for example) average between 25 and 30 million viewers a week. A special occasion (such as the last original episode of *Cheers* in 1993) may attract more than 60 million; even greater numbers worldwide watch some big sporting events.

Until 1948 the motion picture industry's reaction to the TV threat was ostrich like. At one studio it was reported to be forbidden even to use the word *television* in executive conversation. Then the stance shifted to passive resistance through deliberate withholding of the enormous resources of talent and reservoir of product. No actors, writers, or directors under contract were permitted to work for television. No feature films produced by the major studios were offered for airing. Films playing in theaters were not advertised on television. Revenues from the box office continued to decline, of course, and complaints from stockholders about dwindling dividends steadily to increase.

The critical problem was finding access to an audience. Since the production companies no longer owned the theaters, which anyway were being converted into supermarkets or razed to make way for parking lots, their loyalty to the theater owners and resolve to try to protect them from even greater television competition was weakened. When the pressures finally became too great, the studios followed the old industry saw about joining 'em if you can't beat 'em. They began by making available to TV the vast libraries of feature films that had accumulated during the past decades.

The unloading of the vaults, if it set the motion picture industry in competition with itself, was also designed to cause some damage to the enemy. The leasing and outright sale of the hundreds of old feature films was directed toward the independent stations, either directly or through packaging agencies, so as to constitute maximum competition to network programming. The number of features totaled in the thousands and were all disposed of within a couple of years. RKO, after Howard Hughes's withdrawal, and tottering on the brink of financial collapse, was the first major to sell: 740 of its features went to General Teleradio in December 1955. This sale was followed in rapid succession by the sale of feature films owned by Columbia, Warner, M-G-M, United Artists, and the others. Paramount was last to dispose of its great backlog of 750 features, in February 1958.

By 1961 the networks joined the local stations to provide prime-time airing of past major films, which could now be seen in color by an ever-increasing number of viewers. The popularity of theatrical feature films with television audiences has, of course, been enormous. When *The Bridge on the River Kwai* was aired by ABC-TV on Sunday night prime time in 1966, the audience was estimated at 60 million. *The New York Times*, sounding like *Variety* in its excitement, offered to explain "Why 'Kwai' KO'd 'Bonanza' and Ed Sullivan." By the early seventies not only had the backlog of old features been used up, but the supply of recent theatrical film releases was far below the television demand.

The ultimate response of Hollywood to television was to undertake production directly for the tube. It began in 1952 when Columbia Pictures formed the first of the television subsidiaries among the major studios—Screen Gems. This television film making started with the half-hour entertainment series, which became hour-long and, in some instances, even ninety minutes in length, resembling more and more the old "B" pictures that were no longer a profitable kind of production for the more specialized audiences of the theaters. The production for television exerted a gravitational pull towards the West Coast. Soon virtually all nighttime television entertainment was being produced in the Los Angeles area. Only news, documentary and public affairs, and some daytime game shows and soap operas continued to come out of New York. In 1957, Desilu, the company formed by Desi Arnaz and Lucille Ball out of the extraordinary success of their *I Love Lucy* series, shot more film than all the major

Marty ♦ U.S., 1955,
Delbert Mann; Ernest
Borgnine and Betsy Blair.

studios together. By the mid-sixties Hollywood began to make feature films directly for TV rather than for initial theatrical showing.

As television became established people and product began to flow from it into film. Out of the so-called Golden Age of live TV drama in the late forties and early fifties, theatrical feature films were created from the writings of Paddy Chayefsky, Rod Serling, Robert Alan Aurthur, Reginald Rose, Merle Miller, and others. *Marty* (1955), *The Catered Affair* (1956), *Patterns* (1956), *Edge of the City* (1957), *Twelve Angry Men* (1957), *The Bachelor Party* (1957), *The Goddess* (1959), and *Requiem for a Heavyweight* (1962) had all appeared live on the tube. Directors as well as writers came to features from television: Delbert Mann, Sidney Lumet, John Frankenheimer, Robert Mulligan, Sam Peckinpah, Norman Jewison, Ralph Nelson among them. Some of the new stars—Dick Van Dyke, Steve McQueen, James Garner, Rod Taylor—male only, it seems, had also gotten their start in television.

Financial control, studio facilities, story material, production personnel, and performers have continued to move back and forth between film and television. This situation doesn't seem likely to change.

♦ NEW SCREEN PROCESSES

All three major technological additions to the silent black-and-white film—sound, color, wide screen—were around from the very beginning. Their introduction was in every case dependent more upon economic considerations than upon technical feasibility. Whenever the industry is in trouble somebody will say, "There's nothing wrong

with the movies that a few good pictures can't cure." But if producers knew how to
make consistently profitable films, there wouldn't have been any trouble in the first
place. Although popular success can't be guaranteed, technical novelty can be tried.
Sound came in 1927 because of the competition radio then offered for the audiences
of silent films, and because Warner Brothers was attempting corporate expansion.
Technicolor was added to feature film production in 1935 in an attempt to remedy the
continuing Depression slump. In 1952 the failing box office and television competition once again goaded the industry into introducing a number of "new screen
processes." All were designed to offer sights and sounds that the competitive medium
could not duplicate, and to give the screen a greater illusion of depth.

Stereoscopic, or 3-D, feature films first appeared in the fall of 1952. (In the
thirties, there had been a series of M-G-M black-and-white 3-D shorts; polaroid lenses
now permitted the addition of color.) With *Bwana Devil* it seemed to the audience that
a lion was charging them (promotion promised "A lion in your lap"), or a spear being
thrown over their heads.

At first, the 3-D films were extremely successful, but their attraction wore off
within less than a year. It was said that audiences didn't like the special glasses
required. By the time any substantial work was undertaken in 3-D the audience had

Dial M for Murder ♦ U.S., 1954, Alfred Hitchcock, in 3-D; Grace Kelly.

lost interest. Introduced a couple of months after the wide screen had made its appearance with Cinerama, 3-D came and went, while the wide screen has lasted in one form or another ever since.

It was the grandeur the wide screens added (in the late twenties a wide-screen system called Magnascope had been referred to as the "grandeur screen") that caught public fancy. The first of the new wide-screen processes was the biggest and best of them in terms of spatial illusion. *This Is Cinerama* opened in New York City in September 1952. Developed by Fred Waller from 1939 on, it had been used in an earlier version by the Armed Forces during World War II for aircraft identification and mock gunnery practice. The screen, with a 2.85 to 1 ratio of width to height, was deeply curved and vast. A necessarily small audience sitting well forward had virtually everyone's whole field of vision filled by the image. Viewers felt they really were on that roller coaster or on that plane coming in over the Chicago skyline.

Accompanying the visual format of great width and depth was a hi-fidelity, stereophonic, magnetic sound system. Its enormously increased range of frequencies brought sound reproduction much closer to life than the woefully inadequate optical recording in standard use.

The development of Cinerama had been backed by people outside the Hollywood industry—Mike Todd, Louis de Rochemont, Lowell Thomas, and others—but the studio heads could scarcely be blind to its huge financial success. *This Is Cinerama*

Artist's representation of an audience watching *This Is Cinerama* ◆ U.S., 1952, Merian C. Cooper.

was soon numbered among the great moneymakers of all time, and the several features that followed it, playing in only a few specially equipped and converted "legitimate" theaters at live theater prices, consistently appeared high on *Variety*'s box office tallies. The opportunities and problems Cinerama posed for the industry were not unlike those that had accompanied *The Jazz Singer*'s success a quarter of a century earlier. The appeal of this new gadget to audiences, who had been staying away from the theaters in droves, as Sam Goldwyn is said to have remarked on another occasion, was obvious. But the expense of conversion and unfamiliarity with the techniques required by the new system were awesome obstacles.

Cinerama's cumbersome technology and the small audiences that could be accommodated at each showing presented too severe a wrench to existing production and exhibition practices to be contemplated without alarm. Furthermore, the Cinerama films were essentially a group of travelogue shorts anthologized to feature length. The kinds of stories that might fill that monstrous screen seemed extremely limited. An appropriate size and shape for parades down Fifth Avenue, a train speeding across the Mojave Desert, or two boa constrictors copulating, as someone observed, it offered no clear advantage in dealing with individual human beings (who happen to stand upright), unless they were in quantities of thousands. Even more basically, the use of closeups and editing, essential to screen narrative technique as practiced, would be greatly reduced if not prohibited by what seemed acres of image. What was needed was a sort of poor man's Cinerama—one that spiced up but didn't depart too much from the existing standard.

It was Spyros Skouras, head of Twentieth Century-Fox, who performed the trick. The rabbit he pulled out of the hat was called CinemaScope (and better not forget to capitalize the middle S if you were a Fox employee). It was based on a principle worked out in the twenties by a French inventor, Henri Chrétien. Its wide screen was less wide than Cinerama's and curved only enough to accommodate focus. Though wider than standard (2.55 to 1 rather than 1.33 to 1), CinemaScope did not approximate peripheral vision. It was accompanied in its premiere by hi-fidelity four-track stereophonic sound.

Unlike the inauguration of the earlier 3-D, CinemaScope was launched with a feature that probably would have made money no matter what size and shape the screen. As it was, *The Robe*, which opened in September 1953, proved a tremendous success with its De Mille-like blend of spectacle and religiosity. It was followed by a series of expensive and well-made features, musicals and comedies especially, equally designed to show off the attractions of the new screen process; for example, *Gentlemen Prefer Blondes* (1953), *How to Marry a Millionaire* (1953), *A Star Is Born* (1954), *Seven Brides for Seven Brothers* (1954).

Fox was to wide screen what Warner had been to sound, and again the rest of the industry soon followed along. CinemaScope proved the almost ideal compromise between Cinerama and the conventional screen ratio. It required no major change in production technology or even technique, and was simple and inexpensive to install in existing movie houses. Though it favored certain film types—historical spectacles, musicals, westerns—and was awkward for others—intimate romances, social dramas—stories could be told in it, with fewer camera setups and less editing required.

The Robe ◆ U.S., 1953, Henry Koster; Jeff Morrow, holding robe; Victor Mature, standing; Richard Burton, kneeling, without helmet.

Some of the purists complained that the image it offered was like looking at the world through a postal slot, and Jean Cocteau is credited with remarking that he recognized progress when he saw it and henceforward would put paper in the typewriter sideways when he wrote his poems. But who cared about the purists; the box office was registering public response in large figures. As with sound, directors learned to work with CinemaScope, many reluctantly at first. The new technology was incorporated into the medium, with resultant aesthetic shifts and even some gains—like all of the earlier technological additions. In *East of Eden* (1955), for example, director Elia Kazan and cinematographer Ted McCord made stunning and highly dramatic use of the new proportions for what was essentially an intimate story of family strife.

Other wide-screen systems soon appeared. VistaVision, from Paramount, was a good alternative, providing a sharper image than CinemaScope. Todd A-0 was the first to use 70mm film. Panavision is the current trade name for a 70mm system.

But the extremely wide screens didn't become the exclusive shape, as some feared they might when CinemaScope first appeared. Rather, they eventually became reserved for the extravaganza—the big musical (*My Fair Lady*, 1964; *The Sound of Music*, 1965), the block-busting war picture (*The Guns of Navarone*, 1961; *The*

Longest Day, 1962), the historical spectacular (*Lawrence of Arabia*, 1962; *Doctor Zhivago*, 1965). For more conventional pictures what is called the "standard wide screen"—1.85 to 1 its most common ratio—has replaced the former 1.33 to 1 that has remained standard for television sets.

♦ FALL OF THE STUDIOS/RISE OF THE INDEPENDENTS

Another result of the pressures and changes experienced by the industry in the early fifties was a shakeup in production-distribution practices, which also affected the content and form of the films being made. Among the producing companies it was the former giants, now stripped of theaters, that were hit hardest by the dwindling and erratic earnings of their films. The enormous overhead in real estate, sound stages, expensive equipment, and high-salaried technical and creative personnel on long-term contracts could no longer be supported by the fewer, more costly films that current audience response dictated. Whereas M-G-M had once boasted as its greatest asset "More Stars Than There Are in Heaven," expensive nonworking actors, along with the writers and directors, had become a liability. All of the major studios except one were keeping their books in red ink.

That exception was United Artists, which had never owned theaters and didn't even have a studio. Instead, it had acquired films from independent producers and distributed them to theaters owned by others. It would choose from among the projects presented to it, perhaps supervise the scripts, put up some money and go to the bank for more. What it could guarantee to its producers was major distribution, for which it took a healthy cut. Its production overhead consisted mostly of offices, secretaries, and smart lawyers good at contracts and finance. Billy Wilder, one of United Artists' top producer-directors, observed ruefully, "We used to make pictures; now we make deals." A weak competitor in the old days, when the larger studios controlled exhibition, under the new conditions UA prospered and became the model others would imitate.

The rest of the studios freed themselves from employees under long-term contracts, except for skeleton technical crews. The actors, directors, and former staff producers went into production for themselves, or worked for other independents, with corporate profits and shares in the income from a picture replacing salaries. The studios rented out production space and facilities to the independents, financed their productions wholly or in part, and distributed the completed films. Rather than reading simply "Produced by," Paramount or Warner Brothers, opening credits now read "A Judd Bernard-Irwin Winkler Production for Metro-Goldwyn-Mayer" or "A Horizon Picture, Released through Columbia Pictures Corporation," and the like.

The independent companies were by no means totally independent, however, and the kinds of films they produced departed very little from those that had preceded them. The domination once exercised by the heads of five studios (Metro-Goldwyn-Mayer, Paramount, Warner Brothers, Twentieth Century-Fox, and RKO) was steadily being reduced. But the independents still had to play ball with the majors, whose remaining strongholds were their worldwide distribution organizations. This gave them power to exercise substantial control over the choice of subject matter and its presentation.

Another reason there was less change than might have been expected in the kinds of films being made with this new independence was that the smaller companies were subjected to exactly the same necessity for popular appeal as the large ones had been. In fact, in the case of the independents, the pressure was even greater. With only one picture produced at a time on borrowed money, rather than an annual production program of forty or fifty features financed out of studio reserves, each film had to be a success. Hits couldn't pay for flops. In some respects there seemed less room for experiment and risk than there had been under the old system. Many of the former studio personnel who formed their own companies stuck even closer to tested ingredients than the studios had done. Those who had cried for freedom from the repeated formulas of studio production and expressed the desire to strike out into bold new areas, to do something "really worthwhile," settled for the tried and true. To paraphrase G. B. Shaw, there's nothing as timid as several million dollars.

The little "B" programmers of the thirties and forties had sometimes proven an excellent if modest field for trial and error. They had also served as training ground for talent and permitted the careful building of careers. Now the stakes were too high. Bidding on the open market for stories and the services of top-flight performers and directors had reached an unprecedented level. Without the major studios' vested interest in the industry as a whole, there was no one to assume responsibility for developing new creative talent.

Yet, if we have come to reevaluate the studio production of the thirties and forties, and found excellences that weren't as apparent when they were routine, few would want to go back to the old studio system even if that were possible. With picture-by-picture film making there began to be a greater chance, however high the odds, for the strong creative personality to dominate and control a work without ruinous interference from the front office. It is more than coincidental that in those years of the fifties in which the studios were declining, directors were gaining a new status. When M-G-M, once biggest and proudest of the studios, virtually went out of the motion picture business altogether in the 1970s, the film makers who would have worked for M-G-M still found their way to film making if they were smart enough and tough enough—constant prerequisites to creation in motion-picture art. If film artists spent a lot of their time making deals, as Wilder quipped, they were free from the power and overzealous supervision of production chiefs like Irving Thalberg, and from conceptions of God, country, and motherhood as revealed to Louis B. Mayer.

◆ INTERNATIONALIZATION

Along with all the other sweeping changes, there even seemed some danger that Los Angeles might cease to be the film capital of the world, and fall into ruins like Carthage or ancient Rome. American films were in increasing competition with foreign ones—especially with those of Britain, Italy, and France—for audiences abroad and even in this country. Conational productions and multinational crews and casts became commonplace. And "American" films themselves were as likely to be shot anywhere in the world as within proximity of Hollywood and Vine.

The first consideration to prompt this increased internationalization may have been in part an artistic one. Wide screens encouraged special emphasis on authentic and exotic locales. For conventional sorts of love stories that formerly would have been shot on the sound stages and back lots, film makers now journeyed to Rome (*Three Coins in a Fountain*, 1954), Hong Kong (*Love Is a Many-Splendored Thing*, 1955), or Tokyo (*Sayonara*, 1957). Audiences of the fifties began to get moving-picture postcards along with stars and stories. Some of the spectacles made for the wide screen were very much about the places and terrain where the stories took place: *The Bridge on the River Kwai* (1957), the Southeast Asian jungle; *Lawrence of Arabia* (1962), the Middle Eastern desert.

The secondary considerations were exclusively financial. First, by shooting abroad, American producers could more easily assemble a cast drawn from a number of countries to better ensure warm reception of their films in various parts of the globe. Then too, there was the advantage, for the Americans involved, of delayed payment of U.S. corporate and income taxes on work done outside the country. Also, it was thought to be, and in many cases actually was, cheaper to make films abroad. Generally costs were less in Mexico, Spain, or Italy, for example—especially for labor. (A counterargument was that the apparent saving was often canceled out in working with less-efficient crews who used unfamiliar methods and languages.) There was no doubt that the various schemes of subsidy offered by most foreign governments to encourage national production was a real incentive. Many essentially American films were disguised as British, say—their production set up in a way that met minimum requirements for assistance from Britain's National Film Finance Corporation. In addition, where a quota system existed for proportionate release of foreign to domestic films, as in Britain and elsewhere, a film flying the local flag would be assured immediate exhibition there rather than having to wait among the films of other nations. In some cases, India for example, American profits had become "frozen currency" and couldn't be taken out of the country. One way to make use of that money was to spend it on a production which could then be distributed worldwide and earn revenue elsewhere.

Distribution along with production became increasingly internationalized. American companies began to seek income from the distribution of foreign films in the United States as well as elsewhere. Also, as their own production expenses increased and the size of the domestic audience decreased, they attempted to earn back more and more of their costs from abroad. In former years the huge American market could return a profit on a film, and what was earned elsewhere was gravy. Now over fifty per cent of the income from American films came from overseas. More than ever Hollywood courted the world audience.

Finally, the motion-picture industry developed its own equivalent to the plants set up abroad and the multinational corporations that had become common practice among other industries. Not only was there a British M-G-M, as there was an English Ford, but the United States dominated and to some extent controlled foreign financing of production and international distribution. In terms of financial backing and distribution, Antonioni's *Blow-Up* (1966), made in England, was as much an American film as his *Zabriskie Point* (1970), made in the United States American influence began to reach even into films that appeared to be totally French. Jean-Luc Godard's *A Married Woman* and *Band of Outsiders* (both 1964) were financed by Columbia Pictures. Four of François Truffaut's films were financed by United Artists. Though the European Economic Community tried to set up an alternative financing-distribution pattern to counter American domination, little came of the effort.

Given the increased internationalization of film production-distribution-exhibition, American-controlled or not, it became possible for works that did not appeal to the large audience to earn back their costs by playing for six weeks or longer in small theaters in London, Copenhagen, Paris, Mexico City, New York, and elsewhere. This change, along with the increase in independent production, loosened the rigidities and altered the mass-product conception underlying the old industrial patterns. The new system was able, if not so easily as one might like, to adjust to a greater variety of films and to give them wider international distribution than ever before. Sometimes this increased internationalization and Americanization tended to dilute valuable national qualities. At the same time, it served to stimulate film makers and audiences by affording a greater sampling of the total range of subjects and forms than had ever before been available, even in the silent years. The international spotlight began to whirl very rapidly. It was not so much one nation's production calling for attention and influencing other nations' as it was individual film artists jumping across cultural boundaries to demonstrate to each other and introduce audiences to a wide diversity of personal concerns and styles. Together, recently arrived creators and newly sophisticated audiences significantly advanced the art within the industry during the late fifties and early sixties.

♦ LOOSENED CONTROLS ON CONTENT

In the United States, beginning in the 1950s, social controls placed on the content of motion pictures began to be eased. This encouraged, if not always a greater maturity, at least a new freedom and frankness in the presentation of sexual behavior, states of undress, and kinds of language. During those years, the United States Supreme Court rendered a series of decisions that curtailed the activities of state and local censoring bodies. The Motion Picture Association of America liberalized its code of self-regulation and then started to classify rather than regulate screen content. Organized pressure groups—religious, ethnic, political—turned their attention away from what was showing in the theaters to what was appearing ever more widely on the tube. Producers eagerly, some desperately, took advantage of the new freedom to try to attract audiences away from television and to compete with the forthrightness of European films.

In 1952, in *The Miracle* case, the Supreme Court delivered what became a historic decision. The Rossellini short (which had been packaged with Pagnol's *Joffroy* and Renoir's *A Day in the Country* to be shown as *The Ways of Love*) had aroused

The Miracle ◆ Italy, 1948, Roberto Rossellini; Anna Magnani, center foreground.

Catholics in the New York City area, especially a Catholic veterans' organization. A modern parable of Christ's birth, *The Miracle* starred Anna Magnani as a feeble-minded peasant "Mary"; a bearded Federico Fellini appeared as an itinerant "Joseph." After a round of contretemps, including picketing and bomb threats, the New York State Board of Regents, the censoring agency, revoked the film's license on the grounds that it was "sacrilegious." When the case eventually reached the Supreme Court, the Court seemed to reverse its own precedent. In 1915, in *Mutual Film Corporation* v. *Ohio*, it had been held that motion pictures were "business pure and simple . . . not to be regarded as part of the press of the country or as organs of public opinion," and hence not subject to the freedom from censorship guaranteed by the First Amendment to the Constitution. The 1952 Court did not rule on the constitutionality of film censorship as such, however. It simply stated that "sacrilege," particularly one faith's conception of it, was not sufficient grounds for the Board of Regents' action. Nonetheless, the decision suggested some sympathy toward affording the motion picture the same freedom from restraint prior to release as that enjoyed by the other media of communication and art.

There followed a succession of cases the decisions in which seemed to support that interpretation of the Court's position. Then, in 1954, a small distributor of foreign films, Times Film Corporation, decided to further test the Court by failing to submit to the Chicago Police Department for licensing a perfectly innocuous Italian film entitled *Don Juan*. In this case the Court appeared to take a step backward. It ruled that the City of Chicago had the right to license films, just as it licensed automobiles, push carts, and taverns. The clear implication that those films denied licenses were being censored was ignored.

In 1965, in a case brought by an exhibitor, *Friedman* v. *Maryland* (by then one of the few states still censoring films), the Court again advanced in a liberal direction. It ruled that when films were prevented from being exhibited, the burden of proof must be assumed by the government agency, and that legal processes must be expedited so as to create as little hardship as possible for the defendant. Before this decision, contrary to an underlying principle of our legal system, it had been as if a film were assumed "guilty" (that is, obscene) unless proven otherwise. In 1968 the Supreme Court ruled, in *Telsen* v. *Chicago*, that the Chicago film licensing act was unconstitutional.

With a later shift in Court membership toward the conservative, however, a 1973 decision regarding obscenity cases was rendered that many, not just those within the motion-picture industry, regarded with consternation. It altered and clarified the former criteria for determining what constituted obscenity. Specifically, the Court mandated that the affront need be only to local—as opposed to national— community standards, and that local standards were employable in determining appeal to prurient interest. Additionally, the Court withdrew the "utterly without redeeming social value" test and substituted for it a mere lack of "serious literary, artistic, political, or scientific value."

The way now seemed open for every interested local body to impose conflicting sets of requirements on every film released within conceivably thousands of areas of jurisdiction. That this was not an imaginary danger was made clear when, less than a month after the Supreme Court ruling, the Georgia Supreme Court confirmed a ban on *Carnal Knowledge* and the conviction of a theater owner for showing it. While the citizens of Albany, Georgia, were prevented from seeing Mike Nichols's serious dark comedy about sex, the exploitive and frankly pornographic *Deep Throat* was playing to packed houses in other communities across the land. (The U.S. Supreme Court subsequently reversed the Georgia decision on *Carnal Knowledge*, holding that no jury could legally find that film obscene, and indeed it looks tame today.)

During the same years the Motion Picture Association of America was making its own efforts, on the one hand to allow producers greater freedom of subject and treatment, and on the other to fend off attacks from those who protested that what had resulted was license rather than freedom. Since 1934 no important picture had been distributed without the seal of the MPAA's Production Code Administration. In the fifties, when two "A" features of United Artists were denied a Code seal, UA released them anyway, without it. The MPAA, now that the theaters were no longer owned or controlled by the studios, was unable to prevent the films from playing to large audiences. The first, *The Moon Is Blue* (1953), was from a popular stage comedy and would appear today patently moral. It was in fact about Maggie McNamara's successfully resisting the charms of David Niven. But it did contain considerable talk about sex and the words "virgin" and "pregnant" were used. The Code office subsequently conceded that it had been unwise in refusing that film a seal. No such option existed for the second one, *The Man with the Golden Arm* (1955). Taken from the Nelson

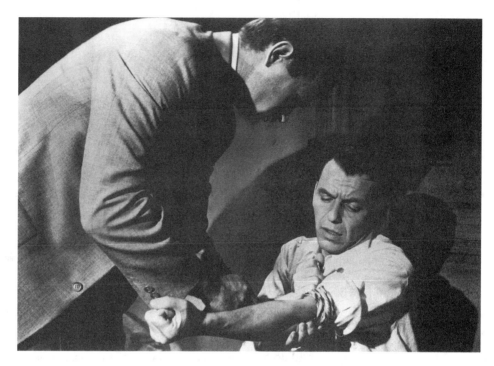

The Man with the Golden Arm ♦ U.S., 1955, Otto Preminger; Frank Sinatra, right.

Algren novel, it dealt directly with narcotic addiction, a subject expressly forbidden by the Code.

Both films were produced and directed by Otto Preminger, who made much of the publicity and set himself up as a champion of free speech. In a show of self-righteous indignation, United Artists withdrew from the MPAA; however, it rejoined after it had collected all its profits from the two offending films. This defiance of the Code administration clearly threatened the whole system of self-regulation, and other production companies, especially the independents, were becoming restive. In 1956 the Code was revised, the main change being to permit the treatment of narcotics.

A decade later Jack Valenti succeeded Eric Johnston as president of the MPAA. Since pressures from producers for increased freedom from restraint had continued to mount, and an ever increasing number of films were being released without the Code seal (distributors of foreign films rarely bothered to apply), one of Valenti's first acts was to further liberalize the Code. Among the concessions in the 1966 revisions were permitting the use of common profanity *(Gone With the Wind*'s famous final line, "Frankly, my dear, I don't give a damn," had required a special ruling in 1939), the treatment of abortion, and justifiable suicide. In general the Code language was softened, with phrases like "good taste" and "dramatic necessity" replacing the strict prohibitions of the earlier Code.

Still, the onrush of new explicitness continued. Inasmuch as the trend seemed irreversible and the outcries provoked were largely on behalf of impressionable children, the MPAA decided that rather than attempt to control screen content, it would regulate audience attendance. The shocking language and sexual intensity of *Who's Afraid of Virginia Woolf?* (1966) were allowed when its advertising carried the statement "Suggested for Mature Audiences." In 1968 the MPAA adopted, not without protest from members of the industry who objected to potential earnings being limited in any way, a system of age classification like those already operating in many countries, the United Kingdom for instance. The rating "G," for "general," meant suitable for all. "M" advised parents that the content was "mature" (subsequently this became "GP" and then "PG"—"parental guidance suggested"). "R" stood for "restricted": those under seventeen had to be accompanied by a parent or adult guardian. "X" indicated that only those eighteen and older would be admitted. (By 1990 the X rating had come to imply the frankly pornographic; it drastically limited distribution, advertising, and hence box-office returns. To avoid the stigma of the X and acknowledge films with adult themes and serious intentions, a new classification was devised: NC-17 [no one under seventeen admitted]. *Henry and June*, about writers Anaïs Nin and Henry Miller in Paris of the thirties, was first to receive it.) What had been the Production Code Administration became the Classification and Rating Administration. Enforcement was left to the theaters.

Much dissatisfaction about classification was expressed. Producers complained when they felt their films had been given a too-restrictive rating. Theater owners resented the encroachment on their domains and the nuisance involved. Organized pressure groups, notably the National Catholic Office of Motion Pictures (which replaced the Legion of Decency), protested that the ratings were too laxly administered. All pointed to the inevitable inconsistencies in the labeling of particular films. Even so, in the face of the continuing threat of legal censorship most of the industry accepted the MPAA classification system as the least of possible evils.

If the freedom of expression of American film makers was still limited (and the vast sums of money involved seemed to require that it be), it was much closer than ever before to that enjoyed by artists working in the traditional arts, and the American screen became among the freest in the world.

◆ SIX DIRECTORS

In 1952 General Dwight Eisenhower, hero of World War II, was elected President of the United States, and again in 1956. It is generally agreed that the Eisenhower years were prosperous, placid, and very "American." The war in Korea ended in 1953. Undercurrents of disaffection that hindsight has revealed didn't surface until the troubled sixties.

Much the same might be said of Hollywood films of the fifties in terms of placidity and Americanism. As shown earlier in this chapter, these years were not as prosperous for the film industry as the preceding decade had been. The six directors whose work will be examined here, however, were among those who were most productive and successful during the period. They are George Cukor, George Stevens, Billy Wilder, Fred Zinnemann, Vincente Minnelli, and Elia Kazan. Though all worked before and afterwards, their work at this time fairly represents the qualities of American film most valued by those within the Hollywood industry, by the major critics, and by the domestic audience.

Of the six, **George Cukor** was the consummate professional, his direction stylish and impeccable. He began in theater in 1919 as stage manager and then director, and his films always had qualities traceable to theater. Invariably his films were praised for their performances, especially those of women: Katharine Hepburn, Norma Shearer, Greta Garbo, Joan Crawford, Judy Holliday, Judy Garland, and Marilyn Monroe among them. Cukor specialized in literary adaptations, sophisticated comedies, musicals, and period pictures. In the 1930s and 1940s most of his major films, many of them produced by David O. Selznick, were based on plays or novels: *A Bill of Divorcement* (1932), *Dinner at Eight* (1933), *Little Women* (1933), *David Copperfield* (1935), *Romeo and Juliet* (1936), *Camille* (1936), *Holiday* (1938), *The Women* (1939), *The Philadelphia Story* (1940), and *Gaslight* (1944).

With *A Double Life* (1947), Cukor began a collaboration with Garson Kanin and Ruth Gordon, the husband-wife screen-writing team, which lasted through six more of their original scripts. *Adam's Rib* (1949), starring Spencer Tracy and Katharine Hepburn, with Judy Holliday in a supporting role, was the first of a series of intelligent, witty, and urbane battle-of-the-sexes comedies. It was followed by *Born Yesterday* (1950), starring Judy Holliday. These performers—Tracy, Hepburn, Holliday—continued working with Cukor in fresh and breezy vignettes of middle-class American life, much of them shot on location, eastern seaboard rather than western. In *The Marrying Kind* (1951) and *It Should Happen to You* (1954), Holliday further developed the lovable zany she had introduced in *Adam's Rib*. In *Pat and Mike* (1952), Hepburn and Tracy, who had been adversary lawyers in *Adam's Rib*, became athlete and manager, respectively. In *The Actress* (1953) Tracy played the beleaguered father of a daughter studying acting in New York City.

With *A Star Is Born* (1954) Cukor was back to Hollywood full-scale, and then some. This CinemaScope Technicolor extravaganza musical-comedy-melodrama was not only shot on the sound stages and back lots, it was about Hollywood. Furthermore, it was a remake, by Warner Brothers, of a 1937 film produced by Selznick and directed by William Wellman. Songs and dances were added; Judy Garland played the Janet Gaynor role and James Mason, Fredric March's. Among its many delights was a superb and innovative use of the new wide-screen shape, with intricate moving camera and rapid cutting. The color, too, was quite exceptional: muted and darker hues, with lots of browns and blues, replaced the standard solid and bright primary colors.

It was also a triumph for Garland and Mason in their roles of band singer Esther Blodgett, who becomes Vicki Lester, a movie star on her way up, and Norman Maine, a movie star on his way down, through a miasma of alcohol. Their love for each other, tender and touching, ennobles Norman's losing battle with himself and the Hollywood system, and permits Vicki to stand up in final dignity, after her husband's suicide, as Mrs. Norman Maine.

A Star Is Born   ◆   U.S., 1954, George Cukor; James Mason and Judy Garland.

Some regard this film as both Garland's and Cukor's finest. Both were deeply distressed, it was said, when Warner Brothers cut it from 181 minutes to 154, deleting two musical numbers along with transitional and motivational narrative material. Almost thirty years later, film historian Ronald Haver engaged in some dogged detective work that unearthed parts of the missing film. With a complete sound track plus added bits and pieces of footage and stills for the irrecoverable scenes, it was reissued in 1983 in a form that at least indicated what had been intended. Cukor, alas, died, at the age of 83, shortly before the reconstruction's first showing.

George Stevens, a native Californian, was in some ways even more firmly placed in the Hollywood aristocracy than George Cukor. Both of Stevens's parents were actors, and he made his debut on stage at the age of five, performing in his father's traveling company. He began work in the film industry in 1921, as an assistant cameraman; he became a cameraman and eventually a director of shorts. He directed his first feature in 1933.

Stevens's films of the thirties varied considerably in genre but were consistently well made. For example: *Alice Adams* (1935) offers some delightful small-town Americana; *Swing Time* (1936) is one of the best of the Astaire-Rogers musicals; *Gunga Din* (1939), based on a Kipling poem, commemorates the British in India. In the forties he made three engaging comedies in succession: *Woman of the Year* (1942), the first film costarring Hepburn and Tracy; *The Talk of the Town* (1942), a distinguished jurist and his landlady joined by a suspected arsonist; *The More the Merrier* (1943), wartime housing shortage in Washington, D.C.

Then in the 1950s Stevens's work seemed to change direction and he made three of his finest films in succession: *A Place in the Sun* (1951), an updated and softened version of Theodore Dreiser's novel *The American Tragedy*; *Shane* (1953), a mythic tribute to the western genre (Stevens's only western); and *Giant* (1956), from the Edna Ferber novel, a celebration and castigation of Texas. These were more serious than his earlier films, with more substantial characterizations (and excellent performances), and a fuller, more exploratory use of cinematic technique.

A Place in the Sun is especially remarkable for its experimentation with sound in relation to sight. Its sound track, rich and detailed, complements the visuals to an unusual degree. A radio, unnoticed by the lonely and pregnant Alice (Shelley Winters), softly plays dance music, adding poignancy to a scene in which she waits in vain for George (Montgomery Clift), who is being drawn away from her by his attraction to the wealthy and glamorous Angela (Elizabeth Taylor). Or again, a portable radio on a deserted lakeside dock carries a newscast of the discovery of Alice's drowning, as George and Angela roar past in the near distance in a powerful speedboat. From time to time, sirens and barking dogs are heard, as they would be in life, contributing to a sense of uneasiness. A loon's cry just before Alice's death is a foreboding.

The film has a sad, romantic glow that sticks in the memory; for example, George and Angela dancing late at night, dreamily in love. In this scene the shots, many of

A Place in the Sun ◆
U.S., 1951, George
Stevens; Elizabeth Taylor
and Montgomery Clift.

them huge closeups, are joined by slow dissolves rather than cuts, holding the delicate, unrecapturable moment before us. The loveliness of Angela, the hopelessness of George's longing for her, given their class differences and his obligation to Alice, are eloquently manifest. Stevens considered *A Place in the Sun* his best film.

Westerns tend to be more closely connected to genre conventions than to the historical or geographical West, but *Shane* seems to be about westerns. Its West, filmed mostly on location in Wyoming, is a lovely valley enclosed by snow-capped mountains seen in expansive panoramic shots (VistaVision and Technicolor). A drab clapboard settlement squats along a muddy street in the middle of it. The farmers settling the valley look real enough and seem to have real problems—with the land and with the ranchers who don't want them on it. Into this community rides the mysterious title character (played by Alan Ladd in white buckskin) at the time the homesteaders need someone to face up to the cattle baron's hired gun, the black-garbed Wilson (Jack Palance). The simple story is seen through the eyes of a boy (Brandon de Wilde) who idolizes Shane. Shane almost becomes part of the community, almost acknowledges the attraction he and the wife (Jean Arthur) of the farmer (Van Heflin) feel for each other. But the gunfight with Wilson is what he has to do. After Wilson's death, Shane rides off into a mountain sunset. When asked where he's headed, he replies, "Someplace I've not been." When asked what it is he wants, he says, "Nothing."

Giant involves ranchers and conflict, too: the clash of landed cattle gentry, represented by Bick and Leslie Benedict (Rock Hudson and Elizabeth Taylor), and the coming technology of the oil and gas industry, represented by Jett Rink (James Dean, who died before the film was released). Its time extends from the 1920s to the 1950s; its scale is large enough to encompass the sprawling Ferber novel. A roundup, a barbecue, the excitement of an oil strike, and myriad details are closely observed and convincing; the huge Victorian mansion on the plain is extraordinary. Like the country, the characters seem bigger, more open, and flatter than life; courtesy and graciousness mingle with hardness and meanness. The awesome size and wealth that feed the legend and the legend itself are captured—*Giant* feels a lot like Texas.

Taken together, these three Stevens films make a large statement about the United States of America. Andrew Sarris labeled them the "American Dream *Sun-Shane-Giant* trilogy." Romantic and mythic they are. Stevens seemed to acknowledge that myths and legends are necessary parts of a culture. He restated them in ways that help us not so much to understand as to recognize values and behaviors that are indigenous, that must nourish us in some way.

As 1951 and *A Place in the Sun* marked a turning point in George Stevens's career, so it was with **Billy Wilder** and *Ace in the Hole* in the same year. This was Wilder's first film after the breakup of his fruitful script writing collaboration with Charles Brackett, which had begun in 1938. Among their many successful scripts were *Ninotchka* (1939), directed by Ernst Lubitsch, and *Ball of Fire* (1941), directed by Howard Hawks. The first of their scripts to be directed by Wilder was *The Major and the Minor* (1942).

With the commercial failure of *Ace in the Hole* (it was rereleased as *The Big Carnival* in an effort to attract more customers), Wilder stopped making "films noir" (discussed in Chapter 10—*Double Indemnity*, 1944; *The Lost Weekend*, 1945; *Sunset Boulevard*, 1950). Instead, he turned mostly to comedies in which dark touches and underlying cynicism were lightened or concealed by laughter.

The first of these, *Stalag 17* (1953), was based on a Broadway hit about American prisoners of war held by the Germans during World War II. (Stalag 17 is the name of the camp.) Its center of interest is an opportunistic POW (played by William Holden) who seems devoted totally to self-interest, even to the point of collaborating with the Germans. Wilder's view of the characters is scathing; the laughter generated is not comfortable. Though it was popular with audiences, some reviewers complained of the film's nihilism and tastelessness.

Sabrina (1954), by contrast, is a Cinderella story that takes place on a lavish Long Island estate. It is about a chauffeur's daughter (Audrey Hepburn) and her romances with the two wealthy brothers her father drives for, the playboy (William Holden) and the stuffy businessman (Humphrey Bogart). Elegant and charming, it is essentially a good-humored joke about class differences and romantic dreams in the United States. Social meaning could be read into it only with considerable, and serious effort.

The Seven Year Itch (1955), a stage-bound, quite amusing film of George Axelrod's play, chucks class differences altogether: Money is no object. The title refers to the sexual longings, fantasies, and guilts of a husband (Tom Ewell) of seven years, inspired by the luscious, kooky blonde (Marilyn Monroe) living in the Manhattan apartment directly above his.

In Love in the Afternoon (1957) much the same sort of material is moved to Paris, as a young woman (Audrey Hepburn) falls in love with an aging American playboy (Gary Cooper). This was Wilder's first film with the screenwriter who would become his second long-lasting collaborator, I. A. L. Diamond.

The above three romantic and/or sexual comedies are very Lubitsch-like, a comparison Wilder readily acknowledged. The next three comedies—*Some Like It Hot* (1959), *The Apartment* (1960), and *One, Two, Three* (1961)—are very Wilder-Diamond-like. In them there is a fusion of the acidic noir films with the joie de vivre of the Lubitsch comedies. Given this understanding of his work, *The Spirit of St. Louis* (1957), Charles Lindbergh's trans-Atlantic flight, and *Witness for the Prosecution* (1958), a courtroom melodrama, seem out of character, though the latter was expertly made and highly profitable.

Some Like It Hot combines elements of the gangster film (two musicians, Tony Curtis and Jack Lemmon, witness the St. Valentine's Day massacre), knockabout farce, fast-paced witty dialogue à la screwball comedy, and transvestism (to escape Spats Colombo, played by George Raft, the two male musicians become "girls" in an all-girl band that includes Marilyn Monroe). Perhaps it is also a critique of American capitalism (at least of organized crime and Florida retirement) and sex (whether hetero- or homo-, male or female, makes not much difference). Confused identities and sexual mismatches are forced to incredible limits. The closing line, delivered by lustful millionaire Osgood Fielding III (Joe E. Brown) when his finacée confesses she's a man, is "Nobody's perfect."

The Apartment, its amalgam of sex and capitalism straightforward by comparison, adds a strong note of poignancy. An accountant for an insurance firm, C. C. "Bud" Baxter (Jack Lemmon), allows company executives to use his apartment for extramarital affairs. This arrangement presents only minor inconveniences, offset by the possibility for advancement, until Bud discovers that one of the users of his apartment, head of personnel (Fred MacMurray), is having an affair with the elevator operator, Fran Kubelik (Shirley MacLaine), whom Baxter secretly cherishes. The evident lack of meaning in the business of the insurance business, the manipulation of people by other people within the bureaucratic hierarchy, the coldness and joylessness of the sexual games being played, cause every laugh to contain some discomfort. Unlike the characters in other Wilder films, Bud and Fran offer the possibility of decency against which the prevailing moral corruption can be measured. Wilder's comments on the way of the world are at least as misanthropic as usual, but the relationship between the principals is one of the tenderest in Wilder's films—one of a very few observed with tenderness.

Any satirical barbs not included in Wilder's work up to this point must be contained in *One, Two, Three* (1961). It is about corporate executives and sex again,

The Apartment ♦ U.S., 1960, Billy Wilder; Jack Lemmon and Shirley MacLaine.

and pleasing the boss, but it invades new territory: politics, on an international scale. The setting is Berlin at the time of the Cold War. (The wall between East and West Berlin was being erected during the shooting of the film; topical references abound.) The protagonist (James Cagney) runs the Berlin Coca-Cola bottling plant. Americans and Soviets are ridiculed evenhandedly; capitalism is shown to be only slightly less obnoxious than communism. Everybody in the film seems self-centered and on the make. When the East German Comrade Piffl asks "Is everyone in this world corrupt?" the Russian Perpetchikoff replies "I don't know everyone." Though very funny, *One, Two, Three* is exceedingly dark.

It is interesting and no doubt significant that these dark comedies of Wilder's were commercial successes during the Eisenhower years, as film noir crime melodramas had been earlier. They allow a side of the Americans to be seen, and a particular view of that side to be taken, that the films of George Cukor and George Stevens do not.

Fred Zinnemann was an immigrant like Wilder. Both were Viennese, Zinnemann a year younger. Both worked in film in Berlin before coming to the United States. In fact, they had worked together on an unusual and interesting semidocumentary feature, *Menschen am Sontag* (*People on Sunday*, 1929), Wilder on script and Zinnemann as assistant, along with Edgar Ulmer, to director Robert Siodmak. All four of those members of the crew subsequently came to Hollywood, Zinnemann arriving in 1929, Wilder in 1934. And there the similarities may end.

Wilder became a satirist, a parodist, a caricaturist; Zinnemann remained close to the documentary impulse of *People on Sunday*. An even more profound influence on his way of thinking about film making and about life in general, he has repeatedly acknowledged, came from his brief association with Robert Flaherty, American documentary pioneer, on an abortive project. In the United States, Zinnemann worked in various capacities on various sorts of films, such as codirector, with Paul Strand, of the documentary *The Wave* (1935), and director of shorts at M-G-M (1937–1942), and from 1942 on, of features.

The Search (1948)—a moving, authentic study of displaced and orphaned children in post-World War II Europe and of Americans in military and relief organizations trying to help them—was the first feature to establish his distinctive qualities. His realistic bent continued in *The Men* (1950), about paraplegic veterans of World War II, and *Teresa* (1951), about conflicts that arose when returning GIs brought home foreign wives, in this case Italian. Both films involved a good deal of location shooting—at a veterans' hospital in the former, in Italy and New York City's Little Italy in the latter—and the use of nonactors in supporting roles.

With *High Noon* (1952) Zinnemann achieved his first big box-office success. This western—produced by Stanley Kramer, photographed by Floyd Crosby, whose credits include most of the major documentaries of Pare Lorentz—is much more conventional than his three films just discussed. But even when directing non-documentary-like fiction, Zinnemann is consistently careful about the particularities of the physical settings, as well as of the psychological situations. *High Noon* is tightly scripted along generic lines and uses only professional actors. In allegorical fashion it deals with an ethical problem important to American society at the time, the political paranoia called McCarthyism (discussed in Chapter 10). Only the sheriff (Gary Cooper) will stand up

High Noon ◆ U.S., 1952, Fred Zinnemann; Lon Chaney, Jr., and Gary Cooper.

against the vengeful outlaw and his gang as other members of the community think of reasons they cannot act. Its script writer, Carl Foreman, was one of those black-listed, following testimony before the House Un-American Activities Committee, and exiled himself in England.

From Here to Eternity (1953), from the best-selling novel by James Jones, was an even bigger box-office success than *High Noon*. It, too, examines the ethical expectations and behavior of Americans and the functioning of an institution, the peacetime army in Hawaii before the Japanese attack on Pearl Harbor. Though Zinnemann used well-known performers, he cast them against type: Montgomery Clift as a committed soldier, Deborah Kerr as the adulterous wife of the captain, Frank Sinatra, in his first straight dramatic role, as the doomed Maggio. Though the film reduces the novel's indictment of the army system to a matter of individual excess, it is about the army system and the hurt done to some men and women connected with it.

During the remainder of the period being discussed Zinnemann never succeeded in recapturing the critical and commercial success of *High Noon* and *From Here to Eternity*, but three films embodied some of the characteristic Zinnemann thematic and stylistic elements.

A Hatful of Rain (1957) is about a drug addict and the effects of his addiction not only on himself but on his family. It was the first film on the subject after the 1956 revision of the Production Code, referred to earlier, permitted it. The location shooting in New York City is noteworthy—the scene in a Lower East Side park in which a pusher is caught by the police, and the night scenes on the streets of the city.

The Nun's Story (1959) concerns the spiritual struggles of a young Belgian nun (Audrey Hepburn) whose desire to nurse the sick and learn more about medicine conflicts with the strict discipline of her order. The first half takes place in the austere convent and deals with the training of the novitiates; the second half is set in the lush Congo jungle and involves an intense and troubling relationship with a surgeon (Peter Finch).

The Sundowners (1960) is a large and sprawling comedy-drama about an Australian family of sheep herders. The exteriors were shot in Australia, and careful attention is given to things Australian—sheep herding and shearing, for example, and a rural horse race.

Though Zinnemann's direction proved expert in various kinds of films (during this period he also directed film versions of Carson McCuller's novel/play *The Member of the Wedding* [1953] and the Rodgers and Hammerstein musical *Oklahoma!* [1955]), he seems at his best when his characters are involved in personal moral dilemmas that relate to a larger social dimension—cultural or institutional. His concerns and his style have been closer to the documentary impulse than have those of other Hollywood directors.

Vincente Minnelli arrived in Hollywood in 1940 after a substantial career as a stage designer and director. Following an apprenticeship at M-G-M, his first film direction was a version of the all-black Broadway musical *Cabin in the Sky* (1943). Minnelli's most distinctive contributions in the forties were his musicals (for example, *Meet Me in St. Louis*, 1944; *The Pirate*, 1948), but he directed noteworthy films in other genres as well (*The Clock*, 1945, romantic drama; *Father of the Bride*, 1950, domestic comedy).

In 1951 Minnelli directed what is felt by many to be his finest film, *An American in Paris*. It was one of a number of especially memorable musicals made between the mid-forties and the mid-fifties by the M-G-M team assembled by producer Arthur Freed. With seasoned talent in every department, music and lyrics of George and Ira Gershwin, choreography and dancing by Gene Kelly, with Leslie Caron as his partner in her first screen appearance, *An American in Paris* nonetheless bears the stamp of Minnelli. The complexity within the coherence of the overall visual design, the expressive use of color and lighting are characteristic of his work in general. In the elaborate twenty-minute daydream ballet sequence, set to the Gershwin music of the title, the changing settings are in the styles of various painters—Renoir, Rousseau, Toulouse-Lautrec, Dufy, Van Gogh, and Manet. Within those artistic worlds, the dancers interpret the feeling evoked by each painter with American energy and grace. It is a dazzling, breathtaking climax.

The Bad and the Beautiful (1952) followed. This movie about Hollywood moviemakers revolves around a producer, Jonathan Shields (played by Kirk Douglas). Though egotistical and ruthless, he has achieved success not only with films he has produced but with careers he has made possible. In a manner reminiscent of *Citizen Kane* (John Houseman, closely involved in the production of Kane, produced *The Bad and the Beautiful* and other Minnelli films), the story is told by three persons whose lives Jonathan has affected and whom he is trying to bring together for yet another

An American in Paris ◆ U.S., 1951, Vincente Minelli; Leslie Caron and Gene Kelly, foreground.

production. We can relish *The Bad and the Beautiful* as exposé; many of its characters and incidents are based on actuality or rumor. It is replete with the glamour and ambition, the mistrust and vulnerability, the wealth and unhappiness associated with Hollywood success. Visually elegant—in stunning black and white with pervasive low-key and high-contrast lighting—its style is faithful to the sort of illusion-making it is about.

    The Band Wagon (1953) is to the musicals of Fred Astaire what *An American in Paris* is to those of Gene Kelly: top drawer. Both films came out of the Arthur Freed group at M-G-M. In *The Band Wagon,* Astaire is joined by Cyd Charisse. It is about theater people, and though rampant egos are kidded, Minnelli's view of them is much gentler and more affectionate than his view of the Hollywood crowd the year before. Yet it has the same roman-à-clef elements, with Astaire more or less playing himself as a former song-and-dance man of the Broadway stage who has gone to Hollywood and attained widespread popularity. In fact, the title, *The Band Wagon*, is that of a 1931 Broadway revue Astaire had starred in. The big number is "The Girl Hunt Ballet," in which Mickey Spillane and New York City private-eye toughness are burlesqued, Fred Astaire dancing a Mike Hammer surrogate.

    Lust for Life (1956) is Minnelli's large dramatic achievement of this period. A biography of Vincent Van Gogh (with Kirk Douglas looking remarkably like Van

Gogh of the self-portraits), it is in wide-screen color. Much of it was shot on location in Holland, Belgium, and France in the regions where Van Gogh had lived. The images, shifting from the real landscape to the famous paintings and back to the landscape, are conceived with obvious sensitivity and appreciation. It is one of the most rewarding Hollywood films about art and artists.

Gigi (1958) is Minnelli's last completely successful musical—it won nine Academy Awards. It has connections with, is in some ways a reprise of, his earlier work out of the Arthur Freed group. For example, it contains: Minnelli's attraction to things French (it is based on the novel by Collette); a script by Alan Jay Lerner (who also scripted Minnelli's *An American in Paris*; *Brigadoon*, 1954; and *On a Clear Day You Can See Forever*, 1970; the latter two from his stage originals); Leslie Caron; color; wide screen; and art, in a way, as the young Gigi in fin-de-siècle Paris is groomed by her grandmother and great aunt to become an accomplished courtesan, as they were.

Much of Minnelli's best work brings art and life together—is about life in relation to art—and is pronouncedly reflexive before the notion of film being about film had achieved currency. This letting the audience in on the spirit of creation adds a playfulness to the musicals; in the serious dramas it provides an irony which amplifies and intensifies the strong emotionality. Minnelli seems an artist's artist: His conception is securely rooted in the expressiveness of art; his filmic statements about life move lightly and gracefully or surely and dramatically along channels that artistic expression makes available. Slightly removed from life, his films nonetheless comment on it in ways that are beautiful and moving.

Elia Kazan, on the other hand, though the stylization in his films may equal that in Minnelli's, used artistic heightening to make life on the screen appear to be that taking place outside the theater. His verisimilitude and dramatic power were achieved primarily through his work with actors. A principal practitioner of "the Method," as the acting style derived from Konstantin Stanislavsky was popularly called, he directed numerous important Broadway productions before and during his work in film (for example, Thornton Wilder's *The Skin of Our Teeth* and Arthur Miller's *Death of a Salesman*). Screen performances directed by Kazan are among the most valued in cinema.

A second striking aspect of Kazan's films is the ways in which they seem to have been connected with the national life, with the political life of the time. Of the six directors discussed in this chapter, Kazan best exemplifies certain of the shifting tendencies in American film generally over several decades. After *A Tree Grows in Brooklyn* (1945) and *Sea of Grass* (1947), both based on popular novels, Kazan directed a body of work that was at the center of the realistic/problem films of liberal sentiments and good causes discussed in Chapter 10. *Boomerang* (1947) and *Panic in the Streets* (1950) were taut crime melodramas which at the same time honored the courageous work of government officials on behalf of the individual and the public in the face of misunderstanding, resistance, and lack of appreciation. *Gentleman's Agreement* (1947) and *Pinky* (1949) were prominent in the race relations cycle. In 1951 he directed the film version of Tennessee Williams's play *A Streetcar Named Desire*, which he had also directed on the stage. Then, in 1952, Kazan was called before the House Un-American Activities Committee, confessed to his own Communist Party membership between 1934 and 1936, and named those he had known as Party members. He placed an ad in *The New York Times* justifying his change of political attitude and calling upon others to join him in confessing past error and denouncing communism and communists.

Elements of self-justification can also be seen in Kazan's subsequent films. *Viva Zapata!* (1952, with a script by John Steinbeck) shows the seeds of corruption taking root within the Mexican revolutionary leader, Emiliano Zapata, and the ultimate failure of the revolution through the adoption of the same totalitarian measures as those of the dictatorial regime which had been overthrown. *Man on a Tightrope* (1953), based on a screenplay by Robert Sherwood, was one of the anticommunist films of the period that dramatized actual events of the Cold War. It recounted the escape of a Czech circus troupe from behind the Iron Curtain.

On the Waterfront (1954), the most powerful and empathic of these social-political statements, is from a script by Budd Schulberg, who also had confessed past Party membership to the House Un-American Activities Committee and named people he had known as communists. It deals with the matter of informing to a government crime commission. Longshoreman Terry Malloy (played by Marlon Brando, who had also played Zapata) comes to realize that in order to stand upright as a moral being he must expose the gangster forces controlling the waterfront labor unions and inform on his former associates. (Lee J. Cobb, who plays the union boss, and Leif Ericson, who plays one of the Waterfront Crime Commission investigators, were others involved in the production who had confessed and named names to HUAC.) The symbolism built around Terry's care and training of his flock of pigeons takes on a special significance when we remember that screenwriter John Howard Lawson, one of the "unfriendly witnesses," had charged that HUAC's "so-called 'evidence'" had come from a parade of "stool pigeons, neurotics, publicity-seeking clowns, Gestapo agents, paid informers and a few ignorant and frightened Hollywood artists."[1]

With these three films Kazan seemed to release his need for broad ideological statement, though *A Face in the Crowd* (1957, script again by Schulberg) concerns a radio-television personality who comes to savor the enormous political power inherent in his mass popularity, and *Wild River* (1960) deals with the individual in conflict with big government in the Tennessee Valley of the 1930s. Instead, he confined himself to individual drama (*East of Eden*, 1955, the finest, starring James Dean; *Baby Doll*, 1956; *Splendor in the Grass*, 1961) which became increasingly personal and even autobiographical. In subsequent years his connection with the Hollywood film industry and with the movie-going public became less frequent and less direct.

The changes that followed in the wake of television's impact on the American motion picture were profound and pervasive—technological, economic, sociological. MacCann, in his view of *Hollywood in Transition*, suggested that they were actually expanded freedoms; but he added that "Freedom is seldom as agreeable as it looks, and never easy." It took the industry time to absorb the changes and to adjust to the newly reduced and more specialized sorts of production, distribution, and exhibition that emerged.

---

[1]Quoted in John Cogley, *Report on Blacklisting I. Movies* (Santa Barbara, CA: The Fund for the Republic, 1956), p. 19.

On the Waterfront ◆
U.S., 1954, Elia Kazan;
Marlon Brando, right.

Changes in the actual content and form of American films during this period—except for those caused by the wide screen, stereophonic sound, and increased use of color—were not nearly so evident. As distinguished as was the work of the six directors discussed above, and of other American film makers in the fifties, it came out of firmly established tradition. Not until the middle and late sixties did American films begin to take on some of the characteristics identified with trends of modern cinema that had begun germinating in Europe from the mid-fifties on.

FILMS OF THE PERIOD

1952

The Bad and the Beautiful (Vincente Minnelli)
Bwana Devil (Arch Oboler)
Five Fingers (Joseph L. Mankiewicz)
The Greatest Show on Earth (Cecil B. De Mille)
High Noon (Fred Zinnemann)
Limelight (Charles Chaplin)
The Quiet Man (John Ford)
Singin' in the Rain
    (Stanley Donen and Gene Kelly)
This Is Cinerama (Merian C. Cooper)
Viva Zapata! (Elia Kazan)

1953

From Here to Eternity (Zinnemann)
Lili (Charles Walters)
The Robe (Henry Koster)
Roman Holiday (William Wyler)
Shane (George Stevens)
The Wild One (Laslo Benedek)

1954

Beat the Devil (John Huston)
Dial M for Murder (Alfred Hitchcock)
On the Waterfront (Kazan)

Rear Window (Hitchcock)
Sabrina (Wilder)
Seven Brides for Seven Brothers (Donen)
A Star Is Born (George Cukor)

1955
Bad Day at Black Rock (John Sturges)
East of Eden (Kazan)
The Man with the Golden Arm (Otto Preminger)
Marty (Delbert Mann)
Rebel Without a Cause (Nicholas Ray)
Summertime (David Lean)

1956
Around the World in 80 Days
    (Michael Anderson)
Friendly Persuasion (Wyler)
Giant (Stevens)
Lust for Life (Minnelli)

1957
The Bachelor Party (Delbert Mann)
Bridge on the River Kwai (Lean)
Funny Face (Donen)
Paths of Glory (Stanley Kubrick)
Sweet Smell of Success
    (Alexander Mackendrick)
Twelve Angry Men (Sidney Lumet)

1958
Cat on a Hot Tin Roof (Richard Brooks)
The Defiant Ones (Stanley Kramer)
Gigi (Minnelli)

The Goddess (John Cromwell)
Touch of Evil (Orson Welles)
Vertigo (Hitchcock)

1959
Anatomy of a Murder (Preminger)
Ben-Hur (Wyler)
North by Northwest (Hitchcock)
Shadows (John Cassevetes)
Some Like It Hot (Wilder)
Suddenly Last Summer (Mankiewicz)

1960
The Alamo (John Wayne)
The Apartment (Wilder)
Home from the Hill (Minnelli)
Psycho (Hitchcock)

1961
The Hustler (Robert Rossen)
The Misfits (Huston)
One, Two, Three (Wilder)
West Side Story (Jerome Robbins and
    Robert Wise)

1962
Lawrence of Arabia (Lean)
Long Days' Journey Into Night (Lumet)
The Manchurian Candidate
    (John Frankenheimer)
To Kill a Mockingbird (Robert Mulligan)
War Hunt (Denis Sanders)

BOOKS ON THE PERIOD

Balio, Tino, ed., *Hollywood in the Age of Television.* New York: HarperCollins, 1991
Belton, John, *Widescreen Cinema.* Cambridge, MA: Harvard University Press, 1992
Byars, Jackie, *All That Hollywood Allows: Re-reading Gender in 1950s Melodrama.* Chapel
    Hill: University of North Carolina Press, 1991
Carr, Robert E., and R. M. Hayes, *Wide Screen Movies: A History and Filmography of Wide
    Gauge Filmmaking.* Jefferson, NC; McFarland, 1988
Hayes, R. M., *3-D Movies: A History and Filmography of Stereoscopic Cinema.* Jefferson, NC:
    McFarland, 1989
Leff, Leonard, and Jerold L. Simmons, *The Dame in the Kimono: Hollywood, Censorship, and
    the Production Code from the 1920s to the 1960s.* New York: Grove Weidenfeld, 1990

Film of the Auteur, the French New Wave, and After

◆ ◆ ◆

1954–

◆ **AUTEURISM**

An article by a young critic named François Truffaut, published in *Cahiers du Cinéma* in January 1954, established the designation and first premise for a critical position that would gain increasing strength both in France and elsewhere in the years to come. Quietly entitled "A Certain Tendency in the French Cinema," Truffaut's piece was against the writer's film—the well-wrought "literary" scenario executed by expert technicians. This "tradition of quality," as he called it, began with the prewar "poetic realism" best represented by the writing-directing team of Jacques Prévert and Marcel Carné; their *Quai des brumes* (*Port of Shadows,* 1938) remained the masterpiece of the method and style, according to Truffaut. During the postwar years emphasis shifted to "psychological realism," and within that style the writing team of Jean Aurenche and Pierre Bost adapted for the screen literary works like *Symphonie Pastorale* (1946), *Devil in the Flesh* (1947), *God Needs Men* (1950), and *Forbidden Games* (1952), which were "illustrated" by such directors as Claude Autant-Lara, Jean Delannoy, and René Clement. Works in this main line were essentially "scenarists' films," Truffaut insisted. At the time of writing, he felt the French cinema had degenerated into films made to win prizes at festivals rather than because anyone had anything urgent or personal to say.

In place of the creations of script writers, Truffaut called for films that would reflect as totally as possible the creative personalities of their directors. He argued that only in this way could French cinema overcome literary stasis and utilize the dynamic filmic potential available. A handful of French directors were capable of this sort of creation, he wrote, and they were the "authors" of their films; that is, in control of, or at least fully involved in, conception as well as execution. He cited Jean Renoir, Robert Bresson, Jean Cocteau, Jacques Becker, Abel Gance, Max Ophüls, Jacques Tati, and Roger Leenhardt as *auteurs* who often wrote their dialogue and some of whom invented the stories they directed. In asking for the elimination of the old psychological realism and dominance by script writers, to be replaced by strongly original directors in creative control, Truffaut declared that he could not believe in the peaceful coexistence of the *tradition of quality* and a *cinema of auteurs.* What his criticism pointed toward was the French New Wave, which would break a few years later and carry him along with it.

The background for Truffaut's manifesto extends at least to Alexandre Astruc's call, as early as 1948, for *la caméra-stylo*—camera as pen; that is, creating the film in its making rather than merely supplying images and sounds for a fully realized and pre-fixed conception. Also, by those early postwar years, the French national film archive and screening center, the Cinémathèque Française, had been thoroughly reestablished, making available a systematic viewing of great amounts of the international history of the motion picture. It became possible to see that the moments of aesthetic excitement among the hours upon hours of films were provided by directorial vision, like that of Griffith or Eisenstein, Murnau or Gance.

Perhaps of even greater consequence was the arrival of the backlog of American films which had been kept from France by the German Occupation. Seeing in rapid succession films produced over a period of years permitted comparisons that provoked new insights. Even among the popular generic entertainments turned out by the big Hollywood studios there were differences, not only of artistic quality but, more important, of artistic personality attributable to certain directors. Both Hawks and Ford made excellent westerns, and yet a Ford western was subtly but nonetheless surely and consistently advancing different themes and offering a different visual style than one by Hawks. The same was true of the musicals of Minnelli compared to those of Donen and Kelly. Further, directors who had been thought of only as having been involved with a few good pictures along with some less good ones could be seen to carry with them a certain special vision; among these were Orson Welles, Fritz Lang, and Alfred Hitchcock. For the young French critics, films by the latter kind of director were much more interesting and rewarding than those of others, however prestigious and expert, whose direction was impersonal. Especially was this so when they regarded all of a director's films together; that is, the director in relation to the total body of work. Even—sometimes especially—the humble action directors working on "B" budgets were able to maintain and articulate their own particular visions: Raoul Walsh in gangster films, Anthony Mann in westerns, Samuel Fuller in war pictures, for example.

It was the application of *la politique des auteurs* to the popular American movie that created the most excitement and controversy. Reevaluations of the total corpus of the American sound film were prompted by the young writers of *Cahiers,* who announced and defended newly discovered masters and masterpieces with enthusiastic rhetoric. As the "auteur theory," it moved westward to the United States in 1961, as evidenced by Andrew Sarris's writing in *Film Culture* and by the appearance of *New York Film Bulletin.* The auteur theory appeared in Great Britain in 1962, upon the publication of *Movie* magazine. Auteurism was attacked by the more conventional critics for ignoring the collective nature of film making, especially Hollywood's, and for turning critical standards upside down by insisting that bad films were good merely because they were made by favored directors.

Whatever the merits of the arguments, the French word *politique* translated badly as *theory;* what it means more nearly is *position* or *policy.* As with Truffaut initially, the auteur critics' positions were partisan and polemical. What they were insisting was simply that, after looking at hundreds of films in relation to who directed them, certain directors they valued and others they did not. The judgments were not based on the importance of the films' statements in humanist terms, nor on their beauty in aesthetic ones. Rather, the criterion was the consistency with which a uniquely personal point of view was expressed through recurring themes, characters, situations, imagery. Pushed to its extreme, the position was that any film directed by Otto Preminger, or Nicholas Ray, or Douglas Sirk (among the auteurists' favorites) was of more value than any film directed by William Wellman, or William Wyler, or Robert Wise. The former were auteurs, the latter merely interpreters, realizers of someone else's conception. What's more, auteurists seemed often to value most those auteur films in which the script was weakest or the content slightest precisely because they allowed the director's creative personality to be disclosed most nakedly, without the cloak of satisfying form.

Quite appropriately, since he had been cofounder of *Cahiers du Cinéma* and patron of Truffaut, critic André Bazin offered the best reasoned analysis of the contributions and pitfalls "De La Politique des Auteurs," in the April 1957 *Cahiers.* In general sympathy with auteurism—largely because it brought cinema into a kind of criticism and onto a level of seriousness longstanding in the other arts—Bazin at the same time pointed out the dangers of excessive zeal. First, film *was* an industrial and commercial art and did not permit anything like the individual control over the work exerted by a Picasso or a Matisse. This should be taken into account, argued Bazin. The ability of the Hollywood production system to provide on occasion fine works within its popular genres, by directors who were not consistent personal film makers (auteurs) should be applauded rather than denigrated. Second, there was the matter of the auteurists' characteristically preferring, for instance, Welles's *Mr. Arkadin* (1953) over his *Citizen Kane* (1941). Since, they insisted, Welles was older when he made *Arkadin,* he must have matured as an artist. And because it was much less a collaborative endeavor than *Kane,* it contained more of Welles's unique artistic sensibility and understanding. Bazin could see that this evaluation followed logically from the auteur position, but maintained that, for himself, though he admired *Mr. Arkadin* and found in it the same gifts as in *Citizen Kane,* the latter opened up a new age of American cinema and *Arkadin* remained a second-rate film.

Elaborating on that example of the *politique* at work, Bazin added:

> *In other terms, they want to retain of the equation, auteur + subject = work, only the auteur, the subject being reduced to 0. Some of these auteur adherents would feign to grant me that, all other things being equal, a good subject*

is obviously worth more than a bad one, but the most frank or the most insolent will admit to me that anything goes, as if their preference were on the contrary for little B films in which the acknowledged banality of the scenario leaves that much more room for the personal contribution of the auteur.[1]

Writing as a friend throughout, Bazin finally embraced *la politique,* not only because it had the merit of treating the cinema with an approach traditional in the other arts, but also because it represented a reaction against the impressionistic relativism which was the basis for most film criticism. There were, wrote Bazin, two symmetrical heresies inherent in film criticism generally: on the one hand, that of applying a critical grid or overlay to all films; on the other, that of considering it sufficient to express pleasure or distaste with individual films. The first position tended to deny the role of taste (auteurs are auteurs are auteurs); the second to set up the critic's taste a priori as superior to that of the auteur (by pronouncing judgment on each work as good or bad). Presenting himself with the inescapable choice, Bazin opted for the more systematic *Politique,* a position that honored the film maker over the critic.

The ideas of auteurism subsequently gained ground internationally. Even the founts of English-language criticism which had been under attack by the auteurists—*The New York Times, The New Yorker,* and *Sight and Sound,* for example—gradually came to reflect their tastes. In 1968 Andrew Sarris consolidated the auteur position in his book *The American Cinema: Directors and Directions 1929–1968.*

◆ THREE AUTEURS

Certain film makers have stood outside the national tendencies at given periods that have served as an organizing basis for this text. In transcending the concerns of their time and place, to the extent that any artist can, they offer analogues to the great creators in the more traditional arts. Three contemporary film artists who cannot conveniently be fitted into a broad historical plan, but whose individual distinction demands recognition, are Robert Bresson, Ingmar Bergman, and Luis Buñuel. Though their creative personalities are markedly different from each other, all three share a preoccupation with basic metaphysical problems, and developed increasingly precise and unelaborated cinematic styles through which to articulate their attitudes. These qualities make their work seem at once old-fashioned and uniquely modern—timeless perhaps.

Bresson was among the French directors Truffaut first cited as auteurs. His important films began shortly after those of the great French film makers of the 1930s and extend to the near present. Throughout his career Bresson has remained an isolated figure, among the most personal of film makers. The austerity of his subject matter, concerned more with moral and theological questions than with psychological

[1]André Bazin, "On The Politique des Auteurs," *Cahiers du Cinéma in English,* no. 1 (January 1966): 14.

analysis, and his insistence on rigorous control over every aspect of production have kept him removed from critical and creative fashion and have limited his output to thirteen films, which stand as monuments to his intellectual and aesthetic integrity. Though Bresson is part of the Catholic humanist tradition, his views take on a particular severity which led to his being called the Jansenist of French cinema.

In *Les Anges du péché* (1943), Bresson's first feature as director, the setting is a convent and the protagonist a young novitiate. Its closed world and struggle for spiritual release into something approximating a state of grace are narrative components present in many of Bresson's films. *Les Dames du bois de Boulogne* (1945) is a dark study of passion and revenge drawn from Diderot's *Jacques le fataliste*. Less typical in its complete secularism and also in its theatricality (dialogue by Jean Cocteau), it has earned a lasting reputation on its own terms.

With *Diary of a Country Priest* (1950), adapted from a novel by Georges Bernanos, Bresson moved into the main themes and mature style of his subsequent work. Set firmly in the midst of French provincial Catholicism, it is concerned not so much with religion as with faith, with the preservation and sharing of belief in God. Further, it is about the misunderstanding and misinterpretation of motives to which the truly saintly are subjected in a world of petty selfishness, rivalry, ambition, and smallness of spirit. Shot on location in the Artois region in bleak fall and early winter weather,

Diary of a Country Priest ◆ France, 1951, Robert Bresson; Claude Laydu, right.

the cast comprises nonactors in many of the roles including the principal one of the young curé.

The next film, *A Man Escaped* (1956), was based on a real incident involving the imprisonment of a member of the resistance and his escape from a Gestapo prison in France in 1943. The film is only indirectly about the war and occupation, however; directly, as with so many of Bresson's works, it is about a human being in isolation, physical as well as spiritual in this case. The inner experience of the protagonist (as in *Diary of a Country Priest*) is refined to a pure, concentrated, intense expression. Again nonactors were used—here the entire cast—directed by Bresson as if they were professionals, with extremely exact and detailed performances obtained through endless repetition.

Pickpocket (1959), a present-day paraphrase of Dostoevski's *Crime and Punishment,* concerns a petty thief locked inside his inchoate and unarticulated feelings. Drawn to his type of crime through obsessive compulsion, he lives emotionally only through the alternating sensations of fear and release accompanying his repeated thefts. The customary nonactors and location shooting were employed. And, as in *A Man Escaped,* Bresson closely observed the physical processes in which the subject is involved and emphasized the objects and sounds which are part of his milieu: documentary means to arrive at nondocumentary ends—spirit through matter.

In *The Trial of Joan of Arc* (1962) Bresson dealt with the same material as had Carl Dreyer, a director with whom Bresson is often compared, in his *The Passion of Joan of Arc* (1928). Like Dreyer's film, Bresson's is based on the actual court records; in his case the dialogue of Joan and her accusers is confined to those words spoken at the trial. This interrogation, this spiritual drama stripped bare, is presented with remarkable austerity even within the context of Bresson's work.

Au hasard, Balthasar and *Mouchette,* both made in 1966, are linked in their examination of the casual, gratuitous inhumanity to which the meek of this earth are subjected: a donkey in the former, a fourteen-year-old girl in the latter. Both films end in the death of their protagonists, as do so many of Bresson's. *A Gentle Creature* (1969) and *Four Nights of a Dreamer* (1971) are based on Dostoevski stories transposed to modern Paris.

Lancelot of the Lake (1974) was the realization of a long-held ambition to film the Arthurian legend. Knightly idealism is set against the clash and clangor of arms on muddy battlefields, and Lancelot emerges as a troubled, tragic hero torn between his love for Guinevere, his religious dedication, and his loyalty to Arthur. It was followed by *The Devil Probably* (1977), which involves suicide, as do other of his films.

Bresson's *L'Argent* (1983), made at the age of seventy-six, concerns the role of chance and predestination so prominent in his work. Based loosely on a story by Tolstoy, it follows a fuel-oil deliveryman who, after unsuspectingly receiving some counterfeit money, loses his job, participates in a holdup, is imprisoned, is abandoned by his wife after the death of their child, and finally commits multiple murders. Remorseless and disturbing, spare and yet almost sensuous in its physicality, it is quintessential Bresson.

While his films have never been widely popular with audiences nor noticeably influential on the work of other film makers, Bresson has emerged as one of the rare examples of a consummate individual stylist. His search for ever greater clarity and simplicty of visual-aural statement, his concentration on only those themes that most deeply concern him, place him among the very select company with which he is being considered.

Almost exactly coincidental with Bresson's major work in France was that of another, even more isolated film artist, **Ingmar Bergman** in Sweden. The uniqueness of his work, as well as that of Bresson, was noted by those advancing the *politique des auteurs.* Of Bergman, young critic and film-maker-to-be Jean-Luc Godard wrote, in the July 1958 *Cahiers du Cinéma,* that he was "the most original auteur of the modern European cinema." To date Bergman stands unchallenged as Sweden's pre-eminent film maker.

In the late teens and early twenties Swedish film had achieved artistic heights and a unique national expression, primarily in the work of Victor Sjöström (*The Outlaw and his Wife,* 1917; *The Phantom Carriage,* 1920) and Mauritz Stiller (*The Treasure of Arne,* 1919; *The Story of Gösta Berling,* 1924). Following this period it descended to a kind of accomplishment appreciated mainly by Scandinavian audiences. The one major director at work in the years between Sjöström/Stiller and the rise of Bergman was Alf Sjöberg. It was with Sjöberg that Bergman began his film career, as script writer of *Torment,* the first postwar Swedish international success (produced in 1944). Coming out of theater, as playwright and director, Bergman continued his theatrical work alongside the cinematic, directing plays in winter and making films in summer. He has said that the theater is his wife, the cinema his mistress.

Bergman's initial film direction was *Crisis* (1945), from his own script, interesting now chiefly as a harbinger of things to come. The first works of stature were *Three Strange Loves* (1949), *Summer Interlude* (1951), *Secrets of Women* and *Monika* (both 1952). All were shown abroad. *The Naked Night* (1953, also called *Sawdust and Tinsel*) marked a turning point; it is a small masterpiece. But it was *Smiles of a Summer Night* (1955), *The Seventh Seal* (1957) and *Wild Strawberries* (1957) that confirmed the earlier promise and set forth fully the thematic preoccupations we associate with the mature Bergman.

For it is what his films are about that becomes the ultimate measure of Bergman's worth. Stylistically he is conservative, somewhat theatrical in manner, with emphasis placed on script and performance. This is not to say that the form of his films doesn't match his intentions perfectly, nor that he is not in absolute command of the medium for his own purposes. His films originate totally with him, from first story idea through the framing of images to the emphasis given a noise laid in on the audio track. We can get at his artistic statements only through the cinematic sights and sounds in which they are embedded. Given the nature of the film medium, of course he worked in collaboration with others. But in addition to providing script and direction, Bergman commanded a devoted stock company of some of the finest performers in film and a crew of technicians who after years of working together had grown accustomed to making tangible his every inclination.

Like Bresson, Bergman deals solely with the questions that obsess him and that he attempts to answer through the creation of his films. They have been seen much more widely than Bresson's and have attracted audiences who have become capable of recognizing and appreciating the essential differences between Bergman and other film makers. To a quite remarkable extent, he (and to lesser degree Federico Fellini) was responsible for inspiring the widespread serious intellectual consideration of film, in the United States at least. Bergman's great appeal to the new kind of audience that began to appear at the end of the fifties was that his films dealt with matters of transcendent importance, and the manner in which he addressed those issues resonated powerfully in modern consciousness.

The familiar image of the game of chess between the Knight and Death in *The Seventh Seal* suggests a visual metaphor for the fifty some films of Bergman. Taken collectively, his work is like a huge chessboard on which a single game is being played. Parts of the game—the characters and themes—may receive his concentration in a particular film, with the rest of the board receding into the background, but most or all are present in each film. This was true at least up through his trilogy—*Through a Glass Darkly* (1961), *Winter Light* (1962), *The Silence* (1963)—in which he claimed to have exorcised his religious preoccupations. In subsequent films he not so much changed his concerns as moved in ever more closely and insistently on those that came to seem most important to him. He conforms to Jean Renoir's observation that a great film maker spends his whole life making a single film.

In *The Seventh Seal* we could see clearly what Bergman felt to be the essential problems confronting humanity, or at least himself. First of all was the human need for God, and His apparent absence, or was it merely silence? Then there was death, the inevitable, unknown and unknowable end. What lay beyond life, if anything; if something, how could we find our way to it? Salvation, for Bergman, had to come through faith rather than knowledge or good works—the young couple Jof and Mia, and their baby, apparently have it and are saved; the Knight and his companions do not and are not (though the Knight, in his one meaningful deed, does distract Death so that Jof's family can escape). If in Bergman's world you can't learn or earn your way to faith, it is occasionally granted to the elect, who are saved. Invariably the faith is simple and unquestioning.

On the other hand, we might see human love, though largely unattainable, as the key to salvation: the love of the young couple for each other and their child in *The Seventh Seal,* and the beginning love of the old doctor for his daughter-in-law in *Wild Strawberries,* which brings him an almost paradisiacal dream. Through love between human beings, faith may come, and from faith, salvation. Bergman's salvation may be merely meaningfulness: answers to the Knight's desperate questions about God and death. If the Knight has to ask them though, of course they can't be answered.

Sex in Bergman's films is not to be confused with love; on the contrary, it is frequently presented as a compulsive and destructive itch (*The Silence*), the scratching of which can sometimes quite literally draw blood (*Cries and Whispers,* 1972). Sex is the field of conflict rather than the source of fulfillment between the sexes (*Smiles of a Summer Night,* 1955, and *The Passion of Anna,* 1970, each in its own different way). Marriages evidently contain their own heaven and hell, but we see much more of the latter (*Scenes from a Marriage,* 1973).

Finally, Bergman is consistently absorbed with the role and function of the artist in society, and even in the cosmos, because, after all, he is a creator, if only with a

Wild Strawberries ◆ Sweden, 1957, Ingmar Bergman; Victor Sjöström and Ingrid Thulin.

small *c*. Bergman sees the artist as a charlatan, a kind of fake who may *almost* achieve understanding of the inscrutable mysteries of the universe and the mysterious ways of humankind. Artists may come closer to this understanding than other people, but thereby suffer more for their ultimate failure and the exposure of their pretensions and pretenses. The artist is invariably subjected to humiliation. *The Magician* (1958) is one of the serious films in which this concern is the center of attention; *Now About These Women* (1964) is one of the comedies. It is hard to say whether Bergman is sincere in this view or whether it is merely an engaging conceit. But in *Persona* (1966), which many regard as the most profound statement of all of his recurrent philosophical/psychological probings, he takes pains to remind us that we are seeing a movie. A projector shines its beam directly at us; a break in the film is simulated; and so on. He has expressed his delight with the basic technology and perceptual illusion on which his medium is based: that about half the time while one is watching a film the screen is in darkness as successive frames are moved into place. In a figurative sense, it's "all done with mirrors," as is said scornfully about certain kinds of magic performances.

In some quarters Bergman is faulted for the narrow range and frequent morbidity of his themes. Increasingly he became vulnerable to this sort of criticism after he abandoned God altogether and concentrated on the ways in which human beings can torture each other out of impulses that may have started as (may still contain some-thing recognizable as) love. It is true that in his pictures there isn't room for the pleasures and positive aspects of human existence celebrated by Jean Renoir, say. Though Bergman's people are mostly physically attractive, intelligent, successful in their vocations, well-to-do, living in pleasant surroundings, they are generally miser-able—the thinking ones anyway. Part of their suffering seems to be caused by their not understanding why they are miserable. In Bergman's films misery seems to come from a lack (an absence of meaning, significance, or fullness) rather than from an active cause. "Ripeness is all," said King Lear, but there is a forbidding amount of spoilage and decay in Bergman's universe.

Fanny and Alexander (1983), which he said would be his last film (as he had said of others), at last offered ripeness. It is like a huge old-fashioned novel. Or, to return to a simile suggested earlier, Bergman here attempts to include most of the chessboard in his view. The well-worked themes are present, but this time Bergman's regard is mellow and, yes, valedictory. Beginning on Christmas Eve in 1907 in a Swedish town that might be Uppsala, where Bergman was born, it is about a large, influential family, a dynasty almost. There are many sharply differentiated characters and varied rela-tionships among those living and visiting in the seemingly vast apartment presided over by the grandmother of the twelve-year-old Alexander and his younger sister, Fanny. It has elements traceable to what we know of Bergman's own growing up, and Alexander serves as the observer. What Bergman seems to be saying finally, if this is finally, is that, though a lot of curious and awful things may happen in this world, and people may torment themselves and each other in strange and pitiable ways, life is colorful and full, rich in its stimulations, tender and tranquil in old age—well worth living.

As a film artist Bergman tends to appeal most directly and strongly to those who aren't interested primarily in film art but regard film from the vantage point of the other arts, especially literature and drama. He has been the first enthusiasm of many people attracted to film who have then gone on to put him aside in favor of more "filmic" directors. But when Bergman has worked his conception completely into cinematic language—when he has created fully and deeply in terms of sights and sounds as well as characters and situations—his films become among the finest and most profoundly moving in all of cinema. Although he has not quite lost himself in the medium, he has transcended its frequent limitations—in regard to what Aristotle in the *Poetics* called Character and Thought—in a way that must be acknowledged. If Judgment Day were tomorrow (a prospect Bergman sometimes seems to entertain), his total body of work, granting the criteria appropriate to it, would entitle him to a place in the company of major artists from all the arts. This can be said of few other film makers in the history of the young art. Bergman is indeed an auteur.

Luis Buñuel was not only a truly independent and therefore isolated artist, like Bresson and Bergman, but his work stands outside a particular national culture. Perhaps one might better say that he carried his Spanish inheritance and later adoption of surrealism with him in films made in a number of countries over a period of fifty-five years.

Buñuel's first work in cinema was in France in the 1920s, as an assistant to Jean Epstein and other impressionist film makers, culminating in his turn to surrealism and collaboration with Salvador Dali on *Un Chien andalou* (1928) and *L'Age d'or* (1930). After a long fallow period spent mostly in the United States—except for *Land Without Bread* (1932), a seering documentary about the impoverished Las Hurdes region of Spain—Buñuel settled in Mexico in 1946. There his production became steady and commercially successful, for the most part, within the popular Latin American genres of melodrama and comedy.

The first exceptional film in the Mexican period was *Los Olvidados* (1950). It extends out of the naturalism of *Land Without Bread*, examining the violence and squalor in a shantytown on the edge of Mexico City as experienced by a gang of juvenile delinquents. An introductory title asserts that the film is "entirely based on actual incidents and all characters are authentic." But, as with *Land Without Bread*, Buñuel's unsparing and unsentimental observation of the horrors created by poverty and the inadequacies or callousness of social institutions in the face of human need moves beyond the usual ways of presenting social problems. As in the earlier Spanish film, reality in *Los Olvidados* becomes *surreal* because we are not used to being forced to contemplate a situation as hopeless as this, or its implications about the structure of society and perhaps the nature of humankind. More conventionally surreal is the beautiful dream sequence in slow motion. Dreams and hallucinations appear throughout Buñuel's work as part of his efforts to capture the irrational drives and fears underlying human behavior.

Other noteworthy films among Buñuel's Mexican work include *Subida al Cielo* (*Mexican Bus Ride,* 1951). As a comedy set in rural Mexico it contrasts strongly with *Los Olvidados,* and a collection of amiable caricatures and bizarre incidents dot its picaresque narrative. In *The Adventures of Robinson Crusoe* (1952) Buñuel turns Defoe's account of individual resourcefulness into a study of the effect of total solitude upon the human psyche, which includes a feverish nightmare mingling Christian symbolism with the sadistic cruelty of Crusoe's father, who will not give his son water to quench his thirst. *El* (1952) deals with the madness of possessive love and the perversions of emotional and sexual expression engendered by the repressiveness of the Catholic Church.

In 1955 Buñuel returned to France and began a body of films, some of them cofinanced by Italian, Mexican, and Spanish sources and shot outside France, which constitute his latter-day career and confirm his position among the great auteurs of international cinema. Among these is *Viridiana* (1961) which, though made in Spain, was denounced and banned in that and other Catholic countries after its completion. *Viridiana* represents Buñuel's most unambiguous attack on what he views as the unhealthy sentimentality and restrictive and warped morality of institutionalized Christianity. The film climaxes as the filthy and deformed, cynical and misanthropic collection of beggars—whom Viridiana has assembled in order to save their souls through prayer—enter into a drunken orgy that includes an outrageous parody of da Vinci's *The Last Supper.* In his own way Buñuel seems to have been as preoccupied with religion—"Thank God I am still an atheist," he would say—as were Bresson the believer or Bergman the agnostic.

Viridiana ◆ Spain, 1961, Luis Buñuel; Silvia Pinal, fifth from left.

The Exterminating Angel (1962) concerns a group of guests mysteriously (miraculously?) unable to leave a sumptuous dinner party for days, maybe even weeks, and the ways in which their enforced proximity to each other brings out the idiosyncracies and destructiveness lurking beneath their conventionally elegant exteriors. In *Diary of a Chambermaid* (1964), based on the novel about the French upper classes by Octave Mirbeau (from which Renoir also made a film, in Hollywood, almost twenty years earlier), Buñuel examines the pervasive evil and moral decadence of an updated, crypto-fascist society. The heroine/protagonist of *Belle de jour* (1967), frigid and sexually unfulfilled with her husband, whom she nonetheless loves, attempts to bring alive her masochistic fantasies of sexual debasement by volunteering her services to a chic brothel. *The Discreet Charm of the Bourgeoisie* (1972) is a loosely structured, amusing and anecdotal attack on the values of polite society. It reverses the situation of *The Exterminating Angel,* with six persons attempting to hold a dinner party which is constantly interrupted. *The Phantom of Liberty* (1974) is a darker companion piece to *The Discreet Charm.* It turns on a series of chance encounters that expose the illogic at the core of modern society.

That Obscure Object of Desire (1978) was Buñuel's last film before his death in 1983. Inspired by Pierre Louÿs's novel *The Woman and the Puppet* (also the basis for Josef von Sternberg's *The Devil Is a Woman,* 1935), it deals with a womanizer's pursuit of a woman who constantly eludes him. It contains Buñuelian themes of obsessive and frustrated desires, fetishism, and the blurring of the distinction between reality and dream.

Throughout Buñuel's work his unflinching contemplation of human cruelty reminds us that he comes from the land of the Inquisition and the bullfight. Some of his films seem clearly to follow the tradition of Goya's horrifying documentation of the human capacity for inhumanity in his series of etchings entitled *The Disasters of War.* (A live reenactment of a Goya painting opens *The Phantom of Liberty.*) On the other hand, Buñuel's surrealism led him to explore the unconscious and powerful forces of sexuality, dangerous and destructive when suppressed, rendering any view of life incomplete and invalid when unacknowledged. His attacks on bourgeois institutions (religion and state, class distinctions, and conventional morality) carry the political charge of the surrealists' revolt. Closer to the anarchist's goal of individual freedom than to the Marxist's credo of cooperative endeavor, yet we can infer from *The Phantom of Liberty* that for Buñuel the concept of individual freedom remained a ghostly one. Buñuel's vision stands as his own, full of endless surprises in its forms of expression while he continually readdresses the themes that concern him most. Along with Bresson's and Bergman's, Buñuel's stature depends on the weight of his moral observations, the way in which his style was refined over the years in order to state his views with increasing economy of means, and his integrity and steadfastness to his own understanding of human nature. Alongside the mature work of these three masters, and out of the critical movement which had placed preeminent value on the director as creative artist, as author of the films, there appeared in France a new national outpouring by new young film makers of very different sorts of talents and preoccupations.

♦ NEW WAVE

Having constructed a critical system exalting the director, it is little wonder the young *Cahiers* critics soon left criticism to become directors themselves. Most of them had from the outset considered criticism only a stepping stone to creation. Still, the ensuing development of a creative movement out of a critical movement is unique in the history of film and seems, to Anglo-Saxons at least, particularly Gallic. In the United States to date, only Peter Bogdanovich and Paul Schrader have come to film directing from writing about film. In France, however, many of the leading film makers of the New Wave, which began at the end of the fifties, were *Cahiers* alumni and auteurists. Aside from Alexandre Astruc and Roger Leenhardt, already established directors at the time they were writing for *Cahiers,* there were among the younger generation of critics-turned-film-makers François Truffaut, Jean-Luc Godard, Claude Chabrol, Jacques Rivette, and Eric Rohmer.

While the critical context of auteurism was being constructed, conditions in the French film industry also came to favor a new kind of film maker. The glut of Hollywood film released during the late forties—a backlog from the Occupation years plus current releases—not only gave rise to its reevaluation by the *Cahiers* critics but also provoked an important series of responses from French producers and government attempting to meet the competition.

Immediately after the war, in 1946, a rather half-hearted quota system was established. Known as the Blum-Byrnes agreement (Léon Blum, President of France, and James F. Byrnes, U.S. Secretary of State), it required French cinemas to show French films at least sixteen weeks of the year. All this did was to establish modest limits on importation. It did not encourage French production, which dwindled in the years immediately following the agreement. In short, it scarcely checked the Americans and further contributed to the stagnation of French film about which Truffaut would complain.

In 1948 a new agreement was reached that stretched the period for exclusive showing of French films to twenty weeks and offered what was intended as temporary government subsidy to the French industry. The aid was financed through a tax on admissions. Money was refunded to the producers in proportion to the amount taken in at the box office. It was a system that favored the established and already successful: the rich got richer while the poor remained poor. Because producers were afraid to risk a share of future admissions, the norm became the repetition of tested ingredients. Kinds of films that had made money in the past were repeated; script writers who had solid success to their credit were hired again; stars who were in public favor had vehicles created for them. But audiences became restive with the standard programming, and the industry soon had yet another crisis on its hands as it became more and more difficult to anticipate public reaction on the basis of the old formulas.

In 1953 André Malraux, Minister of Culture, put forth a new variation on the "temporary" assistance offered to producers. Feature films were given an *avance sur recettes,* a method of funding before the film was finished if the project looked worthwhile to the government advisers. Bresson's *A Man Escaped* (1956) was financed in that manner when he had difficulty finding private backing. Shorts as well as features were covered under the new system, being awarded money in relation to their artistic quality. These *primes de qualité* for the production of short films encouraged directors like Georges Franju, Alain Resnais, and Chris Marker.

Taken together, the developments in France by the mid-fifties—an industry that began to support talented individual film makers, the critical climate created by the *Cahiers* group, the beginning rise of European auteurs such as Bergman plus new works by Max Ophüls, Jacques Becker, Jean-Pierre Melville, and Bresson—prepared an audience to accept innovation and a more personal kind of film making. The dominating script writer's cinema of standard dramaturgy based upon psychological realism began to give way to the director's cinema of eccentric artistic vision and varied style.

At the same time, what would prove to be the precursors of the New Wave began to appear: Alexandre Astruc's *Les Mauvaises rencontres* and Agnes Varda's *La Pointe courte* (both 1955), and Roger Vadim's *And God Created Woman* (1956). The latter, enormously successful and creating a new sex goddess in Brigitte Bardot, also bore—superficially at least—many of the thematic and stylistic marks of the later body of New Wave work. Louis Malle's *The Lovers* and Claude Chabrol's *Le Beau Serge* were so close to the main upswing, in their year of release (1958) and in their artistic character, as to be part of the larger whole. But 1959 was the decisive year and the Cannes Film Festival the appropriate occasion on which three French features signaled to the world the beginning of the first new period of heightened national creativity since Italian neorealism of the late forties and early fifties.

Of the three the most popular was *Black Orpheus,* the second feature of Marcel Camus, who had worked for many years as an assistant director. Based on the Greek legend of Orpheus and Eurydice, shot on location in Rio de Janeiro among Brazilian blacks at carnival time, it became an international success, winning an Academy Award as best foreign picture of the year. However, with its exoticism on the one hand and derivative narrative technique on the other, it belongs to the New Wave only by virtue of its year of release. Camus, in his mid-forties at the time, was part of an earlier generation; he made no other important film after *Black Orpheus.*

The 400 Blows, by François Truffaut, former critic, maker of a few shorts including the delightful *The Mischief Makers* (1957), is a semiautobiographical account of a young boy estranged from his parents, who is caught up in the juvenile judicial and penal system. It began the Antoine Doinel series with the twelve-year-old Jean-Pierre Léaud playing his first role. The subject matter if not the style of *The 400 Blows* also seems closer to what had gone before than to the New Wave films to come. If its

The 400 Blows ◆ France, 1959, François Truffaut; Jean-Pierre Léaud.

warmth and humanity owe something to Renoir, one of Truffaut's heroes, it bears resemblances to Italian neorealism as well, specifically to de Sica's-Zavattini's *Shoeshine*. There are, however, the bravura flourishes—the tracking shots in wide screen and the famous final freeze-frame closeup of the young Léaud—which mark the personal stylist and look ahead to Truffaut's later work.

Last, there was *Hiroshima, mon amour,* directed by Alain Resnais, whose background was in editing and documentary film making. Among the most distinguished of his shorts were *Van Gogh* (1948), *Gauguin* (1950), *Guernica* (1950, on the Picasso painting), *Night and Fog* (1955, about the German concentration camps of World War II), and *Toute la memoire du monde* (1956, dealing with the great French library La Bibliothèque Nationale). The script for *Hiroshima,* by the eminent *nouveau roman* novelist Marguerite Duras, concerns a transient and strained love affair between a French actress and a Japanese architect. The personal relationship is embedded in painful memories of the German occupation of France and the atomic holocaust in Japan. It was *Hiroshima, mon amour* that seemed to many of us in 1959 the most successfully and profoundly new of those three films at Cannes. Its transcendence of temporal-spatial unities, Proustian emphasis on memory, linkage of sexual love and global war were strange and absorbing—and typically Resnais, as it would turn out.

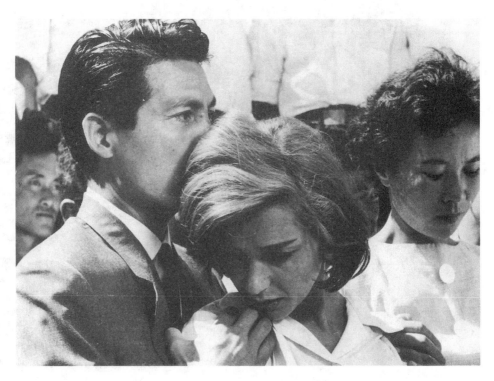

Hiroshima, mon amour ◆ France, 1959, Alain Resnais; Eiji Okada and Emmanuelle Riva.

Also in 1959 were Chabrol's second feature, *The Cousins,* which continued the subtle character studies and preoccupation with moral corruption begun in *Le Beau Serge. The Cousins* set forth fully what would become standard traits of Chabrol's work—the dark fascination with dominance and dependence between characters situated within the modish upper classes, and the elegant, austere visual imagery. Though it examined the contemporary ambience of disenchanted young Parisian intellectuals, as did so many of the New Wave films, *The Cousins,* too, seemed a departure from what had preceded it in degree more than in kind.

Eric Rohmer, another of the *Cahiers* critics, finished his first feature, *Le Signe du lion* (*The Sign of Leo*), in 1959, but it had to wait three years for release. It was his later series of *six contes moraux*—especially *My Night at Maud's* (1969), *Claire's Knee* (1970), and *Chloe in the Afternoon* (1972)—that established him alongside the other major figures to emerge from the Wave.

Released in 1960 were Jean-Luc Godard's first feature, *Breathless,* an idiosyncratic tribute to the American gangster film; Truffaut's second, *Shoot the Piano Player,* with similar generic connections; and Chabrol's *Les Bonnes Femmes,* among his most important films. *Breathless,* though filled with verve and originality in its fragmented storytelling and iconoclastic camera and editing style, seemed somewhat slight at the time. It scarcely predicted the radical experimentation with content along

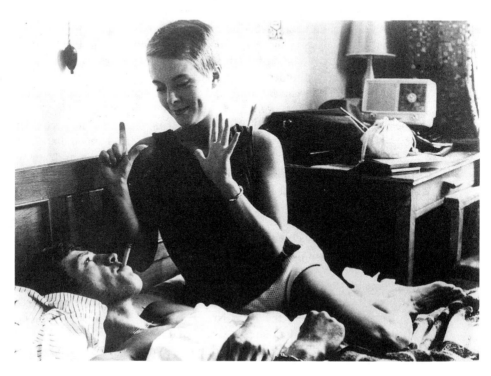

Breathless ♦ France, 1960, Jean-Luc Godard; Jean-Paul Belmondo and Jean Seberg.

with form that would characterize Godard's subsequent output. Jacques Rivette's difficult and puzzling *Paris nous appartient* (*Paris Belongs to Us*), begun in 1958, was completed in 1961. Least popular, most eccentric and obscure of the first of the Wave, it was the subject of admiration by other film makers and thereby influential. Like the other films in Rivette's oeuvre, it remained a special case.

If no one of the seminal films contained all of the most striking or representative characteristics of the New Wave, as a group they outlined its chief concerns and formal innovations. These first films marked the beginning of what was not so much a movement as an explosion. Approximately a hundred directors made their film debuts in France between 1959 and 1962. Naturally the majority of these young and new film makers were less than geniuses and the bulk of their films scarcely master-pieces. When the novelty and excitement began to wear off, self-indulgence and ineptitude became a kind of commercial undertow. Audiences grew increasingly resistant and producers wary. But before the Wave receded an extraordinary number of valuable and/or interesting films were produced that left a permanent mark on the international history of film and established a whole new generation of French film makers.

The term *nouvelle vague* was said to have been coined by a journalist. Used for promotional purposes, it covered a diversity of film makers many of whom had little in common with each other. If the New Wave was not as cohesive a movement as, say, German expressionism in the twenties or post-War II Italian neorealism, still there are certain characteristics that were either shared or that received a new and strong emphasis beginning about 1959 in France.

First was a base in the existentialist philosophy of Jean-Paul Sartre and Albert Camus, especially the latter. Camus's short novel *The Stranger* seems in many ways prototypical of the attitudes and approaches of the new Wave. There is, arguably, a direct line between it and *Breathless*. A distanced, antisentimental stance on the part of their creators typifies both works and much of the New Wave (Truffaut being generally a notable exception). Within those films it is as if no preexisting, external moral codes operate, even to be rebelled against. Events happen that are not prepared for or explained in the usual manner, like the seemingly gratuitous death of the heroine at the end of Godard's *My Life to Live* (1962), and the suicide-murder of two of the three principals climaxing Truffaut's *Jules and Jim* (1961). Characters make decisions that appear arbitrary or lacking in motivation, of a conventional sort at least (Resnais's *Last Year at Marienbad*, 1961, is an encyclopedia of such behavior). They conceive of themselves as responsible only to themselves (Charles Aznavour in Truffaut's *Shoot the Piano Player* is one instance) in a world devoid of logic, justice, or even order.

Then there is the looseness and openness of narrative construction—the pica-resque quality that dominates so many of the films (Godard's *Pierrot le fou,* 1965, a prime example of the general tendency). At the least they are narrative rather than dramtic, more allied to the New Novel than the well-made play. The ascending climaxes of traditional dramaturgy were abandoned, even the ends of narrative threads were no longer neatly tucked in. Randomness replaced the mechanisms of omnipres-ent fate at work in the French films of the thirties noted earlier. Audiences were left to put together the disjointed experience as they exited the theater. Godard, when asked by an exasperated interviewer if a film shouldn't have a beginning, middle, and end, thought a moment and replied, "Yes, but not necessarily in that order."

Accompanying the freedom from strict narrative confines was a tendency to organize time and space according to the dictates of feeling (the film maker's and the characters') rather than the requirements of chronology or contiguity. The intricacies of memory are so dealt with in Resnais's work. *Last Year at Marienbad* seems to contain three tenses—past, present, and future conditional; the real and the imagined are jumbled as the protagonist tries to persuade the heroine and perhaps himself of what had happened between them during the previous summer. The jump cuts, abrupt transitions, and asides of Godard and Truffaut in *Breathless* and *Shoot the Piano Player* similarly defy orderly linear perception.

Finally, many of the New Wave films are about films and film making. Because these young film makers, many of them former critics, felt so at home in their medium, they played with it in uninhibited ways. These included encouraging improvisation by actors (Jeanne Moreau, Jean-Paul Belmondo, Charles Aznavour rose to stardom in their films), taking advantage of the accidents of location shooting, and using new lightweight equipment to attach onto the unfolding action without making it conform to the restraints imposed by the studio method. (*Breathless* was shot in four weeks in indoor and outdoor locations, night as well as day, using "fast" still-photographic stock, a hand-held camera, and postrecorded sound.) There are allusions to other film makers and films, a use of the full range of cinematic conventions, some of them stemming from the silent years (irises, intertitles, masking to change the size and shape of the images), and in-jokes (film friends appearing in apt and amusing bit parts: the director Jean-Pierre Melville as a novelist in *Breathless,* two critics from *Cahiers* as blind men in *A Woman Is a Woman,* 1961). Truffaut's *Day for Night* (1973) is, of course, a summation of this tendency: Its subject *is* film making. Often the films were created as objects for contemplation in their own right rather than as commentaries on the world outside the darkened confines of the theater. These were "movie movies," dedicated to the proposition that if not more real than life, film is a good deal more interesting. In general the New Wave seems not so much art imitating life, as life, at least as it is portrayed in those films, imitating art.

One way of thinking about these aesthetic and stylistic innovations is that the modernism percolating in the other arts since the turn of the century had at last seeped into narrative fiction film. The modernism of the French avant-garde films of the 1920s was allied to and mostly came out of painting and painters. The New Wave modernism was literary in origins, sometimes bearing striking resemblances to what James Joyce had explored in *Ulysses,* published in Paris in 1922. What we now generally think of, in relation to the feature film, as contemporary cinema or modern film can be said to have begun in France at the end of the fifties.

◆ NEW WAVE DIRECTORS

As the New Wave began to roll in the sixties it was Truffaut, Resnais, and Godard who first emerged as the major figures. Like Eisenstein, Pudovkin, and Dovzhenko in the Soviet twenties, the French triumvirate maintained their preeminence. Parallel to their work is that of Chabrol, Rivette, Rohmer, and others.

After *The 400 Blows,* **Truffaut** made *Shoot the Piano Player* (1960), *Jules and Jim* (1961), and the other films (see Films of the Period) which have earned for him the appellation of auteur that he first coined to apply to others. He has written or cowritten all of his films. Generally they are imbued with the sort of romantic realism we would expect from a spiritual godson of Bazin and Renoir. But they also, especially the earlier ones, contain amusing and astute references to the conventions of the medium within which he was working. Throughout there are signs of the well-informed former *cinéphile* and critic, and *hommages* to particular films and favorite film makers, most pointedly to Hitchcock in *The Bride Wore Black* (1967).

Among his later films the most effective and commercially successful was *The Last Metro* (1981). It deals with the theater in affectionate and knowledgeable detail (as *Day for Night* does with film making) and as a means of getting at the strange, muted, complicated, unnerving human tensions in German-occupied Paris of 1942. A wife (Catherine Deneuve) continues to run the Théâtre Montmartre in place of her Jewish husband. But the husband did not flee the country, as was assumed; he hides in the cellar of the theater and observes its continuation, including the addition of a young actor (Gérard Depardieu) with whom his wife has an affair.

Aside from the undervalued *Shoot the Piano Player,* and *Jules and Jim,* which many regard as his masterwork, the Antoine Doinel series (*The 400 Blows;* an episode in *Love at Twenty,* 1962; *Stolen Kisses,* 1968; *Bed and Board,* 1970) may be Truffaut's most distinctive contribution to the history of film. In addition to their worth as separate art works, they represent the closest fictional feature films have come to sustained use of autobiographical material, except perhaps those of Fellini. In *Day for Night* (1973) Truffaut added his own performance to Léaud's to infuse his art with his life. This sort of creation is recognized as the basis for much of the world's great literature, from Cervantes to Faulkner. The idea of a director's life, at least his personal vision, being reflected in his films was inherent in *la politique des auteurs.* Truffaut brought his own experiences more directly to the screen through the evolving Doinel character than any other director has so far done. *L'Amour en fuite (Love on the Run,* 1979) was his farewell to Antoine Doinel. He died in 1984 at the age of 52.

Resnais's qualifications as an auteur are of a different sort. A skilled film maker, his films display a dazzling technical virtuosity and formal elegance that separate them from other New Wave works. Also, his concern with older characters and the past contrasts with the youthful protagonists and current attitudes dominant in the films of Truffaut and Godard. With noteworthy consistency Resnais has pursued his absorption with the processes of memory, his features (*Hiroshima, mon amour; Last Year at Marienbad; Muriel,* 1963; *La Guerre est finie,* 1966; *Je t'aime, je t'aime,* 1968; *Stavisky,* 1974; *Providence,* 1977; *Mon Oncle d'Amérique,* 1981; *La Vie est un roman,* 1983; *L'Amour à mort,* 1984; *Mélo,* 1987) all reveal and insist upon the presence of times past in every present moment. This was true even of the earlier shorts, especially the greatest of them, *Night and Fog.* In *Mon Oncle d'Amérique* the real-life biologist Dr. Henri Laborit, on whose theories the film is based, says "A living creature is a memory that acts." This might be a description of the protagonists of Resnais's films.

Jules and Jim ♦ France, 1961, François Truffaut; Henri Serre, Jeanne Moreau, and Oscar Werner.

The problem Resnais presents in his candidacy for authorship is that on his features he has usually collaborated with strong literary figures such as Marguerite Duras and Alain Robbe-Grillet (who subsequently directed their own scripts), or Jean Cayrol. He has always been generous (perhaps more than) in acknowledging his indebtedness to others, and self-effacing in regard to his own contributions to the conceptions. According to published statements from some of those collaborators, Resnais is almost insistent that the scripts be conceived quite apart from his personal style as a film maker and without special deference to the medium of film. "Give me an original 'literary' work," he seemed to be saying, "and I will make it into cinema."

Resnais's first English-language film, *Providence* (1977), is about literary creation. The script was by playwright David Mercer. Its protagonist, a famous novelist, draws from his relationships with his children and dead wife to shape and reshape scenes intended for his final novel. His characters are at variance with what we are permitted to see of the "real" persons who exist outside his imagination, and the whole, of course, is presented to us in a filmic illusion which is, ultimately, Resnais's interpretation and creation.

His next three films, *Mon Oncle d'Amérique, La Vie est un roman,* and *L'Amour à mort* were scripted by Jean Gruault. A screenwriter rather than a literary figure (his

Last Year at Marienbad ◆
France, 1961, Alain
Resnais; Giorgio Albertazzi
and Delphine Seyrig.

credits include Truffaut's *Jules and Jim, The Wild Child, Two English Girls, The Story of Adele H.,* and *The Green Room;* Rivette's *Paris nous appartient* and *La Religieuse;* Godard's *Les Carabiniers;* and Rossellini's *The Rise of Louis XIV*), his contributions to these three Resnais films must have been central. (The original screenplay for *Mon Oncle d'Amérique,* Resnais's first major commercial success, was nominated for an Oscar.) The first two are complex three-part narratives: the former telling the stories of three quite different modern characters whose lives interact; the latter consisting of three stories set in different times and filmed in different styles which yet connect thematically. Both are based on philosophical propositions: the first relating to the aggression innate in humans and human responses to it; the second to utopias, education and imagination, adulthood and childhood. *L'Amour à mort* is also experimental in its narrative structure and stylized imagery; in this case the philosophical argument concerns the dictates of love.

If the intellectual content of Resnais's films is frequently high, presenting difficulties for the audience, the ideas appear always to be ones that interest him, that he believes in. While the level of achievement may vary, it nonetheless seems clear that as a body of work Resnais's films remain notably coherent regardless of who is credited with the script. We can assume that, whatever the creative relationship between writer and director during production, Resnais is not altogether part of the tradition of writer's cinema about which Truffaut complained.

Perhaps it is **Godard** who represents better than any other single film maker the sort of experimental stretching of the medium that the New Wave provided. In fact, it may be only Griffith and Eisenstein who have contributed as much formal innovation—additions to the "language" of the medium—as Godard. His early work included variations on the melodrama and chase conventions of popular American movies. It is amusing but not surprising that his first feature, *Breathless,* was dedicated to Monogram Pictures, a defunct Hollywood studio of "B" production. *Band of Outsiders* (1964), another "gangster film," has "musical numbers" as well, with Anna Karina singing on the Metro and dancing with two of the petty crooks; in *A Woman Is a Woman* (1961), Karina says she wants to be in a musical choreographed by Bob Fosse.

On the other hand, Godard employed the sort of "distancing" associated with avant-garde theater, or with Bertolt Brecht, whom Godard frequently invoked in interviews. In the famous opening scene of *My Life to Live* (1962) the camera remains mostly on the backs of Nana and Paul, preventing us from seeing their facial expressions as they converse. Its twelve episodes are punctuated by titles, pulling us further out of the narrative, which is already deliberately disjunctive, and suggesting a series of moral lessons (Montaigne furnishes the text for one of the tableaux).

But a new kind of realism was also present in Godard's mixed style. In *Sympathy for the Devil* (1968) and elsewhere, *cinéma vérité* actuality mingles with fictive elements. Godard has said that there are two kinds of cinema, Flaherty and Eisenstein: There is documentary and there is theater; but that ultimately, at the highest level, they are one and the same. Through documentary realism we arrive at the structure of theater, and through theatrical imagination and fiction we arrive at the reality of life.[2] Even when working with actors, as he generally did, Godard observed aspects of their actual personalities as much as the created roles they played. In *Breathless,* Belmondo's energy and toughness, coiled-spring tension and handsome-ugliness were first revealed. Jean Seberg, who had failed badly as Joan of Arc in Preminger's film, succeeded completely in playing a young American in Paris whom we suspect might be rather like herself. The series of films with Anna Karina, Godard's wife for a time, were, among other things, poems to her loveliness and essays on the difficulties of understanding and communicating with her (*Le Petit Soldat,* 1960; *A Woman Is a Woman; My Life to Live; Band of Outsiders; Pierrot le fou,* and *Alphaville,* 1965). In *Contempt* (1963) Fritz Lang played himself as a renowned film director.

As Godard's work progressed, his philosophical observations came increasingly to obtrude, extending from the moral and ethical to the political. Later films (*Made in USA,* 1966; *La Chinoise,* 1967; *Weekend,* 1967) became defiantly expository and didactic. In *Le Gai Savoir* (1969), his first film after the May 1968 uprising in France,

---

[2]*Godard on Godard,* translated and edited by Tom Milne (London: Martin Secker & Warburg, 1972), p. 181.

he abolished narrative altogether (and alienated much of his audience) in an effort to find a revolutionary form suitable to revolutionary content. Concomitant with this move towards philosphical abstraction, the dialogue became denser and was assigned a more significant share of the total communication. In *My Life to Live,* Brice Parain, a philosopher in real life, carried on a long dialectical near-monologue that was only tangentially related to the slight plot. Later in the same film Godard's voice on the sound track reads an Edgar Allan Poe story to the heroine. In *See You at Mao* (also called *British Sounds,* 1969) there is so much speech over the images that the words become incomprehensible.

Godard's absorption with politics and formal rarefactions meant that with the exception of *Tout va bien* (1972) and *Numéro deux* (1975)—both of which received limited commercial distribution—his work disappeared from public view after 1968. Later, however, *Sauve qui peut (la vie)* (*Every Man for Himself,* 1980) seemed to connect back to *Weekend* (1967) and the films that preceded it. The narrative structure and character psychology offer difficulty to be sure—like Resnais's *Mon Oncle d'Amérique* it is built around three characters whose lives become intertwined—but there is a story and there are characters. Formal experimentation is present—video

My Life to Live ♦ France, 1962, Jean-Luc Godard; Anna Karina and Brice Parain.

techniques and stop motion, for example—along with Godard's abiding concern for "the politics of the image," and there is much visual beauty.

If *Sauve qui peut* might be thought of as being about the nature of cinema, as was said at the time, *Passion* (1982) most certainly can be. At its center are two East European film makers making a film called *Passion.* However, their film-within-the-film, and therefore Godard's film, is full of famous paintings (by Rembrandt, Goya, Delacroix, El Greco) brought to life in *tableaux vivant* accompanied by famous music (extracts from Mozart, Fauré, Ravel). Although art and politics are linked in *Passion,* as they are in Godard's thinking, the political problems don't seem to receive as much of his attention as the aesthetic ones. It is then a familiar Godardian jumble of elements treated with philosophical engagement and emotional detachment—a truly "modern" film, we might say.

Passion was followed by *First Name: Carmen* (1983), which won the Golden Lion at the Venice Film Festival. It connects only vaguely with the story by Prosper Merimée on which Bizet's opera is based. Set in modern France, Carmen is a member of a gang of bank robbers; Don José is a bank guard. (Godard plays Carmen's dotty Uncle Jean, a washed-up film maker.)

Hail, Mary (1985) is a modern retelling of the immaculate conception, with Mary a sullen basketball-playing teenager pumping gas in her father's station, Joseph a sexually frustrated cab driver, and the archangel Gabriel an unshaven tough. Of course it aroused religious groups and scared distributors (as had Rossellini's *The Miracle,* of 1948, and would Martin Scorsese's *The Last Temptation of Christ,* of 1988). To many it was "shocking and profoundly blasphemous"; to others it was a continuation of Godard's recurrent meditations on the alluring mystery of woman and her ultimate strangeness, which he began with *Breathless* and *A Woman Is a Woman* twenty-five years earlier.

The fecund originality of Godard's conception, the inventiveness and freedom with which he employs all of the technical and stylistic resources available to the film maker, has not been equalled. It could be argued that no matter what his subject matter, he continues to be preoccupied with formal explorations of the possible combinations of moving images and accompanying sounds. He makes one think of the painter Marcel Duchamp, who outlined so many of the forms of modern art. Godard is like Duchamp, too, in his intellectualism and coolness. If, ultimately, he withholds, or is unable to provide, kinds of aesthetic experience that may be valued most, within the humanist tradition at any rate, the importance of his contributions to an evolving art form and his influence on the work of others is unquestionable.

Claude Chabrol has continued—with increasing strength and control in later years—a succession of cohesive works. Narrow in vision (usually they involve an ill-fated triangle which often ends in death), they nonetheless gain power from their concentration. Overtaking Godard as the most prolific of the New Wave directors, Chabrol has consistently pictured a dark underside of bourgeois morality. Among the most carefully wrought, intense, and disturbing of his films are *Les Biches* (1968), *La Femme infidèle* (1969), *Le Boucher* (1970), and *Just Before Nightfall* (1971). His work would seem to be the most conventional of the New Wave directors—frequently

Les Biches ♦ France, 1968, Claude Chabrol; Jacqueline Sassard, Jean-Louis Trintignant, and Stephane Audran.

following lines laid out by Lang and Hitchcock, whose films Chabrol admires—steadily produced and commercially successful.

Jacques Rivette, following *Paris nous appartient,* while Truffaut, Godard, and Chabrol were being prolific, made only two films in the 1960s: *La Religieuse* (1965) and *L'Amour fou* (1968). In 1971 he completed *Out One* (running twelve hours and forty minutes and never released), which became *Out One: Spectre* (1974), re-edited from the same footage. *Celine and Julie Go Boating* (1974) is his most "accessible" film, whimsical and amusing. All of his films maintain the enigmatic qualities of his first feature, either attacking or toying with the whole notion of illusionistic storytelling. In most of them the characters are in some ways involved in the production of plays from classical drama which are intricately interwoven with the modern stories. Rivette has said that his films "are about theater, about truth and lies."

His most recent work at time of writing, *La Belle Noiseuse* (1991, which seems to mean something like "The Beautiful Trouble Maker"), transfers the central setting from theater to a famous painter's studio, but it explores the process of creation even more intently and the development of characters and their shifting interactions remain linked to drama as in his earlier works. (It is credited as being "Based on the story *Le*

Chef d'oeuvre inconnu" by Honoré de Balzac [that is, "The Unknown Masterpiece."]) Also its length, at four hours, is characteristic. But, while being something of a personal statement, it became the first commercial hit of Rivette's career.

Eric Rohmer's passage has been much smoother, his films much more within the main lines of French production. Though a late bloomer, *My Night at Maud's* (1969), first feature of his "Six Moral Tales" to be released, achieved commercial success and established his international reputation. In Rohmer's work the "literary" is even more conspicuous than in Rivette's (whose films abound in references to books) and even in Resnais's. Whereas Resnais has collaborated with authors, Rohmer is one. His *Six Moral Tales* (published in translation under that title by Viking in 1979) were written as stories before he made them into films between 1962 and 1972. *The Marquise of O . . .* (1976) and *Perceval* (1978) are films of world literary classics. Consistent with this literary quality, the settings within which his characters are placed are observed with a particularity that suggests the term *described;* and his characters talk a lot. The way Rohmer thinks of his films is that they deal "less with what people do than with what is going on in their minds while they are doing it." (They have been referred to as "talking cure" films.) His intricate explorations of what are essentially conservative moral positions—supported by a perfection of performance, intelligent and witty dialogue, subtle and exact psychological observation—continue to intrigue. *The Aviator's Wife* (1980) began a new series which Rohmer entitled "Comedies and Prov-

Celine and Julie Go Boating ◆ France, 1974, Jacques Rivette; Bulle Ogier, Marie-France Pisier, and Barbet Schroeder.

My Night at Maud's ◆ France, 1969, Eric Rohmer; Françoise Fabian and Jean-Louis Trintignant.

erbs," and continued with *A Good Marriage* (1982) and *Pauline at the Beach* (1982), *Full Moon in Paris* (1984), and *Summer* (1986). Truffaut, interviewed twenty years after the New Wave began, when asked about "the new directors in France," said: "The one I like best is Eric Rohmer, but of course he is of my generation . . ."[3] Rohmer was sixty-eight at the time the last of his "Comedies and Proverbs," *Boyfriends and Girlfriends* (1988), was released. *A Tale of Springtime* (1990) launched a new series, "Tales of the Four Seasons."

◆ OTHER CONTEMPORARY DIRECTORS

In his seminal essay of 1954, Truffaut cited **Jacques Tati** as one of the few auteurs of French cinema. He preceded the New Wave with *Jour de fête* (1949), *Mr. Hulot's Holiday* (1953), and *Mon Oncle* (1958). During its height he produced nothing. But

[3]Don Allen, "Truffaut: Twenty Years After," *Sight and Sound,* 48, (Autumn 1979): 225-26.

Mr. Hulot's Holiday ◆ France, 1953, Jacques Tati; Tati.

in his last two films before his death in 1982, *Playtime* (1968) and *Traffic* (1971), he created intricate, oblique, amusing commentaries on contemporary life that have served as texts for postmodernist theorists. The character he conceived and performed, Hulot, remains one of the enduring comic figures of the screen.

Not all veteran French film makers currently at work were part of the New Wave. **Agnes Varda,** mentioned earlier, was associated with the group of intellectuals known as the "Left Bank" directors, which included Alain Resnais, Chris Marker, Alain Robbe-Grillet, and Marguerite Duras. From the 1960s on Varda has had scattered successes. Following *Cleo from 5 to 7* (1961)—close enough to the New Wave to be part of it—there were *Le Bonheur* (1965), *Lion's Love* (1969), *One Sings, the Other Doesn't* (1977). Generally regarded as a more solid achievement is *Vagabonde* (1985), a bleak and existential story of a lonely vagrant, Mona, wandering through the wintry landscapes of the South of France. It won the Golden Lion at Venice.

The output of **Louis Malle,** also on the edge of the New Wave from its beginning, as indicated above, has been varied and innovative, alternating documentary and fiction and, more recently, French and American. He too won a Golden Lion, with *Au revoir, les enfants* (1987), an autobiographical account of a boarding school for upper-class boys in German-occupied France which gave sanctuary to three Jewish youngsters in 1944. Of his French work beginning in the 1960s, *Zazie dans le Métro* (1960) and *A Very Private Affair* (1962) are contemporary with the New Wave and

Cleo from 5 to 7 ♦ France, 1961, Agnes Varda; Corinne Marchand, right.

somewhat related in spirit. The first explores the conventions of film making in a comedy centered around a young girl; the second caricatures the harried movie star (played by Brigitte Bardot). Subsequently Malle frequently selected painful moral situations as subjects: in *The Fire Within* (1963) an alcoholic's descent into suicide; in *Murmur of the Heart* (1971) incest between a mother and a teenage son; in *Lacombe, Lucien* (1973) the ethical ambiguities and tortured relationships existing under German occupation; in *Pretty Baby* (1978) child prostitution. The latter began Malle's U.S.-based films. It was followed by *Atlantic City* (1980), about gambling, crime, and friendship (Burt Lancaster as the aging mobster and Susan Sarandon as the young croupier he protects). *My Dinner with André* (1981) was a surprising success. Visually it consists almost solely of medium shots and closeups of two men of the theater (director André Gregory and playwright Wally Shawn, who cocreated the dialogue) seated in an elegant Manhattan restaurant. Verbally—conversation is the film's main content—it combines sophisticated interests and naive enthusiasms, philosophical conundrums and parody of the sort of talk such a pair might have in life. Clearly Malle was drawn to this subject, and to the subjects of his films in general.

Au revoir, les enfants ◆ France, 1987, Louis Malle; Gaspard Manesse, second from left.

Like other French film makers of his generation, he has seemed able to pursue his personal predilections without loss of force.

Having no connection with the New Wave, following it by some fifteen years, is **Bertrand Tavernier** (*The Clockmaker,* 1974; *Death Watch,* 1980). Tavernier's most popular film, *A Sunday in the Country* (1984), is redolent with charm, attributable to the director and also to a tradition of French film making that goes back beyond the New Wave to Jean Renoir. Even the title recalls Renoir's *A Day in the Country* (1936). Furthermore, it is about an aging Impressionist painter of Renoir *père*'s time being visited by his children and grandchildren and acquaintances, on a summer day in 1910. After this considerable success his progress has been less assured. *'Round Midnight* (1986), an English-language production financed by Warner Brothers, deals with a black tenor sax player in the 1950s. Weighed down by weariness and alcoholism he flees the racism of the United States to try to revive his career playing at the famous Blue Note club in Paris. More recently *Daddy Nostalgia* (1990) returned to the general territory of *Sunday in the Country,* though the time is present and the country the Côte d'Azur. It too is constructed around a visit, of a daughter to her father nearing the end of his life, and like the earlier film is touching and honest in its account of family interactions. *Daddy Nostalgia* was followed by *L. 627* (1992). The title comes from the article of the French Code of Public Health relating to narcotics trafficking. Its protagonist is a committed young investigator, nicknamed

A Sunday in the Country ◆ France, 1984, Bertrand Tavernier; Sabine Azema and Louis Ducreux.

Lulu, in the drug unit of the Paris Police. The film concentrates on the procedures in this sort of police work and on Lulu's relationships with informers and other members of his unit.

Raùl Ruiz, the most recent arrival on the French scene to command worldwide attention, is not French but a Chilean exile. Living in Paris since 1974, he began steady film making for France's National Audiovisual Institute in 1977. His amazingly prolific output, averaging six films a year, has been produced on miniscule budgets at incredible speed. And they are of all sorts: shorts and features, documentary and fiction, and mixtures of modes, most of them made originally for television. Whatever their form they carry avant-garde inflections and a virtuosity that opens up new ways of storytelling, new kinds of imagery, and new interrogations of cinematic language. Though featured at international festivals and in the pages of serious film journals, none of his work has received widespread distribution in the United States. My impressions are limited to a series at the Film Center of the Art Institute of Chicago some five years ago. But even the titles may suggest the fabulous and metaphysical aspects of his work: *Dog's Dialogue* (1977), *The Hypothesis of the Stolen Painting* (1978), *The Territory* (1981), *The Roof of the Whale* (1982), *City of Pirates* (1983). You might think that with *Treasure Island* (1991) you would be on familiar ground. But it turns out to be a wildly mythic and incoherent parody, stories within stories in the form of a child's game, connecting only occasionally with the Robert Louis Stevenson novel.

In any case, Ruiz's films seem related to a Latin Amerian literary tradition that is proving to be a major wellspring for postmodernist narrative explorations—the writing of José-Luis Borges, Carlos Fuentes, Gabriel García Márquez, and others. Like the tales of those authors, Ruiz's films are filled with hallucinatory fantasies, labyrinthian mysteries, and unexpected shifts in character, style, and structure. If his distinctiveness is clear from limited evidence, meaningful description and trustworthy evaluation must await the availability of additional films. Meanwhile, it can only be acknowledged that Ruiz has evoked some of the same critical excitement that Godard and Rivette did in the 1960s and 1970s, and for some of the same reasons.

Though the New Wave as something resembling a movement lasted only a few years, roughly 1959 to 1962, its effects have extended down to the present. It completely revitalized French cinema and spawned most of the major directors subsequently at work. Together with the critical reevaluation of *la politique des auteurs* which preceded it, it gave more emphasis than had previously been the rule to a personal cinema under individual artistic control. Thinking of film as an art, and of the director as the controlling artist, became a predominant view in France and extended widely abroad.

At the end of the fifties, first in France and then elsewhere, the kind of authority with which Bresson, Bergman, and Buñuel had been able to make their filmic state-

City of Pirates ♦ France, 1983, Raúl Ruiz.

ments began to be acquired by a growing number of film makers. Since then an ever-increasing range of distinctive personal styles has enriched the medium and our contemplation of it. What had been thought of largely as commercial entertainment, collectively produced and mass consumed, now appeared, under the right conditions, to be capable of the complexities and subtleties of the traditional arts. Though rarely challenging the box office dominance of more popular forms, this new kind of creation opened up a modest but viable system of distribution and exhibition of "difficult" films for selective audiences. The "art cinema," as it is misleadingly called (as if there hadn't always been art in popular cinema), has been with us since the early sixties, and the French film makers can claim a large share of credit for its emergence.

Further, the influence of the New Wave extended not only to other countries but even into popular cinema. We can point to "new wave" elements in Tony Richardson's *Tom Jones* (1963), Arthur Penn's *Mickey One* (1964, shot by one of the New Wave cameramen, Ghislain Cloquet), the Beatles films of Richard Lester (*A Hard Day's Night,* 1964, and *Help!,* 1965) and his American *Petulia* (1968), John Schlesinger's *Darling* (1965), and Stanley Donen's *Two for the Road* (1967, set appropriately in France). These are only a few among the many films made subsequently elsewhere using styles and themes that first came to the fore during the New Wave. But it was Italy that advanced most immediately and solidly into the breach France had opened in established convention. A dimension and weight were added as well, making modern Italian cinema uniquely contributive to the whole, a rival to the French in competition for creative leadership.

FILMS OF THE PERIOD

1956
And God Created Woman (Roger Vadim)
A Man Escaped (Robert Bresson)

1958
Le Beau Serge (Claude Chabrol)
Black Orpheus (Marcel Camus)
The Lovers (Louis Malle)
Mon Oncle (Jacques Tati)

1959
The Cousins (Chabrol)
The 400 Blows (François Truffaut)
Hiroshima, mon amour (Alain Resnais)
Pickpocket (Bresson)

1960
Les Bonnes Femmes (Chabrol)
Breathless (Jean-Luc Godard)
Paris nous appartient (Jacques Rivette)

Shoot the Piano Player (Truffaut)
Zazie dans le Métro (Malle)

1961
Cleo from 5 to 7 (Agnes Varda)
Jules and Jim (Truffaut)
Last Year at Marienbad (Resnais)
Lola (Jacques Demy)
Viridiana (Luis Buñuel)

1962
The Exterminating Angel (Buñuel)
My Life to Live (Godard)
The Trial of Joan of Arc (Bresson)

1963
Contempt (Godard)
Diary of a Chambermaid (Buñuel)
Muriel (Resnais)

1964
Band of Outsiders (Godard)
A Married Woman (Godard)
The Umbrellas of Cherbourg (Demy)

1965
Alphaville (Godard)
Le Bonheur (Varda)
Pierrot le fou (Godard)

1966
Au hasard, Balthasar (Bresson)
Fahrenheit 451 (Trauffaut)
La Guerre est finie (Resnais)
A Man and a Woman (Claude Lelouch)
Masculine-Feminine (Godard)

1967
Belle de jour (Buñuel)
Mouchette (Bresson)
Playtime (Tati)
Weekend (Godard)

1968
Les Biches (Chabrol)

1969
La Femme infidèle (Chabrol)
My Night at Maud's (Rohmer)
Z (Constantin Costa-Gavras)

1970
Le Boucher (Chabrol)
Claire's Knee (Rohmer)
Tristana (Buñuel)
The Wild Child (Truffaut)

1971
Just Before Nightfall (Chabrol)
Murmer of the Heart (Malle)
Two English Girls (Truffaut)

1972
Chloe in the Afternoon (Rohmer)
The Discreet Charm of the Bourgeoisie (Buñuel)

1973
Day for Night (Truffaut)

Lacombe, Lucien (Malle)
The Mother and the Whore (Jean Eustache)

1974
Celine and Julie Go Boating (Rivette)
The Clockmaker (Bertrand Tavernier)
Lancelot of the Lake (Bresson)
The Phantom of Liberty (Buñuel)
Stavisky (Resnais)

1975
Numéro deux (Godard)
The Story of Adele H. (Truffaut)

1976
The Marquise of O . . . (Rohmer)

1977
The Devil Probably (Bresson)
The Man Who Loved Women (Truffaut)
Providence (Resnais)
That Obscure Object of Desire (Buñuel

1978
Hypothesis of the Stolen Painting (Raul Ruiz)
Violette (Chabrol)

1979
Love on the Run (Truffaut)

1980
Death Watch (Tavernier)
The Last Metro (Truffaut)
Mon Oncle d'Amérique (Resnais)

1981
The Aviator's Wife (Rohmer)
Diva (Jean-Jacques Beineix)
On Top of the Whale (Ruiz)
Le Pont du Nord (Rivette)

1982
A Good Marriage (Rohmer)
Passion (Godard)
A Room in Town (Demy)

1983
L'Argent (Bresson)

First Nane: Carmen (Godard)
Pauline at the Beach (Rohmer)

1984
Full Moon in Paris (Rohmer)
A Sunday in the Country (Tavernier)

1985
Hail, Mary (Godard)
'Round Midnight (Tavernier)
Vagabonde (Varda)

1987
Au revoir, les enfants (Malle)
Jean de Florette (Claude Berri)
King Lear (Godard)
Manon of the Spring (Berri)

1988
Boyfriends and Girlfriends (Rohmer)

1990
Daddy Nostalgia (Tavernier)

1991
Les Amants du Pont-Neuf (Leos Carax)
La Belle Noiseuse (Rivette)

1992
L. 627 (Tavernier)
A Winter's Tale (Rohmer)

BOOKS ON THE PERIOD

Buss, Robin, *The French Through Their Films.* New York: Continuum, 1988

Forbes, Jill, *Cinema in France: After the New Wave.* London: Macmillan, 1993

Slide, Anthony, *Fifty Classic French Films, 1912–1982: A Pictorial Record.* New York: Dover, 1987

Williams, Alan, *Republic of Images: A History of French Filmmaking.* Cambridge, MA: Harvard University Press, 1992

New Italians
and Newer Italians

◆ ◆ ◆

1960–

Like the French New Wave that broke at Cannes in 1959, a new kind of Italian cinema emerged at the Venice International Film Festival the following year. Unlike the French, however, the Italian films were by experienced directors whose landmark works of 1960 were set within careers that extended back into immediate postwar neorealism. The films also pointed ahead to the subsequent development of their directors and to a younger generation that would quickly grow up around them. The films were *Rocco and His Brothers*, *La Dolce Vita*, and *L'Avventura*; their directors were, respectively, Luchino Visconti, Federico Fellini, and Michelangelo Antonioni.

◆ RELATIONSHIPS TO THE NEW WAVE

The Italians shared some of the thematic and stylistic innovations of the French—a reaction against classical Hollywood narrative; a basic orientation that might be called postmodernist—Visconti being the exception. *Rocco and His Brothers* looked back to neorealism even if, like the bulk of Visconti's work, it departed from accepted neorealist tenets in its melodramatic emotionality, its heightening of character and incident. *La Dolce Vita* and *L'Avventura*, on the other hand, contained much identifiable as new in both subject and form.

There was the shared existentialist base, derived from the novels of Cesare Pavese, whom Antonioni much admired, as well as the writings of Sartre and Camus: the sense that life was merely the sum of actions lived, the emphasis on alienation and the failure of communication. There was also a similarity with Bergman, acknow-

Rocco and His Brothers ◆ Italy, 1960, Luchino Visconti; Alain Delon, center, white T-shirt

ledged by both Antonioni and Fellini, in picturing a world in which divine faith has been lost and human love seems unattainable.

Then too, the narrative structure of the new Italian films had the same sort of looseness as the French. Both *L'Avventura* and *La Dolce Vita* are episodic rather than tightly woven, and picaresque. The first is organized around a journey and search for a missing person; the second around a sort of spiritual quest for values amidst various physical settings and social groups in and near contemporary Rome. Much of Fellini's work gives us the sense of being on the road; *La Strada* (1954) is the extreme case, the emphasis acknowledged in the title. Antonioni's films, too, set people in motion through countrysides and across cities. He is resolutely narrative rather than dramatic, and that in a low key of slight action and sparse, inconclusive dialogue. Of all film makers perhaps he is closest to certain tendencies in the modern novel in his attempts to deal with the interior lives of his characters. Since little is accidental in an Antonioni film, significance can be attached to a copy of F. Scott Fitzgerald's *Tender Is the Night* lying open on a footstool in *La Notte* (1961). The characters and themes of his "trilogy" (*L'Avventura, La Notte, The Eclipse,* 1962) suggest Fitzgerald. Perhaps he is closer still to the French *nouveau roman* and a novel like Alain Robbe-Grillet's

L'Avventura ◆ Italy, 1960, Michelangelo Antonioni; Monica Vitti and Gabriele Ferzetti

Jalousie in his efforts to convey feeling states through presentation of the particularities of physical surroundings. *The Eclipse* ends with a seven-minute montage of images devoid of people: places and objects that had appeared earlier, now stripped of anthropomorphic meaning.

Unlike the French, though, new Italian film makers as a whole have shown little interest in manipulating time and space in extra-real, purely filmic ways. Fellini, of course, does make use of fantasy (in *8½*, 1963, and *Juliet of the Spirits,* 1965, for example), in which he plays with the physical laws of the universe as well as with subjective and hallucinatory emotional states, but he clearly sets the imagined and remembered apart from the ongoing present reality. In *La Dolce Vita* and elsewhere, in his approach to the "real world," time and space are dealt with in a perfectly straightforward manner—that is, within the conventions employed in realistic films generally. Antonioni, on the other hand, gets even closer than the conventional to the felt passage of time and experienced movement across space. After seeing *L'Avventura* the filmgoer could make out a complete itinerary, with a journal and a map. Antonioni's long-held shots, with slow panning and trucking, are far removed from the ellipses and staccato jump-cutting of early Godard and Truffaut. Nor do Anton-

La Dolce Vita ◆ Italy, 1960, Federico Fellini

ioni's films ever retreat to the past, let alone advance into the future, as do those of Resnais. Fantasy scenes occur only rarely in Antonioni's work—for example, in *Zabriskie Point* (1969), in the ghostly desert love-in, and the conclusion in which the heroine imagines the destruction of her boss's modern mansion.

Last, the Italians did not indulge in the self-conscious playfulness with the medium enjoyed by the French. Fellini is somewhat an exception to that generalization, but his fun and games are more likely to be drawn from the circus and music hall than from the characteristics of the film medium or the work of other film makers. Antonioni and Visconti, of course, are notably unplayful in every respect, though the former in later work undertaken abroad—*Blow-Up* (Britain, 1966), *Zabriskie Point* (United States), *The Passenger* (Italy/United States, 1975, shot in Algeria, Spain, England, and Germany)—departed sharply from the austerity of his Italian films. *Blow-Up* offers a rich aesthetic, even ontological commentary on the very nature of the photographic image (upon which motion as well as still pictures depend) and its relationship to reality. *The Passenger* so emphasizes the shifting frame area and perspective of a moving camera that it too forces the viewer to consider the cinematic process that adds to the cryptic nature of the events observed.

◆ ROOTS IN NEOREALISM: THREE FILM MAKERS

What the new Italian cinema was moving away from and what toward was consolidated at the Venice Festival of 1960. In an Italy that had recovered with astonishing rapidity from the social-political-economic upheaval and aftermath of World War II, the concerns were with the beliefs one might live by now that life itself and the living of it were more assured and comfortable. One indication of the change was that the new Italian film makers turned their attention from the lower to the upper classes. With their capacity to spend life more or less as they chose, the wealthy made most clearly evident the moral vacuum, the angst, the idle pursuit of meaningless pleasures that had accompanied the "economic miracle." In Italy of the sixties, gone or seriously eroded were, on the one hand, the support of traditional Catholic morality and faith in God and His church, and on the other, the solidarity and militancy of the Left that had infused Italian society and political life in the immediate postwar years. Whatever the differences among their films, Visconti, Fellini, and Antonioni established a newly prominent moral, even spiritual, concern, and redirected attention to individual psyches, rather than collective conditions, in a contemporary Italy.

But reality of one sort or another, psychological as well as physical, has prevailed in the Italian film and precluded the excessive whimsicality sometimes evident in the New Wave. Most likely that is so because of the closely preceding tradition of neorealism. As already noted, all three directors of the major Italian films of 1960 had roots in that tradition.

Visconti, in fact, along with Rossellini and de Sica, could lay claim to being one of the founders and principal practitioners of that movement. His *Ossessione* (1942) was clearly a precurser, with its harshly naturalistic approach to character, theme, and setting at a time when Italian films were either patriotic or escaping the realities of wartime Italy, optimistic or cheery in either case. *La Terra Trema* (1948) is among the great neorealist films, though its overlay of highly stylized studiolike cinematography and staged groupings onto actual fishermen and Sicilian village make us think of Eisenstein of *Old and New* rather than of the other neorealists.

In *Rocco and His Brothers* Visconti in a sense returned to his Southern Italians of *La Terra Trema*, but now they are immigrants in Milan. Though social and economic forces are shown as contributing to the destruction of the family, the drama grows out of the personal conflicts and psychological flaws of the characters. The film employs the emotional intensity and extravagant behavior of classical Greek drama rather than the deliberate understatement and restraint associated with neorealism at its purest. Subsequently Visconti used various sorts of historical and literary materials—initiated in *Senso* (1954) and *White Nights* (1957) and continued in *The Leopard* (1963), *Sandra* (1965), *The Stranger* (1967), *The Damned* (1969), *Death in Venice* (1971), and *Ludwig* (1972). As a nobleman whose distinguished family had figured prominently for centuries in Italian history, Visconti had the deep concern for tradition (at odds with his Marxism) and the cultivated taste you would expect. His penultimate film before his death in 1976, *Conversation Piece*, offers an elegiac commentary on an aristocratic intellectual and art lover forced into uneasy but fascinated contact with

The Leopard ◆ Italy, 1963, Luchino Visconti; Claudia Cardinale, Burt Lancaster, and Alain Delon.

the strident exigencies and vulgarities of modern political and social reality. We can imagine that the protagonist (played by Burt Lancaster, who also had played the prince in *The Leopard*) must have been seen by Visconti as some kind of equivalent to himself.

The Visconti who evolved out of neorealism traveled as far from it in style and subjects as could be imagined. If Marxism and the scenographic baroque combined in his earlier films, the creation of lush imagery (a joy in itself) and re-creation and examination of various forms of decadence, usually aristocratic, seem to carry the main weight in the total body of his work. A film maker of international scope as well as stature, Visconti can be thought of as Italian primarily because of the "operatic" qualities of his films. As a film artist he stands in splendid isolation, his work unique and rather formidable.

Fellini had been scriptwriter on *Open City, Paisan,* and *Europe 51* (for Rossellini), *Without Pity* and *Mill on the Po* (for Alberto Lattuada), and *In the Name of the Law* (for Pietro Germi), among other noteworthy neorealist films. The first works he directed as well as wrote—*Variety Lights* (1951, with Lattuada), *The White Sheik* (1952), and especially the autobiographical *I Vitelloni* (1953)—fell clearly within the neorealist tradition, even if they already began to reflect Fellini's predilection for the popular arts and his own personal experiences as source material. The enormously successful *La Strada* (1954) represented a turning point. Though set amidst the poverty and drabness of small-town rural Italy, its protagonists are vagabonds (a traveling strong man and his female assistant) rather than workers or peasants. And Fellini was onto new themes quite outside the persistently materialistic view of the earlier neorealism. What we care about in *La Strada* is not that times are hard and social institutions culpable, but that Zampanò and Gelsomina learn to give and receive the warmth and comfort of human love.

Fellini's films, more obviously Italian in attitude and subject than Visconti's, departed more gradually from the accepted limitations of neorealism. What attracted him, instead of the historical and literary, was the subjective and fantastic. The only films of his which have literary-historical bases are *Fellini Satyricon* (1969) and *Fellini's Casanova* (1976). In these, as their titles imply, Petronius's ancient Rome and Casanova's eighteenth-century Europe are converted into the director's fantasies of debauchery and sexuality, and into extravaganza. Fellini has remarked of his *Satyricon* that it may be even more autobiographical than his much more obviously autobiographical *8½* (1963). Even the two filmed essays, *The Clowns* (1970) and *Fellini's Roma* (1972), keep the film maker's own interests, experiences, tastes, and yes, fantasies at their center: it is *his* fascination with clowns from young boyhood on, *his* Rome. *Amarcord* (1973) is a sort of compendium of his recollections filtered through the exaggeration and imagination of adolescent perception. *City of Women* (1980) brought together and made quite explicit (as dreams) the sexual fears and desires that appear throughout his work.

From the beginning of Fellini's directorial career the autobiographical elements are present either in foreground or background, and usually both. *Variety Lights* deals with the music-hall milieu which he had experienced first hand. *The White Sheik* satirizes the comic book industry, and Fellini had been a cartoonist. *La Strada* is again about touring entertainers. *Il Bidone* (1955), though perhaps not drawn so directly from experience, contains many of the recurring themes and images, especially the religious ones. *The Nights of Cabiria* (1957) portrays the life of Roman prostitutes as Fellini had come to understand it. A special aspect of Fellini's "personalizing" of his work is that his wife, Giulietta Masina, played in all but one of those early films, as well as in many of the later ones.

Up through *Nights of Cabiria,* however, Fellini maintained that he was still working within the neorealist tradition, that he had simply shifted his concentration from external to internal reality. Certainly his films have much the look of the earlier neorealism. If shot more carefully and intimately, with emphasis on composition and the symbolic reverberations of the images, they are still objective in point of view. *I Vitelloni* is especially remarkable in the feeling it gives that the camera just happened to be there to capture bits of lives as they are being lived. Also, those early films make significant use of actual locations and nonactors and are set among the lower classes, the outcasts and dispossessed. But the poverty that concerned Fellini most was the impoverishment of the spirit. Though in his work, as in the original neorealist films, there are things to be sad about and no solutions are outlined, the hope that is offered for the human condition lies not in working-class solidarity but in the joy and love, in an almost religious sense, that the individual soul is capable of. The ending of *Nights of Cabiria*, with the little prostitute picking herself up after a near drowning and walking down a lane encircled by playing children, is very different in its implications from that of *Bicycle Thief*, with father and son walking hand in hand off into the crowd, however similar the action. Both attest to human resiliency; but Antonio and his son, though comforted by their love for each other, merge into the masses to face another jobless day; Cabiria, through the children, recovers her own optimism and sense of self-worth.

With *La Dolce Vita,* Fellini took a long step farther away from neorealism. It is concerned with the decadent idle rich of Rome and the sensational press that reports their doings to a voracious public. The journalist-protagonist (played by Marcello Mastroianni, who would become "Fellini" in *8½*) is in search of meaning in life and values to live by. His passage through the sort of cafe society life well known to Fellini is like a descent into Dante's *Inferno*. The various pursuits to which he might devote himself—wife and family, business success, sexual excitement, religious fervour, philosophical speculation–are successively shown to be corrupting or insufficient to support meaningful existence. By inference we learn that God is absent from this world, or silent as He was in Bergman's. (The pointedly ironic opening scene of a

8½ ♦ Italy, 1963, Federico Fellini; Marcello Mastroianni, center, arm outstretched.

gilded statue of Christ being hauled by helicopter over the rooftops of modern Rome, and the sequence of a highly publicized fake miracle flail at the hollow and superstitious religion subscribed to by the masses and tacitly approved by the Church.) Though it deals with the upper classes and matters of the spirit, *Dolce Vita* is still in a completely realistic style. It is merely that the locations now include *palazzi* and the nonactors are actual members of the Roman aristocracy.

It wasn't until "The Temptation of Dr. Antonio" episode for *Boccacio 70* (1962) that Fellini turned to fantasy—one of his own, more than likely. Not until $8^1/_2$ did he combine the autobiographical and the extravagant personal phantasmagoria that would depart from neorealism entirely and mark the remainder of his work to date. Certainly his most complex film, $8^1/_2$ may also be his finest. It is a witty and revealing account of a director's harried life and the difficulties he has in conceiving his next film, that is, this one, hence the title: Fellini had directed eight films up to that point. Just to make certain there would be no mistake, Mastroianni wore a wide-brimmed western hat like the one Fellini habitually wears on the set.

In more recent films Fellini has moved away from the autobiographical, with indifferent results. *And the Ship Sails On* (1983), a slight tale unfolding during an Adriatic cruise in 1914, parodies the conventions of early cinema and the inflated emotions of the operatic world. In *Ginger & Fred* (1986) the object of satire is television. A 1930s dance team (played by Masina and Mastroianni, whose dancing is scarcely up to their namesakes', of course) are reunited for a superproduction variety show. *Fellini's Scrap-book* (1987) returns more directly to his own past: to his early days at Cinecittà studios, in fact. It includes an homage to *La Dolce Vita*—Fellini coming full circle, you might say.

Antonioni had served his apprenticeship as a critic (like the French New Wave film makers) and script writer, including work on films in the neorealist tradition such as Giuseppe de Santis's *Tragic Hunt* and Fellini's *White Sheik*. He also directed a number of documentary shorts. But his features, aside from *Il Grido* (1957), which is set amidst working-class surroundings in the Po Valley, treat personal values and interpersonal relationships of the middle and upper classes.

In extreme contrast to Fellini's ebullience is Antonioni's austerity. Though *La Dolce Vita* and *L'Avventura* deal with the same social strata (and both are organized around protagonists on the fringes rather than part of the aristocracy) and contain the same themes (loss of meaning and values replaced by promiscuity and debauchery), these two films and the subsequent work of their respective makers could scarcely be more different from each other. Whereas Fellini's films are informed with a Catholic humanist view of the world (evidently deep-rooted if informal and anticlerical), Antonioni's view is that of a post-religious Marxist and existentialist intellectual. While Fellini exposes the shoddiness of the moral values offered by "the sweet life," at the same time he is clucking moralistically he seems to be enjoying the naughtiness and the glamor.

Antonioni offers no such titillation or spectacle. In *L'Avventura* and his Italian films that follow it—*La Notte* (1961), *The Eclipse* (1962), *The Red Desert* (1964), and *Identification of a Woman* (1982)—he dissected the values he saw operative in upper-class modern Italy with the disinterested precision and functional grace of a skilled surgeon, or perhaps of a weary but alert coroner conducting a postmortem. For the "sweet life" in Antonioni's portrayal of it seems closer to death in that the souls have left the bodies. Not only is meaning lacking, but feeling too, except for the instinctual sexual twitching as bodies refuse to acknowledge what minds know. Eroticism is prominent in the films of Antonioni, as it is in those of Fellini, and Antonioni has described it as "a dominating factor in our civilization." But whereas the orgy at the end of *La Dolce Vita* has some prurient appeal (the strip-tease and the horsey-back ride on the bovine blonde actress), the sexual interludes in *L'Avventura* leave us cold and sad: the early scene with Anna in Sandro's apartment, Sandro with Claudia outside the deserted town and later in the hotel room after his encounter with the young architect, Sandro with the high-class prostitute in the early morning. Never has "sin" looked less inviting. The sensuality, pleasure, guilt, and remorse felt by Fellini's characters are replaced by pervasive ennui and irritability, and a sense of the inability of any person to make contact with another even in the most intimate moments. Sex in Antonioni's world may stem from a desire to communicate, but it frequently takes the form of aggression or tired surrender to habit. Among his characters a life in which the sexual act has meaning or even offers enjoyment seems unavailable and perhaps unimaginable.

But it isn't that dreary human landscape alone, or the sensitivity with which certain kinds of despair are revealed, that account for the fascination Antonioni's films hold for his times. As with any considerable artist it is the enveloping form of his works that gives the themes and insights their unique significance. *L'Avventura* is the rare sort of film that sets forth a whole new range of possibilities within the art that hadn't been sensed before and that can be drawn upon ever afterward. Like *Intolerance,* or *Battleship Potemkin,* or *Citizen Kane,* it closes one era and opens another.

The extraordinary visual surface of *L'Avventura,* and of Antonioni's succeeding work, seems less radical now than it did when it first appeared precisely because it has been incorporated into the language of film as one of the prominent styles. Growing out of Antonioni's artistic intentions and statements, of course, it also took peculiar advantage of the attributes of the wide screen, seems almost to require it. The camera is placed at a medium distance more often than close in, frequently moving slowly; the shots are permitted to extend uninterrupted by cutting. Thus each image is more complex, contains more information than it would in a style in which a smaller area is framed and the shots are briefer in duration. In this respect he harks back to Murnau or Dovzhenko rather than Eisenstein. In Antonioni's work we must regard his images at length; he forces our full attention by continuing the shot after others would cut away.

By demanding that we read the complex meaning of several characters in relation to each other and their surroundings, rather than selecting and emphasizing, he makes us become active observers. The action and dialogue, the settings and circumstances must be comprehended almost as life itself, without the exposition and graduated intensity that usually clue us in fiction. The positions in which the characters stand or sit, the way they walk, the irrelevancies of their conversations, and cool overcast light, the starkness and lack of movement in many of the compositions—all cohere into a total view of a kind of existence. A cold and empty world it is, degenerative not in the mode of marathon orgies but because the values are not substantial enough to sustain life at a level of human warmth and dignity. Love, pursued persistently if lethargically, can't be distinguished from lust. Work has no meaning with the impulse to create atrophied. Diversion and puzzling accidents fill in the time, and characters keep on the move or lapse fitfully into hopelessly self-indulgent self-analysis. If we, the audience, are put in the position of onlookers, what we see is a world in which the possibility of significant action has been lost.

While Antonioni offers us a view in certain respects closer to life than is usual, he is an artist of superb control which extends into and balances every aspect of his films. His method does not include the spontaneity and improvisation of Fellini, nor does it permit the rough edges that Visconti allows to go uncorrected in his impatience to outline a grand plan. Consider, for example, the much-noted island sequence in *L'Avventura*. (See still on page 331.) In it the characters are continually being commented upon, linked, and separated, by their positions in relation to each other and within the frame: their movements and the camera's are choreographed with equal care. The growing awareness and desire of Sandro and Claudia for each other is initially signaled through such means. For instance, one shot begins with the camera looking down on Sandro. Then it tilts up and, on another plane above him, frames Claudia in the distance as she walks toward the camera (and Sandro's position). Or,

The Passenger ◆
Italy-France-Spain, 1975,
Michelangelo Antonioni; Maria
Schneider and Jack Nicholson.

in another shot, there is a slight, slow pan from left to right with Claudia in the background. As the shot proceeds, Sandro enters frame left, mid-foreground. Then there is the *pas de deux* in successive shots when Claudia is trying to avoid Sandro and he, somewhat unconsciously and helplessly, tries to attach himself to her. Sometimes the camera even becomes like a member of the group as it moves ahead of the actors until they catch up with it and walk into frame again.

But with Antonioni, that kind of visual calculation—the framing and movement of actors and camera, the settings (barren rocky island, eerie deserted town), the way the light falls (the cold gray of early morning in the halls of the palatial hotel)—is everywhere designed to enrich narrative. A director like Eisenstein, who planned and executed his films with equal attention to detail, for all of his visual and kinetic brilliance was saying simple things. The complexity in his films resides almost entirely in their visual artistry. Antonioni, on the other hand, has provided the sorts of ambiguity considered proper to narrative art. It is his kind of imagery and storytelling, rather than the more selective and directive method of Eisenstein, that has come to characterize the best of modern cinema and to represent a profound break with what had gone before. It also appeals most strongly to the needs and sensibilities of a new kind of audience which now looks to film rather than to the older arts for the fullest and most satisfying expression of a modern worldview.

♦ OTHER DIRECTORS AND SUBSEQUENT FILMS

Following Visconti, Fellini, and Antonioni, and building on their foundation to greater or lesser extent and in various ways, there appeared a cluster of powerfully talented younger Italian film makers. The first two to be dealt with here, rather than paralleling the then current concerns of the three veterans, returned to some of the earlier neorealist impulses. One had had extensive documentary experience before turning to fiction; the other began his film career as assistant director on a neorealist feature.

Ermanno Olmi's first features contain socially significant themes, were shot on location, and use nonactors as in the earlier tradition. But instead of unemployment and poverty, he deals with jobs that offer little satisfaction and the difficulties of achieving fulfilling lives and relationships within the conformist demands of an industrialized society. What Olmi provides is a subtle and absorbing attention to the individual among the working classes. *Il Posto* (1961) is about a teen-age boy from a small village on his first job as messenger for a large firm in Milan. The tenderness and gentle humor with which the director regards the boy's tentative relationship with a girl, his loneliness at a dreary office party, and his feelings when he first sits at a clerk's desk are uniquely Olmi's own. *The Fiancés* (1963) concentrates on a worker who goes from the North to a new plant in Sicily. The slender story deals largely with his efforts to come to a better understanding of the fiancée he has had to leave behind and of their relationship. In later films, *One Fine Day* (1968) and *The Circumstance* (1974) for example, Olmi moved to the middle and upper classes, from workers to bosses, and fragmented his narrative, the present and recollected past sometimes intermingled with Resnais-like complexity. In *The Tree of Wooden Clogs* (1979),

Il Posto ♦ Italy, 1961, Ermanno Olmi; Sandro Panzeri, second from right.

about the life of a peasant community in Lombardy at the close of the nineteenth century, Olmi returned to his earlier lyrical and unadorned style. But in *Long Live the Lady!* (1987) he mixes his special comedy of behavior, in this case that of ordinary kids, with a fantastic banquet hosted by the incredibly ancient lady of the title. And *The Legend of the Holy Drinker* (1988) is a fable about a tramp in Paris. The 200 francs loaned him by a mysterious stranger helps him rehabilitate himself but he never manages to repay the loan as he had promised and dies, finally, in a drunken stupor, while attempting to.

Francesco Rosi, little known in the United States, is much admired in Italy and in Europe generally. His first considerable achievement was *Salvatore Giuliano* (1962), shot entirely on location in Sicily with an almost exclusively nonprofessional cast. It concerns an actual Mafia leader whose banditry and guerrilla activities are seen as aimed toward achieving Sicilian independence. *Hands Over the City* (1963), in many ways similar in method and ultimate intent, examines the exploitation of capitalist power and political corruption by an unscrupulous housing developer in Naples. *The Mattei Affair* (1972) retains its basis in actuality but extends to a national, even international, scale. Enrico Mattei was an industrial manager who created a state-controlled oil company that loomed large in Italian political-economic affairs and competed against other national and multinational oil interests in the world market. *Christ Stopped at Eboli* (1979) is Rosi's version of the Carlo Levi book about the condition of rural Southern Italy in the 1930s. *Three Brothers* (1981) traces the

Hands Over the City   ♦   Italy, 1963, Francesco Rosi.

fortunes of three sons of a farmer in the Puglia region whose lives mirror the development of post-World War II Italy. It is a meditation on the conflicting values of the South and the North, the rural and the urban, and on the political violence and social fragmentation prevalent in modern Italy. The enigma of power, the pervasiveness of political influence, and the factual source remain characteristic of Rosi's finest work. Of the neo-neorealist directors, perhaps it is Rosi who has made most fully manifest the ideology implicit in the original movement.

His next two films departed from that main line, however. Both are adaptations of masterpieces, one an opera and the other a novel. Rosi's version of Bizet's *Carmen* (1984) was his first substantial success in the United States, partly due to the excellent interpretation and performance and most especially to the compelling sensuality of Julia Migenes Johnson in the title role. It was followed by his version of Gabriel García Márquez's *Chronicle of a Death Foretold* (1987). Though both films follow the neorealist tenet of shooting on location—*Carmen* in the Andalusian region of Spain and *Chronicle* in Colombia—in other respects they are closer to the later Visconti. (Rosi began in film as assistant director on *La Terra Trema*.)

In the work of other directors emerging in the 1960s who were close to the earlier neorealists we can see signs of the changing times. Rather than either Olmi or Rosi, perhaps another two Italian film makers, clearly influenced by the French New

Wave, are more representative of the generation that followed Visconti, Fellini, and Antonioni.

Piero Paolo Pasolini and Bernardo Bertolucci had many things in common. Bertolucci even counted Pasolini as a "father" and was considerably influenced by his films and theoretical writings. Both were strongly committed to the political left, but the new rather than the old, Italian intellectual rather than doctrinaire Marxist. Both used their films as means of exploring the structure of society. Even when the surfaces or foregrounds seem devoted solely to the relationships among individuals, the attitudes of their characters and the kinds of dilemmas they find themselves in have political dimensions. While in France there is an active political consciousness at work among certain film makers and critics, in Italy this sort of concern is almost endemic among those involved with cinema. Much of the critical discussion of a film there—from both right and left—will be devoted to its ideological significance and likely effects on social attitudes.

Pasolini, a novelist, poet, linguist, and film theorist before he directed his first feature, *Accattone!,* in 1961, consistently dealt with the "subproletariat"—beggars and outcasts. Even *The Gospel According to St. Matthew* (1964), his best-known film, conforms to that generalization. In it Christ is portrayed as a revolutionary orator-leader from the masses, of a sort common in the history of the Middle-Eastern

The Gospel According to St. Matthew ◆ Italy, 1964, Pier Paolo Pasolini; Enrique Irazoqui as Christ, center, hand to mouth.

peoples. Shot as if it were reportage rather than re-creation, hand-held camera and nonactors give the Biblical story a feeling of contemporary actuality and urgency. *The Hawks and the Sparrows* (1966), an allegorical comedy, reveals and examines the interdependency between Christianity and Marxism, between religion, ideology, and existence. *Teorema* (1968) and *Pigpen* (1969) include strange mythic evocations of transcendental states, perverse sexuality, and cannibalism in their attacks on capitalist society. Pasolini's ability as a writer and translator led him to attempt new interpretations of classic literary works. Following *Oedipus Rex* (1967) were *Medea* (1970), *The Decameron* (1971), *The Canterbury Tales* (1972), and *The Arabian Nights* (1974). His last film, *Salò—The 120 Days of Sodom,* suggested by a work of the Marquis de Sade and full of violence, was completed just before his own violent death in 1975. Brilliant and multitalented, at the same time idiosyncratic and unpredictable, Pasolini occupied a position of leadership among the new Italians.

Bertolucci, who worked as assistant director on *Accatone!,* achieved a prodigious international success with *Before the Revolution* (1964), which he completed at the age of twenty-four. (His first feature, *The Grim Reaper,* based on a rough draft by Pasolini, had been made two years earlier.) Of the post-Visconti-Fellini-Antonioni generation, Bertolucci has made least use of the neorealist inheritance. His films more nearly resemble those of the later Visconti, in their sorting through of intertwined personal relationships and political attitudes, and in their bold painterly style: *The Conformist* and *The Spider's Stratagem,* both 1970, for example. Arguably his most exceptional work to date, *Last Tango in Paris* (1972), also bears some resemblance to Antonioni thematically and aroused something of the same excitement as *L'Avventura* in suggesting a new sort of film language, or personal idiom at least. In Bertolucci's case his contributions to cinematic expressiveness may lie solely in the style which is the man. Dense and unanalyzable in many respects, it is hard to know just what makes *Last Tango* work so powerfully. If it is too early to tell whether it is an enduring masterpiece, there is no question about its initial impact, the force with which Bertolucci was able to speak to his contemporaries. It was followed by the vast panorama of *1900* (1976), covering some seventy years of life and social conflict in the Emilia region of Italy; *La Luna* (1979), the intimate study of an incestuous relationship between mother and son which occasioned controversy at least equal to that caused by *Last Tango*; and *Tragedy of a Ridiculous Man* (1981), involving a father-son relationship, kidnapping, and terrorism in present-day Italy.

The last three films had mixed critical receptions and weak box office performances. His next, *The Last Emperor* (1987), was a triumph on all counts. A huge multinational production, it tells the story of Pu Yi, the last emperor of China. The film can be seen in several ways. It is a sumptuous visual feast of elegance and display on a colossal scale. As cultural and political history it is less satisfactory; too much is crammed into too little time, with large events hinted at or dealt with obliquely. Perhaps it can best be understood as the story of a person whose emotional life becomes constricted and empty as a result of early traumas. He is torn from his mother and then from his wet nurse; ritual obeisance is substituted for love and nurturing. He is told he is the most powerful person in the world who can do anything he wants, when in fact he is someone who experiences one loss after another. In a sense he is a

Last Tango in Paris ♦ Italy, 1972,
Bernardo Bertolucci; Marlon Brando
and Maria Schneider.

prisoner throughout his life. This aspect of the film is consistent with Bertolucci's persistent fascination with psychological tensions that lead to loneliness and aberrant behavior. He has suggested that his method of film making and each of his films is part of his own psychoanalysis. In any event, the gamble at high stakes paid off handsomely. *The Last Emperor* attracted a great amount of critical attention, won eight Academy Awards, and became an international financial success.

Among the films of the newer Italian film makers especially popular in the United States have been those by the **Taviani brothers,** Paolo and Vittorio. They first became known in this country chiefly for *Padre Padrone* (1977), an adaptation of a best-selling account of the progress of an ignorant Sardinian from shepherd to university professor. *The Night of the Shooting Stars* (1982), shot in their native Tuscany, was based on their own experiences as young boys and on oral accounts of fellow Tuscans. It concerns a group of villagers who in 1944 left their town in defiance of the retreating Germans and resident Fascists to search for the advancing Americans. It was followed by *Chaos* (1984), adaptations of four Luigi Pirandello stories shot in Sicily with a cast that included many nonprofessional actors. Like Bertrand Tavernier, whose success in France led him to *'Round Midnight,* an American-financed English-language film aimed at the international market, the Tavianis were drawn to Hollywood. In fact, their first American film was about Hollywood, though shot mostly in Italy and Spain. *Good Morning, Babylon* (1987) concerns two Italian artisan brothers' involvement in the construction of the massive Babylon sets for D. W. Griffith's *Intolerance* and sundry subsequent adventures. Though a charming fable, the best of the Taviani films return to the emotional territory of neorealism, or at least have their roots in the history and traditional culture of the Italian people. *Night Sun* (1990), set in southern Italy in the eighteenth-century, is a tale of a young nobleman who becomes something of a tortured saint. Though based on Leo Tolstoy's "Father Sergius," the film is richly reflective of the Italian heritage.

Many of the major contemporary Italian film makers appear to be stretching themselves, to be trying out new subjects and new forms. The resulting films don't always make full use of the special talents demonstrated in their earlier work. Yet, seen as a whole, Italian film from 1960 onward represents a range and maturity of statement that has earned wide admiration. Artistic innovation has been tempered by continuing awareness of the role of film in society. A common sense of national identity among the film makers has strengthened individual efforts. In spite of obvious personal and generational differences, contemporary Italian directors share many

Night of the Shooting Stars ◆ Italy, 1982, Paolo and Vittorio Taviani.

aesthetic and political as well as cultural assumptions. That cohesiveness permitted artists of the stature of Visconti and Fellini and Antonioni to have long productive careers. It has also provided a background from which newcomers have emerged to command worldwide attention. The term "Italian New Wave," bandied about at the time of the 1960 Venice Festival, wasn't really appropriate. What was being revealed in the three remarkable films shown there was merely the beginning of another evolutionary stage in an ongoing tradition that has existed in Italy at least since the end of World War II.

On the other side of what Winston Churchill perceived as an Iron Curtain, film history was for a long time characterized more often than not by a resistance to change, especially in the dominant state, the Soviet Union. Recently that situation has changed more radically than could have been imagined by anyone only a short while ago, with an end to Communism and of the Union of Soviet Socialist Republics itself.

FILMS OF THE PERIOD

1960
L'Avventura (Michelangelo Antonioni)
La Dolce Vita (Federico Fellini)
Rocco and His Brothers (Luchino Visconti)

1961
Accatone! (Piero Paolo Pasolini)
Bandits of Orgosolo (Vittorio de Seta)
Divorce, Italian Style (Pietro Germi)
La Notte (Antonioni)
Il Posto (Ermanno Olmi)

1962
The Eclipse (Antonioni)
Salvatore Giuliano (Francesco Rosi)

1963
8^1⁄$_2$ (Fellini)
The Fiancés (Olmi)
Hands Over the City (Rosi)
The Leopard (Visconti)

1964
Before the Revolution (Bernardo Bertolucci)
The Gospel According to St. Matthew (Pasolini)
The Red Desert (Antonioni)

1965
Juliet of the Spirits (Fellini)
Sandra (Visconti)

1966
The Battle of Algiers (Gillo Pontecorvo)
Fists in the Pocket (Marco Bellochio)
The Hawks and the Sparrows (Pasolini)

1967
China Is Near (Bellochio)

1968
One Fine Day (Olmi)

1969
Burn! (Pontecorvo)
The Damned (Visconti)
Fellini Satyricon (Fellini)

1970
The Conformist (Bertolucci)
The Garden of the Finzi-Continis
    (Vittorio de Sica)
Investigation of a Citizen above Suspicion
    (Elio Petri)
The Spider's Stratagem (Bertolucci)

1971
In the Name of the Father (Bellochio)

1972
Last Tango in Paris (Bertolucci)
The Mattei Affair (Rosi)

1973
Amarcord (Fellini)

1975
Conversation Piece (Visconti)
The Passenger (Antonioni)

1976
Fellini's Casanova (Fellini)
The Innocent (Visconti)
1900 (Bertolucci)
Seven Beauties (Lina Wertmüller)

1977
Padre Padrone (Paolo and Vittorio Taviani)

1979
Christ Stopped at Eboli (Rosi)
Luna (Bertolucci)
The Tree of the Wooden Clogs (Olmi)

1981
Three Brothers (Rosi)
Tragedy of a Ridiculous Man (Bertolucci)

1982
Identification of a Woman (Antonioni)
The Night of the Shooting Stars (Taviani)

1983
And the Ship Sails On (Fellini)
Cammina Cammina (Olmi)

1984
Carmen (Rosi)

1986
Ginger & Fred (Fellini)

1987
Good Morning, Babylon (Taviani)
The Last Emperor (Bertolucci)
Long Live the Lady! (Olmi)

1988
Cinema Paradiso (Giuseppe Tornatore)
The Legend of the Holy Drinker (Olmi)

1990
Under the Sheltering Sky (Bertolucci)
Night Sun (Taviani)

BOOKS ON THE PERIOD

Bondanella, Peter, *Italian Cinema:From Neorealism to the Present.* New York: Continuum, 1990.

Marcus, Millicent, *Italian Film in the Light of Neorealism.* Princeton: Princeton University Press, 1987

16

Eastern European Cinema

◆ ◆ ◆

1954–

Throughout the first years of the new revolutionary government in Russia, in the 1920s, considerable freedom and experimentation were present in the arts as well as in other aspects of life. With Stalin's consolidation of power, permissiveness and variety gave way to enormous monolithic control. By the early thirties "socialist realism" was the official and only state aesthetic. Prescribed content was locked into straightforward unambiguous narrative form. The seductive artistry of the Soviet silent films was replaced by the positive, wholesome, uplifting, and bland portrayal of communist heroes whose lives might have some implication for the revolution, or by the presentation of ideologically "correct" modern peasants, workers, and professional people. *Chapayev* (1934) was the prototype. Until recently, with rare exceptions, contemporary Soviet films aroused little interest in the West. Conversely, when Fellini's *8½* was shown at the first Moscow Film Festival, in 1963, it was subjected to violent criticism as a decadent bourgeois work full of "vagueness and morbidity." Only after considerable argument and insistence on the part of the invited western judges was it awarded first prize. Neither it nor other of the new French and Italian films were shown generally in the Soviet Union.

In the communist countries the effect of a film on the audience's social and political attitudes was regarded as more important than the money it brought in. Given this concern, film content was carefully scrutinized and regulated to one degree or another by the state. Consequently film production in the Soviet bloc could be analyzed as a kind of barometer measuring political pressure operating within a society at any given time. A few months before the 1963 Moscow Festival, Communist Party Chairman Nikita Khrushchev delivered an important speech regarding his attitude toward the arts in the Soviet Union. He said, in part,

> *We adhere to class positions in art and resolutely oppose peaceful coexistence between socialist and capitalist ideologies. Art belongs to the sphere of ideology. . . . Abstractionism and formalism, whose right to a place in socialist art is advocated by some of their champions, are forms of capitalist ideology. . . .*

Only within the last few years has this government position changed. The Soviet Union and its break-up will be returned to at the end of this chapter.

In the Eastern European countries within the Soviet sphere, the situation was not as consistently restrictive as within the Soviet Union itself. On the contrary, the idealistic aspects of communism infused with an apparently unquenchable nationalism and exposure to new films from the West accounted for fertile periods of creativity in the cinema of Poland, Hungary, Czechoslovakia, and Yugoslavia.

Prior to World War II the film production of Eastern European countries was negligible in quantity and quality. Few of their films found audiences beyond their own borders, and the small national populations could not be counted on to return the profits necessary to private enterprise. With the establishment of communist governments in those countries immediately after the war, there were new incentives for production, like those in the Soviet Union earlier, and a new base for economic support. It took a few years for the ground to be prepared, but once the state film schools had begun turning out graduates, and film production, distribution and exhibition had been stimulated and coordinated, the Eastern People's Republics were ready to take their places in the international spotlight. These governments wanted films that would inform and indoctrinate, that would interpret events of the immediate past to give a sense of solidarity, and that would instill attitudes contributing to future progress. Replacing the subject of the Bolshevik Revolution, dealt with by the first Soviet film makers, was the resistance to Nazi Germany during World War II. Communism was represented as the only force with the people's interest at heart capable of opposing fascism effectively and offering an alternative, more democratic way of life.

◆ POLAND

Immediately following the war the communist regime in Poland rigidly followed the Stalinist line, including tight controls on the arts. During those years only a few Polish films achieved distinction: Wanda Jakubowska's *The Last Stage* (1948), a tragic account of suffering and endurance in the notorious concentration camp at Auschwitz; and the films of veteran Aleksander Ford (*Border Street,* 1948 and *Five Boys from Barska Street,* 1953), about wartime and immediate postwar problems. At the end of the forties there was established at Lodz the most famous and influential of the new national film schools of the Eastern European republics. As a result of its training and leadership a whole generation of young film makers emerged who would change the nature of Polish film and bring it to worldwide attention.

After Stalin died in 1953 a lessening of Soviet domination, relaxation of internal controls, and growing expression of national sentiment gradually began at the rate of two steps of liberalization forward to one of repression back. In Polish film the three important events of 1954 were the criticism by Jerzy Toeplitz, head of the state film school, of Polish production as oversimplified and uninspired; the reorganization of the national industry into independent production groups; and the appearance of the first feature of **Andrzej Wajda,** *A Generation.* Though the latter contained remnants of the simplistic communist morality tale, the film was full of beauty and idealism, a key transitional work, and a harbinger.

Wajda, who would become one of Poland's major directors, led the sudden upsurge of Polish production which reached a peak between 1955 and 1958. *A Generation* began an unplanned trilogy completed with *Kanal* (1956) and *Ashes and Diamonds* (1958). Together the three films explored the conflicting loyalties, confused politics, bravery and sacrifice that had characterized Poland's sad history during the years following German invasion and occupation to the first days of peace.

Ashes and Diamonds ◆ Poland, 1958 Andrzej Wajda; Zbigniew Cybulski and Adam Pawlikowski.

Though Wajda's romanticism tended to soften and mythologize, his intellectual stance was often antiheroic, probing, and implicitly critical of the leadership and causes for which so many young men his age had died. In *Ashes and Diamonds,* and in his and others' subsequent films, the actor Zbigniew Cybulski frequently portrayed a young man trying to sort out values and create a life amidst the shifting and unclear postwar conditions. He resembled an existentialist antihero more than a working-class hero of orthodox socialist realism. (He and his roles occasioned comparison with his contemporary, American actor James Dean.) Many of the Polish films of the time had in common as major or minor themes the inability of the individual to discover a place for himself in his own national community.

But it is the overall mood and particular images of Wajda's films that are remembered long after their content has receded from memory. The visual style is strong and distinctive—romantic, dramatic, and symbolic all at the same time. In *Ashes and Diamonds,* for instance, there is the scene of Cybulski lighting glasses of vodka lined up along the bar in salute to dead comrades. Then there is the discordant but still stately polonaise danced in the early morning hours, a dreamlike souvenir of former patriotic sentiments now tired and faded. Finally we recall the mortally wounded Cybulski staggering through sheets hanging on a clothesline to fall to his death on a garbage heap. These and other memorable scenes measure the extent of the director's evocative power.

Wajda's career has continued on into the nineties as he has retained his place among what is now the older generation. *Everything for Sale* (1968) was in part a tribute to Cybulski, who was killed accidentally in 1967 as he jumped from a train. It is also Wajda's reflection on his own relationship to life and art. With a film director protagonist and a film within a film, as in works of Fellini and Godard earlier and Truffaut later, it is one of the major examples of this reflexive tendency of modern cinema. In *Landscape After Battle* (1970) Wajda returned to the war, but now the underlying philosophy seemed truly existential and some of the action and imagery almost surreal.

Andrzej Munk directed his first feature, *Man on the Track,* in 1956. It departed from the broad historical settings of other Polish films of the time for a close observation in psychological terms of an old locomotive engineer. Not only is he no positive socialist hero, he is at odds with the new order. With *Eroica* (1958) Munk turned to the war. The first of its two complementary but separate parts is set in the Warsaw uprising of September 1944, the same futile and tragic gesture Wajda had dealt with in *Kanal.* What is amazing about this episode of Munk's film, "A Scherzo in the Polish Manner," is that it completely deprives the rebellion of sentimentality in a macabre and at times hilarious tale of a con man who becomes a hero in spite of himself. The second episode, "Lugubrious Obstinacy," takes place in a German prisoner-of-war camp for resistance fighters. The sham values of the Polish officers frequently compel them to join their captors in a bizarre partnership to maintain a false myth so as not to destroy their own morale. The "heroism" of the title is clearly intended ironically since Munk, even more than Wajda, took a skeptical view of the efficacy of Polish valor. In 1961 Munk was killed in an auto accident while working on *Passenger.* To provide some inkling of its qualities, the material he had shot was

Eroica ♦ Poland, 1958, Andrzej Munk.

pieced together and released posthumously in 1963. From the evidence it might well have been Munk's masterpiece. With a base in the present, *Passenger* reflects on the past of Auschwitz through recollections of a German woman who had been a guard there.

The national traumas of the war were returned to again and again in the films of Eastern Europe generally. Often the social and psychological insights they contained were clearly if indirectly applicable to the postwar societies. Beginning about 1959, however, the Poles began to turn away from war themes. **Jerzy Kawalerowicz,** for example, made two important "period pieces" dealing with non-Polish history: *Mother Joan of the Angels* (1961), based on the incidents of demonic possession and exorcism in a seventeenth-century French convent that inspired Aldous Huxley's book *The Devils of Loudon* and Ken Russell's film *The Devils;* and *Pharoah* (1965), a huge historical re-creation of ancient Egypt.

More typical of the changes taking place in Polish production was the work of two younger directors, **Roman Polanski** and **Jerzy Skolimowski.** Both developed quite personal styles and were preoccupied with the kinds of themes that would shortly cause them to work abroad. After his first feature, *Knife in the Water* (1962), a tight triangle of latent sexuality and violence, Polanski moved on to England (*Repulsion,* 1965; *Cul de Sac,* 1966; *Macbeth,* 1971; *Tess,* 1979) and the United States

(*Rosemary's Baby,* 1968; *Chinatown,* 1974). Skolimowski, after *Identification Marks: None* (1964) and *Walkover* (1965), made his last Polish film for awhile with *Barrier* (1966). The latter is especially remarkable for its abstract and symbolic qualities, a truly avant-garde experiment as well as a highly personal statement. Following *Le Depart* (Belgium, 1967), with its New Wave borrowings unequivocal, Skolimowski returned briefly to Poland to make *Hands Up!* (1967), which he regarded as his best and most mature work up to that time. When it was banned, he again left. He then worked abroad, his most interesting films being done in England: *The Shout,* 1978; *Moonlighting,* 1982; *Success Is the Best Revenge,* 1984. His first American-made feature was *The Lightship* (1985), which costarred Klaus-Maria Brandauer, as captain, and Robert Duvall, as a fleeing criminal, who, along with two henchmen, attempts to force the captain to weigh anchor and move out. The struggle for dominance between two men aboard ship, observed by the captain's teenage son (played by Skolimowski's teenage son), resembles *Knife in the Water,* which Skolimowski had coscripted.

In Poland in 1968 there occurred a violent repression of students and intelligentsia. The film production groups were once again reorganized and controls on film content became tighter. Since that time Poland has not been represented as promi-

The Contract ◆ Poland, 1981, Krysztof Zanussi.

nently on the international film scene as it had been during the heady years of the late fifties. Among the directors working in Poland in the 1970s it was **Krzysztof Zanussi** whose films, along with the continuing work of Wajda (*Promised Land,* 1974; *Without Anesthetic,* 1979), received the most attention abroad. Zanussi stuck to contemporary themes, often dealing with moral and existential issues of corruption, careerism, and exploitation. *Family Life* (1970), *Illumination* (1973), *Camouflage* (1976), and *The Contract* (1981) were particularly noted. In the latter the gathering of diverse people at a wedding party becomes a microcosm of Polish intellectual life. The narrative wanders through this well-heeled throng of bizarre characters and relationships, bouncing one person off another. Its scathing indictment of Poland's privileged classes is presented through wild and anarchic humor.

In 1980 the shipyard workers in Gdansk struck and wrested from the authorities concessions that created Solidarity, Eastern Europe's first independent labor union. The national euphoria that followed was shortlived, but before and during it two of Wajda's films were released that expressed to Poland and the rest of the world the spirit of the times (and also the deeply embedded official distrust that might cause it to end). *Man of Marble* (1977) encompassed the events of 1970, when workers rebelling against food prices were shot down in Gdansk and elsewhere along the Baltic coast. Though it was temporarily suppressed and kept from export for several years, the film had such an impact it is said to have precipitated a government shake-up. *Man of Iron* (1981), its sequel, carried the story into the 1980 events. Its frankness about government control and manipulation of the media and its obvious commitment to Solidarity are breathtaking, particularly in light of subsequent devel-

Man of Iron ♦ Poland, 1981, Andrzej Wajda; Krystyna Janda and Jerzy Radziwilowicz.

opments. It was considered by many to be the most important and courageous film to have been made in Eastern Europe up to that time.

In 1981 martial law was imposed, in part to counter the threat of Soviet invasion, and Solidarity was outlawed. Wajda left for France, where he made *Danton* (1983), about the struggle of that leader of the French Revolution with Robespierre for the freedom of the French people. It had obvious parallels with the struggles being waged in Poland at the time of its making. It was followed by *A Love in Germany* (1983), in which Hanna Schygulla plays a married woman who has a love affair, in violation of Nazi law, with a Polish prisoner-of-war in provincial Baden-Württemberg. The film, though a co-West German and French production, from a German novel, had a screenplay by three Poles: Boleslaw Michalek, Agnieszka Holland, and Wajda.

Joining Wajda and Zanussi was a younger generation whose films were labelled the "cinema of moral concern." **Agnieska Holland** is among these. In addition to scripting for others she has directed her own scripts, including films made outside Poland. *Europa, Europa* (1991), a French-German co-production based on a true story of a German Jew who takes on the identity of a Nazi during World War II, was a considerable international success. *Olivier Olivier* (France, 1991), also said to be based on an actual person and events, deals with the disappearance of a son and his subsequent replacement by an impostor who causes incestual sexual tensions and confusions within the family.

Holland's most recent work at time of writing, *The Secret Garden* (1993), from the 1911 children's classic by Frances Burnett Hodgson, also involves psychological probings into disturbed family relationships. It is different in that it is not from her own script and is her first English-language film, an $18 million production of Francis Ford Coppola's Zoetrope Studio for Warner Brothers. It differs even more from her earlier films in the attention given to the gorgeous surrounding of its characters in a remote Yorkshire estate and countryside, and in the general elegance of the *mise en scène* accompanying precise, detailed, and nuanced performances, especially from the two children principals. Holland seems to be becoming an international superstar writer/director.

The most important, original, and highly respected member of the younger Polish generation, who has remained at home, is **Krzysztof Kieślowski**. His fiction features at first continued the realist, aggressive approach of his documentary shorts. *The Calm Before the Storm* (1976) was about then current Polish working conditions; *Camera Buff* (1979) revealed a reportedly quite accurate picture of the way the filmmaking system functioned in Poland.

Following the 1981 crackdown Kieślowski's *No End* (1984) was much admired. It deals with the private tragedies and public conflicts under martial law as seen through the eyes of a widow whose husband had been a defense lawyer for the accused. Eventually she decides to commit suicide, not being able to bear her personal loss.

No End was Kieślowski's first film coscripted with Kryzysztof Piesiewicz. Subsequently the two created a series of ten films for Polish television based on the Ten Commandments ("Decalogue"). Two of these, *A Short Film about Killing* (Thou shalt not kill) and *A Short Film about Love* (Thou shalt not commit adultery) were

Europa, Europa ◆ France/Germany, 1991, Agnieska Holland; Marco Hofschneider.

released as theatrical features in 1988. The former won a Special Jury Prize at Cannes and an Oscar for Best Foreign Feature. An English-language version of the "Decalogue" screenplay was published by Faber & Faber in 1991.

The Double Life of Véronique (1991) is Kieślowski's first coproduction (French-Polish). In it he and cowriter Piesiewicz imagine girls—one a Polish Veronika, the other a French Véronique—born on the same day, who are alike in all respects including a lovely singing voice and a potentially fatal heart condition. The film moves back and forth between them in their separate countries as one gives up her boyfriend to pursue her singing career and dies, while the other abandons singing, engages in a love affair and lives.

The evolution of Kieślowski's preoccupations over the past decade or so seems remarkable, from a resolute social realism focused on political and societal issues to an increasing concern with moral choices being made by ordinary people well outside the public issues of their time. The core of these films is the individual in relation to other individuals, but there seem to be spiritual overtones as well, almost religious in a general sense. (Someone remarked that Kieślowski's films of the past decade represent an "agnostic mysticism.") Given the favorable audience response to them

A Short Film about Killing ♦   Poland, 1988, Krystztof Kieślowski; Miroslaw Baka, on the left.

this shift may somehow reflect more general changes in the dominant ideas and feelings of post-Communist Poland.

But Polish film does not stand alone among the films of the Eastern European countries. Even during its earlier period of ascendancy in the late fifties Poland had shared the spotlight before yielding it. An upcoming Hungary took advantage of some of the new creative opportunities that then appeared with an increased expression of nationalism on the one hand and of quite personal concerns on the other.

♦ HUNGARY

In 1956 there were uprisings in Poland and Hungary. Both occurred in populations who, having been given a small taste of increased liberty and independence, wanted more. In the case of Poland concessions were made to "the Polish road to socialism." Soviet troops were withdrawn, a new era of greater freedom and nationalism began, and the Polish film flourished. As for Hungary, the Soviet army quashed the rebellion; hundreds were killed, nearly 200,000 fled the country, and the national film flowering just beginning was temporarily ended.

Most prominent among Hungarian directors at work at the time was Zoltán Fábri. His *Merry-Go-Round* (1955) and *Professor Hannibal* (1956), made just before the uprising, moved well outside the confines of prevailing socialist realism. The first dealt with contemporary youth trying to find their way to new attitudes in a changed society. Its humor and lyricism were especially original. The second went even further, taking as target for social satire the question of historical revisionism, a sensitive subject in communist countries.

It wasn't until about 1963 or 1964 that a new era began with the reorganization of the film industry and of the Academy of Film and Dramatic Art. The first works of a younger generation appeared during those same years, including films by András Kovács (it was the later *Cold Days,* 1966, which gained him international attention), István Gaál (*The Falcons,* 1970, his fourth feature, is his best known), and István Szabó (whose *25 Fireman's Street,* 1974, presented a brilliant kaleidoscope of the Hungarian historical experience).

Two major factors were evident among the twenty to twenty-five Hungarian films produced each year. One was their emphasis on life in the villages rather than life in the big city. The other was their strong ties to Hungarian literature. For example, Károly Makk's *Love* (1970), which won a batch of international prizes, was an adaptation of a famous novel by Tibor Déry. A second successful example from this period, *Sinbad* (1971), directed by Zoltán Husárik, was based on novels by one of the greatest Hungarian writers of the twentieth century.

A conspicuous exception to this literary connection was **Miklós Jancsó.** It was Jancsó who—from *My Way Home* (1964), his third feature, on—carried Hungary's banner most prominently out into the world. Dominated by an obsessive subjective vision and intricate formal design that make it unique within Eastern European cinema, his work is coherent and consistent almost to a fault. The strange world of his films has no exact counterpart anywhere, for that matter; reviewers habitually referred to it as "Jancsó country."Among his films available in the United States, besides *My Way Home,* are: *Cantata* (1963), *The Round-Up* (1965), *The Red and the White* (1967), *Silence and Cry* (1968), *The Confrontation* (1969), *Winter Wind* (1969), *Agnus Dei* (1971), *Red Psalm* (1972), and *Hungarian Rhapsody* (1978).

The Red and the White, seen most widely, is typical. Like so many of Jancsó's films, it takes place on a vast windswept plain. The historical setting is the civil war following the Russian Revolution. Armies battle, but the causes seem arbitrary and unavailing in relation to universal and casual inhumanity. Sides cannot be told apart once uniforms are removed; nationalities are not distinguishable except when characters speak. At one moment the Whites are winning, at the next the Reds. Everyone is subject to pursuit, capture, humiliation, and execution.

Applied to this disturbing narrative material, and informing and affecting its meaning profoundly, is an equally extraordinary visual style. Shot in wide-screen black-and-white, the takes are long in duration. Camera movement is almost continuous and exceptionally varied: pans, tilts, dollies, tracking, and helicopter shots all combined. In addition to the insistently moving camera, there is constantly shifting and complex movement within the frame—mainly of men and horses. The movement is unusually frantic, with much running and galloping, and its meaning tacitly ironic. These humans behave instinctively, like other animals; their capacity for reason and emotion merely causes unnatural self-destruction. All of the frenzied activity leads only to death in this land of the still. The highly stylized and decorative visual

The Red and the White ◆ Hungary, 1967, Miklós Jancsó.

treatment applied to ugly human actions formalizes and distances them from us—they form part of a *danse macabre.* The choreographic quality plus the repetition of event, as each side achieves temporary victory or suffers more certain defeat, turns the action into arcane ritual.

In more recent years Jancsó worked mostly in theater and television (including a nine-hour TV series entitled *Faustus Faustus Faustus,* which covers Hungarian political history from its hero's birth in 1927 to his death in 1973). Meanwhile, the films of István Szabó and Márta Mészáros attracted considerable attention outside Hungary.

Szabó's hugely successful *Mephisto* (1981) is concerned with an opportunistic actor in Hitler's Germany who shifts his personal allegiances (including wife and mistresses) and adjusts his principles to conform to the requirements placed on an artist in a totalitarian state. His *Colonel Redl* (1985), with the same star, Klaus-Maria Brandauer, covers similar thematic ground in the earlier Austro-Hungarian Empire.

Meeting Venus (1990) was a British production (David Puttnam producer) about a Hungarian orchestra leader invited to conduct a pan-European performance of *Tannhäuser* in Paris to be broadcast to twenty-seven countries via satellite. The romantic entanglements and bureaucratic travails that nearly scuffle the production seem accurately, and certainly acidly, observed. His most recent film at time of writing, *Sweet Emma, Dear Böbe* (1992), evidently resembles *Meeting Venus* in its portrayal of a dysfunctional social system mired in bureaucracy and petty feuds, and a clandestine love affair with no future.

Mephisto ◆ Hungary, 1981, István Szabó; Klaus Maria Brandauer.

Márta Mészáros is one of the few women directors in the world to make consistently successful films, commercially and critically, that reach an international audience. (Her *The Girl* (1968), *Riddance* (1973), and *Adoption* (1975) are currently available in this country on video.) This success seems all the more remarkable in that her films deal resolutely with the problems of women in contemporary Hungary. The life presented is bleak; the view of it unsparing.

Among the socialist states, which generally demanded of their film makers positive and constructive service in the building of new societies, Hungary allowed surprisingly personal and critical examinations of the shared cultural experience. Hungarian films must speak with a special resonance to a people bearing scars from centuries of conquest, tyranny, and rebellion. Perhaps they provided a kind of national expression and escape valve for feelings that cannot, finally, be either ignored or suppressed.

◆ CZECHOSLOVAKIA

In Czechoslovakia the stirrings of 1956 were quietly quelled by the indigenous Communist hierarchy so that the Czechs neither gained additional freedom and independence, as did the Poles, nor were they subjected to Soviet invasion, as were the Hungarians. It wasn't really until the sixties that the political and cultural climate

The Girl ◆ Hungary, 1968, Márta Mészáros.

warmed sufficiently for the Czechs to freely expand into their own equivalent to the New Wave.

In 1963 a generation of FAMU (national film academy in Prague) graduates that included Miloš Forman, Jaromil Jireš, and Věra Chytilová made their feature debuts. Following these in the "Prague spring" were other features by new young film makers: Forman's *Black Peter* (1964) and *Loves of a Blonde* (1965), Jan Němec's *Diamonds of the Night* (1964), Pavel Juráček's and Jan Schmidt's *Joseph Kilián* (1964), and Chytilová's *Daisies* (1966). But the big international success was *The Shop on Main Street* (1965), by two veterans, Ján Kadár and Elmar Klos. The first Czech film to win an Academy Award, it is made up of known ingredients skillfully and movingly blended. Set in a small town under German occupation it exposed the evils of fascist mentality and its most heinous manifestation in anti-Semitism and genocide. *Shop on Main Street* treats these large themes on an intimate scale. The horrors inflicted upon inconceivable millions are expressed through events occurring in the lives of a simple carpenter, his greedy wife and fascist brother-in-law, and an ancient Jewish shopkeeper. Their paradoxical situation, as the carpenter tries to save the old lady from extermination, becomes credible through the fully rounded performances. Warmly and delicately observed detail and humor mingled with pathos characterize script and direction. Satisfying within its own terms, *The Shop on Main Street* was more conventional than the Czech films that would follow.

One of the leaders of a truly new Czech cinema was Miloš Forman, whose widely seen *Loves of a Blonde* and *The Firemen's Ball* (1967) might be compared to Italian Ermanno Olmi's early work. Like *Il Posto, Loves of a Blonde* is about a young person experiencing the impersonality and loneliness of the industrial world in a first job away from home. Forman uses a similar *cinéma-vérité*-like style and draws the same remarkable performances from casts surely composed largely of nonprofessionals. In *The Firemen's Ball*, Forman's observation of average people and everyday situations is more humorous and satiric than Olmi's. The cross-purposes, confusions, and inarticulateness of the petit-bourgeois characters in their relationships with each other, the tensions and misunderstandings between generations, the hopeless incompetence and self-inflated importance of bureaucracy are all wryly commented on in a totally disarming way. Life goes on, it seems, with its usual bumblings and eccentricities, irrespective of ideologies, governments, and large causes. Forman's co-scriptwriter, Ivan Passer, conceived and directed *Intimate Lighting* (1966) in much the same manner. In it he observes the reunion in a provincial Czech town of two old musician friends, one with wife and family, the other with a mistress.

Of **Jiří Menzel**'s films the best known in the West is *Closely Watched Trains* (1966). (It too won an Academy Award.) Like Forman and Passer, Menzel observes

The Shop on Main Street ♦ Czechoslovakia, 1965, Ján Kadár and Elmar Klos; Ida Kamińska and Jozef Króner.

The Firemen's Ball ♦
Czechoslovakia, 1967,
Miloš Forman.

with careful attention and detached amusement the actions of "the little people."
Though set in World War II and including partisan sabotage of the German-controlled
railway, instead of epic events, *Closely Watched Trains* concentrates on the coming-
of-age of a shy and ineffectual young station attendant and the peculiar sexual
goings-on around him in the isolated post.

The films of **Evald Schorm** have not received the same wide circulation in the
West as those mentioned above—perhaps because he dealt seriously with significant
contemporary themes. Both *Courage for Everyday* (1964) and *The Return of the
Prodigal Son* (1966) ran into censorship trouble, the first withheld for many months,
the second virtually banned on its release. *Courage for Everyday* concerns a politically active youth who attempts to maintain his own integrity in the face of a society
that demands that he be judged by its standards. *Return of the Prodigal Son* treats
sympathetically a talented and successful young artist who becomes depressed and
alienated from those around him, attempts suicide, and is institutionalized. The overall
thrust of Schorm's work would seem to be more like that of his Polish contemporaries
than of his own compatriots in its intense probing of the conflicts between individuals
and society. Called the "conscience" of the new Czech cinema, he died in 1988.

Finally, **Jan Němec,** too, makes one think of the Poles, especially of Jerzy
Skolimowski. *Report on the Party and the Guests* (1966), in which Schorm plays the
role of husband, carries the surrealist impulses of *Barrier* even further. In fact, it is a
sort of political allegory clothed in trappings of the avant-garde—at times it looks like

Closely Watched Trains ♦ Czechoslovakia, 1966, Jiří Menzel; Václav Neckář and Jitka Bendová.

Resnais's *Last Year at Marienbad*—with overtones of Kafka. The party takes place at formally set tables beside a lake in a lonely wood. The characters move and behave as if they are part of some sort of game with arcane rules, frenetic endeavor being followed by somnambulistic languor. The threat of violence and punishment hangs over the whole. Promptly banned upon completion, it was defiantly awarded the Czech Critics Prize a year later. Němec was forcibly exiled in 1974.

Even if unenthusiastic and vacillating, an official liberalization had clearly occurred within Czechoslovakia that permitted statements from film artists which were either openly or covertly critical of the society. The Czechs, like the Poles and Hungarians before them, responded by striving for still more freedom from Party conformity and for self-identification as Czechoslovaks. The years 1966 to 1968 saw the greatest ferment. Then, in the summer of 1968, an uprising was crushed by Soviet tanks, and Czechoslovakia once again became an occupied country for a time. As with the Hungarians earlier, many who weren't killed, imprisoned, or forced underground, fled. Some came to the United States and continued to work here; for example Kadár

Report on the Party and the Guests ♦ Czechoslovakia, 1966, Jan Němec.

(*Lies My Father Told Me,* 1975), Forman (*One Flew Over the Cuckoo's Nest,* 1975; *Hair,* 1979; *Ragtime,* 1981, *Amadeus,* 1984), and Passer (*Cutter's Way,* 1981).

In 1976–1977 there seems to have been a mild "thaw" and some of the leading figures returned to the studios after an absence of five or six years. Jiří Menzel made *Seclusion Near a Forest* and Věra Chytilová *The Apple Game* (both in 1977). Following a reorganization of the studios in 1983, films of somewhat greater boldness began to appear. In 1988 Chytilová's *The Jester and the Queen* was released, in which she evidently pursues her usual fresh and inventive experimentation with narrative. Still, there seems little to compare with the best of recent Hungarian cinema.As far as we in this country are concerned, those Czechs who stayed behind remained largely silent.

In 1993, the country divided itself into its two ethnic components, Czech and Slovak. It is too soon to know what sorts of films will result from this new situation. So far it is mostly the brief "Golden Age" in the late sixties that we remember. How curious and yet fitting that Czechoslovakia's most distinctive filmic contribution has been in celebration and gentle criticism of individual lives lived more or less oblivious to the earthshaking events that have marked its history along with that of its neighbors.

♦ YUGOSLAVIA

Among the Eastern European countries Yugoslavia was special in that its communism was resolutely national. It was also special in that its economy was a compromise between socialist and capitalist. In 1948 it removed itself from the Soviet orbit and maintained its independence in spite of every effort short of invasion to make it return to the fold. Stalin took out his resentment on the other "satellite" nations in severe repressive measures designed to make certain they did not follow the Yugoslav example. After Stalin's death the new Soviet leaders journeyed to Belgrade to offer public apologies for past U.S.S.R. policies. From that time on Yugoslavia's territorial integrity, as the phrase goes, was more assured.

Though the Yugoslavs, following earlier Czech example, developed an animation industry in Zagreb which remained among the most imaginative if not most prolific in the world, its live-action features plodded along the path of socialist realism as doggedly as if still being guided by the Soviets. It wasn't until the late sixties that there appeared a new generation of feature film makers, including Dušan Makavejev, Aleksandar Petrović, Živojin Pavlović, and a cluster of their innovative films (such as *Man Is Not a Bird,* 1965; *I Even Met Happy Gypsies,* 1967; *When I Was Dead and White,* 1967).

Makavejev and his early works seen widely abroad—*Love Affair, or The Case of the Missing Switchboard Operator* (1967), *Innocence Unprotected* (1968), *WR: Mysteries of the Organism* (1971), *Sweet Movie* (1974)—burst on the scene like some sort of Slavic bombshell. His experimental bent went even beyond that of the Pole Skolimowski or the Czech Němec. Makavejev's work makes you think of the most stylistically mixed of Godard's features. Or perhaps a better comparison would be with the Swedish Vilgot Sjöman's *I Am Curious* (1967), with its similar combination of sex and politics, fantasy and fact, fiction and newsreel.

In subject matter *Innocence Unprotected* is quite different from Makavejev's other films; in technique it has aspects in common. An affectionate recall of the first Serbian talkie, made in 1942 during the German occupation, it is subtitled "A New Edition of a Good Old Film." Interspersed with the original are interviews with its surviving creators—who talk about its production—and newsreels of military and political events of that time. *Love Affair, WR,* and *Sweet Movie,* on the other hand, all elaborate on the relationship between sexuality and the social-political restraints and expectations faced by the individual. Wildly funny, bawdy, if not obscene, and irreverent, jumbled and complex, they are finally impossible to describe, even thematically. Of the three, *Love Affair* is the most coherent, with two central characters and a slender thread of plot spun out in flashes forward as well as back, preceded by a lecture on sex and interrupted by another on murder. *WR* includes an informal television-style "profile" of psychologist Wilhelm Reich, replete with interviews of people who knew him, a fragmented account of two zany sexually preoccupied young women and their encounters with men, satirical political references, phallic jokes about Stalin, and other odds and ends including a demonstration by a markedly strange lady making a cast of a penis. Makavejev encapsulated "the message" (in an interview in *Film Quarterly,* Winter 1971–72) as: "the main thing in sexual repression or sexual freedom is actually the political content of human personal freedom." *Sweet Movie* is an even more scabrous, hilarious and at the same time darker mixture of diverse elements, scatology added to sexuality and politics. It throws haymaker punches at both the capitalist and communist mythologies, in about equal proportion, and provoked enraged responses from all sides. *Montenegro* (1981), shot in Sweden, was much more straightforward in narrative form but its content reiterates Makavejev's fascination (obsession?) with sexual homicidal mania. How extraordinary that the kind of film making that in the United States would be confined to the so-called underground, with no viable economic base and seen only by a small audience with esoteric tastes, should ultimately if indirectly be paid for by the taxpayers of a socialist state. But then Makavejev has become increasingly a man of the world. His *The Coca-Cola Kid* (1985), for example, is about an American representative of the title company in Australia. Most recent—not yet seen in the United States—is *Gorilla Bathes at Noon* (1992), reportedly a comic postmortem on life under communism in East Berlin.

A successor Yugoslavian star director is **Emir Kusturica,** whose first film, *Do You Remember Daisy Bell?* (1981), won a Golden Lion at Venice. His biggest success, *When Father Was Away on Business* (1985), won the Golden Palm Award at Cannes and has been seen widely abroad. It is a Bosnian comic drama set in Sarajevo in 1950. Father isn't really away on business but in a political prison camp during the period following the momentous break with the Soviet Union. He has been accused of "Stalinist tendencies." The film examines the family under the pressures

WR: Mysteries of the Organism ◆ Yugoslavia, 1971, Dušan Makavejev; Vica Vidovic, Jagoder Kaloper, and Milena Dravic.

When Father Was Away on Business   ◆   Yugoslavia, 1985, Emir Kusturica.

that stem from the nation at a crossroads. The warmth and understated humor of its observation of individuals and society are in a manner reminiscent of the Czechs. And, in fact, Kusturica, and other Yugoslav directors and cinematographers of his generation, attended the FAMU school in Prague. His *A Time of the Gypsies* (1990) is a sort of folk tale about a homely and unlucky gypsy lad who sets out to steal enough money to marry the girl he desires.

The peaceful breakup of Czechoslovakia into two states was preceded by the dissolution of Yugoslavia into separate republics beginning in 1990, which devolved into bloody civil war among the three main ethnic/religious factions: Serbs, Croats, Muslims. At the moment conditions are such that film production has virtually ceased. It is impossible to predict the outcome of this dreadful conflict for the participants, let alone what kinds of films may emerge when it is ended.

◆ SOVIET UNION AND AFTER

In the dominant power of the Eastern bloc, trends of reform began in 1985 at the 27th Congress of the Communist Party that eventually would lead to the breaking up of the Soviet Union. At that time Mikhail Gorbachev became First Secretary and *glasnost* (openness) and *perestroika* (restructuring) became key terms in his program. By 1986, when Gorbachev announced his commitment to "frank debate," films that had been "shelved," going back as far as 1966, were reexamined and many of them released. One of the most shelved of contemporary Soviet film makers, Elem Klimov, became one of the major figures involved in bringing revision, reassessment, and new latitude into the cinema. Klimov's films include *Rasputin* (1975, released in the United States in 1986), *Come and See* (1985, released in the United States in 1987), and *Farewell* (1983, released in the United States in 1987). Following a tense and significant election, Klimov became First Secretary of the Union of Soviet Filmmakers.

One exceptional find in the reexamination was *The Commissar* (completed in 1967, released in 1987), directed by Alexander Askoldov. Set in the Ukraine during the Civil War that followed the Revolution, *The Commissar* is about an iron-willed Russian woman, who waits out her pregnancy amidst a Jewish family whose house has been requisitioned. Their loving gentleness contrasts with her fierce revolutionary zeal. The compassionate treatment of Jews, including a surrealist vision of the Holocaust to come, is most likely the reason it was suppressed. Askoldov's continuing efforts to have the film released earned him official disfavor. He was branded "professionally incompetent" and not allowed to make another film.

Other noteworthy recent "discoveries" included *Repentance* (1984, Tengiz Abuladze), said to be an allegory of Stalinism; *The Theme* (1979, Gleb Panfilov), which

The Commissar ♦ U.S.S.R., 1967/87, Alexander Askoldov; Raisa Nedashkovskaya, Nonna Mordyukova, and Rolan Bykov.

Shadows of Our Forgotten Ancestors ♦ U.S.S.R., 1964, Sergei Paradjanov; Ivan Nikolaichuk, in tub.

includes reference to a censured writer forced to work as a gravedigger while he awaits the opportunity to emigrate to Israel; and *My Friend Ivan Lapchine* (1984, Alexi Guermann), which presents small-town life during the Stalin era frankly and naturalistically.

Two films made during the period of *glasnost* were especially popular at home and were exported abroad. Both are about young people and contemporary life in the Soviet Union. *Is It Easy to be Young?* (1987), a documentary, offers a broad survey showing the complex and problematic nature of the choices being faced by the young generation. *Little Vera* (1988), though fiction, is both sociological and satiric in its depiction of a working-class family in the midst of a breakdown of moral norms under the pressures of consumerism and the influence of Western pop culture.

One of the most uniquely talented of contemporary Soviet film makers resumed his career after fifteen years of enforced idleness. **Sergei Paradjanov** is known abroad for his *Shadows of Our Forgotten Ancestors* (1964) and *The Color of Pomegranates* (1969). *Shadows* is an extraordinary and unique epic blend of fact, fiction, and poetry in celebration of peasant life, lore, and mythology in a remote part of the Ukraine. Loose and elliptical in construction, "formalistic" and at the same time sensual, it is a film that would seem to stand quite outside the requirements of a modern socialist state, as did Dovzhenko's *Earth* before it. *The Color of Pomegranates* is about Sayat Nova, an eighteenth-century Armenian poet monk who suffers in an alien society. It was shelved after completion and reedited by others, over the film maker's protest, before release in 1973. Paradjanov's subsequent projects were either not accepted for production or not permitted to be completed. In 1974 he was convicted of homosexuality (a criminal offense in the Soviet Union), illegal currency dealings, and "incitement to suicide," and sentenced to six years hard labor. Though tried as a citizen and not as an artist, considerable suspicion was expressed that his real crime may have been his ebullient and rebellious spirit and the individualistic and iconoclastic nature of his finest and most important films.

By 1983 Paradjanov was out of prison and working on *The Legend of the Suram Fortress* (1985). Based on Georgian sources, it apparently contains the sort of folk elements and pagan traditions mixed with Christianity and nationalism, heroism and sacrifice and breathtaking imagery, as did his earlier films. He died of cancer in 1990.

Another contemporary Soviet film maker, to whom Paradjanov's last film, *Ashik Kerib* (1988), was dedicated, managed to escape the dictates of socialist realism and express a strong personal vision through structures and styles more nearly resembling those of contemporary film makers in Western Europe. **Andrei Tarkovsky**'s *Ivan's Childhood* (1962), *Andrei Rublev* (1966), and *Solaris* (1972) all won prizes at festivals abroad. *Ivan's Childhood*, with its strong and clear humanist message carrying along its unusual display of technical virtuosity, was extremely popular at home as well. *Andrei Rublev*, however, a more involuted and complex film about a monk icon painter who lived at the turn of the fifteen century, was held up for several years and then released in a cut version. It seems to bear certain resemblances to Paradjanov's *The Color of Pomegranates*, and to have suffered a somewhat similar fate. Evidently it was suspect because of its religious themes, unorthodox view of history, and scenes of brutality. *Solaris,* a science-fiction film, evoked comparisons with Stanley Kubrick's *2001,* though Tarkovsky eschewed spectacular technology and psychedelic fantasy in favor of the philosophical implications of his vision of the future and its effects on human lives. *The Mirror,* released in a very limited way in the Soviet Union in 1974 and not until nearly a decade later in the United States, is autobiographical as well as experimental, mingling dream and reality, childhood memories with an ongoing marriage.

Tarkovsky's next two films were made in Italy. In *Stalker* (1979) he returned to science-fiction. It is a grim odyssey of two Russian intellectuals led by the title character into "the Zone," a devastated postapocalyptic wasteland sealed off by the authorities. *Nostalgia* (1983), a brooding account of a journey through Italy by a Russian scholar, was made for European television. Its main theme seems to be the impossibility of transcultural understanding.

In 1984 Tarkovsky sought political asylum in the West. His last film, *The Sacrifice* (1986), was made in Sweden with a mostly Swedish crew including Sven Nykvist, Bergman's cinematographer. Erland Josephson, from Bergman's repertory company, is principal actor (as he is in *Nostalgia*). Like Bergman, Tarkovsky tends toward the poetic and the mystical, makes much use of philosophical dialogues and creates his visual style by relying on prolonged takes with a slowly moving camera.

There are similarities other than those just suggested, and the two film makers are known to have admired each other's films.

In *The Sacrifice* a woefully unhappy collection of humans on an isolated estate, most of them family members, torture themselves and each other psychologically. A nuclear war may break out or may be imagined; it may be countered by religious belief or by supernatural forces, if it ever happened. As the sacrifice promised to God for release from his fear of dying, the father burns down the house and is taken away by medical attendants. Though some aspects of the film parallel *Shame* and others *The Seventh Seal,* it is slower than Bergman's films, more attuned to the visual—remarkably so. Tarkovsky seems to be trying to transcend the limitations of plot, character, and dialogue to arrive at pure feeling states; images that don't advance narrative meaning but intensify the desperate dark despair are held relentlessly and returned to repeatedly. It is a strange and troubling metaphysical inquiry.

Tarkovsky died in Paris in 1986. From this short distance his slender body of work looks to be the most important and lasting by a Russian film maker since that of the Soviet artists of the 1920s. It is markedly different from theirs and from the socialist realism that followed, in subject matter and themes particularly—intensely personal and private rather than public and social. The individual preoccupies him

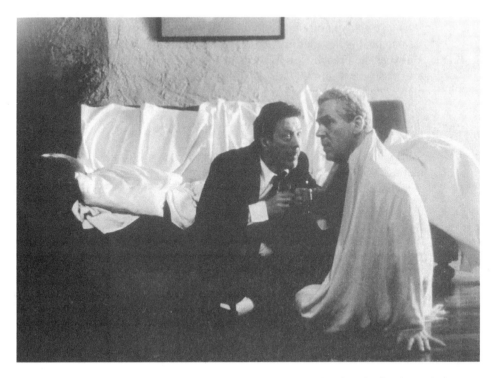

The Sacrifice ♦ U.S.S.R., 1986, Andrei Tarkovsky; Allan Edwall and Erland Josephson, on right.

more than the society; the society is seen only through individuals. So it is not to Eisenstein, Pudovkin, or Dovzhenko that we would compare Tarkovsky; rather, to Bergman and other Western European auteurs, and in many respects his creation seems unique.

But the country from which Tarkovsky emigrated has itself changed more radically than could have been imagined at the time of his death. Following an attempted coup in 1991 aimed at unseating Gorbachev and reversing the changes he had begun, the Soviet Union itself has ceased to exist, being replaced by twelve autonomous republics, and the planned economy of communism has been succeeded by attempts toward achieving the market economy of capitalism. It is not yet possible to see what the effects of this second revolution will be on the film production of the countries making up the former Union of Socialist Soviet Republics except that state monopoly of a monolithic film industry has ceased, more coproductions with Western countries are occurring, and greater efforts are being made to reach international audiences and the financial returns this will bring.

In any case, over the past four decades the films of Poland, Hungary, Czechoslovakia, Yugoslavia, and Russia have had intermittent periods in which critical self-examination, doubt and even despair have appeared. Often the questioning, criticism, and satire seemed remarkably pointed and frank to Westerners whose biases and ignorances may have precluded an understanding of how these nations actually functioned socially and politically. Also, within what we called the Soviet bloc there was an equally surprising amount of experimentation with form and the development of personal styles that include the ambiguous and the obscure. In these societies not only has the French New Wave had an effect on film makers' creation and audiences' responsiveness, but the Eastern Europeans have themselves contributed much to the new in terms of national expression, major film artists, and enduring works of art.

Beginning in the late fifties the Eastern European countries, joining France and Italy, achieved their own versions of a New Wave. Despite prominent differences, one thing common to all of these countries was a new emphasis on personal expression in film with the director as artist. Another was the use of new methods and techniques, defiance of former conventions, and the breaking up of traditional forms. In a general way the most interesting and important films from the countries on the continent, West and East, departed from the usual entertainment "package" as commercially conceived and from earnest Marxist exhortation. Instead they attempted to offer directly the kinds of moral, ethical, and aesthetic sustenance looked for in art works. It is these qualities in total that roughly characterize the New Wave, or Contemporary Cinema, or Modem Film, as the terms have come to be understood.

FILMS OF THE PERIOD

Czechoslovakia
1964
Black Peter (Miloš Forman)
Diamonds of the Night
(Jan Němec)

Joseph Kilián
(Pavel Juráček and Jan Schmidt)

1965
Intimate Lighting (Ivan Passer)

Loves of a Blonde (Forman)
The Shop on Main Street
    (Ján Kadár and Elmar Klos)

1966
Closely Watched Trains (Jiří Menzel)
Daisies (Věra Chytilová)
The Martyrs of Love (Němec)
Report on the Party and the Guests
    (Němec)
The Return of the Prodigal Son
    (Evald Schorm)

1967
The Firemen's Ball (Forman)

Hungary
1955
Merry-Go-Round (Zoltán Fábri)

1956
Professor Hannibal (Fábri)

1963
Cantata (Miklós Jancsó)

1964
The Age of Daydreaming (István Szabó)
My Way Home (Jancsó)

1965
The Round-Up (Jancsó)

1966
Cold Days (András Kovács)
Father (Szabó)

1967
The Red and the White (Jancsó)
Ten Thousand Suns (Ferenc Kósa)

1968
The Girl (Márta Mészáros)

1969
The Confrontation (Jancsó)

1970
The Falcons (István Gaál)
Love (Károly Makk)

1971
Agnus Dei (Jancsó)
Sinbad (Zoltan Husárik)

1972
Red Psalm (Jancsó)

1973
Riddance (Mészáros)

1974
25 Fireman's Street (Szabó)

1975
Adoption (Mészáros)

1976
Budapest Tales (Szabó)

1980
Confidence (Szabó)

1981
Mephisto (Szabó)

1982
Another Way (Makk)
The Princess (Pál Erdöss)

1992
Sweet Emma, Dear Böbe (Szabó)

Poland
1954
A Generation (Andrzej Wajda)

1956
Kanal (Wajda)
Man on the Track (Andrzej Munk)

1958
Ashes and Diamonds (Wajda)
Eroica (Munk)

1961
Mother Joan of the Angels (Jerzy
    Kawalerowicz)

1962
Knife in the Water (Roman Polanski)

1963
Passenger (Munk)

1964
Identification Marks: None (Jerzy Skolimowski)

1965
Walkover (Skolimowski)

1966
Barrier (Skolimowski)

1968
Everything for Sale (Wajda)

1970
Landscape After Battle (Wajda)

1971
Family Life (Krzysztof Zanussi)

1973
Illumination (Zanussi)

1974
Promised Land (Wajda)

1976
The Calm Before the Storm
   (Krzysztof Kieślowski)

1977
Camouflage (Zanussi)
Man of Marble (Wajda)

1979
Camera Buff (Kieślowski)
Without Anesthetic (Wajda)

1980
The Contract (Zanussi)

1981
Man of Iron (Wajda)
A Woman on Her Own (Agnieszka Holland)

1984
No End (Kieślowski)

1985
Angry Harvest (Holland)

1988
A Short Film About Killing (Kieślowski)
A Short Film about Love (Kieślowski)

Russia
1962
Ivan's Childhood (Andrei Tarkovsky)

1964
Shadows of Our Forgotten Ancestors
   (Sergei Paradjanov)

1966
Andrei Rublev (Tarkovsky)

1967/87
The Commissar (Alexander Askoldov)

1969
The Color of Pomegranates (Paradjanov)

1972
Solaris (Tarkovsky)

1975
Rasputin (Elem Klimov)

1983
Farewell (Klimov)

1985
Come and See (Klimov)

1988
Ashik Kerib (Paradjanov)

Yugoslavia
1965
Man Is Not a Bird (Dušan Makavejev)

1967
I Even Met Happy Gypsies
   (Aleksandar Petrović)
Love Affair (Makavejev)

1968
Innocence Unprotected (Makaveiev)
When I Was Dead and White (Živojin Pavlović)

1971
WR: Mysteries of the Organism (Makavejev)

1974
Sweet Movie (Makavejev)

1981
Montenegro (Makavejev)
Do You Remember Daisy Bell? (Emir Kusturica)

1985
When Father Was Away on Business (Kusturica)

1990
A Time of the Gypsies (Kusturica)

1992
Gorilla Bathes at Noon (Makavejev)

BOOKS ON THE PERIOD

Eastern Europe
Balski, Grzegorz, comp. and ed., *Directory of Eastern European Film-makers and Films 1945–1991*. Westport, Ct: Greenwood Press, 1992
Goulding, Daniel J., ed., *Post New Wave Cinema in the Soviet Union and Eastern Europe.* Bloomington: Indiana University Press, 1989
Petrie, Graham and Ruth Dwyer, eds. *Before the Wall Came Down: Soviet and East European Filmmakers Working in the West.* Lanham, MD: University Press of America, 1990

Poland
Michałek, Bolesław and Frank Turaj, *The Modern Cinema of Poland.* Bloomington: Indiana University Press, 1988
Sobansi, Oskar, *Polish Feature Films: A Reference Guide, 1945–1985.* West Cornwall, CT: Locust Hill Press, 1987

Russia
Attwood, Lynne, ed., *Red Women on the Silver Screen: Soviet Women and Cinema from the Beginning to the End of the Communist Era.* San Francisco: Pandora Press, 1993
Galichenko, Nicholas (ed. by Robert Allington), *Glasnost: Soviet Cinema Responds in Transition.* Austin: University of Texas Press, 1991
Horton, Andrew and Michael Brashinsky, *The Zero Hour: Glasnost and Soviet Cinema.* Princeton, NJ: Princeton University Press, 1992
Lawton, Anna, *Kinoglast: Soviet Cinema in Our Time.* New York: Cambridge University Press, 1993
Lawton, Anna, *The Red Screen: Politics, Society, Art in Soviet Cinema.* New York: Routledge, 1992
Taylor, Richard and Derek Spring, eds., *Stalinism and Soviet Cinema.* New York: Routledge, 1992
Zorkaya, Neya, *The Illustrated History of Soviet Cinema.* New York: Hippocrene Books, 1991

17

American Reevaluation and Reemergence

◆ ◆ ◆

1963–1980

Frequently Americans have been slow, not to enjoy but to value what is most vital and characteristic among our own popular art forms. The French, on the other hand, have often responded to the pleasures offered by our entertainment with a serious appreciation which initially may have seemed inflated but later prevailed. It was Baudelaire and the symbolist poets who first exalted that writer of tales Edgar Allan Poe. It was critic and film maker Louis Delluc and the French Impressionists of the early 1920s who early celebrated the virtues of American movies, notably those of Douglas Fairbanks, Pearl White, Mack Sennett, Thomas Ince, and, of course, Charles Chaplin. It was the writers for *Cahiers du Cinéma* who later recognized the merits of unsung auteurs at work among the staple genres of the contemporary Hollywood film who would become principal sources of inspiration and influence for the French New Wave.

◆ REEVALUATION

By 1957, the year of Bazin's critique of *la politique des auteurs,* it had become the principal critical approach of *Cahiers du Cinéma.* Andrew Sarris, American missionary of auteurism, first fully articulated his own views in "Notes on the Auteur Theory in 1962" in *Film Culture,* Winter 1962/63; the Spring 1963 special issue of the same journal comprised the initial version of his herculean effort to organize and assess, by director, the vast output of the American sound film.

The ideas of auteurism subsequently gained ground internationally. Even the established founts of English-language criticism which had been under attack by the auteurists—*The New York Times, The New Yorker,* and *Sight and Sound*—gradually came to reflect their tastes, as did histories of film like this one. In 1968 Sarris consolidated the auteur position in his book *The American Cinema: Directors and Directions 1929–1968.* No work since the much earlier writings of Paul Rotha (*The Film Till Now,* 1930) and Lewis Jacobs (*The Rise of the American Film,* 1939) has done as much to shape our thinking about the history of the American film. "Reshape" would be the better term, since Sarris's book reduced the status of many directors whose work had formerly been most valued, and raised that of others who had attracted little critical attention up to that point. For the films of the directors discussed below released between 1963 and 1980 see "Films of the Period" at the end of this chapter.

Into his "Pantheon" Sarris admitted fourteen directors he felt had "transcended their technical problems with a personal vision," had created "a self-contained world with its own laws and landscapes." Among them were D. W. Griffith, Charles Chaplin and Buster Keaton, John Ford and Howard Hawks, Ernst Lubitsch, Fritz Lang, and Josef von Sternberg, and Alfred Hitchcock. By the time *The American Cinema* was published, almost half of them were dead and others in retirement. All those in Sarris's Pantheon had begun work in the silent period except Max Ophuls and Orson Welles. None of its members is alive today.

In his second category, labeled "The Far Side of Paradise," Sarris included twenty directors who fell short of the Pantheon "either because of a fragmentation of their personal vision or because of disruptive career problems." Like his first category, with only minor quibbles, most of the choices—of the older veterans especially—were acceptable to the more traditional, non-auteur critical approaches; for example, Cecil B. De Mille, Raoul Walsh, Erich von Stroheim, Frank Capra, George Cukor, George Stevens, and Preston Sturges. A number of these men had died by the time Sarris's book was published; all have died since.

But it was another group of directors in Sarris's second category, mainly of a younger generation, who most clearly reflected the contention surrounding auteurism and the evaluative shifts it contributed. These were directors who had seemed to other critics to embody, even epitomize, the excesses of the Hollywood film, its formulas and superficialities, its glossy unreality on the one hand and gratuitous violence on the other. The auteurists celebrated the visions of these directors and the styles in which they were encased as being especially American and distinctively individual. These directors attempted to turn what had been regarded as trivial or meretricious into a consistent and coherent view of life, operating often below the surface or around the edges of the frequently assigned plot material on which they worked.

Heretofore these directors had not been identified with so-called serious film. Conventionally, critics had most valued content of moral substance and social significance dealt with in realistic style. The auteurists generally defended their choices more in terms of manner than matter; it was not what the script had in it so much as what the director made of the subject. In the course of their investigations the auteurists frequently offered evidence of a kind of directorial intelligence and control in operation that had not been acknowledged up to that point.

One of these directors, Nicholas Ray, became a cause célèbre of the auteur theory. Some of the auteurists advanced him as the greatest director who ever lived; some other critics considered him a Hollywood hack. Sarris placed him somewhere between those two extremes. As with most of the directors in his top two categories, Sarris found that Ray had "always displayed an exciting visual style." Sarris noted that Ray, unlike some of the directors of this second category, did have a consistent and important statement running through his work: namely, that "every relationship establishes its own moral code and that there is no such thing as abstract morality." Among Ray's films that transcend auteur enthusiasms and are generally considered major works are: *They Live by Night* (1949)—his first feature (and a precursor to Arthur Penn's *Bonnie and Clyde* and Robert Altman's *Thieves Like Us*); *Rebel Without a Cause* (1955)—which made James Dean spokesman and symbol for his generation; and *Bitter Victory* (1958)—made in France but set in the British Libyan campaign of World War II. Ray's final film, *Lightning Over Water* (1979), is an extraordinary, painful document, part fiction, mostly fact. Co-directed by German film maker Wim Wenders, who finished it after Ray's death, it is about Ray as artist-film maker and about his dying.

The remaining directors in Sarris's "Far Side of Paradise" were equally crucial to the auteur theory and needed similar explication and defense. First, there were the special sort of Hollywood stylists who frequently worked with conventional melodrama, adaptations of popular novels, or sex farces, and used a screen iconography that was strong on clear-cut dramatic composition and assertive color: Douglas Sirk, Otto Preminger, Vincente Minnelli (of the melodramas rather than the musicals), and Blake Edwards. The thematic materials of these films were often so patently the stuff of which mass daydreams are made that most critics dismissed them as vacuous. The auteurists, however, saw in them a deliberate exaggeration and flaunting of the generic elements on which they were based; it was through this kind of hyperbolic excess, they argued, that the auteurs were able to criticize the very values to which the films seemed to be pandering. Usually this alleged sophistication on the part of the films' makers was more apparent abroad than at home.

Other inclusions in the "Far Side of Paradise" that raised critical hackles could be shorthanded as the tough guys, the directors working in the conventional action genres: Anthony Mann, Samuel Fuller, Robert Aldrich. They, too, had made manifest their world views and obsessions through personal styles, but the styles were frequently pared lean and fitted efficiently to the events and themes of their films, which contained a prevailing violence.

It doesn't now seem possible to give more space to the auteurists' reevaluation and contribution to our understanding of the American cinema of the recent past; perhaps it's no longer needed. About the time that Sarris's *The American Cinema* was published, a new sort of creative vitality—new kinds of films and new film makers—began to make itself felt. The emerging artistic characteristics and films of some of the principal present-day creators were at first embedded in a Hollywood response to the sociological and political phenomenon of youthful revolt.

◆ REEMERGENCE

Spread across the sixties were the civil rights movement, with sit-ins, marches, and riots, and the Vietnam War resistance, with demonstrations, moratoriums, and student strikes. Along with these protest movements there arose a youth culture, as it was called. Young people in large numbers disassociated themselves from what they regarded as their parents' too exclusive concern with material accumulation; lack of honesty and decency in dealing with each other; complacency, apathy, and conformity within a society dominated by big business and governmental and educational systems that seemed to be in collusion with it. They signaled their solidarity by letting their hair grow, and by donning clothes that were, by conventional fashion, either sexually indeterminate or outlandish—in either case, not like those worn by the elders and the straights. Their disaffection also took the form of refusal to assume the expected roles of wage earners, husbands, wives, or parents. Some of them "dropped out" of society into drugs, Eastern mysticism, communes. Others became active in attacking the political-economic structure that had dictated our involvement in what they regarded as an immoral war, and which tolerated poverty, injustice, and racial discrimination at home.

The spirit of these times was echoed in a film cycle called the "youth films" or the "now films," which achieved a significant popularity before tapering off—as the protest movements themselves did. The films were about young people and new lifestyles in conflict with the old. They were made for the youthful audiences who were now the principal patrons of the theaters. Sometimes they were even made by young film makers. All of them explored social, and some of them political, problems in one way or another. A few sounded strong notes of dissent. They also combined forms—documentary and experimental styles and subject matter along with those of conventional fiction—in ways that some of the recent films coming from abroad were doing (those of Godard and Makavejev, for example).

The trend started off indirectly in 1967 with three of the most popular releases of that year: *Bonnie and Clyde, The Graduate,* and *Cool Hand Luke.* Though *Bonnie and Clyde* was a sort of gangster film set in rural America of the thirties, encoded within it were themes of current youthful protest: the individual against the system; an unconventional and hedonistic lifestyle that put emphasis on kicks; and the implicit justification of violence directed against the impersonal institutions of society and against the conscientious, middle-aged, and humorless who served them. *The Graduate,* more explicit if less bold and beautiful, expressed other manifestations of contemporary youthful tension and conflict. *Cool Hand Luke* may seem a peripheral case, but it was about another resister, passive protester, who wouldn't buckle under to the demands of his (in that case prison) society.

It took Hollywood two years to contemplate those three films before producing more which incorporated some of the elements that seemed to have been responsible for their success. In 1969 the youth/now cycle proper began with *Easy Rider, Medium Cool, Zabriskie Point,* and *Alice's Restaurant. Easy Rider,* the seminal film, became an immediate favorite with the eighteen-to-twenty-five-year-old audience. Those two young men riding their bikes and getting high on pot and LSD "in search of America," as pop-song lyrics of the time put it (*Easy Rider* used folk-rock throughout for its score), were adopted as youth-cult heroes. Like Bonnie and Clyde, Billy and Captain America were killed by the squares and the rednecks. *Easy Rider* spawned a profusion of features with related themes, some of them much more direct in their criticism of the dominant values of contemporary American society.

Coming up through those years of national turmoil and dissidence were a number of important film makers who maintained a strong interest in critically examining certain aspects of American culture, including the violence so prevalent during our recent history. Some of the five to be dealt with here had established roots earlier; all continued into the eighties and most into the nineties as creators of individual distinction. The choices are Arthur Penn, Sam Peckinpah, Francis Ford Coppola, Robert Altman, and Martin Scorsese.

Arthur Penn seems preoccupied with the meaning of America. Every one of his films to date explicitly examines a facet of American culture. The people who interest him most, however, are the outcasts from this society. Coming out of theater and television, Penn, in his first film, *The Left-Handed Gun* (1958), reinvented the legend of Billy the Kid along speculative Freudian lines. *The Miracle Worker* (1962) considers the young Helen Keller, blind, deaf, and mute, and the teacher who helped her overcome the terrible handicaps and go on to a remarkable life and career. *Mickey One* (1965) explores the fear and threat of violence omnipresent in American cities through the eyes of a paranoid and desperate nightclub comic pursued by the Mob. *The Chase* (1966) follows that same climate of violence into a small Southern town and adds to it the general erosion of sexual morality. *Bonnie and Clyde* (1967), surely among the most influential of American films, sets real-life bank robbers of the thirties in the light of the myth they themselves had helped create. *Alice's Restaurant* (1969), also based on actuality, deals understandingly with troubled American youth of the sixties. *Little Big Man* (1970) moves backward over white responsibility and guilt for the genocide perpetrated on Native Americans in the conquest of their land. *Night Moves* (1975), which includes self-conscious play with the film medium and audience expectations, was of the post-Watergate moment. In its existential detective story the culpable protagonist chases elusive criminals through a confusing society that seems to have lost its moral equilibrium. *The Missouri Breaks* (1976) was a critical and commercial disaster caused in part by contention between its two expensive and demanding stars, Marlon Brando and Jack Nicholson.

Though Penn's preoccupation with things American continued, of the five directors here being considered he seemed to have the strongest attraction to the kind of artistic modernism in film that had been emanating from Europe since the late fifties. *Bonnie and Clyde* was originally conceived by its scriptwriters, David Newman and Robert Benton, for direction by Truffaut or Godard. *Mickey One* and *Night Moves* are the full-scale examples—what the trade would call art movies—experimental and philosophical within their genre trappings. Penn may be the most "intellectual" of the five directors, noteworthy for his integrity in choice of subjects and for his articulateness in discussing his intentions in regard to them. He also is a film maker of considerable skill and sensitivity to the medium.

Bonnie and Clyde ♦ U.S.,
1967, Arthur Penn;
Warren Beatty and Faye
Dunaway.

Sam Peckinpah is another of the crop of directors who came to features from television. He had been a writer-director on several TV western series and remained mostly loyal, even when working in a form that was not outwardly a western, to that most American of film genres. To its basic patterns he added his particular attitudes and absorption with loners and losers, with outmoded responses to cultural change, and with violence. His first feature, *Deadly Companions* (1961), gives special emphasis to the way in which a hostile countryside reflects as well as conditions human motives and actions that are more confused and troubled than those of the classic western. *Ride the High Country* (1962), along with the autumnal beauty of mountain scenery and the raucous, violent humor of a mining camp, offers an essay on the fading myth of the western itself—embodied by the aging characters played by aging western actors Joel McCrea and Randolph Scott. *Major Dundee* (1964), set in the Civil War West of cavalry and Indians, concentrates on the conflict of character between two strong, wrong men. One is a grim, pragmatic Union major, the other, a flamboyant Irishman who had been fighting for the Confederate cause. *The Wild Bunch* (1969) brings violence to the fore—gross in quantity, refined in quality of treatment, gruesome detail combined with poetic reflection. Peckinpah's statement in that film seems at once repellent and profound. It is a highly personal, obsessive, microcosmic view of the kind of society which might emerge when the traditional values that had given frontier violence meaning no longer function.

The Ballad of Cable Hogue (1970), though also a western, attempts to transcend the specificity of the American myth through a curious mixture of comedy and universal, quasi-religious themes symbolically stated. In *Straw Dogs* (1971) Peckin-pah moved to an English village; out of his culture altogether, except for the inclusion of an American protagonist. But its themes are not unfamiliar in westerns, especially those of Peckinpah. It concerns the nastiness and sadistic violence built into human nature, and the need for a good man with gun in hand to face the rest of society, obtain justice, and confirm his manhood. *Junior Bonner* (1972) deals with a modern rodeo rider trying to survive and maintain an anachronistic individualism. *The Getaway* (1972) is a more or less routine chase-thriller set in the contemporary Southwest, which nonetheless manages to continue some of Peckinpah's favorite themes. Some of the potential force of *Pat Garrett and Billy the Kid* (1973), a highly personal interpretation of that legend, was evidently deflected by an excess of the sort of producer interference Peckinpah seems prone to. *Bring Me the Head of Alfredo Garcia* (1974) is a present-day revenge story set in Mexico, in which a down-at-heel piano player fights a smoothly functioning capitalist-criminal system out of a need for self-redemption, a commitment to principle, and feelings for one other human being.

Peckinpah's view of the human animal's struggle for survival in the face of malevolent and cynical forces, with only a professional code for sustenance, is recognizably his own. Though his understanding of the world is scarcely everyone's, it is a view expressed with great technical control, considerable strength, and some beauty, and one that evidently exerts an uneasy attraction for American audiences. The expression of it has ended, however; Peckinpah died in 1984 at the age of 59.

The Wild Bunch ♦ U.S., 1969, Sam Peckinpah; Ben Johnson, Warren Oates, William Holden, and Ernest Borgnine.

Francis Ford Coppola is the first major American director to have graduated from a university film program (UCLA's). Given that academic training, with its emphasis on personal expression, it is interesting that during the first part of his career Coppola largely withheld or concealed his own personality in his work, opting instead for a "professional" range of subjects and styles. *Dementia 13* (1963), a low-budget horror film, was financed by Roger Corman (who has given other young talent their first chance). It was Coppola's second feature, *You're a Big Boy Now* (1967), that caught public attention. A charmingly light and unpretentious comedy, it is about a teenager's attempts to free himself from his parents' domination and find love and sex, in either order. Among its attractions are its New York City location and the handling of bit-players in bizarrely eccentric roles. The next film, *Finian's Rainbow* (1968), a semiblockbuster musical, was a complete switch that offered no threat to the masters of the genre. Over-inflated, rather unlovely and unamusing, it is a stage-bound version of the Broadway hit. *The Rain People* (1969) is something else. Flawed in part, and oddly unresolved, it is nonetheless a serious and quite original attempt to get at the stresses felt by a particular American woman, stresses which cause her to leave her husband, though she is several months pregnant, to try to find herself in a cross-country journey by car.

With *The Godfather* (1972) Coppola's career took off in a rocketlike trajectory. What quickly became one of the great financial successes in the history of film is also a work of enduring value. Expert in every respect, the great appeal of the film clearly comes from the warm glow of people and times remembered, when not only were men men and women women, but families were families, including especially the Mafia. While *The Godfather* satisfied the constant American appetite for the simplicities and verities that a nostalgic view can best afford, the sentiments expressed were especially close to Coppola, who was himself from an Italian-American background. As for the gangster-film tradition, he chose to heighten rather than disturb the myths and to flesh them out with convincing and moving human detail, much of which had surely been observed and felt at first hand. *The Conversation* (1974) slightly preceded Penn's *Night Moves,* and deals even more specifically with the Watergate syndrome. It concerns an electronic eavesdropper who applies his expertise impartially and amorally, gaining his only satisfactions from his considerable skill and the vicarious experiencing of fragments of other lives. *The Godfather, Part II* (1974) expanded on the themes and confirmed the mastery Coppola had demonstrated in the original.

If the direction Coppola has taken since the achievement of *The Godfather* is less than clear, his need for personal expression about important aspects of American life remains constant. His *Apocalypse Now* (1979) will be dealt with in Chapter 20, along with other films about the Vietnam War.

Robert Altman, like Penn and Peckinpah, came to film out of directing for television series. What many of his features have in common is a dissection of the traditional American film genres, in the course of which he pokes fun at, questions, and attacks the values and shibboleths that their conventions support. He has said, and one can infer from his work, that he employs a good deal of improvisation in his direction. *M*A*S*H* (1970), his fast substantial success (which spawned an even more successful long-running television series), rode the crest of the youth/now cycle

The Godfather ♦ U.S., 1972, Francis Ford Coppola; Al Pacino and Marlon Brando.

and launched Altman's subsequent career. An outrageous satire of both the military and medical professions, it simultaneously desecrated our memories of *All Quiet on the Western Front* and *Young Doctor Kildare*. In the same year, *Brewster McCloud* went to work on science fiction and private-eye sleuthing. It is mainly slapstick farce, about a young man who tries to develop an apparatus and muscles that will enable him to fly like a bird.

Brewster McCloud was followed by the visually extraordinary and thematically haunting *McCabe and Mrs. Miller* (1971). Totally unlike Altman's previous work, it is a kind of antiwestern. In place of the conventional assurance, solitary strength, and fast draw with a sure shot, it introduced psychological vulnerability, the need for human companionship, and the impossibility of avoiding one's destiny. Though *McCabe and Mrs. Miller* is somber in what it says about the nature of humanity, Altman's view of the two protagonists remains warm, affectionate, and humorous.

With *The Long Goodbye* (1973), also, the parody is softer and subtler than in *M*A*S*H* or *Brewster McCloud,* and the film works in its own right, not requiring us to know how it contrasts with the Raymond Chandler novel. Altman's point seems to be that the old-fashioned nobility of a whole genealogy of screen Marlowes, however muted in tough talk, is no longer applicable to these unheroic times. Elliott Gould replaces Humphrey Bogart, with a fumbling ineptitude designed to put the legend to rest.

Thieves Like Us (1974), though related to the exploits of the Barrow gang that had been treated in a number of other films, drops parody altogether. In part ironic and distanced, it is yet a serious and sensitive, if quite different, version of the legendary material. *California Split* (1974) has its generic origins in a cycle of films that dealt with what might be described as bonding between men (that had begun with the great success of *Butch Cassidy and the Sundance Kid,* 1969). There are lots of laughs and a happy ending of sorts, but along the way the film explores compulsive gambling, the milieu in which it takes place, and a significant relationship between two contrasting characters.

From the confines of a California casino, Altman moved to *Nashville* (1975), the Middle America capital of country-and-western music, and to numerous characters caught up in that industry and in the presidential campaign of a populist demagogue. The subjects of parody and satire here are popular music and popular politics, the sorts of performance and manipulation involved in both, and the audiences to which both appeal. A big, ambitious film, some regard it as his crowning achievement; Altman himself has referred to it as his "metaphor for America." *Buffalo Bill and the Indians* (1976), based on the play *Indians* by Arthur Kopit, debunks the legend surrounding and exploited by William F. Cody as touring showman. *3 Women* (1977) explores the incomplete psyches and changing relationships of two southern California roommates and their landlady, a painter of mysterious and grotesque murals.

A Wedding (1978) is very like *Nashville* in many ways—they might be thought of as companion pieces. Arguably Altman's most considerable achievements, during this period at least, there are no other films quite like them. *Nashville*'s twenty-four characters have become *A Wedding*'s forty-eight. In *Nashville* all are together at the opening and closing (which occur in public places); in *A Wedding* the same is true (but the places are private [or family] in a sense). In between the film is structured around the separate characters, with narrative threads linking their actions. If *Nashville* is a sort of musical and perhaps a tragedy; *Wedding* is a sort of romance and surely a comedy. Yet it begins near the end; that is, in classical drama (Greek and Elizabethan at any rate) comedies conclude with marriage, tragedies with death. This comedy begins with a wedding (during which it is pointedly implied that the young couple will not live happily ever after) and has one death near the beginning and two deaths near the end that seem to lead to, if not a happy ending, kinds of resolutions and comings together. Though these characters are of high estate—not kings and queens maybe but robber barons and baronesses at least—their tale is being told by a minstrel (as myth) or by a sage (as history) rather than by a dramatist. Much the same could be said about *The Player,* which catapulted Altman into a new prominence in the nineties.

Of the five contemporary American film makers dealt with in this section, Altman was the most prolific, averaging over a film a year following the success of *M*A*S*H.* Through producing as well as directing, he seemed able to control what he said and the way he said it. His accomplishment has been aided by a group of actors appearing regularly in his work: Shelley Duvall, Keith Carradine, Sissy Spacek, Geraldine Chaplin, and Elliott Gould among the stalwarts. And, like Ingmar Bergman, Altman obtains distinctive and compelling performances from his repertory company. Though the potential of each individual film doesn't always seem to be fully realized, Altman

Nashville ◆ U.S., 1975,
Robert Altman; Ronnee
Blakley and Henry Gibson.

achieved a position from which he could carry his own distinctive, sardonic view of American society from one film to the next. This is a considerable achievement in an art which is first of all an industry.

Martin Scorsese is the newest and youngest (born in 1942) of the five directors; Coppola is next (born in 1939), whose career Scorsese's in some ways parallels. Both are from Italian-American backgrounds, which they have drawn upon in their films; both attended university film departments (New York University in Scorsese's case). But there are differences, of course. Coppola has ranged more widely in his subjects and forms; Scorsese has stuck with remarkable and commendable closeness to what he learned while growing up in New York's Little Italy. When Coppola tried his hand at a musical, it was *Finian's Rainbow,* a bit of Irish whimsy replete with leprechaun and pot o' gold at rainbow's end; Scorsese's musical was *New York, New York,* about a self-absorbed tenor sax man obssessed with jazz.

Who's That Knocking at My Door? (1968) was the transitional feature between Scorsese's quite brilliant student shorts and his fully professional career. It sets up the Scorsese world of young Italian-American punks, one of them troubled by yearnings for emotional freedom from the limited lives of the ethnic enclave. The time seems predominantly late at night; much of the action consists of piling into, riding in, or getting out of cars, standing around in cheerless deserted bars, or luring "broads" to a sleazy apartment.

Boxcar Bertha (1972) was an exploitation film directed for Roger Corman (as *Dementia 13* had been by Coppola); it was Scorsese's first commercial feature. Then he returned to Little Italy with *Mean Streets* (1973), a fuller, tougher, more assured development of the same sorts of characters, themes, and milieu that had appeared in *Who's That Knocking*. In *Mean Streets* the protagonist (Harvey Keitel) attempts to reconcile his persistent sense of decency and concern for others with his ambition to succeed in the Mafia-imbued life around him. Specifically, he wants to manage the restaurant owned by his uncle, who demands that he reject both his epileptic girlfriend and his maddeningly irresponsible buddy. The latter role is played by Robert De Niro, who has become a fully participating collaborator in the expression of Scorsese's mythos.

Alice Doesn't Live Here Anymore (1975) broke away from the earlier New York films. Set in small towns and on the road in the far Southwest, its title character, played by Ellen Burstyn, is a thirty-five-year-old housewife with a bumptious twelve-year-old son. After the death of her unsympathetic husband of fifteen years, she pursues her nostalgic illusion of returning home to Monterey and having a singing career. The film centers on Alice's efforts along the way (she never reaches Monterey) to cope with various relationships and a desultory and unrewarding life, wisecracks and humor covering loneliness and confusion. (Apart from its prevailing comedy, *Alice* resembles Coppola's *Rain People* in many respects.)

Taxi Driver (1976) returned to New York City and to what might be seen as an extreme variation on the failed saint figure who appeared as protagonist in both *Who's That Knocking* and *Mean Streets*. Here the character, played by De Niro, is locked into near catatonia, and becomes obsessed with cleansing the world's evil through a bath of blood. The isolation of the De Niro character is truly frightening in its credibility, the homicidal violence shocking and unnerving. It dealt with attempted political

Taxi Driver ♦ U.S., 1976, Martin Scorsese; Robert De Niro.

assassination following a time when our leaders (Martin Luther King, the two Kennedys) had been gunned down. It featured Jodie Foster, obsessive love object of the man who would wound Ronald Reagan.

New York, New York (1977) is not so much a musical as it is a drama with music, or, even more precisely, a funny-sweet-sad love story about two musicians. It salutes the city in the manner of the films of the forties and offers a loving reprise for the music being played at the end of the big band era. De Niro's performance is full of charm and pyrotechnics, from marvelous wacky humor to tight-faced pathos, and the Liza Minnelli persona is softened and warmed in this production. It reasserted Scorsese's affection for and identification with his characters, as well as his obvious familiarity with and control of the medium.

Raging Bull (1980) has the New York City setting and Italian-American context of the earlier films. What is different about it is its tone. The life of fighter Jake La Motta, who rose to become middleweight champion and then descended into dissoluteness and a self-parodic nightclub act, is presented with what seems to be La Motta's own lack of understanding of his animal violence and self-indulgence. The film making is brilliant in control of technique (in black and white) and performance (De Niro received an Oscar). As a case study of a primitive and self-destructive person it is absolutely believable. Lacking is a sense of what Scorsese thinks about all this, and what he wants us to think about it. The same sort of documented material and clinical examination of it would mark another powerful Scorsese film of the nineties, *GoodFellas.*

By 1980, the end of this arbitrary period being considered, the United States had regained its place among the leading nations of film art. It had achieved that position as France, Italy, and the Eastern European countries had done, by giving working space to film makers of originality and distinction—Penn, Peckinpah, Coppola, Altman, and Scorsese among them. But if the United States was once more back within the international artistic spotlight, it was sharing it. If it remained dominant in world commerce, it did so partly through employing the film makers and distributing the films of other countries. Perhaps the clearly identifiable phases of national creativity up through postwar Italian neorealism have given way. In the chapters on the films of Asia, France, Italy, and Eastern Europe that preceded this one, no ending dates were assigned to the periods under consideration. All these cinemas have continued vital and restive. Now it is time to return to Great Britain, which we left in 1963, to bring it up to the present.

FILMS OF THE PERIOD

1963
The Birds (Alfred Hitchcock)
Hud (Martin Ritt)

1964
Cheyenne Autumn (John Ford)
The Killers (Don Siegel)

Major Dundee (Sam Peckinpah)
My Fair Lady (George Cukor)

1965
Cat Ballou (Elliot Silverstein)
Doctor Zhivago (David Lean)
The Sound of Music (Robert Wise)

1967
Bonnie and Clyde (Arthur Penn)
The Dirty Dozen (Robert Aldrich)
The Graduate (Mike Nichols)
Guess Who's Coming to Dinner (Stanley Kramer)
In the Heat of the Night (Norman Jewison)

1968
Hell in the Pacific (John Boorman)

1969
Alice's Restaurant (Penn)
Butch Cassidy and the Sundance Kid
    (George Roy Hill)
Downhill Racer (Michael Ritchie)
Easy Rider (Dennis Hopper)
Medium Cool (Haskell Wexler)
Midnight Cowboy (John Schlesinger)
The Wild Bunch (Peckinpah)
Zabriskie Point (Michelangelo Antonioni)

1970
Little Big Man (Penn)
*M*A*S*H* (Robert Altman)
Patton (Franklin Schaffner)

1971
The French Connection (William Friedkin)
The Last Picture Show (Peter Bogdanovich)
McCabe and Mrs. Miller (Altman)

1972
Cabaret (Bob Fosse)
Fat City (John Huston)
The Godfather (Francis Ford Coppola)

1973
American Graffiti (George Lucas)
Badlands (Terence Malick)

The Last Detail (Hal Ashby)
The Long Goodbye (Altman)
Mean Streets (Martin Scorsese)

1974
Chinatown (Roman Polanski)
The Conversation (Coppola)
Thieves Like Us (Altman)

1975
Alice Doesn't Live Here Any More (Scorsese)
Nashville (Altman)
Night Moves (Penn)

1976
Taxi Driver (Scorsese)

1977
Julia (Fred Zinnemann)
New York, New York (Scorsese)
3 Women (Altman)

1978
Days of Heaven (Terence Malick)
Midnight Express (Alan Parker)
A Wedding (Altman)

1979
Apocalypse Now (Coppola)
Breaking Away (Peter Yates)
The Electric Horseman (Sydney Pollack)
Kramer vs. Kramer (Robert Benton)
Norma Rae (Ritt)

1980
Coal Miner's Daughter (Michael Apted)
Raging Bull (Scorsese)

BOOKS ON THE PERIOD

James, David E., *Allegories of Cinema: American Film in the Sixties.* Princeton, NJ: Princeton University Press, 1989

Palmer, William J., *The Films of the Seventies: A Social History.* Metuchen, NJ: Scarecrow Press, 1987

18

British Film

♦ ♦ ♦

1963–

Apart from the culturally distinctive qualities of the postwar comedies, the social-realist features, and the Gothic horror films dealt with in Chapter 11, British cinema of the sixties and seventies was distinguished by a cluster of sometimes brilliant directors whose films for the most part had an international rather than a national identity. They worked on either side of the Atlantic and for American money in any case. Within the past three decades there has been more interchange than ever. Of the former social-realist directors, Reisz (*Who'll Stop the Rain?*, 1978; *The French Lieutenant's Woman,* 1981) has worked in the United States and on American projects; Richardson (*The Charge of the Light Brigade,* 1968; *The Border,* 1982) and Schlesinger (*Midnight Cowboy,* 1969; *Sunday Bloody Sunday,* 1971; *The Falcon and the Snowman,* 1985; *Madame Sousatzka,* 1988) have alternated between the United Kingdom and the United States. On the other hand, three Americans, long-time residents in England, clearly became English to the extent that Henry James and T. S. Eliot became English, and will be dealt with here.

♦ AMERICANS ABROAD

Joseph Losey, after a modestly successful Hollywood career, exiled himself in 1951 in order to escape the blacklisting of the McCarthy era. In Britain his reputation was first established with a succession of moderately budgeted pictures within conventional idioms that are packed with political meaning and psychological, even philosophical, complexities. *Time Without Pity* (1957), a thriller in which a father attempts to save his son from execution for a murder he didn't commit, goes beyond an attack on capital punishment to examine the individual apathy, selfishness, and lack of social responsibility which support the injustice perpetrated by the judicial system. *Blind*

Date (1959, *Chance Meeting* in the United States) is a detective story which implies that a person's understanding of reality is more likely an illusion predetermined by past experience, including especially that of class. *The Criminal* (1960, *The Concrete Jungle* in the United States), a crime-and-prison picture on the surface, makes clear the ways in which the criminal is a natural part of a society based on power and acquisitiveness, and that the prison community is a mirror image of the one outside its walls. *The Damned* (1963, *These Are the Damned* in the United States) is a science-fiction forecast of the kinds of social malaise—violence and authoritarian-ism—that will erupt in a society which allows itself to come under the threat of nuclear warfare.

With *The Servant* (1963) Losey began his association with playwright Harold Pinter and moved from the partially covert investigation of British society to a more direct observation less restricted by rigid and complex plotting. To be more exact, beginning with *The Servant* a group of Losey's films comment directly upon a culture which he observed with the eye of an outsider who has experienced fresh what others had absorbed from birth. *The Servant* concerns a contemporary young aristocrat who attempts to exercise the prerogatives of his class with the arrogance but without the force that once accrued naturally to rulers of an empire. He is led down into a mire of dissipation and self-indulgence by a malicious and clever servant who in fact becomes master. Though succeeding in the struggle for domination, the servant is no happier as a result and remains subject to class-based feelings of inferiority and impotence. The microcosm of this strange pair living together in a destructive relationship within a Chelsea house must be taken to represent a Britain in which an outmoded class system enervates and embitters all of its inhabitants.

King and Country (1964) is even more claustrophobic in setting than *The Servant* and direct in its sociopolitical comment. It concerns the trial of a deserter during World War I. A simple working-class youth, caught in a war the reasons for which he doesn't understand and that terrifies him, has simply walked back away from the front lines headed for home. Within the military code, the officers-gentlemen have no recourse but to sentence him to execution even while realizing the enormity of the punishment in relation to the crime. As the war seems to the soldier to have little to do with what is important in his life, so his death becomes a pointless irony, another corpse added to the hundreds of thousands already fallen.

In *Accident* (1967) Losey is back with Pinter and in some ways resumes the examination begun in *The Servant* of values and satisfactions inadequate to sustain meaningful, productive lives. Here the characters are middle-class and middle-aged on one side (Oxford dons and their wives) and aristocratic and youthful on the other (an English boy and Austrian girl students). While the plot moves through a complex series of sexual attractions and rivalries, the qualities of these humans at the very apex of the English social pyramid are weighed and found wanting. They are too pallid somehow and too fixed in ritual patterns. Pinter's and Losey's observation is exact; the details of the sort of lives the two dons lead are completely convincing. If very English they are yet as recognizable elsewhere as another American emigré's J. Alfred Prufrock, who measured out his life with coffee spoons.

The Servant ♦ U.K., 1963, Joseph Losey; Dirk Bogarde and James Fox.

The Go-Between (1971, script by Pinter), set in Edwardian times, is an even more muted study of class and sexuality. This tale of passion between an elegant and self-centered young lady and a robust and attractive tenant farmer is refracted through the imperfect comprehension of a thirteen-year-old middle-class summer visitor. Confused and disturbed by the unfamiliar proprieties of the wealthy household and what he can jealously sense of the relationship he becomes party to, his vacation experience proves a shattering one. As an outsider the boy serves as a perfect surrogate for Losey himself, and the tensions that lie beneath the apparent calm of polished upper-class manners are revealed obliquely, with seeming inadvertence. *The Romantic Englishwoman* (1975) continued many of the same concerns.

Losey made other kinds of films as well subsequently, including those made while living in Paris for awhile (*Mr. Klein,* 1976; *Don Giovanni,* 1979). But with his final film, *Steaming* (1985), he returned to Britain and to the sort of social observation he had mastered, in this case of a group of women who convene regularly in a Turkish bath. It is his body of work which surveys aspects of British society in ways that few native British film makers have done that can be regarded as his most important achievement. The subtlety of his technique as well as the refinement of his sensibilities increased until they might well remind us of the mature Henry James, reflecting on the intricacies of cultural and class attitudes that must strike Americans as different

from their own no matter how long they've lived abroad or how closely they empathize with the life of their adopted country. Losey died in 1984.

Richard Lester is a much different sort of American from Losey and was
attracted to a much different kind of England—the rock, the mod, and the trendy in
his case. Moving to London in 1955 (at the age of twenty-three) Lester worked on
television commercials during his first years there, developing the technical facility—
including rapid cutting, freely moving camera, and improvisational performance
style—that is associated with his earlier, and some of his later, work. *The Running,
Jumping, and Standing-Still Film* (1959), a short for BBC-TV's *The Goon Show*, set
forth his special talents in capsule form.

A Hard Days' Night (1964) was his first noteworthy feature, an affectionate
tribute to the Beatles in which they play themselves within a slight narrative. A
heightened *cinéma vérité* style with breathtaking zooms and jump cuts complements
their energetic and irreverent playfulness. *The Knack* (1965) also celebrated the new
youthful lifestyles of a swinging London; and *Help!*, the same year, brought the
Beatles back for a wildly assorted mixture of farcical villains in pursuit of a sacrificial
ring, and musical performances high in the Alps or in the midst of military maneuvers.
With *A Funny Thing Happened on the Way to the Forum* (1966), however, the
directorial style Lester had developed seemed to many observers extraneous to the
requirements of translating a stage musical into film.

A Hard Day's Night ♦
U.K., 1964, Richard
Lester; Paul McCartney,
George Harrison, Ringo
Starr, and John Lennon.

In *How I Won the War* (1967) he brought his dazzling array of techniques to bear on a comic-bitter satire on the inevitable sameness and meaninglessness of all war which, despite the causes and objectives (in this case the immediate one is that of establishing an advanced-area cricket pitch deep in enemy-held territory), consists finally of endlessly repeated deaths. It was the first film in which he attempted to get at themes of the utmost seriousness through farcical means.

Petulia (1968) is an even further departure for Lester and stands alone in his work to date in many respects. His first feature shot in the United States not only appraises the American scene through the revealing exaggerations that California manners and mores offer, but attempts a much more intense and sustained probing of character than any of his other films. *The Bed Sitting Room* (1969) returned to the same sort of satirical antiwar themes as *How I Won the War,* this time tackling the Bomb. The humor is even colder and more distancing than in the earlier film, and it was even less successful at the box office.

After a hiatus caused by the failure of *The Bed Sitting Room,* Lester returned to feature direction in the capacity of clever, intelligent, international entertainer with *The Three Musketeers* (1974). There is little specifically English, or even American-English, in that film or in the others that followed it; for example *Robin and Marian* (1976), another historical comedy; *Butch and Sundance: The Early Days* (1979), his only western; *Superman II* (1981) and *III* (1983), comic strip adventures, etc.; and, full circle, *Return of the Musketeers* (1989). It does not seem possible to predict exactly where his commercial success will lead him. It does appear likely, however, that Lester's contributions, if international in appeal, will continue to be made from a British base.

Stanley Kubrick, who arrived in Britain ten years after Losey, had an even more substantial career before leaving the States. In his American films Kubrick seemed to be setting off in several directions at once, however: antiwar statement (the youthful outcry of *Fear and Desire,* 1953; the mature condemnation of *Paths of Glory,* 1957); gangster film (the experimentally expressionistic *Killer's Kiss,* 1955; the expertly professional *The Killing,* 1956); and even historical spectacle (*Spartacus,* 1960). Beginning with his first film made in Britain, *Lolita* (1962), he began gradually to settle into a consistently cynical, increasingly misanthropic view of humankind. Like Resnais, Kubrick came to depend upon strong literary figures for sources and/or collaboration: Vladimir Nabokov for *Lolita,* Terry Southern for *Dr. Strangelove, or: How I Learned to Stop Worrying and Love the Bomb* (1964), Arthur Clarke for *2001: A Space Odyssey* (1968), and Anthony Burgess for *A Clockwork Orange* (1971). Each of those films is laced with dark humor and enlivened by extraordinary set constructions.

It is interesting and significant that Kubrick's first three British films were not set in Britain. Instead they were situated in a studio-constructed America and dealt fixedly with American themes, problems, and peculiarities—past, present, and future. If almost unprecedented in film, American artists abroad sorting through mixed feelings about their homeland have been a tradition extending at least from James Whistler through James Baldwin. At his worst, or best, Kubrick brought a cold-blooded savagery to his analysis of the American scene; at the same time, and a mark of his consistency, it must be granted that the view *A Clockwork Orange* presents of

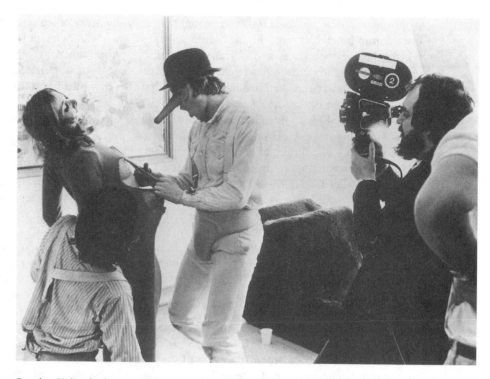

Stanley Kubrick shooting a scene for his A *Clockwork Orange* ◆ U.K., 1971; Adrienne
Corri and Malcolm McDowell.

modern English society is chilling and violent in the extreme. Its Droods exist in a
kind of culture of their own, set within but at war with English culture.

When the production of *Barry Lyndon* (1975) was announced, it appeared that
Kubrick had come round to an identification with the British historical tradition.
Based on a Thackeray novel, the film was written, produced, and directed by Kubrick.
It is, first of all, a massive, elaborate and meticulous re-creation of the look of the
eighteenth century, often with references to the ways contemporary painters saw it:
the verdant countrysides, the formally laid out battles, the interiors of country houses
and gaming rooms, the costumes, even the candlelight (with special lenses for the
purpose). There is much elegance, much beauty. But behind that pleasing exterior, the
life depicted is largely cheerless and more than a little harried. The confines of a rigid
social system are shown to imprison imagination and spontaneity; warmth and gaiety
are absent. The film ends in random and pointless disaster and desolation for virtually
all of its characters.

Barry Lyndon represented no increased "Englishness" on Kubrick's part after all.
In *The Shining* (1980) he returned to (a fantastical) present-day America (created in
the Elstree Studios outside London). Its protagonist is a writer who becomes winter
caretaker of a monstrous, deserted hotel in the Colorado Rockies. It centers around
his descent into madness, including homicidal designs on his wife and young son.

Full Metal Jacket (1987) is a "Vietnam movie" shot in England. Its title refers to a bullet encasement that does not disintegrate when it enters the body. The film follows a young Marine Corps rifle squad from their first days at boot camp in South Carolina to the climax in bloody house-to-house combat in the city of Hue during the 1968 Tet Offensive.

With these last two films the question of national coloring—American or English—seems to have been answered. Though long based in England, Kubrick remains American, "with distance giving a better perspective," as he puts it. Kubrick's legendary absorption with advanced film technology and tireless search for technical perfection (the filming of *Full Metal Jacket* took some thirteen months) never seem to slacken. But perhaps the most conspicuous aspect of his films is the consistency of the world they portray. Of the somberness of this spectacle Kubrick has said "We're never going to get down to doing anything about the things that are really bad in the world until there is recognition within us of the darker side of our natures, the shadow side."[1] If he is not alone in this view, his expression of it remains idiosyncratic and constant.

♦ BRITONS AT HOME

In the early 1980s there was talk of a British film renaissance. *Chariots of Fire,* directed by Hugh Hudson, had become the most successful British film ever released in the United States and won the Oscar for best picture of 1981. In the exhilaration of the moment the cry "The British are coming!" was uttered (by a Brit, admittedly). *Gregory's Girl* (1980), *Gandhi* (1982), *Educating Rita* (1983), and other films were well received by critics and public at home and abroad.

Amidst this bustle of profitable activity two contemporary film makers, who have worked together on occasion, established trustworthy creative credits. One is producer David Puttnam, the other director Bill Forsyth.

Puttnam, of *Chariots of Fire,* has produced first features of a number of directors who have made important films. Though drawn to talent, he does not regard the director as the film artist, nor himself as an *auteur* for that matter. He began his career in advertising, but in the early 1970s he started to produce theatrical features, including Ken Russell's *Mahler* (1973) and *Lisztomania* (1975). Then in 1976 Puttnam formed his own production company, Enigma; its first release was Ridley Scott's *The Duellists* (1977), widely praised in the United States. His first great international box-office hit was Alan Parker's *Midnight Express* (1978), followed by *Chariots of Fire, The Killing Fields* (1984), and *The Mission* (1986).

On the basis of his success he was named head of Columbia Pictures. Though Hollywood has long attracted and imported foreign talent, the appointment of a foreigner as head of a major studio was unprecedented. Given Puttnam's commitment to making films he cared about and his lack of experience with megacorporations

[1]As quoted in Penelope Gilliatt, "Heavy Metal," *American Film,* 12, no. 10 (September 1987): 20–23, 50–51.

Chariots of Fire ♦ U.K., 1981, Hugh Hudson; Ian Charleson, waving.

(Columbia was a subsidiary of Coca-Cola), both the offer and its acceptance were surprising. His acceptance was announced in September 1986; his resignation in September 1987.

During that year Puttnam managed to commission a film by Bill Forsyth, *House-keeping* (1987), whose *Local Hero* (1983) he had earlier produced. Forsyth, a Scot, has worked within what can be described as a revival of the Ealing comedy tradition (see Chapter 11). Like many of the earlier Ealing directors, he began film making with documentaries. His first fiction feature, *That Sinking Feeling* (1979), is a comedy about a bunch of Glasgow slum urchins who engage in an elaborate and preposterous scheme to burgle some stainless steel sinks. His second feature, *Gregory's Girl*, concerns the adolescent infatuation of a gawky lad for a lovely lass who insists on playing soccer with (and plays better than) the boys' team. It also was set in Scotland, as was his third, *Local Hero* (1983). Shot on location in Fort William, *Local Hero* concerns the oil strike in the North Sea and a visiting agent for a Houston oil company. It is reminiscent of the situation in *Tight Little Island* (1949), with an American intruder replacing the earlier English one. In this case, however, the foreigner succumbs to the charms of the villagers and longs to be one of them.

Comfort and Joy (1984) Forsyth described as a cross between *Alice in Wonderland* and *Sullivan's Travels* (the Preston Sturges comedy). Its protagonist is a popular disk jockey on a Glasgow radio station who uncovers an ice-cream war between factions of an Italian family: those who run fish and chips shops attempt to move in on those who are ice-cream vendors.

Housekeeping chronicles the *rite de passage* of two pubescent girls whose mother commits suicide and whose aunt, charming if a bit daft, attempts to look after them. It is narrated by the elder, who is more bonded to the aunt and less able to cope with the world as it exists outside her private universe of loss and pain which the aunt has somewhat ameliorated. It ends without resolution (though the voice-over is that of a grown woman looking back) as the aunt wanders off down the railroad tracks on which she had ridden into town. Forsyth's only American film has much in common with his Scottish ones, except there is more sadness, less humor. It is in fact a sad film—bleak, like the isolated Pacific Northwest town and the lives lived therein which it portrays—but not without sweetness.

Except for *Housekeeping,* Forsyth's films have offered Scottish looks and Scottish ways with a knowing and affectionate humor. Like the work of Ealing Studios, his films manage to celebrate things British in the face of American competition.

Two other highly regarded British directors currently at work are **Nicolas Roeg** and **John Boorman.** Roeg, who had become a topflight cinematographer (on, for example, Truffaut's *Fahrenheit 451,* 1966; Schlesinger's *Far from the Madding Crowd,* 1967; and Lester's *Petulia,* 1968), turned to direction with *Performance* (1970, codirected by its scriptwriter, Donald Cammell). It features rock star Mick Jagger and a plot that intermingles music, drugs, sex, and identity confusions. *Walkabout* (1971), filmed in Australia, is about a teen-age girl and her younger brother, who become lost in the bush. They are saved by an aboriginal youth but eventually become the occasion for his suicide, through failure in understanding and

Local Hero ♦ U.K., 1983, Bill Forsyth; Burt Lancaster and Peter Riegert.

communication. *Don't Look Now* (1973), with Julie Christie and Donald Sutherland in Venice, combines murder, illusion, and perhaps the supernatural somewhat in the manner of Hitchcock's *Vertigo*. *The Man Who Fell to Earth* (1976) is an eerie science fiction featuring rock star David Bowie as the alien being. In *Bad Timing* (1980), Art Garfunkel and Theresa Russell play two Americans in Vienna, he a diffident college professor, she an unrestrained hedonist. They meet in an art gallery; the Gustav Klimt paintings on exhibit suggest the fragmented style adopted by Roeg in this tale of tortured erotic love. Some consider it the peak of his career to date. *Eureka* (1983) is about a prospector (played by Gene Hackman) in northern Canada obsessed with finding gold who, when he does, buys a Caribbean island. The plot is concerned mostly with the miner's attempts to hang onto what he has achieved in the face of others' efforts to take his island away from him. *Insignificance* (1985) is a close adaptation of a play that explores metaphysical issues through a cast of four characters brought into contact with each other in a Manhattan hotel room. The "characters" are in fact renditions of contrasting celebrities—Albert Einstein, Marilyn Monroe, Joe Di Maggio, and Senator Joseph McCarthy. They concern themselves with the nature of the physical universe and the likelihood of nuclear anihilation, stardom, love and its loss, and patriotism (which here is indistinguishable from madness). *Castaway*

Bad Timing ♦ U.K., 1980, Nicolas Roeg; Theresa Russell and Art Garfunkel.

(1986), too, is limited in cast and locale, and about ultimate philosophical, or at least psychological, matters. Its protagonist, who has a Robinson Crusoe-like fascination with living an isolated existence, advertises for a "wife" to live for a year on an island just off northernmost Australia. The film is devoted to the subtle intricacies of their sojourn, which passes through most of the permutations of male-female relationships, of aloneness and togetherness, of isolation and society.

Roeg's films present increasingly complex and dazzling mosaics of structure and style in which logic is transcended; the images, extraordinarily sensual, are cut together in pursuit of feeling, like the stories of Argentinian writer Jorge Luis Borges (who is in fact invoked in *Performance*). Roeg's ambiguities offer many readings, but the consistency of his disturbing vision—the threat of violence that we bring to each other through our mismatchings and misunderstandings—marks a film maker emotionally and artistically clear about what he is saying. His kind of film making, rare anywhere, is unusual indeed in Britain.

John Boorman's connection with film began as a film reviewer. He then worked in British television, first as a film editor, eventually as a director of documentaries for BBC-TV (including one on D. W. Griffith). His first feature direction was *Catch Us If You Can* (United Kingdom, 1965; *Having a Wild Weekend* in the United States), which starred the Dave Clark Five pop group, and then *Point Blank* (1967) in the United States. Subsequently, while remaining essentially an English director, he alternated between America and Britain—*Hell in the Pacific* (United States, 1968), *Leo the Last* (United Kingdom, 1970), *Deliverance* (United States, 1972), *Zardoz* (United Kingdom, 1974), *Exorcist II: The Heretic* (United States, 1977)—before settling in Britain: *Merlin and the Knights of King Arthur* (1980), *Excalibur* (1981), *The Emerald Forest* (1985). In his films, even in the more realistic ones, Boorman has been drawn to mythic and fantastic material; quests, magic, and nature appear strongly in them, especially in his British films.

With *Hope and Glory* (1987) he draws some of the same sorts of themes out of his own remembered past as a nine-year-old during the Blitz in London and subsequently at his grandparents' on the Thames at Shepperton. Observation is concentrated on family members, their friends and acquaintances. The special charm of the film is the way in which it deals with life going on in the midst of bombs and wartime separations. In fact the blitzed London, with its collapsed buildings and rubble, becomes a kind of playground. And when his vacant school receives a direct hit, permitting the boy to return to his grandparents' and the river, he mutters "Thank you, Adolf." It is as if the historical moment chronicled by the British wartime semidocumentaries is overlaid with the amused, gentle, and affectionate spirit of the Ealing comedies. It seems a very English film.

Following and paralleling the work of these established film makers is a flock of directors with important and/or interesting films to their credit. Among them are three who have received wide distribution in the United States; the latter two have made films here as well. All of the films mentioned below and others by them are available on video.

Peter Greenaway began as a painter (his films are very painterly) before becoming a documentary film editor. From 1966 on he made experimental shorts; in 1980

Hope and Glory ♦ U.K., 1987, John
Boorman; Sebastian Rice-Edwards and
Geraldine Muir.

he turned to features. The first of these to receive international attention was *The Draughtsman's Contract* (1982). An extremely clever, mannered evocation of the mores and morals of aristocratic seventeenth-century England, it revolves around seduction and murder in a stately country house. Eventually it becomes a metaphysical puzzle that proves insoluble—at least in terms of the evidence offered. *The Cook, the Thief, His Wife, and Her Lover* (1989) benefitted at the box office from the notoriety earned by its scandalous content: adulterous copulation being carried on mostly in the washrooms of an incredibly posh London restaurant while the title characters are engaged in sumptuous dinners. Its form includes sets and lighting palettes of red, or blue, or dazzling white, and references to famous painters' paintings. It was followed by *Prospero's Books* (1991), a stylish, erudite reworking of Shakespeare's *The Tempest* and starring John Gielgud. It sums up and confirms Greenaway's idiosyncratic talent, his formal and thematic concerns to date. Though not appealing to all tastes, his creation, as a whole and film by film, is nonetheless extraordinarily original and forceful. These are quite amazing art works to emerge from a commercial cinema (and perhaps it is not incidental that the funding for *Prospero's Books* came from the Netherlands, France, and Italy, rather than from the United Kingdom or the United States).

Quite unlike Greenaway, **Stephen Frears** presents the phenomenon of a film maker who has made an unusual number of films that have been generally successful with the critics and at the box office but lack the personal stamp of an auteur; or, in

The Cook, the Thief, His Wife, and Her Lover ♦ U.K., Peter Greenaway, 1989; Alan Howard, Richard Bohringer, Helen Mirren, and Michael Gambon, in foreground.

any case, that seem markedly different from each other in style and content. There's *My Beautiful Laundrette* (1985), his first big hit set in a down-at-heel section of London and dealing with the unconventional relationship, love affair really, between two young men, one of them a reasonably well-to-do Pakastani, the other a working-class streetwise Cockney. It examines sexuality, race relations, and economic problems in the Margaret Thatcher era. Then there's *Dangerous Liaisons* (1988), an elegant, cruel, witty, and very verbal melodrama of eighteenth-century French nobility (John Malkovich, Glenn Close, and Michelle Pfeiffer in the principal roles) involved in a perverse contest for control over each other's affections. More recently Frears has worked in the United States rather than in Britain, and *The Grifters* (1990) and *Accidental Hero* (1992) are both quite American in their subject matter and feelings. The former was successful all the way 'round; the latter not, and after it he returned to England. In interviews Frears seems curiously faceless and self-deprecating; it's as if he thinks the films happened by accident. But, if not exactly an auteur, the combined excellence of his various interpretations has earned him equivalent respect.

At the moment it is **Neil Jordan** who is at high tide following the considerable esteem gained by *The Crying Game* (1992). His background is unusual in at least two

My Beautiful Laundrette ◆ U.K., 1985, Stephen Frears; Daniel Day-Lewis and Gordon Warneke.

respects: he is Irish, living near Dublin, and was a writer before becoming a film maker (he was twenty-five when his collection of short stories, *A Night in Tunisia,* was published; he has scripted most of his films, and most of them are original stories). His first two directorial efforts—*Angel* (*Danny Boy* in the United States, 1982) and *The Company of Wolves* (1984)—are fine pieces of work, distinctive and at the same time very Irish. His third, *Mona Lisa* (1986), was a resounding success. It is set in London and introduces the elements of violence, transsexuality, and racial difference that would characterize *The Crying Game* (the white male protagonist infatuated with a black lesbian female rather than a black transvestite male). The latter film added the element of political conflict, as it begins in Ireland with an IRA kidnapping of a British soldier before moving on to London. Certainly one of the most remarkable things about *The Crying Game* is the tenderness with which the relationship of heterosexual and homosexual is presented; another is the considerable popularity and approval it received within mainstream cinema. Jordan's ability as an extraordinarily powerful storyteller in control of conception and execution is clearly the basis for both. (*The Crying Game* won an Academy Award for Best Original Screenplay.) The willing suspension of disbelief is made to operate fully as we come to identify with characters and situations distinguished by their unusualness—the

The Crying Game ♦ U.K., 1992, Neil Jordan; Stephen Rea and Jaye Davidson.

Outsider, the Other, earning our sympathy and perhaps even some understanding. This quality seems at the center of Jordan's best work; unusual it is, to be sure.

♦ STATE OF THE INDUSTRY

Adding support to the British film renaissance was a television channel, Channel 4 of the quasi-governmental BBC, named in reference to the other two BBC channels plus the commercial channel, ITV. Set up in 1980, Channel 4 went on the air in 1982. In that year it began to finance feature films in the manner of Italian (RAI) and West German (ZDF) state television. *The Draughtsman's Contract* (1982) and *Dance with a Stranger* (1984) were made because Channel 4 was prepared to supplement monies obtained elsewhere as required. In 1984 ten out of twenty-eight British features had financial investment from Channel 4; several of the others were presold to the network (*Insignificance,* for example). In 1985 *My Beautiful Laundrette* was fully financed by Channel 4, as was most of *Wetherby.* The British Film Institute, another partly governmental agency, has also contributed to the financing and cofinancing of a number of British successes.

What seems remarkable about the resurgence of British cinema in the eighties is not only that it managed to retain a national identity, but that its success was due to its national flavor. Many of these films comment critically—directly or metaphorically—on the political, economic, and social stresses that have preoccupied Britain since the midfifties, and this later success seems even more substantial than that of the earlier social-realist features. *Mona Lisa* (1986), *White Mischief* (1987), *Little Dorrit* (1988), *Cry Freedom* (1988), and *Dangerous Liaisons* (1988) are other examples. As American distributors have increasingly shied away from films with subtitles, the English-language British art film has become the dominant entry in the American art-house market. In addition, all of these films have been released on video. There is now a continuity of financial support not seen since the heyday of Michael Balcon's Ealing Studios some fifty years ago.

As regards Ealing's influence, it seems to have come full circle with the biggest British hit of 1988, *A Fish Called Wanda,* directed by former Ealing director Charles Crichton. As for the centrality of television in the recent British film scene, Crichton's co-creator was John Cleese, preeminent star of the *Monty Python* and *Fawlty Towers* series.

But the question, What is a British film? isn't altogether answered by *Wanda,* as redolent as it is with reminders of *The Lavender Hill Mob* and *Fawlty Towers.* Creatively it may be British, but it was an M-G-M movie, financed in Hollywood. Whatever Britain looks like in the atlas, it is no island entire of itself but part of the main. Even its specifically national film types and most distinctive creators fit into an international economic context. It is to other successful examples of distinctive national film expression developed in the face of American hegemony that the next chapter is devoted.

FILMS OF THE PERIOD

1963
The Damned (Joseph Losey)

1964
Dr. Strangelove (Stanley Kubrick)
A Hard Day's Night (Richard Lester)
King and Country (Losey)

1965
Darling (John Schlesinger)
Help! (Lester)
The Knack (Lester)

1967
Accident (Losey)
How I Won the War (Lester)

1968
Petulia (Lester)
2001: A Space Odyssey (Kubrick)

1969
If . . . (Lindsay Anderson)
Women in Love (Ken Russell)

1970
The Music Lovers (Russell)
Performance (Nicolas Roeg)

1971
A Clockwork Orange (Kubrick)
The Devils (Russell)
The Go-Between (Losey)
Sunday Bloody Sunday
    (Schlesinger)
Walkabout (Roeg)

1972
Savage Messiah (Russell)

1973
Don't Look Now (Roeg)
O Lucky Man! (Anderson)

1974
Mahler (Russell)
The Three Musketeers (Lester)

1975
Barry Lyndon (Kubrick)
Lisztomania (Russell)

1976
The Man Who Fell to Earth (Roeg)

1979
That Sinking Feeling (Bill Forsyth)

1980
Bad Timing (Roeg)
The Shining (Kubrick)

1981
Chariots of Fire (Hugh Hudson)
The French Lieutenant's Woman (Karel Reisz)
Gregory's Girl (Forsyth)

1982
The Draughtsman's Contract (Peter Greenaway)
Gandhi (Richard Attenborough)

1983
Educating Rita (Lewis Gilbert)
Eureka (Roeg)
Experience Preferred . . . But Not Essential
    (Peter Duffell)
Local Hero (Forsyth)
The Ploughman's Lunch (Richard Eyre)

1984
Comfort and Joy (Forsyth)
Dance with a Stranger (Mike Newell)
The Killing Fields (Roland Joffé)
A Private Function (Malcom Mowbray)

1985
My Beautiful Laundrette (Stephen Frears)
Brazil (Terry Gilliam)

The Emerald Forest (John Boorman)
Insignificance (Roeg)
A Passage to India (David Lean)
Wetherby (David Hare)

1986
Castaway (Roeg)
The Mission (Joffé)
Mona Lisa (Neil Jordan)
A Room with a View (James Ivory)

1987
Cry Freedom (Attenborough)
Full Metal Jacket (Kubrick)
Hope and Glory (Boorman)
Little Dorrit (Christine Edzard)
Maurice (Ivory)
Prick Up Your Ears (Frears)
Sammy and Rosie Get Laid (Frears)
White Mischief (Michael Radford)
Wish You Were Here (David Leland)

1988
Dangerous Liaisons (Frears)
Distant Voices, Still Lives (Terence Davies)
A Fish Called Wanda (Charles Crichton)
High Hopes (Mike Leigh)

1989
The Cook, the Thief, His Wife and Her Lover
    (Greenaway)

1991
Edward II (Derek Jarman)
Howard's End (Ivory)
Prospero's Books (Greenaway)
Young Soul Rebels (Isaac Julien)

1992
Blue Black Permanent (Margaret Tait)
The Crying Game (Neil Jordan)
The Long Day Closes (Davies)
Orlando (Sally Potter)

1993
The Remains of the Day (Ivory)

BOOKS ON THE PERIOD

Barr, Charles, ed., *All Our Yesterdays: 90 Years of British Cinema.* London: British Film Institute, 1987

Friedman, Lester, ed., *Fires Were Started: British Cinema and Thatcherism.* Minneapolis: University of Minnesota Press, 1992

Hacker, Jonathan, and David Price, *Take Ten: Contemporarry British Film Directors.* New York: Clarendon Press, 1991

Murphy, Robert, *Sixties British Cinema.* London: British Film Institute, 1992

Petrie, Duncan J., *Creativity and Constraint in the British Film Industry.* London: Macmillan, 1991

Petrie, Duncan, ed., *New Questions of British Cinema.* London: British Film Institute, 1992

Pym, John, *Film on Four.* London: British Film Institute, 1993 [*Four* is Channel 4 of BBC-TV]

19

Third-World Cinema and Recent National Movements

♦ ♦ ♦

1959–

Early films from the so-called developing nations which attracted international attention generally expressed a strong sense of nationalism, frequently accompanied by anti-imperialism (specifically anti-Americanism in many instances), and sometimes a call to revolution. Film making in some of the Latin American countries, especially, conformed to these generalizations. Among them **Cuba** was preeminent. With its socialist revolution achieved, it was able to offer inspiration, encouragement, and actual assistance to the independent leftist film makers in the neighboring countries of South America.

The Cuban Revolution of 1959 (against foreign—that is, American—domination as well as the Fulgencio Batista government) brought sweeping changes in the Cuban motion-picture industry. Like Russia following its revolution in 1917, or the Eastern Republics after 1945, Cuba established a government agency to organize and regulate all production, distribution, and exhibition. Called Instituto Cubano del Arte y Industria Cinematográficos (ICAIC), it created first-rate production facilities, and invited Czechoslovakian film makers in to train Cuban personnel.

Consistent with Lenin's advice to the earlier Soviet film makers, the Cubans used newsreels and documentaries to meet the needs of the people as seen by the new state. The leading figure of this nonnarrative short-film output was Santiago Alvarez, whose *L.B.J.* (1968) and *79 Springtimes* (1969, about Vietnamese leader Ho Chi Minh) have been seen on a limited basis in the United States. Their ironic and experimental forms of attack on the violence of the United States, and lyrical portrayal of "the struggle of the underdeveloped and small peoples for their human dignity," as Alvarez has put it, place him among the leading innovators in art used for political persuasion.

As for narrative fiction features, other Cuban film makers have transcended the immediate political requirements. Best known abroad is Tomás Gutièrrez Alea, whose *Memories of Underdevelopment* (1968) was the first Cuban feature to achieve international recognition. Far from serving any obvious agitprop function, it chronicles the spiritual displacement of a bourgeois intellectual within postrevolutionary Cuban culture with a kind of cinematic sophistication and emotional detachment that place it within the mainstream of modern world cinema. His *Up to a Point* (1983) deals with the problems of a long tradition of Latin American *machismo*. The title comes from one of the brief interviews with real workers interspersed throughout this fictional narrative. A young black male questioned about *machismo* laughingly replies, "Oh, they've managed to change my attitudes on that score; I've certainly changed up to a certain point. I'm probably at 80% now. Maybe they can work on me and get me to, say, 87%. But they will never, never get me up to 100%, no way."

Humberto Solás's *Lucía* (1968) also eschews narrow political ends for a broad view of the historical role of women in Cuban society. Actually it is three films in one, and there are three Lucías: the first an aristocrat living in 1895, at the time of the struggle for Cuban independence from Spain; the second a factory worker in 1933,

Memories of Underdevelopment ♦ Cuba, 1968, Tomás Gutièrrez Alea; Sergio Corrieri, on right.

married to a revolutionary during Gerardo Machado's dictatorship; the third a spunky peasant newlywed in Castro's Cuba, whose husband considers her his property. Each historical period is re-created in a different cinematic style. Embedded within the formal pleasures the film offers is the point that, though social and political contexts may have changed over the years, women's struggle to establish independence from male dominance continues.

Then there is *One Way or Another* (1977), a fiction-documentary mix about a young, idealistic social worker who, while trying to teach ghetto kids, falls in love with a local man struggling to break out of the neighborhood's deprived existence. This exceptional film was by Sara Gómez, who died before editing was completed. Nothing of comparable significance from Cuba has appeared in recent years at international film festivals.

In **Brazil**, in an upsurge of nationalism at about the same time as the Cuban Revolution, a cooperative was formed by Glauber Rocha, Nelson Pereira dos Santos (*Barren Lives*, 1963), and Ruy Guerra (*The Guns*, 1964), which produced what they called Cinema Nôvo. This group offered a more applicable model than did Cuba for other Latin American film makers on the left working independently within entrenched capitalist regimes. Rocha was its leader and spokesman; *Black God, White Devil* (1964) and *Antonio das Mortes* (1969) are the two films of his which have

Black God, White Devil ◆ Brazil, 1964, Glauber Rocha.

received widest distribution outside Brazil. Both are set in the barren northeastern region of the country and explore the mythic folk roots of banditry and mystical religion that extreme poverty had bred. *Black God, White Devil*, particularly, is strange and haunting in its combination of severe naturalism and stylized ritual, in its portrayal of violence and madness. It lights up the screen with a kind of savage hallucination totally foreign to the cultural experience of most of us. We can see that it might have represented for Brazilians a revolutionary scream. In any case, in the year of its release there was a reactionary military coup. Following the release of *Antonio das Mortes* Rocha left Brazil and worked abroad. He made films in Europe and Africa which attempted to deal with the problems of a Third World—of underdevelopment, of neocolonialist exploitation—and of the possibilities for political action to bring about radical social change. In 1976 he returned to Brazil, but completed little of significance before his death in 1981.

Post-Cinema Nôvo production has become prolific. A line of leftist criticism has been maintained but added to it is a diversity of popular films. Pereira dos Santos continued the political line in, for instance, *How Tasty Was My Little Frenchman* (1971), *Amulet of Orgum* (1974), *Tent of Miracles* (1977), and *Prison Memories* (1984). For the most part, however, revolutionary Brazilian film makers have blended into the commercial film industry, which has become increasingly visible following the wide showing of Bruno Barreto's *Dona Flor and Her Two Husbands* (1978). Carlos Diegues's *Xica* (1976), *Bye Bye Brazil* (1980), and Argentine emigrè Hector Babenco's *Pixote* (1981) are other examples of Brazilian films that have gone out into the world.

Kiss of the Spider Woman
♦ Brazil, 1985, Hector Babenco; Raul Julia and William Hurt.

Babenco's first English-language film, *Kiss of the Spider Woman* (1985), a U.S.-Brazilian coproduction, met with resounding international success. It centers on the relationship of two very different prison cellmates, a sensitive, imaginative, homosexual "queen" (William Hurt) and a tough-minded Marxist militant (Raul Julia) who come to respect and care for each other, achieving a personal and political solidarity within the repressive society they inhabit. A film-within-the-film, which the homosexual recounts lovingly as we see snippets of it, is a Nazi melodrama cum propaganda about a singer (Sonia Braga) in love with a German superman in occupied France during World War II. Subsequently Babenco directed *Ironweed* (1988) in the United States, the big-budget adaptation of William Kennedy's Albany novel starring Jack Nicholson and Meryl Streep, and *At Play in the Fields of the Lord* (1991), about Yankee missionaries in Brazilian rainforests.

In **Argentina** in the 1960s another group of political film makers set up an independent cooperative, in their case called Cine Liberación. Its principal organizer was Fernando Solanas and its major work his *The Hour of the Furnaces* (1968, codirected with Octavio Getino). This huge documentary (nearly four-and-a-half hours long) is in three separate parts: "Neo-Colonialism and Violence," "An Act for Liberation," and "Violence and Liberation." The first part presents a historical, geographical, economic, and social analysis of Argentina. The content of the second and third parts was developed out of points raised during audience discussion following the necessarily clandestine screenings of the first. Because of the time at which it appeared, its ambitious scope, its formal eclecticism, and the circumstances surround-

The Hour of the Furnaces ◆ Argentina, 1969, Fernando Solanas and Octavio Getino.

ing its production and distribution, *Hour of the Furnaces* has been regarded as the single most influential documentary to have come out of the entire new Latin American cinema movement. With subsequent resumption of military rule in Argentina in 1976, the films of the Cine Liberación group were not only no longer smuggled abroad, they were not shown in Argentina itself, even clandestinely, because of the severe penalties attached to any activities critical of the government.

With the defeat of Argentina in the Falklands War of 1982, the military was weak enough to be opposed. Following the election of a civilian government in 1983, *The Official Story* was produced, dealing with the disappearance of roughly thirty thousand Argentines—the *desaparecidos*—between 1976 and 1983. The first feature of Luis Puenzo, a director of television commercials, it won the 1985 Academy Award for Best Foreign Film. Solanas's *South* (1988) is about a newly released prisoner wandering the night streets of Buenos Aires, reawakening memories and ghosts; *The Voyage* (1991) is a biting comedy-satire of a weak and ineffectual Argentina, representative of South America as a whole.

In **Bolivia**, since the nationalist government of Paz Estenssoro was overthrown in 1964, there have been a succession of military coups and dictatorships. Nonetheless, Jorge Sanjinés and his collaborators in the production group called Ukamau Films

The Official Story ♦ Argentina, 1983, Luis Puenzo; Norma Aleandro.

Blood of the Condor ♦ Bolivia, 1969, Jorge Sanjinés.

managed to produce several features, the best known of which is *Blood of the Condor* (1969). It deals, in semidocumentary fashion, with an alleged campaign of sterilization carried out by members of the U.S. Peace Corps against the native Indians, and urges the preservation of the Indian heritage and cultural identity. Sanjinés's next feature, *The Night of San Juan* (1971), used survivors and witnesses to reconstruct a massacre of striking miners by the army. Soon after its release, in another shift of government towards reaction and repression, film making in Bolivia virtually ceased and Sanjinés fled into exile in Chile. Subsequently he made *The Principal Enemy* (1974) in Peru; he returned to Bolivia in 1979.

In **Chile**, in the 1960s, a group of political film makers had developed in support of Salvador Allende's socialist movement. Their cooperative was called Cinematografia Tercer Mundo and its best known film is *The Jackal of Nahueltero* (1969), directed by Miguel Littin. This was another semidocumentary reconstruction, of a mass murder committed by a peasant brutalized and driven mad by hopeless poverty. After Allende's election in 1970, Littin was appointed head of the newly nationalized Chile Films, which began producing a program of newsreels and documentaries following the Cuban pattern. (Of these, *The First Years*, 1971, made by Patricio Guzman [whose later The *Battle of Chile*, 1973, is even better known], received the widest distribution.) After the military coup of 1973, which deposed Allende, Littin

The Battle of Chile ♦ Chile, 1973, Patricio Guzman.

left Chile and resumed work in Mexico. In Cuba, he finished *The Promised Land* (1973), another fictional account of an incident in Chilean history, in this case the establishment and destruction of a socialist republic in the thirties. Subsequently he lived in Spain and made films in exile. *Alsino and the Condor* (1982), a young boy's view of the Nicaraguan conflict between the Somoza government and the Sandanista rebels, may be his most widely seen film. (It is available on video.)

The climax of South American political film making, reached at the end of the sixties, receded into an unpromising denouement. In the seventies many of the principal film makers were working in exile abroad, without benefit of the strengths they had derived from their native cultures and the national political goals that had infused their work with revolutionary energy. Those at home were forced to remain silent or work within the noncommitted commercial film industries. In the eighties and into the nineties Cuba continued steadily on a modest scale, attracting little attention abroad. Among the other Latin American nations Brazil alone achieved success without eschewing altogether earlier political commitments.

In **Africa**—except Algeria and other Arab countries of the North, where a certain amount of noteworthy production is evident—the development of national film industries has been limited. Sub-Saharan cinema of the late 1950s and early 1960s was little more than the work of a few isolated creators. As in Latin America, their films were socially and politically inspired, post- (and anti-) colonialist, part of what was then called "Third-World Euphoria." Most of the important Black African film makers to emerge since then are from countries that had been colonies of France or Belgium, with French their common language. Senegal assumed early leadership, especially in work of Ousmane Sembène.

Novelist as well as film maker, Sembène has offered a genuine expression of certain facets of African culture and aspiration. With what is evidently deeply felt, painful irony, his first film to be seen in this country, *Black Girl* (1966), attacked the exploitation and racism to which blacks were subjected by the French colonists. In *Xala* (1974), using satire and bawdy humor, he shows how the leaders of the new black state mimic the ways of their former colonial masters to the continued detriment of the people. With *Ceddo* (1977), Sembène continued his attempts to develop a truly African film language, making use of the griot or oral storyteller as the center of the narrative. His next feature after *Ceddo, Camp de Thiaroye* (1987), made with Thierno Faty Sow, deals with an event of World War II in which a group of West African infantrymen awaiting demobilization after active service in Europe were suspected of mutiny and fired upon by the French. Sembène maintains his preeminence as the father and leader of black African cinema.

Following Sembène were a group of younger film makers whose films start from the oral tradition of African narrative and deal with indigenous subjects close to the

Black Girl ◆ Senegal, 1966, Ousmane Sembène.

people. For example, Med Hondo's *Sarraounia* (Mauritania, 1986) recounts the story of the successful resistance against the French in the 1890s led by the queen of the Aznas, who united pagan and moslem Africans to defeat a powerful and well-armed invading force. Souleymane Cissé's *Yeelen* (*Brightness*, Mali, 1987), set in a remote desert area in the sixteenth century, is concerned with superstition and the supernatural invoked in a conflict between son and father, and the impact of these forces on the people. Idressa Ouedraogo's *Yaaba* (*The Grandmother*, Burkina Faso, 1989) takes place in a village near the film maker's home and performances are by the villagers and some of his relatives. It is built around an African tale of the oral tradition, as is *Yeelen*. Both films won the Jury Prize at Cannes; both are in distribution in the United States.

It is beginning to seem possible that this new African cinema, which leaves aside the earler ideological anticolonialist thrust to pursue native themes and narrative structures and styles, may increase interest in African cinema outside Africa, and become the basis for a viable African film industry.

◆ GERMANY

In Europe, while Germany was still divided into East and West, it was West German film that experienced a resurgence, earning it international attention. Like films of the Third World, just dealt with, its successes generally came from political positions on the left. Following the Oberhausen Film Festival of 1962, at which a group of young film makers presented a manifesto denouncing "Papa's cinema" and offering to make better films at half the cost, there appeared a group of directors who soon came to be regarded by the world at large and eventually in Germany itself as the new *Wunderkinder*. Under the leadership of **Alexander Kluge,** the group won government subsidy for the films of young directors and the establishment of a film school. Kluge's own features include *Yesterday Girl* (1966), *Artists at the Top of the Big Top: Disoriented* (1968), and *The Part-Time Work of a Domestic Slave* (1974). The last deals with a twenty-nine-year-old woman trying to achieve some order, meaning, and effectiveness in a life that includes roles as wife and mother, abortionist, and political militant.

Volker Schlöndorff, another member of the German new wave, also made his first feature (*Young Törless*) in 1966 and has remained active since. *The Lost Honor of Katharina Blum* (1975) was written and directed in collaboration with his wife, **Magarethe von Trotta**. It concerns a young woman who spends the night with a fugitive political activist and is, as a result, hounded and exposed to humiliation by the authorities and the sensational press. *The Tin Drum* (1978), Schlöndorff's adaptation of Günter Grass's novel, is his most substantial international success to date. He has, subsequently, become something of a specialist in literary adaptation and also something of an internationalist. His *Swann in Love* (1984) presents part of the first novel of Marcel Proust's multivolume *Remembrance of Things Past*. A French film, its cast and crew were multinational. In the United States he directed the film-for-television *Death of a Salesman* (1985) starring Dustin Hoffman.

Following her initial collaboration with her husband, von Trotta became quite active on her own. *The German Sisters* (1977), *Sisters or the Balance of Happiness* (1979), *Friends and Husbands* (1981), and *Sheer Madness* (1983) explore modern women's lives, and political matters.

Jean-Marie Straub, an Alsatian, was in exile from France for political reasons from 1958 on. He is both much more outspoken in his Marxism and more experimental in his exploration of cinema forms—in the development of a minimalist cinema—than his major colleagues. His later films have been made in collaboration with his wife, **Danièle Huillet**. *Not Reconciled* (1965) probed the ways in which the dominant Junkerism and Nazism of past generations carried over into contemporary German life, accompanied by lingering guilt and continuing need for explanations. *Chronicle of Anna Magdalena Bach* (1967) presents performances of Bach's music with reverence but also attempts to imply the feelings and social ambience that surrounded the life of the composer. *History Lessons* (1973), a freely adapted version of a novel by Bertolt Brecht, combines a Marxist interpretation of the economic motives underlying the usual rendering of the history of ancient Rome with a slow automobile drive through the crowded streets of the present-day city. *Moses and Aaron* (1975) is a faithful rendition of Arnold Schönberg's twelve-tone opera with added ideological emphasis and characteristic straining of the formal conventions of narrative cinema. *Class Relations* (1985), an adaptation of Franz Kafka's *Amerika*, is literary and minimalist, in black and white. Its thesis is that the nature of human relationships is determined by class and capital rather than by individual psychologies. Of the modern German film makers the Straubs are the most "difficult," the least "accessible" to general audiences. At the same time their work is valued by the few as the most innovative in their attempts to analyze and expose the medium itself, and to make it serve the purposes of truly radical, politically committed film making.

The two German film makers who seemed most surely to speak to the pit as well as the gallery were **Rainer Werner Fassbinder** and **Werner Herzog**. Fassbinder, before his death in 1982, worked usually in the idiom of melodrama gone slightly askew, infusing the unfortunate plight of his characters with broad political meanings. *The Merchant of Four Seasons* (1971), for example, about a *lumpen* fruit peddler hounded by the women in his life (mother, girlfriend, wife) into drinking himself to death, is essentially a critique of bourgeois manners. In it wildly incongruous behavior becomes part of everyday reality. *The Bitter Tears of Petra von Kant* (1972), dealing with female homosexuality, explores various permutations of freedom and slavery evident in the women's relationship with each other in an extraordinarily bizarre and artificial visual style. *Ali: Fear Eats the Soul* (1974) is about a sixty-year-old German cleaning woman who falls in love with and marries a much younger immigrant Moroccan laborer and is ostracized by her family and the community because of racial prejudice. A subtitle suggests that "happiness is not always fun." Most widely popular among the forty-one features and television miniseries directed by the prodigious Fassbinder following his first in 1969 was *The Marriage of Maria Braun* (1979). It stars Hanna Schygulla as a woman buffeted by and adapting to the changing social conditions in Germany, from the stressful end of World War II to later affluence. The material success she achieves does not satisfy her hunger of spirit.

The Marriage of Maria Braun ♦ West Germany, 1979, Rainer Werner Fassbinder; Ivan Desny, Gisela Uhlen, Gottfried John, Anton Schirsner, Hanna Schygulla, and Elizabeth Trissenaar.

Werner Herzog first came to notice with *Even Dwarfs Started Small* (1970), in which he offers as political metaphor a ludicrously ineffectual revolt of prisoners, all played by dwarfs, whose hedonistic and anarchic impulses and inability to advance along any clear-cut line of collective action confines them in surrealistic chaos. *Aguirre, the Wrath of God* (1973) is a historical invention about one of Pizarro's conquistadors who leads an expedition into the Amazon jungle in search of El Dorado and ends as sole survivor lost in megalomaniacal fantasy. *The Mystery of Kaspar Hauser* (1974), originally entitled *Every Man for Himself and God Against All*, is about an actual nineteenth-century case of a young man who had been locked in solitary confinement in a dark cellar from childhood on. When he mysteriously appears on the streets of Nuremberg he is without language, without concepts—an instinctual and literally uncultured human animal.

Herzog's *Nosferatu* (1979), a reverent remake of Murnau's 1922 film, lacks the sort of individuality and passion we associate with its maker. *Fitzcarraldo* (1982), on the other hand, was as idiosyncratic and flamboyant a project as anyone could imagine. Huge, costly, beset with misadventures and interruptions, the making of the film in Peru was not unlike the events it chronicles, and Herzog not unlike its obsessed

Aguirre, The Wrath of God ◆ West Germany, 1973, Werner Herzog; Klaus Kinski and Cecilia Rivera.

protagonist. It is about a nineteenth-century rubber tycoon who has a river steamer hauled over a mountain in the course of trying to satisfy his love for opera by building an opera house in the jungle. Herzog has pursued his absorption with the far corners of the earth. *Where the Green Ants Dream* (1984) is about Australian Aborigines protesting a mining company drilling in one of their holy places. *Cobra Verde* (1987) concerns a nineteenth-century Brazilian peasant who becomes a feared bandit and then an adventurer trying to reestablish the slave trade in West Africa. Of all the new German film makers, Herzog may be the most original and imaginative; certainly his work is the most varied.

Following him on the international scene was **Wim Wenders**. We knew him first for *The Goalie's Anxiety at the Penalty Kick* (1972), *Alice in the Cities* (1974), *False Movement* (1975), *Kings of the Road* (1976), *The American Friend* (1977). All of these involve, to one degree or another, individual alienation from society, aimless wandering, cities, and a fascination with the United States. One of the characters in *Kings of the Road* says "The Americans have colonized our subconscious."

Wenders's fascination with America quite naturally took him there. *Paris, Texas* (1984) is the best film to have come out of his stay. Though shot in this country, with a script by two Americans, Sam Shepard and L. M. Kit Carson growing out of the former's *Motel Chronicles*, it was said by many to be a German picture made in America (as had been said of Murnau's *Sunrise* before it). If *Paris, Texas* is a continuation of Wenders's road pictures and of his personal preoccupations, within that body of work, it surely would have to be recognized as one of the finest. It won the Grand Prix at Cannes.

At that festival in 1987, Wenders was awarded the prize for best direction for *Wings of Desire,* his first German-language film in a decade. It is a homecoming in a profound sense, an effort to capture the feeling of Berlin in the years since the end of World War II to the present, including the wounds left by that war. The fanciful elements that distinguish it from anything Wenders had done before are both daring and effective. These include angels (males and females in black overcoats) who fly the heavens and also patrol the streets of Berlin, listening to the unspoken thoughts of its inhabitants. The angel protagonist (played by Bruno Ganz) falls in love with a trapeze artist (Solveig Dommartin) and has to choose whether to continue his spiritual existence or opt for mortality with its attendant pains and uncertainties.

Wenders's films to date may be those most closely attuned to certain cultural traits in modern Germany. In any case, he seems to be trying to sort out his cultural inheritance in a way that is deeply felt, insightful, and engrossing even to those of us who don't share it.

Taken together the contemporary directors discussed here have not only regained for German cinema something of the importance with which Murnau, Lang, and Pabst

Wings of Desire ◆ West Germany, 1987, Wim Wenders; Solveig Dommartin and Bruno Ganz.

had earlier endowed it, they have brought it abreast of the postmodernist tendencies so strong in other leading national cinemas. An intelligence at work on political, social, and economic criticism, together with an aesthetic based on experimentation with narrative form characterize their best work.

◆ SPAIN

In Spain, Buñuel's native land, an easing of censorship that began in the early seventies has allowed a newly serious and critical examination of the national culture. Following the death of dictator Francisco Franco in 1975, a variety of topics that had long been off limits—church, army, sexual relations, the Civil War—have been treated with candor and humor. Spanish politics, from the turn of the century to the present, is the note that recurs most frequently. Three Spanish film makers who stand out clearly are Carlos Saura, Victor Erice, and more recently Pedro Almodóvar.

Saura's *The Hunt* (1966) was one of the first Spanish films to return to the painful experience of the Civil War with an honesty designed to lay bare and perhaps to cauterize the old wounds. It proceeds obliquely, however, from a kind of allegory of a hunting expedition undertaken by a group of friends who had earlier fought together

The Hunt ◆ Spain, 1966, Carlos Saura.

in that dreadful conflict under Franco. In *Cousin Angelica* (1974) Saura also looked back to the 1930s from a modern perspective, with a protagonist who revisits a town for the first time in thirty years and relives episodes of his childhood, especially those centering around his relationship with his cousin Angelica. Saura's distinctive narrative style, combining allusion and association with chronological disruption, the past falling into place alongside the present, grew out of his need to deal with subjects that would otherwise have been taboo. *Hurry, Hurry* (1980) seems to be the first film in which he confronted a present reality, probing the lives of four young delinquents rushing headlong into tragedy. He also directed a stylish "flamenco trilogy" of ballets based on well-known literary works: *Blood Wedding* (1981), *Carmen* (1983), and *El amor brujo* (*Love, the Magician*, 1985).

Erice has directed only three films in twenty years. Best known is *The Spirit of the Beehive* (1973), which takes place in the period just after the Civil War. In it he evokes a strange dream world seen through the childhood games and fantasies of two sisters. There are what seem to be allusions to surrounding events (for example, a fugitive soldier hides in their barn), but mostly it is the mood of unstated tension and fragile unreality which conveys Erice's sense of what it was like living in those first years of fascist rule. Following *The Spirit of the Beehive*, the next film, *The South* (1983), is also about a Spanish provincial family, as seen through the childhood memories of a young woman. It is a tale of mystery and romance in which her father is the dominant figure. *Dream of Light* (1991) chronicles the impossible attempt of

The Spirit of the Beehive ◆ Spain, 1973, Victor Erice; Ana Torrent and Terésa Gimpera.

the painter Antonio López to capture on canvas the moment of golden splendor when the fruit on a quince tree in his garden ripens. An oblique and strange document, it pursues the subtle mystery of an artist and his creation.

Contrasting as sharply as could be imagined with Erice's high seriousness is **Almodóvar**'s playful postmodernism. Also, against the sparsity of Erice's output is the fecundity of Almodóvar's: almost a film a year since his first feature in 1980. And then there is the audience: Erice's small, devoted following; Almodóvar's widespread popularity. Not only was *Women on the Verge of a Nervous Breakdown* the most successful Spanish film in Spain up to that point, it was the highest grossing foreign film in North America in 1989. At present, all eight films he has made since 1982 are available on video in the United States; none of Saura's is, and only *Spirit of the Beehive* of Erice. Critical reaction to Almodóvar's work has varied from critic to critic and film to film, probably because of the paradoxical nature of the films themselves. They grow out of a gay sensibility and yet have women at their centers, played most notably by the actress Carmen Maura. Dark and deviant sexual fantasy and violence (including death) abound. Though situations and characters may seem bizarre, they are treated with a seriousness and sensitivity that enable us to identify and empathize with them. Plot outlines more often than not are straight melodrama, which is then undercut with witty references to pop culture, citations of earlier films (*Duel in the*

Women on the Verge of a Nervous Breakdown ♦ Spain, 1987, Pedro Almodóvar; Julieta Serrano.

Sun, Johnny Guitar), and parodies of the styles of pantheon film makers (Buñuel, Bergman). Perhaps the eclectic mix is most satisfyingly achieved in *What Have I Done to Deserve This?* (1984), *The Law of Desire* (1986), and *Women on the Verge of a Nervous Breakdown* (1987). Clearly the work of an auteur, they may also represent a new Spain—democratic and permissive, sophisticated and irreverent—totally different from the Spain of the Franco years. It can be hoped that the astonishing success of Almodóvar will open the channels of international distribution to films of other Spanish film makers and make them as accessible as they deserve to be.

◆ AUSTRALIA

The country to step into the spotlight most recently is Australia. To some extent its appearance was created by fiat. In 1970 the Australian government established an experimental fund for neophyte film makers, a film and television school, and a national development corporation to provide starting money for film productions. Before that time Australia had been known on the screen chiefly in a few films made by Britons and Americans. Once Australians were able to make their own films, they tended to feature the history and topography of their subcontinent.

In 1975 Ken Hannam's *Sunday Too Far Away*, an engaging film about the lives of itinerant Australian sheep shearers, was shown at the Cannes Film Festival. It was followed the next year by **Peter Weir**'s *Picnic at Hanging Rock* (1975), the first Australian film to achieve great commercial success both in Australia and abroad. It

Picnic at Hanging Rock ◆ Australia, 1975, Peter Weir.

The Chant of Jimmie Blacksmith ♦ Australia, 1978, Fred Shepisi; Tommy Lang and Freddy Reynolds.

is a haunting story of a girls' boarding-school outing on which a number of the students disappear mysteriously. It evokes turn-of-the-century dress and manners and makes stunning use of its country's scenery. Its director became one of the leaders in the new Australian cinema. Weir's *The Last Wave* (1977) is about a white upper-middle-class Sydney lawyer who becomes engulfed by the tribal mysteries of his aboriginal clients. *Gallipoli* (1981), a big-budget spectacular, is about Australians fighting under English command in Turkey during World War I; it ends in senseless slaughter. It was the first Australian film to be distributed by a major U.S. studio (Paramount). *The Year of Living Dangerously* (1982), partly financed by M-G-M, is about an Australian journalist in Indonesia in the mid-1960s, around the time of Sukarno's fall from power. It received worldwide distribution.

Films by other Australian film makers have achieved considerable international success as well. *Newsfront* (1978), directed by **Phillip Noyce**, is about two rival Australian newsreel companies in the pretelevision decade following World War II. Actual newsreel footage is ingeniously woven into its fictional plot. *The Chant of Jimmie Blacksmith* (1978), directed by **Fred Schepisi**, concerns a young half-caste aborigine in 1900 who, after being exploited by whites, turns to violence and revenge.

My Brilliant Career (1979), directed by **Gillian Armstrong**, is based on a novel published in 1901 about a spirited young woman from a poor farming family who persists in her resolution to become a writer. *Breaker Morant* (1980), directed by **Bruce Beresford**, is a powerful drama of court-martial for political reasons of Australian soldiers fighting under the English in the Boer War in South Africa.

Among a newer generation of film makers **Jane Campion** is most prominent. She began with *Sweetie* (1989), a tragicomedy about a pair of bizarre and mismatched sisters. It was quickly followed by *An Angel at My Table* (1989), an internationally acclaimed biography of New Zealand writer/poet Janet Frame, which originated as a New Zealand television miniseries. Both films are available on video.

Concurrent with the films utilizing the history and landscape of Australia were the "Ocker" comedies. These featured a (male) protagonist presented as being "typically" Australian: naive, vulgar, not too bright, good hearted, and down to earth. An early version was *The Adventures of Barry McKenzie* (1972), the first feature directed by Beresford. The pinnacle of the Ocker comedies was *"Crocodile" Dundee* (1986), the biggest box office hit ever in Australia; its closest rival (and not very close) was *E.T.—The Extra-Terrestrial*. Additional alternatives to the dominant historical landscape were the *Mad Max* road warrior movies (1979, 1981, 1985) directed by **George Miller**.

"Crocodile" Dundee ♦ Australia, 1986, Peter Faiman; Paul Hogan.

During the eighties directors of the important Australian films of the seventies began making American films. By 1984 those with international reputations—Peter Weir, Fred Schepisi, Bruce Beresford, Gillian Armstrong—were all working in the United States. George Miller arrived a bit later to direct *The Witches of Eastwick* (1987). Mel Gibson, who had started toward international stardom with Miller's *Mad Max*, had also succumbed to Hollywood. His roles included several in the American films of Australian directors.

Weir's first American film, *Witness* (1985), was particularly well received critically. Among the things written about it was that it was a quintessentially American movie. Weir's next was *The Mosquito Coast* (1987), a relative failure, followed by *Dead Poets Society* (1989), starring Robin Williams in his first serious role, a smashing success, financially and critically, and *Greencard* (1990), from his original screenplay, which he also produced. Weir seems to have become an American film maker, that is to say an international one. Schepisi's success has been less assured; *Barbarosa* (1982) was his first American film. Beresford, on the other hand, has had a steady post-Australian career; *Tender Mercies* (1982) was his first film made in the United States. Armstrong had the most difficulty finding her place here; her first and only American feature was *Mrs. Soffel* (1984). After that she returned home, where she directed *High Tide* (1987) and *The Last Days of Chez Nous* (1990).

In fact, each of the directors mentioned has returned to Australia at some point to make films. Beresford directed *The Fringe Dwellers*, a film about rural aboriginals, in 1986. Schepisi directed *A Cry in the Dark*, based on a celebrated legal case involving the disappearance of a child in the Outback and starring Meryl Streep, in 1988. Weir has done his editing in Sydney; Miller maintains his own Australlian company through which he makes deals with Hollywood studios. In general, the cultural transition from Australia to America seems to have been easier and more likely to succeed than that from Europe or Latin America.

This chapter, surveying newly prominent film-producing countries, began with Third-World nations fired with revolutionary zeal, anticolonialism, anticapitalism, and nationalism. They were followed by West Germany, whose films also leaned leftward politically but consisted more of social and economic criticism, and examination of alienation and angst. In Spain the left-leanings are less pronounced and the view has tended to be backward, over Spanish political history and cultural heritage of the past six decades.

With Australia we return to the mainstream of the international film industry. Australian films, those that reach the United States anyway, are not noticeably left politically; its contemplation of its own culture and past has appeared to be mainly nostalgic (with a few swipes at the former British Empire, to be sure). The problem for Australian films seems to be a familiar one of hanging onto "Australianness" and international success at the same time, in the face of American competition and within the global industry dominated by the United States.

The dominant American industry has always faced the same problem, of course, and has solved it with sufficient success so that what comes from America is popular around the world. In these days of conglomerates and multinationals, financial balance sheets tend more than ever to demand a huge international audience. A film that might be distinctively American or especially personal may have considerable difficulty finding backing. If young American film makers come increasingly from university film departments, the young men and women who really call the shots (heads of studios) come increasingly from schools of business.

The next and final chapter of this history of film is devoted to the present state of the industry we call Hollywood, to a cycle of American films that examines a painful phase of our recent past, to another that looks at the present through the distortions of funhouse mirrors, and to some talented film makers who seem to have found ways to express themselves on film.

FILMS OF THE PERIOD

Africa
1966
Black Girl (Senegal, Ousmane Sembène)

1974
Xala (Senegal, Sembène)

1977
Ceddo (Senegal, Sembène)

1986
Sarraounia (Mauritania, Med Hondo)

1987
Camp de Thiaroye
    (Senegal, Sembène and Thierno Faty Sow)
Yeelen (*Brightness,* Mali, Souleuymane Cissé)

1989
Yaaba
    (*The Grandmother*, Burkina Faso,
    Idressa Ouedraogo)

Argentina
1968
The Hour of the Furnaces
    (Fernando Solanas and Octavio
    Getino)

1983
The Offcial Story (Luis Puenzo)

1991
The Voyage (Solanas)

Australia
1975
Picnic at Hanging Rock (Peter Weir)
Sunday Too Far Away (Ken Hannam)

1977
The Last Wave (Weir)

1978
The Chant of Jimmie Blacksmith (Fred Schepisi)
Newsfront (Phillip Noyce)

1979
Mad Max (George Miller)
My Brilliant Career (Gillian Armstrong)

1980
Breaker Morant (Bruce Beresford)

1981
Gallipoli (Weir)

1982
The Year of Living Dangerously (Weir)

1986
"Crocodile" Dundee (Peter Faiman)

1987
High Tide (Armstrong)

1989
Sweetie (Jane Campion)
An Angel at My Table (Campion)

1990
The Last Days of Chez Nous (Armstrong)

1992
Strictly Ballroom (Baz Luhrmann)

1993
The Piano (Campion)

Bolivia
1969
Blood of the Condor (Jorge Sanjinés)

Brazil
1963
Barren Lives (Nelson Pereira dos Santos)

1964
Black God, White Devil (Glauber Rocha)

1967
Terra em Transe (Rocha)

1969
Antonio das Mortes (Rocha)

1971
How Tasty Was My Little Frenchman
    (dos Santos)

1975
Ogum's Amulet (Pereira)

1977
Tent of Miracles (Pereira)

1978
Dona Flor and Her Two Husbands
    (Bruno Barreto)

1979
Bye Bye Brazil (Carlos Diegues)

1981
They Don't Wear Black Ties (Diegues)
Xica (Diegues)

1982
Pixote (Hector Babenco)

1984
Prison Memories (Pereira)

1985
Kiss of the Spider Woman (Babenco)

Chile
1969
The Jackal of Nahueltero (Miguel Littin)

1973
The Battle of Chile (Patricio Guzman)

1982
Alsino and the Condor (Littin)

Cuba
1968
Lucía (Humberto Solás)
Memories of Underdevelopment
    (Tomás Gutiérrez Alea)

1977
One Way or Another (Sara Gómez)

1983
Up to a Point (Gutiérrez Alea)

Germany
1965
Not Reconciled
    (Jean-Marie Straub and Danièle Huillet)

1966
Yesterday Girl (Alexander Kluge)
Young Törless (Volker Schlöndorff)

1967
Chronicle of Anna Magdalena Bach
    (Straub and Huillet)

1968
Artists at the Top of the Big Top: Disoriented
    (Kluge)

1970
Even Dwarfs Started Small (Werner Herzog)

1971
The Merchant of Four Seasons
    (Rainer Werner Fassbinder)

1972
The Bitter Tears of Petra von Kant (Fassbinder)
The Goalie's Anxiety at the Penalty Kick
    (Wim Wenders)

1973
Aguirre, the Wrath of God (Herzog)
Ludwig: Requiem for a Virgin King
    (Hans-Jürgen Syberberg)

1974
Ali: Fear Eats the Soul (Fassbinder)
Alice in the Cities (Wenders)
The Mystery of Kaspar Hauser (Herzog)
The Part-Time Work of a Domestic Slave (Kluge)

1975
False Movement (Wenders)
The Lost Honor of Katharina Blum
    (Schlöndorff and Margarethe von Trotta)

1976
Kings of the Road (Wenders)

1977
The American Friend (Wenders)
The German Sisters (von Trotta)
Hitler, a Film from Germany (Syberberg)

1978
The Tin Drum (Schlöndorff)

1979
The Marriage of Maria Braun (Fassbinder)
Nosferatu (Herzog)
Sisters or the Balance of Happiness (von Trotta)

1981
Friends and Husbands (von Trotta)

1982
Fitzcarraldo (Herzog)

1985
Class Relations (Straub and Huillet)

1986
Sugarbaby (Percy Adlon)

1987
Cobra Verde (Herzog)
Wings of Desire (Wenders)

1988
Three Sisters (von Trotta)

Spain
1966
The Hunt (Carlos Saura)

1973
The Spirit of the Beehive (Victor Erice)

1974
Cousin Angelica (Saura)

1975
Poachers (José Luis Borau)

1980
La Sabina (Borau)

1983
Carmen (Saura)
The South (Erice)

1984
What Have I Done to Deserve This?
    (Pedro Almodóvar)

1986
The Law of Desire (Almodóvar)

1987
Women on the Verge of a Nervous Breakdown
    (Almodóvar)

1990
Ay! Carmela (Saura)

1991
Dream of Light (Erice)
High Heels (Almodóvar)

BOOKS ON THE PERIOD

Africa **(see also *"Third World"*)**

Diawara, Manthia, *African Cinema: Politics and Culture*. Bloomington: Indiana University Press, 1992

Malkmus, Lizbeth, and Roy Armes, *Arab and African Film-making*. London: Zed Books, 1991

Pfaff, Françoise, *Twenty-Five Black African Film-Makers*. Westport, CT: Greenwood Press, 1993

Shiri,Keith, ed., *Directory of African Film-Makers and Films*, Westport, CT: Greenwood Press, 1993

Ukadike, N. Frank, *Black African Cinema*. Berkeley: University of California Press, 1993

Australia

Dermody, Susan, and Elizabeth Jacka, eds. *The Imaginary Industry: Australian Film in the Late '80s*. North Ryde, NSW: Australian Film, Television and Radio School, 1989

Lewis, Glen, *Australian Movies and the American Dream*. New York: Praeger, 1987

McFarlane, Brian, *Australian Cinema*. New York: Columbia University Press, 1988.

McFarlane, Brian, and Geoff Mayer, *New Australian Cinema: Sources and Parallels in British and American Film*. New York: Cambridge University Press, 1992

Rattigan, Neil, *Images of Australia: 100 Films of the New Austalian Cinema*. Dallas: Southern Methodist University Press, 1991

Germany

Corrigan, Timothy, *New German Film: The Displaced Image*. Bloomington: Indiana University Press, 1994

Elsaesser, Thomas, *New German Cinema: A History*. New Brunswick, N.J.: Rutgers University Press, 1989

Helt, Richard C., and Marie E. Helt, *West German Cinema since 1945: A Reference Handbook*. Metuchen, NJ: Scarecrow Press, 1987

Helt, Richard C., and Marie E. Helt, *West German Cinema 1985–1990: A Reference Handbook*. Metuchen, NJ: Scarecrow Press, 1992

Pflaum, Hans Günther, *Germany in Film: Theme and Content in the Cinema of the Federal Republic of Germany*. Detroit: Wayne State University Press, 1991

Rentschler, Eric, ed., *West German Filmmakers on Film: Visions and Voices*. New York: Holmes and Meier, 1988

Latin America **(see also *"Third World"*)**

Barnard, Tim, ed., *Argentine Cinema*. Toronto: Nightwood Editions, 1987

Berg, Charles Ramirez, *Cinema of Solitude: A Critical Study of Mexican Film, 1967–1983*. Austin: University of Texas Press, 1992

Foster, David William, *Contemporary Argentine Cinema*. Columbia: University of Missouri Press, 1992

Johnson, Randal, *The Film Industry in Brazil: Culture and the State*. Pittsburgh: University of Pittsburgh Press, 1987

Johnson, Randal, and Robert Stam, eds., *Brazilian Cinema*. Austin: University of Texas Press, 1988 [paperback of the 1982 volume]

King, John, *Magical Reels: A History of Cinema in Latin America*. London: Verso, 1990

Mora, Carl J., *Mexican Cinema: Reflections of a Society, 1896–1988*. Berkeley: University of California Press, 1990

Spain

Higginbotham, Virginia, *Spanish Film under Franco*. Austin: University of Texas Press, 1988

Hopewell, John, *Out of the Past: Spanish Cinema after Franco*. London; British Film Institute, 1987

Kinder, Marsha, *Blood Cinema: The Reconstruction of National Identity in Spain*. Berkeley: University of California Press, 1993

Schwartz, Ronald, *The Great Spanish Films: 1950–1990*. Metuchen, N.J.: Scarecrow Press, 1991

Third World (**see also** *"Africa"* **and** *"Latin America"*)

Armes, Roy, *Third World Film Making and the West*. Berkeley: University of California Press, 1987

Downing, John D. H., *Film and Politics in the Third World*. New Yoek: Prager, 1988

Pines, Jim, and Paul Willemen, eds., *Questions of Third Cinema*. London: British Film Institute, 1989

20

Here and Now: United States

◆ ◆ ◆

1975–

◆ THE ECONOMY AND TECHNOLOGY

As for the present Hollywood **economy,** the major studios—Warner Brothers, Universal, Columbia/TriStar, Paramount, Disney, M-G-M/UA, Twentieth Century-Fox, and Orion—have tended to follow the pattern of acquisitions and mergers prevalent in American industry generally. For example, in 1981 United Artists, then owned by Transamerica, was sold to Metro-Goldwyn-Mayer, which had earlier been purchased by Kirk Kerkorian, Las Vegas real-estate magnate. In 1982, Columbia Pictures was obtained by the Coca-Cola Company. Then, in 1985, an incursion of foreign capital began with News Corporation (part of the media empire of Australian Rupert Murdoch) purchasing Twentieth Century-Fox. The major thrust of subsequent foreign investment came from Japan, especially from the electronic industry giants. Sony Corporation acquired Columbia in 1989; Matsushita Electric Industrial Company (which includes brand names like Panasonic, JVC, and Technics) purchased Universal in 1991. These Japanese firms not only had excess capital they wanted to invest, they could see that being able to provide software (movies) for the hardware they manufactured (home videos) made good business sense. Not to be outdone, two American firms, Time, Inc. and Warner Brothers, merged in 1989 to become Time Warner, the biggest media company in the world. It owns/controls newspaper and magazine publishing, a cable television network with more than six million subscribers, the Home Box Office cable channel, the world's largest music company, and the old Warner Brothers studio. This merger mania and takeover fever seem part of a transition to a few global media conglomerates which may well dominate the film industry in the 1990s.

437

Fewer and bigger tends to be the pattern for the pictures produced as well. A major studio that used to produce around fifty films a year now frequently produces no more than twelve or fifteen, or fewer, though it will distribute independently produced pictures as well. What seems clear is that a few movies on which a lot of money is spent can return huge profits; the studios and the independents try hard to make one of those few. Hollywood's ten top-grossing films of all time have been released since 1975. That was the year of *Jaws,* and the beginning year of this final chapter. The extraordinary success of *Jaws* made it a model that has been followed in subsequent films aimed at setting new box-office records.

Superspectacles and science fiction have been dominant among box-office winners. *Star Wars* (1977) set the trend. Its record $185 million in income from domestic rentals surpassed even *Jaws. Star Wars* was followed by its comparably successful sequels, *The Empire Strikes Back* (1980) and *Return of the Jedi* (1983), which completed a trilogy. *Close Encounters of the Third Kind* (1977), *Star Trek* (1979), and *Raiders of the Lost Ark* (1981) cost a lot and made a lot. *E.T.—The Extra-Terrestrial* (1982) was the biggest box-office success up to that point—$400 million gross worldwide.

There have been, of course, extremely successful films that were neither sci-fi nor spectacular: *One Flew Over the Cuckoo's Nest* (1975), *Rocky* (1976), *Saturday Night Fever* (1977), *Grease* (1978); more recently, *Rain Man* (1988) and *Driving Miss Daisy* (1990), both serious films about serious subjects. Then there were spectaculars that were biographical/historical: *Reds* (1981, which cost $30 million), *Gandhi* (1982, $20 million), and *The Right Stuff* (1983, $27 million); and others that were fictional/historical: *Heaven's Gate* (1980, $36 million), *Ragtime* (1981, $25 million), *Havana* (1990, $55 million). *Reds, Ragtime,* and *Havana* were disappointing at the box office. *Heaven's Gate* was a much-publicized financial disaster that led to the sale of United Artists to M-G-M, and shook the industry considerably.

The lesson learned from *Heaven's Gate* was not that less money should be spent on a given film. Film budgets rose from an average of $8.5 million per picture in 1980 to $18 million by the end of the 1980s to $27 million in 1991. But instead of gambling on the vision of a particular auteur/director such as Michael Cimino, the large budgets were allocated to comparatively safe projects. Consistent big money makers were: (1) the "heavy metal" films of Sylvester Stallone (*First Blood* [1984], *Rambo II* [1985], *III* [1988]) and Arnold Schwarzenegger (*The Terminator* [1984], *II* [1991]); (2) gimmicky comedies (*Ghostbusters* [1984], *II* [1989], *Back to the Future* [1985], *II* [1989], *III* [1990], *Honey I Shrunk the Kids, [1989], Home Alone [1990];* (3) corporate genre action adventure pieces *(Die Hard* [1988], *II* [1990], *Indiana Jones and the Last Crusade [1989]);* and (4) comic book adaptations *(Batman* [1989], *Dick Tracy* [1990], *Teenage Mutant Ninja Turtles* [1990], *II* [1991]). *Batman,* playing in more than 2,200 North American theaters at its peak, moved into the top-ten grossing films of all time in a matter of months. Warner Brothers spent $63 million to advertise it, $10 million more than it cost to make. Its sequel(s?) will no doubt have appeared by the time this book is in print.

A final thing to be noted about the present Hollywood industry is the power in the hands of a few stars and the talent agencies representing them. The stars are male, for the most part. Prominent among them: Tom Cruise, Dustin Hoffman, Eddie Murphy, Bill Murray, Jack Nicholson, Arnold Schwarzenegger, Sylvester Stallone. If the agencies don't control their clients, they at least influence them. They can say to a studio: "If you want Bruce Willis for *Die Hard,* you can have him. But it'll cost you $5 million." In numerous instances Creative Artists Agency, for example, has used its commanding control of many of the industry's top names to dictate movie packages. In this respect agents have replaced studio heads. Jack Nicholson's contract for starring as The Joker in *Batman* gave him $6 million up front and 15 to 20 cents on every box-office dollar, boosting his total earnings from that picture to $50 million. Partly as a result, *Batman,* the fifth highest grossing film of all time, was still in the red a year and a half after its release. A helluva way to run a railroad, as used to be said when railroads were a more integral and respected part of our society.

The money being spent and returned (or not being returned) is up, and the **technology** being employed has reached a correspondingly high level. Great advances have been made in special effects. It seems that George Lucas's Industrial Light and Magic company—which was organized in 1975 and created the sophisticated special effects for many of the science-fiction and action-adventure films mentioned above—can make almost anything appear to exist or happen. *Terminator II* (1991) and *Jurassic Park* (1993) are recent, extraordinary examples. Computers have assisted available technology to create these amazing effects.

For live-action cinematography, Steadicam permits the camera to move with a steadiness that formerly would have required a large hydraulic boom or a dolly and tracks. It was first used in 1976 with striking effect in the opening scene of *Bound for Glory* (1976) to follow David Carradine from overhead into a crowd of 700 or 800 in a migrant labor camp; then in *Rocky* (1976) to run alongside Sylvester Stallone up the steps of the Philadelphia Museum of Art. Since that time its use has become commonplace. Arifflex or Panavision cameras, Nagra tape recorders, and location dollies comprise the standard apparatus. In the new look of films, hand-held technique has come a long way, as has the equipment designed for it: cameras are lighter and better balanced; cinematographers have learned to operate them with increased skill.

Since 1984 the colorization process, employing computer technology, has been used to transfer black-and-white film to videotape in approximate color. The motivation for it is admittedly financial—to make profits by re-presenting films from the vaults on television and video cassette. The commercial argument is that audiences raised on color tend to skip black-and-white films (and old TV series) as they flip channels. When the colorized *Miracle on 34th Street* (1947) was shown on network television in 1985 it received the highest audience rating of syndicated films for that year. Colorized cassettes of *Yankee Doodle Dandy, The Maltese Falcon, Topper,* and *It's a Wonderful Life* became available soon after. The colorized *Casablanca* premiered in 1988; *Citizen Kane* may be threatened.

Scholars, critics, and film makers have been loud in their denunciation of colorization's distortions of the creative intentions of the artists who created the films. Director Fred Zinnemann called such tampering "a cultural crime of the first order." He was joined by others expressing outrage including Woody Allen, Martin Scorsese, Warren Beatty, John Huston, Steven Spielberg, and Elia Kazan—along with the

American Film Institute, the Directors Guild of America, the Writers Guild of America West, the American Society of Cinematographers, and the Society for Cinema Studies. The argument still rages but so far money is winning.

Along with the economic and technological developments within the film industry is the excitement and uncertainty of the new electronic means of producing and distributing the moving image accompanied by sound. Videotape, electronic cameras and editing machines are steadily replacing the photochemical system of the traditional motion picture. Electronic transmission and playback possibilities already include—in addition to broadcast television—satellite, cable, video cassette, disc recorders, laser disc players, and now even computers. Widespread availability of feature films for home video began about 1981; by 1987 the home video industry's annual gross rentals exceeded rentals paid for films by the theaters. High-definition-television (HDTV), also introduced in 1981, is still being worked on and debated. Most HDTV systems more than double the number of lines currently available on a video screen (525), giving sharpness and detail of image comparable at least to 16mm projection. At the moment the Federal Communications Commission is in the process of deciding which of five competing systems to choose as the U.S. HDTV standard. With the use being made of fibre optics and the advances toward high-definition-television, in a comparatively short while the motion picture as art form, replete with computer graphics no doubt, will be part of the visual-audio material filling the walls of our living rooms with crisp wide-screen images accompanied by stereophonic digital sound.

Motion pictures made with and for such new technologies, and audience expectations regarding them, will likely be quite different from what we have experienced to date. Another aesthetic jump—like that taken from silence to sound, from black and white to color, from almost square to very wide screen and stereophonic sound—is beginning. It may be bigger and more profound in its effects than any of the earlier technological leaps. Until it has been made and measured, the aesthetician can only conjecture about it. The historian as yet has nothing to say.

♦ SOCIAL CONTENT

American movies frequently wait until after the tensions have somehow been resolved before dealing with large-scale stress and cultural dislocation, or deal with them obliquely. The film industry is loathe to offend segments of its audience by adopting a position on disturbing issues; it is generally believed that the audience pays its admission to experience something other than the serious and worrisome actuality existing outside the theater.

Even allowing for this tendency, the **Vietnam War** is unique in having been absent from the screens of the United States until long after the event; even more puzzling was the sudden appearance of a number of films dealing with the subject five years after the last American troops had left Vietnam. The only earlier exception to prove the rule was *Green Berets* (1968). But for all of its patriotic intentions, it was more a military adventure than a film about our involvement in Vietnam. Not only was there no film that dealt directly and seriously with that war, any oblique acknowledgments of it must have been so heavily coded as to be undetected by most of us.

In 1978 there began a cycle of films about the Vietnam War that included *Go Tell the Spartans, Coming Home, Who'll Stop the Rain?,* and *The Deer Hunter.* In 1979 it reached its climax with *Apocalypse Now.*

Though not as popular as Vietnam films that followed it, *Go Tell the Spartans* (Ted Post) seems in many ways the most scrupulously accurate. Set in 1964, its point of view is that of a frustrated commander (Burt Lancaster) of a group of American military advisers at Penang who leads a platoon to an outpost that had been abandoned by the defeated French a decade before. *Go Tell the Spartans* portrays the shifting demands, the unclear loyalties, and the ethical dilemma that underlay the complex and irregular mode of warfare.

Coming Home (Hal Ashby) and *Who'll Stop the Rain?* (Karel Reisz) deal with those returning from Vietnam combat—the damage the experience has done to them emotionally and its effect on the lives of others at home. *Coming Home* concerns a paraplegic veteran (Jon Voight) who falls in love with the wife (Jane Fonda) of a pro-war Marine officer (Bruce Dern). Though involving no combat—and perhaps sentimental and unreal, as has been argued—it seems an honest attempt to confront the human wreckage left in the wake of war, the aftermath of the Vietnam War in particular. It does not question the war itself so much as the attitudes it had given rise to.

The opening ten minutes of *Who'll Stop the Rain?,* based on the novel *Dog Soldiers* by Robert Stone, offers some horrifying scenes of warfare in the Vietnamese countryside and of corruption in Saigon. Its narrative then centers on a war correspondent who has become so traumatized by the moral degradation he observed in the war that human decency and innocence have lost all meaning for him. He becomes a heroin smuggler. In "a world like this one," he says, "people are going to naturally want to get high."

It was *The Deer Hunter* (Michael Cimino) that seemed to touch the national nerve most directly. It deals with three buddies from a Pennsylvania steel town who volunteer for Vietnam. They experience dreadful violence and torture, physical and psychological. One dies in Saigon, one loses his legs, the other survivor has become truncated emotionally. The use of Russian roulette in prison camp and as a game for Saigon gambling created a furor; Cimino acknowledged that it probably didn't happen but insisted on his artist's prerogative to use it as a metaphor for the war. The ending of the film is ambiguous but exalting, even if it might be argued what exactly is being exalted. At a funeral breakfast the returned veterans begin to sing "God Bless America" as a dirge for their dead friend. As they continue the song becomes a hymn, to this country and to the values it traditionally holds, for which they and others had fought and died. This scene provides a catharsis of sorts; it is a sad moment but also curiously ennobling. Life goes on, it seems to mean, and we Americans may be, or can again become, the Americans we want to be.

Apocalypse Now (Francis Ford Coppola), with its effort to fuse the mystery and gloom of Joseph Conrad's *Heart of Darkness* with the known and awful actualities of the Vietnam War, was the first film to excoriate directly American involvement. A behemoth of a film, it was years and many millions of dollars in the making. Its production became something like a re-creation of the war it was portraying. Shot in the Philippines, it ran over schedule and over budget; most critics and probably viewers found that it did not conclude satisfactorily. Yet it is a chilling and convincing vision of a kind of madness rampant in the American military command: homicidal, conspiratorial, megalomaniacal. It offers surreal experience of jungle and battle; colors and sounds overwhelm the senses, and we may feel that this is the way it must have felt to American soldiers, especially if their sensations were heightened by fear and perhaps drugs. The terrors of warfare and the disordered personalities encountered in that film are frighteningly real and their reality is seen and heard from an intensified perception.

Apocalypse Now seemed to satisfy for awhile our need to deal with that painful conflict, at least in such direct, sustained, and apocalyptic form. Then, after a hiatus of eight years, a second wave of Vietnam films began with *Platoon*, continued in 1987 with *Gardens of Stone, The Hanoi Hilton, Full Metal Jacket,* and *Hamburger Hill,* followed in 1988 by *Good Morning, Vietnam,* and in 1989 by *Casualties of War,* and *Born on the Fourth of July.* Of these, *Platoon* and *Good Morning, Vietnam* received the widest public response, thus, in social terms, seem to be the most significant. (*Full Metal Jacket* was dealt with earlier in the discussion of Stanley Kubrick's work.)

Platoon ◆ U.S., 1986, Oliver Stone; Tom Berenger, Charlie Sheen, and Willem Dafoe.

Good Morning, Vietnam ♦ U.S., 1988, Barry Levinson; Robin Williams

Many people felt that *Platoon* came closest to what the combat experience in Vietnam must have been like of any of the films dealing with the subject. It centers around the experience of a rookie and can be assumed to be autobiographical to a degree. Its writer-director, Oliver Stone, volunteered for the army in 1967 and spent fifteen months in Vietnam. The fragmented structure—a sequence of events rather than a coherent narrative—and number of characters involved—the men of the platoon—add to this sense of actuality. It is a tough film to watch; the violence, the jungle, the heat and the stench, all seem palpable. But there are also mythic elements involved, as in *The Deer Hunter* and *Apocalypse Now:* in this case two sergeants of contrasting temperaments; one has become a hardened killing machine, the other serene and Christ-like.

Whatever it was about the combination of its elements—painfully convincing naturalistic detail and mythic confrontation between representatives of good and evil—its reception was quite extraordinary. Not a film you would expect to be popular or honored, it was a box-office success and won four Academy Awards including Best Picture and Best Director.

Good Morning, Vietnam, written and directed by Barry Levinson, is very different from *Platoon,* and from the other Vietnam films. A comedy set in Saigon in 1965, it focuses on, in fact he's scarcely off the screen, a disc jockey for Armed Forces Radio (the role based on an actual person). Its popularity and much of its charm come from the star performance of Robin Williams. His incessant, fast-paced, irreverent, and wildly inventive patter delivered on and off the air punctures military pretensions and pomposities and exposes the double-speak dishonesty of censorship and official news releases. Though the tone has almost none of the seriousness of the other Vietnam films, it raises questions that remain implicit in them regarding the arguments made for our being in that war, and the motivations and integrity of our leaders. Things laughed at here could otherwise be wept over.

Another cycle of films that paralleled the second Vietnam cycle recall the *film noir* that existed alongside (or underneath, if you like) the realistic, exhortative, liberal films of World War II and immediate postwar (see Chapter 9)—with a difference. This later cycle has the added element of bizarre humor that suggests the screwball comedies of the thirties and early forties (see Chapter 8). Ergo: **screwball-noir.**

The screwball-noir cycle seems to have begun with Scorsese's *The King of Comedy* (1983). In it, amidst New York City setting and characters, Robert de Niro plays an obsessive would-be comic who threatens the life of talk-show host Jerry Lewis to get his big break. It is a venturesome (the film did not do well at the box office), seemingly personally felt, and certainly acerbic essay on show biz and celebrity. Scorsese became one of two masters of this subgenre, and his *After Hours* (1985) could be regarded as one of its two definitive works to date. *After Hours* is about an office worker who, in a casual and innocent search for sexual adventure, becomes helplessly lost in the night streets, apartments, and clubs of the Soho district of Manhattan, encountering wildly assorted, perverse, scary, and unreal aspects of human behavior among its denizens.

The other master of screwball-noir is Alan Rudolph, whose master work is *Choose Me* (1984), followed by its less completely realized sequel, *Trouble in Mind* (1985). *Choose Me* follows a man who casually escapes from a mental hospital, wanders into a bar, becomes involved with—lies elaborately (or maybe tells the truth), kisses, and proposes to—three women. When they react to his precipitous proposals with incredulity, he responds "I only kiss women I'd marry, and when I marry I never cheat." *Trouble in Mind* concerns an ex-cop freed from jail who returns to Rain City (actually Seattle), in some unspecific and unpleasant near-future, hangs out at Wanda's Café (Eve's Bar was the hangout in *Choose Me*), gets involved with some young people who've just come to the big city.

Other films of the mid-eighties with similar ingredients are *Heartbreakers* (1984, Bobby Roth), *Desperately Seeking Susan* (1985, Susan Seidelman), *Lost in America* (1985, Albert Brooks), *Something Wild* (1986, Jonathan Demme), *House of Games* (1987, David Mamet). And this is only a sampling; a considerable number of other films might qualify in whole or in part as screwball-noir. *Brazil* (1985, Terry Gilliam) is fully qualified but British; *Barton Fink* (1990, Joel and Ethan Coen), is, without qualification, a prime addition.

In any case, the criteria for screwball-noir are these: They take place in a mostly urban setting, at night and/or indoors. Their protagonists are young and hip, but they have not exactly arrived where they want to be emotionally. They do not feel fulfilled. They are looking for something and are obsessed with this search. There is more than a suggestion of madness in these films, but it is not altogether clear whether it is the

Choose Me ◆ U.S., 1984, Alan Rudolph; Keith Carradine, on right.

person, the culture, or the society that is mad or the cause of madness. A set of rules and a kind of logic appear to exist but they are elusive, erratic, and inconsistent in their operation. When we think we know what's happening, or what to expect, it turns out not to be what we think, or something we didn't expect.

As the label implies, "screwball-noir" is a mix of genres, techniques, appeals; of distanciation and seduction of the audience; of reality, unreality, and fantasy. The comedy grows out of the incongruous mix of outrageous characters, behaviors, and events. The films are dream-like or nightmare-like, often dreams that turn into nightmares. The threat of violence is pervasive; it may become manifest but more frequently it remains latent—possible, likely, part of the environment of the screen lives being lived.

If there is in fact a screwball-noir as described, or something like it, the question can then be asked: What is it saying to and revealing about our culture at this time? Why is this content (including techniques and styles) recurring with some frequency here and now? Whereas the Vietnam films attempt to address a recent past and current emotional reality through a direct, realistic approach comparable to the post-World War II problem pictures (see Chapter 9), the screwball-noir offer metaphors for the insecurities and fears that underlie our contemporary social fabric. The appearance of these films as cycles suggests that certain emotional needs of the audience are being met, that certain kinds of gratifications are being offered by their plots, themes, and characters. In either their realistic or metaphorical forms, these films cannot be dismissed as escapist entertainment; social analysts would say there is no such thing. Or in any case, what is being escaped to in movie entertainment can tell us something about what is being escaped from in reality if our examination of it is sophisticated enough.

◆ NEW VOICES

Happily, the mainstream industry's preoccupation with high tech, high finance, and blockbusters hasn't completely absorbed American cinema. In some ways, and inadvertently to be sure, it may allow more space for resolute independent film makers appealing to minority audiences. Funding for these independent productions may come from completely outside the industry: from Public Television's *American Playhouse* series, the National Endowment for the Arts, and occasionally German television. Mostly the film makers raise their modest (sometimes minuscule) budgets any way they can: from friends and relatives, huckerstering, delayed payment for services. The films are often premiered and may find distributors at the Independent Feature Film Market in New York City, founded in 1978, and at the United States Sundance Film Festival in Utah, started by Robert Redford in 1981. The latter event has been especially helpful in introducing young talent and unusual new works. The 1993 festival presented more than eighty features and fifty shorts. Among the fiction award winners were *Public Access* (Bryan Singer), *Ruby in Paradise* (Victor Nuñez), *El Mariachi* (Robert Rodriguez), and *Just Another Girl on the I.R.T.* (Leslie Harris). Among documentaries were *Children of Fate: Life and Death in a Sicilian Family* (Andrew Young, Susan Todd, Robert M. Young, Michael Roemer), *Silverlake Life: The View from Here* (Peter Friedman), and *Earth and the American Dream* (Bill Couturie). Represented among these works are female, African American, and homosexual film makers and concerns, which have a new prominence in American film generally.

In Hollywood, sexism has long been notorious, from the storied casting couch to the demonstrable absence of **women** in key administrative and creative positions. The exceptions only prove the rule, and were exceptional in their talent and determination. In the thirties Dorothy Arzner came up through editing and script writing to directing (notably *Christopher Strong* [1933] and *Dance, Girl, Dance* [1940]). In the fifties and sixties there was Ida Lupino, whose success as an actor gave her enough leverage to become an independent producer and director (for example *The Hitchhiker* [1953] and *The Trouble with Angels* [1966]). From the eighties on there has been some change in this situation, or at least a few more exceptions. For example, in an unprecedented appointment, Sherry Lansing became President in Charge of Film Production at Twentieth Century-Fox in 1980.

Among directors Amy Heckerling had a solid hit with *Fast Times at Ridgemont High* (1982), about teen-age growing pains in Southern California, one of the best of type and a big boost in the career of imminent star Sean Penn. Of the films she directed subsequently—four comedies—*Look Who's Talking* (1989), about an unwed mother in search of a perfect father for her baby, was the only one to approximate its success (at least it made a lot of money).

Susan Seidelman's first feature, following graduate film school at New York University, was *Smithereens* (1982). It is an honest, tough-minded, painfully believable film about a near-psychotic young female hustler on the fringe of the punk-rock scene. *Desperately Seeking Susan* (1985), one of the screwball-noir cycle discussed earlier, is about a bored New Jersey housewife (Rosanna Arquette) who pursues a bizarre woman being sought through a personal ad (Madonna). It was a smash hit, advancing the careers of its director and two stars. That considerable success was followed by three comparative failures. *Making Mr. Right* (1987) is a comedy involving an android designed for space travel, created in the image of his scientist creator, and the female public relations agent assigned to promote the project. *Cookie* (1989) from her own script, is a comedy about a mafia chief's daughter who undertakes a life of crime. *She-Devil* (1990) is an adaption of Fay Weldon's feminist novel, *The Life and Loves of a She-Devil,* the comic-book rendering fitting the dark original poorly. In interviews Seidelman has talked about the perils of success and big budgets, and lamented the absence of moderately priced movies that fall midway between blockbusters and independents.

Desperately Seeking Susan ◆ U.S., 1985, Susan Seidelman; Rosanna Arquette.

Martha Coolidge seemed to be typed as a director of teen-age flicks, of which her first, *Valley Girl* (1983), was the most interesting and successful. A departure with her fifth film, *Bare Essentials* (1991), made for television, was a generally agreed disaster. It is about a New York couple marooned on a desert island who, away from the distractions of city life, have little choice but to get to know each other. And then there was *Ramblin' Rose* (1991). In spite of its title (the role was played by Laura Dern, nominated for an Oscar as Best Actress; Diane Ladd, who played Mother, was nominated for Best Actress in Supporting Role), it is really a coming-of-age story recalled by a man who returns home to visit his father in 1971. He remembers Rose, who came to work at their house during the Depression, and the various incidents and involvements growing out of her rampant if innocent sexuality (including the beginnings of his own sexuality, stimulated by her presence). A warm and nostalgic comedy of character and manners, its direction is coherent and controlled.

If it is easier for women to become directors than it was at the beginning of this last period, it is by no means easy. Female directors complain that they don't have access to the "boys' club," that is the predominantly male group of executives who have the power to "greenlight" projects. Moreover, they fall prey to male stereotyping that holds that women can't direct action pictures, can't direct commercial movies, can't control crews, and so on. Male prejudices within the industry are still a formidable barrier, it seems.

Unlike female directors, whose films are not wholly confined to "women's issues," **black** film makers so far have made films about aspects of the African American experience. The breakthrough, in what has become a substantial body of black films, was *She's Gotta Have It* (1986). Its director was Spike Lee, another NYU alumnus, who has become a sort of bellwether for black film making. He writes, directs, edits, and acts in his films and has built up a company of black collaborators, including his father as composer, who have worked with him. *She's Gotta Have It* is not so much about blacks in this culture as about the relationships of Nola Darling with her three lovers and friends. She is a single, sexually emancipated commercial artist living in Harlem. The life she makes for herself includes the relationships available to her, but she maintains an attractiveness and a dignity that are her own. *School Daze* (1988), though it too is a comedy, is about being black, about class and color among black Americans. It takes place at Mission, a fictitious, predominantly black college in the South. The students body is divided into two factions; those who are lighter skinned and aspire to be like upper-middle-class whites, and those who are darker, poorer, first-generation college students—the black underclass.

With *Do the Right Thing* (1989) he created a highly controversial, markedly successful direct attack on the problems of black-white (and Asian) relations in the urban ghetto, in this instance the Bedford Stuyvesant section of Brooklyn. It centers around a Pizzeria owned by an Italian (played by Danny Aiello), his efforts to do business and live amicably in an indigent neighborhood of repressed and angry African Americans. His own anger eventually leads to murder which triggers a race riot started by one of his employees (played by Lee) that includes the burning down of his pizza parlor. The film ends on a note of temporary reconciliation which leaves

Do the Right Thing ♦ U.S., 1989, Spike Lee; Lee and Danny Aiello.

the essential problems of racial discord unresolved, with contradictory quotes on the sound track from Martin Luther King, Jr., urging nonviolent protest, and Malcolm X, approving violence that is self-defense. This was the most talked about film of the year; it became news, with critics and viewers alike taking sides.

The financial success of *She's Gotta Have It* (it grossed $8 million against a budget of $175,000) and *Do the Right Thing* ($28 million against $6.5 million) enable Lee to continue making roughly a film a year (*Mo' Better Blues* [1990], *Jungle Fever* [1991], *Malcolm X* [1992]) and led to a veritable explosion of black films in 1991—some nineteen features were released, first features for most of their directors.

House Party (1990, Reginald and Warrington Hudlin), dealing with black hip-hop culture and rap music, preceded the explosion: it premiered at the Sundance Festival and was distributed by its independent New York production company, New Line. *New Jack City* (1991, Mario Van Peebles) was a gangster ghetto melodrama of crack cocaine drug dealers and rebel cops that seemed in the mold of the blaxploitation films of the 1970s rather than a new direction. *Boyz N the Hood* (1991, John Singleton) was most widely seen and discussed of the black films, apart from Spike Lee's. It's about four young black male high school students with different aims, ambitions, and family situations trying to survive amidst Los Angeles gangs and bigotry. *Straight Out of Brooklyn* (1991, Matty Rich) is much rougher in technique and narrative structure, the most bleak and hopeless of the black wave, yet it has power and conviction. Its writer-director, who also plays one of the characters, was only seventeen when he began it, nineteen when it was completed. It is a look at a struggling black family in Brooklyn's Red Hook housing project. The ghetto is presented as stultifying, occupying and shaping all aspects of life.

So far the emphasis of the black films has been almost exclusively on young black males and their problems. (*Just Another Girl on the I.R.T.*, mentioned above, is a welcome exception.) Perhaps that's as it should be since they are made by young black males; but it must be said that they seem, at least to someone outside the black culture being shown, to be not only dismissive of black women but misogynistic, putting women down to raise men up. The quest for black manhood appears as the dominant concern in so many of these films. One of the most depressing aspects of *Straight Out of Brooklyn* is that it ends by implying that this cannot be achieved—that black men cannot depend on each other to reach their goals, that their efforts in this direction result only in mutual destruction. *Menace II Society* (1993, Allen and Albert Hughes) confirms and makes this charge even stronger. Clearly it's something that needs to be said.

At the end of the eighties prominent films with **gay** or **lesbian** sensibilities came first from black film makers. For example from Isaac Julien, who is British, but whose films have been widely seen and admired here. *Looking for Langston* (1988) is a poetic and evocative study of Langston Hughes, black poet and homosexual of the Harlem renaissance of the 1930s. *Young Soul Rebels* (1991) focuses on the friendship of two young men in London in 1977, one black and gay the other half-black/half-white and heterosexual, who run a pirate radio station that plays black import records. In Marlon T. Riggs's expressionistic documentary *Tongues Untied* (1989) a disparate group of unidentified black gay men relate their personal experiences. Jennie Livingston's *Paris Is Burning* (1990), a more straightforward as well as an amusing and skillful documentary, is about black drag costume balls in Harlem. These films suggest the predominance of male homosexuality within what would be called "New Queer Cinema." Films about male couples and coupling assumed the lead.

Gus Van Sant's *My Own Private Idaho* (1991) was the breakthough feature. It concerns a young narcoleptic male hustler and his passion for an upper-class rich-kid who is part of the scene on the streets of Seattle but really just slumming. It received wide distribution (for such subject matter) and subsequently became available on video. (Van Sant's previous *Mala Noche* [1987] also dealt with homosexual obsessive desire but received only limited distribution. *Drugstore Cowboy* [1989], his biggest hit, had a heterosexual relationship at its center and was concerned with drug addiction.)

Swoon (1991, Tom Kalin) is a reworking of the infamous 1923 Loeb-Leopold case in which two wealthy Chicago eighteen-year-olds kidnap and murder a neighbor's child as a mad extension of their love for each other. *The Hours and Times* (1991, Christopher Munch) is also based on historical incident but in this instance the

My Own Private Idaho ◆ U.S., 1991, Gus Van Sant; River Phoenix and William Reichart.

portrayed action is conjectural, having more to do with myth and memory than with fact. The question, which is elaborated on without being answered, is whether during a trip to Barcelona in 1963 John Lennon had sex with the Beatles' gay manager. In *The Living End* (1992, Gregg Araki) the gay pair—both HIV-positive, thus with nothing to lose—take to the road on a crime spree, one out of rage, the other out of boredom. All of the recent gay films exist under the shadow of AIDS, of course.

Lesbian films and film makers that received considerable attention at festivals and in the press include Laurie Lynd's *R.S.V.P.* (1991) and Sadie Bennings's *Jollies* (1992) and *It Wasn't Love* (1992). Alas, nothing can be written about them or other lesbian films here because there seems to be no easy way to see them. For the most part they have been experimental and documentary shorts available through specialized distribution sources.

Granting this partial limitation, the possibilities now available for gay, lesbian, and bisexual films to be made inexpensively on video and Super 8mm, and for bypassing conventional theatrical, nontheatrical, and television distribution to be sold and rented directly on video tape or disc to persons interested in them, means that they—along with works representing other minority interests—can be created and enjoyed much as literature and the other arts, which have long allowed for the innovative and specialized, and even the unpopular and outrageous. It seems a healthy new dimension added to the formerly, predominantly mass medium of motion picture.

♦ ARTISTRY

Within mainstream production a number of film makers have been able to maintain sufficient control over their films to make personal statements representing their own ways of seeing and feeling. To attempt to pick directors so close to the present in terms of the lasting artistic interest and value of their films, however, is particularly arbitrary and chancy. On the other hand there is little difficulty in deciding whose films have been widely popular during recent years. A list of this sort (adding some directors dealt with in earlier chapters, notably Altman and Scorsese) would include Brian De Palma, Woody Allen, Alan J. Pakula, Steven Spielberg, and Jonathan Demme, arranged in the order in which they directed their first feature.

Brian De Palma's forte has been the skillfully made and highly manipulative thriller dealing with the bizarre and inexplicable—*Carrie* (1976), high school misfit releases telekinetic powers against those who have mocked her; *The Fury* (1978), three people with occult powers—or the bizarre and explicable—*Dressed to Kill* (1980), a transvestite homicidal maniac; *Body Double* (1984), an obsessive voyeur. The latter two, the first very successful commercially, were criticized by many for creating their chilling effects through graphic depiction of violence toward women. What else might be said of these films and of De Palma's work generally—and that of the other so-called movie brats (Francis Coppola, George Lucas, Martin Scorsese, Steven Spielberg, John Milius)—is that De Palma obviously has seen and understood thoroughly a lot of films. Movie genres and movie techniques seem to be what his films are about. His world includes many homages to Hitchcock; *Dressed to Kill* opens with Angie Dickinson in the shower, shot in a way to remind us of the shower scene in *Psycho*. The railway station shootout in *The Untouchables* (1987) draws on

Dressed to Kill ♦ U.S., 1980, Brian De Palma; Angie Dickinson and Michael Caine.

the "Odessa Steps" sequence of *Potemkin,* including a baby carriage descending down the stairs. With *Scarface* (1983) De Palma moved out of the thriller to remake Howard Hawks's gangster film of 1932. *The Untouchables,* based on the earlier long-running television series, covers much the same ground, though with considerably more energy and panache.

If *Casualties of War* (1989) is a generic war drama, like other of the Vietnam War films discussed earlier, it is an unusual one. It is based on an actual rape and murder of a young Vietnamese woman by American soldiers. The awful events are seen through the eyes of an ordinary Midwesterner, Eriksson (played by Michael J. Fox), who refused to participate and later brought charges against the other members of the five-man patrol. *The Bonfire of the Vanities* (1990) may be a genre film of one sort or another; perhaps it is closest to the earlier big-budget studio adaptations of best-selling novels. The source here is Tom Wolfe's acidic observation of the haves and have nots, law and justice, media and privacy in New York City (and our society generally). To most critics it seemed the wrong sort of material for De Palma. Given the elaborate plot and plenitude of satiric detail of the original, its reduction to a two-hour film, plus miscasting in all the major roles, work against the credibility and coherence, render it a thing of pieces, formless. For it is the form of his movies, as it affects audience response, more than their substance that seems most to interest De Palma. If his best films are derivative, their fascination must be acknowledged. A lot of us respond to those forms. It seems likely that he will return to his often absorbing and sometimes original reworkings of the known, the formulaic.

In *Annie Hall* (1977) **Woody Allen** hit full stride with his own special and highly personal brand of humor. Based in New York City, it draws on Jewishness and psychoanalysis, and offers in-jokes about show biz and other films. But most essential to it are the gentle, recognizable, and amusing revelations about certain (male intellectual) sexual insecurities and inadequacies. *Manhattan* (1979), in black and white Panavision, is more of the same. Though the humor is darker, it maintains the same high level of exact observation presented in the perfect nuances of Allen's and Diane Keaton's performances.

Zelig (1983) offered a new and bold line of comic invention. Allen plays Leonard Zelig, the "Chameleon Man," who takes on the identities and abilities of those around him—whatever groups he happens to be associating with at the moment; for example, physicians, politicians, black jazz musicians. It is a delicious satire of 1920s America with its flagpole sitters, home-run kings, movie stars, and gangsters. It is also a delightful parody of film styles and fashions, with re-created newsreels and home movies made and mixed so skillfully with the real thing that it's hard to tell them apart. *Zelig* is more than Allen's usual chic clowning; it is as if he had become a kindly Jonathan Swift trying to characterize an age and a culture.

In subsequent films he has frequently confined himself to writing and directing for others, though the lives he deals with remain part of his personal territory and can be related to earlier films. The films also have become increasingly serious.

In *The Purple Rose of Cairo* (1985) Allen made another conceptual film about an American period and its popular culture—specifically the thirties and the movies. In it the star of the black-and-white movie within the color movie, both with the same

Annie Hall ◆ U.S., 1977, Woody Allen;
Diane Keaton and Allen.

title, steps off the theater screen and leads an adoring fan into a round of romance. Eventually her hero must return to the screen and she to a brutish husband and the Depression in a town whose plant has closed. This commentary on what (some) thirties movies were like and what they meant to audiences (especially female ones in this instance) is engaging. If it is sweet in its innocence and fantasy, it is ultimately more sad than funny. Allen does not appear in it.

Radio Days (1986) has some similarities to *Purple Rose.* Allen is not in it; but he does narrate this story, pretty much his own we may suppose, about a lower-middle-class Jewish family in Brooklyn in the late thirties and early forties. Radio programs are important to their lives—everyone has his/her favorite—and the big-band swing music of the era provides the score.

Unlike *Broadway Danny Rose* (1984), his last performance before it, in *Hannah and Her Sisters* (1985) his role is not the major one. Though it is a comedy in the classical sense of comedy distinguished from tragedy, the unhappiness, which under-lies much of Allen's funnier films (including *Broadway Danny Rose*), is here brought into balance with the humor. Overall, however, it is a wonderfully warm study of an extended family. Since in his non-comic films Allen often seems to be working out of

Ingmar Bergman, it is apt to consider *Hannah and Her Sisters* in relation to Bergman's valedictory *Fanny and Alexander.*

Allen's next two films, *September* (1987) and *Another Woman* (1988), head directly for the earlier, gloomier Bergman (as did *Interiors,* 1978, Allen's first serious drama). His ability to persist in this vein seems commendable, yet the legions of Woody Allen fans and the reviewers favor the romantic comedies set in contemporary Manhattan (*Annie Hall, Manhattan, Hannah and Her Sisters*). The intellectual critics, on the other hand, are drawn to the self-reflexive films about the film maker, film making, and the film being made (*Stardust Memories,* 1980, *Zelig, The Purple Rose of Cairo*).

Crimes and Misdemeanors (1990) has the same sorts of characters and milieu as *Hannah,* but is much, much darker—ending in fact with the Allen figure (a documentary film maker) in despair following the serious moral and religious transgressions of several characters. *Alice* (1990) worked over some of the same moral ambiguities within a Catholic rather than Jewish theological context, with stylized and fantastical elements added. It is one of the "intellectual" creations, as is *Shadows and Fog* (1991), which has an even stranger artificiality. A philosophical/psychological conundrum set in Germany of the 1920s, it flaunts an Expressionist visual style in black-and-white, pointed homage to the films of that time and place, with the music made up of Kurt Weill songs.

Following the release of *Shadows and Fog,* Allen's tumultuous personal life hit the media. The scandal involved Mia Farrow, actress in his films and longtime intimate companion, a child custody suit, and allegations of child abuse. Throughout all this Allen's output continued and audiences continued to respond in spite of widespread misgivings, shock, and some outrage.

Husbands and Wives (1992) connected directly back to *Hannah and her Sisters* and *Crimes and Misdemeanors*: same upper-middle-class urban professional couples, with troubled marriages and infidelities, afloat on a pond of emotional confusion. Though all of Allen's films are autobiographical to one degree or another, with this one, starring Allen and Farrow as husband and wife, it was difficult to keep from connecting the predicaments of the characters to the headlines. (At one point she says, "You think we'd ever break up?,"which they do in the film as in life; at another he says, "I've learned nothing over the years," which some of his loyal fans were beginning to fear was true.) In any case, it is quite extraordinary that Allen has been able to sustain his steady output of a film a year as an independent working in New York City with a resident cast and crew, to draw from his own experience, and to say what he wants to say about it, funny or sad.

Alan J. Pakula began film making as a producer and generally produces the films he directs. They have been noteworthy for their sophistication, seeming to come from an especially modern sensibility and to be dealing with problems of deep current concern. Earlier Pakula films had as subjects loveless sexuality, violence, and fear, in *Klute* (1971); political assassination, in *The Parallax View* (1974); and political culpability, in *All the President's Men* (1976). During this final period he has made: *Comes a Horseman* (1978), about pollution and destruction of the land; *Starting Over*

(1979), divorce and a new life; *Rollover* (1981), international high finance and Arab oil money; and *Sophie's Choice* (1982), the effects of Nazi concentration camps on their survivors, and mental unbalance. Pakula's work is also noteworthy for the way in which a very sure sense of narrative and performance is combined with an elegant and precise visual sensitivity. *Sophie's Choice*—from the novel by William Styron, script by Pakula—seems an ultimate achievement of type: a "literary" film that communicates its feeling for literature through affecting performances, images, and accompanying sounds.

 See You in the Morning (1989) represents a departure in that it is from Pakula's original script. Set in upper-middle-class New York City, it is a love story about two very decent and attractive persons who try to build a second marriage on ground firmer (also less romantic and glamorous) than their first ones. *Presumed Innocent* (1990) is a skillful adaption of an enormously popular novel, which Pakula coscripted. The film preserves the convincing and absorbing legal and political maneuvering, the courtroom tactics and behavior of the original. (Its author was a former prosecuting attorney in Chicago; exteriors were shot in Detroit.) *Consenting Adults* (1992) he coproduced but did not write. This Hitchcockian psychological thriller involves two suburban couples intertwined by one of the husbands whose greed fuels his socio-

Sophie's Choice ◆ U.S., 1982, Alan J. Pakula; Meryl Streep and Kevin Kline.

pathic behavior that results in two murders, and self-destruction all around. It is clever and has some of the broader implications about ethics and morality in the latter part of the twentieth century that the earlier films had; but its main thrust is toward the criminal intrigue and resultant suspense, peripheral to the sorts of concerns Pakula is especially good dealing with.

The phenomenal success of *Jaws* (1975), a dark myth about a white shark preying on a seaside community, fixed the direction **Steven Spielberg**'s career would subsequently take. Its popularity was repeated with *Close Encounters of the Third Kind* (1977), about an average guy who comes in contact with creatures from another planet. The comedy *1941* (1979), set in California in the year we entered World War II, was unsuccessful—because it was unfunny, many said. With the first of the Indiana Jones series, *Raiders of the Lost Ark* (1981)—a rousing, globe-circling action-adventure full of derring-do—he was back on track. *E.T.—The Extraterrestrial* (1982), with its lovable space creature in the midst of suburbia, achieved some sort of pinnacle in public response.

After *Indiana Jones and the Temple of Doom* (1984) Spielberg continued his positive thinking with what would seem intransigent literary material situated firmly in an actuality (both sources more or less autobiographical) quite outside his own experience of life or movie-making. *The Color Purple* (1985), from a Pulitzer Prize-winning book, recounts the growing up (the film spans some forty years) of a black girl in the South during hard times. The book was softened and sweetened, it was felt; the film's interpretation created some controversy. *Empire of the Sun* (1987) is about a privileged English boy who had been living in Shanghai at the outbreak of the Second World War, was separated from his parents, spent four years in a Japanese

E.T.—The Extraterrestrial ◆ U.S., 1982, Steven Spielberg; Henry Thomas and friend.

prison camp, then has to fend for himself at the war's end in Japanese-occupied China as the prison camps are evacuated. Both films received mixed reviews. The reactions seemed to depend on whether the feelings Spielberg was attempting to evoke could be accepted or whether his kind of film making was thought to be contrived and inflated beyond what the content at any given moment warranted.

Following these departures into more "adult" and socially aware subjects Spielberg returned to the popular action series with *Indiana Jones and the Last Crusade* (1989). With the exception of *Always* (1990)—a remake of *A Guy Named Joe* (1944), sentimental patriotic World War II fantasy, a critical and financial failure—he continued with more characteristic material. *Hook* (1991) is a reworking of J. M. Barrie's turn-of-the-century play *Peter Pan,* in the Disney manner. It deals directly with themes implicit in many Spielberg films: a child's fear of growing up, and the possibility that an adult can return to a magical childhood state. By his own admission, and the evidence of his films, Spielberg values the child's view of the world.

Jurassic Park (1993) is heavy on fear; the magic is black. Like *Jaws,* this is a monster film—in this case genetically engineered dinosaurs—adapted from an enormously successful novel. In many ways it seems ultimate Spielberg and will no doubt top the huge amounts of money earned by his first big hit. This raised the ultimate question about Spielberg, the most commercially successful director the world has yet seen. Can these entertainments, constructed with considerable skill and ever-increasing technological virtuosity, be taken seriously as something resembling works of art that somehow contain personal statements? And perhaps the corollaries as well: Does that really matter? What sorts of criteria *are* to be applied to Spielberg's most popular works?

Clearly he is onto mythic material that has a wide, even universal, appeal. Isn't it hard to say that films offering pleasure (that is, aesthetic experience) to millions upon millions of people are less valuable in the general scheme of things than those offering perhaps a more intense pleasure to a much more limited number? Carl Jung, who thought and wrote about mythology in ways that would seem to apply to many aspects of Spielberg's films, might well have opted for the universal.

A second point that might be made about Spielberg's films is that they grow out of the same sort of familiarity with movies that characterizes the "film generation," both the makers and the viewers. Spielberg seems quite content—thinks it proper, even necessary perhaps—to make his films within standard genres. Furthermore, he employs the familiar, the clichéd, with knowing and affectionate expertise; his films are full of "quotes" from other films. At their best, they are movie-movies, as a student film maker might say about them, and surely can be and in fact are no doubt valued in that way by their vast audiences.

Jonathan Demme, like Coppola, Scorsese, and others, began direction with exploitation films for Roger Corman's New World Pictures (*Caged Heat,* 1974, women in prison; *Crazy Mama,* 1975, three women on a crime spree; *Fighting Mad,* 1976, rampaging rednecks—he also wrote the first and last). His first critical success, and first comedy, was *Citizens Band* (1977), a low-key episodic account of people in a small Midwestern town absorbed with the use of the newly available CB radio. *Melvin and Howard* (1980) is another comedy about ordinary folks, more offbeat and very funny, based on a true episode of a working-class guy who picked up eccentric billionaire Howard Hughes hitchhiking as a hobo in the Nevada desert and later sued for a share in Hughes's will. *Swing Shift* (1983), too, deals with working-class characters, in this case an aircraft plant during World War II. It contains much that is accurate about the strained and heightened feelings of those times, with husbands and wives separated, women entering the male workplace, but is said to be much less than it was before star/producer Goldie Hawn took it away from Demme and had it partially redone.

Demme has moved back and forth between fiction and nonfiction (like Louis Malle), which is unusual for American film makers (though Scorsese has made nonfiction films). Best known of Demme's are *Stop Making Sense* (1984), a Los Angeles rock concert of David Byrne's Talking Heads group; *Swimming to Cambodia* (1987), a performance film of actor Spalding Gray in ironic monologue about modern life; *Cousin Bobby* (1992), about Demme's own cousin, an engaging middle-aged Episcopalian priest working in Harlem.

Something Wild (1986) is one of the screwball-noir films discussed above. *Married to the Mob* (1988) has some similarities to it: powerful and somewhat mad female leads escaping from a past life, who finally defeat males in pursuit, including a psychopathic former boyfriend in the former and the mafia in the latter. Both mix the elements of comedy and thriller. *The Silence of the Lambs* (1990) leaves out the comedy. Based on the Thomas Harris novel, it is about an FBI trainee (Jodie Foster)

The Silence of the Lambs ◆ U.S., 1991, Jonathan Demme; Anthony Hopkins and Jodie Foster.

assigned to the case of "Buffalo Bill," a serial killer who skins the bodies of his young female victims. A huge success, with countless awards for picture, performances, direction, it is unquestionably brilliant suspense film making. It took other dimensions as well: as the subject of considerable discussion among feminists regarding the Foster character's functioning in the patriarchal hierarchy of the FBI and as a potential victim of deranged male sexuality. It also was seen, especially in the gay community, as homophobic in its portrayal of "Buffalo Bill" and his insane desire to assume a female identity.

All of Demme's films display a mastery of filmic narrative. Tightly constructed, well made, and compelling, they seem to grow out of intense concentration and an ability to find the exact way in which particular subjects and themes can best be presented. Also, his films are characterized by a kind of hipness, street smarts. He seems to have an intuitive sense of current cultural issues and styles, and sees them with toughness of mind and compassionate humor. His characters are fresh, individual, frequently eccentric, with especial sympathy and understanding given to the female roles. Because they are believable we may even accept as possible the improbable situations they find themselves in.

Like Robert Altman, Demme seems a quintessentially American film maker deeply involved in his culture. Since he's almost twenty years Altman's junior, and his career shows no signs of faltering, we can look forward to having new Demme films available for some time to come.

Since 1975 a crop of new, young directors has appeared. Alas, the space remaining allows for little more than an acknowledgment of those who seem most significant at this moment and a lightly annotated catalogue of their most notable work.

First into the field, scriptwriter, as well as director of his films, who trained as a painter, was **David Lynch.** His *Eraserhead* (1978), which carries its horror in a dark view of the world and deliberately repugnant imagery, has gained a considerable cult following. In *The Elephant Man* (1980) Lynch put his intelligence to work on another man cruelly afflicted with physical deformity. In this case the treatment of the protagonist is remarkable for its sensitivity and delicacy. A quite adequate budget (his first film had been made for a pittance) permitted the re-creation of a convincing Victorian London. *Dune* (1984), a huge, long version of Frank Herbert's fantasy novel, proved a disaster, critically and commercially. *Blue Velvet* (1986), on the other hand, is Lynch's most resounding success to date. It carries his attraction to the mysterious and perverse (it is his original script) into a picture-postcard American small town. Its underside is discovered by two teenagers who become involved with the awfulness they discover.

Nothing Lynch has done since has fulfilled the promise of that film (or of *Eraserhead,* for that matter). He next conceived, and directed some episodes of, the network television series *Twin Peaks* (1990–1991). It offered the same exposure of moral corruption beneath the surface of a small town (in this instance in Oregon, but read American society generally). It also had some of the same mixture of genres (mystery/horror/soap opera) and levels of reality, adding a juggling of narrative time to delve into the past. It achieved a cult following and added to the materials Lynch would continue to explore. *Wild at Heart* (1990) draws on both *Twin Peaks* and *Blue*

Blue Velvet ◆ U.S., 1986, David Lynch; Kyle MacLachlan and Dennis Hopper.

Velvet but takes the form of a (formless, you might want to say) road movie. The couple in this rambling and wildly undisciplined saga, which includes violent and sexual excesses like those of *Blue Velvet,* are deeply into mad love.

Then, returning to the TV series as source, in fact dealing with events in the characters' lives that preceded those of the series, was *Twin Peaks; Fire Walk with Me* (1992). This film seems seriously out of control, however, Lynch indulging his obsessive perversity in an unremitting nightmare of horror which lacks completely the quirky charm and playfulness interlaced with crime, evil, and the supernatural that characterized the series. It is not at all clear where Lynch will go from here, but his avant-garde talent with images and sounds and the intermittent seductiveness of his inverse view of humanity may keep him afloat in the commercial world of film production, as it has done to date.

Lawrence Kasdan debuted as writer-director with *Body Heat* (1981), an extraordinarily polished and involving reworking of *film noir* material including a very sexy woman, arson, and murder. *The Big Chill* (1983), which he also wrote as well as directed, concerns the reunion of a group of college radicals of the 1960s. What it is mainly about is the ways in which they have become very different persons in the intervening years, and the stresses and changes that occur in their relationships. *The Accidental Tourist* (1988) is the most ambitious and accomplished of Kasdan's films so far. Made from Anne Tyler's acclaimed novel, it is especially impressive in maintaining a feature-length narrative about a man filled with depression and uncertainty, a man who is incapable of action—the kind of material thought to be unfilm-

The Accidental Tourist ◆ U.S., 1988, Lawrence Kasdan; William Hurt and Geena Davis.

able, and which might have proved so in other hands. William Hurt, whose perform-ance accounts in part for this achievement, has starred in all three of the Kasdan pictures; Kathleen Turner in the first and third.

I Love You to Death (1990), Hurt again in the cast, was less successful. Based on a true story, it is a dark comedy about a woman who tries to get her cheating husband killed. In *Grand Canyon* (1991) he is back in form. In some ways it can be seen as a successor to *The Big Chill*. Set in Los Angeles, and about that city (and American cities and urban culture), its characters are a diverse group of people involved in relationships with each other (friends, husband-wife, boss-secretary, parents-children) or who have chance encounters (driver of a broken-down car and a tow-truck driver). All are attempting to live satisfying and secure lives in a milieu made up of little that can be assured with eruptions of random and senseless violence. Though the causes of all this are not really explored, it is nonetheless a grim premonition of the riots that would shortly engulf Los Angeles. Since Kasdan has scripted or coscripted most of his films it is worth noting that an element of topicality is common to them, that there seems to be on his part a fixed concern about what we have become and may be becoming. He is a very professional film maker who has achieved considerable success in a comparatively short time.

Jim Jarmusch's *Stranger Than Paradise* (1984) plummeted him into the inter-national spotlight. It won the Camera d'Or at Cannes (for Best New Director) and was voted best film of the year by the (U.S.) National Society of Film Critics. It is an engaging road comedy in which an unprepossessing young man, his emigré Hungar-ian female cousin, and dull-witted friend take off on an odyssey that extends from

New York's Lower East Side to Cleveland to Florida. *Down by Law* (1986) has some of the same qualities. Jarmusch described it as the story of "a pimp, a disc jockey, and an Italian tourist stuck in a Louisiana prison." They break out and wander off into the swamplands until they reach Luigi's Tintop, an isolated eating-joint near the Texas border run by Nicoletta, niece of the late Luigi. She and the Italian, Roberto (or "Bob, 'itsa the same thing"), fall immediately in love. He remains and the other two men wander down the road, then separate to pursue their solitary ways.

Mystery Train (1989) is an assemblage of three stories that occur one afternoon and night in Memphis. The principal characters are foreign visitors: a Japanese teen-age couple arriving to visit Graceland and the Sun Studios, shrines to Elvis Presley and other early rock stars; an Italian woman, who has flown from Rome to identify the body of her suddenly deceased husband, and a young American woman she meets who has just walked out on her British boyfriend; the boyfriend and his two pals. The three sets of characters overlap—they all spend the night in a seedy hotel, listen to the same radio program, frequent the same diner across the street—but they never meet. In the morning they go on their ways. Jarmusch regards this as the last of a trilogy that included his two earlier films. All three involve foreigners exploring American culture on the fringes of society—tourists in a sense.

Stranger Than Paradise ♦ U.S., 1984, Jim Jarmusch; John Lurie, Eszter Balint, and Richard Edson.

Night on Earth (1992) is another anthology. Each of its five stories concerns a cab driver and a fare—in Los Angeles, New York, Paris, Rome, Helsinki. Like *Mystery Train* the encounters take place simultaneously, beginning at 7:07 P.M. in California, which works its way around to 5:07 A.M. in Finland. But there is no tying together of these stories except that they occur at the same time, in taxis, and in large cities. In fact part of the point is that the differences among the cultures determine the ways in which these brief encounters between ill-matched types are conducted. All (except for a death in one of them) end more or less inconclusively. This film shares with the others Jarmusch's offbeat and quite personal sense of narrative structure and visual style, which have earned him considerable respect at home and abroad. At the moment he is a very hot property, as they say.

The **Coen** brothers, Joel and Ethan, also had their first big hit, *Blood Simple,* in 1984. Like Jarmusch, Joel is from New York University; the undergraduate film program in his case. He directed, Ethan produced, they wrote the script together. It is a very clever, slick, highly stylized suspense-thriller in the manner of Hitchcock, or even more that of Brian De Palma. Action-horror is the Coens' label for it and, to be sure, it has considerable shock value. Set in Texas, the beginning of its intricate plotting occurs when a cuckolded husband hires an unsavory character to kill his wife and her boyfriend. Deception and double-cross, a body thought to be dead buried alive, re-killed with a shovel, and the like occupy the remainder. *Raising Arizona* (1987) is a wacky farce about an ex-con husband and police officer wife. When they discover they cannot have a child they kidnap one of the newborn Arizona quintuplets, sons of Nathan Arizona, an unfinished-furniture tycoon.

Miller's Crossing (1990) is an expertly made gangster film set sometime and somewhere in the Prohibition era. It suggests not so much the gangster movies of the thirties, however, as the Dashiell Hammett novels of crime and corruption. The plot, though astonishingly complicated, is devoted essentially to loyalty and betrayal among members of the entrenched Irish boss's gang and their Italian rivals. *Barton Fink* (1991) has already been referred to as a screwball-noir. The title character is a playwright (modeled on Clifford Odets) who, after the success of his leftist play on Broadway, is imported by a Hollywood studio (resembling Columbia Pictures, whose boss could pass for Harry Cohn) to write a wrestling "B" picture to star Wallace Beery. Along the way he has a fragmented relationship with a famous drunken novelist turned screenwriter (who even looks like William Faulkner). In the midst of this parodic and caricatured Hollywood is the eerie hotel in which Barton is staying, and the neighbor who offers him help and friendship, and proves to be a psychopathic murderer. Of the Coen films this may be the most clever and also the most telling in its oblique commentary on art and life.

Though their films are all different from each other they are alike in working out of and around popular genre, and in the evidence they offer of a sophisticated understanding of the movies and movie makers preceding them. The Coens resolutely deny any concealed auteur attraction to subjects or themes, however; instead, they concentrate on craftsmanship and storytelling. Apparently their ambition is to create the perfect entertainment.

David Mamet is also an astute and knowledgeable craftsman, but his craft so far has been more closely related to theater than to movies or novels. He was an

Barton Fink ◆ U.S., 1991, Joel Coen; John Goodman and John Turturro.

established playwright (*American Buffalo, Sexual Perversity in Chicago* [filmed by others as *About Last Night,* 1986], and *Glengarry Glen Ross* [also filmed by others in 1993]) before he became a screenwriter (*The Postman Always Rings Twice,* 1981; *The Verdict,* 1982; *The Untouchables,* 1987), and both before he became a writer-director of his own film, *House of Games* (1987). Its protagonist is a female psychiatrist and author of a best-selling book on compulsive behavior. Starting out to do research on gambling, she is led by her fascination with a charming con artist to try to beat him at his own game—with fatal results. *Things Change* (1988) concerns a low-ranking Chicago mobster who forms a relationship with an elderly Sicilian shoeshine man who agrees to take the rap, for pay, for a murder he didn't commit. The complications occur when he is mistaken for a big-time mafia boss.

Homicide (1991) is a police thriller about a Jewish detective in Baltimore who becomes involved in what may (or may not) have been an anti-Semitic murder in an Afro-American neighborhood. In the course of the investigation he is forced to consult his own subjugated Jewishness in reference to his loyalty to the Homicide Division. Mamet's most "filmic" film to date, it also contains, in addition to considerable suspense, an absorbing moral and ethical examination of the motives and goals of the characters in relation to each other. Like his plays, Mamet's films present problems with contending arguments pitted against each other that are fully reasoned but may not lead to a solution, at least not to one that was expected or desired by anyone involved.

House of Games ◆ U.S., 1987, David Mamet; Joe Mantegna and Lindsay Crouse.

What follows is a postscript to acknowledge that within this last period of American film some actors—superstars, mainly—have stepped forward as important directors. The lead of a film being its producer or coproducer has long been fairly common practice; but actors directing, especially films in which they do not appear, is quite unusual. Earlier exceptions that come to mind are Chaplin, with *A Woman of Paris* (1923) and *A Countess from Hong Kong* (1967), in which he did not appear; and Brando, with *One-Eyed Jacks* (1961), in which he did. Within this final period Warren Beatty has directed three films in which he did appear: *Heaven Can Wait* (1978), *Reds* (1981), *Dick Tracy* (1990). Kevin Costner directed *Dances with Wolves* (1990) and Jodie Foster *Little Man Tate* (1991), in which they appear. Then there is Robert Redford, who has directed three films in which he does not appear: *Ordinary People* (1980), *The Milagro Beanfield War* (1988), and *A River Runs Through It* (1992).

The major instance, however, is **Clint Eastwood,** who has directed films in which he appears and a film in which he does not. His first direction was in 1971, *Play Misty for Me.* Since then he has directed more than a dozen films. Of these, *Bird* (1988) is the only one in which he does not appear, though it grows out of his serious interest in jazz. It is a quite accurate and deeply respectful biography of Charlie Parker, the black alto saxophonist who created the bebop revolution of the 1940s and 1950s—a fine film in many ways. But Eastwood's master work is surely *Unforgiven* (1992). In it he plays the role of a wandering gunman which first brought him to attention in the "spaghetti westerns." (The film is dedicated to Sergio Leone, who directed those

Unforgiven ◆ U.S., 1992, Clint Eastwood; Eastwood.

films, and to Don Siegel, who directed Eastwood's first major American ones.) In *Unforgiven* he not only presents the pervasiveness of violence in American life, and the false masculinity accompanying it, but offers meditations on the western as genre and on his own dominant persona, all of this in a remarkably thoughtful way. It is a very intelligent film as well as a moving one. In a fusion of aging actor and aging genre, he lets us experience the satisfactions of western and stardom while helping us to understand more fully what we are responding to. Quite an achievement.

◆ MULTINATIONALISM

Organizing an international history of film around the concept of national cinemas is much more satisfactory for the earlier chapters than for the later ones. Those national periods of heightened creativity are well into the past, their hegemony widely recognized, and the canon of what films warrant preservation and continued study more or less agreed upon.

A profound change of recent years is the increasing internationalization of the industry, which internationalizes the art—for better or worse. It is no longer possible to draw distinctions among films of different nations with the assurance it once was;

film money, film makers, and film production move across national boundaries. Some of the most important films of recent years are multinational mixes, not only of finance, crew, and cast, but even of subjects, themes, and styles. If we can say that the United States is at the center of the film universe and exerts a gravitational pull (it controls an estimated fifty-six percent of the world film market), it is not that universe.

Speaking of *The Three Musketeers,* its director, Richard Lester, said:

> *It was a film whose producer had a Mexican passport and who was the honorary consul for Costa Rica in Switzerland. The company that employed me was from Liechtenstein, the company that produced the film in pre-production was French; it was a Spanish film when it was made. I found out afterwards that I'd probably made the best Panamanian film ever and in the end it qualified for the British Academy Awards as a British film. The technicians were almost entirely British but the cast were primarily Americans and the film was shot in Spain. The money came from God knows where. All I know is that whenever one asked the producers about profits they started speaking in Russian.*[1]

As discussed in Chapter 18, Lester is an American who lives in England.

What seemed odd in 1974, when *The Three Musketeers* was made, is now commonplace. Among major Academy Award winning films of the recent past *The Last Emperor* (1987) may be the most conspicuous example. Its source was the autobiography of Pu Yi, *From Emperor to Citizen,* published in China in 1964. The screenplay was by Mark Peploe (English) and Bernardo Bertolucci (Italian). It had to be approved by the Chinese authorities before production could proceed. The budget of $25 million was raised by British independent producer Jeremy Thomas from five British and European banks. Principal crew members were Italian: director, Bertolucci; set designer, Nando Scarfiotta; cinematographer, Vittorio Storaro. The cast comprised a substantial number of Chinese-Americans from California, plus Chinese nationals, plus Peter O'Toole (the solitary non-Chinese). Shooting was divided between sixteen weeks in China and five weeks of interiors in the studio in Rome. Its producer said that "it was pre-sold virtually everywhere in the world"—except for China, where the Chinese Co-production Corporation had distribution rights. Interestingly it was distributed by Shochiku-Fuji, a Japanese entertainment conglomerate.

You could also say that Miloš Forman's *Amadeus* (1985) is to all intents and purposes an East European film; Oliver Stone's *Platoon* (1986) is a British production of an American story; *The Unbearable Lightness of Being* (1988), from a Czech novel, was produced and directed by Americans, written with a Frenchman and filmed in France, with cast and crew including British, French, and Swedes. And then there is *A Room with a View* (1986), an American production of a British literary classic set in Italy and made by Merchant Ivory Productions, who have come into this new multinationalism and made excellent use of it.

---

[1]Ferdinand, "Double Takes: Home(less) Movie," *Sight & Sound,* 58 (Winter 1988/89): 42.

The Last Emperor ♦ Italy/U.K./China, 1987, Bernardo Bertolucci.

The earlier collaborations of Ismail Merchant (producer), James Ivory (director), and Ruth Prawer Jhabvala (writer) could be thought of as an adjunct to the Indian film. Though made for the international market, with dialogue in English, their features were mostly about India—particularly about Anglo-Indian relationships. *Shakespeare-Wallah* (1965), centered on a resolutely English family of touring actors in postcolonial India, was their first success. It was followed by *The Guru* (1968), *Bombay Talkie* (1970), *Autobiography of a Princess* (1975), *Heat and Dust* (1983), among others. These films all have a kind of close and subtle observation of surface manners and cultural strains reminiscent of E. M. Forster's *A Passage to India,* or of Henry James (to whom they would subsequently turn with *The Europeans,* 1979), an author who dealt with other cross-cultural exchanges. These concerns are not surprising since the three film makers themselves represent a striking cultural mix: Merchant is Indian, Ivory is American, and Jhabvala is German-born of Polish-Jewish descent married to an Indian.

With *The Bostonians* (1984), from another Henry James novel, Merchant-Ivory launched fully and strongly into multinationalism. Its cast and crew were British-American; it was shot in New England; postproduction was done in London. It too, in a way, deals with tensions between cultures. Set in Boston of the late 1880s it centers on the conflict experienced by a young woman between loyalty to the burgeoning feminist movement and attraction to a handsome, sexist Mississippi gentleman.

The next film was *A Room with a View,* from an E. M. Forster novel. This turn-of-the-century romantic comedy is about a young English woman traveler in

Florence who meets and falls in love with a free-spirited young Englishman slightly below her class. On their eventual return to an English country town she decides to ditch her stuffy official suitor and take off with the less proper young man. Though more British than *The Bostonians,* it received eight Academy Award nominations; made for roughly $3.5 million, it grossed more than $1 million in its first sixteen weeks at just one New York City theater.

Perhaps it was the success of *A Room with a View* that led Merchant-Ivory to other Forster novels. *Maurice* (1987) is about a young Englishman coming to age and coming to terms with his homosexuality in Britain in 1912. This time the success was critical rather than financial. *Howard's End* (1991) is from what many regard as Forster's finest work. Written in 1910, it portrays the moral decay and unscrupulousness in an English society shaken by economic and social change. The film, both a critical and financial success, is replete with the sort of excellences we've come to expect from these film makers. Still, the main point about Merchant-Ivory Productions may be that they have been able to sustain themselves for over thirty years on films of high artistic merit and independent financing. Though the astuteness and talent of Merchant, Ivory, and Jhabvala deserve to be celebrated, the steady continuance of their creation has been made possible by the support of discriminating audiences throughout the world—even of those in the United States, where it has been notoriously difficult for foreign films, including British ones, to win their way.

Room with a View ♦
U.K., 1986, James Ivory;
Julian Sands and Helena
Bonham Carter.

The metaphor pursued throughout this book of a country stepping into the international spotlight with a particularly innovative national contribution to the evolution of film art now has to be modified. Instead of more or less separable national developments, we have films from any country reaching audiences in any other—if not always easily, certainly more readily than ever before.

As the old industry and old audiences give way to the new, individual artists are at last beginning to receive the recognition in film they have always had in the other arts. Yet, the motion picture remains an awesomely difficult medium in which to create. The very characteristics that distinguish it from the older arts often impede the artist: the massive and complex technology, the demands of high finance, the necessity for a huge and diverse audience. But, as the film made for theaters has yielded to television its place as mass entertainer, and as the rigid production-distribution-exhibition systems have been shaken and cracked in many places, art of a new seriousness and difficulty, greater originality and individuality, has begun to appear.

The flexible and subtle eloquence of modern film has been built upon those periods of great national creativity surveyed in this history. The capacity of the medium for handling widely varied personal expression has been added to, bit by bit. Along with the ever-growing richness of the new, it is a further boon that we are able to go back and review the old through the work of film archives and museums, film history courses, retrospective series, and now video cassettes and laser discs. In art there is rarely progress, only change. The works of Griffith, Murnau, and Eisenstein are no less valuable now than when they were created. Each generation of viewers can find something new in them, sometimes more than was seen by the original audiences; Kurosawa, Bergman, Resnais, Antonioni, Losey, Wajda, and Altman have replaced no one. Knowing as much as we can of the sum total of cinema helps us better appreciate the work of every film maker and each individual work. That is the use of the history of film.

FILMS OF THE PERIOD

1975
Jaws (Steven Spielberg)
One Flew Over the Cuckoo's Nest
    (Miloš Forman)

1976
All the President's Men (Alan J. Pakula)
Network (Sidney Lumet)
Rocky (John G. Avildsen)

1977
Annie Hall (Woody Allen)
Close Encounters of the Third Kind
    (Spielberg)

Saturday Night Fever (John Badham)
Star Wars (George Lucas)

1978
Coming Home (Hal Ashby)
The Deer Hunter (Michael Cimino)
Who'll Stop the Rain? (Karel Reisz)

1979
Apocalypse Now (Francis Ford Coppola)

1980
Atlantic City (Louis Malle)
Dressed to Kill (Brian De Palma)

Melvin and Howard (Jonathan Demme)
Ordinary People (Robert Redford)

1981
Absence of Malice (Sydney Pollack)
Body Heat (Lawrence Kasdan)
Cutter's Way (Ivan Passer)
Raiders of the Lost Ark (Spielberg)
Reds (Warren Beatty)

1982
Blade Runner (Ridley Scott)
Chan Is Missing (Wayne Wang)
Diner (Barry Levinson)
E.T.—The Extraterrestrial (Spielberg)
Sophie's Choice (Alan J. Pakula)
Tootsie (Pollack)

1983
The Big Chill (Kasdan)
The King of Comedy (Martin Scorsese)
The Right Stuff (Philip Kaufman)
Terms of Endearment (James L. Brooks)
Under Fire (Roger Spottiswoode)
Zelig (Woody Allen)

1984
Amadeus (Forman)
Blood Simple (Joel Coen)
Choose Me (Alan Rudolph)
Dim Sum: A Little Bit of Heart (Wang)
Once Upon a Time in America (Sergio Leone)
Stranger Than Paradise (Jim Jarmusch)

1985
After Hours (Scorsese)
The Color Purple (Spielberg)
Desperately Seeking Susan (Susan Seidelman)
Out of Africa (Pollack)
Prizzi's Honor (John Huston)
The Purple Rose of Cairo (Allen)
Witness (Peter Weir)

1986
Blue Velvet (David Lynch)
Down by Law (Jarmusch)
The Fly (David Cronenberg)
Hannah and Her Sisters (Allen)
Platoon (Oliver Stone)

She's Gotta Have It (Spike Lee)
Something Wild (Demme)

1987
Broadcast News (Brooks)
House of Games (David Mamet)
Radio Days (Allen)
Raising Arizona (Coen)
The Untouchables (De Palma)
Wall Street (Stone)

1988
The Accidental Tourist (Kasdan)
Bird (Clint Eastwood)
Good Morning, Vietnam (Levinson)
Mississippi Burning (Alan Parker)
The Moderns (Rudolph)
Rain Man (Levinson)
The Unbearable Lightness of Being (Kaufman)
Who Framed Roger Rabbit?
    (Roger Zemeckis and Richard Williams)

1989
Batman (Tim Burton)
Do the Right Thing (Lee)
Married to the Mob (Demme)
Mystery Train (Jarmusch)
sex, lies, and videotapes (Steven Soderbergh)

1990
Crimes and Misdemeanors (Allen)
Dances with Wolves (Kevin Costner)
Driving Miss Daisy (Bruce Beresford))
Goodfellas (Scorsese)
The Grifters (Stephen Frears)
Miller's Crossing (Coen)
Mr. and Mrs. Bridge (James Ivory)
Presumed Innocent (Pakula)
When Harry Met Sally (Rob Reiner)

1991
Barton Fink (Coen)
Beauty and the Beast
    (Gary Trousdale and Kirk Wise)
Boyz N the Hood (John Singleton)
Cape Fear (Scorsese)
Grand Canyon (Kasdan)
Homicide (Mamet)
Hook (Spielberg)

My Own Private Idaho (Gus Van Sant)
Rambling Rose (Martha Coolidge)
The Silence of the Lambs (Demme)
Terminator 2: Judgement Day
    (James Cameron)

1992
Aladdin (John Musker and Ron Clements)
Husbands and Wives (Allen)

The Player (Robert Altman)
Unforgiven (Eastwood)

1993
In the Line of Fire (Wolfgang Peterson)
Jurassic Park (Spielberg)
Short Cuts (Altman)
What's Love Got to Do With It (Brian Gibson)

BOOKS ON THE PERIOD

Anderegg, Michael, ed. *Inventing Vietnam: The War in Film and Television.* Philadelphia: Temple University Press, 1990

Auster, Albert, and Leonard Quart, *How the War Was Remembered: Hollywood and Vietnam.* New York: Praeger, 1988

Corrigan, Timothy, *A Cinema Without Walls: Movies and Culture After Vietnam.* New Brunswick, NJ: Rutgers University Press, 1991

Diawara, Manthia, ed., *Black American Cinema.* New York: Routledge, 1992

Dittmar, Linda, and Gene Michaud, eds., *From Hanoi to Hollywood: The Vietnam War in American Film.* New Brunswick, NJ: Rutgers University Press, 1990

Hillier, Jim, *The New Hollywood.* London: Studio Vista, 1993

Kent, Nicolas, *Naked Hollywood: Money, Power and the Movies.* London: BBC Books, 1991

O'Brien, Tom, *The Screening of America: Movies and Values from Rocky to Rain Man.* New York: Continuum, 1990

Quart, Barbara Koenig, *Women Directors: The Emergence of a New Cinema.* New York: Praeger, 1988

Vineberg, Steve, *No Surprises, Please: Movies in the Reagan Decade.* New York: Schirmer Books, 1993

Wollen, Tana, and Phillip Hayward, eds., *Future Visions: New Technologies of the Screen.* London: British Film Institute, 1993

INDEX

♦ ♦ ♦

This page constitutes a continuation of the copyright page.